MASTERING IMPORT & EXPORT MANAGEMENT

SECOND EDITION

MASTERING IMPORT & EXPORT MANAGEMENT

SECOND EDITION

Thomas A. Cook

with

Rennie Alston and Kelly Raia

- Major Issues in Global Supply Chain Management
- Main Features of the Incoterms® 2010
- New TSA Regulations
- Documents, Operations, & Procedures
- Risk Assessment & Mitigation
- Import & Export Management Tools

AMACOM

American Management Association

New York • Atlanta • Brussels • Chicago • Mexico City • San Francisco
Shanghai • Tokyo • Toronto • Washington, D. C.

Bulk discounts available. For details visit:
www.amacombooks.org/go/specialsales
Or contact special sales:
Phone: 800-250-5308
Email: specialsls@amanet.org
View all the AMACOM titles at: www.amacombooks.org

Library of Congress Cataloging-in-Publication Data

Cook, Thomas A.
  Mastering import & export management / Thomas A. Cook with Rennie Alston and Kelly Raia.—2nd ed.
    p. cm.
  Includes bibliographical references and index.
  ISBN-13: 978-0-8144-2026-3
  ISBN-10: 0-8144-2026-5
  1. Exports—Management. 2. Export controls. 3. Foreign trade promotion. 4. Imports—Management. 5. International trade. 6. Exports—United States—Management. 7. Export controls—United States. 8. Foreign trade promotion—United States. 9. Imports—United States—Management. I. Alston, Rennie. II. Raia, Kelly. III. Title. IV. Title: Mastering import and export management.
  HF1414.4.C665   2012
  658.8'4—dc23

                                                                                2011035514

American Management Association (www.amanet.org) is a world leader in talent development, advancing the skills of individuals to drive business success. Our mission is to support the goals of individuals and organizations through a complete range of products and services, including classroom and virtual seminars, webcasts, webinars, podcasts, conferences, corporate and government solutions, business books and research. AMA's approach to improving performance combines experiential learning—learning through doing—with opportunities for ongoing professional growth at every step of one's career journey.

Printing number
10 9 8 7 6 5 4 3 2 1

Contents

MASTERING IMPORT & EXPORT MANAGEMENT

SECOND EDITION

1

Major Issues in Global Supply Chain Management Today

The book opens with a view of current world events that impact global supply chains, import and export operations, and the entire responsibilities that business executives have in trade compliance management.

2011 and into 2012 have seen a number of shifts in world politics, Middle East stability, and major physical occurrences that have huge short-term impacts on global trade, and these impacts may extend into the future for years to come.

Overview

Physical Events

The earthquake in Japan has rocked the world in a number of ways. Perhaps most important, the long-term utilization of nuclear power is very much in jeopardy.

The impact of the devastating tsunami that followed goes far beyond the tragic loss of life that occurred. The insurance community who insured the risks involved with both events will have to pay hundreds of million in claims, potentially in excess of several billion dollars. This will impact insurance costs and the availability of certain types of insurances in risk-prone centers of the globe as well as for freight that moves on certain trade lanes. Cost and availability will become major issues.

Personnel involved in international shipping and logistics who had freight coming in and out of Japan are witnessing great delays in transit times, limited access to transportation infrastructure, and increases in freight charges.

Shipping managers worldwide have looked at this disaster in Japan and have already begun to access risk management alternatives not only in earthquake-prone areas, but in all corners of the globe where there are significant physical risks such as but not limited to:

- Earthquakes
- Floods
- Tornadoes
- Hurricanes
- Harsh changes from winter to summer weather patterns
- Tsunamis

These are but a few of the major physical exposures that companies who operate globally are now assessing, and they are reevaluating their supply chain decisions to avoid exposure and mitigate risk.

Economic Events

As of this writing, most professional assessments and benchmarks in world trade have shown a betterment in most market segments in the overall economy. Most manufacturing, inventory, and trade indexes have shown increases of 3 to 6 percent in 2011 into 2012.

While most sectors have shown improvement, there is still serious concern over the following areas:

- Stability of global banking and financial infrastructure.
- Housing and unemployment in the United States.
- Political instability in the Middle East.
- Financial issues in an array of countries, such as but not limited to Greece, Poland, Brazil, Venezuela, and the United States.
- The rise in government bailouts and increase in debt worldwide.

All of this impacts global supply chains.

It impacts cost, risk, and choice of global sourcing and offshore manufacturing, and it potentially retards the growth of globalization.

A good example of this in the United States is shown by the number of companies who had sent manufacturing overseas to Asia and the Near East but have moved some or all of it back here to America or to Mexico or Canada (referred to as "near-shoring").

Near-shoring makes a huge statement to the world. It says that from a competitive standpoint there may be better places to locate operations than Asia and the Near East (primarily India and Pakistan)—reversing a major trend of the past thirty years.

In logistics, these economic woes have reduced capacity in the ocean freight market, causing pricing instability and difficulties in locating available containers and chassis for timely, reliable, and consistent bookings.

Companies relying on the ocean freight mode to fulfill a time-sensitive supply chain have been hugely disappointed in 2011 and have had to make major compromises in risk, cost, and choice of carriers.

Political Instability

The events in the Middle East—in Tunisia, Libya, Egypt, and Bahrain to name a few—have rocked the traditional world of dictatorship and kingdoms in terms of historic attitudes in the Muslim community in that part of the globe.

The West, led by the United States, has taken a fairly aggressive role in supporting the move to democratic governments, including military action.

There are costs to supporting these uprisings that add to the economic turmoil, tied into the instability which has caused the price of crude oil to climb in excess of $100.00 US.

This will impact every aspect of the supply chain cost models, from manufacturing, to plastics, freight, and security surcharges due to gasoline increases.

The threat of an increase in terrorism promised from the more radical corners of that circle will place additional stresses on security and oil costs.

Many security analysts also see the West's proactive engagement in these Muslim democratic turnovers as another reason for terrorists to mount more aggressive and frequent attacks, which will include exposure for global supply chains.

The continued presence of the United States and its allies in Iraq and Afghanistan has also increased political stress among the West and the Muslim countries. These stresses impact politics—here and in those countries—which in turn impact the decision-making process as to where and how to ship, source, deliver, and partner.

These issues increase risk and cost.

Airfreight: TSA/Transportation Security Administration and Hazardous Materials

100 percent cargo screening, not just for Americans anymore!

The screening rules of 2010–2012 affected all air cargo destined for a passenger aircraft originating in the United States or being shipped from overseas to the United States. The TSA was charged with this daunting task. While the shipping community doubted the TSA would be able to accomplish the 100 percent screening rule by the initial 2010 deadlines, the TSA proved us wrong. They have accomplished this task and have done it without too many hiccups in the process. This process is still a work-in-process and is being tweaked and modified as we enter 2012.

The fear and overall concern were mainly twofold: the issue of higher costs and the issue of serious delays in the movement of air cargo.

While there has been a cost increase due to the additional layer of security that has been imposed, it has not been dramatic. Nor have the anticipated delays been as serious as we first thought they would be. The program seems to be a success so far.

As the air freight community just began to breathe easy again, here comes another directive. All foreign origin inbound air cargo must be screened at 100 percent. This issue of screening foreign air cargo is not a new development. The primary goal of the U.S. government was to enact the rule for screening of cargo that originates in the United States, and then to ultimately include foreign origin air freight, with a deadline of Y2013 for such foreign origin freight movement.

Then it happened! While we were focused heavily on cargo originating in America that was booked to fly aboard a *passenger* aircraft, terrorists were focusing on freight originating in a foreign country that was intended to fly on an all-cargo aircraft. UPS and FedEx both recently discovered explosive devices in cargo shipments that were ultimately addressed to a synagogue in Chicago. Fortunately, these devices were found prior to the final flight to the United States. Packages with explosives were found in Dubai and in the United Kingdom. The Prime Minister of England stated that it appears the device they discovered was intended to go off in midair, en route to the United States.

The publicity, hype, and exposure of the 100-percent passenger air cargo screening rule was a clear indicator to terrorists that there is a big black hole in the screening program: foreign-origin air cargo coming into our country is not subjected to rigorous screening. While U.S. Customs and Border Protection controls the security of inbound cargo through the C-TPAT program (Customs Trade

Partnership Against Terrorism), the program is heavily focused on ocean freight. And the program is only in effect for commercial import companies who voluntarily join the program.

Remember that goal of Y2013 for screening of foreign inbound cargo? Well, that date was moved to a goal of December 2011, and as of this writing in fall 2011, it looks like it will be achieved.

What should we do if we import air cargo? Will this requirement be a detriment to our ability to import goods timely and cost effectively? Maybe—and maybe not.

How can the importing community proactively respond to this requirement? There are several things we can do to prepare for this monumental task. A good start would be to discuss this pending issue with your freight forwarder/customs broker. The U.S. forwarding and brokerage community must act quickly to ensure a smooth flow of goods across our borders. Service providers here in the states should be advising their foreign agents of this new directive. They should work with their foreign counterparts to ensure that all screening options are reviewed, and to ensure that the options presented are viable for particular business models. For example, how will shipments of perishables and dangerous goods be screened? Will the foreign agent or carrier be responsible for any damage that may occur to the cargo during the screening process, or does additional insurance need to be purchased for this risk?

It is strongly recommended that the import community approach this issue before the rule goes into effect. The proactive approach that we all took regarding the 100-percent screening deadline related to U.S. origin air shipments must be the same approach we take now, as our borders are being pushed back even further. After all, that approach certainly eased the pain here in the United States.

When the first day that the mandatory screening of 100 percent of air cargo destined for a passenger aircraft goes into effect, every single package, prior to being loaded on a passenger aircraft, will have to go through security screening. That is, *every* single package *at the piece level*. For example, you tender a skid containing twenty-five packages. The skid will be broken down and each package on the skid will be individually screened.

There are various methods of screening that are authorized by the TSA. There are also various points in the supply chain where screening can take place.

There are very strict regulations regarding the sharing of information about the programs that are in place to screen packages. Therefore, the information that follows will be basic.

Currently, according to TSA statistics, the air carriers are at their capacity regarding their capability to screen cargo. And currently they are *not* screening at the 100-percent level. That translates to big delays on the near horizon. The bottleneck is anticipated to hinder the current flow of exports and domestic "just in time" distribution systems. In anticipation of this dilemma, the TSA developed a program to allow businesses other than air carriers to perform the screening of air cargo prior to the cargo being tendered to the carrier. Thus, when you deliver the cargo that you have had screened by one of these alternate businesses, the carrier is permitted to proceed with loading of that cargo. BIG time saver! The key is to have an alternate plan. The key is to not rely on the carrier to fulfill the screening requirements.

Even this late in the game, it is not too late to put a screening program in place. This is particularly wise for the shippers of air cargo. A shipper is eligible to participate in the Certified Cargo Screening Program (CCSP). Under the program, a shipper's place of packaging can become a Certified Cargo Screening Facility (CCSF). You may sometimes hear this program referred to as "reverse screening." This name comes from the idea that the screening occurs at time of *packaging*, and not after it is packaged and en route to carrier, a reversal of the usual carrier-performed screening.

This screening program has been available to the community and I find it hard to believe that more shippers have not joined the program. Companies, in tight financial straits due to the faltering economy, fear the cost and labor would be too heavy a financial burden right now. I must say that this line of thinking does not square with the actuality. In my consulting capacity, I have personally assisted many clients with their application to become a screening facility and I can assure you that in almost all cases, the costs were minimal—and the benefit tremendous!

Many freight forwarders are becoming Certified Cargo Screening Facilities to provide their customers yet another option. The concern with having a third-party service provider responsible for screening is the increased risk of damage of the contents of the packages. Some freight forwarders and smaller service providers are performing physical screening, opening every single package to check the entire contents. Naturally, this gives cause for reasonable concerns of increased incidents of damage and subsequent insurance claims.

However, freight forwarders and other transportation service providers are not required to be a screening facility in order to transport screened cargo. That opens the door to yet another program that involves the chain of custody of screened cargo. Transportation service providers can work with the TSA to develop a program that insures the integrity and security of cargo from point of screening to point of delivery to the air carrier. This would probably be the most cost-effective, time-saving option. The shipper should become a screening facility and, at a minimum, the chain of custody program should be in place for their providers.

And just as a side note to all those shippers who are already C-TPAT members, you already meet most of the minimum security criterion. Much of the battle has already been won for you.

Shippers are strongly encouraged to reach out and grab hold of this program. You will be very thankful you did!

What can shippers do to avoid the huge delays that can be incurred by carriers and service providers as they work at meeting this 100-percent screening rule? Become a Certified Screening Facility. The discussion below gives a brief overview of the program. If you wish to obtain more information, or wish to inquire about becoming your own screening facility, contact the TSA through their website: www.tsa.gov.

The Certified Cargo Screening Program

The Certified Cargo Screening Program (CCSP) is a voluntary program—facilities that seek approval as certified cargo screening facilities will be required to meet a variety of rigorous security standards and will be regulated by the TSA.

For example, a CCSP would be required to submit to security threat assessments of personnel, adhere to specified physical security standards, and maintain a strict chain of custody for cargo they screen and forward to the air carrier as a condition of its acceptance as screened cargo by the air carrier.

A key characteristic of the system will be rigorous tracking of the chain of custody, including the use of tamper-evident technology to assure that, once screened, cargo remains secured in transit to the aircraft. Under CCSP, air carriers will continue to have ultimate responsibility for ensuring that cargo has been screened prior to flight. If an air carrier cannot verify that cargo has been screened, the carrier must screen it before allowing it to be transported.

CCSP shippers will benefit from participation in several ways. By screening their own shipments, shippers can significantly reduce the possibility that their cargo may be physically opened. Additionally, they can bypass the potential delays that could occur if all screening is performed only at the airport.

Similarly, Indirect Air Carriers (IACs) benefit by these same measures, and may also continue to take advantage of typical airline reduced rates for cargo tendered in bulk.

By focusing outreach on IACs and shippers using the airports with the highest volume of cargo we have been able to maximize the impact of the pilots and to date we have validated over 200 facilities in the pilot program. TSA plans to ultimately roll out the program nationwide.

Any facility that sends cargo directly to an air carrier or indirect air carrier (IAC) may apply to become a CCSP. This includes:

- Manufacturers
- Warehouses
- Distribution centers
- Third-party logistics providers
- Indirect air carriers
- Airport cargo handlers

TSA Cargo Screening in 2011/12

Have you caught the SNL video of the TSA Enhanced Pat Downs on YouTube? Pretty funny stuff. The TSA certainly has its challenges these days between dealing with air travelers, underwear bombers, ink cartridges, and other cargo. The TSA gave a recent presentation at SUNY Old Westbury on the CCSP program and provided an overview as to what they've done but more importantly as to where they appear to be going. It's pretty obvious to any of us involved in supply chain the future holds only more stringent regulations and screening.

If we look back at the recommendations of the 9/11 Commission that were put in place in August of 2010, Congress required that cargo be screened at a level of security commensurate with checked baggage. In order to accomplish this, the TSA established the Certified Cargo Screening Program (CCSP) described above, and as of November 2010 has certified over 1100 entities. Under this voluntary program, a shipper may screen its own cargo utilizing one or more of several different screening methods as outlined under the screening mandate. Under the program, a shipper could be a shipping facility, warehouse, freight forwarder, 3PL, manufacturer, or independent cargo screening facility.

The TSA accomplished this through various forms of outreach to the shipping community including town hall meetings, webinars, and conferences. The TSA also increased the number of approved pieces of technology and also assisted some facilities in obtaining the equipment for screening.

As August 1, 2010, came around, the deadline was found to be met without too many problems, but was still moved to the end of 2011, beginning of 2012. This was largely due to the airlines preparing for additional screening in the months leading up to August by purchasing additional equipment and through communications with their customers.

One of the challenges currently facing the shipping industry is the limited technologies actually available. It's pretty tough for a small shipper to purchase an explosive trace detection machine. Therefore the smaller companies tend to perform a physical search on the skids, boxes, or pallets. Additional challenges for shippers include those with perishable items, high value, sealed drums, and cold chain handling.

So what's in the future for TSA screening? Well, the 9/11 Act requirement to screen also applies to international inbound air cargo. However, the TSA cannot set up a CCSP outside of the United States. The regulation scope is limited to carriers. This will be a heavy burden for the carriers, who will need to reach out to their foreign shippers and bring them up to speed on changing regulations. This should prove particularly challenging and we can only do our best in educating our foreign business partners as to the importance of security on both sides of the supply chain. For its part the TSA is working with countries that already have existing air cargo security programs to establish mutual recognition agreements that will allow carriers flying directly to the United States to follow the national air cargo programs of that host government. Similar to the implementation steps of C-TPAT, the TSA is focusing on highest volume countries.

So what's compliance professional to do? Stay up-to-date on changes in regulations that may be affecting your shipments. The TSA is continuing to offer information on the CCSP program through their website: www.tsa.gov/ccsp.

Chemical Facility Anti-Terrorism Standards (CFATS): Facility Inspections

On April 9, 2007, the U.S. Department of Homeland Security issued the Chemical Facility Anti-Terrorism Standards (CFATS). Congress authorized this interim final rule (IFR) under Section 550 of the Department of Homeland Security Appropriations Act of 2007, directing the Department to identify, assess, and ensure effective security at high-risk chemical facilities.

As Since then, there have been numerous updates, modifications, and date changes to these regulations.

Accordingly, the Department requires all chemical facilities to comply with regulatory requirements as detailed in 6CFR27 (CFATS). The process includes completing a screening process or Top-Screen for potentially dangerous materials, identifying vulnerabilities through a security vulnerability assessment (SVA), and developing a site security plan (SSP).

Through these implementations, the Department will determine whether or not facilities are high-risk. The acceptable layering of measures used to meet risk-based performance standards (RBPS) will vary according to risk-based tiers ranging from tier 1, which contains the highest risk of covered facilities, to tier 4, which contains the lowest risk of covered facilities.

For facilities that are determined to be high-risk, the Department requires each of the facilities to comply with regulatory measures, including developing and implementing an site security plan (SSP), which describes security measures (both physical and procedural).

In order to ensure compliance with the SSP, the Department will conduct inspections and/or audits at each of the tiered facilities. The Department will inspect high-risk facilities at regular intervals with tier-1 facilities being inspected first and more frequently. Inspectors from the Department may also inspect a facility at any time based on new information or security concerns. Depending on particular circumstances, the Department will provide facilities with a minimum of 24 hours advance notice for compliance inspections, unless specific security concerns or exigent circumstances demand immediate attention.

Facilities that have successfully implemented their approved SSPs and have passed an inspection will be considered as compliant with the required performance standards.

The Department of Homeland Security is committed to meeting the letter and spirit of CFATS to enhance and ensure the security of the nation's chemical industry, a vital component of the nation's critical infrastructure. Inspections of high-risk chemical facilities will help the Department ensure compliance and promote the highest security for the people.

New, More Efficient Emergency Response Procedure

The Department of Transportation—PHMSA (Pipeline and Hazardous Material Safety Administration) has issued a final rule, which was posted in the Federal Register on October 19, 2009, with action dates into 2012.

Basically, this rule clarifies the specific method in which emergency contact information must be identified and entered on the transportation documents.

As freight moves along the supply chain, third-party freight providers may need to transpose data from the original hazmat declaration or shipping paper onto another intermediary bill of lading. These intermediary documents may or may not contain the name of the original shipper. This causes delays for the emergency responders in order to properly identify the customer, the material safety data sheets (MSDSs), and the like.

Here is the summary of this final rule: PHMSA is requiring supplemental basic identifying information to be included on shipping papers. The additional information that will be required is the name of the company that has the contract with the emergency response provider or the contract number that is in place between the shipper and the ER provider. Currently, the shipper is only required to identify a 24-hour emergency response number. This has caused much delay in past incidences where the emergency responders would contact the ER provider listed on the documents. The delays begin when the provider has to painstakingly try to identify who "their" client is, and then access the necessary information to assist in the emergency. These delays have the potential of holding life and death in its hands! Sometimes minutes and even seconds count in an emergency. Emergency responders risk their lives to save our lives. When a responder calls the 24-hour contact number on the documentation, the last thing they want to hear is "Which company? Which product? What's the address of the registered party? Please wait while we try to find them in our database!"

This required supplemental information will enable the emergency response information provider to identify the shipper (the company that is registered with the provider) on whose behalf it is accepting responsibility for providing emergency response information in the event of a hazardous materials incident, and obtain additional information about the hazardous material as needed.

General Trade Compliance and Managing International Business

Food Safety Modernization Act (FSMA)

On January 4, 2011, President Obama signed into law the Food Safety Modernization Act (FSMA). This is the first significant piece of legislation to reform our food safety system since 1938, when the Federal Food, Drug and Cosmetic Act (FFDC) became law, giving authority to the Food and Drug Administration (FDA) to oversee the safety of food, drugs, and cosmetics.

This new law directs the FDA to set up a new system of food safety oversight based upon preventing problems within the food chain resulting in illness within the population. Processors of all types of food will now be required to evaluate the hazards in their operations, implement and monitor effective measures to prevent contamination, and have a plan in place to take any corrective actions that are necessary. The FDA currently has prevention-oriented standards in place for seafood, juices, and eggs and the U.S. Department of Agriculture (USDA) has similar standards in place for meat and poultry as well.

For all the safeguards built into the American food system, a breakdown at any point on the farm-to-table spectrum can cause catastrophic harm to the health of consumers and great disruption and economic loss to the food industry. FSMA will address the food system as a whole, the food safety responsibility of all its participants, and strengthen accountability for prevention throughout the entire food system both domestically and internationally.

The FSMA will enable the FDA to have much more effective enforcement tools for ensuring that its plans are adequate and properly implemented and to establish standards for the safe production and harvesting of fruits and vegetables. It gives the FDA the authority to mandate product recalls if it finds a "reasonable probability" that food is contaminated or misbranded. In the past, the FDA had to negotiate with a company for the withdrawal of potentially contaminated food from the market. The FDA will increase the frequency of inspections, have stronger record access authority, and protect whistleblowers who testify, assist, or participate in a proceeding regarding a violation.

Relevance to Importers

The legislation significantly enhances FDA's ability to oversee the millions of food products coming into the United States from other countries each year. Among the improvements is the requirement that importers verify the safety of food from their suppliers and that the FDA block foods from facilities or countries that refuse our inspection. The FDA will also be working more closely with foreign governments and increasing its inspection of foreign food facilities. The FDA's new import tool kit will have a huge impact on food safety, given that an estimated 15 percent of the U.S. food supply is imported, including 60 percent of fresh fruits and vegetables and 80 percent of seafood.

FSMA gives the FDA for the first time a congressional mandate for risk-based inspections of food processing facilities inspected within five years of the law's enactment and no more than every three years thereafter.

This legislation will build off leading practices used by regulators and the private sector, including a greater focus in areas of risk through an analysis of safety hazards, ingredient safety, food defense plans, traceability, recall procedures, and increased import safety.

Companies with facilities subject to FDA jurisdiction should take immediate steps to review and, where necessary, modify their standard operating procedures (SOPs) and policies. As an example, given the FDA's expanded access to business records, companies should have SOPs in place that anticipate which records they may have to turn over and which they may not. Companies also should anticipate now how they need to change their policies and approaches to mandatory recalls.

Historically, whenever any government agency takes steps to increase its role within a process—be it manufacturing, growth, production, or procurement—there is an immediate rise in the enforcement efforts that is noticed at the point of entry processing and final entry review. The increased role of the FDA in ensuring food safety will have an immediate impact on the FDA review and release process. We can be assured that foreign manufacturer registrations and quality affirmations will be reviewed to a more detailed extent, resulting in common areas of noncompliant declarations due to the absence of previous scrutiny. Importers should review the foreign manufacturer's information in greater detail to ensure that all registrations are in place and in good standing with FDA prior to the procurement process being completed. We can expect more documentary reviews, holds, and request for information as a result of this added food safety verification process.

It's important to remember that we will not see an immediate impact of the law at our tables. This new law sets an important public health foundation of increasing food protection. Because of this new law, all of us will be eating safer food than we have in the past. For those involved in importing these products, we need to ensure we have procedures in place to comply.

Trade Regulations: When Disclosing to a Government Agency

You may have read recently that U.S. and foreign companies have been pursued by the U.S. Treasury Department's Office of Foreign Asset Controls, (OFAC). You have probably seen the huge penalties issued by them in settlement of a company's disclosure. Many of the companies that were fined had voluntarily approached the OFAC to disclose these violations. In a voluntary self-disclosure, the company not only has a burden of researching its past business activities, it has to protect files and documents from being lost or destroyed. In such a disclosure the corporation must admit to the violation and work up a plan to assure the OFAC that the violation will not happen again.

Most of the time when a disclosure is being prepared legal counsel takes time to review what is being disclosed and what documents are included in the filing. Remember that a company must reach deep within its operation in order to get every nugget of information to disclose relative to the violation. In some cases a company employee or officer may forget to include a record or a file, which may be inadvertently omitted from the disclosure. In one case, outside counsel advised the client to withhold a document that turned out to be a costly mistake for the company.

In that case, an aircraft company based in Miami paid a $225,000 settlement to OFAC for lying to the government. This is the maximum penalty allowed for lying to OFAC. The company manager was advised by the company counsel to omit a file that was later found in OFAC's investigation. The actual violation involved the company's illegal shipment of an aircraft engine to Iran, and the penalty for the *violation* has not been levied.

Now this same company admitted to OFAC that they were advised by legal counsel to remove that one letter in the file from their submission. They acted on counsel's advice, but OFAC was not in agreement with the reason behind the omission. Since it was an outside party giving this improper advice, OFAC did allow a 10 percent reduction of the penalty.

The moral of this story is to remember that when a violation is found and your company decides to disclose it, you must reach all the way into your records, correspondence, and possibly your outside parties such as customs brokers and forwarders to verify what information they may have to assist in your research and submission of information. And think twice about excluding information, records, or files.

Include others in the process. Don't make this just a single department's responsibility. Keep all of your work confidential, protecting yourself under the legal privilege whenever possible. But make absolutely certain that you have disclosed all violations to the fullest.

And utilize specialized trade legal expertise when called for.

Viewing the Top Government Agencies and Finding Synergies

One of the mainstays of an ever enhancing import/export compliance program is to become familiar with our industry's regulatory agencies within the federal government. A great way to accomplish this effectively is to learn the various acronyms and their meanings, and to understand the responsibilities of each agency as well as their responsibilities.

This is a snapshot of the most important import/export compliance specific agencies and how they interact together to ensure that goods enter and depart the commerce of the United States in the most efficient and secure manner possible.

These agencies include:

- Department of Homeland Security (DHS)
- Bureau of Customs and Border Protection (CBP)
- Bureau of Industry and Security (BIS)
- Office of Foreign Asset Controls (OFAC)
- The Census Bureau
- Food and Drug Administration (FDA)

Department of Homeland Security (DHS)

The most important mission of this Department, formed on the heels of the events of September 11, 2001, is to lead a unified national effort to secure the country and preserve our freedoms. While the department was created to secure our country against those who seek to disrupt the American way of life, DHS's charter also includes preparation for and response to all hazards and disasters.

The DHS *Strategic Plan* serves to focus its mission and sharpen operational effectiveness, particularly in delivering services in support of department-wide initiatives and the other mission goals. The department uses performance measures at all levels to monitor its strategic progress and program success. This process also keeps the department's priorities aligned, linking programs and operations to performance measures, mission goals, resource priorities, and strategic objectives. DHS is explained more fully in Chapter 8.

Bureau of Customs and Border Protection (CBP)

This agency, operating within the Department of Homeland Security, protects our nation's borders from terrorism, human and drug smuggling, illegal migration, and agricultural pests while simultaneously facilitating the flow of legitimate travel and trade. CBP's mission is responsible for the protection of the American people and the national economy, working to secure the nation's borders both at and between the official ports of entry and also to extend our zone of security.

While carrying out its priority anti-terrorism mission, CBP also facilitates the movement of legitimate trade and travelers. CBP screens all travelers entering the United States using a risk-based approach. Automated advance data combined with intelligence and new biometric travel documents are tools that facilitate travel while keeping our borders safe.

Working on conjunction with other agencies, CBP enforces trade and tariff laws. This helps to ensure that industry operates in a fair and competitive trade environment. Such interagency activities include:

- Collecting import duties, taxes and fees.
- Enforcing trade laws; regulating trade practices to collect the appropriate revenue.
- Working with the BIS to maintain export controls.
- Providing the FDA with an electronic notification upon arrival of all imports in order for FDA to coincide its information with those provided within the import documents.
- Working with the USDA to protect U.S. agricultural resources via inspection activities at the ports of entry.

The security expectations of the CBP are detailed in Chapter 14.

Bureau of Industry and Security (BIS)

The main objective of BIS is to protect the security of the United States. This includes its national security, economic security, cyber security, and homeland security.

BIS works with other agencies of the U.S. government, including the National Security Council, DHS, State Department, the Dept of Defense, Dept of Energy and the Intelligence Community, as well as with state and local governments.

The primary focus of BIS is in the area of dual-use export controls. BIS enforces such controls to stem the proliferation of weapons of mass destruction and the means of delivering them, to halt the spread of weapons to terrorists or countries of concern, and to further important U.S. foreign policy objectives. BIS will intercede where there is credible evidence suggesting that the export of a dual-use item threatens U.S. security.

With regard to export control laws in particular, effective enforcement is greatly enhanced by both international cooperation and an effort to harmonize the substance of U.S. laws with those of U.S. principal trading partners.

Office of Foreign Assets Control (OFAC)

The Office of Foreign Assets Control (OFAC) of the Department of Treasury administers and enforces economic and trade sanctions based on U.S. foreign policy and national security goals against targeted foreign countries and regimes, terrorists, international narcotics traffickers, those engaged in activities related to the proliferation of weapons of mass destruction and other threats to the national security, foreign policy, or economy of the United States. OFAC acts under presidential national emergency powers, as well as authority granted by specific legislation, to impose controls on transactions and freeze assets under U.S. jurisdiction. Many of the sanctions are based on United Nations and other international mandates, are multilateral in scope, and involve close cooperation with allied governments.

OFAC is the successor to the Office of Foreign Funds Control (FFC), which was established at the advent of World War II following the German invasion of Norway in 1940. The FFC program was administered by the Secretary of the Treasury throughout the war. The FFC's initial purpose was to prevent Nazi use of the occupied countries' holdings of foreign exchange and securities and to prevent forced repatriation of funds belonging to nationals of those countries. These controls were later extended to protect assets of other invaded countries. After the United States formally entered World War II, the FFC played a leading role in economic warfare against the Axis powers by blocking enemy assets and prohibiting foreign trade and financial transactions.

OFAC itself was formally created in December 1950, following the entry of China into the Korean War, when President Truman declared a national emergency and blocked all Chinese and North Korean assets subject to U.S. jurisdiction.

More detailed information on BIS and OFAC is available in Chapter 10.

Census Bureau

The Census Bureau serves as the leading source of official data regarding the nation's people and economy. The Census Bureau is charged with providing the following:

- Population and Housing Census (every ten years)
- Economic Census—(every 5 years)
- American Community Survey (annually)
- And many other demographic and economic surveys.

The Census Bureau uses this data to determine the distribution of Congressional seats to states, to apportion seats in the U.S. House of Representatives, define legislature districts, school district assignment areas, and other important functional areas of government. The data is also used make decisions about what community services to provide, such as services for the elderly, building new roads and schools, where to locate job training centers, and how to distribute $300 billion in federal funds to local, state, and tribal governments each year.

The Census Bureau also obtains import and export activity information from CBP and BIS for the purpose of reporting to Congress as to our country's success and position in the world's economy. It regulates the reporting of all export shipments from the Unites States, and is the official source of our official import and export statistics.

Food and Drug Administration (FDA)

The FDA is an agency within the Department of Health and Human Services (HHS), and consists of centers and offices throughout the United States.

The FDA is responsible for protecting the public health by assuring the safety, efficacy, and security of human and veterinary drugs, biological products, medical devices, our nation's food supply, cosmetics, and products that emit radiation.

The FDA is also responsible for advancing the public health by helping to speed innovations that make medicines and foods more effective, safer, and more affordable; and helping the public get the accurate, science-based information they need to use medicines and foods to improve their health.

The FDA works closely with CBP, BIS and DHS to insure that all food and drug products entering or leaving the United States meet the guidelines put forth by each of these jurisdictions. These agencies to work together to insure the safe dissemination of all food and drug products.

How Do These Agencies Work Together?

While each of the departments discussed above has their own direct responsibilities, we've mentioned some of the ways these departments coordinate with each other in order to preserve a safe, secure, and efficient process.

Here are some other examples of interagency cooperation:

- CBP and BIS work under the vast DHS umbrella.
- In order to keep goods flowing, CBP and BIS must work with OFAC to insure that only the proper goods are shipped.
- FDA is also intertwined within this process to insure the safe processing and transfer of food and drugs throughout the world.
- All the agencies feed data to the Census Bureau, which uses it to track our position within the world marketplace.

GAO Undercover Operations Show Continued Vulnerability of Domestic Sales Becoming Illegal Export

In June of 2009, the Government Accountability Office (GAO) detailed their findings from an undercover operation they had undertaken to investigate the availability of military technology and other sensitive dual-use items. They found that these items can be easily and legally purchased from manufacturers and distributors within the United States, often for subsequent illegal export. This poses a serious risk to the United States security.

The task at hand for the GAO was received from the subcommittee. The GAO was asked to conduct an undercover operation. The operation would entail the undercover agents to try to buy these types of items from U.S. companies. Then they were to attempt to illegally export these items without being found out.

The GAO hid behind a front company and various false identities to buy these sensitive items, including night-vision scopes, electronic sensors used in IEDs (improvised explosive devices, or roadside bombs), and parts used in guided missiles and military aircraft. These types of items continue to be used against U.S. soldiers in Iraq and Afghanistan. Access to that type of sensitive military technology could give terrorists or foreign governments an advantage in a combat situation against the United States, the report said.

The GAO was able to export without any questions asked to a country that it identified as "a known trans-shipment point for terrorist organizations and foreign governments attempting to acquire sensitive technology," according to the report. In addition, the GAO was also able to export a number of benign versions of these items using the U. S. postal system.

While the items purchased during this operation were subject to export restrictions under the Export Administration Regulations CCL (Commerce Control List) or the Department of State USML (United States Munitions List), they could be legally and easily purchased from manufacturers and distributors here in the United States. In most cases you only had to give a name and credit card, the undercover operation revealed.

The report suggested that restricting domestic sales of dual-use and military items could be the key to preventing the illegal export of such technology. Currently, there are not even legal requirements for the sellers of dual-use or military technology to conduct background checks on prospective domestic customers. The United States, which currently is the leading producer of advanced military and dual-use technology, has become a primary target for illegal procurement efforts launched by terrorists and foreign governments, according to the GAO report. The issue of illegal retransfers came up again just five days after the release of the GAO report because of the sentencing of Traian Bujduveanu, a naturalized U.S. citizen, who was convicted for his role in a conspiracy to illegally export dual-use aircraft parts to Iran and was sentenced to thirty-five months in federal prison for helping to smuggle parts of F-14 fighter jets, Cobra AH-1 attack helicopters, and CH-53A military helicopters.

You can find the GAO report online at http://gao.gov/new.items/d09725t.pdf.

Revisions to Incoterms

The International Chamber of Commerce (ICC) introduced the first version of Incoterms, short for "International Commercial Terms" in 1936. Today, there are thirteen Incoterms currently in use. Incoterms are revised every ten years in order to reflect international trade developments. Incoterms® 2010 was announced in September 2010 and went into effect in January 2011 but implementation will last into 2012, as companies engage the changes and bring these into use in their global supply chains.

Incoterms® rules explain standard terms that are used in contracts for the sale of goods. They are essential tools in international trade that help traders avoid misunderstandings by clarifying the costs, risks, and responsibilities of both the buyers and sellers. Because the rules are developed by experts and practitioners brought together by ICC, they are globally accepted and have become the standard in the setting of international business rules.

These revisions, ICC's first since 2000, aim to adapt changes that have occurred in global trade over the past ten years. According to the ICC website, the reason for the changes include, "the importance of cargo security, the resulting new obligation on traders, developments in container transport and the 2004 revisions of the United States Uniform Commercial Code , which resulted in a deletion of the former U. S. shipment and delivery terms." Incoterms 2010 provides a more user friendly set of terms reflecting up-to-date practices. In a nutshell, here are the changes:

There will be fewer terms with the elimination of four Incoterms®.

Four Incoterms® were dropped:

- DDU Delivered Duty Unpaid
- DEQ Delivered Ex Quay
- DES Delivered Ex Ship
- DAF Delivered at Frontier

Two new rules were introduced. The two new Incoterms for 2010 were:

- DAT Delivered at Terminal
- DAP Delivered at Place

The Incoterms® 2010 is divided into two sections. One set of rules governs any mode of transportation and the second set includes rules for sea and inland waterway transport.

Any Mode of Transport

- CIP Carriage and Insurance Paid
- CPT Carriage Paid To
- DAP Delivered At Place
- DAT Delivered at Terminal
- DDP Delivered Duty Paid
- EXW Ex Works
- FCA Free Carrier

Sea and Inland Waterway Transport Only

- CFR Cost and Freight
- CIF Cost, Insurance and Freight
- FAS Free Alongside Ship
- FOB Free On Board

In addition to these rules, Incoterms® 2010 includes:

- Extensive guidance notes and illustrative graphics to users efficiently choose the right rule for each transaction
- New classification to help choosing the most suitable rule in relation to the mode of transport
- Advice for the use of electronic procedures
- Information on security—related clearances for shipment
- Advice for the use of Incoterms® 2010 in domestic trade

Seminars and webinars on Incoterms 2010 are offered by training organizations such as those listed below (check websites for current schedules or offerings):

The World Academy: www.theworldacademy.com Frank Reynolds: www.iccincoterms2010.com Unz & Co: www.unzco.com

Incoterms® 2010 ICC Official Rules of the Interpretation of Trade Terms can be ordered directly by visiting the iccbooksusa.com website.

Trade Compliance Management Avoids Fines and Penalties

The Commerce Department's Bureau of Industry and Security (BIS) and the Treasury Department's Office of Foreign Assets Control (OFAC) entered into a joint settlement agreement with shipping giant DHL on August 6, 2009, with regard to allegations that DHL unlawfully aided and abetted the illegal exportation of goods to Syria, Iran, and Sudan and failed to comply with record-keeping requirements of the Export Administration Regulations (EAR) and OFAC regulations. DHL had to pay a civil penalty of $9,444,744 and conduct external audits covering exports to Iran, Syria and Sudan from March 2007 through December 2011.

BIS charged that on a number of occasion in the summer of 2004, DHL caused, aided and abetted acts prohibited by EAR when it transported items subject to the EAR from the United States to Syria, and DHL failed to retain air waybills and other export control documents required to be retained under Part 762 of the EAR numerous times between May and November of that year..

OFAC, in turn, charged that DHL violated various OFAC regulations between 2002 and 2006 relating to thousands of shipments to Iran and Sudan. Like DHL's EAR violations, its OFAC violations primarily involve DHL's failure to comply with applicable recordkeeping requirements.

In addition to the monetary penalty, DHL was required to hire an expert on U.S. export controls laws and sanctions regulations for an external audit of DHL transactions to Iran, Sudan and Syria between March 2007 and December 2009. The external auditor conducted annual calendar year audits in 2010 and 2011 to assess DHL's compliance with all EAR and OFAC regulations, including record-keeping requirements.

No company wants to see what happened to DHL happen to them. Following all the guidance this book has to offer will put you way ahead of the issues and give you the best opportunity to avoid the headaches of fines and penalties.

Contracts of Sale

What is the United Nations Convention on Contracts for the International Sale of Goods (CISG)?

The United Nations Convention on Contracts for the International Sale of Goods is an international trade agreement developed by the United Nations Commission on International Trade Law (UNCITRAL) and adopted in 1980 at the Vienna Convention for the International Sale of Goods. It came into force as a multilateral treaty after being ratified by eleven countries. Countries that have ratified the CISG are referred to within the treaty as "Contracting States.'" The objective of the CISG is to eliminate ambiguity caused by different domestic laws concerning the international sales of goods. The laws within the CISG supersede domestic trade laws and apply to contracts between companies located in different countries. The CISG was entered into force in the United States on January 1, 1988 and on June 1, 2010, Albania will enter into force and become the seventy-fourth party to the convention. The CISG now includes most of the major trading nations and provides "gap filling" rules that govern contract formation and sets forth the rights and obligations of the buyer and seller.

One of the main benefits of the CISG is its unified code of rules and regulations, making importing and exporting and other facets of international trade easier. Rather than dealing with the domestic laws for international trade in numerous foreign countries, companies can readily apply CISG, alleviating misinterpretation of domestic law.

When dealing in international trade it is important to understand the CISG because unless the parties to a transaction specifically indicate that it does not apply, the CISG will be the governing law pertaining to all commercial contracts for the sale of goods between parties having their places of business in different countries which have adopted the CISG. For instance, if a company located in New York has a commercial sales agreement with a company located in Japan, and they do not agree to the contrary, the rules and regulations of the CISG will automatically apply. If the parties should wish to be bound by some other law such as the Uniform Commercial Code (UCC) or local Japanese law, they may "opt out" of the CISG by specifying that the other agreed upon law will apply. This allows contracting parties to remain free to specify whatever law or terms they wish to apply to their transaction. It recommended that when "opting out" of the CISG it is stated in the contract in order to avoid any disputes or misunderstandings.

The CISG does not apply to international sales:

- Of goods brought for personal, family or household use, unless the seller at any time before or at the conclusion of the contract, neither knew nor ought to have known that the goods were bought for any such use.
- By auction.
- On execution or otherwise by authority of law.
- Of stocks, shares, investment securities, negotiable instruments, or money.
- Of ships, vessels, hovercraft, or aircraft.
- Of electricity.

Adoption of the CISG by the United States offers important benefits to U. S. companies as the CISG offers accepted substantive rules on which contracting parties, courts, and arbitrators may rely. However, since there are several important distinctions between the CISG and the UCC (to which your legal department is accustomed) that U. S. companies should be aware of in order to protect themselves prior to getting into international contract negotiations. Differences can be seen in areas such as in the specification of price, revocability of offer, and terms of acceptance, just to name a few. It is crucial that you be familiar with the CISG if you are involved in the international sales of goods.

For more information on the UNCISG visit: www.uncitral.org

Considering a Mock Audit in 2012 for Trade Compliance? Here Are the Reasons Why You Should!

If you have the responsibility for import and/or export compliance for your company, you may be considering conducting an in-house self-assessment of your compliance profile, commonly known as a "mock audit." Regulatory agencies such as U.S. Customs and Border Protection and The Bureau of Industry and Security have acknowledged the efforts of self-policing to be essential to any compliance management program. Many companies would rather have a mock audit performed to test their compliance profile as a proactive exercise in compliance management, rather than undergo an import Focused Assessment or export penalty review and then determine compliance deficiencies. Many companies are facing the tasks of determining the most effective means to conduct an in-house assessment. If your company has specific industry expertise, there may be merit to using internal expertise to conduct these audits to identify, analyze, and correct any found compliance deficiencies. But many companies are reviewing the option of having an outside company perform a mock compliance audit of their import/export supply chain. I will outline the benefits of third-party offsite compliance resource assistance that you may find helpful in your compliance decision-making process.

Little can be more painful than CBP or BIS coming in unannounced to perform a real audit. CBP randomly picks companies in various regions of the country to perform customs audits. Sometimes CBP does this through targeting specific industries. Most companies that go through random CBP audits incur fines and penalties. The fines vary in size depending upon the severity of the breach. Ignorance of the rules and regulations is not a mitigating factor in reduction of these fines. In some cases, if the findings are very serious, CBP can temporarily cancel the import and export privileges of a company while they are performing their investigative audit. This suspension can last for months.

For a company with a sizeable import or export business, this can be a major financial hit.

Every company can budget for a mock audit. A qualified independent consulting firm performing a mock audit will "paint a picture" of your current operation and find the "holes" that need repairing. This is accomplished through on-site interviews with all personnel involved in the supply chain, as well as a review of actual import/export transaction files. Some of these holes can be relatively minor issues such as recordkeeping deficiencies, or more serious ones like shipping to denied parties, improper classification, or not applying for export licenses when they are required. A mock audit done by a professional consulting company can mitigate many serious consequences. No company can budget for the potential fines and penalties and loss of import and or export business. Many companies defer these projects in recessionary times, but the government is not curtailing their efforts, so it is important not to curtail yours.

A mock audit can be helpful in developing standard operating procedures (SOPs). The outside consulting firm can identify specific weak areas within a companies import/export supply chain. Implementation of specific SOPs can mitigate and hopefully prevent future problems (i.e., fines/penalties). Just by having compliance SOPs in place (prepared by a company recognized by CBP or BIS as an expert in the field) and being able to present these to CBP or BIS during a random audit may be helpful in reducing the time government auditors stay at your facility. This is an important component of proving to the government you are meeting your requirement for due diligence and reasonable care standards. These SOPs will set in place procedures from the moment an order is placed until is shipped.

Setting up SOPs is only one step in the mock audit process. Once a company has SOPs in place, it needs to focus on training and educating the staff that carries out these SOPs on a daily basis—training them *how* to execute the SOPs, and educating them as to *why* they have been set up in the first place. Part of this training is making employees aware of their personal liability as well as the company's liability to in ensure the compliance bar is being raised to new heights. When shopping for a firm to perform the mock audit, you should be sure the company has a training program as part of the complete package.

It is recommended that the company performing the mock audit be a completely neutral entity. Part of the process of a mock audit is to review all components of the supply chain for compliance issues. This will include the freight forwarders and customs house brokers a company uses. We suggest that you do not hire these entities to perform this review, regardless of how inexpensively they may price their services when they hear you are seeking an outside firm to work on this project—for they may be part of the problem. It also important to inquire into the experience level of the actual consultant who will be on site conducting the interviews and reviewing files by checking his or her resume. You may end up hiring a top-ranked consulting firm, only to find out that the person heading up this project is new to this field, and possibly does not have the experience required to "turn over all stones."

If you are interested in looking for qualified companies to perform a mock audit for you, please contact the Professional Association of Import/Export Compliance Managers at pacman@compliancemaven.com for a listing of companies recommended by industry professionals.

NAFTA Issues for 2012 and Beyond

A NAFTA form is pretty easy to fill out. The back has instructions that tells you how to complete it and explains all the abbreviations—and before you know it, . . . you've knocked out the form. Exporter, producer, importer, tax identification numbers—no problem! Description of goods, six digits of my HTS (for most products)—no problem! Preference criterion: choose your favorite letter—no, no, no, you do have to put the accurate letter there. Producer: answer yes or no. Country of origin: MX, US, CA. Please, my fourteen-year-old can answer this. Net cost: well, now that I'm actually reading the back I guess the value for export would be wrong so I'll just put "NO" in there because I'm not using my Net Cost on my value for export.

If you're a NAFTA pro, you may be laughing. If you're not, are you looking at these responses and thinking "hmmm, there's more to this than I thought"?

The real problem with NAFTA are those cruel paragraphs at the bottom of the form:

I certify the information on this document is true and accurate and assume the responsibility for proving such representations. I understand that I am liable for any false statements or material omissions made on or in connection with this agreement.

I agree to maintain, and present upon request, documentation necessary to support this certificate, and to inform, in writing, all persons to whom the certificate was given of any changes that could affect the accuracy or validity of this certificate.

Wait a minute . . . where did it say anything about my obligations on those easy instructions for completing the NAFTA Certificate?

I certify the information on this document is true and accurate . . . Under NAFTA, there are specific requirements that must be met in order for the product to qualify for NAFTA. It's not enough to say "it's made in the U.S." It needs to qualify under a precise Rule of Origin in order to qualify. That's what the Preference Criterion is all about.

I assume responsibility for proving such representations . . . made on or in connection with this agreement. All criminal, civil or administrative penalties that may be imposed on U. S. importers, exporters, and producers for violations of the Customs and related laws and regulations also apply to U. S. importers, exporters, and producers for violations of the laws and regulations relating to NAFTA.

I agree to maintain, and present upon request, documentation necessary to support this certificate, . . . The recordkeeping requirement for NAFTA in the United States is five years from the date of the NAFTA Certificate. Keep in mind Canada and

Mexico have their own guidelines on recordkeeping, so if you have an affiliate in either of these countries they need to be following the local law.

I agree to inform in writing all persons to whom the certificate was given of any changes that could affect the accuracy or validity of this certificate. If your sourcing changes and your purchasing people are now importing that gasket from China that used to be produced in Ohio, you will have to inform anyone who has been issued a current NAFTA Certificate by your company for that product of the change.

The NAFTA Certificate is a government document. Would you carelessly complete your CBP7501 or AES filing by guessing in the blanks? NAFTA must be understood to be used. More importantly, if your company obtains NAFTA Certificates from its suppliers to be used to make the case for your own NAFTA certifications, you should be reviewing those certifications to ensure they are accurate.

Here are some things you must know about filling out this form. This won't make you a total expert, but it will give you a leg up.

NAFTA Document Fields

Field 1: If you are the exporter, enter your company name, address, and employer identification number. If you are not the exporter, leave this blank.

Field 2: The intent of this to/from listed here is not to use this as a fax cover page nor a dream getaway destination. If the NAFTA Certificate you are preparing is for a one-time shipment, leave this blank. However, many companies opt to have a NAFTA Certificate apply for a defined period of time so the company doesn't have to issue a NAFTA Certificate per shipment. This can be a time saver but as we remember (*I agree to inform in writing all persons to whom the certificate was given of any changes that could affect the accuracy or validity of this certificate*), any changes to a NAFTA Certificate must be brought to the attention of the person to whom the form was provided to and this creates additional recordkeeping and communication responsibilities. The blanket period cannot exceed one year.

Field 3: There are many options available for this field. If your company is the producer and exporter you can indicate your company name again or just write "same." If you are the producer but not the exporter, indicate your company name. If you are not the producer and wish to keep the producer information confidential you may indicate "available to Customs upon request."

Field 4: If you know the importer information, complete this with the importer's name, address, and tax identification number. If you are preparing this form to use for many customers, you may indicate "various."

Field 5: A brief description should be entered. This description should be a bit more detailed than "part #123." "Stainless steel screws" or "Pencil sharpeners" are certainly more specific and they give Customs an indication that your good might actually be a real item.

Field 6: Indicate the harmonized tariff number to six digits. It's important to keep in mind though that under NAFTA, there are specific rules of origin that require eight digits, which means you have to indicate the eight digit number: "8702.1060 (other motor vehicles)" is a good example of this.

Field 7: The Preference criterion is the crux of the NAFTA Certificate, the sun of our solar system, the core of the . . . okay you get it. This is the basis of the whole NAFTA. For each item we have listed on the Certificate we are now going to have to provide how we made our determination in order to be entitled to preferential tariff treatment.

Preference Criteria A: "wholly obtained or produced entirely" in one or more NAFTA territories. This means NO FOREIGN PARTS! There are few manufactured items that contain no foreign parts so be careful when receiving certificates from suppliers that indicate "A" and double-check with them because Customs may be double-checking you. NAFTA specifically lists examples of wholly originating goods: live animals, born and raised in NAFTA territory; fish caught by a registered flag vessel of a NAFTA territory; mined minerals and space rocks. Yes, I know it's weird. They threw that into the NAFTA to make sure the person reading it is still awake.

Preference Criterion B: "tariff change and regional value content." According to NAFTA, "the good is produced entirely in the territory of one or more of the NAFTA countries and satisfies the specific rule of origin that applies to its tariff classification. The rule may include a tariff classification change, regional value content requirement or a combination thereof." Piece of cake, right?

Speaking of cakes . . . let's talk about fishcakes. Yes, like Mrs. Paul's fishcakes (HTS #1604.20.2000). The fishcakes were made from fresh haddock imported from Scandinavia (HTS #0302.62.0000). We compliance professionals have heard of substantial transformation and possibly even common sense. Well, it's not enough to judge NAFTA without the specific Rule of Origin. So I now look up the Rule of Origin for my product, the fish cake. The rule notes: "A change to heading 1601 through 1605 from any other chapter." Well, my fresh fish falls under chapter 3 and my fishcakes are under chapter 16 so I qualify for NAFTA under Preference Criterion B because I meet the specific Rule of Origin.

Let's throw in a "what if" here. What if I imported the fishcakes and am bringing them into the United States to throw a tomato on top of them. I'm jazzing these up to serve them to Chef Ramsey up in Canada. The tomatoes are from a farm on Long Island (btw: NAFTA Preference Criterion A) but those fishcakes are from Scandinavia. Am I going to qualify for NAFTA under Preference Criterion B? Did I meet the applicable tariff change "from any other chapter" I started in chapter 16 and ended there. No can do.

That example demonstrated tariff change but what is the regional value content and what can be included in regional value content? I'm glad you asked (if you were considering getting a cup of coffee, now would be a good time).

There are two methods of determining regional value content: *transaction value* method and *net cost* method. The net cost method must be used if there is no transaction value or the transaction value is not acceptable.

You must add up the costs involved in making the product. Some costs will be considered originating and some will be excluded. A percentage of the costs is the regional value content. Remember your valuation concepts? Regional value content includes: direct materials, indirect materials, direct labor and overhead.

Direct materials: components physically incorporated into the finished item

Indirect materials: materials used in production of the item but not physically incorporated (for example, safety glasses and gloves worn by employees in manufacturing the item)

Direct labor: salaries of employees directly involved in the production

Direct overhead: overhead costs directly associated with production of those items (for example, electricity)

Once you have determined the appropriate numbers, we plug them into the formulas below. Yes, that's right we're talking formulas and mathematics.

Transaction Value Method

$$\text{Regional Value Content} = \frac{TV - VNM}{TV} \times 100$$

Net Cost Method

$$\text{Regional Value Content} = \frac{NC - VNM}{NC} \times 100$$

Legend

TV: Transaction Value
VNM: Value of Non-originating Material
NC: Net cost

Upon reading the NAFTA rule of origin, you will know the percentage you need to meet in order to qualify. If you meet the percentage for your product, you have qualified and can proudly enter a "B" in Field 7.

We now arrive at **Preference Criterion C.:** "The good is produced entirely in the territory of one or more of the NAFTA countries exclusively from originating materials. Under this criterion, one or more of the materials may not fall within the definition of wholly produced or obtained." While C sounds a lot like A, what the rule says is that if you have an item that was foreign made and that item went through a process that caused it to now be a NAFTA item, you can qualify that product for NAFTA under Preference Criteria C.

For example, if my plant in Mexico imports raw cow skin from Argentina and that cow skin is tanned and manufactured into leather strips, it went through a process in Mexico that qualified as "originating" in Mexico even though the cow skin originally came from Argentina. Now when my plant ships those leather strips to the United States to produce belts, those strips qualify for NAFTA under Preference Criterion C.

Suppose my plant in Cleveland manufactures steel shelving out of steel imported from Japan. The steel is formed into shelving parts in Cleveland, and the shelves are built in Cleveland as well. The parts originate under the applicable tariff shift and regional value content rule. If there are no non-originating materials, the shelves will be originating under Preference Criterion C.

If your company manufactures a product that has 25 different components purchased from different suppliers then your company would have to get a NAFTA certificate from each supplier to qualify your final product under Preference Criterion C. If you are unable to obtain documented proof on each component and raw material, don't claim Preference Criterion C.

Here we have reviewed NAFTA requirements: the NAFTA determination process, preference criterion, recordkeeping, and managing NAFTA compliance. The employee signing the NAFTA Certificate must be knowledgeable, responsible, and have the authority to commit the exporter to the information being submitted on the NAFTA Certificate. Companies must recognize their employees require training to properly complete the NAFTA Certificate and fully understand the parameters and limitations of the information a company has on file for finished goods, parts and components as it pertains to the NAFTA Certificate.

Over the past few months, we have been seeing an increase in both requests for information and NAFTA verification questionnaires. Companies must remain diligent in completing the NAFTA Certificate. At the end of the day, completing a NAFTA Certificate is voluntary. Don't volunteer to complete the form if you can't back up your statement

Freight and Logistics

Shipping to the European Union?

The 27 member countries of the European Union implemented Regulation 1875 on 1/1/2011, with the goal of increasing cargo security.

This new regulation states that for any type of cargo bound from a foreign country to any of the member countries, well as from the Mediterranean and the Middle East, and for all cargo that moves via those ports, an Entry Summary Declaration (ENS) needs to be filed with EU customs twenty-four hours prior to vessel departure.

This rule also affects cargo being transshipped in Europe to other destinations, whether the cargo is off-loaded or remains on board the vessel.

The ENS is the responsibility of the ocean carrier, based on information received on the master bill of lading.

The declaration must contain at least four digits of the H.S. code; however it is recommended that the full six digits be declared to avoid possible additional scrutiny and misinterpretation of cargo description by European customs. In order to comply, carriers will now require the six-digit H.S code to avoid such misinterpretations on cargo descriptions and possible cargo holds, which might force the carriers to roll the cargo to a later vessel. Furthermore, carriers will need this information at the time the AES is being filed with the Census Bureau.

General descriptions of commodities can no longer be accepted. Here are a few examples of not acceptable descriptions vs. acceptable:

Not Acceptable	Acceptable
Agricultural products	Oranges, fish, rice, bread
Auto parts	Automobile brakes, windshield glass for automobiles
Chemicals, hazardous	Actual chemical name (not brand name)
Machinery	Metalworking machinery, cigarette- making machinery, sewing machines, printing machines
Sanitary goods	Towels, buckets, detergents, toothbrushes
Tools	Hand Tools, electric tools

Ocean carriers have made it very clear that not complying with Regulation 1875 will result in the containers not being loaded onto vessels. As of this writing, neither specific penalties and or violations from the European Union, nor a return message of "do not load" instructions, have been set forth.

In the event a bill of lading needs to be corrected this must be done 48 hours prior to a vessel's arrival at the first port of call. Special permission of the ocean carrier must be obtained. Corrections fees might be applied by the ocean carrier, based on a per bill of lading correction.

Air carriers, too, are affected by this rule and must file four hours prior to landing at any European Union airport, and for departures for flights lasting less than four hours.

Cutoff times for freight and documentation will need to be pushed back in order to comply with this new rule.

U.S. Foreign-Trade Zones Support Import Compliance, Cargo Security and Lean Logistics Corporate Initiatives

The Rockefeller Group is a great source for information on Foreign Trade Zones (The Rockefeller Group, www.rgftz.com)

The job of a trade compliance manager is often a thankless role, compounded by current challenges in a strained economy of getting companies to invest in initiatives such as compliance and cargo security. If there appears to be no tangible positive impact to the bottom line, the threat of fines, penalties and delays (the frequent tools of compliance managers) find little favor or are put off in favor of ever existent more urgent priorities.

Foreign-trade zones ("FTZs") offer a creative approach to the problem by saving the company money while integrating trade compliance into business operations and supporting streamlined international supply chains.

There are many ways to save money through use of FTZs and, thanks to some new initiatives by the U.S. Foreign-Trade Zones Board, getting a FTZ can be faster and less costly than in the past. For companies engaged in site selection for a new facility, there are many existing FTZ locations in key industrial markets for consideration.

In terms of FTZ trends, liberalization of trade in certain industries such as the textile quota phase-out have opened up new opportunities to industry sectors that are associated with relatively high import duties and traditionally have not been able to take full advantage of FTZs.

The first step is to quantify the opportunity. Saving money in a FTZ involves duty deferral, reduction, and/or elimination. Instead of paying import duty when a shipment arrives and clears a U. S. port of entry, duty payment is deferred until the merchandise is withdrawn from the zone for consumption in the United States.

In a distribution environment, merchandise from overseas may be deconsolidated and inspected and in some cases repairs, repackaging, labeling, and marking may be performed in the FTZ to prepare the goods for final sale.

Many companies choose to use the FTZ program to support a location in the United States as a global regional hub, supplying the U.S. market as well as other smaller markets in the broader region. For products exported out of the FTZ, import duty is eliminated entirely, replacing administratively burdensome and costly drawback programs or money simply left on the table due to lack of coordination between import and export transactions. Companies also eliminate duty in FTZs by creating an interim inspection point where goods determined to be unsalable are either returned to the vendor prior to Customs entry or destroyed in the FTZ.

For those companies that manufacture, assemble, process, and even kit in a FTZ, duties may be further reduced. With proper authorization from the U.S. Foreign-Trade Zones Board, importers may elect to pay duty at the lower rate of a finished good when applicable as compared to the higher rate of imported components. FTZs encourage value added activity in the United States by equalizing the duty treatment that foreign producers receive when importing finished goods from abroad. While FTZ users may qualify for a lower duty rate, the foreign value remains the same because importers do not have to add the value of any U.S. labor or domestic inputs applied in the FTZ.

In addition to duty savings, FTZ usage as part of an integrated supply chain strategy can result in lower inventory levels and expedited movement of goods to and from the zone. Direct delivery provides for imported shipments to move in bond directly from the port of unlading to a U.S. manufacturing or distribution facility. By not undertaking Customs entry at the time of arrival, certain types of delays associated with entry documentation reviews can be eliminated—although all advance manifest data requirements still apply and all merchandise is subject to cargo security reviews.

Outbound, FTZ users may qualify for weekly entry procedures allowing for one weekly entry summary for all goods shipped from the FTZ over a seven-day period. For high volume, 24/7 operations, weekly entry equates to flexible and just in time delivery schedules to customers as well as fewer Customs entries. Delaying and reducing the number of Customs entries can reduce administrative savings in the form of Customs broker filing fees and merchandise processing fees. By filing Customs entries after goods have been physically received, verified, and shipped, importers find that FTZs support their Customs compliance efforts by allowing for more accurate Customs reporting and reduced post-entry adjustments and amendments.

Companies can also position themselves to realize FTZ benefits throughout the supply chain for inventory moves between facilities using zone-to-zone transfers. Transfer of title can be performed in a FTZ, providing flexibility in support of vendor-managed inventory strategies. For new or expanded capital investments in the United States, certain FTZ benefits also apply to imported production equipment for use in the zone. Given the high value and extended time frame for shipping, assembly and testing of production equipment associated duty benefits can be significant.

Some of the best news about FTZs for importers is that FTZs are flexible and operationally feasible. For most companies, implementation of a FTZ means little or no operational change. For example, foreign and domestic merchandise can be commingled so products can continue to be stored by SKU if recordkeeping and reporting processes support product identities. Recordkeeping approaches such as First-In, First-Out by SKU optimize deferral savings and keep floor operations efficient.

FTZs are secure areas requiring physical security as well as access and inventory controls. Most modern operations have the necessary security already in place as part of Customs-Trade Partnership Against Terrorism (C-TPAT) processes or to protect employees and merchandise. As such, FTZs complement and support secure supply chains. Participants in C-TPAT should know that U.S. Customs and Border Protection recognizes use of U.S. FTZs as a C-TPAT best practice.

For trade compliance managers looking for a carrot instead of a stick to get corporate and operations personnel on board, FTZs may provide a win-win.

Third-Party Logistics; Lessons Learned in 2011/12

The operational and regulatory logistics and compliance requirements that international trade participants have to meet continue to grow in complexity. Many importers and exporters realized that their organizations lacked the internal expertise to meet and manage these requirements. The best practice concept of outsourcing to a third-party logistics (3PL) provider to bring external expertise in house has proved a very sound decision for many international trade importers and exporters. The decision to seek the services of an industry expert as either an on-site or off-site third-party service provider has resulted in more effective management of the international supply chain related to compliance and security management.

There have also been instances in which the outsourcing relationships between

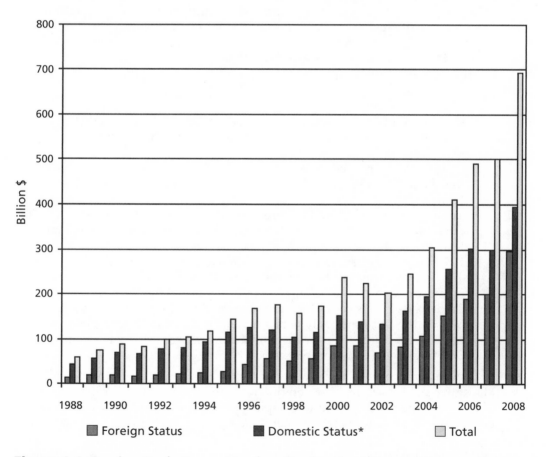

Figure 1-1. Foreign-Trade Zones: Merchandise Received (General-Purpose Zones and Subzones) 1988–2008.

*"Domestic status merchandise" includes both domestic-origin items and foreign-origin items that have been entered for consumption (duty-paid) prior to FTZ admission.

importers and exporters have not gone so well. It is important to understand and learn from the failures of industry partners so as not to repeat the same mistakes in your own profiles. Understanding past efforts of international trade participants will provide learning curve objectives in the development of a successful action plan for those companies who are considering or are in the current operations of a 3PL service relationship.

The five reasons why most 3PL relationships were unsuccessful are as follows:

1. There was a lack of cultural fit of the 3PL personnel into the trade participant's organization.
2. There was a lack of clear deliverables established in the original agreement for the 3PL service provider.
3. The 3PL service provider did not have the automated tools at an operational level to compliment the trade practices of the importers and exporters.
4. The 3PL service provider did not perform to the level of expectation of the trade participant.

The 3PL service provider was too pushy in offering its own operational service solutions, which turned out not to be in the best interest of the client as a result of lack of service or non-competitive pricing. As importers and exporters, international trade participants can consider the above points lessons learned related to oursourced 3PL service provider services. It is recommended that these points be reviewed by your international supply chain team to ensure that your current and future business relationships can be enhanced by avoiding these circumstances.

Best Practice Tools for Outsourced 3PL Success

1. Conduct a full review and diligent process of the 3PL personnel that will be assigned to your account to ensure that there will be a cultural fit to your organization.
2. Trade participants should ensure that all 3PL service proposals clearly outline the deliverables of the 3PL relationship with clear and defined responsibilities.
3. Trade participants should ensure that all 3PL service providers who offer operations or compliance assistance have automated tools at the operational level that will have an immediate positive impact on the participant's ability to manage logistics and to comply with regulatory requirements.
4. Trade participants should incorporate a 3PL performance review on a periodic basis to measure the ongoing performance of the 3PL services.
5. Trade participants should offer an option of bid for service solutions to the 3PL on the basis that only competitive pricing and service options will be considered. Failure to provide consistency in these areas will disqualify the 3PL from the bidding process.

Good management of any process proves to be a best practice tool for success. Managing a 3PL relationship is no different, and requires proactive assessments of not only who is best suited to complete the tasks but also what is required to best complete the tasks. Sometimes, it is also good to know what not to do.

International Logistics: How Can a Shipper Utilize a Transportation Provider (Forwarder and Broker) to Become Trade Compliant

Doing business internationally has become a difficult task in today's complex and ever-changing world. Once recognized only by large multinationals and defense manufacturers, trade compliance is now a mandate for each importer and exporter in this global economy . It is imperative for every business and individual involved in doing business globally; in fact, compliance is now a major factor in maintaining a competitive edge.

Importers and exporters alike have a duty to be trade compliant in order to avoid violations of federal agencies' regulations. Transgressions may result in audits, penalties, fines, seizure of cargo or assets, and revoked privileges as an exporter.

If any of these questions were answered no, you would be considered noncompliant.

A good, reliable, and compliant freight forwarder and customs house broker will be able to assist you in correcting any of the questions you may have answered no to. In addition, they can assist you with other valuable information

Take this quick self-assessment test to see where your company stands with compliance.

A   Does my company have a written Trade Compliance Policy Statement, which was issued by our most senior executive? ☐ yes   ☐ no

B   Does my company have a formal Trade Compliance Department, "Empowered Official," or Designated Trade Compliance Officer? ☐ yes   ☐ no

C   Have our employees been involved in the processing of international transactions and/or completed current import and/or export compliance training (and updates) within the last six months? ☐ yes   ☐ no

D   Has my company properly classified all of its export products with appropriate Export Control Classification Numbers (ECCN), U.S. Munitions List (USML), dual-use and such categories, or import commodities with appropriate Harmonized Tariff Schedule (HTS) numbers? ☐ yes   ☐ no

E   Do our employees that are involved with any export transactions, including in the sales process, check all foreign parties (including banks, freight forwarders, etc.) against the Bureau of Industry and Security's recommended "Lists to Check" (e.g., Denied Persons, Specially Designated Nationals, etc.)? ☐ yes   ☐ no

F   Does my company keep documented import and/or export transactions for compliance and internal audit procedures, and are we aware of what paperwork that involves and for how long we must keep it available? ☐ yes   ☐ no

to ensure that you are fully compliant, thus avoiding a myriad of possible penalties.

What are the qualities of a good, reliable, and compliant freight forwarder or customs house broker? Here are a few questions that you might want to ask your present freight forwarder/customs house broker:

1. How many years of experience in the industry do their operations personnel have?
2. Is there a system in place to monitor quality control and take corrective measures?
3. Have they formalized internal SOPs (standard operating procedures) for dealing with compliance in their operation?
4. Do they have mandatory in-house education and training for their operations personnel?
5. What type of technology (if any) are they using to screen the "denied party lists"

If they don't have long years of experience, or if they answer no to questions 2, 3, and 4, you may want to reconsider your relationship with them.

My experience over the years has shown that while many companies believe they are trade compliant, many times a deeper dive into processes and a mock audit reveals that exporters and importers are, in fact, not compliant or are lacking full compliance.

Utilizing a transportation provider, freight forwarder, or customs house broker with expertise in this important area can be a valuable tool. These issues need to be taken into consideration, in addition to the fees they charge.

Value-added is always a better option than choosing the least expensive!

H.R. 2355: Making Opportunities Via Efficient and More Effective National Transportation Act of 2009

H.R. 2355 is a bill that has been introduced to the House of Representatives.

The short title of this bill is the "MOVEMENT Act of 2009". The objective of the bill is "to establish a National Goods Movement Improvement Fund to provide funding for infrastructure projects that will improve the movement of goods, mitigate environmental damage caused by the movement of goods, and enhance the security of transported goods."

While there are many benefits to the supply chain as a whole, such as decreased damage to cargo in transit, more effective security measures, more cost-effective and efficient infrastructure of the transportation system, after reviewing the bill I had one very pertinent and all too common question: How will these measures be paid for?

The issue of funding is certainly one big pitfall of this bill. If this bill passes, the current Harbor Maintenance Fee (HMF) would more than triple. The HMF is a tax imposed on imports via ocean to the United States and went into effect in 1987. The funds are intended for upkeep of the U.S. ports and harbors.

The current HMF is 0.125 percent of the value of the commercial cargo that is entering the seaport. The bill proposes to increase this amount to 0.4375 percent. That is a staggering 0.3125 percent increase. It is estimated that more than 70 percent of the fees collected would be used by the Department of Transportation for the infrastructure improvement processes.

Be careful to note that if goods arrive by sea to a foreign port, this increase will still apply. For example, goods arrive into port of Montreal. The goods move in-bond via truck into the United States from Canada. This entry would be subject to the HMF. However, to keep consistent with the goal of NAFTA, NAFTA shipments would not be subject to the HMF if the goods *originate* in Canada or Mexico.

If this bill passes, the cost increase to the import supply chain can become dramatic and budgeting adjustments may be in order, so keep your eyes and ears open as this bill progresses through the legislative system. You can direct questions or concerns to industry action groups or your Congressman or Congresswoman.

A copy of the actual bill can be found at the following web link: http://frweb gate.access.gpo.gov/cgi-bin/getdoc.cgi?dbname=111_cong_bills&docid=f:h2355 ih.txt.pdf

President Obama's Export Initiative

In January 2011 President Obama announced an Export Initative Program aimed at reducing export controls. These changes—in what we control, how we control it, how we enforce those controls and how we manage our controls—will help strengthen our national security by focusing our efforts on controlling the most critical products and technologies and by enhancing the competitiveness of key U.S. manufacturing and technology sectors.

In August 2010 President Obama directed a broad-based interagency review of the U.S. export control system with the goal of strengthening national security and the competitiveness of key U.S. manufacturing and technology sectors by focusing on current threats and adapting to the changing economic and technological landscape. The review determined that the current export control system is overly complicated, contains too many redundancies, and, in trying to protect too much, diminishes our ability to focus our efforts on the most critical national security priorities:

- The current system operates under two different control lists with fundamentally different approaches to defining controlled products, administered by two different departments. This has caused significant ambiguity, confusion and jurisdictional disputes, delaying clear license determinations for months and, in some cases, years;
- There are three different primary licensing agencies, each applying their own policies. None sees the others' licenses, and each operates under unique procedures and definitions, leading to gaps in the system and disparate licensing requirements for nearly identical products;
- A multitude of agencies with overlapping and duplicative authorities currently enforce our export controls, creating redundancies and jeopardizing each other's cases; and
- All these agencies operate on a number of separate information technology (IT) systems, none of which is accessible to other licensing or enforcement agencies or easily compatible with the other systems, resulting in the U.S. government not having the capability of knowing what it has approved for export and, more significantly, what it has denied.

The Control Lists

Under the approach outlined by President Obama, agencies will apply new criteria for determining what items need to be controlled and a common set of policies for determining when an export license is required. The control list criteria are based on transparent rules, which will reduce the uncertainty faced by our Allies, U.S. industry and its foreign partners, and will allow the government to erect higher walls around the most sensitive items in order to enhance national security.

Agencies will apply the criteria and revise the lists of munitions and dual-use items that are controlled for export so that:

- They are "tiered" to distinguish the types of items that should be subject to stricter or more permissive levels of control for different destinations, end-uses, and end-users.
- They create a "bright line" between the two current control lists to clarify jurisdictional determinations and reduce government and industry uncertainty about whether particular items are subject to the control of the State Department or the Commerce Department.
- They are structurally aligned so that they potentially can be combined into a single list of controlled items.

To accomplish these tasks, both the U.S. Munitions List and the Commerce Control List need to be fully structured as "positive lists." A "positive list" is a list that describes controlled items using objective criteria (e.g., technical parameters such as horsepower or microns) rather than broad, open-ended, subjective, catch-all, or design intent-based criteria. Doing this will end most, if not all, jurisdictional disputes and ambiguities that have come to define our current system.

Applying the criteria, the existing two lists will be split into three tiers:

- Items in the highest tier are those that provide a critical military or intelligence advantage to the United States and are available almost exclusively from the United States, or items that are a weapon of mass destruction.
- Items in the middle tier are those that provide a substantial military or intelligence advantage to the United States and are available almost exclusively from our multilateral partners and Allies.
- Items in the lowest tier are those that provide a significant military or intelligence advantage but are available more broadly.

This flexible construct will improve the nation's national security and permit the government to adjust controls in a timely manner over a product's life cycle in order to keep lists targeted and up-to-date based on the maturity and sensitivity of an item.

Licensing Policies

Once a controlled item is placed into a tier, a corresponding licensing policy will be assigned to it to focus agency reviews on the most sensitive items:

- A license will generally be required for items in the highest tier to all destinations. Many of the items in the second tier will be authorized for export to multilateral partners and Allies under license exemptions or general authorizations. For less sensitive items, a license will not be required more broadly.

- For items authorized to be exported without licenses, there will be new controls imposed on the reexport of those items to prevent their diversion to unauthorized destinations.
- At the same time, the U. S. government will continue our sanctions programs directed toward specific countries, such as Iran and Cuba.

The restructuring of the control lists and the harmonized licensing policies based on the tier of control will revolutionize our current control system. The preliminary results of deploying this new system highlight this fact.

- Technical experts across the government have completed the overhaul of one category of controls on the U.S. Munitions List and the corresponding entries on the Commerce Control List and have restructured USML Category VII (Tanks and Military Vehicles) into a positive, tiered list.
- The results are significant. Our preliminary analysis is that about 74 percent of the 12,000 items we licensed last year in this Munitions List category will either be moved to the Commerce Control List or will be decontrolled altogether.
- Our preliminary estimate is that about 32 percent of the total may be decontrolled altogether. Of the 26 percent of items that remain on the Munitions List, none were found to be in the highest tier of control, about 18 percent are in the middle tier, and the remaining 8 percent in the lowest tier.

Under the current system, whether a product requires a license depends on which list it falls. The same product may be subject to two significantly different licensing requirements, depending on how it is categorized.

- Examples include brake pads for the M1A1 tank. These brake pads are virtually identical to brake pads for fire trucks but the tank brake pads require a license to be exported to any country around the world, while the fire truck brake pads can be exported to virtually all countries without a license. Still, under our current system, we devote the same resources to protecting the brake pad as we do to protecting the M1A1 tank itself.

Restructuring the control lists and applying the same licensing policies across the government will eliminate these anomalies and allow us to focus our resources on protecting the items and technologies most critical to our national security.

Export Enforcement

Agencies will focus and strengthen our enforcement efforts, including by building higher walls around the most sensitive items. There will be additional end-use assurances against diversion from foreign consignees, increased outreach and on-site visits domestically and abroad, and enhanced compliance and enforcement.

- The President signed an executive order establishing an Export Enforcement Coordination Center that will coordinate and strengthen the U. S. government's enforcement efforts—and eliminate gaps and duplication—across all relevant departments and agencies.

Information Technology Systems

Finally, the U. S. government is transitioning to a single information technology (IT) system to administer its export control system. The Departments of State and Defense are currently being linked to the same IT system and the Department of Commerce will integrate into this system by next year. All relevant departments and agencies will have access to the system. These improvements will create efficiencies within the U. S. government for reviewing applications and ensure that decisions are fully informed. It will also make it easier for exporters seeking licenses and for enforcement authorities to see what actions have been taken.

The Administration's goal is to begin issuing proposed revisions to the control lists and licensing policies later this year. These changes, along with enhancements to enforcement capabilities and information technology systems, will create an export control system that is more effective, transparent and predictable—one that enhances U. S. national security, improves the functioning of the government, and maintains the competitiveness of critical manufacturing and technology sectors.

As we implement these steps, the Administration will continue to work with Congress and the export control community, including on the necessary authorities to consolidate these activities under a single licensing agency and single export enforcement coordination agency.

Technology: Protecting Confidential System Information and Data

Is your company at risk with data getting to the wrong people? Every organization has confidential information that they cannot afford to compromise. Today's business environment, being highly competitive, intensifies the vulnerability and risk. With layoffs and possible disgruntled employees, global operations, and outsourcing projects, your vulnerability spreads. Increasingly popular "mobile" tools for accessing and distributing information, such as the Internet, email and mobile computing devices, increase the risk. The protection of confidential data on laptops is a top priority for both corporations and government agencies today. The impact of stolen or missing laptops is not merely about losing money. It's about losing the unsecured customer data and intellectual property stored on the computers, which can result in the loss of millions of dollars from compliance fines, the costs of notifying customers, not to mention loss of competitive advantage and damage to your brand.

Information vulnerability and risk come from both malicious and unintentional disclosures by employees and partners; unintentional disclosures are usually the larger problem. Reducing these risks and vulnerabilities is now both a business imperative and a legal mandate as recent regulations impose obligations on organizations to protect certain types of information.

Global corporations and government organizations require more than network security and access control to guard their confidential data. They must protect the information itself, inform the behavior of those carrying the information, have visibility regarding where their confidential data resides on their network, have influence over where that data is going, and implement a policy for managing it. A strategy that balances the organization's legal and business needs to protect information with the competing interests to share it is vital.

Eight Best Practice Strategies for Protecting Your Information

1. Set up a team from various departments to evaluate and monitor your SOP.
2. Asses all risks.
3. Identify and classify confidential information.
4. Develop information protection policies and procedures.
5. Deploy technologies that enable policy compliance and enforcement.
6. Conduct data audits so that employees and other stakeholders are held accountable.
7. Integrate information protection practices into all your business processes.
8. Communicate and educate all your employees and other stakeholders to create a compliance culture.

Recommended Steps to Information Protection Strategy Best Practices

- Identify which information should be protected.
- Locate confidential data on the network.
- Distinguish types of confidential information and apply classification(s).
- Determine perceived risks and severity of information loss and develop SOPs to mitigate the risks.
- Identify existing information protection policies, procedures, and practices.
- Determine who has access.
- Demonstrate the flow of information internally.
- Provide evidence of information being sent by and to unauthorized users.
- Identify business processes that may cause information loss.
- Document at-risk confidential data.
- Quantify risk of noncompliance.
- Provide a record of information flow from inside the network to outside the network.
- Research software that creates automated policy builders. They create policies to take advantage of software that contribute to policy compliance and enforcement. These software tools:
  - Protect data wherever it is stored or used.
  - Discover and protect confidential information exposed on file servers, databases, Microsoft SharePoint, Lotus Notes, web servers, Microsoft Exchange, end-user laptops and desktops, and other data repositories.
  - Discover and inventory confidential data stored on laptops and desktops and data repositories.

A cross-functional information protection team works most effectively to synthesize the results of the risk assessment, management survey, and software risk assessment tools. The team typically consists of representatives from Legal, IT and Corporate Security, with involvement from representatives of business units, such as Research and Development, Marketing and Customer Engineering, and representatives from Compliance, Human Resources, Corporate Communications, Audit, Competitive Intelligence, or Risk Management, among others, depending on the contribution that they can make to the priorities of the information protection strategy.

It is not sufficient to rely on software technology to prevent information loss.

An employee who does not respect and protect information will likely put it at risk by sharing it in hard copy, verbally, or in some other manner, even if the technology to prevent unauthorized electronic transmissions is in place. The function of the cross-functional, interdisciplinary team is to ensure the effectiveness of the organization's information.

Section One

The Global Supply Chain

2

Purchasing Management Skill Sets in Foreign Markets

This chapter provides an overview of the skill sets that any supply chain executive would benefit from in any aspect of their import or export activity. However, our focus in this chapter is a review of the skill sets particularly useful to the purchaser who is sourcing goods and material from overseas suppliers.

Purchasing from Foreign Sources

Purchasing managers must look at three issues in determining which overseas suppliers to buy from: costs, specifications, and scheduling.

Costs

There can be quite a bottom-line saving when you purchase product from a supplier located in a country with cheap labor costs, deregulated Occupational Safety and Health Administration (OSHA)-type controls, fewer environmental issues, etc.

An analysis of the "true cost" or "landed cost" will assist in determining this cost issue. One must measure the total of all the incremental costs to then view the final landed cost in determining ultimate supplier options. This analysis requires an experienced eye and tenure in operations, logistics, and negotiation management.

LANDED COST COMPONENTS

- Quoting
- Documentation
- Handling
- Inland freight
- Export clearance
- International freight
- Import costs: license, registrations
- Import clearance
- Duty, taxes, etc.
- Warehousing

- Inland freight and on-forwarding
- Possible repacking, remarking, or relabeling
- Possible further processing, refinements, or manufacturing

The experienced purchasing manager has to evaluate all these parameters to make an intelligent decision in where to source product from.

Meeting Product Specifications

This parameter is relevant no matter where the goods originate. One only need to be sensitive to the differences in language, culture, legal, design metrics, etc. when comparing "apples to apples."

Prior to the 1980s foreign sourcing was always considered shabby. But the influence of western engineering, quality control, and technology on foreign manufacturing in the last thirty years has significantly brought up their capability. As we approach 2012, in some product lines, such as certain consumer products, communication and broadcast equipment, and high-end automobiles, foreign suppliers have proven very capable.

If you are venturing into product lines in which the overseas supplier has little experience, the obvious initiative of being more diligent and exercising greater scrutiny brings on new meaning.

Meeting Delivery Schedules

I witness many importers frustrated when purchasing from foreign suppliers who continually miss shipping deadlines and delivery schedules. It is critical to bring this into the overall formula in evaluating an overseas source, as missing deadlines could prove to have deadly consequences to customer, inventory, or manufacturing schedules. If they can't deliver on time, then "cheap" loses its value.

Importers who have "just in time" inventory controls need to be even more on top of the inbound supply chain and more proactive in the face of potential delays or work flow stoppage. For those importers who hold extra inventory, delays from overseas sources have much less effect.

So cost, specifications, and delivery capabilities are the key governing factors in determining overseas supply options. I know some import purchasing managers who manage all three concerns in a manner that avoids pitfalls and leverages opportunities.

Detail, Detail, and More Detail

Purchasing managers must pay attention to a lot of detail in making sure their inbound supply chains are managed cost-effectively and are competitive. (See Figure 2-1.)

> *In addition, the importer must determine the duties and taxes applicable for an import from that particular country, to analyze the "landed cost," which will allow them to determine the competitiveness of that sourcing option.*

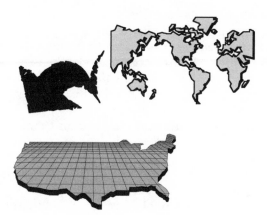

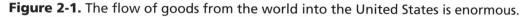

Figure 2-1. The flow of goods from the world into the United States is enormous.

The detail to be managed requires experience, creativity, and an awareness of all the parameters of inbound supply chain management.

Inbound supply chain management is as much an art as it is a science. I mention below a number of areas that purchasing executives ought to consider in their day-to-day responsibilities.

Companies looking to foreign suppliers can create quality purchasing opportunities. However, the importer must go through a number of steps before buying the goods to make sure the deal will work successfully. For example, the importer must make sure that the party overseas is a "legitimate" entity approved to do business with U.S. companies.

Importers have an array of steps they must take to purchase goods from foreign suppliers. Some of these steps are:

1. **Make sure all the entities you are doing business with are legitimate.** Check out your partners, just as you would any party within the United States, before you would enter an agreement. I am always astonished at the lack of due diligence in checking out foreign suppliers in the face of million dollar transactions.

2. **In addition, you should check all the U.S. Government lists—Denied Persons, Unverified, Office of Foreign Asset Control (OFAC) Sanctions, and State Department lists—to make sure the party and individuals you are engaging are not on these lists.** Since the events of 9/11, these lists have grown tenfold. In the appendix, the access to these government sites is provided. It is part of an importer's due diligence to check these lists each and every time.

3. **Make sure that the supplier can meet all your manufacturing and production needs.** I would suggest before moving all your business with the new supplier, you allow some period of "testing and review" before long-term agreements are reached. There should be no reason to rush into a new supplier and arrange a long-term agreement until you are reasonably sure they can meet your needs on a timely and efficient basis. Don't give up your existing supply lines until the new one is solid. You may want to "wean" the new one into full time slowly, while the other is gradually turned off.

4. **Review all vulnerabilities and set up "Plan Bs" and contingency arrangements. Set up a committee with all those engaged in the inbound supply chain.**

Make a checklist of "what ifs" and "vulnerabilities." Then create a new checklist with a proactive strategy to deal with all the issues.

5. **Work with qualified consultants and attorneys, in the United States and locally overseas.** Typical "house" counsel lacks the expertise required and ultimately can cause more harm than good. Check with outside counsel, trade associations, the Internet, and vendors for names of experienced international legal counsel.

6. **Develop contracts that limit exclusivity and that have arbitration agreements in them.** Do not commit to deals that restrict your ability to change or modify the agreement, if not satisfied with your supplier's performance. All disputes to be settled in a neutral setting like in an arbitration panel in London, Toronto, or Sydney and not in the country where you are sourcing your goods.

7. **Do extensive product testing before entering into the U.S. market or using in your full-scale manufacturing.** It can become a real embarrassment when you have a boatload of goods coming in, and the prototypes do not meet specification. Buying from overseas markets requires patience and thorough diligence.

8. **Make sure your suppliers' products meet all regulatory requirements.** Customs, OSHA, USDA/FDA, BATF, DEC, DOT, FCC, CDC, etc., to name a limited few. It is imperative that the importer coordinate the import legal requirements with the various agencies that govern the specific product line. In many cases, there are multiple agencies involved with similar or conflicting regulations.

Larger corporations may have multiple compliance specialists in the various purviews; a pharmaceutical company, for example, might have an FDA compliance person, an OSHA compliance person, and an import compliance manager.

9. **Make sure your new supplier meets all packing, marking, and labeling requirements.** It is an importers responsibility, typically as "importer of record" to ensure the goods entering the United States meet all requirements for how the goods are marked, packed, and labeled. For example, the carton and internal wrapping of a cereal product must meet FDA standards. The outside of the carton must meet United States Department of Agriculture (USDA) guidelines on communicating product handling and nutritional information, etc.

With new security guidelines in place, like the 24-Hour Manifest Ruling (page XXX), the importer must make sure that the details of just what is entering the United States is manifested by the inbound ocean carrier at least twenty-four hours prior to the vessel sailing from the exporters outbound port.

New time frames for air, ocean, and truck shipments came out in 2009 and are still being tweaked as I write (summer, 2011).

10. **Control the inbound logistics by controlling the terms of purchase.** Use free on board (FOB) Plant or Ex Warehouse International Commercial (INCO) Terms. This will give you control of the inbound supply chain. This will typically allow you better pricing, control of delivery scheduling, and all compliance responsibilities.

Many importers have determined, unwisely, that removing themselves from the hassles of the import process and inbound logistics serves their best interest. My group has studied this circumstance for over forty years. Every analysis clearly points out that the importer is always better served when they control the inbound and "importer of record" responsibilities.

The importer benefits by reducing overall logistics costs, managing compliance and security requirements, and maintaining control over the inbound status and disposition of the imported merchandise.

11. **Control who the customs broker will be.** Use your customhouse broker where you can have documentary and compliance controls in place—and where you have the "relationship" to make things happen.

Many importers appreciate being out of the "loop" of the clearance process. Customs has regulations referring to "ultimate consignee" (page 264), which may force you to be the "importer of record" irrespective of who manages the clearance process.

Those importers who control the importing and clearance process are better exercising due diligence and reasonable care, which are dictates of Customs Border and Protection.

12. **Calculate the anticipated "landed costs." This is imperative to make sure you are competitive in comparison to local purchasing or from other sites.** This is covered in more detail on page XXX. Too many times we have seen importers begin to import a product, raw material, or component from a foreign supplier and then get hit with duties, taxes, and inland charges, which make the transaction cost prohibitive.

Do your homework before you import.

13. **Pay attention to detail. Make sure all the minutiae of information—such as valuation, classification, origin, language, invoice data, etc.—is relevant and accurate.** Failure to do so, after the fact, slows the inbound supply chain, adds unnecessary import costs, and exposes you to fines and penalties. Using quality and compliant customhouse brokers will greatly assist you in this endeavor.

14. **Make sure your transaction from point of purchase to point of processing or sale is well documented and all records are maintained for at least five years.** This is a "reasonable care" standard, for which failure can result in serious penalties.

15. **Make sure the shipment is insured for the full value of your potential loss. The valuation for insurance purposes can be calculated to full sales value, including profit.** It is at the time of loss or damage that most companies worry about "cargo insurance." Then it's too late. Set up the insurances to provide "All Risk" "Warehouse to Warehouse" coverage on your imports with a quality third-party insurance company who specializes in international transportation risks.

16. **Pay attention to global and local economic and political events and trends.** Bring these circumstances into your equation for determining the viability of the foreign source you are contemplating. Not paying attention could cost millions. Many foreign companies invested money into construction projects in Iraq, pre-U.S. invasion. Now their investments are worth zero.

With all the turmoil in the Middle East in 2011 (Tunisia, Egypt, and Libya), purchasing managers who have any petroleum-related products are warned to plan for increased costs and potential supply issues.

17. **Look at options closer to home.** As we move into 2012 many companies are looking to "near sourcing" as alternatives to sourcing in China, India, and other Asian markets. Mexico, Canada and certain Central American countries pose potential options that afford more cost-effective "landed costs."

This is due to shorter distances and less expensive freight costs, favorable tax and duty regulations, and the rise in costs with certain Asian manufacturers. Importers and companies who manufacture overseas are well advised to review "near sourcing options" before finalizing purchasing agreements in further away origin sites.

Importers who pay attention to detail and follow the seventeen steps and integrate these into inbound supply chain standard operating procedures (SOPs) will place themselves in the very best situation to always be compliant and secure, cost-effective, and competitive.

Determining the Best Overseas Suppliers

For the most part U.S. purchasing managers will have options when looking at potential foreign suppliers.

The following set of guidelines will help the purchasing executive make the right choice. The overseas supplier should have:

- Experience in manufacturing your specific product
- Tenure in the business
- Experience in servicing foreign markets
- Experience in selling into the United States and/or other destinations you are purchasing on behalf of
- High-quality operations staff
- A number of personnel who speak, write, and communicate well in English
- A willingness to travel to the United States and/or other overseas facilities
- The flexibility to change specifications and meet customer nuances
- The ability to meet all the security and compliance regulations put forth by the U.S. government
- The capability to manufacture, mark, package, and label according to the multitude of various government agency requirements
- Willingness to allow you as the importer to control the freight and logistics into the U.S. market
- Willingness to extend credit
- A policy on returns, defective parts, warranties, and exchanges
- Willingness and ability to assist in market studies, R & D, trade shows, etc., both from afar and here in the United States
- A number of service centers here in the Unites States if applicable
- Noncompete and trade secrets policies
- Exclusivity policies

And . . .

- **The ability to meet basic C-TPAT (Customs Trade Partnership Against Terrorism) supplier guidelines for security and trade compliance regulations here in the United States.** As we approach 2012—and no doubt for years to come—all these regulations will continue to increase for foreign suppliers in all markets around the world.

An importer who uses the above guidelines as a checklist for all import arrangements will reduce the opportunities for current and future problems.

The checklist needs to be reviewed for the specific nuances that are unique to your supply chain and incorporated into your existing business profile. Doing so will greatly assist you in choosing and managing your overseas suppliers

The Trade Compliance Skill Set for the New Millenium and Beyond

Purchasing managers will need to devlop a capability and skill set that deals with all the regulatory issues involved in purchasing goods from foreign sources. Trade compliance management will need to be understood, mastered, and acted on in all purchasing functions.

Trade Compliance Management

This entire subject is covered in various aspects of this book but this section deals with how the purchasing and supply chain management team deals with all the regulatory concerns of governments controls over imports and exports.

Keep in mind that the clear majority of companies that import have exports as well.

While trade compliance has always been a serious concern for U.S. companies engaged in global trade, the events of 9/11 has greatly heightened the regulatory impact and the consequences of noncompliance.

This discussion deals with how purchasing managers can act to structure trade compliance programs in their import and export efforts.

Keep in mind that as we move into 2011 and beyond, imports and exports are becoming an ever increasing aspect of how companies operate in the international arena.

The U.S. Government Mindset in Trade Compliance

U.S. Trade Compliance Regulations which are discussed within every chapter of this book are develped to assist with both security and compliance benefits to the country in whole.

The governemt puts forth a set of standards that companies are requested to follow in order to meet the regulatory guidelines in their import and export supply chains. They are:

- Due diligence
- Reasonable care
- Supervision and control
- Engagement

How we define these is a critical but basic aspect of global trade and trade compliance management.

Due Diligence and Reasonable Care

The government agencies that regulate global supply chains, such as but not limited to Customs Border and Protection (CBP) and The Bureau of Industry and Security (BIS), require that personnel engaged in imports and exports should act with due diligence and reasonable care in handling their day-to-day responsibilities.

For example, employees need to be trained in at least basic import and export controls. They need to take the initiative in finding out what regulations impact their import/export operations and on how to work within these guidelines correctly and compliantly.

In addition, they need to seek out information and use information to be compliant. For example, they must check Denied Persons lists, utilize the correct HTS or Schedule B Number, and so on. Maintaining documentation, using correct valuation formulas, and managing closed party transactions are all examples of how a company act with due diligence and with reasonable care.

Supervision and Control

Government agencies recognizes that many importers and exporters outsource logistics and supply chain responsibilities to third parties. Freight forwarders, customhouse brokers, and TPLs are but a few of the providers that work with principal import and export companies.

The government mandates that even though you outsource work to a third party, you still have final responsibility for their work and **you must supervise and control their activities on your own behalf.**

The various government agencies that regulate trade require that principal import and export companies actually supervise and control every aspect of their global supply chain operations **and those who operate on their behalf** to assure compliance with all trade regulations.

Engagement

While not part of any specific government edicts, this author strongly believes, based upon how government agencies, such as CBP and BIS operate . . . that they expect the personnel for companies that operate globally . . . to be very much engaged in all the initiatives and programs that the government offers as "outreach" or in "voluntary regulatory participation".

Joining C-TPAT (Customs-Trade Partnership Against Terrorism), attending Customs Trade Symposiums and BIS Outreach Conferences would all be examples of how companies might engage themselves proactively.

Trade compliance is now as important a skill set for purchasing managers as finding suppliers and negotiating favorable purchase agreements.

Concluding Remarks

Purchasing management and inbound supply chain management require a unique set of skill sets in global trade. There is an array of considerations and outside influences that could seriously affect landed costs, freight, clearance, trade compliance, and security of the imported goods. This chapter along with the balance of this book provides an encyclopedia of specific information to make this effort doable and possible.

In a new post 9/11 era of increased "compliance and security," control offers the best strategy for mitigating risk, avoiding fines and penalties, and maintaining open inbound supply chains.

3

Freight, Logistics, and Specialized Transportation Issues for Import/ Export Managers

Until we have a Star Trek capability and can move things through space electronically , all freight will have to move physically from point A to point B. And that is what we call logistics.

Managing logistics in the import/export trade is critical because shipping costs and shipping efficiency will determine the bottom-line competitiveness of the transaction. This chapter dissects all the material one needs to know about managing import/export logistics and obtaining great value for all the external services necessary to move products internationally. Specialized international transportation situations are reviewed with an outline of solutions and options.

Using Service Providers

Freight forwarders, customhouse brokers, and third-party services are excellent partners to assist corporations in managing their supply chains. They can be "all things" to all people or you can select among the services they offer. Irrespective of the extent to which you utilize them, they can be of service in your global supply chain. They can make or break your import and export operation. They typically have expertise, qualified personnel, and resources to make your supply chain function in a timely, safe, and cost-effective way. A good service provider can be a tremendous advantage for importers and exporters to partner with to control landed costs and earn sustainability in their global supply chains.

A service provider can make or break a supply chain; a top-shelf one will be an integral component of its success and long-term future.

The chapter also describes in detail the services they offer and how best to use them to obtain a competitive advantage.

Import/Export Trade: Five Key Areas to Get the Best from Your Forwarder

The quality of your freight forwarders and the delivery of the international services they provide is key to the success of your import/export operation. Even though they sometimes seem to be nothing but a necessary evil, forwarders can be your best ally in mitigating the hazards of world trade and assuring successful and profitable international transactions.

Like other key vendors, freight forwarders need to be managed and treated as partners with mutual goals, common direction, and a full understanding of what each party brings to the relationship and ultimately the benefit to each other through the association. Five key points in this regard are presented in this chapter:

1. Selection
2. Logistics consulting
3. Pricing
4. Value-added services
5. Setting performance standards

Selection

There are several resources to help you determine what forwarder to choose:

- Go to other shippers for referrals.
- Ask carriers for recommendations.
- Check the Export Yellow Pages.
- Check the American Export Register.
- Associations such as NCBFAA (National Customhouse Brokers and Freight Forwarders Association, TIA (Transport Intermediaries Association) and AFF (Airfreight Forwarders Association) are also excellent sources of highly qualified service providers in global supply chain options.

Potentially, there are another dozen resources to turn to, including other shippers who have firsthand experience.

To determine if the freight forwarder is suited to meet your needs, you must set up selections criteria.

For example, a large shipper may have a fully staffed traffic department and may be fully capable of executing documentation and negotiating freight rates. In this case, a freight forwarder might be needed for a niche-type activity, special tasks, and overall logistics consulting.

However, a small shipper may require the freight forwarder to execute every document, from the pro forma invoice, the export declaration, and the certificate of origin, to the bill of lading, etc. It is essential to note that even some very large shippers have decided to purchase all services of a freight forwarder in lieu of establishing a fully staffed traffic department. At the same time, some qualified small shippers prefer to do much of the work themselves. You need to survey your needs, which then become the criteria for the selection process.

Freight forwarders vary greatly from one another in skills, capability, and delivery of services. Some forwarders are specialists on certain trade routes, specific commodities, degree of value-added services, etc. Some shippers use two or more forwarders for different areas.

We suggest you create a list of criteria, which would be a reflection of your needs. This should be given to the forwarder to obtain a proposal from him. The proposals from various forwarders will serve as a gauge for evaluation of their services in the areas you have identified to be important. For example:

- Documentation, rating, carrier selection
- Postselection, packaging, insurance, warehousing, electronic data interchange (EDI)
- Knowledge of your product
- Logistics consulting
- Tracking and tracing
- Customs clearance, labeling, hours of operation, rate negotiation
- Import/export compliance management
- In-house education and training
- Technology capabilities

Logistics Consulting

One of the most important services a forwarder can provide is advice and counsel. Most shippers would probably tell you that the single most important factor in freight forwarder selection is the forwarder's experience, resources, and general working knowledge of international trade. The freight forwarder can make significant contributions to your overall sales, marketing, pricing, and distribution choices. If you typically sell on a cost, insurance, freight (CIF) basis and are now venturing into a totally new market, your freight forwarder, based on previous experience, may advise you that the claims experience is horrendous in the importer's airport of entry or port facility and that you should amend your terms to a cost and freight (CFR) basis. This obviously will affect pricing and may be a key factor in making the transaction profitable in the long run.

Another example may be that you are experiencing a frequency of damage claims via a particular mode of transit. The forwarder might guide you to changes in packaging that would better protect your cargo and lead to fewer losses and more satisfied customers.

Pricing

Pricing can vary among different forwarders. We suggest that pricing always be obtained up front. In some situations, it may be impossible to estimate costs exactly, but in most cases a forwarder can provide a fairly accurate estimate. Two basic elements of a freight forwarder's charges are fees and carrier costs.

For ocean freight, you will typically pay what the forwarder pays to the carrier except for consolidations, nonvessel common carriers (NVOCCs), and project work where certain discounts or surcharges may apply. The forwarder will typically earn a commission in ocean freight and will charge handling fees.

In other modes of transit, such as by air, you will pay what the forwarder charges you and not necessarily what the forwarder pays the carrier. This is why the rates in international airfreight tend to be more evenly priced.

Fees will vary among forwarders. Obtaining shipping information, contracting overseas agents, follow-up, faxing, negotiating rates, and preparing documentation all have costs attached. Following is a breakdown of your potential shipping costs.

Domestic Invoice Total–Additional Domestic Costs
(may be part of the forwarder's fee)

- Warehousing
- Inland freight

- Export packing
- Loading charges

SHIPPING AND DOCUMENTATION

- Consularization/notarization
- Export declaration
- Export license
- Certificate of origin
- Packing list
- Bills of lading
- SGS inspection
- Insurance certificates
- Health/sanitary certificates
- Miscellaneous

BANKING AND FINANCE

- Letter of credit
- Sight draft
- Miscellaneous

FREIGHT FORWARDING FEES
INSURANCE
FREIGHT

- Foreign import costs
- Customs clearance
- Local delivery
- Import license
- Fuel and security surcharges
- Miscellaneous

Value-Added Services

A forwarder can provide an array of services that may be considered standard or value-added. For example, you may be entering a new market in a different country. In your analysis, you will need to be supplied with a significant amount of data. Your forwarder may be in a position to review your needs and provide feedback in areas such as:

- Export shipping and mode options
- Costs of shipping
- Documentation requirements
- Packaging considerations
- Warehousing and inland transit options (third-party logistics)
- Legal and government restrictions
- Labeling requirements
- Distribution systems
- Compliance management
- Technology capabilities

Another potential value-added service is providing EDI (technology) capability. This basically entails the retrieval of manual shipping data in an automated format, production of documentation, and tracking in an automated mode. The range of data, equipment availability, and report formatting may vary, but the bottom line is that your forwarder's EDI capability needs to reduce costs and provide shipping data in a timely manner and comprehensively to be considered value-added.

Other examples of potential value-added services are:

- Capability to handle hazardous materials
- Export packing expertise
- Warehousing capabilities
- Expertise in marine exposures and coverages
- Comprehensive office and agency system

Setting Performance Standards

We are strong advocates of making sure that freight forwarders keep their promises and maintain high standards leading to cost-effective service and on-time performance.

Following are five steps that can be used to maintain the forwarder's performance:

1. **Keep all commitments, quotes, proposals, promises, etc., in writing.**
2. **Allocate time frames to all jobs.** Maintain a diary and follow-up schedule to determine responsiveness and accuracy.
3. **Have all jobs quoted.** If there is no time to quote, then have pricing made available as soon as practical.
4. **Have your forwarder submit annual stewardship reports and bring in competitors from time to time.**
5. **Demand regular meetings with your forwarder.** Gain access to senior management. It is also recommended that you meet with all staff and operating personnel and make sure they are familiar with your account, your needs, and the promises made by their salespeople. Knowing who the operation personnel are is key, as they sometimes become far more important to you than the salesperson.

Certain regulations of Customs and Border Patrol now require annual visits of service providers to their clients' offices.

The effectiveness of the forwarder will partially depend on how you manage this valuable vendor relationship. The forwarder should be viewed as a partner who is part of your entire logistics management team. When used effectively, the forwarder can maximize profit, mitigate risk, and spearhead you into successful exporting.

Following is a comparison checklist for choosing freight forwarders. Establish criteria that are specific to your operation and prioritize the salience and importance.

- ✓ Service areas
- ✓ Scope of expertise
- ✓ Ocean, air, truck, and rail
- ✓ Quality of sales and operations personnel
- ✓ Location nearest your main office
- ✓ Pricing

✓ Insurance availability and fees
✓ Warehousing and fulfillment capability
✓ Your own or third-party trucks
✓ EDI capability
✓ Imports and exports and domestic
✓ Export documentation
✓ Tracking capability
✓ Handles small packages
✓ Handles time-sensitive freight
✓ Consulting services
✓ Import/export compliance capabilities
✓ In-house training and education
✓ Packaging, marking, and labeling
✓ Payment terms
✓ Will lay out duties and taxes
✓ Are you just a small fish in their big pond?
✓ Who will service your account? From which office?
✓ Office and agency network
✓ Years in business
✓ REFERENCES

Use of "Consolidators" in Import/Export Trade: A Viable Option for Ocean and Air Freight

Ocean shippers with over 100 trailer exchange units (TEUs) (20-foot equivalent unit, or 20-foot container) per annum are typically at the lower end of the scale but have minimal clout to negotiate directly with steamship lines for rating discounts and relief from standard tariffs. The more volume you move, the more clout you will have in reducing ocean shipping costs. Large exporters with more than 1,000 TEUs are in a great position for favorable ocean tariffs.

Many ocean carriers will only price shipping starting at 20-feet and 40-feet units. Many will not even look at less than container load (LCL) freight. This places the smaller, less frequent shipper at a disadvantage to larger more frequent shippers. Those shippers with small shipment (LCL) sizes have fewer options and will typically pay more. Sometimes an LCL shipper will pay more for a third of a container worth of freight than for the whole container at a full container rate. A good example: A shipper from San Francisco has 12 metric tons of dried vegetables to ship from Port of Oakland to Prague. The LCL rate is $242 per metric ton or $2,904. The 20-foot container, holding approximately 22 metric tons, costs only $3,900 or a difference of $1,000. Add another 3 metric tons and it would be better to buy the full container. Of course. dimensions would play a role but this example is for demonstration purposes only.

Shippers need to investigate this as it may be more cost effective and certainly less risky to ship the full container load (FCL) in certain circumstances. The shipper must become an "educated consumer."

The more practical option is to develop a relationship with a forwarder who accesses an NVOCC or one that is an NVOCC. Those NVOCCs licensed by the Federal Maritime Commission (FMC) act as consolidators, accept LCL freight, and can offer savings to smaller, less frequent shippers that often are not available dealing directly with the actual carriers.

The NVOCC is able to take the volume of "all its shippers" and negotiate with the clout of "many." It can then predict greater volumes with the steamship lines, arranging for tariff relief. These discounts can then be passed off in proportion to the small shipper. The NVOCC becomes a buying cooperative or purchasing group that works on the concept of clout in negotiation. The clients of the NVOCC benefit as the membership grows and the management becomes stronger.

You must be very careful when choosing NVOCCs, as there are many fly-by-night operators in the industry. NVOCCs become a direct extension of the carrier, offer their own bill's of lading, and accept certain liabilities, as if they were the actual steamship line.

When choosing an NVOCC:

Make sure you get referrals and credit references. Many NVOCCs have expertise in certain commodities or trade routes. Make sure the one you chose meets your needs.

- Make sure they carry the proper liability insurance.
- Get all pricing and quotes in writing.
- Identify the specific routing. To save money many NVOCCs will divert freight causing delays and adding unnecessary risk to export cargo.

Four quality NVOCC's are Sea Lion Shipping, Ocean Tiger, Rose Container Line, and EconoCaribe. All four have good reputations and offer competitive pricing and quality service.

NVOCCs can often provide inland warehousing, documentation, and logistics/fulfillment services directly or in conjunction with their forwarding entities or other carrier relationships. NVOCCs and consolidators who specialize in various commodities, specific geographic regions, or trade routes can be valuable in providing export transportation advice and counsel. Ocean Tiger, for example, has expertise in chemicals, perishables, contract freight, and cargo with special needs. EconoCaribe Consolidators specializes in consolidations to the Caribbean and Latin America.

Most ocean gateways, like New York, Miami, Los Angeles, Houston, are homes to many consolidators/NVOCCs. Local port authorities, freight forwarders, world trade clubs, and international associations can be excellent referral sources for NVOCC options.

Some value-added services that these entities can provide are as follows:

- Inland trucking
- Warehousing
- Pick and pack/fulfillment
- Marking/labeling
- Consolidation/repacking
- EDI, exchange of information, and tracking of freight
- Access to freight forwarding services
- Worldwide agency network
- Hazardous material or perishable capability

The concept of consolidation and NVOCC services also extends to airfreight. Companies such as ACI and Air Consolidators International, based in New York and Los Angeles with satellites in other cities, can offer airfreight shippers competitive pricing, particularly important to smaller shippers and those who ship less frequently. Typically these air consolidators will receive freight at air gateways like New York, Miami, and Los Angeles and certain days of the week will move freight to a particular city in a foreign country. Their move is typically an airport-to-airport basis, with the terminating airport city being a major inbound gateway to that country, not a smaller inner city point. Examples would be: in Australia, Sydney; in Germany, Frankfurt; in Brazil, Sao Paulo; in China, Beijing or Hong Kong. U.S. importers use airfreight consolidators on inbound imports frequently and with success.

Airfreight consolidators will typically book space in advance based on prior experience of freight volumes. They will usually obtain competitive rates. This space then becomes available to the clients of the airfreight consolidator as required, with some portion of the rate discount passed back to them. Often freight forwarders with high volumes of airfreight will arrange their own consolidations as needed or prearrange consolidations for predictable clients and trade routes.

Consolidation and the effective use of NVOCCs can be a lucrative method to control exporting costs.

Potential Increases in Airfreight Rates

In 2010, many exporters saw a decline in the cost of shipping goods by airfreight. Competitive pressures afforded such a situation and benefited those needing to move international freight by air. By the beginning of 2011 rates stabilized but as we approach mid year 2011 rates on certain trade lanes have shown an increase.

All indications point to a continued rise of up to 8 to 10 percent, depending on trade routes and carriers. Many U.S. carriers, such as American, Continental, United, and Delta, have taken steps to initiate rate increases on certain of their international trade routes. Foreign carriers like Alitalia, Lufthansa, British Airways, Air France, and JAL have hardened their pricing structures, and the trend will no doubt continue as fuel prices rise. Integrated carriers like United Parcel Service (UPS), DHL, and Federal Express have also responded with higher rate structures and tariffs.

It is important to note that most airlines have formed "alliances" with synergistic carriers and increased their overall freight capabilities. The size of commercial aircraft has been downsized, and this has been a factor in the overall freight market.

While airfreight is a more expensive option than ocean freight it still is a very viable option for time sensitive and special need shipments. Unfortunately commercial capability for numerous reasons has continued to decline into 2011 and many are concerned that the larger integrators will eventually dominate all airfreight traffic. This would reduce competion and cause freight rates to increase dramatically.

Freight forwarders, who often act as the intermediary between exporters and the actual airfreight carriers, are witnessing increases of 8 to 10 percent, and higher in some areas. In consultation with their clients, they are preparing for this trend to continue for some time. Following is a discussion of the reasons for this expected increase.

There is a global increase in airfreight utilization that stresses current airfreight capacity. Some trade routes, the United States to Europe and the Far East are two good examples, are experiencing rate increases because of supply/demand issues. Why such demand? There are many factors. One factor is the growing need for speed. Everyone wants everything today. As the world shrinks, so does the supply chain process. UPS used to deliver from the United States to major European cities on a two- to three-day basis. Years ago, this was acceptable; now clients want it delivered the following day by 8:30 AM—and many carriers can now respond to this demand.

The practice of or "just in time" (JIT) purchasing, production, and inventory management often reduces the inventory and streamlines the distribution process, resulting in a demand for quicker shipping that only airfreight can provide.

World trade is on the rise, and all modes of transit are benefiting, particularly airfreight. The elimination of tariffs (General Agreement on Tariffs and Trade [GATT]), the creation of new trading alliances (North American Free Trade Agreement [NAFTA], Mercosur, Euro, etc.), and, for a while, the strength of the U.S. dollar all have been favorable for exports for U.S. companies. U.S. products are in great demand in overseas markets. Contrary to popular opinion and a misguided media, most international businessmen know that U.S. products do well in overseas markets. Airfreight has benefited from this, placing a greater demand on airfreight services, and in the meantime causing backlogs, delays, and increased tariffs.

Some airfreight analysts point to the reduction in cargo capacity as another reason for rate increases. The reality is that the airline industry, being "passenger oriented" first, and "cargo oriented" second, has reduced the size of fleets and the individual carrying capacity of the planes. There used to be more than twenty 747 jumbo jets from JFK airport to Europe each night. Now there are fewer than twelve, a 40 percent reduction Newer planes also carry less cargo than the jumbo 747s. The integrated air carriers now control a substantial portion of wide bodies and cargo freight.

During the last ten years, airlines, along with some dedicated freighters, have reduced their fleet size and cargo capacity, causing the system to stress. Many airlines have recently upgraded their aging fleets, which has caused significant capital expenditures. They are now attempting to recapture these costs. The additional cost of fuel, which has increased over 70 percent in the last ten years, will cause carriers to pass on these increases through direct price increments and surcharges. In conjunction with this, many trucking companies have passed on their fuel cost surcharges. Keep in mind that these factors will affect airfreight as well, because there is typically an inland leg to all international airfreight shipments.

All of these factors have contributed to the rise in the costs of airfreight. Those who have been planning or budgeting responsibilities should be prepared for increases ranging from 6 to 15 percent through 2012—and perhaps beyond. But all is not lost. As in all global trade issues, there will be some exporters who might see airfreight decreases or at least stability and fare better than others. There are things you can do to minimize the effects of this global airfreight rate increase trend.

Market your shipping needs. Bring in competition. You will be amazed by the results. While loyalty and service are critical components of international partnerships, they can always be factored into the negotiation process.

Look to maximizing your clout with one or two carriers. Many of the worldwide carriers like United, Continental, Delta, Lufthansa, British Airways, and Air France can service the world through their main hubs, if not directly, then through their line haul carrier agreements with other airlines. And as these carriers continue to merge, there may be even greater savings to the wise shipper.

Placing all your business with a "main" air carrier will provide clout in the negotiation process. Many carriers have formed partnerships to enhance their service parameters. Examples of such arrangements include Northwest and KLM as part of Delta. Now the shipper in Chaska, Minnesota, can route cargo with Northwest/Delta to Bombay. Northwest/Delta may not yet go to Bombay, but will forward the freight to Detroit (one of its hubs), then through its partnership agreement with a foreign carrier will forward the freight to Amsterdam for eventual on-forwarding to Bombay. It's a "win-win" for everyone. The shipper can drop in Chaska and have his freight move all the way to Bombay, under one bill of lading, with one source for tracking and tracing. Another example is the exporter in Detroit, Michigan, shipping freight to Jakarta, Indonesia. He can now drop his freight in Detroit with Northwest/Delta Airlines. Northwest/Delta will route it to Minneapolis where it will be transferred to its worldwide partner, who through its hub in Amsterdam, will on-forward to Jakarta. Such arrangements work well for both unsophisticated and more experienced exporters. Work with airfreight consolidators who can often provide competitive rates not available directly with the carriers, particularly for smaller shippers. Consolidators typically target particular markets and trade routes and you need to know this. Your freight forwarder holds the key to these contacts.

Look to specialized airfreight forwarders who will allow access to their airline contracts, typically at better rates than you might be able to obtain on your own. Keep in mind that larger forwarders maximize their clout with carriers based on commitments of the "total business" of their clients' exports.

Combine your total freight purchasing with third party logistic providers. Combining all your transportation purchasing with these providers might provide greater strength in negotiation and economies in the entire distribution process.

Manage inventory, purchasing, and international sales in a way that will take advantage of other modes of transit, like truck, rail, or ocean, that might provide lower freight pricing. Airfreight for shipments in excess of 500 pounds should always be a last resort and saved for occasions when no other options exist.

Analyze option "gateways," such as Miami and Dallas, that might provide lower airfreight rates than other gateway cities, such as Los Angeles, New York, and Chicago. Sometimes the cost of moving the freight by truck to the gateway, plus the airfreight rate will be less than dropping at the nearest local airport or international gateway.

These are but a few of the options to consider when dealing with the problem of potential increasing airfreight rates in the coming years. Keeping these options in mind as rates rise will provide the best hope for dealing with the problem while maintaining profitability and growth.

Negotiating International Freight Rates

Acquire the Skills to Negotiate Global Transit Costs

Importers and exporters who face the reality that the better they negotiate their freight rates, the more competitive their products, and the result will be greater opportunities to make higher profits.

Rate negotiation is an art. It usually takes years of experience. Viewed as a purchasing management function, it can control the ultimate success or failure of any export operation.

Regardless of who pays directly for the freight costs in an export sale, the customer will eventually pay for it. By controlling the cost, you will favorably affect customer satisfaction. Because you get what you pay for, let us consider the first step.

There is an array of services that transportation service providers and carriers will provide:

- Documentation
- Export packing
- Door to door
- Inland transit
- Licensing
- Insurance
- Routing
- Storage
- Consolidation
- Loading/unloading
- Rate negotiation

As the exporter, you must decide what services you require, what services you will keep in-house, and which ones you will have your carriers provide. Once these are determined and you have let the carrier know, then you have taken the first step in the negotiation process.

Determine the Field of Vendors/Suppliers

The second step is a difficult one because personal and long-term relationships will come into play. We suggest you choose one or two forwarders and give them access to the market. You may want to bring one consolidator and/or nonvessel operating common carrier into the bid process. And you may want to go to one or two carriers directly. This will afford you access to the broadest spectrum of the available market.

Keep in mind, however, that all this requires an allocation of resources, time, and effort. If you have a limited availability of all three, you may want to only go to one or two forwarders affording them, with direction, the access to all market options.

Experience has shown that exploring all the options will maximize your opportunities for the best rates.

Provide Quality Information

It is key that you provide both quality and up-to-date shipping information. We recommend the following as basic data:

- Specific descriptions of products (provide schedule B numbers).
- Advise points of origin and times of availability.
- Identify packaging and unitization (pallets, slip sheets, D containers).
- Give net, tare, and gross rates.
- Give dimensions, including unitization pieces (i.e., pallets).

- Identify all shipping needs, who is to prepare documents, insurance required, clearance needed.
- Advise on any tangible information (e.g., perishable, fragile, hazardous).
- Provide all pertinent consignee and delivery information (e.g., address, telephone number).
- Any special documentation requirements.
- Advise terms of sale and payment. This includes the use of the INCO Term which has been updated in 2010, effective to all global trade on 1 January 2011. INCO Terms are discussed in more detail in Chapters 9 and 10.

Taking the time and making the effort to provide good shipping information will pay off in multiples as vendor efforts will not be wasted in renegotiations or correcting misdirected quotes.

Put Everything in Writing

It can be very frustrating to have billing disputes between exporters and carriers after freight has been shipped. For this reason alone, we recommend that all quotes be put in writing. This prevents future headaches and can limit litigation potential when disputes occur.

In the best scenario, it is recommended that a "quote sheet" be established between the exporter and the transportation vendor, whether it be a carrier, forwarder, or otherwise. What this entails is to have a profile of all the shipping data, as outlined previously, provided to the carrier by the exporter. This immediately begins the process of vendor accountability because it cannot be argued as to what the carrier based the quote on. We also recommend that this is transferred via EDI, e-mail, fax, or other electronic means. This affords timely and cost-effective communication and ease of inventorying the massive amounts of "paper" associated with an export transaction. It should also contain a reference number for current and future identification and tracking.

The transportation vendor should have a system in place to acknowledge the quote request and advise the time frame for response, ask additional information, if required, or obtain edification on any area requiring it.

The carrier would then send the quote back electronically. This closes the circle of accountability, as the exporter has the quote in "black and white," as does the carrier. The room for error or misunderstanding is minimized. The billing should match the quote.

While setting up these systems causes pain at first, has a learning curve, and usually comes with employee reluctance, in time they usually work well and provide richer rewards than the efforts expended.

Contingency Plan

In international shipping, no matter how well you prepare or plan, there are always going to be some variables that will come into play for which you will have difficulty budgeting. After years of experience in international trade, one learns about new variables every day. It is one of the things that makes the field challenging.

An example of a cost that might show up after the shipment has been dispatched that would not have typically been budgeted for is "waiting time."

Trucks or inland carriers dropping off containers at the pier or freight at the airline terminals will give the exporter about one hour to accomplish this. If they are held up by the carrier, they will pass off waiting charges in the range of twenty to eighty dollars per hour. Delays of an entire day could greatly increase the cost of shipping.

Discrepancies might arise from negotiating letters of credit, and a bank will charge fees and penalties to correct the documentation or the letter of credit. There is additional expense in the communication and time delays as the discrepancy is being corrected.

Changes in duties, taxes, reclassification of cargoes, all can lead to unexpected costs in international shipping.

Not figuring the differences between actual and dimensional weights causes discrepancies. In LCL freight, the carrier will have a right to charge the tariff rates against the actual or the dimensional weight. If you have an item with a low weight that has bulk, you may be budgeting in the 1,000-kilo actual weight, when in fact the dimensional weight is 1,500 kilos, adding approximately an additional 30 percent to the shipping charges. This is where total and quality information with pieces, weights, and dimensions must be given to the carrier to minimize the opportunity for this to occur.

In all these areas, it is almost impossible to budget for the expenses. It is recommended that regular shippers develop a slush fund and put a minimum of 1 percent of international sales into it to handle any potential or unexpected costs. If the money from the fund is not used, it can be cleared out periodically and used in the regular flow of operating expenditures.

The Impact of the Ocean Shipping Reform Act of 1998 (OSRA)

Lower pricing is the "silver" medal, but service can be the "gold!"

OSRA was signed into law in 1998 and became effective as of May 1999, affecting all ocean shippers into the new millennium.

Many international shippers have already achieved significant benefits in lowering their shipping costs as a result of the confidentiality features that the new law provides. While saving freight costs is critical to better competitive global sales, there is a secondary benefit of OSRA, which is the ability to freely negotiate service parameters from the ocean carrier and the terms agreed to within the tariff and bills of lading. Gaining competitive advantage in global sales is not only achieved through direct savings in freight costs but now can be achieved through an array of flexible issues afforded under the OSRA, including:

- Carrier liability: terms and amounts
- Positioning of containers and availability
- Payment terms
- Pricing exclusive of accessorial charges, like the terminal handling charge (THC) and bunker adjustment factor (BAF)
- Long-term contracts
- Collect freight arrangements
- Logistics services

Carrier Liability

Ocean carriers limit their liability in the wording on the bills of lading and tariffs and by law (e.g., Carriage of Goods by Sea Act [COGSA], etc., which usually is

$500 per package). In addition, when you analyze the exposures or risks for which they are liable, it is evident by these factors along with legal precedence that the carriers are actually "liable" for very little.

Carrier liability can now be negotiated, with carriers assuming greater risks or limits. While it is still unclear how litigation might be affected, this entire area is subject to modification and change by the ocean carriers for the benefit of shippers. Holding the ocean carrier to a higher standard of accountability and liability will help to make them perform better because they will not be able to hide under prior defenses. This potentially affords the shipper significant commercial advantages.

Container Positioning

Shippers will be able to negotiate ocean service contacts that will enable them to have containers available where and when needed for better control of inventory and supply chain management timing. World trade is increasing. The ocean carrier capacity to maintain internal support infrastructures of equipment has not kept up with demand. This sometimes stresses the demand requirements of shippers, particularly exporters, to have containers positioned at their facilities on a timely basis.

The further away you are from outbound gateway centers, the more difficult the situation. You may have to arrange container positioning as much as a week in advance. Now this can be easily negotiated as part of the overall carrier agreement, and you can have containers positioned on a basis that serves your need and not the supply/demand facility of the carrier.

This could greatly improve the management of your outbound export supply chain process.

Payment Terms

Carriers typically held short leashes on exporters' payment terms, typically due on a cash basis in seven working days and rarely as much as thirty days. Today, with OSRA, you can negotiate the payment terms as part of the overall carrier agreement and obtain terms that meet your internal cash flow needs. Thirty days is a given, and depending on volume and pricing, there is a potential for forty-five to sixty days with more flexible carriers, NVOCCs, and forwarders.

Accessorial Charges

I have witnessed some exporters obtain all-inclusive pricing structures that eliminate the individual surcharge accounted for by certain carriers on a line-item basis, like BAF, currency adjustment factors (CAFs), Panama toll charges (PTC), container service charge (CSC), and THC. Instead, the carrier provides a pricing structure without these potential additional costs on a line-item basis. This assists with standardization and affords more consistency in establishing shipping costs on specific trade routes.

Long-Term Contracts

Some exporters with long-term projects or lengthy sales contracts might want to look into the possibility of negotiating ocean freight costs for more than a year.

Commitments can be obtained from ocean carriers, NVOCCs, freight forwarders, and logistics providers that expand contracts for up to three and even to five years. Most will allow some flexibility for annual price adjustments, but they are preagreed at fixed or standard terms and levels based on reasonableness.

Collect Freight Arrangements

Many exporters struggle when ocean freight terms are collected, as many carriers are reluctant to provide the capability to all service areas or charge exorbitant fees. This is a serious point of negotiation. Carriers now, more then ever, are willing to provide collect capabilities throughout their service network and the "collect fees" are negotiable and can be kept reasonable.

Logistics Services

The increased flexibility offered carriers under OSRA allows ocean carriers to become better partners in providing third-party logistics services. Areas like pick 'n' pack, fulfillment, packing, warehousing, domestic distribution, bonded capabilities are but a few of the value-added capabilities being offered more easily.

Ocean carriers within their own infrastructures and with establishing close vendor ties are capable of offering an array of third party logistics services completing a very important aspect of integrating the international supply chain process.

Overall, exporters benefit with OSRA in that carriers can now price competitively and offer an expansion of services. That is where the "gold" is won, and with competitive pricing the more easily the ocean carrier also can add value.

Controlling Shipping Issues in the Entertainment, Communications, and Broadcast Industries: Key Practices

The entertainment, communications, and broadcast industries have a unique set of requirements for their logistics needs. Perfection is a priority. Tolerance for late deliveries is nonexistent. Damages must be few and far between. Time sensitivity is critical. The potential loss of revenue for late deliveries is serious and has consequences. Only a handful of logistics service providers are available to handle the delicate needs of these industries.

Use Experienced, Reputable Carriers

Handling the shipping needs of the entertainment, communications, and broadcast industries is both an art and a science. Above all it requires experience. Experience can best be determined by a quality reputation, which is obtained through the following:

- Consistent performance
- Safe, secure deliveries
- 'Round-the-clock service
- On-time pickups and deliveries
- Worldwide capability
- Personalized service

- Flexible service parameters
- Competitive pricing
- Tenure in business

When determining your transportation carrier, seek out referrals from quality sources. Firsthand experience is often your best guide. Bigger is not always better. More so than in other industries, the entertainment and related businesses require a lot of attention, often not available with large transportation carriers where you are just one small fish in a very large pond. This industry also requires a lot of flexibility, again not typically available in more structured and rigid larger carriers.

The key is to find a carrier that is large enough to provide the necessary resources and capabilities, but structured with flexibility and personalized service enhancements.

Time is typically critical in this industry. Carriers with an understanding of that issue with systems in place to make pickups and deliveries at any time in any place are rare commodities, but there are a limited number of companies that do specialize in this area and can respond to those specific needs. The entertainment industry is global, therefore, the transportation company used must have capabilities that encompass every corner of the world.

Make Sure the Shipment Is Insured

A shipment that is lost or damaged and is not insured can be a total nightmare and provides the potential for financial ruin. Carriers typically limit their liability. The limit can be determined by reading the service contracts, tariffs, or the bills of lading. These limits will usually fall far below the value of the goods shipped and the agreed upon terms will often limit exposures that fall out of their control, like "acts of God and inherent vice."

Shippers have options to protect their interests. The best is to purchase an independent transportation policy that covers all shipments, worldwide, at the broadest insuring terms available, that is, "all-risk."

Carriers will also afford you the ability to declare higher values and/or purchase insurances through them. They will charge additionally for this service and coverage availability.

It is critical for you to know first where you stand, then arrange for the necessary coverage. There are specialized insurance brokers and underwriters geared up for the entertainment, film, broadcast, and communication companies that have the knowledge and the expertise to provide competitive options and assist and mitigate in the recovery of claims.

You should have all the necessary information with you, particularly when off site, for the purpose of mitigating a loss or processing a claim. This insurance will prove to be money well spent and will save lots of dollars in the long run.

Pack and Label the Freight

Improper packing and labeling can account for almost 70 percent of all losses in transit. It is the shipper's responsibility to make sure the freight is properly protected for the intended journey. The more remote the ultimate destination, the greater the need to provide adequate levels of packing, marking, and labeling.

If you are unable to take care of this, specialized carriers will often provide these services and charge you accordingly. The bottom line is, as the shipper, whether you package or pass it on to a third party, you must make sure the freight is addressed.

Carriers and freight forwarders are often good sources for packing advice. The fragile and expensive nature of communications and broadcast equipment requires the need for a high standard and level of packing. Once your shipping needs are known, the case manufacturers can provide packing that conforms to international standards.

Because equipment will be handled repeatedly, sometimes with degrees of carelessness, shipping globally will require enhancements to handle these increases in exposure. Airfreight is often the mode of transit. Though typically safer than by truck, rail, and ocean forms of transit, handling and abuse can often occur. Equipment must be protected from shock through the use of cushioning mediums that have a high degree of resilience. Outer casings must be rigid and provide protection against handling, stowage, and transit exposures.

Fiberboard is often a packing choice. We recommend minimal standards of double wall, with moisture protection additives and at least 200-pound plus in bursting strength. For international shipments, triple wall will offer better results.

Unitization, palletizing, consolidation, and containerization should be considered when practical. Stretch and shrink-wrapping are excellent enhancements. This will prevent loss and damage by reducing access to freight (larger units are more difficult to pilfer) and will afford handling by forklift rather than manual movement. Often you can load containers or unit loads at origin, then secure the unit until it reaches the ultimate destination. This maximizes security, reduces opportunity for loss and damage, and usually will provide the best potential for freight arriving in the intended condition.

In addition, unitization will often reduce shipping costs as carriers will provide rating discounts. In airfreight and ocean freight, the use of LD3 containers or 20-foot and 40-foot steamship containers will reduce shipping costs as much as 30 percent over standard "loose and break bulk" modes.

Labeling all pieces with the shipper's name, address, contact names, and telephone numbers is critical. Even when you unitize/consolidate several pieces as one shipping unit, it is important to label each piece in the event, by mistake or otherwise, that the consolidation unit is broken down.

Product names sometimes have value, but more often than not, it is best to keep product or brand name identifiers hidden. Advertising during transit provides little public relations but does call out to potential thieves.

We recommend that all boxes and cases provide some barrier to moisture and contaminants. Once the goods leave your care and custody, you lose control. Carriers could leave your freight out in open areas while awaiting transfer and expose the cargo to the elements. Stretch and shrink-wrapping provide excellent loss prevention measures. Opaque wrap will also cover brand names.

Using the proper packaging and adequate unit loads will increase up-front costs slightly, but in the long run will always reduce the cost of shipping and all its related and intertwined expenses.

Competitive Bidding

There is absolutely nothing wrong with obtaining two to three bids from competitors in the transportation services area. There are many integrated carriers, transport providers, and freight forwarders who will be more than willing to provide competitive bids. Even if you are satisfied with your current carrier, it pays to keep that carrier honest and/or reconfirm that your deal is a good one.

Having said that, certain guidelines should be followed in the bidding process:

- Long-term relationships and favorable track records should always be given certain advantages in the proposal process.
- Price is important, but if the freight is lost or arrives damaged, then the best price has little value. We recommend that you find a balance between service and price. To accomplish that, determine the best carrier by service, then negotiate the pricing. Even go as far as to request a proposal that only outlines services. Once you have reviewed all of the proposals, choose the best one or two, then work on the pricing.
- Stick to the bid deadlines.
- Make sure you compare "apples to apples."
- Get the opinions of others in your organization. Particularly those who interface with the shipping function sector.

Following these guidelines will maximize the bid process to get a good price and "the best value for your transportation dollar."

Form Partnerships with Your Carriers

There is no better way to maximize carrier performance and control shipping costs than to form partnerships with the transport management team handling the servicing of your account.

Bring them into your management thought process. Afford them access to the same information and future planning that you have. You will be surprised to see how, by treating them as a "partner," their performance will increase and they will start affecting the pricing favorably; they will act as if it were their own dollars expended.

It requires a lot of trust, usually accomplished with an existing relationship or a highly recommended one. The following are necessary for it to work successfully:

- Payment for services must be adequate.
- Communication must be excellent.
- Trust factor must be absolute.
- Dialogue must be straightforward, no-nonsense.
- Goals must be clearly defined.
- Time frame for goal completion must be realistic and doable.
- The carrier must be made part of budgetary process.

The smaller shipper may not need such a comprehensive relationship, but larger and more frequent shippers will find that this is an excellent option to have when seeking to maximize carrier performance and control shipping costs.

Dealing with Time-Sensitive and Specialized Freight Needs

The communications industry has specialized needs. Often the shipments are time-sensitive and arrangements for pickups and deliveries have unique times and features. The pickup could be in London at midnight, following the broadcast of the Olympics with delivery the following day in Los Angeles. Or the pickup could be at 5 AM outside an arena in Las Vegas for 800 pounds of anvil cases to be delivered the same day to New York City for retooling, then out again for next-day delivery in San Juan, Puerto Rico.

The shipment may be transiting overseas on a temporary basis and require an international carnet to assist the clearance, duty, and tariff issues. You may require local assistance in a city on foreign shores. You may need counsel and support on foreign documentation needs.

The transport companies you use must be able to handle these special needs and have experience in all these matters, along with a network of foreign offices and/or agents.

The bottom line is that while the shipment of freight and equipment may sometimes be frustrating, and we accept that there are certain things we cannot control, the process can be controlled to certain acceptable tolerance levels and the costs can be managed.

Shipping Equipment Internationally on a Temporary Basis

Many individuals and companies who operate on a global scale from time to time have the need to move equipment, samples, or trade show material on a temporary basis to and from countries overseas and then back to the United States. These situations often can lead to mass confusion, shipping uncertainty, additional costs, and delays at customs. Ignorance of workable options in conjunction with improper preparation is usually the cause. The shipper has the following three options available:

1. Carnet (ATA)
2. Local Leverage
3. Temporary Import Bonds (TIBs)

Carnet (ATA)

The carnet is usually considered the best option in shipping goods worldwide on a temporary basis. It affords shippers the opportunity to temporarily import goods without having to pay duties and taxes in the countries of destination and upon its return to the United States. It also eases customs entry and formality and will reduce the overall cost of customhouse services.

Carnets are classified for issuance in the following categories:

- Professional equipment
- Commercial samples
- Exhibitions and fairs
- Consumable items, gifts

Goods for sale are not acceptable for carnet application.

The United States Council for International Business, with offices in various U.S. cities, is part of a worldwide association, the International Chamber of Commerce, which administers the issuance of the carnet. In the process of obtaining the carnet, there is a bonding requirement that the council also administers.

The fees vary for "carnets, but average around $400. The bond costs will vary depending on the value of the equipment but are approximately 0.4 percent of the total value. Other factors that might affect the overall availability and cost of the carnet include the following:

- Financial integrity of the applying company
- Time available to process the carnet application
- Number of countries to be visited
- Time frame overseas

An application form is easy to complete. The general list that must accompany the application is a bit more detailed, requiring the following information:

- Description of all equipment
- Manufacturer's name; serial, and/or model number
- Quantity and weight of each item
- Value of each piece listed

You should allow at least five to seven days to process a carnet. However, for an additional fee, some carnets can be processed the same day or overnight, but this is the exception and not the rule. You are better off allowing as much time as possible for processing.

For frequent users of the carnet, arrangements can be made with the U.S. Council for Ease of Applications, Expedited Carnet Processing and Surety Arrangements.

Not all countries are carnet available. Countries are periodically added to a list that includes the United States, Algeria, Australia, Austria, Belgium, Bulgaria, Canada, Croatia, Cyprus, Czech Republic, Denmark, Finland, France, Germany, Gibraltar, Greece, Hong Kong, Hungary, Iceland, India, Israel, Italy, Japan, Korea, Latvia, Lithuania, Luxembourg, Malaysia, Malta, Mauritius, the Netherlands, New Zealand, Norway, Poland, Portugal, Romania, Russia, Senegal, Singapore, Slovakia, Slovenia, South Africa, Spain, Sri Lanka, Sweden, Switzerland, Turkey, the United Kingdom, and others.

The country list (see Table 3-1) is fluid and always changing due to a number of political reasons, economic events, and forces involved in the international arena. One should always check with the U.S. Council for updates.

The U.S. Council is always looking to improve service. Fax and on-line services have been available for some time for carnet processing, and the Council is continually working to add countries that are carnet approved. The period of the carnet can vary slightly, but usually is for a period of one year, but the surety can remain open for as long as thirty months.

The carnet document travels with the equipment and is signed in and out of the countries upon entry and departure. Among European Community countries, it only needs to be signed in and out once. The carnet document, once used, is returned to the U.S. Council, and if all papers (vouchers and counter foils) are completed, the carnet is closed out. The premium for the bond is nonrefundable, but the bond may remain open until a later date to assure there will be no claims following the return. The carnet headquarters of the U.S. Council for International Business is located at 1212 Avenue of the Americas, New York, NY 10036. Phone: (866) 786-5625 or (800) 5DUTYFREE (538-8937) ; fax: 212-944-0012; website: *www.uscib.org;* e-mail: atacarnet@uscib.org.

Local Leverage

When carnets cannot be used, a good second option is to obtain local leverage in the country of destination by working with the local customs office to afford

Table 3-1. Carnet Members Countries and Their Territories

Algeria	France	Luxembourg	Russia
Andorra	French Guiana	Macao, China	Senegal
Antarctica	Germany	Macedonia	Singapore
Aruba	GibraltarGreece	Malaysia	Slovakia
Australia	Greenland	Malta	Slovenia
Austria	Guadeloupe	Martinique	South Africa
Balearic Islands	Guernsey	Mauritius	Spain
Belarus	Guam	Mayotte	Sri Lanka
Belgium	Hong Kong	Melilla	St. Barthelmey
Botswana	Hungary	Miquelon	St. Martin (Fr. side)
Bulgaria	Iceland	Moldova	St. Pierre
Canada	India	Monaco	Swaziland
Canary Islands	Iran	Mongolia	Sweden
Ceuta	Ireland	Montegegro	Switzerland
Chile	Isle of Man	Morocco	Tahiti
China	Israel	Namibia	Taiwan*
Corsica	Italy	Netherlands	Tasmania
Crete	Ivory Coast	New Caledonia	Thailand
Croatia	Japan	New Zealand	Tunisia
Curacao	Jersey	Norway	Turkey
Cyprus	Korea	Pakistan	UAE
Czech Republic	Latvia	Poland	Ukraine
Denmark	Lebanon	Portugal	United Kingdom
Estonia	Lesotho	Puerto Rico	United States
European Union	Liechtenstein	Reunion Island	Wallis and
Finland	Lithuania	Romania	Futuna Islands

*TECRO/AIT Carnets are accepted for goods traveling between Taiwan and the U.S. only.

Nonmember* Areas
Caribbean Islands

Anguilla	Cayman Islands	Roadtown	St. Vincent
Antigua	Dominica	St. Croix	Tortola
Bahamas	Grenada	St. John	Trinidad and
Barbados	Grenadines	St. Kitts-Nevis	Tobago
Barbuda	Jamaica	St. Lucia	Turks and Caicos
Bermuda	Netherlands Antilles	St. Thomas	Islands

Others

Fiji Islands   South and Central American Nations

*ATA Carnets may be accepted here, however, the United States Council for International Business (USCIB) will not guarantee their acceptance.

temporary entry. Often the best circumstance is when your local contacts can provide influence over their local customs officials.

For example: You are planning to exhibit in a trade show in a noncarnet country. Often in these circumstances the local management group handling the show, sometimes the hotel where the show is being held, has made prior arrangements with customs to afford ease of entry and a reduction or elimination of duties and taxes.

Another example: You are sending show equipment to a "shoot" in a noncarnet country. Often the managers of the shoot can influence the local customs officers, prior to the equipment arriving, by approaching the local agency involved with the promotion of the entertainment business. Many countries have ways to handle temporary imports when it can be demonstrated to benefit the local economy.

Many times the answer lies in maximizing local clout and resources in the country of destination. It is amazing what can be accomplished with a little creativity and effort.

Temporary Import Bonds (TIBs)

These are typically a last resort and could be quite expensive. Local customhouse or insurance facilities often can provide third-party access to financial guarantees to local authorities in the country of destination. Typically, these need to be arranged up to sixty days ahead of arrival and can cost up to 20 to 30 percent of the value of the goods. Certain Latin American countries have 100 percent surety requirements. Many times the surety guarantee is not refundable, proving to be quite expensive.

Often your U.S. insurance broker or underwriter can assist in arranging for the TIB along with the customhouse broker in the importing city of destination.

The high cost of the TIB, along with the timing and difficulty of arranging it makes the TIB an option of last resort.

When using the TIB or other noncarnet means, one must consider the return to the United States. All equipment should be registered with U.S. Customs before the original departure. This is usually done hours before the equipment is loaded aboard the international transit conveyance. There is a specific U.S. Customs form for registration. Similar to the carnet list, it identifies piece count, value, origin/ manufacturer, serial numbers, etc., accompanied by export bill of lading details.

The equipment is subject to inspection by customs officials, requiring you to have the freight available for inspection when Customs signs the registration certificates. Some U.S. Customs officers will require you to drop the equipment at the exporting carrier before signing off. All export points in the United States are manned by customs officers who will be able to assist you in the registration process.

If many pieces are shipped, the contents of each box or package should be clearly identified to match the lists or information provided to authorities. This will greatly ease the inspection process if you are inspected. All pieces should also be clearly labeled with the destination address, contact names, and telephone numbers for communication purposes.

Exporting equipment temporarily can be done easily when you know the options and prepare in advance. Your freight forwarders, customhouse brokers, foreign agents, and U.S. Customs are excellent resources for assistance. The U.S. Council, with its qualified and responsive staffing, can also provide assistance.

Shipping Perishable Freight

Shipping ice cream is not that different from shipping computer parts, it's just that the temperature range variance is narrower and failures are more immediately obvious. Fresh meat, ice cream, frozen dough, medicine, milk, and candy are but a few of the many products shipped globally that will spoil if not handled under the almost perfect standards for shipping perishable freight. Perishable products have more critical tolerances than general cargo, but the principles apply to both.

The exposures for perishable freight include the following:

- Time
- Weather
- Adverse handling
- Poor documentation and labeling
- Poor communication
- Bad insurance

The shelf life of most perishables is reduced when the product is handled out of the required environment. Ice cream may be sellable within a year of manufacturing, but only if it is kept frozen. A maximum operating temperature range must exist for the product to hold its value. Too warm, it will melt. Too cold, it will freeze. It is important for the frozen product to be maintained at a temperature within the appropriate range.

This goes for just about any product shipped, in that there is a maximum and safe operating temperature for it to be handled and stored in. That range is typically the smallest for perishables. But having said that, any extreme in temperature will most likely cause harm to the majority of international freight. Depending on the time of year and the course of transit, the parameters of temperature fall between zero- and 100-degrees Fahrenheit. Obviously this can change by 20 to 30 percent depending on the variables of the season and location (e.g., New Delhi in August is *hot*).

For most shippers, using that guideline will determine the exposures to their freight. Shippers in consultation with their forwarders, carriers, customers, and government weather resources can identify the specific needs surrounding the distribution and supply chain requirements. Once identified, these details will provide the necessary steps to be taken to provide safe transport.

Any issue that will delay delivery will cause potential harm to perishable freight. While not all perishable freight is specifically time-sensitive, it does by its very nature have a conflict with time.

Therefore, perishable freight must be shipped with time in mind (i.e., the most expeditious and safe method possible) with obvious cost efficiencies in place. Always keep in mind what happens when things go wrong.

Perishable freight could adversely affect the conveyances in which it is carried. This brings in an additional consideration to the transport company and a potential liability to the shipper. Melting butter in the hold of a 747 freighter could cause damage to the airplane, at great expense. Decaying meat in a 40-foot ocean container could cause great harm to the container in cleaning, fumigation, and recouping expense; hassles with customs, food and agricultural authorities; and total loss of freight to the "unhappy" importer.

Adverse handling will negatively affect perishable freight. Temperature-sensitive cargo usually requires special handling. An example would be an airfreight shipment of frozen ice cream samples packed in dry ice. During terminal stays and particularly if a flight is delayed, the freight should be kept in refrigerated or frozen reefer space when available. This requires the carrier to accomplish an additional physical movement. With certain carriers and certain carriers' personnel, this is an easy task. In many instances, however, it is a burden and difficult to accomplish. The bottom line is the difference between the ice cream melting or staying frozen.

A 20-foot steamship container loaded with chocolate and shipped at ambient temperatures will provide a safe haven for the freight. However, place that container on the deck of a vessel, under direct sunlight, with no steps taken for ventilation, in ambient temperatures of 80-degrees Fahrenheit and the internal temperature of the container could exceed 110-degrees Fahrenheit. At that temperature, the chocolate could spoil. Think about your car in the parking lot during summer months. Keep the windows closed, return a few hours later, and you're set for a "too hot to sit in" car with the air conditioning blasting. That's how hot it will be inside that ocean container.

Following is a discussion of recommendations that should be considered when shipping perishable freight.

1. **Samples should be shipped with the same urgency and quality operational procedures as commercial freight.** Just because a small quantity is shipped does not mean it is not susceptible to harm or customs scrutiny. A lot of this sample freight is shipped by integrated carriers, like UPS, Federal Express, or DHL. On certain trade routes consideration should be given to alternative options in dealing directly with forwarders, carriers, or courier companies. Samples are a test for regular shipments as well. Don't "nickel and dime" the sample shipment, because it has low value. The sample is an extension of your operation, and it's safe, timely arrival will increase your opportunity for concluding a much larger order. Therefore, use the best method of shipping, which may mean paying a fair transportation cost.

2. **Communicate with all parties involved in the shipment.** Use your resources and learn all the shipping, documentation, and handling requirements before executing the order. Make sure all parties understand the shipping requirements.

3. **Set up a system that affords ease of tracking the status of the shipment and allows all potential problems to be communicated as soon as possible so mitigating steps can be enacted quickly.** When structuring the details of the shipment logistics, communication lines must be included as a priority. All parties involved in the storage, handling, forwarding, and transport must be advised to communicate shipment status and problems as soon as possible. Use of written communication is key. Fax, e-mail, and letters of instruction should all be used. Telephone and fax numbers, key personnel, and emergency response actions need to be communicated and documented in the process.

The bills of lading, which become the contract of carriage between you and the carrier, are an excellent source to communicate the special shipping requirements associated with perishables. For example, keep away from heat, dry ice required, maintain temperatures between 10- and 40-degrees Fahrenheit, use ventilated containers only, sensitive to extremes or sudden changes in temperature, product must be stored in freezers during terminal stays are but a few of the clauses that would be placed on bills of lading. By doing so, two things are accomplished: (1) Special needs are communicated, which hopefully the carrier will comply with, and (2) by including these clauses you establish a line of accountability to hold the carrier liable in the event the freight is damaged due to their lack of or incorrect actions.

Besides communicating to the carrier via the bill of lading, calls should be made to operating personnel, which help to make sure on a more personal basis that directions are understood and will be complied with. While all this sounds logical, you would be surprised at how many times these simple steps are not followed because many shippers take the approach "out of sight, out of mind."

4. **Identify carriers and staff that have the expertise and previous operating experience to handle perishable freight.** There are independent companies and individuals within the trucking, warehousing, freight forwarding, steamship lines, and air carrier industries that are specialized in the care and handling of perishable exports. To name a few—trucking: Glacier Express; air: Lufthansa; sea: Maersk; warehousing: Norbert Dentressangle; and freight forwarder: American River Logistics. They all have offices and agents in major U.S. gateway cities with sales and operating personnel to assist you with your shipping needs. To obtain freight orders, many carriers will misrepresent their perishable capabilities. You will need to discern this. Ask for referrals and *check them diligently*. A review of carrier's capabilities must include the quality of their tracking and overseas office and the agency network to mitigate the potential problems that will occur over time.

5. **Keep current with government and overseas customs regulations to assure accurate documentation requirements and timely clearance and delivery.** While sources exist in booklet form to identify export documentation, these are not a good idea, since the information is usually outdated by the time it is published and certainly not current at the time of your shipment. Rules, regulations, and local practices vary greatly from country to country, city to city, and import customs officer to officer.

Instead, you should communicate with your customer and your freight forwarders office/agent in the country of importation to identify not only the documentation requirements, but also the rules and regulations for packaging and labeling just prior to shipping. This will offer the most current information and provide the greatest opportunity to reduce import problems.

At the same time identify local nuances that might affect your perishable export by asking the following questions: Are cold store facilities available during terminal stays and clearance delays? Will certain carriers work better than others shipping into a particular port or airport facility? As the exporter, is there anything you can do prior to shipment that will make it easier for your customer to facilitate import, etc.? Perishable exports that involve food and medicines are typically under some degree of scrutiny by government officials in every country. This may involve interaction with many different government agencies in the importing country. Foreign equivalents of U.S. Customs; Food and Drug Administration; Department of Agriculture; and federal, state, and local health agencies will all be factors affecting the perishable export. Many times the entire process will be in a gray area and certainly confusing. Countries in the Middle East will bring religion into the equation. Certain countries such as Mexico are not absolutely clear on packaging and labeling requirements and show inconsistencies at various border crossings. Western European (EURO) cultures are becoming more Americanized in their product liability concerns, and this will directly affect U.S. perishable food and medicine exports. Some countries such as Poland, Russia, the Czech Republic, and Slovakia do not have clear and concise regulations for perishable imports and are struggling with their transportation infrastructures, causing logistical problems for safe and timely deliveries.

6. **Insure all shipments on an "all-risk, warehouse to warehouse" basis to cover any of the potential risks and exposures you will face in exporting perishables.** This includes refrigeration breakdown. Many marine insurance companies will provide full coverage, but will have amendments to the policy restricting coverage for perishable freight. One such clause, "24-Hour Reefer Breakdown," implies that the conveyance, like a steamship 20-foot container, can retain the required temperature for at least twenty-four hours once the temperature control unit has broken down. This may or may not be correct. As the insured, you need to determine if these policy amendments/endorsements exist and how they might affect your ability to get paid if a loss occurs. Most underwriters will provide a tailored marine policy to cover your specific needs for a premium that you must negotiate.

Another factor affecting the underwriting of perishable exports is that of preshipment conditions. Marine insurance coverage is designed to cover insured risks during transit. It is presumed that the goods are sound prior to export. For example, an export of frozen meat, upon defrosting at destination, is discovered to have an awful "taint." When all the documentation is reviewed by underwriters, on presentation of a claim, if they do not identify anything that shows how the loss occurred during transit, they will deny the claim on the basis that the goods were probably not sound prior to shipment, what is sometimes referred to a preshipment condition.

Some underwriters, for a consideration, will provide terms that give "prima facie" evidence that the goods were sound prior to export, upon issuance of certain plant or third-party inspection certifications. One such certificate, the MID Certificate, is provided by the Department of Agriculture, Meat Inspection Division (MID). Inspectors from the MID will inspect shipments prior to export and plant departure and certify the quality and status for export. Upon the issuance, the marine underwriter, who extends this coverage, is acknowledging that the goods were sound prior to export and this in return will make it easier to negotiate on a concealed damage claim.

This is an important consideration for all perishable exports and an essential ingredient in a complete export strategy. The marine underwriting community is professional, competitive, comprehensive, and accommodating to the needs of U.S. exporters and are prepared to tailor policies, terms, and conditions to meet some of the demanding needs of perishable exporters.

Insurance companies like Great American, Continental/MOAC, CIGNA, Fireman's Fund, the Hartford, and Washington Mutual are just some that have quality staff and capabilities to insure perishable exports. John Rowney is President of

Great American, Marine Division, which I have great respect for as one of the best marine underwriting sources for insuring U.S. perishable exports.

7. **Certain precautions should be taken in the shipping process.** For air-freight shipments, make sure that samples are packed with enough dry ice to accommodate the tenure of the flight: 5 pounds of dry ice for each 20 pounds of product per transit day is a guideline. For a 40-pound shipment going from Chicago to Hong Kong with an estimated transit time of two days plus adding one day for something to go wrong, one would need $3 \times 5 \times 2$ or 30 pounds of dry ice. Specific product requirements will need to be considered as well as what packing is used.

Styrofoam boxes covered on the exterior by fiberboard provide adequate protection. Keep in mind that dry ice is preferable to blue ice and regular water ice, but product and time considerations need to be evaluated. All flaps, corners, and openings should be sealed with tape. The exterior of the box should be Haz-mat labeled DRY ICE CLASS 9, identified as a perishable, and any special handling requirements should be clearly outlined. You are also well advised to use the language of the importing country.

Dry ice is classified as a Haz-mat and requires "Haz-mat" labeling and will have certain restrictions and limitations on carriage and handling. New technology is developing with experimental chemicals and "blue ice" that can hold temperatures for longer periods of time than dry ice, but another one to two years for experimentation is needed before this author will make any recommendations for consideration. CROYPAK Corporation in San Diego, California, has some new products available to replace dry ice.

For airfreight shipments, make sure that the specific airplane is not booked to carry live animals. The carrier cannot combine a shipment with dry ice with live animals, which means that the perishable will get bumped at the time of loading. Dry ice rapidly absorbs oxygen when exposed to air. In a small space, like a cargo hold, this could prove deadly to any living thing in the cargo hold.

Use airfreight carriers with capabilities to store product in reefer areas during terminal stays and customs delays. Direct flights are preferable, when available.

For ocean shipments use only reputable carriers with the most direct routing. Transfers of perishable freight are often a cause of spoilage claims. In evaluating ocean carriers of perishable goods, look to their perishable equipment capability and inventory. How old are the insulated boxes and the refrigeration units that keep them cool? What is their maintenance program? Do they have a game plan when reefers break down on route? Can they replace broken units quickly?

Time, which is the biggest enemy of the perishable exporter, is always adversely affected by weather. While this is almost impossible to specifically control by shipment, it can be generally controlled by the overall strategy of supply chain management. If you know that airfreight becomes crowded from Thanksgiving to New Year's Day, then attempt to ship before or after this time. For ocean shipments from the United States, the winter North Atlantic can provide havoc and potential delays. When possible, you may want to limit the volume of shipments at this time.

Perishable exports can reap high awards and profits when the risks are mitigated. The steps outlined in this chapter are all feasible and can be easily followed. The recommendations are critical to the safe and timely delivery of all perishable exports.

Use Specialized Carriers and Forwarders for the Best Service and Rates

No international forwarder or carrier can be all things, all the time, to all parts of the globe. There tend to be common traits, however, among forwarders and carriers that specialize in certain trade routes, commodities, and service levels. Knowing who these forwarders and carriers are and having some level of working relationship with the sales and/or operating management will show results in the long run. Larger shippers often will have their international business split among several carriers and forwarders to take advantage of individual areas of expertise. While you may not want to contend with ten transportation vendors, working with two to four may prove beneficial.

In this evaluation, consolidators and NVOCCs should be brought into the profile of options, as they tend to specialize in certain geographic zones and or commodities. They also can bring competitive rates to the table, particularly for less frequent shippers and all LCL exporters.

Develop Relationships with Your Carriers and Forwarders

All carriers and forwarders have sales or account representatives. Get to know these people well. They usually can bring a significant amount of resources to your favor. They are often the critical link to operations, which ultimately will be responsible for how the carrier services your account. Know who the key operating personnel are in case you have to reach them directly. Know who the general or senior manager is for those more difficult or time-sensitive problems.

Visit the carrier operations offices to meet the operating personnel personally. Face-to-face meetings will bring about a better working rapport. Operations personnel, who can be inundated with problems on any given day, will work harder for you when they know who you are, have "broken some bread" with you, and there is some basis of friendship.

Knowing the key players, their strengths and weakness, their idiosyncrasies, etc., will better enable you to maximize utilization of their services, particularly at critical transportation times—which occur all too frequently.

Know Your Commodity Classification

Ocean transportation rates are controlled by many key factors, one of which is the commodity. Often subtle differences in how you "describe" the commodity will affect the freight rates. While you do not want to be dishonest, you do often have room to offer a different commodity classification that will enable you to obtain a better freight rate. Your sales agent and/or freight forwarder can assist you in determining the correct, best option.

Review the Logistics

The typical ocean move will have several legs of the journey. Minimally you will have two inland transits and an ocean leg. When the freight rates are being quoted, have them quoted with and without the inland transit; you may be able to obtain better land rates on your own, depending on an array of factors.

Check Out Intermodalism

Sometimes combinations of rail (piggyback or container or flat car [COFC]), truck, and ocean will provide better rates than more direct modes.

Develop Negotiating Skills and Bring Them into Practice

In any purchasing management function, developing skills that afford greater control of vendor prices will prove cost effective, particularly with carriers and forwarders. Once you have received a rate proposal from your transport vendors, unless you know absolutely that the rates quoted are the best, go back and ask for better pricing. Even if you get nowhere, you are better off for asking. The most likely result is that you will get pricing anywhere from 5 to 20 percent better just because you took the time to ask.

Compromise on Little Things to Win Bigger Issues

Be persistent and have persuasiveness. Do not give in. Be stubborn and maintain your demands. It may take several meetings to bring in the results you want.

Many times in the proposal stage, the transport vendor might ask you to divulge what rates you are looking for or what rates you currently are paying. Use great discretion when responding. Divulge this information only in the best of long-term relationships. You would be better off telling the carrier to give its best rates. Once this has been done, you can always work with the carrier to bring them in line with what you need, if the rates quoted are higher. The downside, however, might be in the case where your current rates or expectations are high, and the carrier knows this and offers rates just low enough to beat the competition, when they could have offered even lower rates. You lose.

Remember that negotiation is as much an art as a science. It takes a great deal of effort, skill, and persuasiveness to be on the winning side consistently. In exporting, having the best rates gives you a significant competitive advantage, resulting in more satisfied customers, increased sales, and higher profits.

Customer Service in Freight and Logistics

Service providers need to maintain high standards in handling all the customer service needs of import and export global syupply chains.

Here are nine considerations in making sure the customer service bar is raised:

1. One must never forget how important quality customer service is. We must always remember in dealings with vendors, carriers, etc. how much we appreciate quality customer service.

2. While "price" will always be a 'driving" factor in the logistics business. Quality customer service is what will "drive" maintaining and satisfying client needs.

3. Customer service has many "faces." What I mean is that in different situations, with different personalities, one must meet the specific combination of cus-

tomer service skill sets that are unique to that client or for that situation. For example:

- Some clients like a more personalized touch. They first want to talk about personal issues: their kids' first day at school, a disagreement with their husband, etc.
- Some respect timely responses. Some are "nitpickers" for detail, some hate detail. Some want you to call with every minute piece of detail. Some say you take care of it, call me only when you absolutely need to.
- Some deal well over the phone. Some want to see you once a month, have lunch or whatever.
- The bottom line is that you have to recognize the individual needs and provide a customer service approach for that unique client.

4. Good customer service is creating a "perception" that you are always working in the best interest of the client. In reality, this happens if one works to accomplish that. So the perception becomes reality and the customer is satisfied.

That is where "respect and trust" is developed between you and the client. When they know you are working on their behalf and giving it 150%.

Honesty, integrity, always taking the "high road" are critical traits here.

5. One must continually "turn stones over" when seeking options for the client. Shortcuts are killers. Going the extra yard will pay off in spades.

6. Never be greedy. From a transactional perspective, one could lose revenue on a specific file or even do well. But at the end of the day, value for services rendered at a fair competitive price should be the governing factor. I have heard it said: Pigs get killed, hogs get slaughtered. Greed is a "killer".

7. Problems are going to occur, particularly in international freight and logistics business. At some point in time, freight will be lost, missing, misrouted or otherwise. Always take the high road. Work with companies that are proactive and up front with status, updates, mitigation steps, disposition, etc.

The problem will not go away with no activity or poor communication. Be proactive, work to resolve the problem, take every action possible, offer options in mitigation. And most importantly, communicate with them first. Don't wait for their call. Update them regularly, even if it is no news or bad news.

Managing problems proactively will differentiate between an understanding customer and one that is livid with distrust.

8. Never be complacent. Complacency is the silent killer. One won't know it's coming. You just won't get any shipments anymore—they go away quietly. You wake up one morning and they are gone.

I deal with this in my own business, working always to be conscious of not developing a complacent attitude. I ask myself almost every day. I'm always thinking: "What can I do to be better at my responsibilities and how best to make my business a more customer service friendly for our clients?"

Customer service is a very integral aspect of freight and logistics management and must be another skill set to be learned, developed, cultured and managed in all global supply chain functions.

The Choice of Transportation: Air Versus Ocean

Exporters are always being confronted with making shipping decisions for which the choice between air and ocean is a critical factor. The many factors affecting the decision-making process are:

- Cost
- Time sensitivity/delivery requirements
- Nature of product and size of order(s)
- Customer needs, origin, and destination location(s)

Cost

Ocean shipping is generally less expensive than airfreight. This would be true whether determining calculations by volume or weight. Most shippers consider shipping by air a "premium service" left for high priority and urgent shipments only.

Shipping 20,000 pounds of electronics from New York City to London might cost $3.500 by ocean compared to $11,000 by airfreight, a cost savings of 68 percent. Obviously there is a great difference in the time frame: the air transit on a door-to-door basis might be two to four days compared to twelve to twenty days by ocean. Also the ocean leg might bring on greater exposure for damage during transit and all the hazards associated with vessel transit across the North Atlantic Ocean.

The savings on a cost comparison basis only is diminished as the size of the shipment lessens. In other words, an LCL by ocean transit does not produce as great a savings compared to airfreight. There is no exact size to determine that the savings/benefit issue balances itself out as all trade routes and commodities have wide variables; however, once the shipment weighs less than 1,000 pounds or 454 kilos, you need to take a serious look at airfreight pricing, as it would probably, on a door-to-door basis, be very close to ocean transportation costs.

It's important to keep in mind that the commodity, its density, dimensions, and the trade route will all have an affect on the breakpoint for a responsible comparison of air versus ocean.

It's also important to look at the trade route at particular points, for example, the United States/South American corridor. Currently, there is a heavy amount of airfreight that comes from cities like Bogota, Rio de Janeiro, Buenos Aires, and Caracas to various American cities through gateways such as Chicago, Miami, and New York. There is also a lot of competition among airfreight companies. The effect of all this is that a shipper can negotiate favorable airfreight rates for higher and lower weight breaks. In comparison with ocean freight, this would bring up the potential breakpoint to weights as high as 5,000 pounds or 2,268 kilos, or less.

Time Sensitivity/Delivery Requirements

Airfreight will always provide a better option on time-sensitive freight. Major cities in the world can all be reached within one to four days from all gateway points in the United States. Depending on outlying points of final delivery and the infrastructure of the importer's country, you may need to add another one to four days for local clearance and delivery. Ocean freight can take up to as much as seven to forty-five days to reach most port cities, not including time for clearance and inland transit.

A vendor filling orders on a JIT inventory management basis may only have two to three days to move the inventory supplies from their Chicago manufacturing plant to the customer in Brussels. Ocean transit is not an option. Airfreight becomes the only answer and is very doable.

More exporters are considering airfreight, even with its increased transit expenses, as a lucrative overall logistics option because savings can be had that outweigh the additional freight expenditure. These savings include the following:

1. Reduced cost of inventory, storage, and insurance costs
2. Less expensive packaging and handling outlay
3. Lower transportation (marine) insurance
4. Greater productivity of manpower and use of time

Nature of Product and Size of Orders

The size of the shipment will dictate carrier options. In simplest of terms, it does not pay to send a 10-pound package by ocean. The economy of small packages is in airfreight. Integrated carriers, along with the U.S. Postal System, have numerous options for small packages less than 30 pounds.

Integrated carriers such as UPS, DHL, and Federal Express and freight forwarders are excellent options on midrange freight from 30 to 500 pounds. Once 500 pounds is reached, you should review ocean freight as a potential option. Most shippers, however, make the "break" at 1,000 pounds.

However, larger freight by weight and dimension pose several logistical problems to air carriers. The size of the aircraft plays a key role in determining service availability. The openings in the cargo hold are an important element. For instance, a 737 passenger carrier that takes freight in the belly will typically restrict the weight of one piece to 300 to 350 pounds and the height or width to no more than 42 inches.

Compared to a 747 freighter, which can handle up to 35,000 pounds per piece, the actual determining factor would be density per square foot. The 747 has forward lower door openings of 104 by 64 inches and a front nose loader with 7- by 10-feet capability.

There are commercial aircraft in the Hercules class that can handle up to 100,000 pounds per piece. The actual determining factor would be density per square foot with a nose opening in excess of 20 by 30 feet. There is an array of carriers and forwarders that specialize in heavy lift cargoes. You would have to look at the air carriers, their aircraft, and their trade routes to determine just how large a piece they could carry. It is also important to understand that the larger aircraft, particularly one with heavy weights on board, needs plenty of runway to land safely. Not all airports have this capability. You may be able to get the cargo on the plane in JFK/New York but there may be no capability to handle the larger aircraft in Durban, South Africa, with its shorter runways.

The nature of the product will also determine carrier options. You would not ship scrap metal by air. Its value against a high density and volume affords only ocean freight as a competitive option. If you are moving an entire oil platform, its size restricts you to the vessel mode. And you would not ship precious artwork with very high value by ocean. The risks and time frame are too great. These are but a few of the examples involved when considering the options.

Customer Needs, Origin, and Destination Issues

The customer may dictate carrier options. These options may be part of the sales negotiations and ultimately part of the sales contracts being clearly identified in the commercial documents, like the letters of credit. In certain developing countries, the importer may require shipments by ocean to be with their national carriers. In this case you may have little option as to the carriers used once the mode is agreed upon. The customer's inventory and purchasing management systems may dictate need. The location of the shipping point and the origin point will dictate mode of transit. For example, an exporter to Latin America, located near Miami, will have lots of less expensive airfreight options compared to an exporter located in Pocatello, Idaho. Shipping to Guam makes all modes expensive because of its remoteness. The closer an exporter is to port cities like New York City, Los Angeles, Seattle, and New Orleans, the lower the inland costs. The river system presents potential lower inland costs than trucking, but still, the closer you are to the port, the lower your overall transportation costs.

The opening of the Eastern Bloc led to new opportunities for exporters in Russian ports, like Moscow, Irkutsk, Omsk, and Igarka. But exporters are also finding that there are high transportation costs into these areas, great risk of theft, pilferage, and damage, and very few options by air and ocean with reasonable and consistent delivery schedules.

Exporters to the Caribbean find both ocean and air viable options on smaller shipments. There are many LCL carriers with ocean consolidations at competitive prices.

Airfreight to the Far East is expensive compared to ocean freight, where there is a high volume of traffic and many competitors. The transit times are continually being improved with faster vessels, better scheduling, and new intermodal methods such as the mini land bridge, which moves freight by rail from eastern and central points to the West Coast and then onto vessels destined for the Far East.

The bottom line is that there are many factors that must be considered when deciding the best options. Forwarders, carriers, transportation consultants, traffic clubs, and international trade organizations, along with several key transportation periodicals, are usually the best resources for gathering data to make informed decisions. Informed decisions lead to better shipping and greater profits in exporting.

Ocean Freight Rates Are Increasing: Buyers Beware!

Over the last couple years importers have seen wild fluctuations in rates on a global platform. When you break down the rate scenarios of a single major trade lane—for example, inbound China to the U. S. West Coast—you can see the dramatic shifts in pricing.

The volatility in rates can be blamed on the economic downturn, but at the end of the day how we handle it affects how our customers perceive us and the profitability of our organizations.

Not even two years ago we looked at eastbound ex China rates slipping below $700 per foot equivalent unit (FEU), with carriers scrambling for market share and jockeying for position as the imports slowed a bit due to onset of the recession. There was a predominant thought that volume would cure all and would allow the strongest carriers and alliances to survive.

This downward turn in rates caused a price war that this industry may have never seen before. With the import and export business in flux on the global stage due to the worldwide recession, many eyes were focused on the China eastbound trade. As the U. S. economy and buying patterns go, so does much of the industry decision-making process. With so many carriers shifting their vessels to the trade lane to support the demand, steamship lines pulled capacity away from other markets that had already experienced the downturn in attempt to create some stability. With the China eastbound lane struggling and the profits drying up, importers and the consumer were all feeling the pinch as carriers reduced their inventory of ships servicing this important lane, causing delays in restocking shelves and eventually increasing freight rates.

Enter the rate stabilization era. As steamship lines suffered massive losses they had to do something. At the same time, theyhad to act responsively and ethically without colluding. What transpired was the age of coupled general rate increases (GRI) supplemented with peak season surcharges (PSS) in an attempt to bring rates to a breakeven point. As a consequence, within six calendar months of these unbelievably low rates, rates skyrocketed to over $2000 dollars per FEU, an increase of almost 300 percent! This was simply a result of supply and demand. This left importers scratching their heads, looking to protect their profit margins. With ships running at low capacity the lines were losing money and making it hard to justify rate increases. Steamship companies simply took to parking vessels at anchorage in various ports around the world, slowing vessels down, changing routings, and creating a capacity demand.

Those of us importing had to find unique and inventive ways to refigure our landed costs factoring in these skyrocketing rates, with GRIs and PSS charges eclipsing the $3000 mark in the summer of 2010. The combination of less container availability and the likelihood of our cargo not making a vessel forced importers and freight forwarders to become more creative in their processes of securing containers and locking in a price. Even those of us fortunate enough to belong to a shipping association were looking at other avenues to secure a container—even if it meant paying almost double our contracted rate.

At the time of this writing, the average rate from China to L.A. is in the mid $2000s per FEU. With the numerous changes in rate, service, and transit times it makes it even more important to select the right service providers. With these wild rate and service scenarios we must have freight forwarders and steamship lines we can rely on. Importers need to align themselves with service providers that are proactive and not reactive. We need to address a variety of issues with these providers, such as customer service, tracking and tracing capabilities, and pricing, and we must ensure that they are helping us to operate in the most compliant manner.

As an importer we need to be a partner to our service providers and make sure they stand behind the rates we commit to. The term "logistics partner" has taken on a completely new meaning from the old days: no longer just taking a booking and making a delivery—now our partners must ensure that our supply chain is protected in an ever-changing world and economy; they must protect us from the volatility we have experienced in the past two years.

Dealing with Strikes in Purchasing Transportation Services: The 1998 United Parcel Service Disaster and Los Angeles/Long Beach Issues Teaches Us a Few Lessons

The freight forwarding, trucking, and air carriers industry has never been so busy as it was in 1998, when the Teamsters-led strike was activated against the leading small package carrier, UPS.

The effects on shippers and carriers from these events has been long-lasting. The small package industry will never be the same. Many exporters, importers, and domestic shippers were greatly affected. They will not operate on a similar basis again, although some never learn from their mistakes!

On reflection, five suggestions have been identified that exporters and, for that matter, all shippers should consider in lieu of a revisit to an equally grand fiasco as witnessed in the UPS strike.

Don't Put All Your Eggs in One Basket

Having sold freight services for many years, I often came across the traffic manager who had no reason to see me as he was "very happy with the current carrier, thank you." Hogwash! While I fully recognize that it's not necessary to see every freight vendor who calls on you, the UPS strike clearly demonstrated the need to have and continually develop relationships with several providers.

You may decide to have one primary vendor, but you should have options and/or at least relationships with potential vendors so you can act quickly if necessary.

Many diehard UPS shippers frantically called Federal Express, Airborne, DHL, or their friendly freight forwarder looking for a last-minute option only to find out that they were first servicing existing accounts, reluctant to open new accounts, or charging retail plus prices, leaving you at a significant disadvantage. Too bad!

Maintain a Portfolio of Options

Spend at least 5 to 10 percent of your time meeting new vendors, attending networking sessions, visiting trade associations/trade shows, etc. While they might not have short-term advantage, they will provide long-term advantages: when options are needed, they are just a call away.

While we all have busy schedules and are expected to accomplish more with less, an integral ingredient to success in global trade is to network oneself with an array of service providers, friendly competitors, and exporting colleagues to maintain a dossier of options for potential future needs. The effort will pay off in spades and prove a successful ingredient in your overall export operation.

Develop a Contingency Plan

The UPS strike proved that the inevitable can happen. We should not wait until it happens again before planning a contingent strategy. The UPS strike could have been foreseen. The media started to report the potential problem more than six months before the strike started, which was more than enough time to seek alternatives.

Many companies were crippled by the strike. UPS who at the time allegedly carried 80 percent of all small package freight in the United States would never be replaced in the short term, in the best of circumstances. This strike affected all modes of transit, strained the entire transportation infrastructure both within the United States and for our exports. No one alternate carrier or group of alternates could totally replace the shipping requirements of the UPS client base.

This called for strategies that reach into:

- Manufacturing
- Production
- Inventory management
- Corporate planning

The possibility of a similar strike calls for a very intensive organized effort for larger companies and a focused charge for smaller organizations, which goes way beyond just thinking of freight movements but instead of "total global logistics."

The worse case scenario must be predicted and alternate plans found that offer some degree of fail-safe.

A company would best be served by meeting with key operating and sales staff, forming a committee that would review the consequences of a potential UPS strike, and developing a strategic Plan B to prevent a potential disaster from occurring again.

Maintain Quality Communications

The disruption this strike caused for many companies strained vendor-client relations. Timely, accurate, and quality communication between the shipper and the consignee could help. Here is a checklist of things you can do to mitigate such an event.

✓ Make sure the consignees are aware of the problem early, so they can consider other options for shipping or alternate supply sources.
✓ Suggest the consignee adapt to the situation and have you ship only critical goods in the short term.
✓ Let the consignee know you are doing all you can and *keep* them informed.
✓ Let the consignee know ahead of time that the cost of shipping may increase, and work out options to share the additional costs.

All this will go a long way in maintaining long-term client relationships.

Change the Logistics

Many exporters of small packages found an option by retiming their shipments and sending larger orders. This opened the door for a host of options with consolidators, freight forwarders, and specialized integrated units to deal directly with air, truck, rail, or ocean carriers.

Keep in mind that there are small package carriers and package carriers that carry heavy weights (from 100 pounds to 20 tons and more). By increasing your shipping weights, you now have an array of options, competitors, and vendors who can move your freight.

The strike proved fruitful for some companies who thought UPS was the only option. Many shippers found numerous choices by common carrier, freight forwarder, or by integrated competitors.

Often what appears to be a disaster can offer many long-term benefits. Being forced to search for choices now opens the door for potentially better shipping methods and logistics that can prove more cost effective to the exporter.

Solid Wood Packing Treatment Guidelines

The USDA APHIS (Animal Plant Health Inspection Service) adopted an international standard on wood import regulations.

This standard, which is referred to as IPPC (International Plant Protection Convention) calls for wood packaging material to be either heat treated or fumigated with methyl bromide and marked with an international mark certifying treatment.adopted the IPPC guidelines because they represent the current international standard determined to be effective for controlling pests in wood packaging material use throughout the world in global trade.

In 1996 a connection was discovered between the Asian long-horned beetle and the death of trees in Chicago and New York. In 1998 APHIS issued regulations mandating all wood packaging from China required a certificate stating the wood had been properly treated. The acceptable methods of treatment were by heat treatment or by fumigation.

Since that time, solid wood packing regulations have affected import shipments into other countries, including Australia, Brazil, and the European Community.

The IPPC guideline also requires that the treated wood packaging be visibly marked. The mark follows an approved standard and includes identifying the treatment facilities, country, and producer codes.

These regulations can be found on the APHIS website (www.usda/aphis.gov).

Hazardous Materials and Handling Issues

The import/export supply chain managers on domestic and international shipments have an array of regulations when shipping materials with hazardous properties.

It is critical to determine the nature of the product. This is best determined by having technical personnel, engineers, chemists, etc. work with material safety data sheets (MSDS) in conjunction with government regulations to determine the hazardous qualities of the cargo and it's proper classification.

This can be as much an art as a science, and it requires a specific level of hazardous material expertise. Proper training and education in hazardous materials regulations is a critical element of any compliance/safety programs.

Once the nature of the cargo is determined, the logistics personnel must incorporate the packing, marking, labeling, storage, and shipping process with various regulatory agencies, such as but not limited to:

- Department of Transportation (DOT)
- Coast Guard
- Federal Aviation Administration/Transportation Security Administration
- International Air Transportation Association
- National Transportation Safety Administration
- International Materials Dangerous Goods Commission
- Nuclear Regulatory Agency
- Federal Communications Commission
- And an array of local, state, and foreign regulatory authorities

While the DOT sets the overlying standards for hazardous materials in the United States within Code of Federal Regulations (CFR) Title 49 depending upon the mode of transit, the from and to, specific products, and quantities, there maybe several governing agencies that the importer and exporter must be aware of and make sure they are managing the freight within the supply chain in a compliant manner.

The following ten suggestions will help keep most companies out of trouble:

1. **Train, train, train!** Everyone and anyone in your organization should have up-to-date training in each mode of transport that your organization uses to move your hazardous materials. Additionally, each organization, at each location, should have the current set of mode-specific regulations or SOPs (standard operating procedures) for transporting Haz-mat.

2. **Put a specific person in charge.** Every organization should delegate the main compliance, safety, and security issues concerning Haz-mat to a designated employee. That employee should be trained every year, regardless of what is mandated by law. Haz-mat laws change during the year and the person "in charge" needs to be kept current on any pertinent changes. This person should be available to all Haz-mat employees for the purpose of support, review, and assistance. Some companies also engage consultants to provide necessary support capabilities.

3. **Perform an in-house audit.** There are record keeping requirements that are mandated by the Haz-mat regulations and law. A quarterly, or at least biannual internal audit should be conducted by the "person in charge" or an independent third party such as a consultant mentioned above. They should be checking that AT LEAST the shipping papers pertaining to Haz-mat transportation are properly filed, but should also spot-check transactions for accuracy and compliance with all regulations.

4. **Always use UN specification packaging.** Almost every Haz-mat shipment requires packing in UN Spec packaging, developed in accordance with the guidelines of the United Nations Committee of Experts on the Transportation of Dangerous Goods. Always be certain that the manufacturer that you purchase UN Spec packaging from includes the instructions for use, AND THAT THOSE INSTRUCTIONS ARE FOLLOWED by the employee charged with the task of packaging the material. During a DOT audit, you may be asked to produce the instructions from the manufacturer. (See Figure 3-1.)

5. **Use The Material Safety Data Sheets (MSDS).** The Occupational Safety and Health Administration (OSHA) requires that MSDSs be made immediately and readily available to all employees who handle or who are subjected to Haz-mat materials. This is not a Haz-mat requirement. However, it is a good tool for double-checking. (Some carriers require the MSDS be sent with the shipment, and they have the right to impose this requirement under their own Haz-mat safety plan). It is helpful to include these when sending shipments to a freight forwarder or other carrier or trucker. If you are the actual manufacturer of the product and prepare your own MSDS, it is extremely helpful to add a "transportation" section that lists the proper shipping name, class number, and UN or ID number. Any compliant MSDS will include this information.

6. **Provide an emergency response telephone number.** This is a requirement of U.S. law (CFR49 parts 100–185). This number must be operative 24 hours a day, 7 days a week, and 365 days per year. It cannot be voicemail, a pager number, or a message machine. Someone who has knowledge of handling a spill or other emergency must be immediately available to the authorities. Country code and city codes must be included in the emergency response number if it is an international shipment. The ER number for international shipments may NOT BE TOLL FREE unless the number works internationally. The Haz-mat person in charge also needs to be linked to this number for emergency response support.

Welcome to HAZMAT SAFETY...

Figure 3-1. The Office of Hazardous Materials Safety of the DOT is user friendly and available to help all supply chain managers with hazardous materials safety programs, access to government resources and access to eapertise that can help then through the maze of government regulation.

7. **Be on top of your inventory.** Each organization who ships Haz-mat should take frequent inventory of their packaging, label, and especially their placard supplies. In most cases it is the shipper's responsibility to offer the applicable placards to the driver, at time of pick up. It is a direct violation of U.S. law if the shipper does not provide the driver with placards when they are required by Tables 1 and 2 in CFR49 part 172.504. Your shipment could be unnecessarily delayed if your inventory is not kept current. This will also eliminate the temptation of the shipping or packaging department to use noncompatible UN Spec packaging. Older stock in your inventory might need updating.

8. **Know the storage rules.** Proper separation and segregation are critical to safety. Be certain that all Haz-mat employees in your organization who are involved in storage, inventory, and loading of Haz-mat have the "segregation" chart readily available. It is imperative to safety that certain substances not be stored next to or near other substances. For example, Class 3 flammable liquids should not be stored with any oxidizing substances. In the event that the flammable liquid caught on fire, the oxidizer would feed a fire, which is exactly what happened on May 11, 1996, in the ValuJet disaster in South Florida, where 110 people died. CFR49 provides all the criteria for proper segregation.

9. *Be conscientious with your ORM-D materials.* ORM-D ("Other Regulated Mail–Domestic") is an exception that the U.S. Regulations have put in place for consumer commodities that are packaged with the intention of, or suitable for sale through retail sales agencies for, consumption by individuals for personal care or household use. ORM-D IS NOT INTERNATIONALLY RECOGNIZED. If you are shipping your goods to a domestic location for on-forwarding to your international customer, you will need to follow the IATA (air) or International Maritime Dangerous Goods (IMDG) (ocean) regulations. ORM-D for domestic ground transportation does not require any shipping papers indicating the class, proper shipping name etc. Other than ground transportation, the documentation

must be changed, and a shipping paper or dangerous goods declaration must be prepared, typically as a Limited Quantity shipment. If you ship ORM-D goods and know they are going to be transported in any other mode than ground somewhere along the line, you as the shipper must comply with the documentation requirements for that mode of transport.

10. *Review your Haz-mat security plan regularly.* Since September 2003, it has been a federal requirement (CFR49 172.800 and 172.802) that each Haz-mat employer have a security plan. Consult the regulations for a list of the components of the plan that must be in place, and who the mandatory security plant applies to. You can also find these sections at the DOT web site.

Most corporations and manufacturers have hazardous materials risks. It is not limited to pharmaceutical, chemical, and food companies. For example, batteries, certain types of aerosols, and certain paints all can be classified as Haz-mat, depending upon specifics. These risks extend to all the service providers, carriers, and vendors/suppliers.

Quality hazardous materials loss control programs include SOPs and participation from all the parties in the supply chain.

A key website for hazardous materials is http://hazmat.dot.gov/. An excellent consulting contact is Randi Keenan, who is part of the teaching staff at the World Academy and can be reached at: Randi@Worldest.com or 904-693-9772.

DOT Issues Lithium Battery Safety Advisory to Increase Aviation Industry Awareness

In its continuing effort to promote the safe transportation of lithium batteries, the Department of Transportation in Washington, D.C. has **issued a safety advisory in the Federal Register targeting shippers and carriers responsible for compliance with hazardous materials regulations covering both passenger and cargo aircraft.**

The Pipeline and Hazardous Materials Safety Administration, in coordination with the Federal Aviation Administration, published the advisory to highlight recent aviation incidents involving lithium batteries, outline the current regulatory requirements for the safe transportation of lithium batteries, and announce that the two agencies are stepping up enforcement of the safety standards. The agencies are particularly concerned with undeclared shipments of lithium batteries and in bringing enforcement action against those responsible for offering them in transportation.

"This advisory puts all shippers on notice that non-compliance with the safety regulations is not acceptable," said Secretary Ray LaHood. "I have asked the department's enforcement personnel to increase their inspections and step up enforcement where necessary."

Since 1991, more than 40 air transport-related incidents involving lithium batteries and devices powered by lithium batteries have been identified. Many of these incidents were directly related to the lack of awareness of the regulations, risk and required safety measures applicable to the shipment of lithium batteries.

More DOT Security Scrutiny for Haz-Mat Shippers

Shippers and carriers of certain highly hazardous materials were mandated to have operating antiterrorist security plans in place by September 24, 2003 that continue into 2011. The plans were mandated under a March 2003 final rule issued by the Transportation Department's Research and Special Programs Administration (RSPA). The RSPA rule also requires hazardous materials shippers and carriers to assure that their employee training includes a security component.

Notice of the security plan and employee training requirement was published in the March 25 Federal Register and the rule became effective that same day. RSPA said in the notice that persons subject to the security plan requirement have six months from the effective date to implement their plans.

To recap RSPAs March 25 notice, the agency said its final rule adopts the following revisions to the Hazardous Materials Regulations:

- Shippers and carriers subject to the registration requirements in CFR49 part 107 or who offer or transport select agents and toxins regulated by the Centers for Disease Control and Prevention must develop and implement security plans.
- Haz-mat employers must provide security training to their Haz-mat employees. Haz-mat employees of companies required to have a security plan under this final rule must be trained in the plan's specifics. All Haz-mat employees must receive training that provides an awareness of the security issues associated with hazardous materials transportation and possible methods to enhance transportation security. This training must also include a component covering how to recognize and respond to possible security threats.

RSPA said that when federal inspectors conduct inspections at shipper and other facilities, they will look for security plans and training records related to security. The agency noted that in public comments, critics said the security requirements would not have prevented the September 11, 2001 terrorist attacks and that the requirements fail to strike an appropriate balance between security and economic goals.

A complete copy of the RSPA hazardous material security rule can be found at the following web site http://hazmat.dot.gov/68fr-14509.pdf.

What to Do When the Hazmat Inspector Comes to Call?

I would have to say that the greatest peace of mind in the world of global commerce is to be *totally* compliant with security regulations. If we were totally compliant in every area of our business practice, we would welcome the inspector when he/she came to call! Unfortunately, perhaps, that's not the reality. Even in the largest of companies where resources are plentiful, a noncompliant act is going to occur at one point or another.

This is even more true today in 2012, when the myriad of regulations that a global logistics professional must navigate are abundant, and change continually as the face of the landscape in the global arena changes.

The best thing you can do to be prepared is . . . be prepared. Although the chances of a Haz-mat inspection is not great, you should still anticipate that the possibility is real. Especially now, when federal enforcement programs are helping each other enforce all of these intricate regulations and when new inspectors are continually being added to the enforcement staff, you must be prepared!

Here are answers to ten basic questions that can help in any inspection situation, not just Haz-mat compliance.

1. **When the inspector knocks on our door, what do we do first?** Always ask for credentials. This should include the inspector's name, agency name, telephone number and address of the inspector's place of business, fax, and email address. Call their office to verify that the inspector is truly with that agency. A good inspector will appreciate this verification effort on your part.

2. **Who will be the point person for the inspector?** This should always be someone at a senior management level. Establish this point person in advance, prior to an inspection.

3. **What if a senior manager is not available?** It's okay to ask for the inspector to come back at a time when the contact person will be present. Some companies inform their legal department, to give legal an opportunity to participate.

4. **What should we do first, once the inspection begins?** Once the inspection begins, try to ascertain the scope and purpose of the inspection immediately. Try to find out what caused the inspection (e.g., leaking package, employee complaint, customer or carrier complaints).

5. **Once the scope is determined, how should we proceed?** Once you have determined exactly what the inspector wants to see or know about, keep it limited to that subject only. It's not in your best interest to offer any more information than what is required. For example, do not offer them a facility tour—although, of course, if they request it, you should not refuse.

6. **Take good notes!** Be sure to take good notes of all issues discussed. Don't be afraid to ask the inspector to give you time to write as you discuss the issue(s).

7. **How should you answer questions asked by the inspector?** Keep your answers truthful and factual—and say as little as possible. Do not volunteer any additional information unless specifically asked. But be sure to always be polite.

8. **What if the inspector asks us to sign something?** The answer is NO! The only thing you should sign is possibly an acknowledgement of receipt of something given to you by the inspector. There have been times where an inspector will word their own statement in such a way that would be incriminating and most certainly binding, without you knowing you are being led into this admission of guilt. Don't sign!! Insist politely that the request to go through the legal department, and give the inspector all the necessary contact information. (Be sure to give legal a headsup.)

9. **What if the inspector asks to make copies of documents for his records?** Again, ask politely for that request to go to the legal department. You should not give copies of documents to anyone who will be taking them outside the company. The legal department or a similar department within your organization should first approve this request.

10. **What should you do after the inspector leaves?** The notes taken during the inspection should be immediately transposed into a report form. This report should be as detailed as possible. It should include the people the inspector spoke with, date/time of visit, the main scope of the inspection, notation of any samples or photographs taken by the inspector. The report should include the potential violation(s) your company is facing, and you should attach any and all documentation left with you by the inspector. Finally, the report should advise what the next steps your company must take, according to the inspector. Send this report immediately to legal counsel and/or any other supervisory person who will be affected or involved in resolving the issue(s).

COMMENT: If you have other facilities that could have the same potential violations, be sure to copy those facilities' management on the findings, mitigation, and resolution of the inspection. This will help avoid a repeated offense.

Any government inspection causes anxiety and fear. However, if you are prepared with a good compliance program, are keeping your employees current with their hazmat training (and with good recordkeeping practices of such training), and are compliance minded you should rest assured that you are doing better than the majority. This is all very much in your favor when mitigating a fine or penalty. If you are compliant in general, and try to remain compliant continually, then the chance of a major enforcement action is not likely.

Transport providers work within agency networks.

Importers and exporters who are likely to use service providers need to recognize that these providers use an agency network of logistics, supply chain, warehouse and tyransportation companies here in the United States and overseas.

Developing, growing and managing these networks is a critical component of freight and logistics management.

As companies grow and expand into both domestic and international markets, a key ingredient to their success is how they find, utilize and manage an agency network.

This discussion is structured to provide a "Best Practices" Guide on how to accomplish that task.

The key topics are as follows:

- Should I utilize agents or grow organically?
  - Pros and cons
  - Making the Right Decision
- Securing and qualifying great agents
  - Lists and referral networks
  - due diligence
- Maintaining financial and regulatory integrity
  - Fiduciary exposures: identifying and mitigating
  - Managing regulations: FMC, IATA, DHS/Customs, TSA, Foreign, etc
- Long-term performance guidelines: domestic and international
  - Quality control
  - Paying attention to detail
  - Relationship building

Should I Utilize Agents or Grow Organically?

The utilization of agents is critical for most growing companies.

- Pros and cons
- Making the right decision

The costs to set up an independent agent network or proprietary office system would be too harsh for most companies and I would question whether that would be monies well spent when one of the big advantages of accessing an already existing network is so readily available.

This makes the most obvious "pro" for utilizing or working an agency network: Both cost and ease of access.

The transportation capabilities, manpower, purchasing clout, and convenience of an existing agency network are more reasons that this becomes an obvious option for transportation companies in having satellite capabilities.

The agency network opens up access to carriers, service providers, warehouses and other related services that might be denied to newer or smaller companies from the outset or might require them to provide significant financial worth.

The key issue here is not to consider an agency network, because that is an obvious choice. The key issue is making the right decision when choosing agents, which is what we will address in this section.

Choosing wisely will determine the success of your agent program. It is as much an art as it is a science.

Securing and Qualifying Great Agents

- Lists and referral networks
- Due diligence

The best practices for securing quality agents are as follows:

- Turn a lot of stones to determine an array of options.
- Take time and apply plenty of due diligence to qualify potential agents.
- Obtain at least 5 referrals and call them. Ask a lot of questions and don't be shy about what you ask. Levels of responsibility and accountability must be able to be determined in this process.
- Obtain detailed financial references and qualify financial standing.
- Make sure all insurance liability details are available, clear, concise and transparent.
- Read all agreements and contracts and use discretion in utilizing expert advice and counsel from trade attorneys and transportation specialists.
- Set clear lines of communication, expectations and deliverables with a system for assuring compliance with all points agreed.
- Qualify adherence to all laws, regulatory matters, trade compliance and related matters.

This part requires patience, paying attention to detail and crossing your "T's" and dotting your "I's". Your level of detail will directly impact the opportunity for favorable outcomes.

Skip a step and it will eventually be very costly.

Maintaining Financial and Regulatory Integrity

- Fiduciary exposures: identifying and mitigating
- Managing regulations: FMC, IATA, DHS/Customs, TSA, foreign, etc.

It is critical to identify exactly what financial or fidiucary exposures you have in your agency relationships.

For example, they arrange a transport on your behalf on a prepaid basis to themselves. They bill you, you pay, but they never remit funds to the carrier. Do you then have to pay twice?

What if it is duties and taxes to a customs authority?

What if they make an incorrect statement to a government regulatory authority, such as The Department of Commerce/Bureau of Industry and Security, leading to a fine or penalty. Who would then be liable?

In addition to all of this, agents often act as a liaison between you, the principal client, and government agencies where potentially significant transfers of information are taking place. Who then is responsible, liable and has ownership of these related responsibilities?

Due diligence includes obtaining information very accurately that answers all of these questions and putting agreements in place that proposes compliance, clear lines of responsibility and actions to avoid issues with the regulations one needs to manage when handling domestic and international shipments.

Today, issues with the FAA, TSA, DOT are enough to have a full person engaged in compliance. Add in Customs (CBP), Treasury and Census to name a few of the many agencies that regulate freight movements and you can easily see that managing regulatory concerns needs focus and commitment.

You must be on top of all these issues with your agents, proactively, not reactively.

Long-Term Performance Guidelines: Domestic and International

- Quality control
- Paying attention to detail
- Relationship building

Companies that utilize agents in a proactive management mind-set establish systems for accountability and responsibility or what we refer to as . . . quality control.

A basic agreement will include expectations and deliverables.

Quality control systems set up business processes that manage to assure the delivery of all the promises and expectations.

An example would be an audit system that checks actual freight carrier bills against agency billing of third parties.

Another example would be on-site periodic audits and reviews that allow access to agency files and records.

Paying attention to detail in relationships with agents is a sure-fired way to maintain sustainability and long term association between parties.

Making sure that all agreements are detailed and comprehensive of what is being accomplished is important.

Relationship Building

One of the most important aspects in successful agent relationships is the commitment that both parties make to develop and sustain effective working relationships.

You can spend a lot of money on a legal document created by the best legal minds; that will not "mean a darn," when things go wrong, if the relationship is not there or it is now soured.

Good, effective working relationships allow parties to go through difficult conflicts and problem with favorable outcomes and resolutions.

In a tenured relationship, over time it is certain problems and conflicts will arise in the best of agency networks. Many times, these cannot be controlled or minimized.

It is how we deal with these difficult times, which will occur at some point, that will determine the long term value of the relationship.

Good relationships can see their way through most conflicts. When no quality relationship exists, problems become magnified and present barriers that sometimes are too difficult to navigate to resolve.

Breaking bread, getting to know the agent and working towards strong business but personalized relationships will go a long way to assuring the ability to work out most problems and create the best opportunity for profits, growth and sustainability.

Spend time and money on all the legal, due diligence and regulatory matters we discussed . . . but also spend a lot of both on that "relationship"!!

Summary: Creating "Win-Win" Relationships

Utilizing agents is a very viable and cost effective options for transportation companies looking to grow and expand into other cities, markets and even on a global basis.

The key is to manage this option by selecting and qualifying the very best.

Integrating financial and regulatory controls into the relationship provides mitigation of inherent risks and provides a balance for profits.

Setting up systems for quality control, paying attention to detail and maximizing both business and personal relationships will create a formula that has tried-and-tested results for success.

At the end of the day you are building an agent network that develops a "Win-Win" for all parties. This reduces risk and maximizes profits and sustainability for the long term.

The most successful supply chains recognize the importance of service providers and their agency networks that provide an array of varied freight and logiustics services to principal import and export operations both on a domestic and global basis.

The more we understand and support these agency networks the better we can operate sustainable and profitable supply chains.

INCO Terms, Revenue Recognition, and Transfer of Title

An issue facing companies involved in global supply chains—and typically one that always causes confusion—is the relationship between INCO terms, revenue

---

Proper Packaging Is Key! And Is Typically the Shipper's Responsibility

The buzzword of the new millennium is "third party logistics," meaning to purchase the services of a third party transport carrier to work on your transportation needs. Taking this concept to a more enhanced state is to have that relationship on a higher level or "partnership."

recognition, transfer of title, insurance tisk, trade compliance, and, to a smaller extent, freight and payment terms.

To frame the issues . . .

All companies who export and import have seven areas that are "**different but connected,**" which need to be managed by strict SOPs within the supply chain. These SOPs will also have an implication on related matters associated with global trade compliance, logistics management, SOX, and the FCPA for companies who engage in world trade.They are:

- INCO terms (terms of sale)
- Payment terms
- Freight
- Insurance
- Title
- Revenue recognition
- Trade compliance management

While these areas have certain aspects of "connectivity" and are "related" to one another in an export and import sale or purchase, transfer pricing, revenue earning, etc., they are also very distinct issues that need to be resolved and worked out on their own merit.

You must also keep in mind that there is the strict interpretation of rules and regulations from the IRS, SEC, IAS, SOX, and many others, but there is also the functionality of dealing with theses rules and regulations while still operating our supply chains compliantly, securely and cost effectively.

Before acting in any regard to the material contained in this section, due diligence dictates professional consultation with internal and external accounting, financial and legal expertise before making final decisions in any of these areas.

Each supply chain operates differently. Each supply chain interprets regulation and practice to be compliant but to work to their favor. This paper establishes a reference point for discussion, not implementation.

The purpose of this paper is to frame the issues and create a starting point of dialogue between appropriate corporate personnel for the eventual construction of SOP's and business process that will protect the company's interests.

INCO Terms

INCO terms primarily address a point in time in which responsibilities and liabilities pass between an exporter and an importer located overseas. It does not specifically address freight, title, payment, and revenue recognition, . . . though "by default" it may have bearing.

The INCO Terms do concern itself with liability for loss and damage, but depending upon how payment is made, which must be factored in, when looking at "functional" supply chain management issues. The best example of this is the question of exactly when responsibility and liability pass to an importer where credit terms have been extended, as in a FOB/FCA port of export sale where sixty-day open account terms are also provided.

What would happen if the shipment was lost or damaged? How would the exporter protect themselves?

There are various options available to the exporter, but they would depend upon how the supply chain operates. But here I am showing the conflict between the term of sale and the term of payment where a point in time has passed between seller and buyer but exposure still exists for the seller.

Every international executive should have an INCO Terms manual on their desk. It is a foundation issue in global trade. Go to www.iccbooksusa.com for your copy.

Payment

Whatever both parties agree to fits in here. Just keep in mind that receivable exposure may exist and is an area that can be insured and your interests protected.

Payment in advance, drafts, open accounts, letters of credit, and credit cards are but a few of the options. It is a point of negotiation, irrespective of the INCO term.

But you must be sensitive not to create an INCO term and a payment term that causes conflict and exposure without means of mitigation.

Freight

Whatever both parties agree to fits in here, but the intent of freight payment should coincide with the INCO term and be built into the cost of goods sold to your foreign buyers and or to your purchasing group, accounted for and line-itemed in your purchase order or commercial invoice.

Freight also can be prepaid or collect; this will have bearing on potential financial exposures.

Demurrage and other ancillary freight expenses can be also become issues when these are not spelled out clearly in the contract of sale.

The INCO term tries to clearly spell out who has responsibility to arrange freight to a specific point in time. This will usually dictate then who will pay for the freight.

Sellers and buyers be aware—make sure you fully evaluate your landed costs to make sure the chosen INCO term provides you with the best logistics and the most competitive transportation costs.

Insurance

Responsibility for risk of loss and damage is dictated by the INCO term. However circumstances can arise, as outlined above, that dictate that the payment term can impact risk, therefore creating exposure to an exporter beyond the time outlined in the INCO term.

It is critical that risk be assessed in each import or export transaction and that a specific decision be offered to accept, mitigate or transfer that exposure.

We see too many corporations not address risk until a claim has already risen and created financial exposure.

Marine insurance—also known as cargo coverage—is readily available and relatively inexpensive on a transactional basis.

In the area of insurance is the concern over "products liability." Typically, as in the United States, most countries will dictate that the "importer of record" is the "manufacturer of record" and responsible locally for any product liability issues.

This then impacts choice of INCO term directly, to minimize a company's liability exposures in the area of product liability.

Also, there may be some exposures within the Foreign Corrupt Practices Act (FCPA) as a result of the correct choice of INCO terms. Typically the legal department will have some influence or controls in place regarding this.

Title

Title is not determined by the INCO Term. It is determined by the sales contract, agreement or what you have in the commercial invoice. It should only pass on an export, once the contract has been satisfied . . . meaning you have delivered and they have paid.

This needs to be expressly written into your contract of sale or on the commercial invoice.

The INCO terms prologue specifically states: "**Although incoterms are extremely important for the implementation of sale, a great number of problems which may occur in such a contract are not dealt with at all, like transfer of ownership and other property rights.**"

Most companies need to control title by additional wording in the contract of sale or the commercial invoice or both, wording that transfers ownership at a point in time, when both parties have met their obligations, that is, **you shipped, and they paid!**

Possession, responsibility for, and ownership are three very different issues.

Revenue Recognition

This is a more complicated area for an export. It is primarily covered and interpreted under GAAP/IAS (Generally Accepted Accounting Principles/International Accounting Standards). For export revenue to be recognized, as a responsible SOP . . . there must be four things in place, which are generally accepted:

1. An order exists, best evidenced in writing such as through a purchase order.
2. The order can be completed . . . work in process, inventory, etc.
3. There is a reasonable expectation that funds will be collected.
4. Delivery has been made

From prior rulings and established precedence, there is also an onus on the corporation to be "consistent" in their revenue recognition practice. This has a potential major impact on SOX compliance matters.

The more difficult area of the component is "delivery." In most situations this is highly interpretative and subjective. Most companies, however, have successfully defined term, as a result of court precedence, as when the goods are either loaded on the international conveyance or handed over to the inland carrier for international transport or when they have an international bill of lading in their possession. This is where there is a connection to the INCO term.

Important in this choice of the deliver term is that it be consistent and that documentation exists that an export will happen. Tie in the other two factors—contract completion and payment—and a company can meet this standard.

An example: Many companies have fallen into trouble with the IRS and the SEC where an export has happened, but the nature of the sale was one of goods on consignment or ones that were placed strategically in an overseas warehouse, available for the importer to access, but prior to sale. But in reality the final sale is specifically not made until a purchase order exists and the goods are removed from local inventory and shipped to the customer locally.

The INCO term of the sale was FOB port of export and delivery has occurred, but the nature of the "deal" changes how this sale is really being made. The company takes the sale when the goods are exported, but really should not have done that till the goods have been extracted from inventory. Many companies have had major issues over this type of export where revenue is recognized prematurely.

Trade Compliance Management

Trade compliance management is a very important by-product of all this discussion. It is a necessary component in a "best practices" initiative and a corporation is required to meet the government's guidelines of:

- Due diligence
- Reasonable care
- Supervision and control in their global supply chains

In exports we have the USPPI (United States Principal Party in Interest) concern. This entity is the company that receives the primary benefit in an export transaction and is responsible for export compliance, in other words, the information passed onto the government: where the goods are shipped, who they are going to, and how they will be utilized.

The government does not care if the INCO term is Ex Works, FOB or FCA; they will still hold the manufacturer responsible for trade compliance. So then why would a company allow a third party not under their control to handle the shipment? If they do, they are creating significant compliance exposure.

So this too must be factored in when deciding what INCO term to utilize.

In imports in a DDP (Delivered Duty Paid) transaction, the U.S. company is the "ultimate consignee," but not responsible functionally to manage the import clearance process.

This could then make the consignee responsible for trade compliance in the import, such as but not limited to matters of *valuation, origin, HTS, recordkeeping, payment of duties and taxes, to name a few*. But if that consignee has a third party appointed by the supplier to manage the import clearance process, they have not chosen a a very diligent option.

2010 Changes

INCO Terms typically change every ten years and in September 2010 the changed with an impact date of 1 January 2011.

Changes are supposed to reflect betterments and simplifications in the INCO Terms and in some analysis this was accomplished with the new changes.

Four INCO Terms were eliminated: DES, DEF, DEQ and DDU. Two new ones were added: DAT and DAP—delivered at terminal and delivered at place.

Most trade professionals are comfortable with the ones eliminated and most agree that DAP has basically replaced DDU, which was a very commonly utilized trade term.

The INCO Terms book was reorganized into two sections . . . those terms that are for ocean freight only and those for all modes of transit.

The World Academy (theworldacademy.com) and The U.S. Council for International Business (USCIB.org) run numerous classes on the 2010 changes which the author highly recommends for anyone to take ASAP who are engaging in global trade practice.

Summary

Everything lies with your choice of INCO term. Hopefully you realize that the choice has far-reaching implications within a company and must be decided as an integrated solution to numerous areas of concern.

Sales personnel, along with purchasing managers must be trained in how best to manage the INCO terms, not only to reduce risk, but more importantly to take advantage of them.

Most corporations do not address these seven areas as responsibly and thoroughly as they should, which leads to logistics and compliance issues in their global supply chain.

To manage successfully, company personnel must become informed, have access to external expertise, learn regulatory concerns, and develop integrated and connected SOPs that work for all the varied import/export interests a company has.

In global supply chains corporations attempt to accomplish the following:

- Safe shipments
- Timely delivery
- Cost-effective freight

Your choice of INCO term will impact all these areas and ultimately determine the effectiveness of your logistics operation.

International Logistics for Imports and Exports Impacts Issues with Sarbanes-Oxley

Unfortunately too many public corporations leave the global supply chain out of their SOX governance which is really a serious mistake that could lead to issues with the governing agencies, such as the IRS and the SEC.

The accounting scandals of the late 90s set the stage for the Congress to pass legislation to control the bad corporate accounting practices and lack of responsibility on the part of corporate officers. The Sarbanes-Oxley Act of 2002 (SOX) has dramatically changed the fiscal landscape of American corporations.

SOX requires very strict lines of communications and better fiscal accounting practices within a public corporation.

These regulations have had a huge impact on American public corporations, and they have had to create SOX operating guidelines and procedures. SOX regulations absolutely and unequivocally extend into global supply chains.

With SOX now in place, the chief executive and the chief financial officer will be held accountable and responsible. The law states that both must sign off on and can be held accountable for:

- All financial statements, both internal and external, such as those published and distributed to shareholders, the Securities and Exchange Commission and analysts. These include quarterly and annual forecasts, 10(k) and 10(q) filings, and other statements.
- Accounting practices and standard operating procedures, or SOPs.

- Certification from internal and external auditors validating that SOP documentation and practices are legal and accurate.

The company must make itself available for scrutiny by outside auditors, the SEC, and government investigators. If wrongdoing is uncovered, company officials can trade their pinstriped suits for a striped uniform of another kind. They will no longer be permitted to say, "I didn't know about . . .; it was his responsibility!"

This increased scrutiny goes beyond the boardroom. For years, while senior management strategized upstairs with MBAs and high-priced analysts, the "grunts" toiled down in the warehouse, making sure products got in and out on time. Not only did the chief executive or chief financial officer not know this was taking place, most of the time they couldn't even find the dock!

For years, Customs and Border Protection, Bureau of Industry and Security, Census, and other governmental agencies have required companies to submit import-export documentation that includes: Entry Summary forms 7501 and 3461 (for imports); Automated Export System (AES), an electronic version of the Shipper's Export Declaration (for exports); commercial and pro-forma invoices; certificates of origin; correct HTUS/Schedule B classifications to determine duty rates and taxes; letters of credit and money transfers; applicable licenses or permits; quota documentation; and packing lists.

This documentation and related shipping-receiving SOPs authenticate a company's trustworthiness to conduct international business. It is only natural that these processes be infused into the SOX Act's requirements. With millions of dollars expended daily in this area, you can bet it will ultimately be an audit point and as ripe for prosecution as misleading financial statements.

One can easily see a dotted-line progression of the Customs-Trade Partnership Against Terrorism (C-TPAT covered in Chapter 12) into the SOX arena. As the fallout continues from the 9/11 Commission Report, one might contemplate that if the new information czar position heads all these related programs SOX and C-TPAT will result in a new era of self-audit and overall business compliance and scrutiny.

Keep in mind that in December of 2004, a new intelligence agency was authorized by Congress and signed into law by President George Bush that will have ramifications, not only in compliance and security, but also for applications to the new SOX regulations. In 2011, the Obama administration supported by Congress still prioritizes all matters regarding supply chain security and trade compliance.

Companies have found that C-TPAT participation has helped them with their supply chain management. Many corporations have created import-export compliance departments that usually report directly to corporate counsel or internal audit departments, and have an important say in supply chain, manufacturing, and risk management decisions. These professionals have become the de facto watchdog over the entire supply chain.

Many companies with limited staff retain consulting firms to manage their compliance programs. Not only does the consultant monitor supply chain, manufacturing, and risk management issues, but also broker and service provider relationships.

Corporations are discovering the importance of a safe, competitive, and secure global supply chain. Operating within the SOX guidelines has become another skill set that must be mastered by logistics, traffic, and warehousing managers as well as chief executives and chief financial officers. A company's success in their import and export operation may depend on it.

The FOB INCO Term 2010 and Global Logistics Management

Freight and logistics providers and their principal import and export companies need to be wary of the utilization of the new 2010 definition of the INCO term "FOB" when shipping goods globally.

A potential issue has come up recently regarding the use of the FOB INCO term, due to the difference between the 2000 and the 2010 edition of INCO terms.

Trying to keep this simple: An exporter arranges an international sale with freight originating in Chicago being shipped to Brussels utilizing the FOB Baltimore INCO term.

The intent of this INCO term is to have "delivery" and the passage of risk from the seller to the buyer occur when the goods are loaded on board the oceangoing vessel (typically nominated by the buyer) in Baltimore.

The main difference between the 2000 and 2010 INCO term is that in the 2000 edition the point of transfer was when the goods passed the ship's rail, whereas in the 2010 edition the transfer takes place when loaded on board.

The issue at question here is what happens if reasons out of the control of the seller the goods get delivered to the ocean freight terminal as instructed, but loading on board cannot be accomplished due to some unforeseen reason, such as but not limited to the carrier rolls the freight to the next loading, strike, weather, dispute between buyer and carrier, etc.

The seller made a best effort to affect delivery and notified the buyer, but at the end of the day is not able to place the goods "on board."

The INCO term appears—and we use that word "appears" cautiously as the wording is not absolutely 100 percent clear as to interpretation—to indicate that when a seller delivers to a terminal and notifies the buyer appropriately that the goods cannot be loaded on board due to circumstances not as a result of anything the seller did, then the buyer is deemed to have taken delivery and risk and loss are transferred, now premature to the original intent.

Some related concerns/issues here:

1. This means that the time of delivery and the time of risk transfer is impacted by actual events that take place at the pier, events that influence when the loading actually happens and exactly when the goods are considered "loaded on board."
2. It requires sellers to closely track their shipments and to communicate to the buyers in a timely manner as to the shipments' status and any potential delays. Buyers will also need to track inbound shipments prior to the intended delivery point and stay on top of and manage the delivery process with greater diligence.
3. Risk of loss and damage is now also dependent upon circumstances that occur at the pier and on provisions made by both parties to cover, transfer, or mitigate risk potentials.
4. The term "on board" must be clearly defined in the sales contract or the purchase order so the vagueness of the words that term can be more strictly interpreted.

5. Carriers must be chosen carefully and with prudence, in particular in light of their record in honoring intended loading arrangements. This may mean that price becomes less of a factor and on-time performance a more meaningful factor in choice of ocean carriers, NVOCCs, freight forwarders, and other transportation providers.
6. Banks and finance companies that loan or pay against documents under drafts, L/Cs, etc., must be more careful in how they review and accept documents for making payments.
7. Insurance brokers and underwriters along with transport providers who provide cargo insurance must be more careful in how they assess risk and exposures in global trade.

Overall the use of FOB along with all the other INCO terms must be made with a high degree of judgment. You must exercise caution in moving ahead, and focus clearly on when delivery and risk "actually pass" from the seller to the buyer. Sometimes intent is not what it appears to be.

Free Trade Zones and Bonded Warehouses

Importers and exporters are always searching out better and more cost effective options for moving goods on a global basis.

Their goal is typically to lower the landed cost, which is the accumulation of expenses attached to a commercial invoice amount, such as but not limited to: freight, duties, taxes, handling and storage charges. A tried and proven method to lower these fixed costs is to utilize both bonded warhouses and foreign trade zones, discussed below:

Making the Free Trade Zone Work for Your Import/Export Supply Chain

Free Trade Zones (FTZs) are economic free areas where goods can be inventoried without entering the commerce of the country they are in. More importantly, FTZs allow a domiciled company to "work" on goods in these areas for various benefits.

One benefit is that taxes and duties are deferred until such time as the goods are cleared and entered into that country, which could be months after initial arrival. Cash flow is the obvious advantage.

A secondary benefit of the FTZ is that local labor works on the goods, adding local content and value. For example, a manufacturer imports watch components, but the finished timepiece is assembled in the FTZ. The goods are ready for sale, quality controlled, packed, and shipped. In many countries that have FTZs, tax relief is provided to the importer who adds local value to the imported timepieces

This could save the importer literally millions of dollars in tax liabilities, making the FTZ a significant cost-saving tool for lowering the landed cost for the imported goods.

All countries have different rules on how the FTZs operate. There are national and international FTZ organizations that are conduits for information on worldwide locations and capabilities. Additional information can be obtained from the websites in the Appendix.

A third benefit is that the freight is positioned in the foreign market, which will shorten the delivery schedule in your global supply chain. This mitigates the advantages of local competition.

An additional benefit tied into local positioning is the ability to have showrooms. Touchy, feely on-site capabilities can prove advantageous with certain product lines, like automobiles, cosmetics, computers, etc.

Areas in Europe, Asia, and Latin America are developing FTZ capabilities in numerous gateways, like, but not limited to Monterey, Mexico; Singapore, Montevedio, Uruguay; Amsterdam, the Netherlands; and Panama City, Panama.

U.S. exporters, in working with their agents, distributors, direct customers, and subsidiary facilities are finding FTZs mean gaining competitive advantage, while providing local economic benefit. This has short- and long-term political and economic advantages for the United States and the local country operating the FTZ.

Working with preferred FTZ organizations, like the Rockefeller Group in Mt. Olive, New Jersey (973-347-9100; www.rockgroupdevelopment.com/nj/itcnj .html), is an excellent way to acquire quality expertise and account management. The advice and counsel of these organizations combined with side development is *well* worth the effort.

What Supply Chain Managers Should Know About Custom-Bonded Warehouses

Custom-bonded warehouses (CBWs) provide many of the same benefits as FTZs. The difference between FTZs and CBWs is that in most countries bonded warehouses are more temporary and typically limit access to the freight. One cannot typically change the nature of the product in the bonded facility. One might be able to view the cargo, relabel or repack it, but its form, shape, or makeup cannot be changed.

There are a number of uses for CBWs for exporters. They can be made into a foreign consolidation center. Goods are held in bond, in that they have not entered the U.S. economy. A U.S.-based manufacturer/distributor may be selling to Latin America, but sourcing products from the United States and Europe. The U.S. company could import product from Europe into a bonded facility, say in Miami. The product would be held at this facility until it is combined with the domestic sourced/manufactured product and then shipped to Latin America with the cost benefits of a consolidated shipment.

A U.S.-based importer may bring in product with the eventual purpose of exporting a portion to Mexico, Canada, or the Caribbean. A CBW could be used as a warehouse to hold the freight, deferring tax/duty obligations until a decision is reached to import into the United States or export. The goods that are imported have the benefit of tax deferral until the time of actual import, and the exported goods never entered the U.S. economy, so no taxes/duties would be obligated. For the export, the goods would transit from the bonded facility to the outbound port by a bonded carrier, then by international carrier to the overseas market.

Custom facilities also can serve a "holding pens" during disputes with customs or until final determinations are made as to where and when the goods will be exported.

Exporter's need to look into CBWs in conjunction with their logistics departments, freight forwarders, third-party providers, and carriers to determine the benefits applicable to their export operations.

4

Risk Management in International Business

Understanding the exposures of international business is a skill set required for supply chain executives. This chapter explores the risks associated with international shipping: receivables, loss and damage, political risk, etc., and it discusses various insurance products and services available to transfer the exposures to third parties. We talk about some of the private and governmental insurance concerns that are readily available to provide various products for exporters to use to reduce risk and make them more competitive in world trade. In addition, this chapter provides insight into the skill set of risk management, which is vital for the continuation and growth of export trade. Risk management on global supply chain in 2012 is becoming one of the most critical concerns of senior management.

The Logistics of Political Risk Management in Exporting

As importing and exporting continues to make the world smaller, it can make it more complicated. The more complicated it is, the greater the risks. U.S. companies are increasing investment and trade activities in all parts of the world. Where there is certain political instability, like Egypt, Libya, Tunisia, Sudan, Afghanistan, Iraq, Israel, Lebanon, Russia, Haiti, Nigeria, and Korea, to name a few "hot spots," there is a growing demand for corporations to analyze exposure, adopt risk transfer options, and provide loss control alternatives; in other words, do "political risk management." What are we saying, or, in better terms, what are we asking when we talk about "the realities of political risk management"?

These risks and exposure questions are germane to companies large and small, and must be considered by the very experienced and the brand-new export company alike. Political risk management must become a function of the overall logistics management responsibility. Following are seven areas that should be reviewed thoroughly when evaluating the risk management functions of "political risk" before goods are shipped.

1. **Limited Marketplace.** There are only a handful of markets here and abroad that can provide political risk coverage. The U.S. government's Overseas Private Investment Corporation (OPIC), the Export-Import Bank of the United States (Ex-Im Bank), along with private companies like the Foreign Credit Insurance Associ-

ation (FCIA), and COFACE are definite options, which can be explored using a corporate insurance broker.

2. **Terms and Conditions.** Boilerplate policies are not adequate. The policy must be written to follow the nature of the specific trade, transaction, or contract occurring in the foreign market.

3. **Situation Analysis.** Risk managers must consider the social, economic, political, and financial situations of the foreign buyer or partner, the host country, and the world situation in general. This is key to determining exposure!

4. **Loss Control Options.** You must look at options to minimize loss using engineering, contract wording, transaction planning, etc. In many instances, the purchase of insurance can be avoided by executing other options that are more secure and less costly.

5. **Retention.** Political risk covers financial loss. Typical exposures like confiscation, nationalization, expropriation, and deprivation (CNE&D), contract frustration, unfair calling of financial guaranties, etc. require the risk manager to consider a coinsurance factor and a substantial waiting period that become the retention levels for the corporation.

6. **Corporate Communication.** The nature of overseas sales, the bureaucracy of a large corporation, and the time and distance involved often leave "risk management" as an afterthought. The realities typically have the risk manager review a contract after it has been signed, sealed, and delivered. The risk manager needs to communicate to its operating divisions (1) what the exposures are, (2) what the risks are, and (3) how to access the terms before goods are shipped! This is key to a "total approach" effort for successful risk management.

7. **Brokerage Selection.** Your choice of political risk broker may be a difficult one. The specialization of political risk requires not only basic insurance knowledge, but knowledge of international trade, political science, banking expertise, and contract analysis. There are only a handful of specialized brokers in political risk who are spread throughout some of the major brokerage houses and some small specialty facilities. Marsh (merged with Johnson & Higgins), Frenkel, and Willis Faber are but a few of the experienced and qualified brokerage organizations.

These seven areas provide an overview for the exporter to consider before merchandise is shipped. It is key to remember that the U.S. government is committed to promoting exports and investment abroad, thereby reducing the deficit and enhancing our economic stability on foreign shores.

Using finely tuned risk management will enable the exporter to deal with the realities of political risk exposure worldwide. Taking steps as part of the logistics process will help the U.S. exporting industry compete successfully in world markets.

Political Risk Insurance Update: 2010 and Beyond

As the twenty-first century enters it's second decade, U.S. companies continue increasing their overseas trade and investment activities. However, the recent wars in Iraq, Sudan, and Afghanistan and others in Bosnia, the Persian Gulf, the Caribbean, and Central America (Panama) heightened executives' concerns over the risk of political instability. During the last thirty years, Bosnia, Argentina/England, the Tiananmen Square incident, instability in Indonesia, the turmoil in

Central and West Africa, and similar events have caused many a sleepless night for senior corporate executives. And most recently disruptions and turmoil in countries like North Korea, Tunisia, Egypt, and Libya are all calls for concern. American and global interest are at great risk when major political upheaval and problems arise.

Political risk insurance is available to ease these concerns and provide stable international activity and investments. There are a host of willing brokers and underwriters anxious to manage and deal with political risk exposures. This chapter reviews the insurance options.

History

To understand the current political risk insurance arena, it is helpful to understand some of the history of this relatively new line of insurance. The first modern political risk policies were written in the early 1960s. Over the years, political risk policies have become clearer and more specific regarding the intent and scope of coverage. In some instances, these changes broadened coverage, while they made the policies more restrictive in others. The marketplace has also undergone changes over time. Twenty to twenty-five years ago there were many insurers and reinsurers participating in the political risk insurance marketplace; today there are only a handful.

Perhaps the greatest change in political risk insurance since its inception is the underwriting approach used. Today, underwriters have strong skills in international trading, finance, and banking combined with underwriting expertise in international insurance. A political risk insurance underwriter must understand international trade first and underwriting second. To underwrite the vanilla-type of political risk policy, like one covering confiscation and nationalization, only a basic understanding of international trade is necessary. For more complicated risks like counter trade, currency inconvertibility, and contract frustration, the underwriter must be highly educated in the art and science of international trade. Knowledge of banking, letters of credit, foreign contract negotiation, and international law is a prerequisite for successful underwriting. Because there are no formal schools that provide training in political risk insurance, insurers have developed their own training and education programs, and many of them are excellent.

Today's highly educated underwriters require much more information than did their counterparts twenty and more years ago. They ask hard, detailed questions. They also review copies of contracts and terms of trade to completely understand the transaction before issuing binding coverage.

While the political risk insurance marketplace has waxed and waned over the years, the future looks bright. The insurers are positioned for effective underwriting and creative marketing to respond to the needs of U.S. companies engaged in international trade.

Spread of Risk

As with any line of insurance, it is important for insurers to achieve a spread of risk in their insurance portfolios so that they can offer stable pricing and policy terms. Unfortunately, however, the buyers of this insurance have a natural tendency toward adverse selection, that is, corporations with sales or assets in a variety of markets or countries tend to insure only the political risks associated with those areas of the world that present current political instability. The tendency of exporters/insureds to retain "easier" risks while transferring "hot spots" to insurers frustrates insurers' attempts to maintain a diverse spread of risk.

However, there is an inherent flaw in this philosophy of insuring only the difficult risks and retaining the less risky exposures. If an underwriter is provided with a broad spread of risk, a reduction of rates and more liberal underwriting terms may be obtained. The greater the spread of risk presented to an underwriter, the lower the rate that will be used to develop premium, up to a point. This may allow the insurance of more risk for the same premium than would be charged to cover only those countries, projects, or products that present the most exposure to the exporter.

There are several ways an exporter/insured can provide insurers with a spread of risk when buying political risk insurance, including the following:

Diversification of Countries. Consider insuring all export sales, even sales to countries with a tradition of political and economic stability.

Diversification of Products. Insure all products and not just those presenting the highest risk of loss.

Terms of Sale/Payment. Some methods of sale and payment present greater exposure than others. The most secure type of sale is one that has some form of guarantee, security, or collateral from an independent third-party facility, such as a letter of credit where a third-party banking facility guarantees the financial aspects of the transaction. However, a significantly higher exposure is presented to the exporter/insured when sales are done on an open account, sight draft consignment, or other terms whereby the customer in a third-world country is likely to receive the merchandise before being obligated to pay. By insuring secured sales along with those that have no third-party guarantee, the spread of risk is increased.

Timing. Spread of risk can be increased by making shipments over an extended period as opposed to adhering to a compact shipping schedule. This approach allows time for some shipments to be paid before other shipments are delivered. Adjusting the timing in this manner avoids exposing the entire value of the transaction at one time. Shipping schedules encompassing a one- to three-year period are viewed favorably by many underwriters, but some types of transactions will benefit from a longer period (e.g., seven years).

Political Risk Coverages

There are several types of political risks:

- Confiscation
- Currency inconvertibility
- Nationalization
- Devaluation
- Expropriation
- Unfair calling of financial guarantee
- Deprivation
- Trade disruptions
- War, strikes, riots, and civil commotion

- Terrorism
- Contract frustration

There are a number of different types of political risk coverages. In many respects, political risk insurance is similar to export credit insurance (and some people might include export credit insurance in the list). However, there are some distinct differences between these two categories of insurance. Basically, a political risk loss results from a peril originating out of a political or government eventuality, whether the consignee is a sovereign or private entity. An export credit risk, however, is typically defined as the credit exposure emanating solely from the actions or inactions of the private buyer.

The main distinction is that credit exposures emanating solely from private buyers are inherently more volatile than those that depend on the action of a governmental entity. This results in fewer insurers willing to write export credit coverage. When it is provided, a substantial volume of underwriting and credit information is required, the rates are high, and the coverage terms are restrictive.

Incidents like the Egyptians' anti-government uprising, military action between North and South Korea, the Gulf War, and Bosnia caused many people to focus on war and terrorism coverage. Virtually all property insurance policies contain war exclusions, making it clear that damage caused by a war between two or more countries is excluded. The application of a property insurance policy to terrorist acts may not be so clear-cut, but some form of basic coverage is provided for terrorist acts by many property insurance policies. The approach used in the war exclusion of the latest Insurance Services Office, Inc. (ISO) is that commercial property forms are commonly used even in nonbureau forms. Such policies exclude only damage from war, rebellion, revolution, civil war, or warlike action of a military force. Property policies containing exclusions of this nature would typically be deemed to cover damage caused by most terrorist acts. However, some property insurance policies also exclude damage caused by a hostile or warlike action of an agent of a foreign government. Under this language, an insurer might be justified in excluding coverage if the terrorist act was proven to be inflicted by an agent of a foreign government.

ISO War Risk Exclusion

The ISO will not pay for loss or damage caused directly or indirectly by any of the following war and military actions:

1. War, including undeclared civil war
2. Warlike action by a military force, including action hindering or defending against an actual or expected attack, by any government, sovereign or other authority using military personnel or other agents
3. Insurrection, rebellion, revolution, usurped power, or action taken by a governmental authority in hindering or defending against any of these

Coverage for the excluded property damage exposures is available in the political risk insurance marketplace in the form of a war risk, civil commotion, and terrorism policy. The need for this coverage is dictated largely by the stability of the regions in which the insured's facilities are located and the scope of the war risk exclusion in the insured's property insurance policy. Of course, war risk exclusions can vary considerably from policy to policy and must be carefully analyzed when evaluating the need for separate coverage.

Confiscation, nationalization, expropriation, and deprivation (CNE&D) are the most commonly purchased political risk coverages. They are needed by organizations with assets, like refineries or manufacturing plants, that are permanently located in other countries. The policies respond when these assets are taken over by governmental action, as recently occurred in Libya, Iraq, and Venezuela and, in the more distant past, Chile, Vietnam, and Iran.

Nationalization takes place when the host government simply takes over an asset. Deprivation is said to occur when the host government interferes with the foreign entity's access to or use of its asset without actually taking possession of it. In either situation, the property owner can suffer a substantial financial loss. Confiscation and expropriation are similar actions; the host government takes over the foreign asset with the intent of returning it to the owner in the future. However, the time frame is usually not specified and often extends over several years, causing financial loss to the foreign-based property owner. Because of the similarities between these exposures, the best approach to structuring CNE&D coverage is to insure all four perils in a single policy. This approach minimizes the problems that could otherwise result from disputes with insurers as to whether a particular action falls into one category or another.

Another common political risk for which insurance is available is contract frustration. This entails the nonperformance or frustration of a contract with a host governmental entity or private buyer in a third-world country as a result of an invalid action. An invalid action is an activity detrimental to the U.S. interest that would be considered inappropriate or illegal in the United States. It can be further defined as an action that wrongfully invalidates an overseas transaction in such a manner that the exporter is unable to obtain payment for its product or recoup its assets.

As an example of the contract frustration exposure, assume a U.S. company has a contract with a third-world government to supply custom-designed parts for the construction of a factory. However, the third-world government cancels the contract without a valid reason prior to delivery of the product. In such a situation, it would be common for the company to have spent a substantial sum on the initial design and preparation to manufacture the parts. Because the project involved a custom design, it's unlikely that another buyer for the parts could be found, and the exporter would suffer a financial loss.

Currency inconvertibility is an increasing concern for U.S. exporters, particularly those that sell on open account or provide open terms of payment. This type of loss occurs when the insured's customer pays in local currency, and the local government is unable to exchange the local dollars into foreign currency. Examples of countries where this can be a problem are Colombia, Brazil, Nigeria, the Philippines, and Mexico.

Currency inconvertibility has become a particular problem in countries that underwent a tremendous expansion in the past fifty years because of foreign oil sales and the growth of foreign direct investment. When oil sales began to decline in the 1980s and the Organization of Petroleum Exporting Countries (OPEC) could not agree on pricing and sales quotas, affected countries suffered a trade imbalance, causing more hard dollars to leave the country than were arriving. This made it difficult for the national banks of these countries to convert the local currency into the currency of other countries because the banks were not able to purchase foreign dollars, yen, Swiss francs, euros, etc., with hard currency. In other words, the banks may not possess an adequate amount of U.S. dollars or other currencies to make the exchange. Ultimately, what typically occurs in these situations is a rescheduling of the country's debt over a multiyear period, implementation of strict economic controls internally within that country, and involvement by various international entities, such as the International Monetary Fund (IMF), World Bank, and General Agreements on Trade and Tariff (GATT).

When insuring a trading activity in a country that commonly has problems converting its currency, underwriters typically will write the policies with a waiting period that corresponds with the time frame over which the conversion will occur. This waiting period ranges anywhere from 60 to 720 days. The purpose of the waiting period is to ensure the coverage applies only to fortuitous loss.

An often overlooked exposure of many companies doing business overseas is the risk of an unfair calling of a financial guarantee. This risk usually arises with large transactions that take many months or years to complete. In such a situation, it is common for the buyer to make a down payment (e.g., 15 percent of the contract price), followed by periodic installment payments as the project progresses. The buyer would typically require the seller to post a letter of credit or other financial guarantee against these payments, and the buyer would be able to draw down on that letter of credit in the event something occurred that caused the supplier to default. The unfair calling of this financial guarantee is an exposure to the exporter/supplier, and unfair calling insurance protects the exporter against this risk.

Trade Disruption

Another exposure that companies involved in international trade often overlook is the business interruption exposure that is caused not by physical damage to a plant or other facility but by a political event. Both importers and exporters face this loss exposure. For example, assume a manufacturer relies on a single supplier in a third-world country to provide raw material that it imports for its U.S. manufacturing plants. A political occurrence, like a war, strike, change in government, confiscation of the supplier's assets, change in politics, or change in law occurring in the source country, could disrupt the flow of that raw material into the United States. The manufacturer's ability to produce the finished product would be impaired, and a substantial financial loss may occur if an alternative source of the raw material can not be found. In a similar fashion, an exporter can experience a loss when the product is not delivered on time because of some event beyond the control of the exporter. Such exposures are insurable in the political risk insurance market.

It is important to understand that most executives tend to view their potential loss as the value of the physical product, failing to consider the potential loss of earnings, extra expense, loss of profits, and loss of market in the event a physical and/or political eventuality occurs. Trade disruption coverage can provide protection for these losses.

Markets

The political risk insurance marketplace can be divided into two basic categories: governmental markets and private markets. In the United States, the principal governmental market is the FCIA (now part of the Great American Insurance Company), which was authorized by the U.S. government via Ex-Im Bank. With headquarters in New York City and satellite offices throughout the United States, the FCIA provides many types of political risk coverage and export credit insurance for U.S. exporters shipping U.S. products to approved countries. Most countries in the world that have favorable trading status with the United States are considered approved.

In the past, the FCIA was considered bureaucratic and unresponsive to the needs of most exporters. However, in recent years, this has changed, and the FCIA has become more responsive by offering competitive and comprehensive programs, like the bank letter of credit and new-to-export buyer programs.

OPIC is the other U.S. government-sponsored market for political risk insurance. OPIC insures U.S. nonmilitary investment exposures, like confiscation and nationalization, in developing nations throughout the world. Its terms and conditions are broad, and the rates are as competitive as the FCIAs. However, only assets located in nations having favorable trade relationships with the United States qualify for coverage with OPIC.

There are two drawbacks to the U.S. government's programs. First, they are subject to U.S. diplomatic and trade policies. When the U.S. government is following a restrictive trade policy with a particular country, the Ex-Im Bank and other governmental facilities tend to follow suit, thus reducing the availability of coverage or restricting coverage terms for that country. Likewise, when the government eases trade restrictions with a country, coverage availability and terms will increase.

While this may be good politics, it sometimes restricts coverage availability for transactions with countries that, while not on favorable trade terms with the United States, might present good business opportunities and be excellent credit risks for individual businesses. For example, a number of U.S. companies have been successful in trading with the Russia, Poland, and other Eastern Bloc nations over the last few years and have been paid regularly and responsibly. However, because of its unfavorable trade relationship with the United States, transactions with the Russia and the CIS states are generally not eligible for most of the U.S. Government's insurance programs. The second drawback to U.S. governmental markets is that they only cover U.S. companies and/or products. As an example of how this restricts availability, consider a company located in New York City staffed by U.S. personnel that exports Canadian products into Europe on an open account basis, thus creating an exposure that could be covered by export credit insurance. This company would not be eligible to buy credit insurance from the U.S. governmental facilities because the product is not manufactured in the United States.

Of course, this limitation of coverage availability is fundamental to the underlying purpose for which Ex-Im Bank and OPIC was created: to encourage and support the exportation of U.S. products and services. These facilities are not always profitable, but they provide an indirect means of subsidizing U.S. business interests overseas. At this time, the U.S. government will only subsidize activity that directly benefits U.S. interests, products, or services.

Most other Western nations also have established facilities similar to the Ex-Im Bank and OPIC to insure export sales to other countries. U.S. companies with divisions domiciled in these nations can often access these local governmental programs.

The private insurance market provides coverages that are not available from the governmental markets, and it is not bound by the diplomatic policy of any one nation. This market is basically made up of some U.S.-domiciled insurance companies and London markets. The principal U.S. companies that write political risk insurance are Chubb, COFACE, and American International Underwriters (AIU), but there are a handful of other insurers that occasionally write various types of political risk coverage. Most U.S. insurance companies with marine capability will write war, strikes, riots, and civil commotion coverages on overseas transactions. Along with Chubb and AIU, other underwriters include CIGNA and Great American. Being commercially driven, U.S. insurers will write insurance in those areas where there is an opportunity for profit. The natural downside of this tendency is that it is difficult to obtain insurance from these insurers in countries where the possibility of loss is significant. In general, U.S. insurers offer broad policies and competitive rates and are willing to write on a spread of risk basis affording the exporter a complete program covering all overseas sales.

The London market is composed of Lloyd's of London, Institute of London Underwriters (ILU), and other insurers. This marketplace is as competitive as its U.S. counterpart. In addition, the London insurers typically are willing to put out more capacity and are more agreeable to manuscripting policy forms. London underwriters also have different perspectives on certain areas of the world than their U.S. counterparts and may provide coverage in areas where U.S. insurers are reluctant to do so.

Be careful in choosing an agent or broker to access the marketplace. The broker should be large enough to bring a substantial number of international resources to the table and have a staff that is knowledgeable in international trade and the political risk marketplace.

Loss Control

There are a number of loss control tactics that U.S. companies doing business overseas should consider using. These measures help reduce exposure and secure more competitive pricing and more comprehensive terms from political risk insurers.

Political risk exposures are heavily influenced by the contracts underlying the business transaction. Contracts often are executed on overseas transactions without review by insurance advisers. Knowledgeable insurance advisers often can suggest alterations that will substantially reduce the exposure, making the transaction easier and less costly to insure. For example, underwriters view the inclusion of arbitration clauses favorably because such clauses substantially increase the likelihood that the exporter will get a fair hearing in the event of a dispute, as opposed to arguing its case in the local courts. Consider a situation in which an exporter is fighting the government of a third-world country on an unfair calling of a financial guarantee in that country's court. There would be a serious disadvantage to the U.S. company in that situation compared to an arbitration proceeding in Zurich, London, or some other city outside that government.

Another consideration is to give the local government an interest in the overseas venture. For example, assume a U.S. company builds a plant in a third-world country.

Involving local personnel in the management and operations of a local venture can also reduce the political risk exposures. When a foreign-owned facility employs many local citizens, the government is less inclined to cause a disruption of its operations.

Careful consideration should be given to the currency transactions specified by the contract. A transaction that runs into problems because it requires that local currency be converted into U.S. dollars might flow more smoothly if some other currency, like yen or euros, could be used to complete the deal. The alternative currency might then be used in other international trades or converted to U.S. dollars.

It is also important to set up contingency plans to follow in the event a political eventuality occurs that would disrupt the venture or transaction. This involves developing specific strategies for dealing with potential political problems.

A critical element of loss control is to access timely and comprehensive sources of political and economic data that can be used in making decisions on how we sell or source overseas.

Information used constructively can be the most important element of any political risk loss control program.

How to obtain information, how to analyze it, and how best to put it to use are all necessary skill sets in the risk management arena of global supply chains.

Conclusion

In the last few years, there has been a dramatic increase in U.S. exporting and importing activity. In 2010, President Obama put forth various export iniatatives for the purpose of increasing export activity as a method to reduce the deficit and increase jobs. In 2011 and into the future, the trend is that exports have increased by more than 6 percent and as export controls are lessened, exports will continue to grow.

More U.S. companies than ever are making investments overseas and importing raw material or finished products from their overseas subsidiaries. These activities present substantial risks not faced by organizations operating solely in their home country. Once these exposures are identified, they can be insured by government-sponsored facilities or in the domestic and London insurance marketplaces.

Political Risk: Not for the Fainthearted

In the last thirty years, the primary market for political risk insurance had many players, most of them new. Today, there are fewer underwriting options but there is greater market capacity. Reinsurance capacity is adequate. The demand for coverage is moderate and rates are on the increase. The marketplace has changed from thirty years ago but is working to assist companies in covering the foreign political and economic exposures that are now contemporary risks to global trade.

In the mid-1980s insurers encountered significant losses. "Hot" areas like Lebanon, Nicaragua, Libya, Iraq, and Iran produced frequent and large claims in underwriting exposures because of war, terrorism, confiscation, nationalization, expropriation, deprivation, and currency inconvertibility.

In addition, the worldwide debt problem brought substantial and numerous claims in currency inconvertibility, devaluation, and contract frustration. Because of claims in countries like the Philippines, Brazil, Argentina, Mexico, and Nigeria, insurers experienced an increase in loss frequency. As a result, many private insurers withdrew or significantly restricted coverage in certain geographic areas.

In the early 1980s to the late 1990s, insurers had written broad policies containing terms that should have been black and white but that actually were gray. One of these areas was related to currency devaluation. However, it did not take too many losses before underwriters made it clear that this exposure was to be excluded under their insurance terms. Today, a few underwriters provide this coverage but the terms and conditions are very limited.

Ultimately, as a result of the losses that hit the marketplace and fears of more in the future, the marketplace sorted itself out. There are a number of new underwriters, including those who write niche policies under speciality banners, that can be accessed via corporate insurance brokers.

Some major players, like Lloyd's, COFACE, and Chubb, provide substantial capacity, although these insurers now write the risks in a more detailed and comprehensive manner than they did before. Lloyd's has undergone a changing of the guard. Many Lloyd's leaders that were in this business in the early 1980s to the end of the 1990s remain today in 2011, but others who attempted to write political risk insurance have abandoned it.

In addition, although the efforts were minimal, many marine underwriters in London did attempt to extend their policies to cover certain types of political risk. And war risk underwriters in London were, and still are, major players in CNE&D risks.

For example, during the last thirty years banks have attempted mostly unsuccessfully to enter this market as insurers, brokers, or major assureds. In examining political risk insurance in 2011, we must consider the increasingly major role now played by governmental facilities. Most westernized trading nations have some sort of governmental agency that provides insurance on export sales. Typically, these programs are designed to promote export trading and foreign investment. Often they are politically motivated.

The United States has OPIC and the Ex-Im Bank. OPIC primarily responds to fixed investments in third-world countries, while the Ex-Im Bank responds to all U.S. exports worldwide. The Ex-Im Bank is more inclined to help a U.S. trading or exporting company and provides a full range of political risk and export credit insurance programs.

Another quality insurer is the FCIA. At one time the FCIA was underwritten by a consortium of private insurance companies, but sometime between 1980 and 1982, because of poor loss experience, the programs became completely underwritten by the U.S. government's Ex-Im Bank in Washington, D.C. The FCIA offers an array of programs and services via a professional staff of marketing, underwriting, and claims executives. It is now a private underwriter and is part of the Great American International Companies.

In the early 1990s, the Ex-Im Bank was accused of being just another governmental agency with lots of red tape and bureaucracy. But in the past five years it has upgraded its staff, streamlined its procedures, modernized its programs, and is becoming a lucrative option for exporters with programs that are designed for large and small companies, first-time exporters, and financial institutions.

> *One cannot discuss political risk insurance, which is part of the system of international trade, without including institutions in trade finance and banking, which play a major role in the whole process.*

It is important to note that banks in Ex-Im Bank programs can receive their funds promptly when losses occur and not get caught in trade dispute problems that curtail cash flow. Consequently, the Ex-Im Bank should become an even more important player as the U.S. government continues to emphasize U.S. exports and provides the resources to promote them. The agency's challenge is to meet the needs and demands of the U.S. exporter and to make its programs known and easily accessible.

The demand for political risk insurance will grow in the next few years, primarily because U.S. companies will increase their exports to third-world and developing countries. To compete with foreign and domestic suppliers, U.S. companies will sell on extended terms, increasing their credit exposures.

The political risk underwriter will need to extend coverage to commercial credit risks. Currently, only a handful of underwriters will provide the export credit cover. Other markets willing to provide political risk exposure cover should step up to the plate and provide some sort of protection for sales to private buyers and the accompanying credit risks. Governmental insurance programs, which must meet requirements for "American" content, will have to be modified to address the need for "foreign" content as well.

Because of these particular needs, the development of appropriate underwriting skills in credit analysis, political risk review, and international trade also must proceed. The political risk underwriters of the future must be multifaceted and have talents beyond those required by "normal" underwriting. They must also be well versed in letters of credit, foreign banking practice, and current events on a multinational basis and should have an eye for hidden exposures covered by international trade terms.

Because political risk insurance is a unique exposure, special relationships exist. Numerous markets that may be involved in this area but do not make that information public make accommodations to suit their clients.

In addition, the seriousness of the political risk exposure calls for more of a partnership between the insured and the underwriter than do more traditional forms of insurance. The contract of sale between the exporter and the foreign buyer becomes the building block of the policy, ensuring terms and conditions. The insured and the underwriter must communicate openly, develop a complete understanding, and make certain that the "intent" of the policy is made clear. This is essential because the intricacies of international trade are not always black and white.

U.S. and some major foreign banks, which have played a functional role in political risk insurance, will also continue to be an integral part of the market. Many of the banks that have set up export trading companies to become directly involved in international transactions will attempt to become first-party insurers as well. Because banks continue to face legal challenges to their right to become involved with insurance, this development process will be tedious and slow, but definitely will continue to evolve. Banks first will attempt to buy and control brokers that can handle these risks, eventually becoming direct underwriters themselves.

Other Players

Europe, Hong Kong, and Japan will supply other players, in addition to the United States and London. For example, Pan Financial, a company formed in

London as a result of a triventure of Skandia, Yasuda, and Continental, would underwrite certain classes of political risk and credit exposures The trading nations of the world recognize the need to provide insurance for exports, and both governmental and commercial resources will respond to this need

Foreign markets will be particularly important for reinsurance because domestic capacity for these risks will remain limited. (The U.S. reinsurance market appears to have determined that the class is too difficult and that it has tremendous loss potential.) Reinsuring this class of underwriting calls for a different mentality from that required for reinsuring commercial covers. Political risk insurance has no set underwriting guidelines or rating structures. It does not have decades of loss tables or loss experience to measure trend on. It is a totally free market that depends solely on capacity and negotiation.

Insurance Against Political and Credit Risk Exposure for the Small and Medium-Size Enterprise

To grow and expand their worldwide market share and continue to have a high degree of profitability, small and medium-size U.S. companies must increase their activity in the world market. This increase in activity will heighten the exposures faced by these trading enterprises, which can be broken down into four basic areas: export sales activity, personnel, corporate liability, and financing.

Overseas Sales Activity

U.S. companies are also selling more of their product abroad. A considerable amount of this business consists of exports to our Western friends, however, we have also seen an increase in sales to secondary trading partners and third-world countries. Many small and medium-size companies have contributed to this increase.

Another exposure facing companies involved in foreign trade is that of the buyer not honoring the terms of a payment, thereby extending the accounts receivable. Whether or not a product is sold to a Western and/or third-world country, the buyer, being a private organization, may not uphold its obligation to the seller. If this situation occurs, it is very difficult, if not impossible, for the seller to collect on the account receivable as the means available to do so are extremely limited. The less economically advanced the nation is, the more difficult it is to collect. American companies can insure these accounts receivable exposures, referred to as *export credit risks*, with various governmental and private resources. For smaller companies, the FCIA or Ex-Im Bank is a favored option. Larger risks can approach private sources like COFACE, CIGNA, and Chubb.

Particularly in third-world countries, one of the major exposures for U.S. sales activity, primarily in accounts receivable situations, is that of currency inconvertibility. This risk becomes reality when a private organization honors its obligation and pays for goods in local funds, but a foreign government is unable to transfer these funds into U.S. dollars. Numerous losses of this type have occurred in countries like the Philippines, Nigeria, Mexico, Brazil, and Venezuela due to the tremendous debt-related problems of these countries. Slow currency convertibility in Russia and other former Soviet (CIS) countries is becoming a major detriment to trade to these nations as this problem grows into a serious dilemma for U.S. exporters.

For example, companies who need to do business in Russia often have no alternative but to sell on terms that create an account receivable. (Typically, this requirement means a sight draft of sixty or ninety days.) Following the arrival of goods and clearance via Russian customs facilities, the Russian customers pay in rubles. Most exporters wait six months to a year for the Russian government to transfer the rubles into U.S. dollars. In some cases this conversion has taken more than three years. Exporters with export credit insurance policies have been able to receive their funds just ninety days after the default has occurred. In these instances, the insurance company will subrogate against the host government and wait for the funds to be transferred. Under typical third-world moratorium debt conditions, underwriters are likely to see the funds in two to seven years, thereby suffering only a cash flow loss.

Personnel

With the increased activity of companies doing business overseas, there are more and more American personnel traveling to foreign countries. They are exposed to damage and/or loss of life. Statistics show that in between 1994 and 2004, for example, almost 40 percent of all worldwide terrorism has been directed at American interests. The U.S. company can provide some level of protection using kidnap and ransom insurance. This insurance provides a third-party indemnification for any kidnap and ransom money that may need to be expended, but more important, it allows insurance company professionals to intervene and mitigate any loss that may occur.

The most recent events in Libya and Egypt have shown the increased exposure for expatriates and personnel serving abroad in unsecure countries. Under turmoil many are fleeing these countries to avoid further exposure to arrest, harm, and loss of freedom.

When a U.S. national traveling on business was kidnapped in a South American country a few years ago, the company appealed to the U.S. government to intervene. Governmental agencies, however, were unable to provide timely and/or comprehensive assistance, and the company did not know how to proceed. At that point, the professional staff of the insurance company providing the kidnap and ransom insurance stepped in and obtained local talent who understood the situation and were able to negotiate the employee's release. Approximately sixty days after the event, the employee was released, upset and emotionally damaged, but in good physical condition. The employee later remarked that it was specifically the insurance company's intervention that enabled the crisis situation to be resolved as smoothly as it was.

Another issue concerning personnel traveling overseas is that of the health insurance they require. Companies must ensure that their insurance policies extend indemnification and support services to foreign countries. Companies must also ensure that related insurance, like workers' compensation, disability, and life insurance, cover employees' travel abroad. The question is: If an employee goes to the hospital, who pays and how? Clearly these kinds of risks increase the more the exporter travels in areas with specific problems. The use of a specialized facility that assists U.S. nationals abroad called SOS Assistance Corporation, located in Philadelphia, Pennsylvania, is highly recommended.

Liability Insurance

In the United States, companies are familiar with the exposures they face in the U.S. court and litigation system for third-party liability, especially as it relates to their product liability exposures for domestic sales. American companies in particular have experienced a dramatic increase in product liability lawsuits. With augmented sales of American products overseas, more and more domestic companies are exposed to legal action in local litigation systems abroad or in the United States. As a result, American companies must ensure that general liability policies extend coverage to overseas sales. Small and medium-size companies can lose substantial amounts of money that will affect bottom-line results.

American companies must also consider the fact that foreign governments often take highly unfavorable stands on questions of the U.S. company's liability when doing business in their country. In certain nations, executives can be held personally liable and subject to heavy fines and imprisonment for the activity of their company in that country

Companies must be are aware of local law and legislation and that their insurance policies provide indemnification in the instances to which the laws apply. It is just a question of asking a few questions.

Financing

Small and medium-size companies typically have difficulty finding financing for their export activity, particularly financing with extended payment terms and for trade with third-world countries.

By using insurance as a tool, exporters can structure trade finance situations to expand their business. Once the bank or financing facility develops a comfort level using insurance as a fallback, they become more willing to extend financing for export transactions.

The banks can become "named insureds" or "loss payees" as their interest appears. Export trade financing for $25,000 to $25 million has been arranged for an array of small and medium-size trading companies, enabling them to successfully complete transactions and compete in world trade. While the asset base is important, the comfort level and the exporter's trade finance experience become an important part of determining how much new business the exporter can take on.

Basic Steps to Protection

In general, trading companies have many types of exposures when they conduct business on a multinational basis. There are three basic steps a company should follow to protect its interests overseas:

1. **Companies should acquire in-house expertise or retain it.** Acquiring expertise on a transaction-by-transaction basis is possible as an alternative to having in-house staff spend more time than is currently warranted. Some transactions carry the full cost of the expertise. For others, consultants with fees independent of the transaction may be needed.

2. **American companies must remain fully apprised of all possible options available to minimize or transfer risks abroad using governmental programs**

and private organizations. Knowing which governmental program to approach or how the balance shifts between governmental and private sector programs as conditions change means staying on top of the market.

3. **Corporations operating multinationally must practice loss control measures like, but not limited to: contract review, use of local services in foreign countries, monitoring currency exchange laws and international trade trends, and being aware of political activities worldwide.** Using these means to gauge the climate of the international marketplace, some forecasting can be accomplished that will reduce the risk of a political event damaging successful world trade activity.

Although the many exposures inherent in world trade complicate the trading environment, most transactions are completed, and for those companies that have prepared in advance, the responsibility for the problem items can be shifted to experts who are prepared to resolve them.

Basics of Insuring Against Political and Credit Risks

To grow and increase global market share while maintaining a high degree of profitability, corporations around the world must increase global scale activity. But of necessity this also heightens the exposures faced by such multinational enterprises in the areas of fixed investments, sales activity, personnel, and corporate liability.

Numerous companies are purchasing or building factories, offices, and other operational facilities overseas. The major exposure such companies face abroad, particularly in third-world countries, is the possibility of the host government's confiscating, nationalizing, expropriating, or depriving the venture of its interest. Many Western companies have witnessed this in Iran, Libya, Peru, Nicaragua, and some African nations.

For example, prior to the fall of the Shah in 1979, a company had a contract with the Iranian government to establish facilities to provide local telephone and related communication services to the Iranian people. Following the Shah's departure, and with it the fall of the pro-Western regime, the government confiscated all of the company's supplies, equipment, and fixed property for its own use. The company was uninsured at the time and lost between $10 and $15 million, which had to be absorbed internally. Had this client taken advantage of an option to insure such overseas exposure, the loss could have been transferred to an insurance company and been indemnified for 100 percent of the loss.

With an increase in the number of governments worldwide that are unfriendly to foreign interests, including nations in Latin America, the Middle East, Asia, and Africa, the multinational with fixed investments overseas should take steps to provide political risk insurance against these exposures.

In addition to making fixed investments in the world market, foreign companies are also selling more of their product abroad. In particular, from the 1990s to 2011, U.S. companies demonstrated the highest increase in exporting activity. And while a considerable amount of this business consists of exports to Western friends, there has also been a significant increase in sales to secondary trading partners and third-world countries. Since 2001, U.S. firms are also increasing manufacturing and business activity in many developing nations. Global outsourcing and offshoring have made tremendous gains.

Exporters from various countries also encounter other types of exposure, including embargo by the exporting government or the government of the country to which the merchandise is being shipped. For example, in 1985, a company had arranged to sell its product to Nicaragua when the U.S. government suddenly declared an embargo on trade activity with that country. This client had developed a product line specifically designed for a customer in Nicaragua, and all the sales literature, packaging, etc. had been designed specifically for this company. The goods were not shipped because such a shipment would have broken U.S. trade law at the time. The product had to be retooled and repackaged for shipment elsewhere. The expense exceeded $1 million. The company submitted a claim under the embargo provisions of its political risk insurance policy and received full indemnification.

Political Risk Coverage Analyzed: Ten Critical Steps for Risk Managers

With more corporations making direct investments overseas, increasing foreign sales activities, and dealing more frequently with third-world countries, the political risk exposure has increased, creating a need for risk managers to direct attention to this subject area.

Political risk exposures generally refer to losses emanating from governmental or political sources. They include confiscation, nationalization, expropriation, and deprivation of assets by foreign governments, and include events such as import/export license cancellations, currency inconvertibility, war, strikes, riot, civil commotions, embargo, contract cancellation/repudiation, and boycott. Losses emanating from business dealing with private entities abroad are generally classified as export/credit exposures. Insurance can be purchased against one or all of these risks. Following are ten critical steps that a risk manager should take when purchasing political risk insurance:

1. **Selecting a Broker/Underwriter.** The choice of a broker is perhaps the risk manager's most important concern, because the broker is the first line of contact. There are many brokers who can talk around the subject of political risks, but there are few who can perform adequately in a limited insurance market.

There are few options in the choice of underwriting market today, but, the number is increasing rapidly as more insurance companies enter the political risk arena to meet the demands of American businesses.

A properly selected broker and underwriter combination will maximize risk management effectiveness. Establishing broker/underwriter rapport will help accomplish mutual understanding, reliable service, continuity of coverage, and increased opportunities for competitive pricing.

2. **Service Requirements.** In the process of selecting a broker and underwriter, an analysis must be made of what the corporate entity is looking for in the relationship. Aside from arranging the protection of assets, other services available include:

- Export financing
- Filing of applications
- Political risk intelligence
- Loss control and claims handling

- Contract and exposure review
- Communication of coverage to divisions, subsidiaries, etc.

The servicing area for political risk varies greatly among brokers, underwriters, and specialty consultants. Commissions and fees that affect the bottom line should reflect the services provided and the ultimate decision in a choice of broker and market.

3. **Combining Risks.** Risk managers should combine various political risk exposures under one policy. This will maximize underwriting clout in obtaining favorable terms and conditions and will greatly help to reduce premiums. Underwriters will favor a spread of risk and react positively toward being the corporation's only political risk market.

Because of the limited number of markets, minimal capacity, and a relatively small underwriting/brokerage political risk community, it makes good risk management sense to concentrate risks into one market and not continually seek competition.

Risk managers also should combine other international risks in a coverage like kidnap and ransom, difference in conditions, business interruption, marine, construction all-risk, etc. Underwriters favorably view combining these insurance coverages in a package policy, because they typically are more stable and predictable than other political risks and help provide more reasons for the market to perform.

4. **Communication.** Because political risk insurance is unique and cannot be explained to the layman as easily as other conventional property/liability coverages, there is an absolute need to establish comprehensive communication channels between the risk manager's office and operating units, such as international sales, treasury, corporate finance and credit, and legal to name a few. The following actions are recommended:

- Set up in-house seminars to educate and inform employees.
- Establish formal communication systems, including updates and weekly status reports.
- Appoint local coordinators to become familiar with the subject area and operating plan if, because of distant operating units, logistics present problems.
- Consider having brokers communicate directly with the divisional and operating personnel. This might expedite information transfers and provide additional support. However, the risk manager should always be kept informed of activity.

5. **Contract Review.** The typical method of providing underwriting data to the market is by questionnaires. This is an excellent starting point; however, a thorough review should always include analysis and review of the contract, terms of sale, terms of payment, and other documents relating to the exposure. This will help assure that the proper coverage is obtained, the underwriter thoroughly understands the risks, and any questions as to intent are answered clearly.

Changes often can be obtained by altering contract wording, terms of sale, etc., which could greatly reduce exposure and/or increase underwriting ability.

6. **Political Risk Intelligence.** Political risk insurance focuses on economic, social, and political events. To assess the need for coverage, the exposures must be understood, and understanding the exposures requires information. There are numerous sources of international intelligence including the U.S. State and Commerce Departments, private information services, banks, trade associations, embassies, and the media. As part of brokerage services, qualified facilities will assist in the area of information support and provide up-to-date intelligence on world conditions.

7. **Rates, Terms, Conditions.** Consider that each market's standard policy is different and that manuscripting is a necessity if proper coverage is to be provided. The exact exposure should be explicitly defined, and coverage should be tailored to meet the risk, whether it be for nationalization, currency inconvertibility, license cancellation, war, etc. Other areas that should be addressed are:

- Deductibles and coinsurance.
- Waiting period.
- Rescheduling.
- Warranties and exclusions.
- Method of reporting exposures.
- Coverage for business interruption and protection of profits.
- Loss of market, delay.
- Changes or fluctuations in currency. Note that this is an area for which it has become increasingly difficult to arrange coverage.
- Currency for claims payments.
- War risks.

Cost, which appears to be controlled by market conditions, current economic and political situations, and quality of presentation, is typically a significant corporate expenditure.

Premiums vary greatly with each risk, but one must be assured that apples are not being compared with oranges. Compiling checklists comparing quotas is a good method for fair evaluation.

8. **Export Credit.** Most political risk coverages exclude export credit (the proximate cause of loss emanates from the private buyer). Risks like nonpayment and contract frustration are significant exposures that exist when dealing with private buyers. It is important to determine whether the ultimate buyer is private or governmental as interests may be jointly held. The time to make this determination is before the policy is secured and not after a loss has occurred.

Markets for export credit coverage are more limited than for political risk, requiring specific underwriting details about the creditworthiness of the buyer and the payment track record. Obtaining this insurance is often a tool for increasing foreign sales, because account receivables are protected and banks are more apt to provide lucrative export financing.

9. **Loss Control.** Insureds should seek measures to minimize opportunity for loss and to entice the interest of local businesses. Such measures include:

- Use of local management, personnel, etc.
- Development of sales that require continuing support, like providing service, maintenance, spare parts, accessories, etc.

- Development of rapport with local officials by joining business associations, trade groups, etc.
- Review of opportunities for local financing of the import or project
- Analysis of the contract to further protect interests or secure favorable treatment from the host country
- Information gathering, another key ingredient

All of these will help control the fate of your venture in the event of a loss.

10. **Claims Procedure.** Before a loss, written procedures should be developed addressing the who, what, when, where, and how of handling claims. List all personnel of the broker and the underwriter and include their home telephone numbers. Contingency plans should be developed to provide options in the event of loss so that business will stay on track with little interruption. Run drills and have meetings with key personnel. Procedures should be agreed to ahead of time to arrange for arbitrators in the event of contractual and/or claims disputes.

Use a Specialist to Arrange International Protection

From the Export Trading Act of 1982 to the Obama Export Initiative of 2010 and, other recent trade regulatory changes have made it easier for the small to medium-size company to do business overseas. To be competitive, these companies have to sell on terms where credit is extended beyond transfer of title or alternative credit and financing terms are offered. This poses two significant exposures: contingent marine and political/export credit. The inexperienced exporter typically overlooks these exposures until there is a loss. In addition, U.S. exporters are selling on terms where the importer is controlling insurance (i.e., cost and freight (CFR), free on board (FOB), free alongside (FAS), etc. and has terms of payment extended beyond the ocean voyage or after arrival at the ultimate destination.

The marine insurance problem arises when a loss occurs that is discovered at the final destination, and the buyer refuses payment or partial payment based on the fact that not all the merchandise has arrived or is not in 100 percent sound condition.

The exporter will advise the buyer that the full quantity of a sound product was shipped, and that the buyer should seek payment from its insurance company. However, the buyer may never have arranged insurance, or may have limited terms and conditions not covering this type of loss, or the policy may have a huge deductible. Whatever the reason, the buyer has the merchandise and has not paid for it. Other than litigation, there are few other means to seek indemnification from the loss. This is where the marine insurance policy can play a strategic role.

An exporter who sells on terms where it does not control insurance and can sustain a financial loss as a result of physical loss or damage can arrange a "contingency cover" that will respond to the loss as if the exporter were insuring the cargo as a primary interest.

There are numerous insurance brokerage companies that specialize in managing these exposures.

This insurance is known as "unpaid vendor" coverage and can be easily arranged as part of the master cargo policy or on an independent special risk basis. This area is where most exporters leave the door open for exposure and most brokers and underwriters miss the boat. It takes a unique and specialized understanding of marine cargo logistics to do it well.

Specialized insurance brokers highlight other exposures like political risk/export credit that may even be more significant as it is a primary and direct source of loss, not "contingent."

The risks faced come under a multitude of titles: import export license cancellation, private buyer guarantees, currency inconvertibility, confiscation, expropriation, war risk debt rescheduling, contract frustration, letter of credit drawdown, consequential damages, nationalization, deprivation, strikes, riots, and civil commotion.

Increasing those exposures is the U.S. exporter's need to deal with the third-world political events in Libya, Egypt, and Iran. Afghanistan, Lebanon, Mexico, Nigeria, and Brazil have increased the demand for facilities to allow exporting corporations to transfer their risks.

There are numerous governmental and private insurance companies available to underwrite the political and export credit exposures. Lloyds of London underwrites a multitude of U.S. exporter exposures.

An increasing number of U.S. companies are participating in foreign governmental purchases and investments. The contracts involved have inherent political risk exposures. What if a foreign government, after placing a $3 million order and after ten months of production (generating expenses of $1.5 million), experiences a coup d'etat? The new government cancels the contract. Because of the nature of the sale, only $250,000 of the $1.5 million already expended can be salvaged, bringing the net loss to $1.25 million. This risk could have been insured.

What about the U.S. exporter who sells on consignment to Central America and ninety days after arrival the private buyer has not paid or, the customer has paid, but because of a trade deficit the state bank is unable to convert currency? Where does that exporter turn for collection? These risks are insurable.

Political and export credit insurance can be expensive and developing underwriting data is time consuming; However, the exposure warrants the effort and expense because of the protection it provides from potential disaster.

Policies typically have deductible and coinsurance levels with long waiting periods between time of default and underwriters claim payment. These terms should be negotiated in accordance with your contractual obligations.

Terms and conditions vary from underwriter to underwriter and competent brokerage support is mandatory to negotiate the most comprehensive coverage for a particular client's needs. There are only a handful of competent insurance brokers. When choosing a broker the exporter should review the broker's capability to place the coverage and also provide a country risk analysis, analyze sales contracts, work with international marketing executives, service the account daily, and assist in claims settlement.

Many U.S. exporters have used their policies in conjunction with export financing facilities to arrange lucrative export financing and have found this transfer of risk to be an avenue to increased foreign sales.

An exporting executive has the responsibility to protect the corporation's assets. The application of contingent marine insurance and political risk/export credit covers are prudent steps in the overall functions of exporting management. The bottom line is protection of assets and profit and the opportunity to become more competitive in international sales.

Transporters and Exporters Need Political Risk Coverage

Political risk is an issue of rising concern for the transportation industry. As world trade becomes more extensive, especially with third-world countries, the need for political risk insurance is obvious. Although the political risk insurance market is tightening, with rising rates and shrinking capacity, coverage is available.

Shippers and transportation companies should be very aware of the fact that there are exposures, and that there are ways to transfer or minimize those exposures. Most companies doing business overseas are exposed to political risk and in need of coverage, from Fortune 500 companies to one-man trading companies. There are many companies unaware of the need for or the availability of political risk insurance.

Traditionally, the U.S. government has had export insurance programs, but those programs are not the only options. U.S. private markets and Lloyd's of London also provide protection. The most pressing political risk coverage needs are fixed assets exposure and accounts receivable exposure. As an example, the exposure to political risk for a steamship company with overseas operations can be far-reaching. Terminals, cargo handling equipment, and other overseas terminal area assets may be at risk if the political climate in the country in which the company is operating changes. Industrial mishaps or political revolutions can leave an overseas company with substantial losses.

CNE&D coverage is available for such an exposure and will reduce losses that threaten an international company.

Fixed assets coverage for assets on land in an unstable or politically turbulent foreign country is largely unavailable. Companies managing to obtain on-land fixed assets coverage will meet with limited terms and very high prices.

Coverage is available by any mode of transit, and underwriters limit terms in most cases and prices vary considerably. However, insurance is always available at a price.

Underwriters have suffered tremendous losses during the last thirty years. As a result, there has been a tightening up of the market with insurance contracts becoming more detailed. The political risk market has incurred losses in such countries as Iran, Mexico, the Philippines, Brazil, Lebanon, Nicaragua, Russia, Korea, and El Salvador, and more recently in Afghanistan, Egypt, Liberia and Iraq with similar areas indicated as "potential hot spots."

In addition to fixed assets exposure, companies doing business overseas, especially exporters and transporters, are subject to accounts receivable exposure. Export credit insurance is available for those political risks.

When a company exports goods or services to a country with an unstable economy, receiving payment is often a problem. The shipper can become a victim of inconvertibility of foreign currency. In countries where foreign exchange is controlled by the local government, conversion can take many months or, in some cases, years. If a foreign government makes a decision to hold back on its foreign exchange of currency, an exporter can suffer a substantial loss. When the proximate cause of a loss emanates from a government or a political eventuality it becomes a political risk exposure.

An exporter of goods or services also can suffer losses due to an action on the part of the U.S. government, thus creating a political risk exposure. When the U.S. government canceled all export licenses to Libya, a company that had contracted to build a telecommunications system took a great loss. Because that loss was the direct result of a political decision on the part of the U.S. government, political risk insurance was needed to cover the loss.

There are numerous brokers and underwriters who are prepared to provide extensive loss control advice for political risk customers. In the case of an accounts receivable exposure, a company may be advised to bill using a foreign subsidiary where the foreign exchange climate may be more agreeable than that between the United States and the country to which goods are being exported. It may be easier to convert the local currency of a third-world country into Swiss or British currency than into U.S. dollars. Billing using a third country could, in some cases, minimize a risk.

There should also be loss control measures in place for political risk clients with fixed assets exposure. A variety of measures are available. Exposure can be reduced by involving local management in the operation of an overseas facility. If a plant is run by nationals, rather than by foreigners, the company is in a whole different ballpark.

In addition, if a local government has an interest in an operation within its borders, political risk is lessened. It is recommended that corporate contingency plans for companies operating overseas to insure against loss of a plant or loss of future production be put into place.

While political risk capacity is shrinking due to recent losses, the need for coverage is growing. As the globe continues to shrink with more and more third-world countries becoming part of the international commerce scene, the growing need for political risk insurance for shippers and transporters will continue.

Getting More from Marine Insurance

U.S. corporations in international trade are expanding their activity to increase overseas market share. Companies previously involved only in domestic sales are looking to foreign markets to increase greater growth and productivity. With this heightened activity, the requirements for comprehensive marine insurance programs are increasing, and the distribution manager's role in arranging these programs is becoming more vital.

When buyers are not buying, when capital is scarce, when profits dwindle to a fraction of their former selves, distribution managers are put in a tough position. To put it more bluntly, it becomes time for them to cut their costs or pack their bags. When budgets must be trimmed to realize short-term economies, consider-

---

In dealing with political risk, a specialized insurance broker is essential. A political risk expert who is able to determine what coverage is needed, where a risk may be placed, and what kinds of loss control measures are needed to minimize political risk exposure is needed.

ation of long-term benefits (other than job security) often goes out the window. One of the first casualties of these spontaneous purges is insurance. When people are forced to cut in any area they can, one of the first things they do is shop around for a less expensive insurance program, and they may end up leaving an insurance company they've been with for thirty years to go with a new agent who does not know them as well. While this may result in lower premiums, it also results in having an agent who will not cooperate as well when there is a large claim or the company does not have fifty years of premium payments to support paying the big claims. That means there is a better chance of foot-dragging when claims service is needed down the road.

Another favorite budget-trimming technique used by under-the-gun exporters is changing transportation packaging to take advantage of cut-rate carriers. If the exporter has used a U.S. flag conference carrier, a third-world carrier—from which the opportunities for claims recovery are minimal—may be considered. Once again, from an insurance standpoint, the short-term savings may be far outweighed by the procedural problems that are likely to crop up down the road.

The shipper must recognize that insurance is not designed to yield short-term dividends. Insurance is not meant to be used that way. Manipulating insurance coverage to milk savings for the short run will defeat the ultimate goals of the best-laid insurance plans.

The mission of the distribution manager in the current market with regard to marine insurance should not be one of concentrating on reducing the premiums or on downgrading packaging and carrier standards that protect cargo from the need for a claim in the first place. Rather, the emphasis should be on customizing insurance programs to take advantage of the opportunities to protect corporate assets, thereby affecting the bottom line of transportation costs. Cost-effectiveness can be improved not only by cutting initial costs, but by getting a greater return on the money your company has been investing all along.

Clearly, there are a number of steps an international shipper can take to help achieve the short-term and long-term insurance objectives of its company.

Terms and Conditions

"All-risk" and "warehouse to warehouse" are standard conditions offered in marine insurance policies.

You have inland transit lanes that are brutal to the cargo, justifying the need to insure the cargo from door to door. When you're moving cargo to, for example South America, a major market in the new millennium, and a new focus for U.S. companies in 2011, the most severe leg of the entire journey is the inland transit on the import leg.

Overland movement subjects cargo to a different set of stresses than does an ocean leg, something that many shippers overlook as they design packaging to protect their cargo for an ocean shipment.

While the majority of loss and damage comes from rough handling, most shippers must protect their goods against more exotic causes of damage. All-risk insurance coverage provides a broad base of protection, but does have exclusions including delay, inherent vice, willful misconduct of the assured, and loss of market. For example, if an electronics manufacturer is shipping high-technology equipment overseas and the anticipated voyage includes outside storage and the product becomes rusted or deteriorates as a result of outside storage, underwriters could take the position that the loss is uncovered because it would inherently happen if the cargo was stored outside and was not properly protected against the environment. Distribution managers should make sure that product lines that are susceptible to "inherent" loss travel under policies that are properly endorsed to provide that kind of protection.

Another type of risk is loss of market, which is covered by loss of profits or business interruption insurance. It provides coverage for cargo that is lost at sea, delayed, or damaged at the time of arrival with the result that the shipper loses a sale, is unable to complete a project, has an installation delayed, etc. Under this policy, the shipper can still recoup its financial losses.

Brokers and Underwriters

There are plenty of insurance brokers and underwriters around, but very few of them are specialists in international transportation insurance. The search for such a specialist is one of the essential tasks distribution managers must undertake when insuring assets.

If a company is shipping overseas, it should deal with a forwarder that specializes in overseas shipments. When dealing with a claim that originates overseas, the company will then be dealing with an attorney who is a specialist in international law. In the same way, when insuring an international shipment, a specialist is needed.

Corporate insurance and finance departments are good sources of advice on the selection of brokers and underwriters. It is important that the distribution manager carefully select the broker who will place and arrange insurance programs, and that the underwriter be a well-established marine agency with worldwide servicing capabilities and a staff of professionals for in-depth backup and expertise.

Brokerage companies such as Roanoke, Willis, Marsh, AON, ACE, Wells Fargo Insurance Services, etc., all have high-quality brokerage capability in international and marine risks.

Insurable Interests

On an FOB New York export sale, according to international trade definitions as interpreted by International Commercial (INCO) Terms, it is the buyer's responsibility to insure the cargo once it has been placed on the vessel. The terms of sale dictate the insuring responsibility.

However, the terms of payment can also come into play and determine insuring responsibility. A corporation could have an FOB New York sale, and terms of payment could be sight draft sixty days. The U.S. corporation's insurable interest would be up until the day it receives payment.

The vessel could sail from New York destined for Rotterdam and sink three days out. When the corporation attempts to collect payment from the buyer who was responsible for insuring the merchandise, it may discover that the buyer did not insure, has limited terms and conditions, high deductibles, or other factors that will retard the company's opportunities to collect full or partial payment.

Third-world nations are having an increasing effect on the insuring responsibilities of foreign shippers by implementing local regulations that require shippers to insure their cargoes in the local market. Failure to do so can result in fines or even seizure by governmental authorities. This necessity often burdens U.S. shippers with insurance policies that are characterized by high premiums and narrowly defined terms. In that case, a contingent or difference in conditions policy, which sits above anything that has to be purchased locally, should be obtained. This provides protection in case the policy purchased locally falls short or if the buyers did not purchase the required insurance.

Contingency coverage is particularly useful when a shipper's products have been sold on an accounts receivable basis. In this case, the risk is not only that merchandise will be lost, but also that payment will never be received. The potential problem for shippers with this type of sale is that if part of the shipment is lost or damaged on its way to the buyer, the buyer may rightfully refuse payment. However, because the exporter shipped sound goods, it will expect payment and will advise the receiver to recoup the loss from the insurer. However, the buyer may not be sufficiently insured or may be carrying a huge deductible. Apart from legal action, the only way for the exporter to recover its loss in the event of such standoffs is by contingency insurance. The underwriters will expect you to seek payment from the buyer or the buyer's insurance company and will only pay for the loss on a loan basis, but if settlement cannot be made, the loan becomes a final settlement.

The bottom line to the dilemma, insurable interests versus insuring responsibility, is to attempt to control the insuring function at all times, whether you are selling or buying merchandise to or from overseas.

Competitive Markets

Shippers who feel compelled to reduce their premiums should be able to do so without sacrificing the relationship they have built with their current insurance company. Most of the worldwide marine insurance market has been soft for the past decade, and this continues into the year 2011 which means that extremely competitive rates, terms, and conditions can be achieved at this time. This could be beneficial to the distribution manager who is trying to reduce transportation costs. In other words, lower premiums may be there for the asking while insurance companies struggle to maintain their customer base.

The marine insurance market may harden in the near future if conditions follow the "harder" probability/liability market of the past few years.

Reduced Paperwork

Computerization and technology/EDI of insurance reporting has not been among the most vigorously waged campaigns in the computer revolution. In most cases, the technology is ready for action, but shippers have not applied computer technology to more than a few specific tasks. Unfortunately, insurance reporting is not one of those tasks.

There are so many companies, including some of the biggest in the world, who duplicate and reduplicate paper for the reporting of insurance. Some have import/export order entry systems, and all the information they need is in those computer systems. The same information included on invoices is also needed for insurance reports, but many companies are taking this information, which is computer-generated for billing, and are copying it by hand into their insurance reports instead of generating those reports by computer as well.

One bright spot on the international documentation front has developed with regard to certificates of insurance that are often used to meet commercial banking and customer requirements. Much has been done to eliminate the requirements for these certificates by using preprinted invoices and/or preprinted "sticky-backs" which affix to the commercial documents that serve as proof of insurance.

Settling Fees

Marine insurance typically is rated by the shipper's experience, meaning that actual claim experience will determine what premium rates the shipper will pay for marine coverage. Thus, the greater the claims activity of the shipper, the higher the premium rate will potentially be. There are ways to minimize costs in advance of actual losses that can save cash in the short-term on individual loss settlements and in the long-term in the form of lower premiums.

Expenses associated with claim activity include overseas settling fees for agents of the underwriter who handle the claim and survey fees incurred when ascertaining the nature and degree of loss or damage. Some studies have indicated that these expenses range from 5 to 25 percent of claims dollars. That means that for every $100 of claims paid, $20 of that amount could be associated with just handling or settling the claim. Many times a small claim overseas, say $100, will have a $150 survey fee attached to it.

The opportunity exists to prenegotiate settling fees with overseas agents by using U.S. brokers or underwriters on a reduced-account or bulk basis. The old saying, "If you don't ask, you won't get," holds true. There's no reason not to ask for a consideration on reducing settling fees. Limits also can be determined, like for losses under $500, for which surveys can be waived and claims can be paid with the processing of a few documents.

Buy-Back Deductibles

Many shippers dislike the idea of deductibles on principle. They note that many claims are for relatively small losses. Without first-dollar coverage, the shipper pays for the entire loss out of its pocket and never recovers anything from the expensive insurance programs.

The insurer's side of this is that a deductible program is more cost-effective and mitigates nuisance claims and costs.

Insurance and Creative Financing: Down Payments in Solving a Huge Impediment to Trade

Opportunity exists with the political risk insurance organizations to help companies compete globally.

Recently, a potential U.S. exporter had a problem common to many U.S. companies that have cutting edge technology that is in great demand globally. The company's foreign buyer wants to order $100 million of the U.S. company's product and has been asked by the would-be U.S. exporter to make a 30 percent down payment.

Now the foreign buyer is willing to make a $30 million down payment and additional progress payments to enable the purchase of this valued U.S.–made equipment. In the words of the buyer to the seller however: "How do I know that you and your wife will not take my down payment and catch the next plane to Brazil?" There is a solution for this imbroglio in international business and it is called a "counter guarantee."

The foreign buyer asks for a guarantee from the buyer with respect to the down payment. The amount of the requested counter guarantee is normally between 5 and 10 percent of the down payment or progress payment amount. The guarantee takes the form of a standby letter of credit whose effect is to guarantee the foreign buyer that the down payment will be used to manufacture or obtain the goods for export.

Many SMEs(small and medium-sized enterprises) cannot afford the cash collateral that their banks routinely request in order to issue a standby letter of credit. In addition, the 100 percent cash collateral that banks require in order to issue a standby letter of credit restricts the amount of cash available to a company for its working capital, capital it desperately needs to source materials and manufacture the goods.

This dilemma can be solved with a working capital guarantee from the U.S. Ex-Im Bank. The working capital guarantee provides a guarantee to a lender and the wherewithal for the U.S. exporter to borrow at an advance rate of 75 percent against the inventory designated for export, including work in process, and to borrow at an advance rate of 90 percent against the foreign receivable, once the goods are shipped.

While working capital guarantees generate considerable cash flow, the need to cash-collateralize counter guarantees can easily wipe out the working capital of a firm. The solution to this dilemma lies within the structure of a working capital guaranty facility, wherein a sublimit can be established for the issuance of standby letters of credit for this purpose. When guaranteed by the Ex-Im Bank's working capital guarantee facility, the lender's collateral requirement is reduced to 25 percent of the amount of the guarantee. The 25 percent is negotiable. The difference in availability of working capital to the U.S. exporter, assuming 10 percent of the amount of the down-payment, at 25 percent collateralization, in our example, is $2,250,000.

The cost of a WCG facility includes a facility fee of 1.5 percent and a bank interest rate that is negotiable and reasonable because the lender receives the full faith and obligation of United States in the form of the Ex-Im Bank guarantee.

In summary, working capital guarantees are an effective means of obtaining significant down payments and counter-guaranteeing such down payments while retaining sufficient working capital to fulfill the project.

This process utilizes the available market supported by our government resources, and it provides a new way of funding trade opportunities, making U.S. exports more competitive, in keeping with President Obama's Export Initiative of 2010.

Another government program offers "expedited buyer financing" for U.S. manufacturers and service providers. Here's an example of how expedited buyer financing might work:

A U.S.-based exporter of equipment manufactured in the United States had a problem resolving an export opportunity. The manufacturer had a $7 million order destined for Brazil that requires multiyear financing. The exporter preferred that financing be arranged for the buyer in Brazil and asked whether there was an expedited way of doing the deal. The U.S. exporter expressed a pressing need as foreign competitors are vying intensely for this business opportunity.

In response, he was introduced the buyer to a program offered by PNC (Pittsburgh National Corporation), one of the United States's premiere trade finance institutions whose relationship with the U.S. Ex-Im Bank provides U.S. exporters with a unique ability to quickly realize their export opportunities. PNC arranged for the bank's officers in Sao Paulo to visit the buyer and obtain the buyer's financials in order to arrange a multiyear loan. PNC is one of many banks like Citibank, Chase, Wells Fargo, Bank of America, etc., that have access to these programs.

The underlying financing that is being made available to the Brazilian buyer has some characteristics that are important to consider:

- Financing is extended directly to the foreign importer without the need for local bank guarantees or the issuance of expensive letters of credit.
- Financing is free of liens on equipment and other assets.
  A grace period for the installation and set up of equipment is provided.

This type of financing is based on the bank being provided insurance by Ex-Im bank. The financing has the following basic requirements:

- **Loan Amount:** From $350,000 USD and up. The amount may include multiple shipments made from more than one supplier/exporter.
- **Financed Amount:** The lesser of 85% of the sales contract or 100 percent of the U.S. content under the sales contract.
- **Term:** Usually five years (up to seven years for special cases).
- **Repayment**: Semiannual installments of principal and interest.
- **Interest Rate:** Option of fixed or variable interest rate. The variable interest rate fluctuates based on six-month LIBOR plus a preestablished and competitive spread.
- **Ex-Im Bank Risk Premium:** Established by Ex-Imbank, based on the terms and conditions of the loan and the country risk (Please see article in the Managing Imports and Exports of _____ featuring the use of the Ex-Im Bank calculator)
- **Bank Fees:** Based on size and type of credit and competitive

For U.S. manufacturers and providers of the following products and services, expedited financing is available to the foreign buyers of your products:

- Agricultural product
- Broadcasting equipment
- Chemicals/plastics
- Construction
- Food processing
- Franchises
- HVAC
- Printing
- Heavy equipment distribution and leasing
- Manufacturers
- Medical
- Oil and gas
- Packaging/corrugated boxes
- Telecommunications/cable TV

- Textiles
- Transportation equipment

Some engineering and consulting services associated with goods may also be eligible for financing. At the end of the day these programs create significant opportunity for companies looking for competitive advantage in the international marketplace.

5

Technology in Global Trade

The future of international trade lies with the greater use of technology. The execution and management of e-commerce sales, fulfillment, logistics services, payment options, and more using technology is discussed in this chapter.

> *Supply Chain technolgy is becoming an increasingly important component of world trade and international logistics.*

Import/export transactions handled totally by technology is here now. It is not a pipe dream. Those companies that are not spending time, money, and resources on automating import/export operations will not be in global trade for long. The efficiencies gained in import/export/supply chain technology automation will make one company substantially more competitive then another. Guidelines and options for the use of technology in global trade are outlined in this chapter with an emphasis on documentation, tracking, and information management.

And even more importantly technology is now a very critical component of an importer's and exporter's responsibilities in managing global trade compliance management.

Using Technology to Gain a Competitive Advantage in Global Trade

U.S. importers and exporters can gain significant competitive advantage in global trade by the use of technology. Access to new markets, more cost-effective sales efforts, and less costly logistics are but a few of the immediate benefits.

Global technology as it relates to international trade is changing and growing every day. There are many options available to the large, medium, or small import/export company. Hook up a personal computer (PC), secure a modem, and you are ready to go for less than U.S. $2,000. An in-depth review of global technology reveals more than thirty specific tools available in this technological era.

Many software and service providers provide extensive data on businesses overseas. These resources are governmental and commercially based. Using electronic data interchange (EDI) or the Internet, one can log on and find an array of information on the following:

- Market data on overseas opportunities
- Names and contact data on overseas companies (compliance and security management)
- Names and contact data on resources, support services, and service providers
- Research profiles on products, services, and demographics
- Specific product and prospect opportunities

Many of these data providers, like Bureau of National Affairs (BNA), *Journal of Commerce* (JOC)/PIERS, and Trade Compass based in Washington, D.C., have become serious information providers. Others, like the Department of Commerce, AT&T, and Dunn & Bradstreet, have been providing the service a long time, but have greatly expanded their individual capabilities.

Today, companies have developed their own web pages to advertise the products and services they sell. This can be accomplished by the smallest of companies for under U.S. $25 per month. Very extensive and more elaborate web sites can cost tens of thousands of dollars and have electronic commerce capabilities that offer the customer the ability to place an order on the web site, among other services.

E-mail affords a cost-effective, timely communication between sellers and buyers. It can replace the fax or enhance it. It has "broadcast" capability that allows the user to form one message and send it to a wide audience automatically at times when usage rates are the lowest, allowing very cost-effective communication.

It allows marketing and sales pieces to be forwarded without the expense of overnight mail and express services. It allows more flexibility and "tailorability" to individual client needs, in different languages, or with different presentation designs to allow for cultural, ethnic, and religious nuances.

Letters of credit, which are heavily used in global trade, can be transacted via automation without the need for all the historical paperwork. Wire transfers, sight drafts, and other means of documentary credit devices can now be accommodated via EDI. Many of the world's leading financial institutions have begun various initiatives independently and in conjunction with various banking service providers to establish:

- Common EDI means of communication
- Secure methods of protecting confidential data
- More timely paperless transactions
- Global links between foreign companies in an array of countries with local and international banks

Successful logistics providers now view their role as information and communication providers and companies that move freight.

The integrated carrier, the freight forwarder, the customhouse broker, the ocean and air carriers, etc. who are making the investments in technology will be the only ones who will survive into the twenty-first century.

The logistics industry is enhancing its use of technology by:

- Developing defined EDI or Internet interfaces with its customers' import/export order entry systems
- Providing linkage into warehousing, inventory management, and shipping functions

- Establishing systems for tracking freight and to deal with customer service issues
- Becoming an integral partner with its clients as an information resource
- Having programs that ease the knowledge of preparation and execution of international documentation
- Affording access to governmental reporting requirements and export licensing matters
- Providing "cloud" capabilities for integration of all technology functions within a corporation's structure

The integrated carriers like DHL, FedEx, and UPS along with the larger and boutique-like freight forwarders and air/ocean carriers have generally taken taken the lead in offering various competitive products.

Many logistics providers are expanding the array of services they are providing because technology has afforded options not previously available.

Compliance and Security Management

Global supply chains can use technology in managing some of the compliance and security responsibilities, like but not limited to:

- Documentation accuracy
- Denied Parties Screening/Office of Foreign Asset Controls (OFAC)/Department of State (DOS)
- Export license requirements (Department of Commerce and Department of State)
- Screening of vendors and unverified parties
- Country profiling
- Documentation transfer
- Data security
- Retrieval of compliance and security information from both private and governmental databanks

These are but a few of the areas that a technology interface could be used to assist a corporation in managing the security and compliance responsibilities. There is an array of software providers, as outlined in the appendix, that can provide these services to various extents. In addition, many service providers, including freight forwarders, customhouse brokers, and banks, offer software solutions as part of their overall service packages.

Automation Takes the Pain out of International Trade Documentation

At the start of the second decade of the twenty-first century, we find that exporters and importers are now exchanging their arduous, painstaking, transactional documents via the Internet or some other EDI capability in over 80 percent of global transactions..

International documentation typically proves ownership, facilitates transportation, and reacts with customs for entry into the buyers' country. Some documents are used for other purposes, like an insurance certificate in case of loss or damage.

For many international transactions and the accompanying documentation, much of the detail is the same from document to document. Pieces, weight, commodity description, value, from/to, commercial and pro forma invoices, certificates of origin, shippers export declarations, and bills of lading are the key export/import facts and documents—all with loads of repetitive data.

Today, documentation is also utilized to meet numerous government regulatory controls in import/export trade such as AES, C-TPAT, Forms 7501 and 3461, FDA requirements, etc.

Automation affords the most cost-effective approach to creating these documents and managing their distribution and use.

The U.S government is taking an aggressive approach to import/export trade automation. For more than twenty years the government's import initiative, the Automated Brokerage System (ABS) has been very successful, basically automating the import transaction for customs brokers and U.S.-based importers. While the system still has numerous bugs that are being worked on, it can be declared a success. Customs is also now looking at a web-based customs entry system that would do away with any of the current formal and massive systems that are currently in use.

Over the past decade, a combined effort of U.S. Customs and Border Protection, the Census Bureau, and the Bureau of Industry and Security (BIS) has resulted in the Automated Export System (AES). The AES is designed to automate the exporter's requirement to send a shipper's export declaration to the government. This can be done manually at the time a shipment is dropped off with the outbound carrier. By the end of 2009, only electronic Shipper's Export Declaration (SED) transfers were allowed, with very few exceptions. By 2004, all exporters, their forwarders, or agents had to be online with U.S. Customs to report export SED data. While the details of the process, timing, and substance of the transfer of this data are still being modified, the responsibility to report some SED information came in 2001 and the overall process is still being tweaked more than ten years later. This has led exporters to automate other aspects of their export operation, which will have immediate and long-term favorable effects as we move into 2012 and beyond. The government agencies that regulate trade have clearly recognized the benefits of technolgy, particularly in interface with huge amounts of data moving between multiple parties.

Automation allows cost-effective export administration and an EDI-based tracking capability. It affords ease of transfer of export data between various company units (export to accounting to shipping) and allows interface with forwarders and carriers.

Eventually, it will allow consistent transfer of data directly to customers, their overseas agents, and their host customs entity. This will do away with "hard copy," which is expensive and difficult to manage successfully.

Keep in mind that many individuals and companies shy away from exporting because of the problems associated with managing export documentation.

Technology in the documentation supply chain creates the opportunity to ease this task, facilitating import/export activity. It also provides numerous benefits in reducing the cost of the transaction, tracking the logistics/transportation, and providing useful data for future management utilization.

As we progress into 2012, technology will be an excellent foundation for all aspects of global trade including import/export compliance management.

EDI—What to Expect from the Carrier

Importers/exporters searching for timely information, tracking capabilities, and methods of reducing the cost of supply chain logistics are depending increasingly on carriers with EDI (electronic data interchange) facilities. What products or services is EDI offering? What methods is EDI using to deliver these products and services to customers?

Some exporters consider forwarders an extension of the cargo carriers. In this case, the forwarder will be considered a carrier. Forwarders also have taken a leadership role in maintaining a competitive advantage by the use of technology.

Many transport providers believe that EDI communications is the single most important element in providing value added services and vendor differentiation.

Basic EDI Services the Carrier Provides

- Automated bills of lading
- Routing and booking
- Pricing
- Tracking
- Documentation information
- Trade compliance

Most carriers provide electronic bills of lading. This readily reduces the cost of executing shipments, particularly for frequent or repeat exports. Integrated carriers like UPS, DHL, and FedEx have responded to exporters by providing automated processing of bills of lading associated with export transactions. Most larger freight forwarders and steamship lines can also provide this service. Some air carriers have a limited capability. Others, like United Airlines, American Airlines, Delta, and Lufthansa have updated their capabilities for this service.

Many carriers have enhanced their services to assist a shipper to find out about levels and routing options. These advanced carriers allow easy booking, another cost-saving measure.

Shipping rates are available online with some carriers, with the exception of integrated carriers, on a limited basis.

Tracking is critical to the overall evaluation of a carrier's performance. Airlines and integrated carriers have taken the leadership role in this area. Steamships have made great strides but are behind in providing automated data. Compared to airfreight, ocean freight is more complicated to track.

Carriers, particularly freight forwarders, are required to adhere to documentation procedures for export transactions. Integrated carriers like FedEx have automated the process with newly developed software programs for both PCs and Macs. Today, alerts to iPhones, Droids, Blackberrys, and similar handheld and portable devices are very much available.

While there are governmental and private written sources on documentation procedures, these are often outdated. Automation facilitates the ability to update changes in a timely and trade compliant manner.

Delivery Systems

The means used for communication is as important as the information provided. Many carriers, particularly major ocean and air carriers who often provide 800 telephone numbers, are automated internally. A customer service representative at a computer terminal should answer questions based on information in the computer. This is an acceptable option for small shippers.

This does not work for frequent shippers, however, who need to be able to obtain information online.

Some forwarders and carriers with in-house EDI systems deliver the data via fax. This may work in some cases, but direct interface is more cost-effective. Most carriers allow limited access via modem, which is a quick and reliable means for transferring data between carrier and shipper. From the carrier's perspective it also allows control over access to the entire system.

Some systems provide interface from mainframe to mainframe. This system is more expensive, but provides quick detection of viruses, which could have devastating effects if undetected. Many companies use third-party facilities (called *firewalls*) that interface between carriers and shippers. This slows the process of data interchange but the trade-off guarantees security. Many of the third-party facilities act as conduits for carriers before the transfer to the shipper. Teledyne Brown is one such third-party facility that interfaces with various air carriers and feeds the information to forwarders and shippers. The direct interface includes bills of lading, booking, tracking, billing, payment transfers, exchange of documentation information, costing and rating data, and e-mail.

What one expects from the carrier is governed by need and competition. Carriers are being forced to respond to the need to provide extensive data and services on a direct interface basis with its shippers and exporters.

EDI has become state-of-the-art for carrier/exporter communication and services provided. The exporter should demand the services afforded by technology and keep the pressure on during this revolution that is taking place in international trade.

Where Is My Export Freight?

You have completed a $225,000 transaction with a buyer in Thailand and shipped the freight via an air carrier just three days earlier for delivery on Thursday. You walk into your office at 0845 on Friday morning and find an e-mail from an irate new customer screaming, "Where's my freight?"

You call your freight forwarder or integrated carrier and it takes all day Friday to track the shipment. You find out that it had arrived on Wednesday, but it has been delayed in customs, awaiting documentation from the shipper, and you knew nothing about it. Customs is closed in Bangkok on Saturday, so you have to wait until Monday to begin to resolve the problem. In the end, the freight is delivered on Tuesday, five calendar days after the scheduled date. Not a great scenario, but also not atypical.

In the better scenario, you ship the freight on Monday, as before. On Tuesday, you look in your computer, which is directly linked to your air carrier and note that the shipment is confirmed on a flight to Tokyo to meet a transfer flight to Bangkok. On Wednesday, when you come into the office, you have a message from the air carrier or forwarder, advising you that the freight arrived last night, but the invoice was missing from the pouch of documents attached to the master air waybill. Your agent in Bangkok advises you to fax or e-mail a copy, and he will clear with that document. You do as advised. On Thursday, you receive a confirmation on your computer that the freight was out for delivery at 1500 local time in Bangkok. On Friday the communication from your new client advises that all has arrived and he appreciates that all was in order and delivered on time.

Obviously, the second scenario is one that quality exporters would prefer. With certain international carriers, forwarders, and integrated transportation companies, this can be a reality. The carriers that have this capability will survive and thrive in the twenty-first century. Those that do not get onto the bandwagon and cannot provide quality, proactive tracking and tracing will not be in business in the year 2010 and beyond. Many smaller and unresponsive, nonforward-thinking companies have already fallen by the waysidebecause they have not participated in the race for the information superhighway.. EDI is here to stay and will become the measure of the more qualified, service-oriented transportation companies. There are four key areas that EDI will play a role in:

1. Transfer of shipping information to organize and execute international exports
2. Tracking and tracing shipments
3. Management information and reports
4. Trade compliance management

Transfer of Shipping Data

Everyone involved in export is aware of the voluminous documentation they are required to produce. Much of the information is repetitive and the time required to produce these documents could easily be reduced using an electronic interface.

Freight forwarders have taken the lead in this regard. Many large and medium-size freight forwarders have spent the time and money and made the effort to link their in-house computer systems with their customers' systems. This affords ease of communication and allows electronic transfer of data that would normally travel by fax, mail, courier, or other means. This speeds up the documentation turnaround time, provides greater accuracy, and may provide other ancillary benefits like control of inventory, accountability systems, and easier quality control management.

Because of the repetitive information in an export order(for example, the shipper and consignee address), having information in a system's memory to access when you are preparing an invoice, a packing list, an export declaration, a house bill of lading, or other document could speed up the execution of these documents. With a specialized export document program, many additional variables, such as number of pieces, weights, product codes, clearing agents, and shipping instructions, also are readily available and reproducible in all the various required documents.

In elaborate systems, many documents can be forwarded ahead of the shipment via an EDI database, affording the foreign clearance agent the opportunity to clear the goods before arrival. This expedites delivery and makes customers happy.

The banking, governmental, and shipping communities entered this arena long ago via such organizations as the National Committee of International Trade Documentation (NCITD), attempting to standardize shipping EDI needs and to speed up document transfers and payments.

Tracking and Tracing

Integrated carriers like UPS, Federal Express, and DHL have taken great strides in this regard. Their efforts still are evolving, but are light-years ahead of where these companies were a mere decade ago.

Steamship lines and air carriers, including United Airlines, American, Continental, Sealand/Maersk & K Line are but a few of the carriers that use 800 numbers to give clients the capability to track and trace their shipments. Airlines maintain exact data because of the more time-sensitive nature of their shipping clientele. Steamship lines have quality systems that afford basic tracking and updates of estimated time of arrivals (ETAs) around the world. The problem with airlines and steamship lines is that they depend on people to input data in a timely and accurate fashion. They all could use better input quality control management and systems. In addition, there is a syndrome that the people who use the computer to track and trace develop that I have named *the ugly track face syndrome*. What happens is that they depend on the computer 100 percent and forget that the computer is tracking something physical. For example, a shipper calls the 800 number of an airline to find out why the freight has not shown up in Brussels.

The shipper needs someone at the airline or the integrated carrier to find out why the computer is wrong and to do a physical search. This always becomes a struggle and is one of the reasons many shippers turn to forwarders, who will usually do this arduous work for them.

The computer, which was supposed to resolve the problem, can become the bone of contention and cause more harm than good. Many carriers are looking to more modern methods of tracking and tracing. UPS, DHL, and FedEx drivers have coding devices to provide up-to-the-minute data. They are good examples of companies that are using the latest in technology to stay ahead of the competition.

Steamship lines and long-haul trucking companies that enter Mexico and Canada are using satellite or GPS tracking devices to locate containers and trailers. Many transport companies are barcoding freight to track its position as it passes through the various checkpoints in the transit cycle.

High-technology carriers on specialized reefer transport loads are using sophisticated equipment to monitor the performance of refrigeration units and measure the temperature of the stow. Some have limited capability to make changes necessary to protect the cargo from loss or damage.

Many forwarders from abroad have "banded" their resources to form technology networks. They interface and exchange data to the benefit of their mutual clients. This gives them the capability to compete with larger forwarders and integrated carriers. Almost all transport carriers provide in-house computers to their clients, offering varying degrees of EDI capability interface.

In evaluating what serves you best, identify your needs and then your best scenario case. Do not be fooled by buzzwords and fancy names or slogans. Find substantive points, get referrals, and call them.

Management Information and Reports

Once all this information has been recorded and saved, it can be made available to management to dissect, discuss, and draw conclusions. Once the quality of data has been qualified with acceptable degrees of accuracy, management needs to identify the usefulness of it in various formats. Most carriers, integrated companies, steamship lines, and truckers fall down in this area. It is the forwarders and logistics management companies that can deal with all the raw data and provide useful reports for management to evaluate. The following you can generate with the proper use of shipping data:

- Sales by carrier and mode.
- Shipper on-time performance.
- Volumes by customer, country, and mode of transit
- Shipping costs by various units of measure. (You might want to know, for example, that it costs $0.20 per kilo to ship to Asia, whereas it costs only $0.17 per kilo to ship to Europe. Then you can figure out why.)
- Loss and damage reports by carrier and mode of transit.
- Shipping expenditures by carrier, mode, and areas of the world.
- Outturn reports showing differentials in shipped and received weights.
- Inventory and quality control reports.
- Trade compliance statistics.

The number and type of reports are endless. As long as the data is available and of an acceptable level of accuracy and can be captured, manipulated, and formatted, the value for management and operating personnel is extensive.

While EDI has involved in most industries, shipping and international supply chains have sorely lagged behind. In most recent years from 2006–2011 there has been a surge of EDI advancements in international freight services to meet the new demands of shippers and their suppliers, customers and trade partners.

E-Commerce: Export Logistics

E-commerce has become a large phenomenon in global trade. The fulfillment and logistics segments for domestic sales have incorporated e-commerce successfully. But in international trade, statistics point to huge rates of failure in the attempt to incorporate e-commerce.

The following problems remain to be resolved:

1. **While ordering can be achieved in e-commerce from almost anywhere in the world over the Internet, there is still the need to deliver the freight.** All the exposures this book has talked about in global trade exist for e-commerce, but perhaps more so.

2. **Electronic ordering can be built into the system, but not electronic delivery**—unless the product itself is digital, like e-books, songs, and movies, and games and programs for your computer that you can download.

3. **Whatever system is structured for ordering, there is a basic premise in international business that you need to know who your customers are.** Does e-commerce allow this? The Bureau of Industry and Security (BIS) requires U.S.-based exporters to know who they are selling to, what the customers are using the product for, and to protect against transshipment. Does the e-commerce system afford this control?

Failure to comply has the consequences of not being able to export and/or heavy fines and penalties.

4. **Payment needs to be made.** Credit cards work up until the first dispute. Then you realize how useless credit cards can be in international sales, when you do not know the other party.

5. **Someone must make sure the customer understands the risks, liabilities, and costs under International Commercial (INCO) Terms.** Professionals rarely understand them, how would the general public? Then who would be responsible for local clearance and delivery? Do they have local custom's representation? Has

power of attorney been authorized? And keep in mind INCO Terms were recently updated in 2010, impacting all shipments globally after 1 January 2011.

6. **Returns need to be handled correctly.** How will the e-commerce system manage returns?

E-procurement is making greater headway in 2011 and is now a viable option for company procurement managers to find and benchmark sourcing options, but it is a new skill set and one that requires significant training and processing controls.

The questions are frightening. Thus far, no one company has successfully worked out all of these issues on a global basis with e-commerce. The bottom line is that the e-commerce supply chain in exports must be set up to respond to all these issues. It will require large EDI operating platforms of standard operating procedures (SOPs) by country, with compliance performance and all logistical concerns dealt with successfully.

A nuance to global trade is that successful logistics requires a lot of handholding and a lot of flexibility. I am not sure anyone involved in export e-commerce could achieve this without a great deal of tweaking.

Technology Impacts Importers in 2011 and Beyond

Importers Security Filing (ISF) Program (Previously 10 + 2)

Many importers are currently dealing with the anxiety of change as they adjust to the new Importers Security Filing program, which was implemented on January 1, 2010, with maturing modifications in 2011/12. It is important to structure internal actions for proper proactive compliance management to ensure compliant ISF processes, procedures, and import SOPs.

Technology advances in the supply chain between foreign manufacturers and suppliers, freight forwarders, customhouse brokers, and CBP have allowed ISF to move forward throughout 2010 and into 2012.

Unlike all other regulatory standards, the ISF program requires importers to demonstrate informed compliance and reasonable care to meet the standards of ISF compliance. The informed compliance effort includes a proper comprehension of the program's requirements in conjunction with the ability to source, verify, and declare all elements of the additional ten data elements from the specific knowledge of an importer's import supply chain process.

There is a lot of data being collected here which technology makes happen much easier.

At issue is not just the ability to know what to file to meet the program requirements but also what is necessary to file the information in a timely manner to meet the twenty-four-hour preload requirement consistent with the Container Security Initiative platform requirements.

Ten Steps to Proactive Compliance Management

We recommend that companies tackle this problems posed by the new ISF rules by following ten steps of proactive compliance management.

CBP anticipates that importers act in three ways in managing their inbound global supply chains:

- Reasonable care
- Due diligence
- Supervision and Control

These ten steps in concert with technology advances will help importers be compliant with the new ISF regulations:

Step 1: Have a strong compliance program in place. A strong compliance program will contain necessary elements necessary to ensure that timely filing is being achieved, inclusive of proper supervision and control of data transmission through record retention practices. A strong compliance platform will have an automatic benefit in a company's efforts to move forward toward compliance performance in this added regulatory category.

Step 2: Ensure connectivity between the logistics management and purchasing functions. If there is connectivity between the logistics management department and the purchasing department to allow for advanced capture of purchase order information, the advanced manifest filing process will be much more manageable from a compliance perspective. Access to P.O. data earlier in the supply chain process will allow the importer to provide manifest level information sooner to the ISF filing agent.

Step 3: Maintain control of international freight decisions and third-party freight forwarding services. The importer should seek to control the international freight decisions, including the selection of freight forwarders and carriers. The control of these decisions will compliment the efforts of compliant and timely filing as the importer will have direct access to advanced shipment details provided by a service provider with their direct interest as a primary responsibility. Technology is key to the words "timely."

Step 4: Maintain control of the container loading process. It is imperative that the importer control the container loading process to ensure that the container is not offered for loading before a proper and compliant advanced manifest declaration has been tendered to CBP in an automated process.

Step 5: Be proactive in your harmonized line item review process. A comprehensive harmonized line item review should be completed by all importers to ensure that correct harmonized tariff schedule (HTS) information is being provided at the purchase order level to the foreign shippers and sellers; it must be available twenty-four hours prior to the loading of ocean containers on vessels destined for the United States.

Step 6: Initiate proactive discussions with your current manifest filing parties. Importers should conduct proactive discussions with the international supply chain participants that are currently filing twenty-four-hour manifest information on their behalf to determine their specific service offerings relative to the ISF program. You can make an informed decision on the best action to take once you know all your options.

Step 7: Determine the best option for ISF filing for each importer. You should conduct an informed compliance review of the options available for ISF filing, inclusive of the stand alone AMS, stand alone ABI, CF 3461 automated filing, and the CF7501 automated filings for *each* of your importers.

Step 8: Determine the automated options available from your current service providers such as freight forwarders and customs brokers. You should conduct a performance and cost analysis to determine the financial impact that this new program will have on your company's bottom line. This will enable you to make a best practice judgment on the most compliant and cost-effective solution available to meet the ISF requirements.

Step 9: Develop post-filing audit functions to ensure timely filings are being realized on a shipment-by-shipment basis. Every importer must have the ability to manage the post declarations filing information to conduct self-assessment reviews to ensure that proper filing information is being transmitted in a compliant and timely manner.

Step 10: The "good faith" intent to comply with ISF rules and regulations must begin at the top. Senior management must endorse the company's effort to meet the new compliance requirement. The good faith intent will be mirrored at the operations level if such commitment is demonstrated from the top down throughout the organization.

Today, CBP and DHS is looking for new ways to utilize technology for managing trade compliance issues, such as ISF. The importer who is proactive in developing technology resources and utilizes providers and carriers with significant technology capacity will have better managed supply chains—

- Piers: www.JOC/Piers.com
- Bureau of National Affairs: www.BNA.org
- The World Academy: www.theworldacademy.com
- E-Global Logistics: www.stephens.com
- Global Logistics Solutions Worldwide Outlook: www.ARCWeb.com
- Capstan: www.capstan.com
- ClearCross: www.clearcross.com
- Express Action: www.expressaction.com
- American River International: www.americanriverintl.com
- From 2 Global Solutions: www.from2.com
- iLink Global: www.ilinkglobal.com
- myCustoms: www.mycustoms.com
- NextLinx: www.nextlinx.com
- Vastera: www.vastera.com

Some of the key issues in selecting a provider in supply chain logistics, e-commerce, or import/export management are as follows:

- **Tenure in Business.** There are a lot of one-night wonders.
- **Flexibility.** The ability to adapt to different situations.
- **Quality** of programming personnel.
- **Integration** capability.
- **Tailorability.** The ability to provide specific tailoring to individual nuances.
- **State-of-the-Art.** The ability to stay ahead of the market place.
- **Proactive versus Reactive.** Many companies respond to competetive pressures in innovating and designing e-commerce solutions. You want to look for a company that is not a follower, but a leader—an innovator. One who is ahead of the curve and making changes that "lead the pack!"
- **Comprehensive.** The ability to integrate multiple needs into one solution.
- **Trade Compliance Capabilities.**

We have found that in selecting potential technology solutions, a viable option is to work with your service providers, like your freight forwarder, carrier, and customhouse broker, who may have in-house technical capabilities that you can access as a "partner" in the logistics relationship. Often they can build the cost of the technology interface into the freight relationship, and they are often on the cutting edge of capability.

This could easily be a more cost-effective option in lieu of significant proprietary or third-party technology solution options.

Technology Utilization for Denied Party Screening Allows Corporations to Comply in a Comprehensive and Timely Manner!

If you are a principal exporter, importer, or involved in any aspect of providing international transportation services (i.e., freight forwarder, NVOCC, steamship line, etc.), you need to be conscious of the government's requirements to check a number of "lists" prior to exporting.

Technology can be utilized to manage the checking of these lists and assuring the highest standards of trade compliance in an organization operating in the international marketplace.

The primary "list" we need to be aware of is the Denied Party List (DPL), which is controlled by the Bureau of Industry and Security (BIS). The BIS reports into the Deptartment of Commerce. This list identifies individuals and companies both in the United States and abroad that we (American citizens) are not allowed to do business with. A U.S. citizen or company may make this list by being involved in transshipments of products that were destined for an acceptable country (or end-user) but somehow ended up in the hands of an entity that was on the DPL. Or perhaps this U.S.-based individual or company was involved in shipping goods to a banned country through another intermediary.

Whenever an export is being arranged, it is part of best practices to check the names of all parties involved in the transaction on the DPL, which is available online. There are a number of software solutions that enable instantaneous scanning of all government lists (OFAC, Department of State List, European Sanctions List, Entity List, Unverified List, Terrorist List, and others) to expedite the screening and to ensure that you meet compliance regulations.

The BIS also controls a list called "Unverified List." This list identifies parties that the BIS was not able to acquire enough evidence to have them listed on the DPL but there is enough evidence to require due diligence to be performed before an export is facilitated. To get an idea of the potential fines and potential loss of export privileges that companies have endured by not following these best practice SOPs, just visit the website for the BIS at www.bis.doc.gov.

Another list the government controls that has been getting much attention is the OFAC (Office of Foreign Assets Controls) list which is part of the Department of the Treasury. This department controls the money transfer that is involved in an export or import transaction. Here's an example of a potential problem if this list is not checked: If you are a U.S. exporter and your overseas customer (who may or may not be on the DPL) is paying you through a letter of credit issued through a bank that is on the OFAC list, the electronic payments between the overseas bank and your bank can be confiscated by the U.S. government. If this were to happen, not only would you be out the money for the transaction, but the government can also issue fines and penalties on you and your company.

One potential penalty can be the loss of export privileges. If exports represent a significant amount of business to your company, the loss of this privilege for months can be devastating (especially given the current difficult economic situation most companies are facing).

Checking the OFAC list is particularly important for all NVOCCs and steamship lines, since, as part of the supply chain you are required to ensure that you are not carrying products from companies that are involved in transactions that may have OFAC exposure. These providers need to be very diligent about checking the OFAC list.

In our business practice we are seeing more and more steamship lines looking to be proactive about performing a "scrubbing" for the OFAC list on all companies and banks they deal with to take proactive approach in this regard.

Being proactive allows a fixed cost to control a potential unknown expense associated with a fine, penalty, and legal expenses that could be astronomical.

Exporters and importers must exercise due diligence, reasonable care, and supervision and control in their global supply chain. DPL governance is an integral component of that business process.

SOPs need to be created by all companies engaged in international trade to best assure trade compliance. This ties into training and education and the development of trade compliance skill sets that are taught at a number of schools such as The World Academy (www.theworldacademy.com) and the American Management Association (www.amanet.org). Companies can budget for these software solutions, whichcan mitigate many potential problems. You can't budget for the unknown: fines, penalties, bad public relations, and loss of export privileges.

Technology makes this responsibility much easier to manage. It reduces human error. It allows huge scans of data quickly and allows for electronic recordkeeping, which can assist in overall regulatory oversight responsibilities.

Best practices, world class and Sarbannes-Oxley (SOX) concerns in trade compliance can be very favorably impacted with the use of technology in the global supply chain.

Concluding Remarks

Technology controls the future of global commerce, and importing, exporting, and supply chains are a major part of that formula. Taking the initiative to develop software solutions and manage the global supply chain with technology will go a long way in securing your business future. Following the guidelines and options in the use of technology in global trade—from documentation to e-commerce—provided in this chapter will support the importer/exporter in achieving this goal.

The role of technology in trade compliance management is also another key ingredient of technology's utilization and value in the global supply chain.

6

Global Personnel Deployment and Structure

Managing an import and export strategy is difficult enough without personnel issues, but they are inevitable. This chapter presents a review of how to maximize your personnel resources, attract quality personnel, and use both developing and seasoned international executives with global skill sets to their best advantage.

Successful International Sales: Future Managers Will Require Numerous Skill Sets

The global sales executives of the twenty-first century will require a vast arsenal of skill sets to make them the top in their fields. They will need to speak three or four languages and have a graduate degree in international marketing from a top-notch school. In addition, they will need fifteen to twenty years of experience in all phases of global operations, cutting-edge negotiation skills, an understanding of the diversity of cultural and ethnic backgrounds in more than sixteen countries, and be able to function without sleep. They will also need to be widely traveled, an expert in currency exchange rates, have superman understanding of all legal issues in any one of the importing countries, be a mega-salesperson in the intimate marketing needs of all the global markets you sell in, be willing to get up at all hours to coordinate sales activity in the Near and Far East, tolerate all the inconveniences of three-week overseas adventures, and so forth.

In addition, the future executive must understand global logistics, international freight rates, trade compliance, consequences of political events such as we witnessed in Egypt and Libya, local customs regulations, and a host of specialized skill sets in World 101.

That is somewhat of an exaggeration, but the reality is that at any one of these special skill sets may be called upon at any time with the expectation that the executive will rise to the occasion and be all knowing and all showing. Even a working knowledge of "social media" and being minimally functional will be a critical skill set.

International business is complicated and the international sales executive is the engine of the operations train, which leads to successful global trade. This means that to be successful the international sales executive must possess a wide array of skill sets, numerous talents, and instantaneous access to varied resources.

Patience and Commitment

Most of the world works on a "relationship basis" first. This means that foreign customers want to have a relationship with an individual before they buy from his or her company. This requires persistence and patience. Sales in the United States can be developed from a cold call and closed on the first visit. This does not happen in most overseas markets. The process of developing the relationship, over several meetings, over several months to years may be required to create the opportunity.

Commitment is one of the keys to success. The process is time-consuming, traveling is costly, and all the related peripheral issues have associated costs: sending samples, product registration data, answering questions, going back and forth with international communications and global courier services, etc. All this takes a toll—and all of it takes time. Only the executive who is committed, patient, and persistent will survive this process.

Developing Resources and Networking Channels

Global sales are complicated, diverse, extensive, and no one can go it alone. There is no way one person could know all the cultural, political, logistical, and economic issues in all the countries they deal with. Complicating the issue is the fact that the situation is fluid and can change at any moment (for example, the political upheavels in Tunesia, Egypt, Libya, and Syria; piracy off of Sudan; and the world economic downturn from 2007–2011). Developing relationships with high-quality service providers—bankers, attorneys, freight forwarders, air and ocean carriers, accountants, consultants, and trade associations, etc.—with expertise in world trade can be of support and assistance in your global development efforts.

Working with the national and district Export Councils in concert with the Department of Commerce in Washington, D.C., and in all major cities is also a great opportunity for skill set development and resource networking.

Understanding the Landed Cost

The terms of sale determine the extent of the costs associated with a foreign transaction. For example, a free on board (FOB) plant sale minimizes costs and liabilities compared to a cost, insurance, freight (CIF) sale, in which the exporter bears most costs and liabilities associated with the transaction to the port of entry.

However, irrespective of the terms of sale, the international executive needs to know that the importer (your customer) has numerous expenses associated with the transaction to complete the entire supply chain process.

Inland freight and handling, air or ocean freight, import licensing and product registrations, warehousing/storage, freight insurance, customs clearance, value-added taxes (VAT), duty and taxes, inland cartage are a few of the overall costs that the importer needs to calculate into the landed cost to determine the competitive pricing to the end-user.

Anything that the international salesman can do to favorably impact any of these areas reduces the landed cost, thereby making the importer more competitive. This then becomes a competitive advantage for everyone.

Increased sales, greater market opportunities, maximizing margins are all benefits of reducing the landed costs to foreign buyers who are now more satisfied customers.

Here's an example of how to calculate the landed cost of goods originating in a warehouse in Milwaukee for a sale to a customer in Paris, France.

Ex works price:	$499,000.00
Inland freight:	1,000.00
FOB Baltimore:	500,000.00
Ocean freight:	3,000.00
Insurance	500.00
CIF Paris	503,500.00

The customer in Paris has additional costs to bring the goods to point of sale or utilization.

Duties and taxes (20%)	
VAT (4.5%)	
Clearance	$125.00
Handling	$225.00
Import license	$325.00
Inland freight	$750.00
Warehousing and deconsolidation	$335.00

When the French customer is calculating his landed costs he must include all the costs to bring the goods from origin to destination, whether under the specific control of the exporter or not.

But having said that, many variables on how, what, and where the exporter does what he is supposed to do will impact these costs, such as but not limited to:

- Choice of carrier and service provider
- Quality of export documentation
- Marking, packing, and labeling
- How payment is demanded

All these and a host of other issues can impact the landed costs to the importer. It requires very tight and communicative colloboration to reduce costs and maximize efficiency in a global supply chain. Working with your service providers, such as freight forwarders and customhouse brokers, will lead to the most cost-effective logistics—and reduced costs all around.

Creative Marketing Skills

Global competition comes from many sources, from domestic companies to an array of sources from all four corners of the globe. Marketing is another key to maintaining or achieving a competitive edge. The following are some creative marketing ideas:

1. Using free trade zones to position in local markets products ready for immediate entry and delivery to the importing country, but not subject to duty and taxes until the order is processed is one idea. Reducing delivery time and lower entry costs can be a great advantage.
2. Offering credit terms can be a significant convenience. Selling on an open account, even at a higher price, can be a valuable tool in the marketing

approach and, when backed by export receivable insurance, can reduce overall exposure and provide entry into markets with current financial problems, like many in Africa and South America and in certain Asian countries.

3. Offering in-country support in sales and marketing on behalf of the importer to the customer base can be critical.

Running product seminars, sales campaigns, making time to go on sales calls, etc., can be invaluable to developing local knowledge, leading to more orders. This will inevitably mean using a variety of approaches, strategies, and plans tailored to the nuances of the culture, the economy, the logistics, and the politics of the market.

The Power of Networking in International Trade

One of the great advantages of membership and participation in the various export trade associations is the ability to interface with professionals who offer a wealth of information on international business.

One of the greatest challenges in international business is dealing with the array of exposures that are encountered compared to domestic sales. Forces of nature, customs authorities, political risks, currency adjustment factors, shipping logistics, legal, and insurance are but a few of the issues to be negotiated in the arena of international trade.

Each discipline requires expertise. It would be almost impossible for any individual to develop an expertise in all the disciplines. The better option is to develop a basic understanding of all areas and then align yourself with one or two experts in the field who you can call on once the specific need develops. These could be lawyers, air and ocean carriers, custom brokers, insurance brokers, accountants, freight forwarders, bankers, or other importers/exporters.

Networking in international business involves an investment in time, money, and resources. Successful people in international trade invest at least 5 percent of their time networking. International trade associations are great sources of networking. Every major city and gateway have associations involved in exporting, such as but not limited to the District Export Council, World Trade Club, PACMAN Professional Association of Import and Export Compliance Managers, the National Institute for World Trade (NIWT), National Association of Export Companies (NEXCO), and the Small Business Exporters Association (SBEA), which are all excellent options for international business networking.

Payback may not always be immediate. The need for a contact or resource may not occur for two years after a contact is made. Someone who needs counsel or assistance often calls a consultant whom they met two or three years earlier.

The ability to get answers quickly can make you a hero, close the deal, and/or reduce some of the risks! Networking affords ease of access to timely resources and responses, which often can mean the difference between getting the order or not. Power networking or maximizing resources can reduce liabilities and increase the opportunities for profit. Responsible and timely advice on international trade can mitigate all the inherent problems of global business.

International networking has other benefits. It provides the opportunity to meet interesting people who are world travelers and good social partners and friends. Many of the networking organizations sponsor social functions like lunches, dinners, golf outings, seminars, and cocktail parties.

There is also a matter of altruism. By networking, you have the ability to contribute to everyone's advantage, and in return you will receive the benefit of everyone else's contributions.

Matured Export Departments: Review and Analysis

Many corporations experience difficult learning curves before structuring the export sales and operating units successfully. Some operate for more than twenty or thirty years without the proper structure.

Improper structure might not mean nonprofitability, but it does affect cost-effectiveness negatively, which leads to less than adequate results or a bottom line that could be better!

The starting point of a good export operation is a commitment from senior management. This is supported by an individual who is strong in international sales and operations and takes ownership of the entire export supply chain. That person will have direct responsibility for or significant influence over all aspects of sales, marketing, production, inventory management, and logistics.

He or she will control all the links in the export supply chain:, Having control over all the aspects makes the chain strong. Not having control opens the door for possible weak links, which can make the entire supply chain ineffective:

- You can sell it right, pack it right, but if it does not get there on time, it may be of little value!
- You can do the right marketing and logistics but if you do not get paid, all was for naught!
- You can have the best product, at the right price, but if the packing does not hold up and the freight is damaged there will be a dissatisfied customer, and no future orders!

The point is, everything has to be working correctly for the export supply chain to produce consistently high returns. The best chance at managing is to give the entire process to one owner. The "owner" may delegate many of the day-to-day responsibilities, but at the end of the day the responsibility rests with that person.

Another characteristic of a quality export operation is continuous staff education and training. Exporting is a fluid circumstance. The more growth and development, all the time, the better off you are.

A special characteristic of quality export operations is that of taking the high ground. Exporting leaves a lot of room to cut corners, take shortcuts, and be a little "shaky." And since 2001,with Customs and Border Protection (CBP), the Bureau of Industry and Security (BIS), Department of Transportation (DOT), U.S. Food and Drug Administration (USFDA), U.S. Department of Agriculture (USDA), State Department, the Bureau of Alcohol, Tobacco, Firearms (BATF), Transportation Security Administration (TSA), and more in our faces, the high ground is a better place to be! And it is in those circumstances that I have observed the best import/export operations.

Attracting Quality Personnel

Attracting quality personnel with international experience may be the greatest challenge in the coming decades. Corporations with successful export programs are doing their best to hold onto existing staff. "Golden Handcuffs" for senior executives and incentives for middle management tied into competitive compensation packages are the steps keeping most personnel loyal.

There are other things a corporation can do to make itself more attractive than its competitors:

- Offer compensation packages with tax-free incentives.
- Offer overseas trips with families in tow, particularly in the summer months.
- Offer significant comp time to balance out the long overseas trips.
- Rotate personnel into different markets to prevent burnout and/or stagnation.
- Maintain high standards for continuing education, allotting proper time for responsible attendance.
- Encourage employees to learn several foreign languages.
- Develop compensation packages that offer incentives for profit sharing.
- Provide "ownership" of specific markets, products, or trade lanes, affording empowering your employees and affording them liberal freedoms.
- Develop clear paths for growth, promotion, and advancement.
- Keep employees in the loop with timely, responsible communication so they know what is going on.
- Adopt a direct, straightforward, no-nonsense approach to performance and overall responsibilities.
- Add training and education components to their responsibilities.
- Add off-site conference and symposium attendance several times a year to keep them networking, fresh, and engaged.

Implementing all or some of these recommendations, combined with the specific nuances of your business will not only maintain existing international personnel, but it will attract other professionals as the word spreads about your career programs in export trade.

The International Import/Export Compliance Manager

Corporations are finding their way to support a new management position with the primary responsibility of keeping the company compliant in its global supply chain.

I like to use the term *point position for customs*. What I mean is that no matter how big the corporation, no matter how many different operating entities engaged in global trade, there should be one person, perhaps supported by a committee, who will be the only person to "talk" to CBP or other governmental agents and decipher information provided by and to authorities.

The last thing a company under the magnifying glass wants is to have nonqualified personnel talking to Customs and providing information without it being screened or edited for accuracy and content. While a company must cooperate with authorities and provide answers to inquiries, the manner in which this information is disseminated could be a critical aspect of the ultimate disposition of the matter being challenged.

A company would always want to put its best foot forward and by being centralized, with one person in control, it can meet this standard operating procedure. CBP as well prefers a "point" person so they do not have to chase down a lot of varied individuals to obtain answers to inquiries.

The compliance officer will typically come out of a supply chain responsibility, like traffic management, inventory control, or logistics. There is no ''best'' place. Personnel with legal or regulatory background will also present viable options. The key qualities are:

- Understanding the relationship among logistics, transportation, and security/compliance regulations
- Ability to communicate well
- Ability to muster expansive resources
- Knowledge of how best to use technology
- Deep understand both of the product and the company's supply chains
- Ability to deal with ''fiefdoms'' and ''political barriers'' within corporations
- Ability to work in an atmosphere where the responsibilities are sure to exceed his or her authority

As corporations have compliance officers engaged in the Occupational Safety and Health Administration (OSHA), FDA, and hazardous materials, they will have them in their supply chains, as well.

PACMAN (www.compliancemaven.com) offers programs and certificates for corporate compliance managers to enhance and sharpen their skill sets to manage current and future compliance and security responsibilities.

Keeping Out of Trouble

Personnel engaged in global trade have both direct and indirect responsibilities to both their corporations and various government agencies for trade compliance regulations.

Penalties are stiff: as low as $11,000 per incident to as much as ten times the value of the transactions involved.

But the more serious penalties are not necessary financial; there can be civil and criminal prosecutions, and when they occur:

- They cost the company tons of money in legal expense.
- They are bad for publicity.
- They can lower stock price.
- They can distract management and staff from revenue producing and customer opportunities.
- They can irritate customers, vendors, and suppliers.
- They can end a career.
- And they can lead to jail time.

So personnel in global trade are best served by having a detailed understanding of the basic trade compliance issues and making sure they and their companies are taking the high road.

Global Supply Chain Management Personnel Deployment: Import/ Export Compliance Guidelines

Global supply chain personnel must have the skill sets necessary to handle all trade compliance issues. The following are some of the more important steps that must be deployed by sales and operating personnel.

Awareness

Supply chain individuals must become aware of what all the issues are and how they might affect the specific import and export supply chain they are responsible for.

Awareness means having a consistent inbound flow of information so we know what the issues are, what the most recent modifications are, and ultimately what options we have in mitigating these matters in our supply chains.

Senior Management

All corporations have profit and cost centers managed by individuals with personalities and egos, each with their own interpretations and ideas on how various responsibilities should be managed.

When you discuss issues regarding terrorism, compliance, and security with uninformed executives you will find a natural resistance to any infrastructure change recommendations put forth by compliance and security personnel.

This is where the support of senior management is vital. Their support of the compliance and security initiatives will break down the resistance and allow for constructive review and implementation..

Analysis and Review

In order to determine where your company stands, you must conduct a facilities review, which is a detailed analysis and mock audit of your supply chain and operations.

This is typically best accomplished by engaging an independent consultant. This will afford a third-party analysis where "others" do it outside the corporation. They have no specific agendas that conflict with personnel or career matters and will have external reference points to utilize as "benchmarks" for where your company is.

Team Approach

Irrespective of the size of the corporation or the supply chain, one person should be responsible for managing the risks of terrorism, compliance, and security. This person can be part of any profit or cost center: logistics, manufacturing, purchasing, legal/regulatory. We do recommend, however, that this person work within a team approach.

Gaining cooperation will be more easily achieved, when all interests— manufacturing, purchasing, customer service, logistics, etc.—feel that they will have influence, their ideas will be heard, and they can provide constructive input.

Action Plan

Once the analysis is done and the compliance person chosen, a plan will have to be developed. We recommend using an Excel spreadsheet that has four columns.

The action plan will eventually lead the company and the individuals in charge of compliance and security into creating Standard Operating Procedures (SOPs).

SOPs

The importance of SOPs cannot be underestimated. They offer three vital advantages:

1. Creating SOPs commits the process to a written format that clearly outlines how a company will function in its supply chain.
2. These SOPs then become a benchmark to meet the government's requirements of exercising due diligence and reasonable care.
3. Should supply chain personnel move on, there are written guidelines for new personnel to follow.

These brief discussions present just a few of the key guidelines to help you become a compliant import/exporter. Compliance is perhaps the most important skill set that responsible and effect supply chain personnel must master.

Concluding Remarks

The better we manage our corporate export and import infrastructure, the better we can run our global supply chain. The quality of our export/import business is directly related to the quality of the personnel we hire. This staff will require numerous skill sets in global business. We will have to find experienced staff or we will need to train them. In any case the entire personnel and deployment issue will need to be managed.

However, no matter how much training and education is provided, the staffs of international business will never know it all, partially because global trade is always changing. What it takes to clear and deliver freight in Laredo, Texas, today, might be different tomorrow. Resources are needed to keep advised of current events in global trade and to find answers to the numerous questions that challenge us every day while managing our export affairs. This chapter provided many suggestions for good management based on the author's experience with hundreds of export companies.

Developing the needed skill sets will be the key to allowing the international sales executive to navigate to the destinations of successful global trade.

> *Networking can be a powerful discipline . . . ain't it so!!! Always taking the high ground will come back to you in the long run.*

7

Developing Resources in the Import/Export Supply Chain Management

This chapter focuses on the trade assistance that is available to importers and exporters. In addition, the types of information that many organizations involved in trade assistance can provide are presented. Developing resource assistance in importing and exporting is a critical step to successful global supply chain management. The various government agencies engaged in trade compliance expect importers and exporters to be informed and have regular means for updating and current events in regulation. In addition to the contact information in the text, I have included an extensive list of agencies and other resources at the end of this chapter.

Chambers of Commerce

Many chambers of commerce provide services for members interested in importing and exporting. Services range from providing certificates of origin to supplying contacts with foreign companies and distributors. More active chambers of commerce are involved with international trade promotions and import and export workshops. They also provide access to business executives experienced in international trade.

The American Chambers of Commerce Abroad office (202-463-5460; www.uschamber.com/international/directory) is a valuable source of market information in any foreign country. It can supply leads on local trade opportunities, actual and potential competition, and periods of trading activity. Detailed service is supplied free to members of affiliated organizations; nonmembers usually are charged for some services.

A particularly active chamber, the U.S. Hispanic Chamber of Commerce (800-874-2286; www.ushcc.com) has established a network of trade opportunities throughout Hispanic-speaking countries.

State Governments

Export development programs are rapidly increasing at the state level and, in some cases, county and city levels. The assistance these groups offer includes education, identification of potential markets and trade leads, and help with obtaining financing and vehicles to promote exporting, like trade missions and trade shows.

U.S. Department of Commerce

The scope of services provided by this governmental agency is vast. The International Trade Administration (ITA) is a part of the Department of Commerce and deals with U.S. exports. The ITA has many divisions, each with a variety of services and products to help companies planning to export. Working with the Department of Commerce used to be daunting, but the process has been streamlined. Now, all that is necessary is to contact the U.S. Foreign Commerical Service district office nearest you (export.gov/eac/index.asp) for information on everything from financing aid to sales leads. There are sixty-eight Department of Commerce district and branch offices throughout the United States and Puerto Rico.

U.S. businesses can participate in trade shows and trade missions sponsored or supported by the Department of Commerce. Trade missions target specific countries or groups of countries with promising export opportunities. For a description of the various trade shows and trade missions the Department of Commerce participates in, go to www.export.gov. This official site can also provide additional information on upcoming trade events.

Exporters can advertise U.S.-made products or services in *Commercial News USA*, a catalog/magazine published ten times a year to promote U.S. products and services in overseas markets. *Commercial News USA* is disseminated to business readers worldwide by U.S. embassies and consulates and international electronic bulletin boards, and selected portions are reprinted in certain newsletters. Advertisement fees are based on the size of the listing. For more information call ABP International, visit the *Commercial News USA* website at www.cnewsusa.com, or contact your local Department of Commerce District Office.

U.S. exporters can also advertise in the International Broadcasting Bureau (IBB), which is part of the Broadcasting Board of Governors (BBG) (202-203-4400; www.bbg.gov/about). IBB is the umbrella organization of Voice of America (VOA), Worldnet TV, and Radio Free Europe/Radio Liberty. VOA broadcasts almost 700 hours of programming to an estimated audience of 86 million each week, and can be accessed online as well. They can peg a company's ads to different language broadcasts about a particular subject (e.g., science and technology, health and medicine) or target the ads to a specific region or country. For additional information, contact the IBB.

The Department of Commerce also provides private and public trade leads from its offices around the world. These leads are available at www.export.gov. The *Country Directories of International Contacts* provides lists, categorized by country, of foreign directories of importers (showing name, address, telephone number, etc.), governmental agencies, trade associations, and other organizations in countries where the Commercial Service maintains a presence. This list represents the primary sources of contact information that each Commercial Service post thought was useful and does not represent an endorsement of any of the services listed.

The Agent/Distributor Service is a customized search on behalf of U.S. companies seeking foreign representation. U.S. commercial officers abroad conduct the agent/distributor search based on requirements specified by the requesting company. The search for agents and distributors takes sixty to ninety days and average costs $250 per market. This service can be ordered from your local Department of Commerce District Office.

The Gold Key Service is custom-tailored for U.S. companies planning to visit a foreign country. It combines orientation briefings, market research, introductions to potential partners, interpreter service for meetings, and assistance in developing a marketing strategy. The local Department of Commerce District Office can provide more information on this service.

The International Buyer Program supports major domestic trade shows featuring products and services of U.S. industries with high export potential. U.S. and Foreign Commercial Service offices worldwide recruit qualified foreign buyers to attend the shows. The shows are extensively publicized in embassy and regional commercial newsletters, catalog/magazines, foreign trade associations, chambers of commerce, travel agents, governmental agencies, corporations, import agents, and equipment distributors in targeted markets.

More information about the Agent/Distributor Service, Trade Opportunities Program, Gold Key Service, International Buyer Program, and other programs of the U.S. Commercial Service is available on the Commercial Service website (www.ita.doc.gov/tic) or by calling a trade specialist.

The Department of Commerce also organizes certain overseas events to promote U.S. businesses, including the following:

Trade Missions. Focusing on one industry or service sector, trade missions provide detailed marketing information, advanced planning and publicity, logistical support to participants. They also arrange appointments with potential buyers, governmental officials, and others. Participants pay between $2,000 and $5,000 depending on locations and number of countries visited. The missions usually consist of five to twelve U.S. business executives.

Product Literature Center. Trade Development industry specialists at ITA represent U.S. companies at various major international trade shows by distributing product or service literature. In addition, trade specialists at these centers identify potential customers for companies displaying their literature.

Reverse Trade Missions. The United States Trade and Development Agency (USTDA) does not fund traditional trade missions to foreign countries, but it may fund visits to the United States by high-level foreign governmental officials to meet with U.S. industry and governmental representatives. These foreign officials represent procurement authorities of specific projects interested in purchasing U.S. equipment and services. The missions are usually cofunded by U.S. industry.

U.S. Pavilions. About eighty to a hundred worldwide trade fairs are selected annually by the Commerce Department for recruitment of a U.S. pavilion. Selection priority is given to events in viable markets that are suitable for new-to-export or new-to market "export ready" companies. Fees range from $2,500 to $12,000.

Small Business Administration (SBA)

The SBA's programs assists new and existing exporters who want to expand their operation. The SBA provides eligible companies with export information, financial assistance, legal advice, and training from its field offices in cities throughout the United States.

World Trade Centers

A world trade center brings together many kinds of businesses and governmental agencies involved in foreign trade and supplies a variety of services from trade research and opportunities to information on governmental regulations and training programs. There are currently eighty world trade centers worldwide. A list of world trade centers is available at the World Trade Centers Association www.wtcaonline.com.

Commercial Banks

Approximately 300 large U.S. banks have international banking departments. Located in major U.S. cities, these banks maintain correspondent relationships with smaller banks throughout the country and with banks in foreign countries. Banks frequently provide consultation and guidance free of charge to clients, because their income is derived from loans to exporters and from fees for special services. Banks are sources of advice on export regulations, currency exchanges, and collection of foreign receivables. In addition, they can assist with export financing and provide credit information on potential overseas buyers.

International World Trade Clubs

Clubs for those involved in international trade banks, traders, shippers, forwarders, customs brokers, and other service organizations conduct educational programs and organize promotional events to stimulate interest in world trade. Membership in a local association gives a company access to knowledgeable advice and benefits like services, discounts, and contacts in affiliated foreign clubs.

Trading Companies

Trading companies can take full responsibility for the export end of the business, from market research to documentation. This can relieve you of all details except filling the orders.

Universities and Major State and Community Colleges

The databases maintained by state colleges and universities often are a valuable resource. Contact the international business department or the business school to inquire if it has information relevant to your situation. You may be able to hire a graduate student to help with market research, as many schools have programs that grant course credit to students involved in this type of extracurricular work. The World Academy (www.TheWorldAcademy.com) is an excellent educational resource.

Other Advisers

International trade consultants can advise and assist a company with all aspects of foreign marketing, from market identification to establishing contacts with necessary resources like advertising agencies, product service facilities, and local attorneys. Trade consultants usually specialize by product category and global area. When using a trade consultant, determine the consultant's level of experience, ask for references and agree on the fee in advance.

This association provides significant access to supply chain security and compliance regulatory information. It runs a semiannual program on teaching import/export security/compliance management with "testing and certification."

Key Periodicals

You must develop a number of resources that provide timely information on competitors, vendors, service providers, governmental issues, and industry trends. I read more than sixty magazines, newsletters, and periodicals every month. Below is a recommended sampling that is useful for import and export supply chain executives.

> The Export Practioner: (202) 463-1250; www.exportprac.com
> Managing Imports and Exports (MIE): (877) 265-0070; www.theworldacademy
> .com
> Logistics Management: (847) 390-2377; www.Logisticsmgmt.com
> American Shipper: (212) 233-3589; www.americanshipper.com
> Supply Chain Brain: (516) 829-9210; www.supplychainbrain.com
> Inbound Logistics: (212) 629-1560; www.inboundlogistics. com
> The Journal of Commerce: (888) 215-6084; www.joc.com
> Air Cargo World: (770) 642-9170; www.aircargoworld.com
> Technology Services Industry Association: (858) 674-5491; www.tsia.com
> JOC Sailings: (800) 991-9994, ext. 123; www.jocsailings.com
> PACMAN Association: (877) 722-6268; www.compliancemaven.com
> Supply Chain Management Review: (800) 375-8015; www.scmr.com

There are an array of other options that might fit your specific needs better. In our Internet listing on the following page, a number of other sources are identified.

Recommended Schools in Import/Export Supply Chain Management

> The World Academy: (800) 524-2493; www.theworldacademy.com
> PACMAN Association: (877) 265 0070; www.compliancemaven.com
> American Management Association: (212) 586-8100; www.amanet.org
> Global Training Center: (800) 860-5030; www.globaltrainingcenter.com
> Farmingdale State University:(631) 420-2246; www.farmingdale.edu
> Global Maritime and Transportation School: (516) 773-5161; www.gmats.usmma
> .edu

Key Internet Websites

> 1travel.com: www.onetravel.com
> AAPA Directory—Seaports of the Americas, an Annual Publication of the
> American Association of Port Authorities: www.seaportsinfo.com

ACW (Air Cargo Week): www.aircagoweek. com
International Addresses and Salutations: www. bspage.com /address.html
AES Direct (Automated Export System): www.aesdirect.gov
Africa Online: www.africaonline.com
AgExporter: www.fas.usda.gov
Air Cargo World: www.aircargoworld. com
AIRCARGO News: www.aircargonews.com
Airforwarders Association: www.airforwarders.org
Airwise (for toll-free airline numbers and websites): www.airwise.com
American Association of Port Authorities (AAPA): www.aapa-ports.org
American Computer Resources, Inc.: www.the-acr.com
The Global Offset and Countertrade Association (GOCA): www.globaloff
    set.org
American Institute for Shippers' Associations (AISA): www.shippers.org
American Journal of Transportation (AJOT): www.ajot.com
American River International: http://www.americanriverintl.com
American Shipper: www.americanshipper.com
American Short Line and Regional Railroad Association (ASLRRA): www.aslrra
    .org
American Stock Exchange: www.amex.com
American Trucking Association (ATA): www.truckline.com
Associated Press: www.ap.org
ATA Carnet (Merchandise Password): www.atacarnet.com
Aviation Week: www.aviationnow.com
Bureau of Customs and Border Protection: www.cbp.gov
Bureau of Industry and Security (BIS): www.bis.doc.gov
Bureau of National Affairs: www.bna.com
Small Business Advisor: www.sba.gov
Cargo Systems: www.cargosystems. net
Cargovision: www.cargovision.net
Census Bureau, Foreign Trade Division: www.census.gov/foreign-trade/
Central Europe Online: www.einnews.com/centraleurope/
Inside China Today (news from China in English): www.einnews.com/china
Classification Schedules: www.census.gov/foreign-trade/schedules/b/index
    .html
Commerce Business Daily: www.cbd-net.com
Commercial Carrier Journal (CCJ): www.ccjdigital.com
Commercial Encryption Export Controls: www.bis.doc.gov/encryption/
Compliance Consulting of Importers/Exporters: www. compliancemaven. com
Correct Way to Fill Out the Shipper's Export Declaration: www.census.gov/
    foreign-trade/regulations/index.html
Country Risk Forecast: www.controlrisks.com/html/index.php
Create Your Own Newspapers: www.crayon.net
Culture and Travel: globaledge.msu.edu/resourcedesk/
Currency: www.oanda.com
Database at the UN World Bank: www.worldbank.org/data/onlinedatabases/
    onlinedatabases
Department of Transportation: www. dot.gov
Diverse languages of the modern world: www.unicode.org
DOT's Office of Inspector General: www.oig.dot.gov

Dun & Bradstreet: www.dnb.com
Economic Times (India): economictimes.indiatimes.com/
Economist: www.economist.com
Electronic Embassy: www.embassy.org
Embassies & Consulates: www.embassyworld.com
European Union (EU): www.europa.eu/
Export Administration Regulations (EARhttp://ecfr.gpoaccess.gov/cgi/t/
    text/text-idx?sid = 256c971f2e9cb547e32ac24ffc861acb&c = ecfr&tpl = /
    ecfrbrowse/Title15/15cfrv2_02.tpl#730
Export Assistant: www.export.gov
Export-Import Bank of the United States (Ex-Im Bank): www.exim.gov
Export Legal Assistance Network (ELAN): www.exportlegal.org
Export Practitioner (Export Regulations): www.exportprac.com
Federal Register Notice on the Status of AES and AERP: www.census.gov/
    foreign-trade/regulations/fedregnotices/index.html
Federation of International Trade Associations (FITA): www.fita.org
Financial Times: www.ft.com
For female travelers: www.journeywoman.com
Global Business: www.gbn.com
Global Connector: www.kelley.iu.edu/connector/gc_home.cfm
Global Business Law Review: www.globalbusinesslawreview.org
Glossary of Ocean Cargo Insurance Terms: www.tsbic.com/cargo/glossary
    .htm
Hong Kong Trade Development Counsel (TDC): www.hktdc.com
iAgora Work Abroad: www.iagora. com/IMEX Exchange: www.imex.com
Import-Export Bulletin Board: www.imexbb.com/
Inbound Logistics: www.inboundlogistics. com
Incoterms 2010: www.iccwbo.org/incoterms
Independent Accountants International: www.accountants.org
Information on Diseases Abroad: www.cdc.gov
Inside China Today: www.einnews.com/china
Intellicast Weather (4-day forecast): www.intellicast.com/LocalWeather/
    World
Intermodal Association of North America (IANA): www.intermodal.org
International Air Transport Association (IATA): www.iata.org
International Association for Medical Assistance to Travelers (IAMAT): www
    .iamat.org
International Business: Strategies for the Global Marketplace Magazine:
    www.international-business.com
International Chamber of Commerce (ICC): www.iccwbo.org
Lex Mercatoria (international commercial law and e-commerce): www.jus.uio
    .no/lm/
International Executive Service Corps (IESC): www.iesc.org
International Freight Association (IFA): www.ifa-online.com
International Maritime Organization (IMO): www.imo.org
International Monetary Fund (IMF): www.imf.org
International Society of Logistics (SOLE): www.sole.org
International Trade Administration (ITA): www.ita.doc.gov
International Trade Shows and Business Events: global.broad.msu.edu/events

International Trade/Import-Export Jobs: www.internationaltrade.org/jobs/index.html

Intershipper: www.intershipper.com

IWLA: www.iwla.com

Journal of Commerce Online: www.joc.com

Latin Trade: www.latintrade.com

Libraries: www.libraryspot.com/librariesonline.htm

Library of Congress: www.loc.gov

Local Times Around the World: www.times.clari.net.au

Logistics Management & Distribution Report: www.logisticsmgmt.com/

London Stock Exchange: www.londonstockexchange.com

Medical Conditions Around the World: wwwnc.cdc.gov/travel/content/yellowbook/home-2010.aspx

NAFTA Customs: www.nafta-customs.org

National Association of Foreign Trade Zones: www.NAFTZ.org

National Association of Rail Shippers (NARS): www.railshippers.com

National Business Travel Association: www.nbta.org

National Customs Brokers & Forwarders Association of America (NCBFAA): www.ncbfaa.org

National Institute of Standards and Technology (NIST): www.nist.gov

National Law Center For Inter-American Free Trade: www. natlaw.com

National Motor Freight Traffic Association (NMFTA): www.nmfta.org

New York Times: www.nytimes.com

North American Industry Classification System (NAICS): www.census.gov/nacis

Office of Anti-Boycott Compliance: www.bis.doc.gov/complianceandenforcement/antiboycottcomplian ce.htm

Online Chambers of Commerce: www.online-chamber.com

Online Newspapers: www. onlinenewspapers. com

Overseas Private Investment Corp. (OPIC): www.opic.gov

Pacific Dictionary of International Trade and Business:

PACMAN: www.compliancemaven.com

PIERS (Port Import/Export Reporting Service): www.PIERS.com

Professional Association of Import/Export Compliance Managers: www.compliancemaven.com

Resources for International Job Opportunities: www.dbm.com/jobguide/internat.html

Reuters: www.reuters.com

Russia Today: www.rt.com

SBA Office of International Trade: www.sba.gov/oit

SBA Offices and Services: www.sba.gov/about-sba-services/199

Schedule B Export Codes: www.census.gov/foreign-trade/schedules/b

Service Corps of Retired Executives (SCORE): www.score.org

Shipping News (Singapore): www.businesstimes.com.sg/shippingtimes

SIC Codes: http://www.osha.gov/pls/imis/sic_manual.html

Small Business Administration (SBA): www.sba.gov; www.sbaonline.sba.gov

Small Business Development Centers (SBDC): www.sba.gov content/small-business-development-centers-sbdcs

Telephone Directories on the Web: www.infobel.com/en/world/

The American Exporter: www.exportermagazine.com

The International Air Cargo Association (TIACA): www.tiaca.org
The Times: www.thetimes.co.uk
The Trading Floor: www.thetradingfloor.co.uk
Tokyo Stock Exchange: www.tse.or.jp
U.S. Trade and Development Agency (TDA): www.ustda.gov
Trade Compass: www.thetradecompass. com
Trade Information Center (TIC): www.export.gov
HG.org (legal directories), trade law website: www.hg.org/trade.html
World Trade Point Organization: www.tradepoint.org
Trade Statistics: tse.export.gov/tse/tsehome.aspx
Trading Floor Harmonized Code Search Engine: www.foreign-trade.com/ref erence/hscode.htm
Transportation Intermediaries Association (TIA): www.tianet.org
Transportation Jobs and Personnel: www.quotations.com/trans.htm
Travlang: www.travlang.com
UN Conference on Trade and Development: http://www.unctad.org
UN International Trade Center (ITC): www.intracen.org
United Nations (UN): www.un.org
United States-Mexico Chamber of Commerce: www.usmcoc.org/
Universal Travel Protection Insurance (UTPI): www.utravelpro.com
U.S. Business Advisor: www.business.gov
U.S. Census Bureau: www.census.gov
U.S. Census Bureau Economic Indicators: www.census.gov/econ
U.S. Census Bureau Foreign Trade Division Harmonized Tariff Classification Schedule: www.census.gov foreign-trade /schedules/b
U.S. Council for International Business (USCIB): www.uscib.org
U.S. Customs Services: www.cbp.gov
U.S. Department of Commerce (DOC): www.doc.gov
U.S. Department of Commerce Commercial Service: www. trade.gov/cs/
U.S. Department of Commerce International Trade Administration: www.trade .gov
U.S. Export Assistance Centers (USEAC): www.export.gov/eac.html
U.S. Export Portal: www.export.gov
U.S. Federal Maritime Commission (FMC): www.fmc.gov
U.S. Foreign Trade Zones: www.ia.ita. doc.gov/ftzpage
U.S. Government Glossary and Acronym of International Trade Terms: www.ustr.gov/about-us/trade-toolbox/glossary-trade-terms
U.S. Patent and Trademark Office (USPTO): www.uspto.gov
U.S. State Department Travel Advisory: www.travel.state.gov
U.S. Trade Representative (USTR): www.ustr.gov
USA/Internet: www.usa.gov
USDA Foreign Agricultural Service (FAS): www.fas.usda.gov
USDA Shipper and Export Assistance (SEA): www.fas.usda.gov/agx/ship_ doc_req/ship_doc_req.asp
USDOC Trade Information Center: www.export.gov
Wall Street Journal: www.online.wsj.com
Wells Fargo: www.wellsfargo.com
World Bank Group: www.worldbank.org
World Chambers of Commerce Network: www.worldchambers.com
World Customs Organization (WCO): www.wcoomd.org

World Factbook: www.cia.gov/library/publications/the-world-factbook
World Intellectual Property Organization (WIPO): www.wipo.int
World Newspapers Online: www.world-newspapers.com
World Trade Analyzer: www.trade-compass.com
World Trade Centers Association (WTCA): www.wtcaonline.com
World Trade Magazine: www.worldtrademag.com
World Trade Organization (WTO): www.wto.org
World Wide Shipping: www.shipping-worldwide.com

Engagement and Resource Development: The New Trade Compliance Mandate

The government principally has two primary government agencies, CBP and BIS, which have always required that companies operate their global supply chains with the following mandates or guidelines:

- **Due Diligence**
- **Reasonable Care**
- **Supervision and Control**

These guidelines involve areas such as the creation of Standard Operating Procedures (SOPs), training and education, learning and applying applicable trade regulation and law, governance in sales and operations, senior management support, managing and supervising service providers, technology, etc.

There are an array of areas in trade compliance that all managers need to pay attention to, such as but not limited to: valuation, documentation, recordkeeping, harmonized classification or schedule B number identification, export licensing, AES, denied parties review, etc. In the past few years we have identified and studied a new area which we call "engagement." Engagement requires the development of resources, information, and the necessary skill set to meet the basic government trade compliance standards. Scouring the websites, magazines, and newpapers, and being an active member of trade groups—along with networking—is now imperative for supply chain management.

What we mean by this is pretty simple: corporations and the executives and managers who operate global supply chains must be proactive in government initiatives to be considered fully trade compliant. In specific, your corporation must:

- Have a business process in place that actively seeks out and engages government initiatives and works within them. One such initiative would be C-TPAT (Customs Trade Partnership Against Terrorism), a successful program that now covers about 80 percent of all the products that are imported into the United States started just after 9/11. A company voluntarily enters in the program, which provides numerous benefits and advantages to those that participate.
- Have personnel directly interface with government agents who are involved in trade compliance regulation, application, and enforcement and develop relationships and communication channels that can be beneficial in both the short and long term.
- Continue to raise the bar, create best practices, and acknowledge that there is "a vested stakeholder interest" in participation.

The proactive executive must search out what the government expectations are. These can be easily developed by attending the CBP and BIS outreach programs, which are available on their websites (www.cbp.gov and www.doc.bis.gov).

You can also acquire the necessary knowledge by attending trade symposiums offered by industry organizations, reading communication pieces, such as *Cargo Business News,* and going to supply chain programs, such as those run by The World Academy (www.theworldacademy.com),

Proactive engagement is state of the art and the new trade compliance initiative. Trade compliance requires above all a focus on information gathering.

Some key areas to focus on for information are mentioned below.

For a corporation to be successful in its trade compliance program, the individual in charge must be well informed about what is going on with the various regulatory agencies. Departments of State, Treasury, Homeland Security, and Commerce are key government agencies that control what goes on in global supply chains and in the world of importing and exporting.

Other agencies, such as The International Trade Administration (ITA), Customs Border and Protection (CBP), Food and Drug Administration (FDA), Transportation Security Administration (TSA) are but a few of other key government agencies that trade compliance executives need to pay attention to.

Many of these agencies and departments offer outreach programs to the public. These can be best viewed by going into and learning to navigate some of their websites, which are somewhat user friendly and contain "oodles" of data, lists of resources, and other useful information.

Many of the websites allow for direct communication to the agency and provide an online interface. We have found the government personnel involved who manage the websites to be responsive and helpful.

Here is an overview of some of these important websites, with a brief listing of what you will find there:

www.aesdirect.gov (Automated Export System)
   AES filing direct on line
   Look up processing results, print SED
   Frequently asked questions
      http://www.aesdirect.gov/support.html
   Harmonized numbers that cannot be used for export
      http://www.aesdirect.gov/support/invalid_hts.html

www.census.gov/foreign-trade
   Schedule B search engine
      http://www.census.gov/foreign-trade/schedules/b/index.html
   Census regulations
      http://www.census.gov/foreign-trade/regulations/regs/
         regulations20080602-federalregister.pdf

www.bis.doc.gov (Bureau of Industry & Security)
   Actual denied party listings (links to all 5 lists)
      http://www.bis.doc.gov/ComplianceAndEnforcement/
         ListsToCheck.htm
   Export regulations
      Commerce control list
      http://www.access.gpo.gov/bis/ear/ear_data.html

Violations page
http://www.bis.doc.gov/news/index.htm#prs
Current news/updates to regulations
http://www.bis.doc.gov/Whatsnew.htm
Export Management System (SOP outline)
http://www.bis.doc.gov/exportmanagementsystems/
emsguidelines.html

www.cbp.gov (Bureau of Customs & Border Protection)
Current Customs news
http://www.cbp.gov/xp/cgov/newsroom/news_releases/
C-TPAT (Customs Trade Partnership Against Terrorism)
http://www.cbp.gov/xp/cgov/trade/cargo_security/ctpat/
CROSS (Customs Ruling Online Search System)
http://rulings.cbp.gov/
Harmonized tariff numbers
http://www.usitc.gov/tata/hts/bychapter/index.htm
Informed compliance publications (many)
http://www.cbp.gov/xp/cgov/trade/legal/
informed_compliance_pubs/Recordkeeping
Reasonable care
Tariff classification
Marking
http://www.boskage.com/index/index_index.php;
http://bookstore.gpo.gov/
Government publications including HTS, Export Regulations, Customs Regulations
www.trade.gov/td/tic (ITA or International Trade Administration)
Country information
Documentary requirements
Customs requirements
Foreign tariff rates
NAFTA
www.bna.com (Bureau of National Affairs—not a government agency)
Country information
Documentary requirements
Customs requirements
Login/password required
http://www.fda.gov
FDA drug labeling requirements
International Traffic in Arms Regulations
Ocean carriers
Vessel schedules
Login/password required
www.piers.com (Port Import Export Reporting Service)
Trade reports
Login/password required

www.fas.usda.gov/agx/exporter_assistance.asp (USDA Foreign Agriculture
Service)
Exporter assistance food products
Wood packing rules for export

www.uscib.org (U.S. Council for International Business)
    Issues carnets
www.compliancemaven.com (Professional Association of Import/Export Compliance Managers)

These are but a few of the hundreds of websites available for trade compliance professionals to access for critical and timely information on managing their global trade supply chain management responsibilities.

Most of these sites perform for free. Some have nominal or annual access fees; typically, they are well worth their costs.

Information gathering and utilization of the aforementioned websites have become necessary weapons in the arsenal of trade compliance management and make the trade compliance manager a better resource for his or her organization.

Avoiding fines and penalties and running the import and export operation more successfully are the bottomline benefits.

Examples of Some Key Trade Compliance Issues to be Aware of in 2011/12

Some of the pressing issues to be aware of in 2011 and in 2012 are:

- Implementation of ISF Penalties
- EU Advanced filing rules
- Incoterms 2010
- Cargo security

While ISF (Importer Security Filing) became effective in January 2009, the penalty phase for ISF was delayed by customs but is now in place in 2011. For importers that do not comply with rules for ISF filing the fines can be substantial— as much as $5,000.00 per entry. CBP announced in spring of 2010 that being member of the C-TPAT program in good standing could mitigate fines up to 50 percent. Until fines are actually assigned, it is prudent for all importers that deal with ISF filing to review their monthly ISF "report card" to gauge how they or their customs brokers are handling their filings.

Since January 1, 2011 exporters shipping into the EU have to deal with an advance–filing rule that went into effect. The rule is similar to the version in effect on imports into the US with the exception that instead of having a single agency responsible for oversight, as we do with US Customs, enforcement will be handled by individual EU countries. This means you could have to deal with one or more government agencies in up to 27 different countries (representing all 27 individual EU members). The ruling affects ocean freight shipments arriving in the EU regardless if it is being transshipped to another country or just remaining on a vessel. For air freight shipments, data must be filed by the air carrier four hours prior to landing at an EU based airport or upon departure of the flight for flights that are less than four hours in duration. There is a genuine concern in the trade community that many shippers are not aware of this new rule and this could cause major delays and frustrations to customers based in the EU.

Incoterms, which are the foundation of global trade, are updated every 10 years. Incoterms 2010 which were announced in September of 2010 went into effect on Jan 1, 2011. As mentioned elsewhere in this book, there have been significant changes to the Incoterms. Four Incoterms have been dropped (DAF, DES,

DEQ, DDU). Two new terms have been added (DAP—Delivered at Place, DAT—Delivered at Terminal). There have also been changes made to the use of Incoterms related to the modes of transportation utilized.

It is imperative that as an importer or exporter you become familiar with these international terms as they affect many important aspects of international trade, such as which party is responsible for trade compliance, freight and other related issues.

100 percent screening of cargo being transported on domestic passenger aircraft has been in place since August 2010. Due to recent attempted terrorist attempts to blow up cargo aircraft with concealed bombs, we will see changes on how freight is inspected on cargo aircraft as well. Rep. Edward Markey, D-MA who authored the original legislation requiring the 100% screening on passenger aircraft has already announced plans to introduce legislation to inspect 100% of the cargo being moved on cargo aircraft. As importers and exporters who may utilize cargo aircraft to move our goods (more than half the airfreight shipped in 2009 was on cargo aircraft), we need to be aware of this and prepare for potential added costs and delays that the impending regulations will cause the supply chain.

As we enter the new decade, let's also ensure we have procedures in place to deal with these issues and the numerous other issues that have been in place in this post 9/11 world.

Information and engagement are very critical aspects of global trade management. Common sense, best practices and government regulation all require this. The education and awareness process with understanding import/export compliance issues is ongoing and seems to change on a daily basis! By reading the trade journals, scouring the relevant governmental websites, and using the Internet, you will insure that you, your staff, and your company will be in complaince with all the regulations and requirements—until they change again!

8

Essential Overview of Import/Export Compliance and Security Management: Post 9/11

The focus of this chapter is to define all the old and new compliance and security regulations that supply chain managers engaged in importing and exporting will face into the new millennium, most as a result of the tragedy of September 11, 2001.

More than a decade after this attack on American soil, the impact of the events of that day rings loud with every import and export manager operating global supply chains in every corner of the planet.

Overview

Compliance and security have always been issues that supply chain executives have had to contend with. Introduce the unfortunate events of September 11, 2001, and compliance and security management is raised to a entirely new heightened level within all import and export organizations, transportation carriers and providers, overseas ports/terminals, vendors and suppliers and, in reality, almost every entity that is touched within the global supply chain.

Compliance has to do with corporations managing their governmental regulatory obligations in their import/export supply chains, such as but not limited to documentation, recordkeeping, valuation, classification, etc. Security has to do with protecting the interests of the corporation and the citizenship from potential harmful acts such as terrorism, war, civil commotion, etc.

Having defined both, the important issue is that they are also one in the same, for the most part. One cannot be secure and noncompliant, nor compliant and nonsecure. They go "hand-in-hand."

An example is a new security procedure, the 24-Hour Manifest Requirement. This procedure mandates that, on inbound freight into the United States, Customs and Border Protection (CBP) receives a detailed manifest sent electronically, twenty-four hours prior to ship departure from the foreign port of just what will be entering the United States. Failure to comply could result in import refusal, seizure of goods, and/or fines and penalties. This is a new security procedure. However, it also has a compliance element, in that there is a regulatory aspect to the requirement with a financial consequence, and there is a recordkeeping component to the overall process.

Another example is when we export goods from the United States via air cargo, we have a "Known Shipper/FAA" onus that the shipper complete certain Transportation Security Administration (TSA) and Federal Aviation Administration (FAA) forms enabling them to drop freight off with the carrier. This is a security regulation. However, the recordkeeping and consequences aspect of the regulation builds in a compliance element to the security aspect.

Whether compliance or security, the events of 9/11 have added a whole new dimension to supply chain management, that forces the executives in charge to pay attention to a whole new array of regulations and legal processes.

In this foray has come a new set of compliance and security acronyms. The key ones are listed below.

Automated Export System (AES)

The Automated Export System (AES) is covered in great detail in Chapter 9. Basically, it is an electronic system for reporting the shippers export declaration (SED) data to the Department of Census. This process will be an integral component of the export security procedures and mandates from the Department of Homeland Security (DHS) in controlling what is exported from the United States. For more information, go to *www.aesdirect.gov*.

Advance Passenger Information System

The Advance Passenger Information System (APIS) comes under the Aviation Transportation Security Act of 2001 and the Enhanced Border Security and VISA Reform Act of 2002. It is a mandate for the electronic transmission of passenger and crew manifests for inbound and outbound commercial air and commercial sea carriers to the APIS system. It provides another level of security against terrorism.

Trade Act of 2002

The Trade Act of 2002, which gave the president "fast track" authority to negotiate trade agreements, also requires exporters to submit shipping documents no later than twenty-four hours after cargo has been delivered to a marine terminal and at least twenty-four hours prior to a vessel's departure. The act makes it illegal to tender improperly documented shipments to carriers and requires exporters and importers to file customs data electronically. It also establishes a task force to develop procedures for screening and monitoring imports prior to arrival.

Homeland Security Act

The Homeland Security Act passed by Congress in November of 2003 created the Department of Homeland Security, which is charged with preventing terrorist attacks, reducing the country's vulnerability, and assisting in recovery from attack Besides U.S. Customs, the Transportation Security Administration and the Coast

Guard will now be part of DHS. The act does protect customs revenues from diversion to other parts of the new department.

Container Security Initiative

The Container Security Initiative (CSI) is set up to potentially identify high-risk cargo in steamship containers before they arrive in the United States by placing U.S. Customs inspectors at foreign ports where they work with local authorities to screen U.S.-bound containers. To date, over 40 of the world's seaports have signed on, and China has agreed in principle to participate. The program also promotes the use of high-tech detection and security devices. For more information, go to www.cbp.gov/xp/cgov/trade/cargo_security/csi/.

Customs Trade Partnership Against Terrorism

The Customs Trade Partnership Against Terrorism (C-TPAT) requires participants, including importers, carriers, and customs brokers, to document their security procedures. Companies that are accepted into the program also must help overseas suppliers raise their security standards. Participants' shipments qualify for expedited processing and exemption from physical inspections. See Chapter 12 for more information on C-TPAT. Details are available at http://www.cbp.gov/xp/cgov/trade/cargo_security/ctpat/what_ctpat/ctpat_overview.xml

Free and Secure Trade

FAST is a joint program between the Canada Customs Revenue Authority (CCRA) and CBP. FAST streamlines the customs clearance process along the shared border allowing for an expedited clearance while enhancing the security efforts of both countries. The FAST program harmonizes some of the requirements for participation in C-TPAT and Canada's Partners in Protection (PIP) program. Participants receive unique indentifiers that make them eligible for expedited processing at the U.S.-Canadian border. The motor carrier and the individual driver of FAST shipments must be preapproved.

To qualify for FAST expedited clearance the shipment must meet the following requirements:

1. The shipment must be entered by a member of C-TPAT or PIP.
2. The shipment must be carried by a FAST/C-TPAT approved carrier.
3. The shipment must driven by a FAST approved commercial driver.

There are two cargo release methods for FAST shipments. The FAST release is a paperless processing achieved via electronic data transmissions and transponder technology. The prearrival processing system (PAPS) release is a release using bar code technology. The invoice and manifest information is faxed ahead to the border, notated by a bar code. When the truck arrives at the border, customs scans the bar code to determine if an exam is required.

For more information, go to www.cbp.gov/xp/cgov/trade/cargo_security/ctpat/fast/fast_driver/.

Vehicle and Cargo Inspection System

The Vehicle and Cargo Inspection System (VACIS) is a mobile x-ray truck set up to inspect trucks and containers as they pass through American borders. It views the contents of the cargo in the "box." This capability expedites the inspection process because manual unloading and reloading was the alternative. Primarily used in the southwest, it has proven to be a successful deterrent to illegal and clandestine cargo movements. For more information, go to https://help.cbp.gov/app/answers/detail/a_id/317/~/technology-cbp-uses-for-enforcement-vehicle-and-cargo-inspection-system.

Automated Commercial Environment

The Automated Commercial Environment (ACE) is the new import system that is being implemented by customs. The old system was developed in 1984 and could not meet the steadily growing demands of growing trade. ACE is revolutionizing customs and has already automated much of the data collection process, making CBP better able to share information with governmental agencies. The cargo tracking aspects support such security measures as CSI, CTPAT, and Operation Safe Commerce initiatives to capture advance data from the international supply chain and processes it.

Transportation Security Act of 2002

The U.S. Maritime Transportation Security Act of 2002 requires the Coast Guard and local port security committees to conduct vulnerability assessments at U.S. ports. It authorizes the Coast Guard to conduct assessments at foreign ports and to deny entry to vessels from countries that do not meet security standards. It also mandates background checks and identification cards for some personnel, authorizes grants for security improvements at U.S. ports, and orders the development of standards for container seals and locks and a cargo tracking, identification, and screening system for ocean containers.

For the full text, go to www.tsa.gov/assets/pdf/MTSA.pdf.

24-Hour Manifest Rule

CBP's 24-Hour Manifest Rule requires most ocean carriers and consolidators to file cargo manifest data with customs electronically at least twenty-four hours before U.S.-bound cargo is loaded on a vessel at a foreign port. A total of sixteen individual pieces of information are required under the rule, which took effect December 2, 2002. .

Four-Hour Advance Notification

U.S. Customs and Border Protection (CBP) has decided that, like the twenty-four-hour advance manifest rule for ocean, air shipments should have a mandatory electronic reporting period.

The first proposed time frame was twelve hours prior to the flight time, which was introduced as the "strawman" proposal. CBP now states that the "strawman" proposal was merely put out to generate comments from the trade community.

Nevertheless, the new proposal outlines an electronic manifest notification to take place at "wheels up" or at a minimum of four hours prior to the arrival of the importing aircraft.

If for any reason customs is concerned about the safety of the contents in relations to a terrorist threat, the landing rights of the entire aircraft could be denied. There will be no prescreening of merchandise in this proposed process, unlike the twenty-four-hour advance manifest for ocean in the CSI ports of lading.

Importer Security Filing Program

U.S. Customs and Border Protection (CBP) realizes that carrier manifest requirements such as the 24-hour manifest rule lack critical security elements not available to ocean carriers and consolidators, which are, however, necessary for proper security supply chain verification and scrutiny. CBP has initiated a program—originally entitled "10 + 2"—that places the compliance responsibility on the U.S. importer of record to provide additional security information to CBP twenty-four hours prior to the loading of ocean containers in the foreign port of loading. The program is entitled Importer Security Filing (ISF) There is a very strict policy of enforcement for importers who fail to meet this regulatory requirement of advanced manifest security filing, with fines of $5,000.00 per container for late or erroneous ISF filings.

It is imperative that importers proactively secure the information necessary for the advanced security filing so that they can file such data with CBP in a timely manner.

Patriot Act

The USA Patriot Act was passed by Congress following September 11, 2001 and was temporarily extended in early February 2011. The Patriot Act expands the government's investigative abilities and its authority to track and intercept information. This act is viewed as a necessary tool by governmental enforcement agencies as in some cases it creates federal laws for investigating business records and money trails. While the purpose of the act is to focus on terrorism and money laundering, the act remains a controversial point for civil libertarians.

Operation Safe Commerce

Operation Safe Commerce is a joint initiative between the Department of Transportation and the Bureau of Customers and Border Protection (CBP) to fund business initiatives designed to enhance security for container cargo.

DOT's Transportation Security Administration (TSA) appropriated $58 million that are being used to evaluate various technologies that have been developed. The information gathered will ultimately be used to create standard security procedures for companies involved in international shipping.

Subcontractors are working with international shippers at the ports of Seattle, New York/New Jersey, and Long Beach/Los Angeles. There are currently eleven pilot projects being headed by companies like Unisys, Boeing, and Maersk to name a few.

The subcontractors work with the importer to functionally use various technologies to monitor the security of the supply chain in actual import shipments. The test program will have an added benefit in "working out the bugs" and creating a "usual standard" for import security programs.

Some of the technologies being considered are digital photography, radiation detectors, container tracking by GPS satellite and smart seals equipped with radio frequency tracking technology.

Each of these technologies has its obvious benefits in securing supply chains. However, until the time these solutions are mandated by the government, importers will not be running to purchase these technologies, due to their high cost. Aside from providing security, many companies do not see a direct benefit in purchasing these technologies, thus requiring implementation of governmental mandates to "sign on" and incorporate these technologies into their supply chain.

Department of Homeland Security (DHS)

Building a Secure Homeland

The creation of the DHS is the most significant transformation of the U.S. government since 1947 when Harry S. Truman merged the various branches of the U.S. Armed Forces into the Department of Defense to better coordinate the nation's defense against military threats.

DHS represents a similar consolidation, both in style and substance. In the aftermath of the terrorist attacks against America on September 11, 2001, President George W. Bush decided that the twenty-two previously disparate domestic agencies needed to be coordinated into one department to protect the nation against threats to the homeland.

The new department's first priority is to protect the nation against further terrorist attacks. Component agencies analyze threats and intelligence, guard our borders and airports, protect our critical infrastructure, and coordinate the response of our nation for future emergencies.

Besides providing a better coordinated defense of the homeland, DHS is also dedicated to protecting the rights of American citizens and enhancing public services, such as natural disaster assistance and citizenship services, by dedicating offices to these important missions.

What Is the Mission of DHS?

The many men and women who daily protect our borders and secure our country are committed to the safety of our homeland. The DHS helps them do their jobs better with increased communication, coordination, and resources. Specifically, the DHS has three primary missions:

1. Prevent terrorist attacks within the United States.
2. Reduce America's vulnerability to terrorism.
3. Minimize the damage from potential attacks and natural disasters.

To accomplish these three goals the DHS focuses on creating the new capabilities discussed in the July 2002 National Strategy for Homeland Security. The National Strategy pointed out that at the time no one single governmental agency had homeland security as its primary mission. In fact, responsibilities for homeland security were dispersed among more than a hundred different governmental organizations. America needed a single, unified homeland security structure that would improve protection against current threats and be flexible enough to help meet the unknown threats of the future.

DHS has realigned the former confusing patchwork of governmental activities into a single department, giving state and local officials one primary contact instead of many, an important advantage when it comes to matters related to training, equipment, planning, exercises, and other critical homeland security needs. It manages federal grant programs for enhancing the preparedness of fire-fighters, police, and emergency medical personnel. DHS also sets standards for state and local preparedness activities and equipment.

What Was the Plan for Creating the New Department Time Line

In 2012, the Department of Homeland Security has grown to be the second largest government agency after the Department of Defense and has many sub-agencies that are directly involved in managing trade and compliance issues impacting the act of importing and exporting.

As far back as November 25, 2002, the President signed the bill creating the new DHS and on January 24, 2003, the DHS came into existence. On November 25 the President also submitted a Homeland Security Reorganization Plan to Congress. Ninety days after this plan was submitted, the component parts of DHS were free to move to the newly created department. By law, the DHS Secretary has one year from the time the department became effective to bring all of the twenty-two agencies into the new organization. The President stated in the reorganization plan that he anticipated most of the component parts would move into the new department by March 1, 2003.

DHS Transition Team

A Homeland Security Transition Planning Office (TPO) was established in late June 2003 to work with Congress on the legislation and to coordinate planning for DHS. About 50 representatives from the tapped agencies, Office of Personnel Management, the Office of Management and Budget, and the White House were brought together to develop options that would allow DHS to achieve the new and enhanced capabilities in the most effective and timely manner.

The TPO is structured around several different teams that parallel the structure for the DHS: Border and Transportation Security, Science and Technology, Emergency Preparedness and Response, Intelligence and Infrastructure Protection, United States Secret Service, Human Resources, Systems, Legal, Communications, and Budget. The primary role of these teams during the transition process was to map out logistical options and reorganization details for the incoming DHS leadership who ultimately make the substantive policy decisions on these issues. The goal, to the greatest extent possible, was to make the reorganization a collaborative effort with the tapped agencies, employees, unions, Congress, state and local entities, and the private sector.

Building a Strong Department

The following are elements that we believe are important to ensuring a smooth and successful employee transition into the DHS:

- A commitment to provide up-to-date information about the progress of the DHS transition team
- Openness about the process and results
- A pledge to build the DHS culture on the foundations of the cultures of the agencies moving into the new department
- A commitment to distribute paychecks on time and to ensure that services like technical support, legal support, and human resources are not disrupted

DHS Has Five Major Divisions (Directorates)

1. **Border and Transportation Security (BTS).** BTS is responsible for maintaining the security of our nation's borders and transportation systems. It is the largest of the Directorates.
2. **Emergency Preparedness and Response (EPR).** This Directorate ensures that our nation is prepared for, and able to recover from, terrorist attacks and natural disasters.
3. **Science and Technology (S&T).** This Directorate coordinates the department's efforts in research and development, including preparing for and responding to the full range of terrorist threats involving weapons of mass destruction.
4. **Information Analysis and Infrastructure Protection (IAIP).** IAIP merges the capability to identify and assess a broad range of intelligence information concerning threats to the homeland under one roof, issue timely warnings, and take appropriate preventive and protective action.
5. **Management.** This directorate is responsible for budget, management, and personnel issues in DHS.

Besides the five directorates, several other critical agencies folded into DHS or were newly created:

- **United States Coast Guard (USCG).** The Commandant of the Coast Guard reports directly to the Secretary of Homeland Security. However, the USCG also works closely with the Directorate of Border and Transportation Security and maintains its existing independent identity as a military service. Upon declaration of war or when the president so directs, the USCG would operate as an element of the Department of Defense, consistent with existing law.
- **United States Secret Service.** The primary mission of the Secret Service is the protection of the president and other governmental leaders, and security for designated national events. The Secret Service is also the primary agency responsible for protecting U.S. currency from counterfeiters and safeguarding Americans from credit card fraud.
- **Bureau of Citizenship and Immigration Services (USCIS).** While BTS is responsible for enforcement of our nation's immigration laws, the Bureau of Citizenship and Immigration Services (USCIS) dedicates its full energies to providing efficient immigration services and easing the transition to American citizenship. The Director of Citizenship and Immigration Services reports directly to the Deputy Secretary of Homeland Security.
- **Private Sector Office.** Part of the Office of Policy, the Private Sector Office provides America's business community a direct line of communication to DHS. The office works directly with individual businesses and with trade associations and other nongovernmental organizations to foster dialogue

between the private sector and DHS on the full range of issues and challenges faced by America's business sector in today's world.

- **Office of Inspector General.** The Office of Inspector General serves as an independent and objective inspection, audit, and investigative body to promote effectiveness, efficiency, and economy in the DHS's programs and operations, and to prevent and detect fraud, abuse, mismanagement, and waste in such programs and operations.

Who Is Part of DHS?

The agencies who are part of DHS are housed in one of four major directorates: Border and Transportation Security, Emergency Preparedness and Response, Science and Technology, and Information Analysis and Infrastructure Protection.

The Border and Transportation Security directorate brings the major border security and transportation operations under one roof, including the:

- Customs and Border Protection (formerly, U.S. Customs Service, Department of Treasury)
- Immigration and Customs Enforcement (ICE) (formerly, Immigration and Naturalization Service (part), Department of Justice)
- Federal Protective Service (General Services Administration)
- Transportation Security Administration (Department of Transportation)
- Federal Law Enforcement Training Center (Treasury)

The Emergency Preparedness and Response directorate oversees domestic disaster preparedness training and coordinates governmental disaster response. It brings together the:

- Federal Emergency Management Agency (FEMA)
- Strategic National Stockpile and the National Disaster Medical System (Department of Health and Human Services)
- Nuclear Incident Response Team (Department of Energy)
- Domestic Emergency Support Teams (Justice)
- National Domestic Preparedness Office (FBI)

The Science and Technology directorate seeks to use all scientific and technological advantages when securing the homeland. The following assets are part of this effort:

- Chemical, Biological, Radiological, and Nuclear (CBRN) Countermeasures Programs (Energy)
- Environmental Measurements Laboratory (Energy)
- National Biological Weapons (BW) Defense Analysis Center (Department of Defense)
- Plum Island Animal Disease Center (Agriculture)

The Information Analysis and Infrastructure Protection directorate analyzes intelligence and information from other agencies (including the CIA, FBI, DIA, and NSA) involving threats to homeland security and evaluates vulnerabilities in the nation's infrastructure. It brings together the:

- Critical Infrastructure Assurance Office (Department of Commerce)
- Federal Computer Incident Response Center (GSA)

- National Communications System (Defense)
- National Infrastructure Protection Center (FBI)
- Energy Security and Assurance Program (Energy)

The Secret Service and the Coast Guard are also located in the DHS. These agencies remain intact and report directly to the Secretary. In addition, the former INS adjudications and benefits programs report directly to the Deputy Secretary as the Bureau of Citizenship and Immigration Services.

Radioactive Cargo Requires Security

The act's requirements focus on compliance with the regulations, particularly on "high risk" vessels and facilities. These enhanced regulations have caused delays at ocean ports across the United States.

In 2002 the container ship *Palermo Senator* was delayed when radiation was detected during a routine inspection of the ship. Following three tense days of testing, the source of the radiation was determined to be a container of clay tiles.

Many products naturally emit low levels of radiation. Importers are not aware that their products containing these trace amounts of radioactivity raise red flags when shipped in bulk. These trace amounts build up, causing a shipment that was manifested as nonradioactive cargo to be the focus of intensive examination by CBP, Department of Energy, and even the Federal Bureau of Investigation.

One way for shippers to avoid delays is by testing cargo for radioactivity prior to shipping to make sure the levels fall within the regulatory guidelines. Using a forwarder who specializes in handling radioactive shipments can also ease the burden of unforeseen delays. Finally, it is important for shippers to keep themselves current on changing regulations and updates they may receive from industry organizations.

Green Customs Project

Many importers are aware of the Convention on International Trade in Endangered Species of Wild Fauna and Flora (CITES). CITES regulates and enforces the Endangered Species Act, protecting habitats, animals, and environments at risk. These regulations are enforced by customs agencies throughout the world.

A program encompassing CITES and other such international environmental regulations have been created by the United Nations Environment Program (UNEP). The purpose of the Green Customs Project is to train customs officers to detect and apprehend criminals trafficking in banned environmental commodities, like hazardous waste and illegal chlorofluorocarbons.

Criminals circumventing these regulations and illicitly trading these natural resources earn by some estimates over five billion dollars per year. Changed manifests, smuggling, and corruption are just a few of the means used by such traffickers.

The United Nations formed the UNEP to coordinate efforts between the international agencies monitoring environmental regulations. These agencies include Interpol, the World Customs Organization, and other UNEP member groups, like CITES.

Customs officers stand at the world's borders. Customs agents will receive specific training on intercepting these illegal cargoes based on the experience and training methods within the various agencies. By using information sharing, training, and combined energies of these agencies, officials hope to see a decrease in these types of trafficking activity. For more information, go to www.greencus toms.org.

Verification of Government Contracts

Import shipments destined for the U.S. government are subject to the usual customs entry and examination requirements. These same import shipments may qualify for preferential tariff treatment under Chapter 98, provided the governmental contract is current.

The imported product will be classified under the appropriate harmonized tariff schedule number. The import entry will reflect this preferential tariff number and the alternate tariff number that would have been applicable had the product not been classifiable in Chapter 98.

Importers may advise their broker the shipment qualifies for such preferential tariff treatment and declare the shipment as such to customs, only to receive a Customs Form 29 some months later advising a rate advance. The reason for the rate advance is due to the fact the governmental contract information was invalid.

Therefore, it makes good sense to confirm the status of a governmental contract prior to such import. This can be done by contacting the specific governmental agency and speaking with the acting contracting officer.

Import/Export Recordkeeping Is Serious Business

A civil penalty is imposed on an exporter in the amount of $10,000 for violation of 15 CFR 762.2. Is this a penalty for fraud, incorrect valuation, improper marking? No, this penalty is for a recordkeeping violation under the Export Administration Regulations. In addition, the Bureau of Industry and Security (BIS) Office of Enforcement can issue this penalty for *each* document missing from the file.

CBP is just as tough on importers. For willful failure of the importer to maintain, store, or retrieve the demanded record, the importer is subject to a penalty for each release of merchandise, not to exceed $100,000 or an amount equal to 75 percent of the appraised value of the merchandise, whichever is less. In cases of negligence the penalties for the same violation are a bit less at $10,000 for each release or an amount equal to 40 percent of the appraised value of the merchandise, whichever is less.

U.S. Customs spells it out in 19CFR162.1a, records mean statements, declarations, books, papers, correspondence, accounts technical data, magnetic discs and tapes, computer programs necessary to retrieve information in a usable form, and other documents that pertain to any importation in connection with the entry of merchandise that:

- Are of a type normally kept in the ordinary course of business.
- Are sufficiently detailed.
- Establish the right to make entry, correctness of entry, liability of any person for duties and taxes due, liability of fines, and penalties.

CBP and BIS have a statement that is signed by every importer/exporter (filing a shipper's export declaration) which is paraphrased: "I certify the above information is certified true and correct." Whether or not the broker is signing the statement on custom form 7501 or the forwarder is signing the shipper's export declaration, a statement is being submitted on behalf of the company. If that statement is found to be a false statement, a penalty will be assessed. And that is before the auditor even opens the transaction file.

The foundation of a CBP/BIS audit is to review files. Customs clears import shipments via Automated Broker Interface (ABI) and BIS receives information from the Automated Export System (AES) transmission. This information is supported by documentation. A customs auditor may request files to support previous statements made to customs, whether on a custom form 28 (request for information) or proof of payment to a supplier (was the declared amount the actual amount paid). A BIS auditor may check to see proof of payment received by a customer and if the denied lists were checked.

Recordkeeping is a serious issue for importers and exporters. Importers and exporters must exercise care, supervision, and control over their customhouse brokers and freight forwarders. This can best be demonstrated by standard operating procedures (SOPs) issued to supply chain personnel, letters of instructions to brokers and forwarders, and copies of all correspondence for each shipment. It is only by supporting documentation that an importer/exporter is able to display they have taken steps to reasonably supervise their agents.

Importers/exporters must create SOPs within the immediate company and ancillary offices, and with their brokers and forwarders. The SOPs can be a "catch-all" for all divisions with specific procedures spelled out for each individual site and working unit. The SOP should be workable and reviewed by the key personnel for functionality. This will also prevent resentment when a SOP is prepared and implemented without input from the actual users.

Most importantly, if an importer/exporter is going to create and implement a SOP, there had better be internal controls in place to confirm the SOP is being followed correctly. An existing SOP to which no one is adhering, can be an aggravating factor in the event of an outside audit by customs or the BIS. There is now hard evidence that although a SOP was created, which demonstrates there is an awareness of the rules and regulations, it was ignored for whatever the reason. This is an immediate strike during an audit.

During our facility review process, recordkeeping is a consistent problem. "Accounting has that invoice." "Sales keeps those order forms." "Our broker holds that for us." "That gets filed in my wastebasket, was it important?" "Never saw it, never heard of it." "The woman who used to work here said we didn't need it." If any of these answers sound familiar, your company is not alone.

So where are the company's records being kept? To get started, evaluate the supply chain and the sales process. These documents are hiding somewhere. They will be found and it is highly likely to not be where they are expected. The prudent importer/exporter exercising reasonable care and supervision over their brokers/forwarders is also exercising reasonable care and supervision over their own personnel. A good SOP will include recordkeeping practices within the company.

In cases where the importer/exporter is not receiving complete documentation from their broker/forwarder, a written letter of instruction should be given to the company's agents. In addition to handling procedures, the letter should include which documents will be required and when they will be required. The letter should be signed by the broker/forwarder with a copy to the office of the compliance officer.

So, there is now a letter of instruction in place. Now what? A letter of instruction is only as good as the follow-up procedures in place. Someone with the company needs to make sure the instructions are being followed. Are the documents being received timely and in the manner described? Once again, a letter of instruction on file demonstrates the company is aware of the regulation requirements. Is there diligent follow-up by the importer/exporter? Failure to follow-up shows lack of reasonable care, another strike.

We know why recordkeeping is important and have some idea as how to control the recordkeeping process internally and externally. How does a company know what documents to keep? The answer is very simple: EVERYTHING.

Certain privileges provided by CBP, such as drawback and temporary import bond (TIB), require detailed recordkeeping establishing the basis for utilizing these programs. Incomplete records could lead to false claims, interpreted as fraud, which carry severe penalties.

Similarly, the BIS is just as clear in their regulations (15CFR762.2): export control documents, memoranda, notes, correspondence, contracts, invitations to bid, books of account, and other records pertaining to the types of transactions (exports) made by the exporter. The BIS recordkeeping is far-reaching to also cover foreign subsidiaries and any U.S. person working in a foreign company.

Licensing determination must be documented. Were the denied lists reviewed? Were the country charts taken into account? If the answers to these questions are yes, but the tasks were not documented and John Smith on the denied list received a shipment from the company, this is a serious issue (Figure 8-1).

The record retention period is five years for CBP and BIS—five years from the date of entry for customs and five years from the date of shipment for BIS.

CBP has approved electronic methods of recordkeeping in certain instances, now that they are satisfied with the system and retrieval processes. All electronic recordkeeping processes must be approved by customs prior to formalized acceptance (19CFR163.5b).

Specific commodities are also subject to the jurisdiction of other governmental agencies. Hazardous materials, pharmaceuticals, food, cosmetics, animals, and animal products are subject to the additional requirements of the Department of Transportation, FAA, Department of Agriculture, Plant and Health Inspection Services, Food and Drug Administration, and Fish and Wildlife Services and may require additional records.

In summary, *all* records for *every* import/export transaction must be kept for

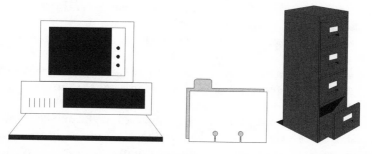

Figure 8-1. Manual records with electronic backup are an excellent import/export recordkeeping procedure.

five years. It is the responsibility of the importer/exporter to maintain all of these records. The conscientious importer/exporter will have a checklist to review all documents received and files created and will periodically perform in-house audits. Outside audits by experienced and knowledgeable consultants can be beneficial in resulting recommendations and may bring out other compliance issues that may arise as a result of the audit process. Recordkeeping may appear to be a time-consuming process, but once the key elements have been established, recordkeeping is doable and manageable.

We also recommend a redundancy system be established in another venue, off site, so if the records are destroyed, there is at least one backup option. The events of September 11, 2001, meant a lot of different things to people who were directly involved with the New York World Trade Towers. Those companies who had offices there lost valuable and cherished personnel in the building's collapse. Those that had no off-site secondary system for recordkeeping further lost documents, records, and files forever, with little opportunity for replacement.

Successful Supply Chain Complaince Management

The events of September 11, 2001 created a whole new set of skill sets for the American Supply Chain Executive. Suddenly the logistics professionals are faced with a new glossary of terms:

CSI (Container Security Initiative)
C-TPAT (Customs Trade Partnership Against Terrorism)
24-Hour Manifest Ruling
USPPI (U.S. Principal Party In Interest)
Deemed Exporter Rules
Homeland Security
Bureau of Customs and Border Patrol

Presently, any logistics professional anywhere in the world doing business in or out of the United States is becoming familiar with these new compliance and security terms. The world is being forced to fall in line with the new U.S. government "initiatives" in post 9/11 security and compliance.

President Bush and his administration took an aggressive approach to protecting the United States, its citizens, and overseas interests. This approach has affected every global supply chain in the world. President Obama continued this assault on terrrorism, as manifested by our support and military action in Libya, the continuation of the war in Iraq and Afghanistan—and the death of BinLaden on May 1, 2011 in Pakistan.

The war on terrorism has added cost and time to international transportation, some argue as much as 20 percent, but I feel it's closer to 6 to 8 percent. It has required supply chain executives to reevaluate the logistics process, which might be unique to their company and add an additional step to the many considerations of importing and exporting..

Documentation, production and inventory control, finance, customer service, and logistics were every supply chain manager's chief concerns. Now added to the list is **security and compliance management**.

In many organizations, the issues are so consequential that new internal positions have been created to address these security and compliance concerns.

Supply chain SOPs have been updated to include procedures outlining how their company will deal with the new security and compliance issues.

One of the new supply chain actions of Customs and Border Protection is the Container Security Initiative (CSI), a proactive and preventive outreach program. CBP believes that if a container were to arrive at a U.S. port with a dirty bomb or a biological weapon on board it would be too late for authorities to deal with the problem.

Therefore, the CSI was created, which extends U.S. custom's reach into foreign ports, enabling customs to inspect foreign supplier facilities and container loading/ handling operations in foreign ports well before the goods are shipped into the United States.

Tied into this effort is the twenty–four-hour manifest requirements that requires importers and their inbound carriers to declare the contents of all import containers at least twenty-four hours before the vessel sails from the foreign port.

U.S. importers have had to significantly change their suppliers and import alert and documentation process to accommodate these new requirements. The U.S. Government, particular in interface with the Departments of State, Census, Customs, and the BIS. is now enforcing rules regarding the USPPI (the U.S. Principal Party in Interest) and Deemed Exports.

The government on all export SEDs require that the USPPI be identified and take compliance responsibility for the export. The USPPI is defined as the entity that receives the primary financial benefit for the export transaction. In most cases this would be the manufacturer. So irrespective of contractual obligations, routed freight shipments or International Commercial (INCO) terms of sale, it is very likely by mandate that the manufacturer has to apply a much higher level of due diligence in export compliance. And for public companies, Sarbanes-Oxley exposure ties directly into export compliance responsibilities and raises the bar for supply chain action.

Knowing the end use, the end user, how the goods or equipment will be used, valuations, and schedule B numbers are but a few of the necessary control items that will fall back onto the responsibility of the USPPI, which is likely to be the U.S. manufacturer. And this ruling potentially applies to foreign subsidiaries, as well.

Deemed Exports is another issue that are not relatively new, but post 9/11 has seen a significant increase in governmental scrutiny. Deemed Exports is the concept of what constitutes an export.

The government holds that the term "export" is not only related to the physical transfer of freight, but also applies to the passing of information, technology, and software, which can all be exported and, therefore, controlled as "exports."

The deemed export rules extend to situations when "foreign nationals" come and visit a plant or facility in the United States, where they are provided technical information or training with the intent for them to bring this information or training back to their country. It applies to foreign employees, as well. This transfer of information, data, training, or technology is a "deemed export" and has the same export controls in place, as if it were the physical export of a product overseas.

Our supply chains all include foreign subsidiaries, contract manufacturers, and channel partners with whom we share technical and proprietary information. But, are we doing it with an "export control process" in mind?

These are but a few of the issues facing supply chain executives in the post-9/11 world. The best supply chain managers are incorporating several new concepts into their global supply chains. We are outlining these actions as our recommendations to make for the most successful import/export supply chains:

1. Identify a "point" person for security and compliance. Spend money and resources for this person to develop the necessary skill sets to make your company compliant. This person can be part of any unit of an organization, but somewhere in the supply chain command, is a feasible place.
2. Develop resources. The supply chain and all the surrounding compliance and security issues are evolving as we read this. So supply chain executives must keep themselves in the loop of current information, by developing various resources, to be timely and comprehensive in the management of their responsibilities.
3. Develop an internal set of SOPs for import/export compliance and its role and functionality in your global supply chain.
4. Train and educate all your supply chain personnel, not only in logistics management but also in the skill sets of compliance and security. Keep the training current and build it into your human resources function.
5. Develop effective relationships with global service and third party providers that prioritize compliance and security into their supply chain relationships with your organization.
6. Build compliance and security SOPs into your vendor contracts with various levels of performance guarantees.
7. Engage in government iniatitives such as C-TPAT that demonstrates interest and participation, which CBP and other government agencies will view favorably. It will also go a long way in mitigating givernment scrutiny and potential fines and penalties.

Global supply chain executives are working in a new world, post 9/11. Those that operate by building an international logistics structure that integrates compliance and security will mitigate the risks of fines, penalties, and work stoppages, and overall create the most comprehensive, cost effective, and best managed supply chains.

And at the same time this international logistics structure is nationalistic and part of the U.S. Government's programs and initiatives in Homeland Security.

Concluding Remarks

Compliance and security management is covered throughout this book and in detail in Chapters 9 and 10. The supply chain manager that recognizes the critical importance of building compliant and secure supply chains and is proactive, not reactive to implementing cost-effective strategies in dealing with the new regulations will maintain his/her company's competitiveness. Failure to heed the necessary regulations will stop the import/export supply chain.

Section Two

Export Operations

9

Export Issues

New Guidance on Use of ITAR Licenses and Exemptions

Many importers who import articles under the International Traffic in Arms Regulations (ITAR) rely on the expertise of their service providers to guide them on issues related to the import and export process. This has been a challenging task, as many service providers operate based on common practices within the industry that were adequate in the past—but no longer. It is important to note that the management of ITAR-regulated items has recently been nationally formalized by U. S. Customs and importers and exporters need to be aware of the new changes.

It is imperative to understand that in order to properly manage the reporting of the ITAR licenses and exemptions on imports and exports, specific training and education is required. Merchandise that is controlled by the Department of State Directorate of Defense Controls under the International Traffic in Arms Regulations is a challenging compliance topic for even seasoned compliance professionals. The export and import procedures are enforced by U. S. Customs and Border Protection (CBP). Many shipments of defense articles face increased scrutiny by the regulatory authorities and are often detained or seized as a result of the incorrect entry declaration of a license or license exemption.

The CBP memorandum to the field is titled "Paperless Entries and ITAR Licensing Procedures." It advises the following:

1. Imports subject to a DSP-61 Temporary Import License or a DSP-73 Temporary Export License must be cleared using a hard copy Customs entry. The entry and license must be presented together to CBP at the port prior to release for review, release and license defragmentation.
2. Imports subject to an ITAR exemption, such as those in 22 CFR 123.4(a), may be submitted electronically using the Automated Broker Interface. This means that the entry may be released electronically ("paperless"). The entry

> *In the past, the enforcement community functioned with an inconsistent pattern of regulatory enforcement, creating an environment of different practices at different ports of entry and exit. CBP has addressed this common practice issue by providing specific guidelines for handling imports and exports that are subject to the ITAR license and exemption process.*

documents must cite the ITAR exemption and contain the statements required by the ITAR to support the exemption.

3. At the time of export, the ITAR exemption must be cited on the Electronic Export Information filed in the Automated Export System and the export documentation must cite the Customs entry number on which the exemption was declared on import. CBP may request a copy of the Customs entry and accompanying documents to verify that the exemption was properly claimed at the time of import.

4. If the appropriate ITAR exemption was not claimed on the Customs entry, CBP will detain the export shipment. The exporter must disclose the violation to DDTC and use a DSP-5 Permanent Export License as authority for export. (Note the recently published DDTC Web notice on temporary import violations that may apply to these circumstances.) After making the disclosure and obtaining a DSP-5, the exporter can petition CBP to release the shipment for export.

5. The memorandum states that first-time violators of these procedures will be issued a warning and allowed to make the necessary corrections. The memorandum goes on to say that "subsequent violations *are not* technical violations and will not be treated as such by the ports."

6. The memorandum also states that the importer may use a continuous-entry bond in connection with entries of ITAR shipments. Some ports had previously required single-transaction bonds for these entries.

The fines and penalties associated with goods regulated by ITAR are quite high therefore it is imperative that importers and exporters, in addition to the service providers, be aware of these newly established procedures and process for obtaining the customs clearance on inbound and outbound shipments.

Affirmation of the proper declaration to CBP must be managed by importers and exporters and they should not solely rely on the expertise of their service providers, as that can be a costly liability. Importers and exporters need to take control of this process and ensure that the proper information is relayed to the service provider and subsequently to CBP.

Through this program, CBP works with the trade community to adopt tighter measures throughout their international supply chains. In exchange for adopting these stronger security practices and after verification by CBP that the measures are in place, CBP generally affords C-TPAT members reduced inspections. C-TPAT is a voluntary program with a "trust but verify" focus and, as such, the program must take immediate action to suspend or remove members that are not in compliance with the program's minimum security criteria.

AES and the FTR (Foreign Trade Regulations)

Most of us who are involved with exports are aware of most of the "working" parts of the FTR as it relates to AES and EEIs. For example, we know that we must file within specified time frames, prior to export, depending on the mode of transport. We understand that accurate and timely filing is one way to avoid fines and penalties. We check, we double-check, we change anything that is incorrect, and once all is in order, we add the EEI/AES to our recordkeeping process and call it a day.

But did we ever really take the time to actually read the FTR (15CFR part 30) to get the "whole picture" of these regulations? Are there any other requirements that we must adhere to, other than the obvious? Most of us have not delved in deeply, but we should. There are various key parts of the FTR that most of us are unaware of. It is my intention to identify just a few of the commonly "overlooked" parts of these regulations.

For example: At some point in your exporting career you may have been (or may be) asked by someone overseas to provide them with a copy of the AES transmission for their specific shipment. Did you know it's a violation of the regulations (15 CFR 30.60) for you to share the AES information with foreign entities? If you share the AES with foreign entities, you are subject to civil penalty actions.

Or, how about this one: In a routed export, we are probably all aware that the written authorization comes from the foreign principal party and is issued to the U. S agent of that FPPI. But did you know that as per section 30.3(e)(1) of the FTR, if you make an agreement with the FPPI that you (the USPPI) will file the AES in a routed export transaction, then you (the USPPI) must have *written* authorization from the FPPI that gives you authority to file AES in this situation.

Another gem that is contained within these regulations is found in section 30.3(e)(2). Here we read that in a routed export, the USPPI has the right to request a copy of the written authorization that was given by the FPPI to the U. S. authorized agent who will be filing the AES. This is your *right* as a USPPI and you should be obtaining a copy of this authorization for your records. This should become common practice and should be included in your export SOP.

Or, how about the proper valuation of export shipments according to the regulations? Those of us who are involved in import activities are probably aware that valuation is a science under the CBP regulations (19 CFR) that involves five main principles. Well, on the export side, there is a similar requirement of valuation. The value of an export shipment for purposes of filing AES is found in the definitions section in 30.1(c). Here it states that the export value on your EEI will be: "The value of the goods at the U. S. port of export. The value shall be the selling price (or the cost if the goods are not sold), including inland or domestic freight, insurance and other charges to the U. S. seaport, airport or land border port of export . . ."

The moral of this story is to dig deeper! Learn all that you can, read all that you can, and you will be amazed at how quickly you can become an expert in yet another area of export compliance.

Best Practices: Routed Exports Transactions

Routed exports may pose particular problems for those companies engaged in export transactions if they are not managed properly. Many of these problems can be resolved through a "best practices" initiative, standard operating procedures, and training and education of personnel.

A routed export transaction is a transaction in which the Foreign Principal Party in Interest authorizes a U. S. agent to facilitate the export of items from the United States on its behalf and prepare and file the Electronic Export Information via AES.

Routed exports create issues for those exporters who believe that if they are out of the functional loop of the export process, they eliminate work and reduce exposure. Neither of these are true.

Let's dissect the issues:

USPPI

In the filing of export documentation, particularly the AES transmission, the USPPI (United States Principal Party in Interest) is the company/individual/entity that is responsible for export compliance in the specific transaction.

In a routed transaction the company that derives the primary financial benefit is the USPPI (typically being the manufacturer, seller or order party).

In a routed transaction, the USPPI is left vulnerable as they are handing off functional responsibility for the export to the foreign buyer and their named forwarder located in the United States. The U. S. government will potentially hold the USPPI responsible for the AES information transfer and other compliance requirements, such as: denied parties screening, recordkeeping, and scrutiny of the end use and end user of the product.

Shipping Control

In a routed export transaction the USPPI relinquishes control of all the functional forwarding and logistics of the shipment to a third party not contracted by them and possibly, even unknown to them.

The government requires that the USPPI act with due diligence, reasonable care and supervision, and control of the export process. This could prove quite difficult in a routed transaction, as the party who has the care, custody, and control of the export has contractual responsibility only to the FPPI, and none to the USPPI, which also needs their interests protected.

If the USPPI does not take a proactive interest in managing routed export transactions, the goods could easily be diverted and end up in the wrong hands. For certain commodities that have military or dual-use functionality, this can result in a breach of national security and noncompliance with U. S. government rules and regulations. This will have an impact on the company, its personnel, and the United States.

The USPPI can take these steps to provide a "best practices" approach to reduce their vulnerability in routed exports.

1. Request from the forwarding agent a copy of the written authority or power of attorney provided to them by the FPPI authorizing them to file AES on their behalf.
2. Provide the forwarding agent with a written Shipper's Letter Instruction containing all the pertinent information required for the forwarding agent to file the AES transmission.
3. Obtain a copy of the filed AES transmission from the forwarding agent, review for accuracy and timely filing, and retain for recordkeeping purposes.
4. Place the Destination Control Statement on your proforma and or commercial invoice.
5. Train sales and customer service personnel.

Eliminate Ex-Work and Routed Transactions

You can implement standard operating procedures and business processes that avoid routed export transactions, and consider eliminating Ex-Work transactions all together.

1. **Place contractual controls into sales contracts that will provide security measures.** If you absolutely need to have routed transactions, build contractual obligations that allow you to complete or control the AES transmission. For instance, the FPPI can authorize the USPPI to file AES on their behalf. This authorization is provided in the same manner the FPPI provides authorization to the forwarding agent, by written authorization or a Power of Attorney.

Mandate in your sales contract that a copy of the international bill of lading and AES transmission be provided to you. This will enable you to see the country of ultimate destination and consignee information. You can also arrange for confirmation of delivery to the intended party. These steps will help you mitigate the risks of due diligence and reasonable care.

2. **Train sales and customer service personnel.** All personnel operating in the global supply chain should be trained in export compliance and Incoterms in order to properly manage routed export transaction. This will enable them to protect the company's interests and eliminate any risks, and exposures relative to trade compliance and security.

BIS Update

Are you looking to acquire new resources, renew old acquaintances, and receive the latest information on the export front? If yes, then you should plan on attending the annual BIS Update.

For anyone who's new to export compliance or just climbed out from under a rock, the BIS Update happens every year in Washington, D.C. In 2010, the update title and theme was "Export Controls in Transition."

The 2010 Update began with opening remarks (recorded) by President Obama. The opening remarks and presentations by key Commerce leaders all focused on the Export Control Reform Initiative. This was followed by breakout sessions which included OFAC, BIS Export Enforcement and Dept of State. As always, there were many other government agencies on hand at the conference.

Although some of the presentations were similar to those presented before, it is always of interest to hear the audience questions answered by government. The "what ifs" and the "I had this happen . . ." are all questions and answers many of us may have as questions in our own minds. The presenters at the presentations in which I attended were all well-versed, interesting and in some instances entertaining. One of the new breakout sessions, Parties to the Transaction Panel, provided a breakdown of the restricted party lists among the government agencies. Call me a compliance nerd, but I enjoy the nitty gritty details of the lists as well as how one actually may come on and off the lists. One disappointment: While the ITAR Update breakout session was interesting, it seemed odd there wasn't a licensing person providing a presentation or available for direct questions.

As to the big question of the update. . . . when will all of this reform take place? Well if we based it on the amount of time CBP and Census took to nail down Mandatory AES and the Foreign Trade Regulations that answer might be not in our lifetime. That said it is an interesting concept to see the government considering combining lists, redefining the USML into a positive list and moving to a potential three tier criteria. It would simplify the lives of compliance personnel across the U.S. if the lines between the lists were drawn to 'clarify jurisdiction'. At least they're talking about it!

Other items from the conference: Good news: Census advised the reporting system capability will be back up and running shortly with enhanced and more efficient data look-ups. Additionally, Census will be adding the reference number to the look-up search within 60-90 days. Bad news: there will be a revision in the regulations to post-departure filing. Current post-departure filers will have to reapply for Option 4 privileges once the regulation is updated.

The BIS does a great job in their outreach efforts. This conference is proof of that. If you are fortunate enough to sign-up and will be attending next year . . . drop me an email and we'll meet up!

Dramatic Changes to Gift Parcels for Cuba

On September 3, 2009, the U. S. Department of Commerce Bureau of Industry and Security (BIS) amended the Export Adminstration Regulations (EAR) to make it easier for Americans to visit Cuba and to send gifts and donations.

In the past, gift parcels could only be shipped to the sender's immediate family. Now, gift parcels can be sent to individuals or any independent religious, educational or charitable organization in Cuba. Also, the value limit for gift parcels increased from $400 to $800. Finally, instead of being able to just send one gift parcel a month per household, donors can send one gift parcel a month to individuals, even if they are in the same household.

The amendment also revises licensing policy to ease exports needed to establish telecommunications links between the United States and Cuba. This includes links established through third countries, and also includes the provision of satellite radio or satellite television services to Cuba.

For more information, check the BIS website for a complete set of FAQs. (http://www.bis.doc.gov/news/2009/cubaqa.htm).

Export Prospects, Partners, and Profits:

If you aren't exporting already, you're missing out!

In today's global economy, businesses can't afford to miss out on international opportunities. Think about it: more than 70 percent of the world's purchasing power is outside of the United States. If you're not exporting, it's highly likely that your competitors are or will be selling internationally. For many of our clients, free trade agreements, ease of transportation, and the Internet have really helped to simplify the export process.

One of the most important things about exporting is that it enables firms to diversify their portfolios and help weather changes in the domestic economy and world economies. By spreading the risk, you boost your competitiveness and bottom line.

Contrary to what many people think, it's not just the big companies that export. By far, the vast majority of exporters are small and medium-sized businesses with fewer than 500 employees, yet we know that only a very small share of businesses export. And nearly 60 percent of all exporters only sell to one foreign market, so many of these exporters could boost their business by expanding the number of countries they sell to.

Commitment Is the Key to Successful Exporting

Companies must have a long-term perspective and top management commitment to make the move into exporting. Exporting can be rewarding, but challenging, and companies need to be in it for the long haul. A track record of successful selling in your domestic market is very helpful. Companies also need to assess their internal resources for doing business abroad, and the U. S. Department of Commerce can help them do that.

U. S. Department of Commerce Offers Useful Programs for Exporters

Local educational programs are available from the U. S. Department of Commerce in every part of the United States, providing companies with a gateway to world markets. The "team" there includes a seamless web of 250 commercial service offices around the world, including American embassies and consulates in eighty countries. Different companies have different needs, and the value of its assistance is tailoring to the individual needs of that company.

Their goal is to help find finding qualified business partners, distributors, agents, representatives, or end users in foreign markets. For example, the U. S. Commercial Service's Gold Key Service provides customized meetings for U. S. businesses with prescreened agents and distributors in those countries. The Department of Commerce also supports U. S. exhibitors at trade shows and events around the world, conducts due diligence on potential international partners, and offers a host of other services. If you don't have the ability to travel to your markets of interest, the International Trade Association's can do a remote control version of the Gold Key Service, called the International Partner Search. Same companies, same due diligence, but you get a list instead of meetings. The U. S. Commercial Service also offers a very popular program, the Featured U. S. Exporter program (FUSE), which allows you to advertise on its international office website, with a link to your website.

Common Pitfalls to Avoid

Do your homework first. Smaller companies will assign the international sales or shipping to one or two people, yet the sale impacts the rest of the company. For example, the accounting department may not understand how the company could be more competitive if they only gained an understanding of finance options for export sales. The sales people are severely limited on what they can offer a foreign buyer. That's because they may not understand international terms of sale, or Incoterms, or what the seller and buyer responsibilities really are once they've agreed to a sale. Also, be prepared to protect your intellectual property in advance. The Commerce Department has resources ready to help you.

Relying on Your Forwarder/Carrier for Export Compliance

We've already discussed in some detail the settlement DHL signed with BIS and OFAC. When I first read about the settlement, I couldn't help but think about the shippers who effected these shipments with DHL. The trickledown effect in action! How many times do we hear colleagues, industry buddies, and international professionals discuss their reliance on the great job their forwarder does for them?

While there are many express consignment courier divisions that provide great service and compliance, there are many more out there that are just pushing the freight through the system. Whether it is an import or an export, the focus is the quick clearance and delivery to the consignee. We accept this because the pricing for this service is "all-in." Let's admit it: we like it quick, cheap and easy; the less aggravation the better, right?

The reality is when we stop and think about it, we are jeopardizing our compliance record by not taking control and managing the import/export process.

"They have my records and always give me them when I ask for them."

"I gave them a letter of instruction so I'm off the hook."

"I'm not the importer of record, so I don't need to be concerned."

You may be reading these statements and agreeing with them. However, if you are a truly compliant company, these statements have the ring of fingernails on a blackboard.

If you are a compliant company, how can you be using service providers that are noncompliant? Do you think CBP really believes that Federal Express is the real importer of twenty pallets of those circuit boards, health monitors, or pineapples?

The Customs Modernization Act of 1993 may seem like ancient history but remember there was a reason for these regulations being put into place. Companies were not following regulations; brokers were providing customer service and getting clearances but not necessarily by the book.

CBP's implementation of mandatory AES and the current Foreign Trade Regulations were created for the same reason. Forwarders and exporters were too happy indicating "machinery parts" and "equipment" on their Shipper's Export Declarations. It was pretty obvious there had to be a better way to monitor what was truly being shipped and to gather accurate statistical data.

Over the years, I have dealt with companies tolerating noncompliant actions of their brokers because "they're nice, helpful and don't bother me too much." Imagine not being able to present accurate documentation to CBP and telling them that is the reason!

Brokers, forwarders, and express consignment carriers must be held accountable for their actions. It is the responsibility of the importer/exporter to supervise and control the actions of their agents.

The key is to manage your relationships with your forwarders and brokers. Provide letters of instruction to your brokers and forwarders, review the documentation you receive back from them, affirm they are doing the right thing, and you'll keep your company compliant.

For express consignment carriers, choose "broker select" options and set up a standard operating procedure that allows your company, as the importer of record, to decide who will be clearing the shipment on your behalf. Supply a broker letter of instruction and make sure the shipment is turned over to the broker of your choosing.

If you are exporting under a routed export, follow the Foreign Trade Regulations in regards to obtaining a Routed Export Letter or obtaining AES authorization to file AES on behalf of the foreign consignee. If you are the USPPI, make certain you are utilizing an Export Letter of Instruction.

Regardless of whether it's an export or import, ensure your service provider calls you with any question as to the shipment and does not make any entry or export decisions on your behalf. Always keep a copy of these communications and of course maintain records in accordance with the appropriate import/export regulations.

A compliant importer/exporter chooses compliant service providers for their team!

Best Compliant Practices for Freight Forwarders

International freight forwarders play a significant role in ensuring the security of the global supply chain. Without their supervision and control over the export process, in addition to the exporter's role, there could be possible breaches of security. Many exporters rely solely on their freight forwarder's expertise and truly believe that the responsibility of compliance and global security falls on the freight forwarder's shoulders. Having a compliance program in place is a good selling tool for a freight forwarder and also demonstrates to the U. S government their commitment to being compliant however; even with these measures in place, however, a customer's lack of knowledge in the compliance area can leave a freight forwarder vulnerable and susceptible to fines and penalties if extra steps are not taken. Having best practices in place can further assist a freight forwarder in avoiding these pitfalls.

Freight forwarders may have compliance responsibilities under the Export Administration Regulations even when their actions are based on information and or instructions provided by the exporter. Freight forwarders should be formally trained in U. S export regulations so that they are able to scrutinize the information being provided and minimize their exposure as well as their customers'. Hiring a freight forwarder to perform these actions does not relieve the exporter of their compliance responsibilities, however, and if an error is not identified or rectified prior to export, the exporter may actually place blame on the freight forwarder for not catching their omission or error. This may lead to both parties being exposed to possible fines and penalties and, perhaps even a loss of that customer to the freight forwarder. Freight forwarders are responsible for the information they file via the Automated Export System on behalf of their customer and it is important that they understand their obligations under the Export Administration Regulations, as no person, including an agent, may proceed with any transaction knowing that a violation of the EAR has occurred or is about to occur.

As freight forwarders, we must all understand our client's needs but it is also critical to determine their level of knowledge and or possible shortcomings in all areas of the global supply chain, particularly in the compliance area. While routine freight forwarder procedures (i.e., tracing and tracking, customer service, etc.) complement a client profile, best practices will further enhance those processes and will offer protection for both parties against compliance deficiencies. Utilizing best practices is one of many ways in which a freight forwarder can offer their support to the export controls that are in place necessary to ensure global security.

Best practices can vary from freight forwarder to freight forwarder dependent on their client base, of course; however, the best practices outlined below pertain to the global supply chain as a whole regardless of a freight forwarder's customer base, regardless of the specific commodities. Any gaps and deficiencies within a freight forwarder's current operating procedures should be identified (such as lack of formal training, no written procedures in place, etc.), addressed, and rectified—and best practices implemented.

- As outlined on the BIS website, best practices are based on the following four principles: Industry and government should work together to foster secure trade that reduces the risk of diversion of items subject to export controls.

- Secure trade will reduce the diversion of dual-use items to prohibited end-uses, end-users, and destinations.
- Secure trade will encourage the more expeditious movement of legitimate trade through borders and ports
- Industry can achieve secure trade objectives through appropriate export management practices

Here are the specific best practices exporters, reexporters and trade facilitators, and freight forwarding companies should all be implementing, as provided by the BIS's website(www.bis.doc.gov/complianceandenforcement/frbestpracmts req5_16.html):

- Each company should develop a written policy against allowing its exports or services to contribute to terrorism or programs of proliferation.
- Each company should identify one person who reports to the CEO, general counsel, or other senior management official as the ultimate party responsible for oversight of the company's export control compliance program.
- Each company should create an export control compliance program. A company should integrate this compliance program into its overall regulatory compliance, security, and ethics programs.
- Each company should ensure that relevant company personnel receive regular training in export control compliance responsibilities.
- Each company should seek to utilize only those trade facilitators / freight forwarders that also observe these best practices.
- An exporter or reexporter should classify each of its products according to the requirements of the EAR and should communicate the appropriate Export Control Classification Number or other classification information for each export to the freight forwarder and the end-user involved in that export.
- A company should screen all parties to proposed transactions for the presence of parties who are: subject to an order denying export privileges; on the Unverified List; on the Entity List or on any list of U. S. government–sanctioned parties; and should maintain a record of such screening.
- A company should have procedures in place to detect and report suspicious transactions to the appropriate authorities.
- A company should pay heightened attention to Red Flag Indicators on the BIS website.
- When a company encounters a suspicious transaction, such as those outlined in the BIS "Know Your Customer" Guidance and Red Flag Indicators, it should inquire further and attempt to resolve any questions raised by the transaction.

All freight forwarders should implement best practices as their due diligence in the support to secure the global supply chain and prevent weapons of mass destruction and other sensitive goods and technologies from falling into the hands of proliferators and terrorists as the benefits will be reaped by all within the industry and the nation.

For more information regarding general best practices you can visit the Bureau of Industry and Security's website www.bis.doc.gov.

Five Best Practice Measures for Exporters

On a weekly basis, I meet with exporters all over the country through training seminars. Within the context of the training or during sidebar discussions we discuss compliance and logistics issues. While I could repeat "relying too heavily on service providers" five times and be done with this article, there are other mistakes made by newbie and seasoned exporters that I come across most frequently.

1. **Incorporate denied party screening throughout the supply chain.** Exporters must incorporate denied party screening into their sales, finance, and shipping departments. The smoothest method to manage screening is to incorporate an electronic solution. There are programs available that include documentation and compliance programs. These programs are relatively inexpensive and can save your company from fines and loss of export privileges.

2. **Utilize a forwarder letter of instruction.** Issuing a standard or per shipment letter of instruction safeguards your shipment and compliance efforts by effectively communicating the shipping requirements and regulatory requirements for your shipment. The letter should be clear and simple. It doesn't have to be on the Shipper's Letter of Instructions format we've seen for the past thirty years. A simple one-page instruction is sufficient. Make certain to include a clause that requests all documentation for the shipment to be sent to you following shipment.

3. **Work with a forwarder who has invested in technology.** Working with a forwarder who has "cutting edge" technology—access to billing, shipment status, proof of delivery, etc.—will free up your time and allow you to manage your exports by exception rather than managing each export movement individually. Some forwarders will even let you piggyback on their own denied party screening and HTS/Schedule B search engines. If you don't ask, you won't get! If they don't have these programs, consider their competition!

4. **Establish a recordkeeping and audit process.** Compliance is about doing things right and ensuring you continue to do so. We must schedule self-audits and reviews for export documents and denied party screening, and we should consistently evaluate our compliance efforts to ensure procedures are being followed. If your systems aren't working to protect you, your customers, and your country, determine why and what steps must be incorporated to make certain your processes work functionally.

5. **Get involved early in the process.** Have sales bring you into the scope of a new sales territory or a new line of products early in the process. You can then assess potential risks, licensing requirements, and logistics issues proactively rather than reactively.

All of the above should be incorporated into your corporate compliance manual.

Training should be included whenever it is warranted for specific subject matter and on a yearly basis as an overview.

Exports Control Including Reexports

Many exporters are not aware of their their compliance management duties and responsibilities regarding reexports of goods from foreign countries. The United

States Department of Commerce regulates exports and reexports of "dual-use" items, i.e., goods, software, and technologies with commercial and proliferation/ military applications, through its Export Administration Regulations (EAR). If you are outside the United States and wish to export or reexport an item that is of U. S. origin or that has a U. S. connection, your product may require a license from the Bureau of Industry and Security.

You must determine whether your item is subject to the Export Administration Regulations. Your item is subject to the Export Administration Regulations (EAR) if it:

1. Was produced or originated in the United States.
2. Is a foreign made product that contains more than a specified percentage of U.S. controlled content.
3. Is a foreign made product based on certain U.S.-origin technology or software and is intended for a shipment to specified destinations.
4. Was made by a plant or major component of a plant located outside the United States, and if that plant or major component of a plant is the direct product of certain U. S. technology or software, and your product is intended for shipment to specified destinations.

You may need to obtain a license to "reexport" an item that was produced or originated in the United States. A "reexport" is the shipment or transmission of an item subject to the EAR from one foreign country (i.e., a country other than the United States) to another foreign country. A reexport also occurs when there is "release" of technology or software (source code) subject to the EAR in one foreign country to a national of another foreign country. Many items subject to the EAR do not need a license to be reexported from one foreign country to another. But certain items are controlled and will either require a license or must qualify for a License Exception. License requirements apply particularly to items controlled by multilateral export control regimes. In addition, some destinations and persons (individuals or groups) are subject to comprehensive export controls, including controls on widely traded consumer products.

To determine whether your U.S.-origin product requires a license you will need the following three pieces of information:

1. The Export Control Classification Number (ECCN). Certain items, notably those controlled by multilateral export control regimes, are on the Commerce Control List (CCL) (part 774 of the EAR) and are included in a specific ECCN. If your item is not on the CCL, it may be classified as EAR99. EAR99 is a general category of goods and technology that encompasses many widely traded consumer and industrial items. The ECCN in the CCL will also tell you the reason(s) for control.
2. The ultimate destination of the item. You will need to match the reason(s) for control listed in ECCNs on the CCL (part 774 of the EAR) with the country of ultimate destination in the Country Chart (part 738 of the EAR). The reason(s) for control, when used in conjunction with the Country Chart, will help you to determine if a license is required to the ultimate destination. If you determine that your reexport transaction requires a license, you should review the EAR to determine if any License Exceptions are available (part 740 of the EAR).
3. The end-user and end-use for the item. Even if you determine a license is

not required based on the ultimate destination (or a license is required but a License Exception would generally apply), you may need to apply for a license because of the end-use or end-user. There are certain special restrictions that apply to persons (or entities) identified in the EAR, as well as to persons whom you know or have reason to know are involved in weapons proliferation activities. In most instances, a license is required to persons identified in part 744 of the EAR for the reexport of all items subject to the EAR (i.e., all items on the CCL and all items classified as EAR99).

In certain instances, if your reexport transaction requires a license, you may be able to use one of the License Exceptions set forth in part 740 of the EAR. A License Exception allows you to reexport an item without applying for a license, provided your transaction meets all the terms and conditions of the License Exception.

You may not reexport an item subject to the EAR to a party whose export privileges have been denied by BIS. Please note that U. S. persons may be subject to additional restrictions under the EAR (see section 744.6 of the EAR). U. S. persons may also be subject to restrictions under other U. S. government regulations, such as those issued by the Office of Foreign Assets Control (OFAC) of the U.S. Department of the Treasury or other U. S. government departments or agencies.

The Department of Commerce has enforcement and protective measures available to it to ensure that recipients of items subject to the EAR comply with the reexport license requirements of the EAR. If the Department of Commerce determines that you have not complied with these requirements and restrictions, it may institute administrative enforcement proceedings, resulting in the possible imposition of civil penalties and/or denial of your eligibility to receive U. S. exports (part 764 of the EAR).

If your reexport requires a license and is not eligible for a License Exception, you may apply for a reexport license electronically through the Simplified Network Application Process Redesign (SNAP-R).

In addition, you may contact the Office of Exporter Services, Bureau of Industry and Security, directly at:

Outreach and Educational Services Division
Room 1099D
14th Street & Pennsylvania Ave., N.W.
U.S. Department of Commerce
Washington, DC 20230
Phone: (202) 482-4811; Fax: (202) 482-2927

10

Export Management
Incoterms, Documentation, Compliance, Operations, and Export Supply Chain Skill Sets

Export documents are import documents. This simple statement is the foundation of a successful export program. Rushing a shipment out the warehouse door should not undermine the importance of documentation, packing, marking, and labeling. Falling down on any one of these elements risks customs delays, monetary penalties, and a dissatisfied customer. There is also the added responsibility of export compliance. Managing an export compliance program requires diligence, recurring training, and senior management support. This chapter offers a guideline of the basic fundamentals to operate a functional and compliant export program. With President Obama's Export Iniatitive it is likely that exports will increase and become a more important and increasingly critical aspect of USA based supply chains. Therefore learning vital skill sets outlined in this chapter will become even more important.

Overview of Incoterms

The Incoterms provide definitions for terms of international trade. The terms are universal as they apply to all trading nations under all circumstances. They transcend language, cultural, and legal issues regardless of the country. The exporter can feel comfortable that an Incoterm in the United States will have the same meaning in Japan, Brazil, or South Africa.

The various terms of sale have significant consequences regarding responsibilities, liabilities, and costs to both the importer and exporter. The Incoterms combine documentary and transactional requirements for transfer of risks and costing. There are many hidden costs involved in international trade that Incoterms set out to define. The Incoterms advise which party is responsible for arranging transportation services, payment of freight charges, arranging insurance, etc. The exporter should be aware that terms of sale directly affect costs and, therefore, may affect an exporter's competitive advantage. The more responsibility assumed, the higher the costs involved. For example, the price might be $4,500 from the plant dock, $4,800 to the U.S. port of export, and $5,800 delivered to the customer's door overseas.

Name the Incoterms and the Point of Shipment

When using the Incoterms, a named place *must* be used. Too many times international transactions contain terms reading "Net 30 days, FCA." While this designates payment will be made in 30 days, it does not designate "free carrier" (FCA) to where?

Is it FCA seller's warehouse, FCA forwarder's warehouse Jamaica (N.Y.), FCA JFK Airport?

> **FCA Seller's Warehouse.** The seller packs the goods for export, makes the freight available at his dock, and is responsible for loading. The seller is required to clear the goods for export.
>
> **FCA Forwarder's Warehouse Jamaica.** The seller packs the goods for export, makes the freight available at his dock, arranges the inland transportation, loads the goods onto the inland carrier, and delivers the goods to the forwarder's warehouse. The seller is required to clear the goods for export.
>
> **FCA British Airways JFK Airport.** The seller packs the goods for export, makes the freight available at his dock, arranges the inland transportation, loads the goods onto the inland carrier, and delivers the goods to the airport, not unloading the goods. The seller is required to clear the goods for export.

It is easy to see the additional costs incurred and responsibility assumed as the named location changes.

If an exporter sells FCA seller's warehouse, risk will pass once the freight has been loaded on board the inland conveyance. This means that the buyer will arrange to pay for the inland transportation. The buyer will also assume responsibility for loss or damage to the freight during transit.

Choosing to sell FCA forwarder's warehouse Jamaica, requires that the seller arrange for the inland freight. The seller will then assume all transit liabilities until the freight is delivered to the forwarder's warehouse.

The third example has the seller assuming all liability until the goods are transferred to the international carrier.

Terms of Payment and Insurance Considerations

An export sale has been created and is now ready to ship. The terms of sale are free on board (FOB) Port of Miami, net 60 days. The shipment is made with the terms of sale calling for a payment from the buyer in Paris in sixty days. The shipment arrives missing three of ten pieces. This amount represents $12,000 of the total invoice value for which the buyer discounts the bill. The seller argues that risk passed in Miami, therefore the responsibility of insurance was with the buyer at the time the freight was loaded on board the vessel.

The buyer argues that the shipment showed up short and that under no circumstances, if the U.S. exporter is to keep the account, will the buyer contribute to the loss, holding the exporter fully responsible. According to this scenario, while the terms of sale appeared to offer less exposure to the exporter, the terms of payment, allowing 60 days, provided greater exposure. The position of the buyer, while unreasonable and incorrect is common when the buyer holds the advantage of not yet having paid for the freight.

Without contingency insurance or unpaid vendor protection, the exporter may have to sue to collect at the cost of losing a customer, unnecessary aggravation, and great expense.

The conclusion to be drawn is that in most export situations, the exporter should control the terms of the sale and the terms of payment. Every factor must be considered in this evaluation, such as, but not limited to the following:

- Price and Payment Terms
- Competitive Pressures
- Forwarder and Carrier Options
- Opportunities for Loss and Damage
- Previous Experience with the Buyer
- City and Country of Destination
- Customs Clearance in the Buyer's Country
- Current Economic and Political Situation in the Buyer's Country

Controlling terms of sale offers the exporter both short and long term options for maintaining competitiveness. If the exporter chooses to sell on terms where all shipping, documentation, insurance, and freight choices are in his control then he has the ability to affect the cost, insurance, and freight costs. The exporter is not forced to accept a particular insurance company whose marine rates may be higher than could be obtained in the open market, but is free to choose steamship lines, having the option to look at possible non-conference carriers that might produce lower shipping costs. Each element and variable of the international transaction must be evaluated. Controlling the option to evaluate will afford the most competitive choices, which will work to the exporter's advantage.

Another important consideration in determining the terms of sale is to understand the pitfalls of attempting a "door-to-door" sale. Customs in some countries, like Brazil, work to the disadvantage of the exporter. Customs has afforded the importer a better opportunity to arrange clearance than with the exporter's agent. The exporter's freight forwarder's local relationship with foreign clearance agents plays a vital role in this regard.

The current political and economic situation in the buyer's country is critical as well. Take the situation in certain areas of Eastern Europe. While there is a big demand for U.S. products, payment is difficult at best. 2012 is becoming the best year for exports from the U.S.in the last forty years. To make the sale, the U.S. exporter may not be able to sell completely on secured terms but may be willing to sell on a collect or sight draft basis. This arrangement might meet the need of the importer and reduce some of the exporter's exposure.

The key word is "reduce," not "eliminate." The exporter will need to make arrangements, with the freight forwarder or the carrier, not to release the freight until the payment is made to the local representation. Quality local representation, good communication and tight monetary controls are critical to the successful execution of this option.

Incoterms do not deal with pricing, method of payment, transfer of ownership or the consequences of a breach of contract. Each of these issues should be dealt with in the contract of sale.

Insurance is another often overlooked issue that is not generally addressed within the Incoterms, with the exception of Cost, Insurance and Freight (CIF) and

Carriage and Insurance Paid To (CIP). While these two Incoterms make mention of insurance, the procurement of such insurance has limitations and in most instances procuring insurance outside of these Incoterms is a better option for exporters.

Quality marine insurance affords protection to the exporter in all situations. The marine insurance contract should have features that protect the exporter, regardless of who is responsible to insure and where risk passes. Unpaid vendor or contingency insurance can be part of any successful export program. It will afford the exporter mitigation of transportation expenses in cases where they are not responsible for insurance but may be exposed due to payment or contract terms.

The bottom line is that the exporter must evaluate many issues in determining the best terms of sale for a particular export transaction. In any case, the exporter should negotiate a controlling advantage that will mitigate potential loss and maximize protection of profits.

A Review of the Eleven Standard Incoterms

The International Chamber of Commerce's *Incoterms 2010* includes eleven trade terms that specify the buyer's and seller's responsibilities, and transfer of risks and costs when those terms are made part of the international transaction.

1. **Ex Works: EXW (insert named place of delivery).** Any mode of transport; seller makes goods available to buyer at seller's premises or other location, not cleared for export and not loaded on any collecting vehicle. The buyer bears all risks and costs involved in taking the goods from the seller's premises and thereafter.

2. **Free Carrier: FCA (insert named place of delivery).** Any mode transport; seller delivers goods, cleared for export, to the carrier named by the buyer at the specified place. If delivery occurs at the seller's premises, the seller is responsible for loading. If delivery occurs elsewhere, the seller must load the conveyance but is not responsible for unloading. The seller is responsible to clear the goods for export.

3. **Free Alongside Ship: FAS (insert named port of shipment).** Sea and inland waterway only; seller delivers when the goods are placed alongside the vessel at the named port of shipment. The seller also clears the goods for export.

4. **Free on Board: FOB (insert named port of shipment).** Sea and inland waterway only; seller delivers when the goods are loaded on board the vessel at the named port. The seller clears the goods for export.

5. **Cost and Freight: CFR (insert named port of destination).** Sea and inland waterway only; seller delivers when the goods are loaded on board the vessel. The seller pays for bringing the goods to the foreign port and clears the goods for export, however the risk passes at the point of delivery to the carrier.

6. **Cost, Insurance, and Freight: CIF (insert named port of destination).** Sea and inland waterway only; seller delivers when the goods are loaded on board the vessel. The seller pays CFR for bringing the goods to the foreign port, obtains insurance against the buyer's risk of loss or damage, and clears the goods for export, however the risk passes at the point of delivery to the carrier.

7. **Carriage and Insurance Paid to: CIP (insert name place of destination).** Any mode of transport; seller delivers the goods to the carrier at an agreed place

and it also pays the cost of bringing the goods to the named destination. The seller also obtains insurance against the buyer's risk of loss or damage during carriage and clears the goods for export. The risk passes at the point of delivery to the carrier.

8. **Carriage Paid To: CPT (insert named place of destination).** Any mode of transport; seller delivers goods to carrier at an agreed place and pays costs of bringing goods to the named destination. The seller also clears the goods for export. The risk passes at the point of delivery to the carrier.

9. **Delivered at Terminal: DAT (insert named terminal at port or place of destination).** Any mode of transport; seller delivers the goods once unloaded from the arriving means of transport and placed at the disposal of the buyer at a named terminal at the named port or place of destination. The seller clears the goods for export.

10. **Delivered at Place: DAP (insert named place of destination).** Any mode of transport; seller delivers when the goods are placed a the disposal of the buyer on the arriving means of transport ready for unloading at the named place of destination. The seller clears the goods for export.

11. **Delivered Duty Paid: DDP (insert named place of destination).** Any mode of transport; seller delivers goods to the buyer, cleared for import (including import license, duties, and taxes) but not unloaded from the means of transport.

Export Documentation

The number one reason export problems occur is incorrect documentation. A missing certificate of origin, a spelling error, deleted language, or an inaccurate number of copies will cause substantial delays in obtaining customs clearance, resulting in additional costs to complete the clearance process overseas. Wasted time and money cut into profits, annoy customers, and frustrate your export staff.

In addition to knowing the required documents, the exporter will also need to know the correct language, required number of copies, required signatures, appropriate format, notary seals, consularization stamps, shipping instructions and any specific documentary requirement due to the type of commodity.

The best sources for information are the customer, the customer's agent, and the freight forwarder being used. A company may ship to Brazil once a month, but the freight forwarder may be moving shipments to Brazil daily. Relying on the forwarder's expertise and their depth and reach can eliminate many export headaches. Additional resources for documentary and customs requirements may be found in the Appendix.

While the documentation process can be complicated to master, the right approach together with support from several resources can simplify the process and remove the inherent obstacles. Many of the necessary documents required for an export transaction are as follows:

- Invoice
- Packing List
- Electronic Export Information (EEI)
- Bill of Lading
- Certificates of Origin
- Payment Instrument (Letter of Credit [L/C], Sight Draft)

- Health/Sanitary Certificate
- Export/Import License
- North American Free Trade Agreement (NAFTA) Certificate
- Societe Generali Surveillence (SGS) Inspection Certificate
- Carnets
- Certificate of Insurance
- Certificate of Quality/Analysis
- Free Trade Agreement Support Certificates

FIVE HELPFUL HINTS

1. Check with several sources for documentation requirements. This double check will assure correct compliance.
2. Documentation files should be set up for each country to facilitate continuity on repeat or future sales. These files should be updated regularly as laws, customs practice, and regulations change frequently.
3. Scan/e-mail or fax all documents ahead of export execution to give your customer an opportunity for review. If changes are necessary, this will permit sufficient time to manage the modifications.
4. Develop systems to check and recheck the original documents before they leave your premises.
5. Make sure that at least one complete and legible set of documents is retained on file and accessible in the unlikely event that the originals are lost.

Documentation and Letter of Credits (L/Cs)

An important function of export documentation is to assure the exporter receives collection proceeds according to the agreed terms of sale and payment.

In a typical L/C transaction, the exporter anticipates receipt of funds once the goods are shipped. While this may be true in theory, in practice the exporter will only receive payment once the required documentation is received and approved by the confirming bank. This process can be difficult if errors are found, documents are incomplete or documents are presented outside the agreed upon time frame.

The bank scrutinizes the documentation so thoroughly because it never sees the freight. Discrepancies in documentation create extra expense, payment delays, and aggravation. The following is a list of ways to minimize L/C problems:

- Select banks with which you have a working relationship.
- Construct L/C checklists that detail the necessary documents, their format, and all pertinent information. This list should be reviewed and managed as part of the export process to ensure accuracy and conformity with the L/C requirements.
- Before a deal is concluded make sure all requirements of the L/C can be met, such as last ship dates and production demands; that all costs of compliance have been taken into consideration; and responsibility has been assigned regarding payment for changes or discrepancies within the L/C.
- For L/Cs from third world countries that are confirmed by their banks in the United States, you should make sure that you understand not only the L/C requirements, but also the interpretations of potential gray areas, as these can prove to be problematic.

- It is critical when L/Cs are used for international transactions that the terms of sale conform to the INCO terms and the Uniform Customs and Practice (UCP) 600 for payment terms.

Electronic Export Information and Automated Export System

The Electronic Export Information (EEI) is a Department of Commerce form that is required by the Census Bureau to compile official export statistics for goods leaving the United States under the Foreign Trade Regulations. The EEI serves a secondary purpose, as it functions as an enforcement tool for other governmental agencies, such as the Bureau of Industry and Security (BIS), Bureau of Customs and Border Protection, and the Department of State.

The EEI is required for export shipments where the value per Harmonized Tariff Number/Schedule B Number is over $2500.00. For shipments requiring an export license, there is no value threshold; an EEI is required regardless of the value per line item.

The statistical information accumulated within the EEI concerns transportation details, commodity information and specific transaction details and specific commodity information. Key section to the EEI includes: U.S. Principal Party in Interest (USPPI), Schedule B Number, and Value.

The EEI is submitted to the carrier electronically prior to the shipment being exported. is submitted electronically, the exporting carrier receives the information in the same format. The export transportation document must cite the Internal Transaction Number (ITN) indicating the EEI was transmitted and accepted through AES by Census.

If the goods in the shipment are controlled for export and there is an applicable Export Commodity Control Number (ECCN) for the items, the ECCN, licensing information or license exception must be included in the AES transmission. If the goods are controlled for shipment under the International Traffic in Arms Regulations (ITAR) that information must also be reported as part of the EEI, including the applicable U.S. Munitions List Category, licensing information, Dept of State registration number, license number, etc.

An EEI is not required for shipments destined to Canada that are not covered by an export license. An EEI is required for shipments to Puerto Rico.

If an EEI is not required due to low value or Canada as the destination, the export transportation document must cite the specific citation from the Foreign Trade Regulations as to why an EEI is not reuiqred.

A listing of EEI requirements is included in the Appendix.

Information contained on the EEI must be true, accurate, and complete. Late EEI filings and false statements made on these documents may result in a violation. The violations begin at $1,000 per day for late filings up to $250,000 or twice the value of the transaction for each violation of the Internaional Emergency Economic Powers Act (IEEPA). For criminial violations, violators may be fined up to $1,000,000 and/or face up to 20 years of imprisonment. Additionally a company may lose its export privileges for violating export control laws.

As part of the recordkeeping requirement for exports, exporters must maintain a copy of the submitted EEI transmission. The forwarder is required to supply a copy of the export declaration upon request by the exporter. Exporters should have a standard instruction letter to their forwarder that a copy of the completed

EEI is given to the exporter along with a copy of the air bill/ocean bill of lading/ transportation document and the forwarder's invoice, if applicable.

Many exporters experience difficulty in obtaining a copy of the EEI for routed export transactions. Even in the situation of a routed export transaction, the forwarder must provide a copy of the EEI to the exporter when requested to do so. A copy of this regulation, 15CFR30.3(e), is contained in the Appendix.

AES

The AES is the joint venture between the Bureau of Customs and Border Protection (CBP), Bureau of Census, Bureau of Industry and Security, and the Department of State. It is the electronic means of filing the EEI directly to Census and CBP. The AES has been designed to improve trade statistics and assure compliance with the export laws. Each of these government agencies has the ability to view the detailed information on an export transaction prior to departure from the U.S. This enables a given agency the opportunity to inspect and/or stop an export prior to departure.

There are two different types of numbers used in the AES transmission process, the internal transaction number (ITN) and the external transaction number (XTN).

The ITN is generated by the AES system. It is the receipt that the information transmitted has been accepted by AES. The ITN changes each time data is changed and resubmitted to AES, signifying a new receipt of the new information. The XTN is the number that is unique for each EEI filed. The XTN never changes.

An important compliance issue for exporters to keep in mind is their loss of control over an export shipment that was sold under the Incoterm ex-works (EXW). In an ex-works transaction the seller is responsible to make the freight available at their dock, packed for export, and no more. Many exporters fail to recognize that while they may be meeting their responsibility under the Incoterm they still have a responsibility to ensure compliance with U.S. export regulations which are not covered under an Incoterm.

These types of transactions, commonly called routed export transactions, still require a U.S. seller to know their customer, provide accurate information to the customer's forwarder to prepare and submit the EEI and to relay any potential ECCN information to the customer's forwarder.

Export sellers should implement the following steps to be compliant with U.S. export regulations under this particular Incoterm:

Utilize a shipper's letter of instruction to the customer's forwarder.
Obtain proof from the customer's forwarder that they are duly authorized to handle the export shipment.
Request and receive a copy of the completed and accepted EEI from the customer's forwarder.
Review the EEI for accuracy based on the data elements provided by the seller.

In the even the EEI information is not correct, the seller should advise the forwarder verbally and in writing to make the appropriate changes.

In our post 9/11 world, EEIs are an important enforcement tool that CBP can use to target particular export commodities, destinations, or any other criteria they create.

Advanced Manifest Filing Rules

October 2003 brought about a new requirement by Customs and Border Protection for Advance Electronic Cargo Data Reporting. The rule represented the further evolution of cargo security regulations in that it covers outbound cargo.

Export shipments require advance notification to customs by means of the AES. Export data is required to be filed prior to departure within the designated time frame for that particular mode of transport. The time frame for air export is two hours prior to departure, rail is four hours prior to departure, truck is one hour prior to departure, and ocean is twenty-four hours prior to departure.

There are some deviations for these rules depending on the circumstances. For example, air exports to Canada, Mexico, Central America, and the Caribbean must be submitted no later than take off. Trucking companies and shippers that participate in the Free and Secure Trade (FAST) program may send information up to thirty minutes before arrival at the border.

Once again we see where the availability of advance cargo data provides CBP the opportunity to screen cargo deemed to be a security risk by using a targeted system. CBP has attempted to strike the right balance between security concerns and business without encumbering supply chains.

USPPI

June 2008 marked the publication of the new Foreign Trade Regulations and with this mandatory AES for all shipments requiring same.

The USPPI is the entity in the United States that receives the primary monetary benefit from the export transaction, typically the manufacturer, distributor, order party, or a foreign buyer located in the United States. The forwarding agent cannot be the USPPI, unless acting as the order party for the importer.

This places a potential greater onus on the "manufacturer" to be held responsible for the export even though they may not be functionally responsible for the mechanics of the export.

The USPPI is responsible for:

1. Providing the forwarding or other agent with the export information necessary to complete the EEI record.
2. Providing the forwarding or other agent with a power of attorney or written authorization to complete the EEI record or signing the authorization block printed on a shipper's letter of instruction. It should be noted that the latter signing is only valid on a transactional basis. Furthermore, in a routed export, the forwarder should be obtaining the written authorization from the Foreign Principal Party in Interest (FPPI).
3. Maintaining documentation to support the information provided to the forwarding or other agent for completion of the EEI record.
4. Retaining records for the required recordkeeping period.

Areas like, but not limited to, who is the buyer, ultimate country of destination, ultimate utilization, choice of carriers, etc., all could fall back on the manufacturer as a regulatory consequence, if an export compliance problem is encountered.

Schedule B Numbers and Harmonized Tariff Schedule

Schedule B Numbers are based on the same numbering system as the Harmonized Tariff Schedule of the United States (HTSUS). The HTSUS is the U.S. version of the harmonized tariff system and is issued by the U.S. International Trade Commission. Schedule B numbers are issued by the Census Bureau. This classification resource is used to identify all commodities by a ten-digit number.

Schedule B numbers and harmonized tariff numbers consists of a ten-digit numerical format composed of a four-digit heading, a four-digit subheading, followed by a two-digit statistical suffix. Schedule B and harmonized numbers share the same first six digits, but at the ten-digit level the codes can be different.

The primary difference between the HTS and the Schedule B numbers are HTSUS are required to be used for import. On the export side the Schedule B number or the HTSUS number may be used when reporting to AES.

Valuation

The value is defined as the selling price by the USPPI to the foreign buyer or cost if not sold, plus the cost of inland freight, insurance, and other charges incurred in moving the goods from their U.S. point of origin to the U.S. port of export.

Many exporters fail to report the correct FOB/FCA value on the commercial invoice, particularly for samples, repairs, and company material. The value stated has to have a resemblance to real market value. The value must be accurate and correct by the party filing the EEI certifying that all information is true and correct.

Efforts to comply with the EEI requirements must be made by shippers, carriers, and freight forwarders. Federal authorities have the authority to fine shippers/forwarders/carriers up to $10,000 for filing late EEIs. Shipments can be detained for noncompliance of SED requirements, which may result in difficulties far greater than a penalty fine.

HIGHLIGHTS OF EXPORTER AND FREIGHT FORWARDER SED REQUIREMENTS

- The exporter must provide accurate and complete information on the EEI. The exporter is responsible even if an authorized agent prepares the EEI.
- The exporter must provide the forwarder with a formal power of attorney or the less formal written authorization as stated on the EEI in transaction where the seller is choosing the forwarder.
- The forwarder must submit the EEI to the exporting carrier prior to exportation.
- Forwarders must provide the exporting carrier with statements or citations when an item or shipment is exempt from EEI requirements.
- The exporter or forwarders must report corrections, cancellations, or amendments to information reported on the EEI to customs at the port of exportation as soon as the need for such changes is determined.
- The exporter or forwarders must maintain all records relating to the exportation for a period of five years under both the Foreign Trade Regulations and the Export Administration Regulations.

Power of Attorney

Freight forwarders, customhouse brokers, agents, etc. all sign/submit documents on behalf of the exporter and make statements/declarations to authorities and the U.S. Government. The service provider typically signs these documents *as agent for* the USPPI. Therefore, to perform these functions they should have authorization from the exporter to do so. The device used to provide this authorization is the power of attorney. The Appendix includes a standard power of attorney.

While a Shippers Letter of Instruction (SLI) contains a block that authorizes the forwarder to submit/file the EEI on behalf of the exporter, this authorization only pertains to the one transactional shipment for which the exporter prepared the EEI. Authorization to submit/file the EEI must then be obtained on a shipment-by-shipment basis if there is no standard power of attorney on file with that particular forwarder.

Export Compliance: It Is Everybody's Business

BIS

In April 2002, the Bureau of Export Administration was renamed the *Bureau of Industry and Security* to better reflect the broad scope of the agencies' responsibilities. Administering export controls on dual-purpose items remains a core BIS responsibility, but the BIS also coordinates all of the Commerce Department's homeland security activities, leads the federal government's outreach to the private sector regarding critical infrastructure protection and cyber security, and assists U.S. industry in complying with the Chemical Weapons Convention and other international arms agreements. The agency also spearheads the Department of Commerce's efforts in defense trade advocacy and monitors the health of the U.S. defense-industrial base.

The mission of the BIS is to advance U.S. national security, foreign policy, and economic interests. Its activities include regulating the export of sensitive goods and technologies in an effective and efficient manner by enforcing export control, antiboycott, and public safety laws, cooperating with and assisting other countries on export control and strategic trade issues, assisting U.S. industry to comply with international arms control agreements, monitoring the viability of the U.S. defense industrial base, and promoting federal initiatives and public-private partnerships across industry sectors to protect the nation's critical infrastructures.

The BIS is responsible for enforcing the Export Administration Regulations (EAR). The EAR cover all items in the United States, all U.S. origin products whether in the United States or abroad, all U.S. origin parts, components, and materials incorporated abroad into foreign made products, and foreign made direct products of U.S. origin technology or software. These regulations include export licensing, denied parties screening, antiboycott compliance, and the list goes on. The BIS maintains its focus on promoting U.S. exports while protecting U.S. security. This is a delicate balance at best.

This is a heavy responsibility for exporters, but it is manageable. A solid export compliance program can ensure a company's exporting future, as the penalties for violations of export law can be severe ranging from monetary fines, imprisonment, denial of export privileges, and bad publicity.

The BIS is not the only agency exporters need to be concerned about. There is also Census, Customs and Border Protection, Department of State, Office of Defense Trade Controls (DTC), Fish and Wildlife Services, Bureau of Alcohol, Tobacco, Firearms (ATF), Food and Drug Administration (FDA), and more. Exporters must enact their compliance program early in the process to guarantee compliance with export regulations.

The penalties for violating export laws are stiff, consisting of civil and criminal fines, imprisonment, denial of export privileges, and the bad publicity associated with the discovery process. Under the Freedom of Information Act (FOIA) the government posts the company names, types of violations, and in some instances the name of the individual who committed the violation. The Appendix contains many examples of these web site postings.

Commerce Control List / Export Commodity Control Number

The BIS maintains a list of items that are under their export control jurisdiction. This list is called the Commerce Control List (CCL).

What is my product? Are there any possible dual use purposes to my product? Does my product require governmental approval before I ship?

The government recognizes that a salesperson or shipping manager may not have the complete knowledge to be able to fully answer these questions. Therefore, it may be necessary to seek the advice of an in-house engineer to correctly answer and assist in reviewing the CCL and assigning an Export Commodity Control Number (ECCN). If an engineer is unavailable, the BIS has a process for companies to submit a commodity classification in which they will review the product specifications to determine the correct ECCN.

Once the ECCN has been assigned, the export compliance program can be set up to guarantee that before a product is shipped proper authorization, whether by an export license or use of a license exception, is obtained. If the product does not fall within the ECCN description, the product may be shipped No License Required (NLR) as long as all other compliance steps, like denied party screening, have been taken into account.

CCL Structure

CATEGORIES

0 Nuclear Materials, Facilities and Equipment and Miscellaneous
1 Materials, Chemicals, Microorganisms, and Toxins
2 Materials Processing
3 Electronics
4 Computers
5 Telecommunications and Information Security
6 Lasers and Sensors
7 Navigation and Avionics
8 Marine
9 Propulsion Systems, Space Vehicles, and Related Equipment

GROUPS

A Equipment, Assemblies, and Components
B Test, Inspection, and Production Equipment
C Materials
D Software
E Technology

REASONS FOR CONTROL

Antiterrorism (AT)
Chemical and Biological Weapons (CB)

Crime Control (CC)
Chemical Weapons Convention (CW)
Encryption Items (EI)
Firearms Convention (FC)
Missile Technology (MT)
National Security (NS)
Nuclear Nonproliferation (NP)
Regional Stability (RS)
Significant Items (SI)
Short Supply (SS)
United Nations (UN)
Computers (XP)

Exporters can design a product matrix to reflect potential destination countries that require licensing prior to export. This important compliance component can be brought in early in the order entry process to ensure timely shipment of a product. If a license is required prior to shipping, a company may not ship without a license. An exporter does not want to find out a license is required the day the shipment is dispatched with the customer eagerly awaiting delivery.

An applicable ECCN does not signify a license is required, only that the product is considered dual use and additional steps must be taken prior to exporting the product. There may be a license exception available that allows the exporter to forego the licensing process. License exceptions can be based on the destination country, value or the circumstances of export, such as on a temporary basis. When a license exception is used, there may be additional reporting requirements that must be adhered to, such as Wassenaar reporting and/or certain encryption exception reporting.

All exports, reexports, and activities covered by the Export Administration Act are subject to the general prohibitions. There are ten general prohibitions. An exporter may not export a shipment without obtaining a license if any of the general prohibitions are applicable. General prohibition numbered 1 to 3 are based on the ECCN. General prohibition numbered 4 to 10 are based on the transaction.

General Prohibitions

General Prohibitions 1 to 3

Without a license or license exception, you may not:

1. Export or reexport controlled items to listed countries if the item is covered by an applicable ECCN and that designated ECCN requires a license to the country of destination.
2. Reexport foreign made items incorporating more than a de minimis amount of controlled U.S. content, if the item incorporates more than the de minimis amount of U.S. content, is covered by an applicable ECCN and that designated ECCN requires a license to the country of destination. The de minimis rule is 25 percent of U.S. content for items being exported to a "regular" destination. The de minimis rule is 10 percent of U.S. content for items being exported to an "irregular" destination.

3. Reexport foreign produced direct product of U.S. technology of software. Items may not be reexported from abroad to Cuba, Libya, Turkmenistan, Ukraine, Uzbekistan, and Vietnam.

General Prohibitions 4 to 10

Without a license or license exception, you may not:

4. Engage in actions prohibited by a denial order. These denial orders include transfers within the United States. Check those denial lists.
5. Export or reexport to prohibited end-users or end-uses.
6. Export or reexport to embargoed destinations (15CFR746).
7. Support of proliferation activities.
8. Ship in transit shipments and items to be unladen from vessel or aircraft via Armenia, Azerbaijan, Belarus, Cambodia, Cuba, Georgia, Kazakhastan, Kyrgyzstan, Laos, Mongolia, North Korea, Russia, Tajikistan, Turkmenistan, Ukraine, Uzbekistan, and Vietnam.
9. Violate any order, terms, and conditions of a license or license exception.
10. Proceed with a transaction with knowledge that a violation has occurred or is about to occur.

License Exceptions

A license exception is an authorization to export or reexport without a license. Some license exceptions require notification, review, or supporting documentation prior to use. Use of all license exceptions should be authorized by the company compliance officer. License exceptions may not be permitted in certain circumstances including, but not limited to, each of the following:

- License Exception Suspended or Revoked
- General Prohibitions 4 to 10 Apply
- Item Is for Surreptitious Interception

License Exceptions are broken down as follows:

Shipments of Limited Value (LVS)
Shipments to Country Group B Countries (GBS)
Civil End-Users (CIV)
Technology and Software Under Restriction (TSR)
Computers (APP)
Temporary Imports, exports, and Re-Exports (TMP)
Servicing and Replacement of Parts and Equipment (RPL)
Government and International Organizations (GOV)
Gift Parcels and Humanitarian Donations (GFT)
Technology and Software Unrestricted (TSU)
Baggage (BAG)
Aircraft and Vessles (AVS)
Additional Permissive Exports (APS)
Encryption Technology, Commodities, and Software (ENC)
Agricultural Commodities (AGR)
Consumer Communication Devices (CCD)

If it appears your export transaction requires an export license look to the license exceptions and all applicable regulations cited within the license exception citation. It could save you and your company time.

Know Your Customer/Denied Parties Screening

An exporter has determined their product is NLR (No License Required). The next step in the compliance program is to run that customer against the various denied party lists maintained by the various government agencies. These agencies include the Department of Commerce, Department of Treasury and Department of State. All parties to the export transaction should be screened using these lists including financial institutions.

The denied party listings are maintained separately by each governmental agency. The best way for an exporter to eliminate the painstaking actions of reviewing each list is to utilize an export software package that incorporates screening of all the denial lists in one shot and is updated on a real time basis.

Denied party screening should be incorporated into every facet of a company's international operation: from an initial sales inquiry coming into a company from the Internet, to the request for quotation, to the processing of the order to the preparation of the actual shipment.

Within the EAR there is a requirement that if an exporter knows an export is for nuclear, chemical, or biological end-uses that they apply for a license. Therefore, the exporter must determine if there are any red flags to the transaction and know their customer and the customer's intended use for the product.

1. Decide if there are red flags. Is there anything fishy about the transaction?

- The customer or purchasing agent is reluctant to offer information about the product end-use.
- The product capabilities do not fit the buyer's line of business.
- The customer has little or no business background.
- The customer is willing to pay cash for a very expensive item when the terms of sale call for financing.
- The customer is unfamiliar with the product's performance characteristics, but still wants the product.
- Routine installation, training, or maintenance service are declined by the customer.
- The delivery dates are vague, or deliveries are planned for out-of-the-way destinations.
- A freight forwarder is listed as the product's final destination.
- The shipping route is abnormal for the product and destination.
- The packaging is inconsistent with the stated method of shipment or destination.
- When questioned, the buyer is evasive or unclear about whether the purchased product is for domestic use, export, or reexport.

2. If there are red flags, inquire. Weed out any bad answers or information that doesn't seem right.

3. Do not self-blind. Do not avoid bad information by salespeople not speaking with operations staff. Should a violation occur, self-blinding is an aggravating factor in an enforcement proceeding.

4. Establish clear policies and compliance procedures so employees understand what they are looking for. Knowledge of a violation by an employee can make the company liable for a violation.

5. Reevaluate all information. Review all the facts that have been uncovered. Have all questions been resolved and answers verified to the point that the compliance officer is comfortable with moving along with the transaction? If yes, the transaction may proceed. If not, hold back the shipment and contact the local BIS office.

All export personnel must be trained in identifying the "red flags" and how to respond legally.

Deemed Exports

An export is the physical movement of a product from point A to point B. An export can also be the transmission of data by fax, telephone, Internet, or other means, like a conference or plant visit.

Consider a physical product that requires an export prior to licensing. The technology or engineering used to create this product may require a license if it is demonstrated, displayed, or discussed with a foreign national whether overseas or here in the United States.

Foreign nationals may visit their U.S. parent company plant in the United States. During a plant tour, the foreign national is shown controlled technology on how the company product is manufactured. When the foreign nationals return to their country, they are taking the information back with them. This is an example of a "deemed export."

Companies must encompass deemed exports within their compliance program. The level of control for the product on the CCL will be the guideline on what information needs to be restricted during plant tours, symposiums, and by interoffice communications. Company databases shared among international subsidiaries should also be considered when reviewing for potential deemed exports with a company.

Antiboycott Compliance

One compliance component that is often overlooked in the export supply chain is screening for boycott statements. The United States has strict regulations regarding any unsanctioned boycott but these rules are primarily geared towards the Arab League boycott of Israel. These rules apply to all U.S. persons including individuals and companies located in the United States and their foreign affiliates. The laws cover U.S. exports and imports, financing, forwarding and shipping, and other activities that may take place entirely offshore.

The regulations require companies to report, on a quarterly basis, that they have received requests to take action to comply with and support an unsanctioned foreign boycott. The Appendix contains examples of boycott requests.

For each violation of the Export Administration Regulations, including antiboycott regulations, export privileges may be denied and fines may be imposed up to $11,000 per violation. When the Export Administration Act is in lapse, penalties for violation of the Antiboycott Regulations are governed by the International Emergency Economic Powers Act (IEEPA). Penalties under IEEPA provides for the greater of $250,000 per violation or twice the value of the transaction for administrative violations and up to $1 million and 20 years imprisonment per violation for criminal antiboycott violations.

Recordkeeping Requirements

A successful compliance program has been implemented and is functioning well within a company. Aside from trouble-free exports, how is a company to prove it has a functioning compliance program? Records. The BIS requires all documents relating to the export transaction be maintained for five years. Required documents include the purchase order, payment receipts, correspondence, E-mails, invoice, packing lists, EEI copies, transportation documents, license applications, export licenses, everything!

An additional compliance step is the inclusion of a destination control statement on all commercial invoices. "These commodities, technology, or software were exported from the United States in accordance with the EAR. Diversion contrary to U.S. law prohibited."

The destination control statement lets the foreign consignee know the products were legally exported and are subject to U.S. regulations. This statement helps to mitigate penalties to the USPPI, should the foreign consignee illegally divert the product.

Office of Foreign Asset Controls (OFAC)

The Office of Foreign Assets Control (OFAC) administers and enforces economic sanctions programs primarily by countries and groups of individuals, like terrorists and narcotics traffickers. The sanctions can be comprehensive or selective, using the blocking of assets and trade restrictions to accomplish foreign policy and national security goals.

These regulations not only affect exporters, but importers, banks, insurance and securities brokers, and tourists. OFAC governs a number of U.S. economic sanctions and embargoes that target geographic regions and governments such as Cuba, Iran, North Korea, Sudan, Liberia, Syria, and Myanmar, as well as other programs targeting individuals or entities that could be anywhere.

The fines for violations can be substantial. Depending on the program, criminal penalties can include fines ranging from $50,000 to $10,000,000 and imprisonment ranging from ten to thirty years for willful violations. Depending on the program, civil penalties range from $11,000 to $1,000,000 for each violation.

OFAC regulations often provide general licenses authorizing the performance of certain categories of transactions. In addition, in some circumstances, U.S. law exempts certain transactions from embargoes. OFAC also issues specific licenses on a case-by-case basis under certain limited situations and conditions.

A license is an authorization from OFAC to engage in a transaction that otherwise would be prohibited. There are two types of licenses: general licenses and specific licenses. A general license is a provision contained in the regulations that authorizes a particular type of transaction.

The OFAC continues to catch companies dealing with Specially Designated Nationals (SDN). The SDN list contains over 10,000 names of financial institutions, importers, exporters, freight forwarders and individuals of whom U.S. companies are forbidden to engage in financial transactions.

Many U.S. companies are aware of these regulations and must screen parties involved in their financial and business transactions against these lists to ensure they are not in violation.

The laws that are violated consist of the Trading with the Enemy Act (TWEA), The International Emergency Economic Powers Act (IEEPA), and the Foreign Narcotics Kingpin Designation Act (FNKDA), to name a few.

OFAC posts a monthly listing of violations on their web site as well. The site will list the name of the violator, the violation, and the penalty amount. A recent perusal of the site listed names like Amazon, Wal-Mart, and the New York Yankees, with fines running the gamut of $2,000.00 to as high as $250,000.00.

Companies should incorporate OFAC screening into their standard operating porcedures (SOPs), keeping in mind other governmental agencies maintain their own lists, and no department within the company should be excluded from performing this screening.

International Traffic in Arms Regulations (ITAR)

The Arms Export Control Act authorizes the President to control the export and import of defense articles and defense services. The President shall designate which articles shall be deemed to be defense articles and defense services.

License or other approval may be granted only to U.S. persons and foreign governmental entities in the United States. Application for license or requests for other approval will generally be considered only if the applicant is registered with Defense Trade Controls.

Any person in the United States who engages in the business of manufacturing or exporting defense articles or furnishing defense services is required to register with DTC. Manufacturers who do not engage in exporting must nevertheless register. Registration is a means to provide the U.S. Government with necessary information on who is involved in certain manufacturing and exporting activities. Registration does not confer any export rights or privileges. It is generally a precondition to the issuance of any license or other approval.

An article or service may be designated to be a defense article if it specifically designed, developed, configured, adapted, or modified for a military application; does not have predominantly civil applications, and does not have performance equivalent (defined by fit, form, and function) to those of an article or service used for civil applications. In addition, an article or service is specifically designed, developed, configured, adapted, or modified for a military application, and has significant military or intelligence applicability such that control under the ITAR is necessary.

Any person in the United States who intends to export (temporarily or permanently) or import temporarily a defense article must obtain the approval of DTC prior to the export/import, unless there is an applicable exemption.

A company's internal process in using license exemptions should be the same as if the company were applying for an export license from DTC. The company must be registered with DTC and must be aware of the conditional requirements of using an exemption. The ITAR lists exemptions for specific circumstances. Use of license exemptions must be documented and the company compliance officer should only authorize the use of exemptions.

The recordkeeping requirements under the ITAR are for all documents related to the export transaction to be maintained for five years from the date of expiration of the license.

In processing a shipment under a Department of State license, the export documentation must be presented to Customs and Border Protection as required. In addition, the export documentation must cite the destination control statement for the Department of State.

"These commodities are authorized by the U.S. Government for export only to (country), for use by (end-user). They may not be transferred, transshipped on a noncontinuous voyage or otherwise be disposed of in any other country, in their original form or after being incorporated into other end-items, without the prior written approval of the U.S. Department of State."

The penalties under the ITAR are severe and include seizure, forfeiture, criminal penalties, and civil penalties. Any attempt to export from the United States any defense articles in violation of the ITAR may result in seizure or forfeiture. In addition, an attempt to violate any of the conditions under which a license was issued may also result in seizure.

Any willful violation of any provision of the Arms Export Control Act and in a registration, license application including an omission of material fact, or issuing an untrue statement of a material fact may result in a three-year debarment, criminal fines not to exceed $1,000,000 per violation and/or imprisonment not to exceed ten years per violation, and civil penalties not to exceed $500,000 per violation.

The United States Munitions List (USML) consists of twenty-one categories. Defense articles and defense services fall within the categories listed below. As part of the licensing process, a company must be able to identify which category best describes their article or service.

Category I Firearms, Close Assault Weapons, and Combat Shotguns
Category II Guns and Armament
Category III Ammunition/Ordnance
Category IV Launch Vehicles, Missiles, Rockets, Torpedoes, Bombs
Category V Explosives, Propellants, Incendiary Agents, and Constituents
Category VI Vessels of War and Special Naval Equipment
Category VII Tanks and Military Vehicles
Category VIII Aircraft and Associated Equipment
Category IX Military Training Equipment
Category X Protective Personnel Equipment
Category XI Military Electronics
Category XII Fire Control, Range Finder, Optical Guidance Equipment
Category XIII Auxiliary Military Equipment
Category XIV Toxicological, Chemical and Biological Agents, and Equipment
Category XV Spacecraft Systems and Associated Equipment
Category XVI Nuclear Weapons, Design, and Testing Related Items
Category XVII Classified Articles, Technical Data, and Defense Services
Category XVIII Directed Energy Weapons
Category XIX Reserved
Category XX Submersible Vessels, Oceanographic and Associated Equipment
Category XXI Miscellaneous Articles

Definitions under the ITAR include:

Defense Article. Any item or technical data designated in 121.1 (Munitions List) of the ITAR. This term includes technical data recorded or stored in any physical form, models, mockups, or other items that reveal technical data directly relating to items designated in 121.1. It does not include basic marketing information on function or purpose or general system description.

Defense Services. Furnishing of assistance (including training) to foreign persons, whether in the United States or abroad in the design development, engineering, manufacture, production, assembly, testing, repair, maintenance, modification, operation, demilitarization, destruction, processing, or use of defense articles; the furnishing to persons of any technical data controlled under the ITAR whether in the United States or abroad; military training of foreign units and forces, regular and irregular, including formal or informal instruction of foreign persons in the United States or abroad or by correspondence courses, technical, educational, or information publications and media of all kinds, training aid, orientation, training exercise, and military advice.

U.S. Person. Lawful permanent resident who is a protected individual. It also means any Corporation, business association, partnership, society, trust, or any other entity, organization or group that is incorporated to do business in the United States. It also includes any governmental (federal, state, local) entity.

Foreign Person. Any natural person who is not a lawful permanent resident or is not a protected individual. It also means any foreign corporation, business association, partnership, trust, society, or any other entity or group that is not incorporated or organized to do business in the United States, and international organizations, foreign governments, and any agency or subdivision of foreign governments (e.g., diplomatic missions).

Export. Sending or taking a defense articles out of the United States in any manner, except by mere travel outside of the United States by a person whose personal knowledge includes technical data, transferring registration, control, or ownership to a foreign person of any aircraft, vessel, or satellite covered by the USML, whether in the United States or abroad; disclosing (including oral or visual disclosure) or transferring in the United States any defense article to an embassy, any agency or subdivision of a foreign government; or disclosing (including oral or visual disclosure) or transferring technical data to a foreign person, whether in the United States or abroad; performing a defense service on behalf of, or for the benefit of, a foreign person, whether in the United States or abroad.

TYPES OF LICENSES

DSP-5 is an application for permanent export of unclassified defense articles and related unclassified technical data.

DSP-61 is an application for temporary import of unclassified defense articles.

DSP-73 is an application for temporary export of unclassified defense articles.

DSP-85 is an application for permanent/temporary export or temporary import of classified defense articles and classified technical data.

DSP-94 gives authority to export defense articles and defense services sold under the foreign military sales program.

Additional Export Considerations

Consularization and Legalization

Many countries require export documents to be consularized and legalized. This process adds additional time constraints and costs to the export shipment. Documents must be presented to a central consulate office, which then performs a brief review and applies a signature stamp to the documents. This is generally done for a fee anywhere from $75 to $300.00.

Exporters must be aware of the destination country's requirement for consularization and legalization. The requirement may be different based on the commodity, quantity, or value. An attempt to import a shipment in the destination country without the proper legalization can result in storage fees imposed by local customs and the carrier and financial penalties.

Solid Wood Packing Material (SWPM) Certificates

In response to the U.S. import requirement of certification of treated wood pallets, other countries have implemented their own import policy on accepting shipments moving on such packing materials.

China, the European Community, and Australia have current regulations regarding the type of pallets and packing that may enter their countries. An untreated pallet can result in additional costs of fumigation in the destination country.

Societe Generali Surveillence (SGS) Inspections

Customs authorities in certain countries require goods be inspected prior to shipment.

The inspection may cover verification of quality, quantity, market price, value for customs purposes, customs classification, and import eligibility. Societe Generali Surveillence (SGS) is a general inspection company that performs this function. They have cargo surveying and inspection capabilities that enable them to mobilize a qualified cargo inspector to certify a cargo for count, accuracy, meeting quality specifications, documentation, or other issues related to a foreign importer's purchase order.

North American Free Trade Agreement Certificates

The North American Free Trade Agreement (NAFTA) formed a trade partnership between the United States, Canada, and Mexico. One of the benefits of this partnership was the reduction of duties for goods qualifying under the applicable NAFTA criterion. Therefore, it is not unusual for a customer to request the exporter issue a NAFTA certificate to accompany the export, considering the financial benefit of paying lower duties or in some cases no duties at all.

To issue a valid NAFTA certificate a company must be certain the product meets the applicable NAFTA criterion. This can be done by verifying the origin of the product and following the rules of origin relevant to the product. These rules of origin may be found in the Harmonized Tariff Schedule of the United States (HTSUS).

NAFTA certificates are frequently validated by customs. There are fines and penalties involved for incorrectly completing the NAFTA certificate so companies must be diligent in preparing this form.

Developing Resources

Every export shipment is unique. Whether it is the product type, the destination country, the potential use of a product, there are many factors that can impede the timely and cost-effective delivery of a company's export. With that understanding, exporters need to develop a dossier of resources in export documentation, export control, and foreign customs requirements. The best resources are a company's forwarder and the customer. A company can ride on the back of the forwarder's experience and worldwide office/agency network to provide documentation requirements in every gateway and relying on their expertise with export compliance concerns. The foreign customer usually has the responsibility to deal with their local customs clearance issues and typically have previously imported.

The Appendix includes a detailed listing of sources for export documentation and compliance including the:

EEI
Decision Tree for U.S. Exporters (Part 732, Supplements 1 and 2)
Commerce Country Chart
CCL

Case Studies in Export Compliance

CASE STUDY 1—THE WRONG WAY

Flying Free is a Connecticut-based distributor of aircraft spare parts. A few of their products are subject to the Commerce Control List (CCL) as they are considered "dual use" items and are subject to export control regulations.

Donna Bisori, the salesperson, receives an e-amiled request from a potential new customer, Trois Avion, located in Paris. The e-mail contains a request for an order of XKY2. XKY2 is one of the products distributed by Flying Free that is listed on the CCL.

The order is a high value order and the biggest order Donna has ever received in her three years working with Flying Free. Donna processes the quotation and sends the standard documents by e-mail to Trois Avion. These documents include a credit application and an end-use statement by Trois Avion.

Trois Avion accepts the quotation, returns the credit application, and requests the order be shipped immediately. Donna grows concerned that the quantity requested is a large order for Flying Free and they may not be able to process the order timely. Donna contacts Trois Avion by phone and speaks with Monsieur Mauvais Gars. Monsieur Gars understands this is a large order and offers to pay cash to expedite the order.

Donna arranges to accept the wire transfer of funds on behalf of the company and waives the credit application. She contacts her warehouse manager and begins to coordinate the materials for shipment. Donna advises Monsieur Gars the order will be processed within the requested time frame. At this time, Donna advises Monsieur Gars that Flying Free has a field engineer working another job in France and that the field engineer can be scheduled to demonstrate the installation of the parts to Trois Avion personnel.

Monsieur Gars informs Donna that Trois Avion is declining the field training. Monsieur Gars e-mails Donna a letter of instruction. The destination address is for a freight forwarder located in Paris, France. There is also a notation on the letter of instruction to include installation instructions in Arabic. Donna calls Monsieur Gars to advise instructions in Arabic are not available and hopes this is not a problem. Monsieur Gars advises the shipment should just ship out as instructed and not to be concerned about the instructions.

Donna receives a call that the order will be ready to ship on Thursday afternoon. Donna confirms accounting has received the payment for the shipment. Donna is anxious for the order to ship as she is scheduled to leave for a long planned vacation in Las Vegas on Friday morning. This sale has also put Donna into the "Silver Sales Group" entitling her to a substantial bonus.

On Friday morning Donna contacts her shipping department and is advised the order was picked up by Flying Free's forwarder and will be shipped on a flight on Friday evening. Donna instructs her shipping department to forward the flight information to Trois Avion. Donna phones Monsieur Gars to advise everything is moving on schedule. Donna is relieved the shipment is moving and departs on her flight to Las Vegas.

On Friday afternoon, the airline carrier contacts Flying Free's forwarder to advise the export shipment has been seized by Exodus, which is the enforcement arm of CBP for exports. Trois Avion is listed as a Denied Person by the BIS.

On Monday morning, an officer from the BIS is waiting to meet with senior management at Flying Free. The BIS officer requests to see the export transaction file for the XKY2 order and a copy of the export compliance procedures for Flying Free. The senior manager at Flying Free is only able to produce a copy of the faxes and e-mails Donna sent and received from Monsieur Gars. Clearly missing from the file are a copy of the denied party screening, end-use statement, export license, and any conversations regarding the various red flags that should have been raised within the transaction dialogue.

Flying Free pays civil penalties of $35,000 and is denied export privileges for one year. As part of their settlement, Flying Free is required to spend an additional $15,000 in implementing an export compliance program including training, to prevent future incidents. Upon Donna's return from vacation she was seeking employment elsewhere, but not in the aircraft industry.

CASE STUDY 2—THE RIGHT WAY

A Florida firm, PSC, receives a request from an engineering consulting firm in Italy. The engineering consulting firm is looking to purchase an industrial pump to be used in Libya. The compliance officer for PSC requests details from the engineering firm, including the name of the end-user in Libya and the details of the transaction, like the final use and type of project for which the system will be used.

Mario Biaggi, the buyer for the engineering firm submits the requested information to PSC's compliance officer. PSC receives the information and screens the names and locations of all involved parties by their compliance software. The names and addresses come out with no hits found.

The compliance officer receives a copy of Mr. Biaggi's purchase order from his sales department. The salesperson is questioning a statement contained within the purchase order requiring a certificate of origin for the product. The salesperson's question arises from an additional detail required on the certificate of origin. "Certificate of origin should state goods are not of Israeli origin." The compliance officer advises the salesperson this is indeed a boycott statement and advises the salesperson to request a new purchase order with this language removed from the purchase order. The compliance officer advises his accounting office of receipt of the boycott statement, so they can add to their IRS report. The compliance officer makes a notation of receipt of the statement, copies the file, and diarizes the item for his quarterly report to the Office of Antiboycott Compliance.

The compliance officer follows up with the salesperson the following day and is advised a new purchase order has been received and the boycott language has been removed from the purchase order.

The compliance officer next receives a telephone call from his customer service manager. The customer service manager has received a set of shipping instructions for the pump. The instructions include a request to move the shipment to Libya transshipping by United Arab Emirates.

The compliance officer is aware that this transshipment point is a potential red flag and decides to contact Mario Biaggi directly to inquire about the transshipping. Mr. Biaggi is reluctant to disclose any information about the request and advises the compliance officer to just send the product.

The compliance officer thanks Mr. Biaggi and ends the discussion.

The compliance officer then contacts his local export enforcement office of the BIS. The compliance officer advises the BIS of the all details of the transaction. The BIS officer asks the compliance officer if PSC would be willing to cooperate with the BIS in their investigation of the engineering firm. The compliance officer agrees and arranges to ship the goods to the United Arab Emirates under the direction of the BIS.

The shipment is moved per Mr. Biaggi's instructions. Upon arrival in the United Arab Emirates, BIS operatives and local customs authorities are able to apprehend a terrorist cell that was looking to use the pump to manufacture chemical weapons.

The compliance manager receives a phone call from the Chief of Export Enforcement thanking him for his cooperation in the investigation. The compliance manager is glad to see PSC's compliance program is effective.

The compliance manager understands that if he did not report the transgression that the culprit would have found another U.S. supplier with no due diligence process.

This type of effort follows the export regulations and is in the spirit of cooperating with the government in fighting terrorism.

Summary of Export Compliance Issues

Various governmental authorities are moving to mandatory compliance of all export regulations.

Exporting has always been associated with intense documentation, bureaucracy, and much frustration. With the increased government scrutiny exporters may find themselves:

- Processing additional paperwork and/or electronic filings for each export shipment
- Needing to automate compliance within the export transaction
- Implementing procedures to ensure compliance with regulations and avoid fines and penalties
- Creating extensive recordkeeping

I have most recently followed numerous cases where exporters have received significant fines for not complying with various export regulations. These cases are on the increase as the various governmental agencies gear up for enforcement by technology, manpower, and mandates for stricter controls take priority. In the Appendix is an update of fines and penalties issued by the BIS against U.S. exporters for various violations of U.S. export law.

I am also witnessing a time when many corporations, both mom and pop and Fortune 100s, are just not paying attention to these export compliance matters as seriously and diligently as is necessary. The consequences are serious and costly. Compliant exporters who have learned to pay attention to these important issues, like export packing, marine insurance, quality documentation, and successful logistics, will now be spending time, money, and resources on compliance issues to survive in global trade.

Incoterms in Exporting

I have always felt that while Incoterms are the foundation of global trade that they are also the most misunderstood aspect of global trade. In most U.S. companies, a salesperson or sales division, agent, or distributor begins the sales process. This is also where the terms of sale are generally introduced. It has been my experience that most international sales representatives, though they have the responsibility, do not understand the ramifications of Incoterms, particularly as it relates to who is responsible for various transportation costs associated with the export and who is responsible to manage the execution of the export documentation.

The consequences of not comprehending the Incoterms can sometimes lead to internal aggravation between operations, finance and sales due to the potential of additional or unaccounted transportation expenses.

An example might be where an export salesperson in Cincinnati has an internal EXW base price of $30,000.00 US dollars and is asked to deliver the freight to an ocean gateway, such as Baltimore.

Technically the sale has now changed to FOB Baltimore, in lieu of EXW Cincinnati. This now puts the burden of the transportation costs of the inland leg (from Cincinnati to Baltimore) back to the exporter. Unless this has been figured into the base costing or as a line item surcharge, after the fact, it will be difficult to account for or recover the cost from the buyer unless this cost was identified up front. This is where the internal strife begins to escalate.

Most exporters do not realize that FOB and CIF terms are terms that are meant for sea and inland waterway transport only. The other nine terms are multi-modal and may be used for all modes of transportation. I regularly see FOB USA airport and CIF destination airport, which is technically incorrect.

The other issue with Incoterms is that an Incoterm, like CFR by itself, is not complete. An Incoterm term is complete when tied in with a "named place" (i.e., FOB Port Elizabeth, CFR Oakland, CIP Rotterdam, DDP Tokyo). An international salesperson who offers FOB, CIF, CPT terms, without the "named place," is only addressing part of the equation and leaving out an integral component, leading to confusion.

A critical issue I will address with respect to Incoterms is that they are the standard terms of sale to describe what would be considered a "typical international transaction." There are eleven terms. However, normal trading practice will afford variations of the eleven leading to countless options and some combinations, which challenge the senses.

For example, you could have an export sale via ocean freight, FOB Charleston, but sales agrees to prepay the ocean freight to the importers domestic gateway, say Copenhagen, Denmark, billing the ocean freight charges back to the importer, by the EXW invoice cost. While from appearances purposes, this might not make sense, it could be accomplished by any agreement reached between the two trading parties. For tax or sales or inland distribution reasons, the importer might best be served by incorporating the international freight costs, so the exporter accommodates the client, by formally selling FOB Charleston, but functionally selling CIF Copenhagen. The paperwork shows one thing, but a side agreement creates another. One most always be careful when doing side agreements or extensions to make sure you are not creating an illegal transaction or a future compliance headache. The reality is that international salespersons, agents, and distributors are always agreeing to provisions in the export transaction, which will alter the ramifications, liabilities, and costing as determined by the actual Incoterms.

The last issue I will address regarding Incoterms is that they are terms of sale that run in conjunction with a related but completely different subject, the terms of payment. And that could be where confusion lies and potential pitfalls.

For example, an exporter sells FCA O'Hare Airport in Chicago. Basically the exporter is accepting responsibility to the point at which the goods are loaded onto an aircraft at the designated airport. They pass liability and costing once the goods are loaded on board the plane.

But the terms of payment are Sight Draft 60 days. The plane crashes. According to Incoterms, technically the risk of the international leg was for the account of the buyer. Now the buyer having not received the goods, is still obligated to pay. Will they? What will it cost for you to collect? The more third world the transaction, the less likely your opportunity to collect. These are all true, very serious every day issues. So international sales and operations must pay attention to the potential conflicts that arise in exports, between the terms of sale and the ultimate terms of payment.

On a side note, in the above example the exporter could have arranged for contingency/unpaid vendor insurance, which would of provide "All Risk" protection in the event they were unable to collect from the buyer.

It is also imperative to remember, as previously mentioned in the chapter, that irrespective of the Incoterm, the USPPI, which would typically be the manufacturer or seller, may be held responsible for compliance with the export regulations.

The BIS

As a 35 year veteran of international trade, I never spent as much time on export controls as I do now, in all three areas of my business: consulting, education and training, and logistics management.

The reality is that the government has stepped up its enforcement efforts, not only on issues typically engaged in national security, but now with our mainstream exporters in areas like with the accuracy of the EEI filings, the overall consistency, conformity, and trueness of the exporter's invoice, packing list, certificate of origin, overall recordkeeping, and the due diligence process in determining what can be exported to whom and where.

The EAR (Export Administration Regulations) is complicated. Understanding the regulations in detail is cumbersome but can be boiled down to these basic questions framing the parameters of the export transaction:

- **What are you shipping?**
- **What quantity/what value?**
- **Where?**
- **To whom?**
- **For what utilization?**

In the simplest of explanations, this is what I believe the Bureau of Industry and Security is requiring each exporter to answer before they can be compliant in their export operations. And a key factor here is that the BIS requires that in each transaction, each export relationship, etc., there is a "SOP" starting with proper due diligence, accountability, recordkeeping, and compliance before an exporter can successfully export.

Ignorance of the rules and regulations is not an acceptable excuse. The fines and penalties can be severe and harsh. Both civilly and personally, with prosecution, suspension/revocation of export privileges, and imprisonment as potential consequences.

One just needs to visit the BIS website to see the results of export enforcement efforts by the BIS and CBP in a proactive mode to catch potential noncompliant individuals and corporations.

- Corporations showing different values between the EEI and the commercial invoice or showing a lower value on the commercial invoice then was the transaction actually accounted for have been fined by the BIS.
- Corporations shipping freight to destinations knowing that a potential transshipment or third party sale will occur to a prohibited country have been penalized.
- Corporations shipping to individuals or corporations on the denied parties lists have had their export privileges revoked or suspended, temporarily or permanently.
- Corporations have had their goods seized for showing that the goods are of U.S. origin, on the export documents, when they were originally imports into the United States.
- Technology companies appearing to export innocuous software only to learn that their products require export licenses, in that the technology has applications for national security exposures.
- High-tech companies finding out that their products are licensable due to the fact that by minor retooling, like with laser equipment for alarm systems, could be retooled for laser weaponry.

The bottom line is that there are hundreds of reasons that the exporter must pay attention to for the level of scrutiny that the BIS is executing on export compliance. This is to avoid serious fines and penalties, prevention of export privilege suspensions, prosecution of the corporation and individuals, and to avoid the expense associated with litigation, mitigation, and the inability to export successfully.

I have observed many corporations ignoring their export compliance requirements and/or procrastinate on dealing with them. For many, this delay or inaction has been very costly.

The activity of the BIS is not waning. It is growing. From the actual outbound ports to the corporate transaction, files are under stiff review and scrutiny.

The BIS decision tree documents the steps an exporter must use to make sure that they can export the product to a particular country, to a specific entity, and for certain utilization. The process must be documented, maintained for at least five years, and be retrievable under any potential audit.

The BIS has established "red flags" or potential occurrences or observations made to the export company, from the potential foreign buyer, that are supposed to cause the exporter to raise their level of diligence, till the inquiry/diligence is successfully mitigated, closed out, or favorably rectified.

For example:

- The foreign buyer wants to pay cash.
- The foreign buyer uses freight forwarder for the delivery sight.
- The foreign buyer is in a completely different line of business.
- The foreign buyer purchases a product that requires installation and training, but tells you not to provide it.
- The foreign buyer is not cooperative with details, delivery sights, dates, etc.

There are numerous other "red flags" that the BIS has identified that the U.S. exporter must learn to understand and react to before completing the export transaction.

Corporate management would be "shocked to learn" the multitude of onus on them in the execution and diligence of their foreign sales.

Exporters must learn the regulations, maintain and update the changes, and have SOPs in place to deal with all the export compliance issues. They must employ specialists on staff or delegate the responsibilities to third parties under contract who are well qualified to provide the export compliance management response necessary. Law firms, freight forwarders, and consultants are the three major types of third party service providers that can offer export compliance expertise.

When the Occupational Safety and Health Administration (OSHA) was developed and expanded in the 1970s to 1980s, many corporations resisted this new governmental intrusion. Some thirty years later, it is well entrenched into corporate America. I view what happened with health and safety issues in corporate America back then to be very similar to what is happening now with export compliance. We can argue about it, we can fight it, but it is here now and apparently here to stay. We need to deal with it constructively, like a necessary evil.

I firmly believe that those corporations and individuals who embrace export compliance proactively will benefit immensely, as those that defer will be at a loss with export operations that are handicapped.

In establishing its export compliance program, the corporation has nominated its corporate compliance officer and created a set of SOPs.

The key to bringing the program to fruition is to establish an internal education and training program.

Importance of Internal Education and Training

Internal education and training will enable the corporation to develop its own in-house expertise. As the compliance officer matures in his new role he will be developing outside resources on which to expand his knowledge. At the same time, one of the many responsibilities of the compliance officer is to disseminate information regarding the compliance program and newly established procedures.

A good export compliance program outlines the framework for the training. Compliance training should begin with senior management for several reasons:

- Compliance is directly related to the company's bottom line.
- Senior management will understand the importance of compliance and, therefore, support the efforts of the compliance manager with additional funding and giving the "hammer" to be used by the compliance officer to enforce the new standard.
- Senior management will provide guidance on the execution of the agreed strategies to be used throughout the company.

Middle management and support staffing must also be included in training. There should be a company directive stating that newly hired employees with specific supply chain responsibilities will require an export compliance overview within thirty days of date of start in the new position. This type of directive requires the cooperation and assistance of the human resources department. It can be incorporated as part of the new employee's indoctrination schedule along with their becoming familiar with the latest benefit plan, for example.

Degree of Training

The levels of training will vary depending on the import/export responsibilities of the employee. As a minimum, all company personnel should be included in a basic compliance class. Everyone in the company including shipping, receiving, accounting, customer service, and sales should be required to attend. Everyone in the company would then be made aware of the compliance program in place within the corporate structure and that senior management is on the same page backing the program.

Accounting, sales, customer service, and operations training should include INCO terms, letters of credit, types of payments, risks of global trade, and denied parties screening. Operations, shipping, and receiving training should include import/export documentation, NAFTA procedures, packing, marking and labeling, and valuation issues.

Training topics should also encompass regulations under other governmental agencies like the FDA, U.S. Department of Agriculture, Department of State, and Department of Transportation, to name a few. Whatever the topics, they should cover the specific needs of the organization.

Sources of Education and Training

Training programs and seminars are offered using different venues. Some programs are offered in connection with international trade organizations like the Society of International Affairs, Professional Association of Import/Export Compliance Managers, American Management Association, International Compliance Professionals Association and The World Academy, etc.

The government also sponsors compliance and regulations seminars throughout the U.S. as well as overseas to provide an opportunity for companies to gain the government perspective on training.

One of the many benefits of attending these seminars is the access to the governmental personnel who are approving license applications, dispensing advice, and enforcing the regulations. These personnel represent an important resource to the compliance manager and are available for in-house visits via their agency outreach programs.

Resource Development

As the compliance officer further defines his role and networks himself with outside organizations he must funnel that information to the troops.

The corporate compliance officer must continue to update the supply chain. CBP and the BIS have daily updates in today's post-9/11 environment. Employees that have received training and are familiar with their day-to-day responsibilities need to be informed of the latest changes. Is United Parcel Service going on strike, will there be port delays in Long Beach next month?

A company web site with a "compliance corner" may offer some corporations a good solution. Other companies may choose to broadcast updates by e-mail to appropriate personnel within the supply chain.

Magazines and newsletters once read should not be tossed away but should make their way around the office. Notable web site links should be sent to all in the company address book.

The corporate compliance officer is also a resource within his company. He must advertise his position to make sure the appropriate person is answering the compliance questions.

Procedures in place, corporate support and the nomination of the corporate compliance officer are the fundamentals of the compliance team. The corporate compliance officer is part of a team and part of a team effort. The best strategy will not work if the team is not working together. It is said "a dedicated team is the fuel for progress and growth." The same lies true for the corporate compliance officer and his supply chain "team."

Is Your Company RoHS Compliant?

RoHS COMPLIANCE FAQ

1. **What is RoHS?** RoHS is an acronym for the Restriction of Use of Hazardous Substances regulations, and refers to European Union directive 2002/95/EC, which limits or bans specific substances—lead, cadmium, polybrominated biphenyl (PBB), mercury, hexavalent chromium, and polybrominated diphenyl ether (PBDE) flame retardants—in the production of new electronic and electric equipment. RoHS applies to these products when destined for the EU market.

2. **What is RoHS compliance?** RoHS compliance means acting in full accordance with RoHS regulations and documenting your testing for RoHS controlled substances. The specified materials are hazardous to the environment, pollute landfills, and are dangerous to workers during manufacturing and/or recycling.

3. **What is RoHS training?** RoHS training involves teaching yourself and your employees about the RoHS regulations as well as the correct testing procedures for these RoHS controlled substances. Ignorance is not considered an excuse for RoHS noncompliance. It is important to familiarize yourself and your employees about the existence of RoHS and how it applies to your company.

4. **Is my business affected by RoHS?** If you are involved in selling, manufacturing, exporting, or importing electric or electronic equipment or parts to any member of the EU, you are most likely affected by these regulations and you should familiarize yourself with RoHS.

5. **When did RoHS regulations become effective?** RoHS regulations went into effect in the EU in July 2006. They remain in place, which means that all electric and electronic equipment being made today must meet RoHS directive rules.

6. **How do I know whether my products are RoHS compliant?** In order to ensure that products are RoHS compliant, careful testing and documentation must be done in accordance with RoHS Directive regulations. There are many resources that can assist businesses ensuring RoHS compliance. For more information, go to www.rohs.edu.

7. **What are the consequences for noncompliance with RoHS?** Failing to make products RoHS compliant or refusing to comply with requests for documentation can result in heavy fines. In some cases, businesses can be denied export of their products. Specific penalties vary from country to country, but noncompliance is always far more costly for a business than compliance.

8. **What is WEEE?** WEEE (Waste from Electrical and Electronic Equipment) is a directive that controls how electric and electronic equipment is handled and recycled. Most businesses that must ensure RoHS compliance must also ensure WEEE compliance as well.

Antiboycott Requests Outside of the Arab League

The antiboycott provisions of BIS's Export Administration Regulations (EAR) were designed to prevent U.S. individuals and companies from participating in or promoting foreign boycotts that the United States does not support.

The Arab League boycott of Israel is the principal foreign economic boycott that U.S. companies must be concerned with. However, the antiboycott laws apply to all boycotts that are imposed by foreign countries that are unsanctioned by the United States, and violations have been reported regarding boycotts of Bangladesh, Indonesia, and Malaysia.

The antiboycott provisions of the EAR apply to all U.S. persons even if they reside outside of the United States, as well as to companies located in the United States and their foreign subsidiaries. While it is more common or more widely known, the Arab League boycott of Israel should not be the only boycott U.S. companies should be concerned with. All companies should be made aware of the possibility of a request to boycott other countries, such as Pakistan and India. These requests may come in many different forms and relate to the sale, purchase or transfer of goods or services, including information, within the United States or between the United States and a foreign country.

For example, companies doing business in Libya before the ouster of Libyan leader Muammar Qaddafi were requested not to do business with companies of Swiss nationality. The tensions between Libya and Switzerland resulted from an incident in the summer of 2008 involving the Swiss police and Qaddafi's son, who was arrested after two hotel employees from Tunisia and Morocco accused him and his expectant wife, Aline, of beating them with a belt and a coat hanger. The Swiss police held the young Qaddafi in custody for two days while his wife remained under police supervision in a clinic in Geneva. They were later released on $490,000 bail. This created an uproar in Libya and resulted in Libya's boycott of the Swiss companies.

It is necessary to stay abreast of current events which could possibly have an affect or an impact on your business. EAR antiboycott issues may arise when dealing with any country and close attention should be paid to countries such as Indonesia, Bangladesh, Pakistan, Iran, India, Ethiopia and Eritrea. Other countries also to be taken into consideration that may require the submission of boycott requests are China, Taiwan, and Serbia. It is important that U.S. companies actively engage their compliance staff to analyze any boycott-related language or request received, regardless of the countries involved.

While it may be difficult to determine if the request you received is actual boycott language or perhaps you are not certain if the request is in violation of U.S. law due to the countries involved, for instance in the case of Libya and Switzerland, it is important to clarify any doubts you may have before acting on any such request. Fines and penalties for complying with boycott requests can be quite high and could result in general denial of export privileges.

In addition to reporting boycott requests to the Department of Commerce, depending on the nature of the request, it may also be reportable to the Department of Treasury. The Department of Treasury has a separate set of antiboycott laws and the basis for the Treasury Department's antiboycott penalties (the Ribicoff Amendment to 1976 Tax Reform Act-Section 999 of the Internal Revenue Code) were issued before the antiboycott regulations contained in the EAR.

You can obtain clarification or more information from the Office of Antiboycott Compliance by visiting this page on their website: www.bis.doc.gov/compliance andenforcement/antiboycottcompliance.htm#requestform.

Foreign Corrupt Practices Act (FCPA)

The U.S. Foreign Corrupt Practices Act (FCPA) of 1977 prohibits U.S. companies, their subsidiaries, as well as their officers, directors, employees, and agents from bribing foreign officials. It also requires that U.S. companies which issue debt or equity maintain internal accounting controls and to keep books and records that accurately reflect all transactions.

The anti-bribery, recordkeeping, and internal accounting controls provisions are applicable to all global operations. The FCPA is enforced jointly by the Securities & Exchange Commission (SEC) and the U.S. Department of Justice (DOJ).

Companies operating globally must create procedures and train personnel in how to avoid participating in any form of activity that could create an FCPA exposure.

Concluding Remarks

The export supply chain as identified in this chapter will run more safely, timely, and competitively when the export manager pays attention to detail and operates in a fashion integrating "compliance" into all facets of the export trade. From creating the sale, to processing the order, to collecting payment are all integral issues that need to be paid attention to, and when they are, will assure successful exporting.

Section Three

Import Operations

11

Future Import Issues

Assist Value Management

In these current times of economic uncertainty described by many as a global economic downturn, many companies are looking for creative ideas, thought processes, and directions to cut expenses and have a positive effect on the corporate bottom line. Companies who participate in international trade activities such as global sourcing and importing are no different. Importers of foreign-sourced merchandise face the same economic challenges that have affected the global economy. In an effort to complement company efforts to cut expenses sourcing, purchase and acquisition expenses are closely reviewed to ensure that the best products are sourced for the most economic price. It is very common in such efforts to minimize expenses of internationally sourced materials, that companies discover alternative sourcing options for raw materials, components, dies, molds, tools, engineering and design work and provide such items to the manufacturers of their foreign-sourced materials at a reduced cost or free of charge. This creative sourcing practice controls the raw material expenses of the manufacturing cycle as well as complements the quality of products from the point of production while protecting the expense of the importing entity's bottom line.

This sourcing strategy is very common for the reasons outlined above as well as for others, such as limited sourcing options in the country of manufacture or production. The commonality of this practice is well known in the import community as a best practice of cost and acquisition control. In such instances however, there lies a responsibility of the importer of record to ensure that Customs valuation regulatory practices are implemented relating to the value declaration of articles that were produced with the assistance of the materials provided to the seller from the buyer at no charge or reduced cost.

Customs valuation regulations are defined and clear—outlined in the Customs Federal Regulations CFR Title 19 Part 152.102—that the cost of any materials, dies molds, tools, engineering work, or design work undertaken outside the United States provided to the seller by the buyer in connection with the production of imported merchandise must be included in the calculation of the correct transaction value of imported merchandise.

This is a regulation that is often overlooked in the valuation computation of imported articles for various reasons.

One common reason that this regulation is often overlooked—regardless of the compliance controls of many sophisticated companies with knowledge of compliance management—is the lack of connectivity in the information flow between different business units related to the sourcing and acquisition decisions for import companies. The disconnect, and lack of awareness that CBP defines the proper valuation concept as all cost incurred in bringing the imported merchandise up to and on board a vessel, vehicle or aircraft in the port of exportation destined for the United States, including the value of materials provided to the seller at a reduced cost or free of charge, results in the common practice of omitting such dutiable values. It is Custom's position that the cost of these materials and the cost of transporting them to the seller to be used in manufacture and production are part of the transaction value. These values are categorized as "assist" values.

The challenge to ensure that assists are identified is the first step towards a compliance practice to properly declare the value of imported articles. World class compliance practices include a company's ability to educate and inform the people in their organization involved in the import supply chain process of the regulatory concept of assists. This informed compliance effort complements the efforts of compliance management and establishes the foundation of a true and comprehensive discovery process by including business units in the opportunity and effort of valuation identification and categorization of assist declaration eligibility. Many companies utilize the outsourced efforts of customs consultants, brokers, and attorneys who specialize in customs law to affirm assist circumstances in cases where they are uncertain of specific computation inclusions and exemptions.

The responsibility of proper valuation declaration is the defined responsibility of the importer of record. Assist valuation declarations are traditionally not disclosed because it is commonly not included on the import commercial invoice as originally prepared. This is because the seller or manufacturer of the products often is not aware of the specific acquisition cost or purchase prices of materials provided to them free of charge or at a reduced cost. The lack of this information prevents such sellers from indicating this cost on the commercial invoice. Even if they knew the acquisition costs or original purchase price of the materials provided to them in the production process, it is common for such sellers not to charge the buyer for materials that the buyer provided to them. However redundant in theory or concept, the reporting of assist values is a regulatory requirement.

Many importers find blind comfort in the absence of assist reporting in past practices due to the perception that this valuation regulation is hidden in the confines of the regulatory guide CFR. This is not the case at all. The importance of an importer's ability to identify assist values is critical to the compliance profile of your import organization. In an effort to protect the revenue of your companies through internal controls linked to SOX standards, companies should note the consequence of default. The failure to properly report imported values such as assist will result in liquidated damages and penalties to the importer of record. Customs and Border Protection is very familiar with the common practices of failure to report assists. CBP includes specific language on entry inquiry request for information entitled Custom Form 28. CBP also requires that every importer endorse a statement of commitment on every import entry form CF7501 that all prices and cost provided to the seller at a reduced cost or free of charge is included in the import declaration value and that any information showing a different state of facts from the originally declared value will be immediately communicated to U.S. Customs and Border Protection by the importer once discovered. The visibility of assist enforcement is present in daily entry supervision and liquidation practices of CBP.

As an international trade consultant, I witness firsthand many instances of unintentional oversight of assist circumstances. I encourage companies to begin the dialogue and effort to identify assist acquisition practices for possible valuation declaration amendment practices. As business divisions such as procurement, technical engineering, and research and development continue to find creative ways to complement the quality of products for a more competitive price, practices such as outsourcing of raw materials, components, molds, tools, and design work will continue to be a best practice. Complement that creative process with a compliant world class practice of assist management.

Customs Enforcement Actions for C-TPAT Noncompliance

Many members of the international supply chain community have taken the positive step towards the enhancement of their global supply chain security management process by joining the Customs Trade Partnership Against Terrorism program. The C-TPAT program is one layer in U.S. Customs and Border Protection's (CBP) multilayered cargo enforcement strategy. Through this program, CBP works with the trade community in adopting tighter security.

The C-TPAT program has had large success in its membership enrollment and certification process. It is very important to note that a continued commitment to all elements of the minimum security criteria is mandatory in this voluntary program. This is not a one and done effort that only requires attention to detail at the initial point of certification. The C-TPAT program requires a diligent effort on a continued basis to monitor and enhance a company's security management process related to their international trade supply chain activities through its direct supply chain process. CBP has a definitive enforcement and appeal process for program participants that are found to be in noncompliance with the C-TPAT security criteria.

Many members of the international trade community are utilizing their influence to ensure that their business partners participate in the C-TPAT program to compliment their international supply chain relationships. Careful diligence continues to be enhanced by such business partners such as the monitoring of the status verification interface data (SVI) information which is designed to provide current enrollment, certification, and validation information for program participants. It is critical for participants to keep current their certified or validated status in the program with a dedicated effort towards security compliance.

It is very important to note that C-TPAT members may be suspended or removed from the program for several reasons including, but not limited to, the following: narcotics seizures or other security-related incidents such as human smuggling; failed validations or lack of compliance with C-TPAT requirements regarding supply chain or other security measures; failure to provide required information or filing false or misleading information; or actions or inaction that shows a lack of commitment to the program. The authority cited and provided for in the SAFE Port Act provides limitless ability to the Commissioner of Customs and Border Protection to take actions to protect the national security of the United States. Importers must note that a continued dedication to C-TPAT management is essential.

The C-TPAT Headquarters (HQ) Program Director makes the final decision to suspend or remove a member based on all available information, including reports and recommendations made by C-TPAT Field Managers. In certain aggravated circumstances companies may be immediately removed from the program, for example, when they are found to have provided false information, have demonstrated inadequate security, or have demonstrated a flagrant disregard for the program's requirements. In other instances, which may not be as egregious, but are nonetheless significant, a company may be suspended from C-TPAT with an opportunity to resume membership once it comes into compliance with program requirements.

To be reinstated into the program after an incident or violation, the company must agree to a corrective action plan, which identifies specific objectives and time frames within which those objectives should be reached. In addition, the company must consent to unannounced visits by C-TPAT staff to monitor progress. In the case of a failed validation, the company must demonstrate that it has successfully addressed all vulnerabilities and complied with all other requirements before being fully reinstated.

If a company is suspended or removed, it has the right to appeal this decision to CBP headquarters. Appeals must include all relevant information that demonstrates how the company has addressed the issues that resulted in the suspension or removal, or provide corrected factual information in the case where a company claims that a mistake of fact or other misunderstanding has resulted in the suspension or removal. CBP will decide the appeal in a timely fashion upon such review and determination of the facts.

The only way to avoid suspension or removal is for C-TPAT members to ensure they are in full compliance with the minimum security criteria and be aware of, and responsive to, mandated time frames established by CBP relative to requests posted in their individual C-TPAT web portal for such deliverables as validation response transmissions, written affirmation of compliance request to security procedure elements of their profile, previously confirmed action item statements, and validation action items.

CPSC at the Port

So, you are importing a shipment of goods into the United States and you suddenly hit an unexpected speed bump: your shipment is being held for exam.

Upon further review, U.S. Customs and Border Protection (CBP) tells you an agency called "CPSC" is responsible for the delay. Who and what is this? Well, you are about to find out.

CPSC, better known as the U.S. Consumer Product Safety Commission, is an independent federal agency created in 1972. The CPSC is charged with protecting the public against unreasonable risks of injury or death associated with consumer products.

CPSC's mandate involves protecting the public from injury and death from thousands of types of consumer products. That means most everything in your home from mattresses, extension cords, furniture, televisions, and cigarette lighters, to children's sleepwear, toys, ATVs, and household appliances. (Popular items CPSC does *not* have jurisdiction over are tobacco, food, and drugs; firearms; motor vehicles; workplace products; and medical devices.)

Each year there are thousands of deaths and millions of injuries associated with consumer products which cost the American public millions of dollars.

Jurisdictional authority for CPSC is covered in several Acts. In 2008, the Consumer Product Safety Improvement Act (CPSIA) added to CPSC's existing jurisdictional authority as originally provided by the Consumer Product Safety Act. The CPSIA gave CPSC increased authority, including the authority to require a Certificate of Conformity for all regulated products and higher standards for children's products.

The Consumer Product Safety Improvement Act of 2008 also established the Import Surveillance Division. This Division co-locates CPSC investigators, like me, with CBP at various ports around the country. We are focused on port-of-entry enforcement of consumer product laws, regulations and standards.

Our exam process is similar to any other agency. We work jointly with CBP using various methods to stop and examine shipments. Depending on the product type, a field screen is performed during the exam process and, if needed, a sample is taken for further testing and compliance determination. Reviews of port of entry documents, product labeling, and test records also take place as part of the exam process. If no sample is needed and the product documentation is in order, the shipment could be released the same day. If a sample was collected the shipment will be detained by CPSC for up to thirty days while the testing is being conducted. When a final sample determination is complete, CPSC will either release, release for reconditioning, seize, or refuse admission of the shipment.

Frequently, importers ask me how they can avoid entry delays when it involves CPSC-regulated products. Although it may not always help, here's a checklist of things to keep in mind when CPSC is examining one of your shipments:

- ✓ Make entry documents, and specifically Certificates and test records, readily available upon request.
- ✓ Ensure goods are classified/invoiced appropriately.
  Include product detail on invoices.
- ✓ Some products require certain agency approvals prior to importation, like action plan for ATVs or prototype review for cigarette lighters. Make sure the third-party testing body is recognized by CPSC
- ✓ Sign up for ISA (Importer Self Assessment program).

As you can see, CPSC is integrated into the import community. You may have even experienced CPSC's role firsthand. In either case, I hope you welcome the agency into this community since both you and your families are potentially at risk from unsafe consumer products. Please feel free to contact me with any questions or concerns you may have regarding the role of CPSC at the ports.

ISF Enforcement Deadline

The majority of importers are aware that Customs and Border Protection's delayed enforcement of the Importer Security Filing (ISF) program began on January 26, 2010. CBP announced on November 4, 2009 that they would take a commonsense approach toward the issuance of fines and penalties and would review all cases in CBP headquarters prior to penalty issuance to ensure that fair and just objectives are achieved. CBP began to assess penalties beginning January 26, 2010, and continues to do so.

It is important for members of the import supply chain ensure that full comprehension is in place internally and externally in the operations management profiles of their third-party service providers. Misconceptions and misstatement of program details can result in unwarranted actions which may develop into a penalty situation. CBP has issued ISF report cards since June of 2009 that details specific areas of noncompliance relative to ISF filings to date. There is a monthly report card issued to the ISF filing agent that must be reviewed to afford the importer and the filer an ability to work through found errors to date.

The penalty structure in place remains at $5,000.00 per entry filing for late or errant filings and became effective on January 26, 2010. The importer of record will receive the penalty for all ISF filing violations and remains responsible to ensure that filing information is provided to all ISF filing agents in a timely manner.

There exists mitigation guidelines related to an importers ISF filing history since January 26, 2009. CBP will take into consideration mitigation for companies who have tried to file and get the information in through historical filing information. There is a direct benefit for importers who are C-TPAT members. The mitigation guidelines in place that will afford C-TPAT companies that are in good standing in their C-TPAT profiles 50 percent mitigation towards such fines and penalties, which makes it very important for companies to participate in the voluntary program as soon as possible if not already a member.

A very common error being received is late filings, which is normally the result of the filing agent getting the information from the importer or importers representatives abroad too late to meet the twenty-four-hour advance loading deadline. There exist additional common errors such as discrepancies in the bill of lading information, shippers, sellers and ship-to identification information.

A "best in class practice" related to ISF management is that the importer controls the affirmation of the data elements for filing. The importer then ensures that the information necessary for filing is documented, dated, and filed with the filing agent no later than forty-eight hours prior to intended date of loading to afford the filing agent an ability to meet the twenty-four-hour advanced time frame.

It is important to note that the ISF responsibility and liability remain that of the importer of record. The importer may assign a freight forwarder or broker to file the information to CBP on their behalf, however the timeliness and correctness of information remains the responsibility of the importer. ISF management should now be incorporated within every importer's compliance management process.

FDA Announces Mandatory Affirmation of Compliance Codes

During a July 2010 webinar, the FDA announced that it would make certain Affirmation of Compliance (AofC) codes mandatory during the transmission of entry data.

The transmission of AofC codes has always been a voluntary process with the added benefit of expediting shipment screening and review. As of this writing, the FDA has not specifically advised which AofC codes they intend on making mandatory. Affirmation of Compliance codes are identified by their three-character code representing the reporting of a specific type of commodity and is accompanied by a "qualifier" code which is typically a quantity amount, other type of measurement amount, model number, or producer/manufacturer name.

While the provision of detailed information will greatly benefit and assist importers in the clearance of their goods, this is certainly a reminder to manufacturers, shippers, and importers that all goods arriving into the United States should knowingly be imported and accounted for in advance. In addition, the codes will certainly influence the data transmitted at the Prior Notice level.

Prior Notice, an act put into place in 2002, requires that the FDA be notified prior to the arrival of shipments containing food products and that those food products be appropriately identified before they arrive within port limits of the U.S. port of arrival.

It appears that the direction that FDA is heading towards is in obtaining as much "statistical" information as possible as the agency gears up for the implementation of PREDICT, which stands for Predictive Risk-based Evaluation for Dynamic Import Compliance Targeting and is, as of this writing, the new risk assessment platform set to replace the current OASIS (Operational and Administrative System for Import Support). This will also allow the FDA staff to search for products through an automated database look-up. Therefore, valid information is key to ensuring that the proper products are being identified for review.

Imports: Take Your Time and Get it Right

U. S. Customs and Border Protection has announced in their five-year strategic plan that includes among other components a greater focus on post-entry activity of import entry transactions. This increase on post-entry information will undoubtedly result in greater scrutiny of the specifications of data details of existing compliance regulatory components such as but not limited to valuation, special tariff treaty eligibility, and commodity classifications.

It is common in the import declaration process to emphasize time-efficient entry declaration to take full advantage of entry pre-file privileges. Importation trade professionals believe this to be a best practice: taking advantage of C-TPAT benefits while ensuring that Customs release is attained as soon as possible. CBP has noted as well that a best practice of importers is to take advantage of pre-file filing process to expedite the ability of the global security and cargo selectivity process prior to the arrival of imported merchandise.

It is important however to ensure that the compliance supervision and control process is implemented as far back in your international supply chain process as possible to afford your compliance program process an opportunity to make sound decisions relative to valuation determination, special tariff treaty program eligibility, and HTS classifications. A world class practice is to implement compliance controls from the point of the purchase process that will proactively complement the ability of your compliance team to manage import entry declaration affirmation regardless of volume and mixed class or kind of goods. This proactive effort adds more time to the compliance process to allow the the importer and the customs brokerage provider to ensure that information is complete and accurate prior to entry filing. Customs compliance management should not be rushed by the ability to present information sooner. "Take your time and get it right" is my suggestion to industry professionals who are often influenced by production demands, manufacturing deadlines, customer performance agreements, and contractual obligations. By putting more time on the front end of your international logistics process, compliance professionals increase their ability to discover, amend, and correct information prior to entry, avoiding post-entry review findings by Customs and Border Protection. The use of import letters of instructions and automated affirmation of concurrence with suppliers invoices, packing lists, and certifications of origin and conformity are additional examples of world class customs compliance practices that complement many well-established compliance profiles.

The benefits of automated filings of ISF and Customs entry declarations affords the import community ever-increasing opportunities to provide information sooner to CBP. Importers and brokers must incorporate greater proactive compliance management effort within the supervision and control process.

Greater advanced submission of data creates increased reactive issues unless the same advancements are also included in compliance management on the front end of our import entry supply chain process. Take the time necessary to verify, validate, and affirm information before authorizing brokers to submit entry information. This will protect your compliance profiles. You will be able to take full advantage of pre-file process and enable your supply chain to operate in an efficient and compliant manner.

Harmonized Tariff Classification Requires Constant Supervision and Control to meet Reasonable Care Standards

Many companies involved in international trade practices often rely on third-party services providers such as customs brokers and freight forwarders to classify their imported and exported products. This common practice has been in place for years and has not traditionally been challenged until an issue arises such as a high duty rate assessment or an inquiry by regulatory authorities namely, U.S. Customs and Border Protection. It is important that international trade participants identified as importers of record (IOR) and United States Principle Parties of Interest (USPPI) recognize that there is a regulatory responsibility of reasonable care that must be demonstrated in the derivation and declaration of the Harmonized Tariff Schedule of the United States (HTSUS).

U.S. Customs and Border Protection outlined this reasonable care responsibility in the Modernization Act of 1993. If your company does not have positive affirmations to the five basic questions related to reasonable care management, which we discuss below, you are not meeting reasonable care standards and are subject to customs penalties in the event of customs action of enforcement.

Merchandise Description and Tariff Classification

The highly technical questions listed below are in service of the fundamental question: "Do you know or have you established a reliable procedure or program to ensure that you know what you ordered, where it was made, and what it is made of?"

1. Have you provided or established reliable procedures to ensure you provide a complete and accurate description of your merchandise to CBP in accordance with 19 U.S.C. 1481? (Also, see 19 CFR 141.87 and 19 CFR 141.89 for special merchandise description requirements.)
2. Have you provided or established reliable procedures to ensure you provide a correct tariff classification of your merchandise to CBP in accordance with 19 U.S.C. 1484?

3. Have you obtained a CBP "ruling" regarding the description of the merchandise or its tariff classification (see 19 CFR 177), and if so, have you established reliable procedures to ensure that you have followed the ruling and brought it to CBP attention?
4. Where merchandise description or tariff classification information is not immediately available, have you established a reliable procedure for providing that information, and is the procedure being followed?
5. Have you participated in a CBP pre-classification of your merchandise relating to proper merchandise?

It is very important that international trade participants realize that the HTSUS number is a crucial element of compliance management. The utilization of the HTS number was expanded with the implementation of the Importer Security Filing program (ISF), whose enforcement period began on January 26, 2010.

It is the trade participant's responsibility to be knowledgeable about the HTSUS classification principles and to provide correct information to CBP. Education and training on HTSUS guidelines is imperative to the success of a compliance management program. Familiarity with CBP rulings process and pre-classification efforts are essential to a company's ability to defend the HTS classifications being utilized within their international supply chain process.

Importers and exporters should move away from traditional common practice delegation of HTS classifications such as using database information without annual update verifications or HTS line reviews. It is recommended that diligence in affirmation be demonstrated by detailed commodity awareness efforts and classification supervision and control as a standard operational objective for all compliance personnel involved in the import and export process.

Focused Assessment Audits Now Include Global Security Parameters

Importers are facing challenging times relative to new government initiatives such as the Importers Security Filing program, the Lacey Act, and Consumer Products Safety Act supervision and control issues. There are also existing challenges facing the import community related to issues that are not new government initiatives. Customs and Border Protection is enhancing existing programs, such as the Focused Assessment audit process (FA) to increase the efficiency and effectiveness of various initiatives in their efforts to secure the borders of the United States and maintain a compliant process of regulatory reporting of import data with each import declaration.

The Customs audit or Focused Assessment audit is a very intense process that has not lost its momentum, despite the popularity of the C-TPAT program and Custom's focus on global security initiatives. The Customs audit process has long been an effort that has caused anxiety for many importers. One of the benefits of C-TPAT membership is the ability to forgo an onsite audit—which is allowed because you joined C-TPAT. You also attain certification into the Importers Self-Assessment program, a very popular import compliance strategy that is responsible for many C-TPAT applications. CBP has now included global security topic parameters in their Focused Assessment review practices as an effort to gain global security information on companies that may not already be involved in the C-TPAT program.

Many importers are upset that global security questions are now included in the FA process. Many feel that a voluntary program such as C-TPAT should keep separate the concepts of its minimum security standards if in fact C-TPAT is truly a voluntary effort.

However, all must realize that CBP is responsible for both compliance and security. There is also the belief on the other side of this issue that holds that the concepts of how well a company is managing the security profile of their supply chain is within reasonable bounds of inquiry for U. S. Customs scrutiny. Whether your firm is in agreement or not, CBP has included global security criteria in the Focused Assessment process and importers need to be prepared. Preparation is the key to managing all compliance issues—now including global security—related to the import supply chain.

Import compliance manuals should now include a reference section for global security management to meet this compliance inclusion of process in the newly amended scope of the Focused Assessment profile. Increased education and training should be included in compliance departments to ensure that effort to meet CBP global security requirements are implemented in the compliance policies and procedures of importers.

How to Self-Audit

So you've implemented procedures, executed training, freight is moving inbound and outbound, no calls from CBP or knocks on the door from BIS. Your compliance program is moving full steam ahead. It's time to check out those vacation brochures and take a load off, right? Absolutely!

When you've finished patting yourself on the back and applying aloe to sunburn from that time away, it's time to get yourself back on track through internal auditing.

Step 1: If your company has an internal audit department, they may be the ones who have to handle the auditing. Make sure they have a good understanding of the issues and know how to recognize potential issues. If they're not handling the audit, no problem, you only have to work the audit into your schedule. Easily said, not easily done.

Step 2: Approach the audit in a palatable manner. Many people become paranoid when they feel they are being scrutinized. They feel they are under deep analysis and make take the word "audit" as a personal affront. You may want to consider using the word "benchmarking" or "review" as an alternative to avoid the negative connotation of an audit.

Step 3: Have a game plan before you start auditing. Are you looking for particular types of files, or problem accounts, or are you performing a general review? Keep plenty of notes, make copies, and ask questions where you need answers.

Step 4: Be respectful of the individual's file and style. There are some people who choose to staple a file on the right side rather than the left side. Why? I don't know, but you're not there to audit the file because it should look like mine. If the file is neat, compliant, and accurate, don't sweat the small stuff unless the company has a strict policy. Also be respectful of the individual's time. Be accommodating of the individual's work flow. The end of the month or end of the fiscal year is probably not a good time to be scheduling "time to talk and review."

Step 5: Give the individual the time to ask you questions and reveal any potential issues of which they are aware. In my own experience, I often hear "this may sound like a dumb question but . . ." This is the time when some people feel most comfortable asking that question. Make certain you give them a good answer and don't respond with a laugh or eye roll no matter how tempted you may be to do so!

Step 6: Follow up with any suggestions and recommendations. Carry out training on the spot where necessary. Let the individual know this is an area "we can improve upon." A philosophy of "we're in this together" and "I'm not looking to create more work for you" leaves the individual feeling positive about the experience.

Step 7: Wrap up the meeting with your formal list and let the individual know when you intend to submit your report for review to senior management.

Once you have prepared your report, you will truly be able to ascertain the success of your compliance program. Each self-audit is an opportunity to better understand the day-to-day functions of those working in the supply chain and for those individuals to better understand where those functions fall in line with compliance.

Compliance Importance of Invoice Content

Import documentation is a very important component of the international supply chain process. The commercial invoice is the nucleus of the documents required for import customs clearance. The invoice represents the details of the international sales transaction, shipment specifications, and details necessary for regulatory verification of several key elements such as article description, quantity, and value. The commercial invoice which is prepared by the foreign shipper, seller, or manufacturer has traditionally been viewed as the single source of affirmation in the import documentation package without scrutiny on true and correct information. This common practice has over the years resulted in a degree of acceptance for errors and incorrect data due to business practices such as purchase order amendments, price adjustments, logistic routing amendments, and order fulfillment obstacles to name a few. A recent survey conducted researched the responses of importers of record on the issue of the percentage of discovery of errors found on commercial invoices. The results were quite astonishing: 65 percent of invoices contained a basic reporting error related to their individual business practices.

U.S. Customs and Border Protection relies on the commercial invoice to represent true and correct facts that will be summarized on the import declaration and customs entry summary submissions. Errors on invoices lead to errors in the import declaration. This process easily has a snowball effect on the correct HTS classification and duties, fees, and taxes due. According to CBP, their strategic plan is to implement a greater emphasis on post-entry reviews in an effort to facilitate trade to a higher degree. Post-entry reviews will undoubtedly include a greater level of scrutiny on import documentation as invoices.

Many importers are not aware of the specific invoice requirements regulated by U. S. Customs and Border Protection and have relied on the common practices of documentation content accepted in the past.. As proper compliance awareness and informed compliance rewards clearly show, the proper invoice content resource is 19 CFR 141.86. t is important that compliance professionals review this detailed list of invoice requirements to ensure that your internal controls incorporate a checklist process to keep incorrect commercial invoices out of your import documentation package, Customs entry, and follow-up summary process.

Compliant invoice reporting elements complement the areas of valuation, classification, and manifest quantity verification that are key components of global compliance and security management.

The regulatory listing of invoice contents as per 19 CFR 141.86 is as follows:

(a) General information required on the invoice:

(1) The port of entry to which the merchandise is destined;

(2) The time when, the place where, and the person by whom and the person to whom the merchandise is sold or agreed to be sold, or if to be imported otherwise than in pursuance of a purchase, the place from which shipped, the time when and the person to whom and the person by whom it is shipped;

(3) A detailed description of the merchandise, including the name by which each item is known, the grade or quality, and the marks, numbers, and symbols under which sold by the seller or manufacturer to the trade in the country of exportation, together with the marks and numbers of the packages in which the merchandise is packed;

(4) The quantities in the weights and measures of the country or place from which the merchandise is shipped, or in the weights and measures of the United States;

(5) The purchase price of each item in the currency of the purchase, if the merchandise is shipped in pursuance of a purchase or an agreement to purchase;

(6) If the merchandise is shipped otherwise than in pursuance of a purchase or an agreement to purchase, the value for each item, in the currency in which the transactions are usually made, or, in the absence of such value, the price in such currency that the manufacturer, seller, shipper, or owner would have received, or was willing to receive, for such merchandise if sold in the ordinary course of trade and in the usual wholesale quantities in the country of exportation;

(7) The kind of currency, whether gold, silver, or paper;

(8) All charges upon the merchandise itemized by name and amount, including freight, insurance, commission, cases, containers, coverings, and cost of packing; and if not included above, all charges, costs, and expenses incurred in bringing the merchandise from alongside the carrier at the port of exportation in the country of exportation and placing it alongside the carrier at the first United States port of entry. The cost of packing, cases, containers, and inland freight to the port of exportation need not be itemized by amount if included in the invoice price, and so identified. Where the required information does not appear on the invoice as originally prepared, it shall be shown on an attachment to the invoice;

(9) All rebates, drawbacks, and bounties, separately itemized, allowed upon the exportation of the merchandise;

(10) The country of origin of the merchandise; and,

(11) All goods or services furnished for the production of the merchandise (e.g., assists such as dies, molds, tools, engineering work) not included in the invoice price. However, goods or services furnished in the United States are excluded. Annual reports for goods and services, when approved by the port director, will be accepted as proof that the goods or services were provided.

(b) *Nonpurchased merchandise shipped by other than manufacturer.* Each invoice of imported merchandise shipped to a person in the United States by a person other than the manufacturer and otherwise than pursuant to a purchase or agreement to purchase shall set forth the time when, the place where, the person from whom such merchandise was purchased, and the price paid therefore in the currency of the purchase, stating whether gold, silver, or paper.

(c) *Merchandise sold in transit.* If the merchandise is sold on the documents while in transit from the port of exportation to the port of entry, the original invoice reflecting the transaction under which the merchandise actually began its journey to the United States, and the resale invoice or a statement of sale showing the price paid for each item by the purchaser, shall be filed as part of the entry, entry summary, or withdrawal documentation. If the original invoice cannot be obtained, a pro forma invoice showing the values and transaction reflected by the original invoice shall be filed together with the resale invoice or statement.

(d) *Invoice to be in English.* The invoice and all attachments shall be in the English language, or shall have attached thereto an accurate English translation containing adequate information for examination of the merchandise and determination of duties.

(e) *Packing list.* Each invoice shall state in adequate detail what merchandise is contained in each individual package.

(f) *Weights and measures.* If the invoice or entry does not disclose the weight, gage, or measure of the merchandise which is necessary to ascertain duties, the consignee shall pay the expense of weighing, gaging, or measuring prior to the release of the merchandise from Customs custody.

(g) *Discounts.* Each invoice shall set forth in detail, for each class or kind of merchandise, every discount from list or other base price which has been or may be allowed in fixing each purchase price or value.

(h) *Numbering of invoices and pages—*(1) *Invoices.* When more than one invoice is included in the same entry, each invoice with its attachments shall be numbered consecutively by the importer on the bottom of the face of each page, beginning with No. 1.

2) Pages. Except when electronic invoice data are transmitted to CBP under the provisions of part 143 of this chapter, if the invoice or invoices filed with one entry consist of more than two pages, each page must be numbered consecutively by the importer on the bottom of the face of each page, with the page numbering beginning with No. 1 for the first page of the first invoice and continuing in a single series of numbers through all the invoices and attachments included in one entry.

(3) Both invoices and pages. Except when electronic invoice data are transmitted to CBP under the provisions of part 143 of this chapter, both the invoice number and the page number must be shown at the bottom of each page when applicable. For example, an entry covering one invoice of one page and a second invoice of two pages must be paginated as follows:

Inv. 1, p. 1.
Inv. 2, p. 2.
Inv. 2, p. 3

(i) Information may be on invoice or attached thereto. Any information required on an invoice by any provision of this subpart may be set forth either on the invoice or on an attachment thereto.

(j) Name of responsible individual. Each invoice of imported merchandise must identify by name a responsible employee of the exporter, who has knowledge, or who can readily obtain knowledge, of the transaction.

Elevate your compliance capabilities by including invoice content reviews in your self-assessment practices, policies, and efforts. Communicate errors to the preparers of the invoices as a measurement of corrective action efforts. In the event that your commercial invoices contain errors that cannot be easily amended, as importer of record you are in many cases capable of preparing a pro forma invoice in place of the errant commercial invoice. This added element of supervision and control will prove to be very beneficial as CBP increases their efforts of post-entry verifications.

C-TPAT Members Gain Mitigation Benefits for ISF Enforced Compliance Penalty Structure

- Many importers are concerned about potential fines and penalties that will be implemented on the effective date of enforced compliance of the newly implemented program entitled Importer Security Filing (ISF) program also known as $10 + 2$.

  The C-TPAT program continues to evolve with respect to providing benefits to its partners in return for proof of strong supply chains. This is evident in the recent announcement that C-TPAT partners will be eligible for increased benefits regarding mitigation of potential fines associated with the ISF enforcement. This is an additional benefit of partnering with CBP in the C-TPAT program if your firm is not already involved as a certified or validated program participant.

  Under the ISF mitigation guidelines, certain C-TPAT partners will be eligible for additional mitigation—up to 50 percent of the normal mitigation amount. However, this benefit is available only to those partners who have excelled in their commitment to supply chain security and in their partnership with CBP.

  This is another very good reason for all C-TPAT members to strive for excellence and continued improvement related to their global security program, procedures, and process.

  Since its inception C-TPAT has made important strides in developing program benefits and will continue to explore new benefits that are relevant to a security focused program. CBP encourages its C-TPAT members, as its trusted partners, to ensure full compliance with the ISF.

Convincing Senior Management to join the C-TPAT Program

In the chaotic months following the September 11, 2001, terrorist attacks, when the newly formed government agency, Department of Homeland Security (DHS), through its Bureau of Customs and Border Protection (CBP) division, developed and announced the implementation of their voluntary security Customs-Trade Partnership Against Terrorism (C-TPAT) program, most of the import community seemed to largely ignore this initiative. Given that CBP was constantly rolling out pilot programs in the hopes of acceptance, most of the importing community viewed this as just another program and figured it would go away.

Well, as of this writing, this program is in its eleventh year, suffice to say this one isn't going away any time soon! In fact, not only has the import community embraced this program, over 10,000 U. S. companies of all shapes and sizes, in various industries, have enrolled in the program, with many more submitting applications every day via the CBP's Web Portal. Add to that, importers and CBP have forged an excellent working alliance to enhance the program's benefits to make it more attractive for companies to join.

More and more companies are becoming savvy to the strategic and competitive advantages of joining this program that they're making it a corporate initiative to do so. Companies also realize the importance of being recognized by CBP as a good, conscientious and proactive "Corporate citizen."

The benefits of the C-TPAT program include:

- Immediate re-access to U. S. ports after the mandatory shutdown period following next terrorist attack on the United States.
- Reduction of inspections by CBP at the ports.
- Immediate mitigation of fines/penalties.
- Reduced probability of being audited or received a Focused Assessment
- Access to other CBP programs such as the Importer Self-Assessment (ISA) program.

The government welcomes proactive engagement, which this program affords. With all this forward momentum to being a member of the C-TPAT program, then why haven't more companies joined? While most, if not all, import/export compliance professionals seem to understand these benefits, many have struggled with gaining support at the senior management level.

What Are the Obstacles and How Can These "Perceptions" Be Averted

In today's very tenuous economy, the general philosophy of most U. S. companies is survival and the focus is, understandably, geared toward different objectives. As such, often senior management doesn't recognize the need or importance of compliance and security initiatives in their company, such as C-TPAT. As companies remain focused on manufacturing and selling their products while reducing expenses to improve their balance sheets, inefficient compliance and security efforts and the penalties for such inadequacies can easily offset any such measures.

Senior management may have some other concerns or "pushbacks" which can include:

- Ignorance of the benefits of the C-TPAT program.
- An onerous enrollment process that can drain already stretched staff and capital resources.
- The belief that being in the C-TPAT program provides no real competitive advantage in the marketplace.
- The perception that by volunteering a security profile information, CBP may be prompted to make a "house call," resulting in a Focused Assessment or fines and penalties based upon the information provided.

While these are all seemingly viable reasons for not joining the C-TPAT program, savvy and informed import/export compliance professionals should easily be able to talk through each concern and convince senior management of the overwhelming upside to getting into the program. To provide some guidance, here are some suggested steps to take to help convince senior management to reconsider their position:

- Alert them to the consequences of noncompliance and lack of security. Failure to maintain solid compliance and security programs can often lead to fines and penalties levied by CBP.
- Cite some "real-life" examples: Many of America's top companies are being fined every day for compliance- and security-related issues (Ford, Boeing, and Pratt & Whitney to name a few of the better known offenders).
- Reinforce the potentiality of loss of import and/or export privileges for egregious compliance and/or security breaches.
- The import/export community mistakenly assumes these privileges to be a right, but they are **NOT!** Importing or exporting goods into or out of the commerce of the United States is a privilege and may be revoked at any time by CBP or the Bureau of Industry and Security (BIS).
- A very effective analogy is the "sprinkler system" argument. Compare the benefits and consequences of maintaining strong compliance and security programs to the merits and inherent disaster potential of constructing a building without installing a sprinkler system. We wouldn't even consider not having a sprinkler system in the building. Why would we ever consider entering into the import/export arena without having compliance and security programs in place for our own protection and to mitigate risk and exposure?
- It is very effective to arrange for a meeting with an outside consultant to deliver an "executive overview" to senior management. The use of an outside agency will typically add credibility to the cause and will increase the opportunity for success.

However, as there may still be resistance, where can you go to get some help to plead your case? Thankfully, there are many helpful options available to provide assistance!

One of the easiest and quickest places to go is to visit the CBP website (www .cbp.gov). By typing in C-TPAT into the search field, you will access a litany of information and resources from which to obtain valuable information pertaining to the C-TPAT program. You may even submit questions online or call CBP directly to speak to a professional equipped to provide all the information you may need. In extreme cases, a local CBP representative may even be available to pay a visit and provide assistance and support for such conversations.

Another useful website is www.compliancemaven.com. **Subscribe to trade publications!** Read! Read! Read! Review various trade journals such as the *Journal of Commerce* and the *American Shipper*, to name a few. Articles pertaining to the C-TPAT are frequently found in these publications which may provide some information to be used to fortify your case.

Hire a consultant! As mentioned above, another very valuable resource available to provide assistance and support would be consulting firms. An experienced import/export consultant, knowledgeable and conversant in all facets of the C-TPAT program, from the enrollment process to the benefits, can provide valuable assistance to support the case to join C-TPAT.

Don't hesitate to tap the consultant's knowledge and use his or her resources to provide valuable assistance. Most consultants can provide documentation, develop a Power Point presentation, or, as mentioned above, meet with senior management to provide support for joining the C-TPAT program.

For the most part, consultants will not charge a company for any of the aforementioned services, but may campaign to handle the Security Profile Evaluation and Application process for which they would charge a fee. However, keep in mind that any such project fees are usually negotiable.

The C-TPAT program is a very important partnership that all importers should flock to join to proactively display their desire to protect and secure the U. S. supply chain. With the many resources available to help educate the uninformed, gaining senior management support may be a much easier task than you had thought.

12

The Import Supply Chain
Purchasing, Operations, Documentation, and Compliance Management

Imports represent over 70 percent of the global supply chain. Almost all exporters import. Almost all exporters have returned merchandise. For these reasons it is very important for all importers, exporters, and supply chain executives to understand what U.S. Customs Border and Protection regulations are and the best inbound supply chain options. Import operations are complicated and the aftermath of the events of 9/11 has raised the bar of regulation and control which has severely impacted how companies bring merchandise in to the United States from overseas markets.

Import Compliance: A Necessary Evil!

The Customs Modernization Act of 1993 puts a much greater onus on importers than had existed previously. Customs spent the next five years in a program called informed compliance. They set out to educate the importing public as to what the rules were and how to administer their import responsibilities.

Since 1997, Customs has now entered into the enforced compliance phase, which is an aggressive effort to hold importers and service providers responsible and accountable for import compliance with severe fines, penalties, and consequences.

Under a mandate from Congress, the Customs Modernization Act outlined strict interpretations of U.S. import rules and regulations and a procedure for strict enforcement. It also funded the enforcement effort. As a side note, many industry analysts see this whole effort as a way for customs, which has steadily been losing tax and duty revenue due to worldwide treaties and agreements eliminating them, to maintain its revenue from new fines and penalties.

Regardless of the rhyme or reason, exporters need to understand this new customs policy because many exporters are also importers—they have returned goods, and circumstances often arise where goods are being brought into the United States.

Now add in the events leading to and following September 11, 2001 where the regulatory, compliance, documentary, and operational guidelines for import supply chains have become convoluted, comprehensive, and have added potential expense to the final "landed cost."

Import compliance management has taken on a new energy requiring a new sophistication and focused initiative of the importer that is unprecedented.

CBP has announced in their Strategic plan of 2009-2013 to pay more attention to compliance enforcement through several different efforts of increased activity. CBP will focus more on post entry enforcement issues to determine common practices of inacurrate import declarations which often result in lost revenue for CBP in the form of duties, taxes and fees. The import community is already realizing the impact of this new effort as they are experiencing a rise in Custom Form 28 Request for Information and Customs Form 29 Notice of Actions.

Customhouse Brokers

These companies are typically part of freight-forwarding organizations and/or international transportation service providers. They are licensed and sanctioned by customs to clear goods through the border for a fee on behalf of importers.

They are required to be an extension of customs, upholding import law and regulations and collecting duty and taxes on their behalf.

Brokers do not have to be utilized in clearing your goods, as a company can do this itself, but it typically makes commercial sense to employ a broker to work on your behalf. They should know the laws, common practice, and functionality of the clearance process to assure timely and accurate release of your product from customs. Although they charge for their services, they are usually a cost-effective option in the long run.

There are large customhouse brokers: Eagle Logistics, Schenkers, Expeditors, Panalpina, and BDP, in addition to many small and midsize brokers. Some smaller-size, but quality brokers include: Newage, American River Brokerage Service, and Northeastern. It is imperative for you to find a broker that is conducive to your size and needs.

You certainly want a broker that is automated broker interface (ABI) compliant, meaning they have an automated relationship with customs and can interface with your automated systems for ease of clearance and less paperwork. It is considered a world class practice to also ensure that the customs broker that is used also interfaces and particpates in the Automated Commercial Environment (ACE) program, which has several state of the art automated benefits made available to importers and brokers alike. Friendly competitors, carriers, international trade organizations, and customs in your inbound gateway can all be sources used to assist you in making the right selection.

While customhouse brokers help you manage the clearance, and you will certainly delegate many of the clearance responsibilities to them, you cannot defer all liability associated with proper compliance to them because customs does not allow you to delegate ultimate control and supervision of their activity. Thus, it is important that all importers understand the basics of import regulations and how it applies to their specific inbound activity.

Duties and Taxes

All duties and taxes must be remitted to customs within ten days of clearance. These are determined by two key factors: the origin of the goods and the description as identified by the appropriate Harmonized Tariff Classification number (HTC). Secondary issues might be utilization of goods (like in the case of samples or promotional items), the value, and who the ultimate consignee might be.

Using various web sites, publications, and resources available from customs, one can obtain classification assistance in determining the applicable duties and taxes. This information also can be obtained from a customhouse broker or local customs office. Importers are responsible for providing Harmonized Tariff Schedule of the United States (HTSUS) classifications to the broker.

Selecting a Customhouse Broker

Customhouse brokers are considered to be industry experts in the customs business. There are considerable risks involved in the selection of a customhouse broker. A broker is required by customs law to maintain a valid customs power of attorney to conduct any and all customs business on behalf of the importer. This power of attorney legally authorizes the customhouse broker to act on behalf of the importer legally binding the importer to many legal obligations. Extreme care needs be exercised in this selection process. Customs purports that many brokers are operating below the reasonable care and compliance standard that is legally expected of them. This lack of reasonable care and compliance equates to fines and penalties for the importer and broker. It is essential to carry out the following points when choosing a customhouse brokerage service:

- Verify that the brokerage operation has qualified customs brokerage personnel with more than five years of operation experience on all levels of customs entry processing.
- Verify that the key licensed person in charge of brokerage operations has licensed support personnel within the brokerage office conducting your customs business.
- Verify that the operations staff has proper and exact experience in valuation issues.
- Verify that the operations staff has proper and exact experience in classification issues. Often they will use the wrong HTSUS classifications based on information the importer has supplied. This will cause potential fines and penalties for both parties and delay the import process.
- Verify that the brokerage operations has representation in all ports in which they claim to conduct customs business. It is important that a third party broker to whom the importer has not issued a power of attorney to act on its behalf is not processing his entries. Importers are to make the decision of who conducts their customs business, not an intermediary broker.
- Verify compliance knowledge with the brokerage operations.
- Make personal visits to the broker's office to note working conditions and automated capabilities.
- Always select an ABI broker who has an operating software package that is not more than five years old. Many changes have taken place in the automated arena of customs business, which makes it crucial to keep pace for clearance advantages.
- Monitor brokerage communications procedures related to "shared" information being given to and received from customs by your broker. All com-

munications need to be forwarded to the importer. Verify the procedures in place to accomplish this goal.

Internal Supervision and Control

Importers of record are responsible for development and maintenance of internal standard operating procedures (SOPs), which directly relate to the customs clearance declaration process. Internal supervision and control represents a standardized measure to control the correctness of information being tendered to customs and all other governmental agencies in relation to entering the commerce of the United States. These procedures should monitor all communications made on behalf of the importer of record in reference to all clearances by the broker and importer themselves.

Traditionally, it has been a common practice for importers to rely on the increased services offered by third party service providers as a luxury. The mindset has been that the greater the service of the brokerage provider the less day-to-day work the importer has to perform related to the specifics of the import declaration. For example, if the overseas vendor sends the import notification to the broker then the broker can execute customs clearance on behalf of the importer and merely send back up notification of the declaration with the billing package. This practice is simply noncompliant. There are many decisions that must be made prior to and at the time of entry. These decisions must be monitored, supervised, and controlled by the importer of record. It is a lack of supervision and control to allow a brokerage provider to make entry decisions on behalf of the importer like valuation verification, country of origin verification, and harmonized tariff classification among others.

Importers who are exercising supervision and control have established an import notification process to validate the shipment as authentic. An authentic shipment is a shipment in which the importer is expecting arrival or can substantiate the validity of the overseas shipper or vendor as being credible in relation to all rights to ship. This validation process is crucial to monitor global security guidelines. The brokerage provider is unable to make this validation on his own. Importers match up purchase order numbers and land invoice transactions to properly validate the shipment.

This validation is usually done and confirmed when the importer sends a letter of notification to the broker authorizing customs clearance. Once the broker receives this letter of notification and instruction, entry may be created and tendered to customs. All supervision and control measurements will have been met in relation to this initial declaration due to this practice.

The entry process has only just begun at this point. The importer must remain in a supervisory role over the entire entry process. If there are any adjustments to the entry including but not limited to value, origin, classification, description, and quantity, the importer must be aware of any and all amendments to the entry. This should be controlled in a proactive manner by the use of electronic notification and validation from the broker to the importer for review and validation. Failure to implement such a process will result in entry corrections and amendments without the knowledge of the importer.

Customs Business

The term *corporate compliance activity* was recently added into the Customs Regulations. This definition has been added to resolve the controversy over customs' previous findings on what constituted customs business.

Customs business was and is still defined as *activities involving transactions with customs concerning the entry and admissibility of merchandise, its classification and valuation, the payment of duties, taxes* but also including *the preparation of documents . . . intended to be filed with Customs.*

Customs issued a ruling in 2001 stating that no one can conduct "customs business" without having a customhouse broker's license. However, under the 1993 Customs Modernization Act, importers were required to exercise "reasonable care" in making entries with reasonable care including knowledge of product classification and valuation.

This ruling created a problem for parent company compliance offices across the country, as it required *each* subsidiary office would have to have its own licensed customs broker on staff, as customs business included *advice*.

Summer 2003 brought about a revised ruling making it possible for a parent company compliance office to give advice to its subsidiaries. In addition, the definition of "customs business" was amended and now states ". . . customs business does not include a corporate compliance activity."

And just what does customs consider corporate compliance activity to be? "Activity performed by a business entity to ensure that documents for a related business entity are prepared and filed with Customs using 'reasonable care' but such activity does not extend to the actual preparation or filing of the documents." This change allows importers to draw together reasonable care and product knowledge to make their companies succeed in the total import compliance picture.

Harmonized Tariff Classification

Importers are responsible to ensure that every harmonized number declared on the import declaration is accurate based on the guidelines established in the HTSUS. Importers are also responsible to know the principles of classification to monitor and control the advice tendered by third party service providers like customhouse brokers.

Classification of commodities is a very detailed process. The responsibility lies on the importer to ensure that all classifications being tendered in relation to their imported products are accurate. This entails a specific knowledge prerequisite that the importer is expected to have to validate such harmonize classifications. The principles of proper classification are not a simple process, yet it is an attainable goal. Specific training on classification principles is needed to properly navigate the HTSUS.

Many importers have again relied on the internal expertise of the brokerage provider to select the classifications for the entry declarations. This common practice is noncompliant and represents a lack of supervision and control, and a failure to meet import reasonable care standards. The importer is responsible to give the broker full and complete information to properly make entry or provide advice as how to make entry. This includes the harmonized tariff classification information as crucial information required for entry.

It is also a common noncompliant practice that brokerage providers rely on a list provided by the importer to classify their imported commodities, without validation that the numbers are accurate on its derivation and applications. Customs' position is that the importer knows the import products specifications better than the broker. There may be details omitted from the standard commercial invoice that do not properly represent the full and complete description enough for the broker to properly classify a product. In this case it is imperative that the importer manage the harmonize classification process to ensure correct reporting information.

Failure to properly supervise this process will result in false information being tendered to customs. This false information is legally viewed as a possible penalty case under the framework of a false statement, act, or omission.

Importers must demonstrate an ability to classify their imported commodities. Formal training in the proper principles of classification can only attain this ability from a qualified industry expert who specializes in customs classification education and training. Once trained, the importer can accurately provide the broker with this full and complete information required for harmonized classification declaration.

Global Security Management: Customs Trade Partnership Against Terrorism Participation

A nationwide invitation has been sent to the importing community for voluntary participation in the Customs Trade Partnership Against Terrorism (C-TPAT). There are significant advantages to voluntary participation that will expedite the customs clearance process. Management of your import supply chain security procedures is a crucial part of the participation process. Development and enhancement demonstrating control measures that effectively monitor the safeguarding of cargo entering the commerce of the United States is the goal.

We are a very different society post-September 11, 2001. Our import practices have been put under a microscope of review to examine the vulnerability of the common import process. Customs realizes their responsibility to protect the borders of the United States against possible future terrorist activity. Importers are responsible to view their own import process and analyze their security strengths and weakness.

The C-TPAT program is a voluntary partnership that customs has introduced to allow the trade community to share each individual analysis with customs to critique, monitor, and advise with any and all recommendations going forward. There is a specific process outlined for voluntary enrollment into the C-TPAT program that includes an Agreement to Voluntarily Participate and a Security Questionnaire. Once enrolled there are specific benefits that the importer will qualify for like Fast Track customs clearance and the Importers Self-Assessment (ISA) program. The ISA is a program that will allow an importer to perform internal audits on behalf of the customs service and provide reports to customs on compliance standards. This privilege is only given and afforded to C-TPAT participants.

C-TPAT is a very good program and initiative to join. It is recommended to carefully review your global security process for the overall good of your company and not just as a C-TPAT initiative. Each importer must review their import supply chain carefully to monitor possible holes in the security process. Careful steps must be taken by importers, with the assistance of senior management, to address these issues in a timely manner. Import validation is a crucial step as previously outlined and detailed. Careful supervision and control of where merchandise is sourced and background checks on overseas vendors should be implemented. A detailed knowledge of the storage and handling of all imported cargo is the responsibility of the importer, even when delegating such services to outside service providers like freight forwarders and common carriers.

Customs has begun to inspect merchandise in overseas ports prior to the merchandise being loaded on a vessel destined for the United States to ensure an increased level of security. Importers need to expand their supervision and control abroad as well to truly take the reins of responsibility in reference to global security. The more globally secure an importer becomes, the higher the comfort level each customs will have with each importer.

Commercial Invoice Requirements

Commercial invoice requirements as established in the Code of Federal Regulations 19CFR141.86 are a very major concern for the Customs Border Protection. The invoice is the engine that drives the international shipment and clearance procedures. Misleading and misstatement of facts could circumvent the governing authorities from properly exercising control of our borders and result in major devastation of domestic property and even lives.

Correct import declaration reporting information is founded on the contents of the invoice. Every importer is bound by Basic Bond Conditions under 19CFR113.62 for providing a complete entry and entry declaration information.

Most importers are unaware of the requirements for invoices. It is a common practice to judge a complete invoice by the amount of information that is contained on a document without looking closely to see if all of the required information is included. Customs is very concerned that required information is being left off invoice documents. This practice of submission of incomplete information is noncompliant and illegal which may result in a costly fine or penalty as a liquidated damage amount of the value of the merchandise plus estimated duties.

There are two types of invoices associated with an import transaction described first as a commercial and second as a *pro forma* invoice. The foreign shipper or manufacturer prepares a commercial invoice. The *pro forma* invoice is prepared by the U.S. importer of record in the event the commercial invoice lacks the required information needed to meet the customs regulatory standards as established in the 19CFR141.86. Customs prefers the first type of invoice as a commercial invoice to be accurate reflecting the details of the import transaction.

The importer is expected to monitor the contents of the invoice to ascertain the correctness of information on a transaction-by-transaction basis. Random audits in a postentry format do not meet the regulatory requirement of supervision and control. Brokers use these invoices as the key source of reference in the import declaration. The information contained in each invoice must be properly reviewed prior to submission to the brokerage provider and well before the customs entry declaration process. This is viewed as a possible delay in many import supply chain operations. Effective incorporation of this process is mandatory for compliance and security concerns.

The importer should ensure the following information is contained on each invoice:

1. The name and address of the foreign shipper or manufacturer.
2. The name and address of the importer of record and consignee.
3. A full and accurate description of the imported merchandise.
4. Quantity of the merchandise being imported with net weights and measures included.
5. The unit price of the imported commodity.
6. Terms of sale associated with the international transaction.
7. Invoice date.
8. Invoice number and purchase order number.
9. A detailed breakdown of any and all prepaid freight and insurance charges associated with the transaction of sale.
10. All discounts offered and or taken.
11. Any commissions must be detailed on the invoice.
12. Invoice must be in English or have an attached translation.
13. Any royalties that exist must be indicated on the invoices.
14. A complete invoice value.
15. Country of origin of the imported merchandise.
16. A name of a responsible person as the preparation party of the invoice.
17. A statement of use is recommended to establish special entry procedures.

There are additional requirements that may be associated with specific imported merchandise. Customs generally accepts nonoriginal documents for shipments that do not require special entry procedures like quota merchandise. Fax copies may be submitted in connection with your import clearance entry as long as all information is legible and accurate.

Duty Payment Management

Every importer's first bond condition is to pay duties, fees, and taxes on a timely basis. It is the importers responsibility to establish and verify that all duties, fees, and taxes are being submitted in accordance with 19CFR113.62 (a).

The liability for payment must be met in most cases within ten days from the date of customs clearance. The payment may be made directly from the importer to customs via check or electronic payment methods of the Automated Clearing House (ACH) Debit or ACH Credit accounts.

Many importers use as a common practice, the services of the brokerage provider to submit duty payment to customs on their behalf. It is another luxury that the brokerage provider advances the duty payment on behalf of the importer as a service. Most companies like this added service that the brokerage community offers as it minimizes the strain on the importers accounting practices to validate correctness of information and issue payment to customs within a ten-working day time frame. Since the broker is advancing the duty payment the importer can take their time in the validation process as most brokers afford thirty-day payment terms with their importers.

It is important to note that the use of this service does not relieve the importer of their responsibility to pay duties, taxes, and fees. The supervision process of how the duty payment process is being handled is the responsibility of the importer. Records of timely payment are maintained by the broker in cases where this advancement is being handled. Copies of the receipts of payments need to be reviewed and retained by the importer.

There are various methods that can be used to achieve this goal, yet it must be met. In a customs audit an importer will be asked how they manage the duty payment process. It is an unacceptable answer to simply state, "my broker pays the duty for us." A system of accountability needs to be implemented to ensure that timely payment is being handled and a level of understanding of just how it is being managed needs to be attained by the importer.

Copies of the final ACH statement copy will serve as proof of payment. Copies of checks with a receipted copy of the CF 7501 Customs Entry summary will also represent timely payment. A stamped copy of the 7501 in itself is not proof of payment, only entry submission. Be careful that the brokerage provider provides a written explanation of the duty payment process.

Informed Compliance

It is the responsibility of every importer, as established in the Customs Modernization Act of 1993, to meet and maintain "Informed Compliance" standards of increased and current education and training on industry specific topics associated with the duties and responsibilities of importers of record.

Many importers have not gone out to seek formal education and training on industry specific issues associated with their day-to-day job responsibilities. There are many issues being handled on a common practice method with knowledge of the specifics of rules and regulatory procedures established by customs in the CFR Customs Federal Regulations.

There are qualified individuals and institutions that provide quality education and training on import specific topics of compliance and global security. It is the law that each importer seeks out this formal training and elevates their internal expertise in reference to the customs regulatory procedures.

Many companies rely on the knowledge of a select few internally within their organization for compliance awareness once the level of informed compliance has been achieved. This is a legally accepted practice, however, operationally an importer can never be overtrained or overeducated. Informed compliance is about remaining current in reference to the on-going changes in the import environment. Current is a difficult place to be without a schedule and action plan of continued education.

Knowledge of reference of the Customs Federal Regulations and the Harmonized Tariff Schedule of the United States (HTSUS) is essential to the demonstration of compliance awareness. The avenue to attain those skills is called informed compliance. External training seminars have proven to be very productive for many importers.

The growing concept of "in-house training" is another very attractive option.

In-house training allows an importer to gain access to high-level expertise at the importers' place of business. It is a cost-effective manner in which to train more staff for less money.

Informed compliance is mandatory to minimize and eliminate costly fines and penalties associated with an audit or operational practices below regulatory standards.

Every importer should use resources available to elevate the level of import awareness and regulatory knowledge.

Reasonable Care Standard

Under the reasonable care standard an importer:

- Should seek guidance from customs for proper compliance using the formal rulings program.
- Should consult with "qualified experts" like a customs broker or attorney, or a consultant specializing in customs law.
- If using a broker, must provide such broker with full and complete information sufficient enough for the broker to properly make an entry (import declaration) or for the broker to provide advice as how to make an entry.
- When appropriate, obtain analyses from accredited labs to determine technical qualities of an imported product.
- Use in-house employees like counsel, a customs administrator, or if valuation is an issue, a corporate controller, who has experience and knowledge of customs laws, regulations and procedures.
- Must follow any binding ruling requested and received from customs.
- If importing any textile or apparel product ensure that the products are accompanied by documentation, packaging, and labeling that are accurate as to its origin.
- Cannot classify own identical merchandise or value own identical transactions in different ways.
- Must notify customs when receiving different treatment by customs for the same goods in different transactions or at different ports.
- Must examine entries (import declarations prepared by the broker to determine accuracy in classification and valuation.

Record Retention

Importers of record are responsible to establish a record retention system that maintains all records relative to an import transaction for five years from the date of entry of the merchandise into the commerce of the United States. Many importers do not keep satisfactory records as established in the 19CFR163.

Customs finds multiple errors of practice associated with many audit proceedings as a common error. Importers must be aware of all documents that they are responsible to maintain as outlined in the (a) 1 (a) listing in the 19CFR163.

All records associated with the import transaction from the point of the purchase inquiry throughout the customs clearance process up to the final disposition of the merchandise at the ultimate place of delivery needs to be retained. Once all of the required documents are identified every importer needs to create a standard operating procedure to ensure that these documents are properly collected on a transaction-by-transaction basis.

Third party service providers, like brokers and freight forwarders, need to be a part of this process to ensure that all documents that are generated by their services are duly tendered to the importer. The importer is responsible to keep all of these mentioned records. This legal obligation cannot be delegated to the third party customs brokerage service provider. Each broker has their own recordkeeping requirements and legal obligations to meet. Many brokers themselves are not properly advising importers of the full obligation to maintain exact records in the process.

The importer is not only responsible to keep the records, they must also be able to retrieve the records in a reasonable amount of time. Records that are maintained yet unattainable do not meet the customs regulatory standards of compliance. Record retrieval processes should be implemented to exercise an importers ability to control any and all request for additional or duplicate documentation made by customs on any customs entry declaration so tendered within the scope of the past five years.

Valuation

Importers of record are responsible to ensure that proper valuation principles are applied to each import transaction and subsequent declaration, as outlined in the 19CFR152. Falsely declared values corrupt trade statistics and possibly defraud the government out of revenue. Valuation verifications and the knowledge of valuation principles are crucial to safeguarding your company from unforeseen customs penalties for misstatement of valuation facts.

There are many variables to valuation declarations that are important to customs at the entry level of declaration. The ability to recognize all of the elements of valuation is the responsibility of the importer of record. Customs holds the importer liable for misstatements of fact on each and every entry. It is the importers' responsibility to correct any and all declarations previously made should the importer discover new information that will change a previously made declaration.

There are instances of accounting that importers use in generally accepted accounting principles that are not acceptable to customs. For example, defective merchandise shipments that are credited between a buyer and seller of imported merchandise in some cases are amended by simply replacing the items at no charge. The next shipment will arrive with a value for a portion of the merchandise to offset the defective values previously imported. General accounting principles would allow such a practice, but the position of customs is clear that the second shipment should be valued at its full price regardless of the credit situation as a result of the defective merchandise circumstance.

Customs valuation is mentioned in the Customs Federal Regulations Part 152 and defined extensively. Importers are responsible to know the regulations and applications of the valuation principles and concepts on a transaction basis.

Customs has several methods of valuation that can be used to value imported merchandise:

- **Transaction Value:** Price paid or payable between the buyer and seller
- **Transaction Value of Identical or Similar Merchandise:** Price paid or payable between another buyer and another seller of imported merchandise imported at or around the same time from the same region of the world
- **Deductive Value:** Price after importation and U.S. resale minus all nondutiable charges
- **Computed Value:** Price of the labor, raw materials, assembly, etc.
- **Value If No Other Value Can Be Determined.** An assigned appraised value by customs

Most transactions are handled on the basis of the transaction value method. Customs does have the authority to use alternative methods as described above to determine a more accurate value than the original value declared.

Importers are responsible to know the methods of valuation to properly assess whether or not imported merchandise has been properly liquidated and agreed to by customs. There are several other valuation concepts that are very crucial to the import declaration including but not limited to commissions. There exist two types of commissions:

- Buying Commissions
- Selling Commissions

Buying commissions are not subject to duties and do not have to be included in the import declarations value. Selling commissions are dutiable and must be included in every import valuation declaration.

Details of valuation are complex and with each and every variation of a sales agreement, there are issues of valuation compliance that must be reviewed. The notion to over declare is a noncompliant practice. Customs is interested in accurate reporting information.

Country of Origin Marking

Importers are responsible to ensure that all merchandise is properly marked upon entry into the United States, as referenced in the 19CFR134. Documentation must also indicate the proper country of origin on all shipments, as a separate requirement.

Many importers are not aware of the specific requirements of marking that states that all goods imported into the United States must be marked to indicate to the ultimate purchaser the country of origin of the merchandise.

There are different country of origin rules for different commodities. The importer must first be aware of the definition of country of origin. For most articles with the exception of textile apparel products, the country of origin is the country of growth, manufacture or production.

A permanent marking unless exempted there from is required on each imported article.

In cases where the item itself cannot be individuially marked, customs may accept the marking on the outer carton as it will indicate to the ultimate purchaser the country of origin of the product. There is a complete listing of exempt articles to the marking requirements in the 19CFR134 known as the "J list."

It is recommended that importers use the customs ruling process to ensure that proper markings are associated with sample products prior to full import activity where there is doubt as to the validity of legal marking status.

In cases where customs believes imported merchandise does not comply with the legal requirements, the importer may be demanded to redeliver imported merchandise previously released from customs custody up to thirty days from the date of customs release. If the merchandise has not been released customs can detain the merchandise by the seizure process and demand that goods be properly marked before release into the commerce of the United States. Customs can also however, release the goods to the importer to be marked at the importers establishment pending proof of such marking.

Power of Attorney Management

All importers should properly manage the number of customs brokers that are conducting customs business on their behalf. It is imperative that proper control be established and maintained to ensure that qualified persons are presenting all declarations.

Many importers do not realize that the power of attorney is established for the protection of the importer of record to control the brokers who are conducting customs business on their behalf. There is a rule that a customs broker, who is authorized to conduct customs business on behalf of an importer, must have a valid power of attorney to conduct such business or face a penalty of up to the value of the merchandise or loss of license.

Many importers have several brokers who, once issued a customs power of attorney, become an extension of the traffic department of the importer. This authority is dangerous when not properly managed. Too many customs brokers create an increased liability for error and mismanagement. Supervision and control over your brokerage providers becomes an unattainable goal when there are an unmanageable number of brokers with customs powers of attorney for an importer.

Importers should perform extensive reviews of all brokerage services to critique the internal expertise being given to each and every entry. They should look closely at the average years of experience that are present in the operational levels of the brokerage service that handles over 90 percent of the work volume associated with the clearance process.

It is the responsibility of the importer to properly manage the performance of the broker and regulate the brokers who meet satisfactory levels of compliance with the customs power of attorney issuance management process. Only compliant and operationally effective brokers should be allowed to conduct customs business on behalf importers.

Importers have the power of attorney management as a tool to implement this requirement. Any broker who falls below the importers standards of compliance will have their power of attorney revoked by letter of revocation sent to the Port Director of Customs at the port of entry.

All powers of attorney should be dated with a date of expiration not to exceed an initial period of thirty days for renewal pending proven performance. Once the importer is satisfied with the broker's performance, power of attorney should not be issued for a period that exceeds one year.

Ultimate Consignee

On most import transactions, the importer of record and the ultimate consignee are the same. The opinion of customs is the ultimate consignee caused the import to occur and is one of the responsible parties to the import transaction. Therefore, the ultimate consignee can be held accountable for regulatory requirements.

This can have serious consequences for a company that purchases goods on a delivered duty paid (DDP) or free domicile basis. This term of sale dictates the seller is responsible for the payment of duties and freight and customs clearance. Ultimate consignees mistakenly believe they can avoid the normal importing process and liabilities that go along with importing.

Customs requires that if a buyer causes the import, the buyer must have the usual records required to import. This includes the bill of lading, entry documents, purchase order, and invoice. Records must also be retained for the usual five year period.

What You Should Know About "Drawback"

Drawback is a privilege granted by customs, which allows an importer to collect 99 percent of duties previously paid by exporting the merchandise from the United States or destroying the imported goods under customs supervision. It is important to note that drawback is a "privilege" that can be taken away if customs considers the drawback claimant in constant fraudulent violation concerning their drawback claims for refunds.

There are three main types of drawback:

1. **Unused Merchandise Drawback.** A 99 percent refund of duties paid on imported merchandise that is exported in the same condition as when imported and remains "unused" in the United States. The importer may claim a drawback for three years from the date of importation.
2. **Rejected Merchandise Drawback.** A 99 percent refund on imported merchandise that is received not conforming to the importer's standards of approval and/or the standards of any governmental agency (i.e., Food and Drug Administration [FDA], Department of Agriculture, FCC, Fish and Wildlife Service, and customs). The importer may claim a drawback for three years from the date of importation.
3. **Manufacturing Drawback.** A 99 percent refund of duties paid on imported merchandise that is received and is to be further processed or manufactured in the United States. Customs will allow a 99 percent refund of duties paid on the imported merchandise for a period of up to five years from the date of importation.

It is key to note that unless given prior permission, all merchandise must be examined by customs prior to export to qualify for the drawback privilege. A filer notifies customs of their intent to file a drawback claim in reference to a drawback by filing a "Notice of Intent" CF 7553.

An importer must allow at least five working days prior to the export of the merchandise. Customs will notify the drawback claimant within two working days of their intent to examine or waive the examination.

Drawback is a fantastic opportunity to recover previously paid duties on exportation and/or destruction. Careful attention must be paid to time limitations and correctness of information declared to customs.

Customs can pursue costly fines and penalties against a drawback claimant for incorrect claims submitted for refund. It is automatically reviewed as a fraudulent act, punishable by a penalty up to the domestic value of the merchandise.

A frequent drawback claimant needs to consider a complete drawback program, containing adequate recordkeeping procedures for proper filing.

Necessary Drawback Documentary Requirements

Following is a list of necessary drawback documents:

- Letter Requesting a Drawback Claim to Be Filed on Behalf of Exporter
- CF 7501 Entry Summary
- Import Commercial Invoice
- CF 3461 Entry/Immediate Delivery
- Import Packing List

- Export Invoice
- Export Packing List

Careful consideration for drawback eligibility must be maintained by industry experts. This is a very trade-specific area of expertise. Assistance from specialized brokers and consultants is a necessity.

Returns and Repairs: The Most Cost-Effective Options

Many exporters have merchandise returned for repair with the intention that once it is repaired, it will be reexported. The best situation to be in as an exporter in this circumstance is to control the entire export/import process from beginning to end. Because certain documentation has to be presented to customs at both ends, to prevent duplication of payment of duties and taxes one party should handle both transits to ease the process. One forwarder/carrier has the export and the same entity handles the import and then the reexport of the repaired piece. This will provide the best economies of scale, ease of document/clearance handling, and the lowest costing.

Too often, returned freight just shows up at the border. The exporter is alerted late, has to pay demurrage, and the whole process gets complicated. The use of one forwarder/carrier eliminates most of the problems. Returned freight still has to be cleared through customs, but if handled properly; one will not have to pay duties and taxes on the value previously exported.

The key is to provide communication and shipping instructions to your overseas customer so they will know whom to contact for shipping instead of just sending it by any means available. For merchandise that is just being returned, one must go through a clearance process and no duties or taxes will have to be paid if the documentation and clearance is processed correctly. Using qualified forwarders and customhouse brokers will make the return process run more smoothly and protect your need for competitive pricing.

Quality logistics becomes an integral component of your customer service capability and provides a competitive advantage.

Import Goods Damaged During Inspection

In today's security-conscious environment, importers have found themselves with damaged shipments following inspection. This is concerning on several fronts, as the damage could have been caused due to the nature of the inspection. Did inspectors feel the shipment contents were lethal, like a bomb? Did inspectors deem the package might have contained drugs or other contraband?

If it is found by the importer that the shipment was damaged during inspection, the importer must follow the governmental guidelines for filing a claim. However, if the government is able to substantiate its case that there was good reason to handle the inspection in a destructive manner, there will be no way to recoup that loss with this venue.

An importer's best practice is to ensure the description of the goods on all documents is correct. The packing should be like would normally contain such product. Tracking the shipment, from point of pickup from the supplier to carrier loading and monitoring the customs clearance must be done. Aside from a reasonable care requirement, this is an importer's best assurance to keep track of their shipment and to be able to track if damage occurred due to an inspection.

Concluding Remarks

Hopefully, this chapter has raised awareness of all the import issues and presented the best resolutions to manage import compliance and inbound supply chain effectiveness. The ultimate measure of import success in the successful importation, without hassle, in compliance and in a costing structure which allows for high profit margins, which all can be accomplished following the thoughts outlined in this section.

Ultimate consignees must be aware there may be an obligation to customs even when they are not the importer of record. There has been a general increase in CBP's scrutiny of this "ultimatee consignee" issue. Importers beware!

13

Import Strategies in Maintaining a "Compliant and Secure" Inbound Supply Chain

It is critical for importers to maintain compliant inbound supply chains. Since 9/11, it has been made clear that importers who are forever noncompliant will sacrifice their privileges to import. This chapter views the corporate strategies to balance the need to maintain compliant supply chains, but balanced off with competitive landed costing.

Internal Compliance Management and Internal Audit

Most companies are not capable of performing a self-audit on their own import/export operations and logistics division. This is due to lack of internal expertise related to the regulatory guidelines, and to the fact that common practice knowledge has plagued the operational process for far too long, and corporate culture cannot separate compliance from common practice.

Many companies seek the professional services of third party service providers who can objectively perform an audit and do not have any conflict of interest in providing accurate assessments of all service providers, vendors, and internal operational functions.

The purpose of internal audit and compliance management is to effectively monitor the compliance measures in place and ensure that operational functions are within the guidelines of those established procedures.

Senior Management Endorsement

For any compliance management program to be effective in the operational aspect of any importer/exporter, it is imperative that senior management endorses the actions and efforts of the compliance department. A centralized center for compliance management is only as good as the hammer that it may place down to effectively identify risks and implement change.

Once the senior management team "buys in" to the concept that compliance is a known cost and noncompliance is an unknown cost, companies are able to effectively implement compliance measures designed to minimize and eliminate risk factors that exist in the import/export supply chain process.

Ownership

There needs to be a person or party delegated to take ownership of the compliance responsibilities for the importer/exporter. This party will be the go-to person for the entire organization on all regulatory affairs related to Bureau of Customs and Border Protection, Bureau of Industry and Security (BIS), Food and Drug Administration (FDA), U.S. Department of Agriculture (USDA), and Transportation Security Administration (TSA), etc.

With the above-mentioned endorsement of senior management, this compliance department will have the authority to implement change and procedures designed to elevate the overall compliance levels of the company.

Customs, other governmental agencies, vendors, and third party service providers will have an immediate centralized contact party to address all inquiries and concerns. This centralized department will be able to control the information being requested and provided on behalf of the company. This level of supervision and internal control is a key element in the compliance management effort. Government agency control officers appreciate a company with a "compliance point person," and it can mitigate their view of a potential problem.

Education and Training

The talented group of individuals that make up the compliance department are only as good as the tools with which they are provided to aid and assist them in their daily activities. The most valuable tool that can be provided to a compliance department is updated and on-going education and training.

It is very important that all persons involved in the compliance management responsibilities fully understand the total risks involved in their day-to-day operational functions as an importer/exporter. Rules and regulations are constantly being amended to reflect the changes of the world's environment.

The ability to stay current is only found in education and training. Many individuals rely on industry articles to keep abreast of the latest changes affecting the trade community. This is a good tool, yet an individual must not just rely on industry articles for their education and training.

Compliance Management Structure

1. **Validation Process.** Every compliance structure should have a validation process to properly analyze the purchase process and valuation structure and the shipping and receiving practices of the transactions. This validation function must be supported by various departments like but not limited to purchasing, accounting, logistics, operations, shipping, and receiving.
2. **Internal Supervision and Control.** The ability to supervise and control the import/export logistics process is a degree of measure of compliance control. If an importer/exporter can demonstrate that there is a control factor in the shipping and receiving process by each respective importer/exporter, they will be regarded as a compliant department. Cases in which companies

rely solely on third party persons to advise and assist without the capability to independently monitor those third party logistics company (3PL) service providers are noncompliant. An importer must be able to demonstrate that it had full knowledge of the shipment from the point of purchase order notification up until it was released from customs authority and domestic disposition of the cargo. It is the exporters' responsibility to know where their goods are being shipped and, as a compliance measure of supervision and control, how the goods will be used and who will use the goods in the country of receipt or destination.

The ability to control the actions of the broker and freight forwarder is a compliance strength. Know your third party service provider's strengths and weaknesses to avoid delays in service and potential fines and penalties. Inquire about specific expertise that all service providers have in handling your commodities.

3. **Classification Structure.** Every importer/exporter is responsible to properly classify all items entering and or leaving the commerce of the United States. Cases in which the importer/exporter relies on the broker or freight forwarder to classify goods are examples of noncompliance. Participants must demonstrate the ability to classify within their own establishment and provide the third party service providers with accurate commodity classifications. The participant must have knowledge of the Harmonize Tariff Schedule of the United States and the online version and the automated process. The ability to audit your transactions to ensure the proper classifications are being used will lead to higher compliance standards.

4. **Power of Attorney Management.** Every importer/exporter is to be fully aware of all parties who have an existing power of attorney on their behalf. Failure to properly identify all parties with this power is a lack of supervision and control and a compliance deficiency.

5. **Record Retention.** Every effective compliance/audit management department will have the ability to create, implement, and audit internal centralized recordkeeping practices of the company. It is essential to the compliance effort that all records be maintained for five years from the date of entry. Ensure that all records are properly received from those parties who generate the records in the original form as when they are created. All amendments to forms and or documents must also be maintained in this effort.

6. **Global Security Management.** Compliance management is a vital partner in the efforts of global security. The Customs Trade Partnership Against Terrorism (C-TPAT) responsibilities may fall under a different department

---

- *Supervision and control is a transaction-by-transaction real-time audit function.*
- *Knowledge of the operational process is a strength in the audit process.*
- *Demonstrate knowledge of the existence of shipments prior to arrival into the United States.*
- *Demonstrate knowledge of the disposition of the merchandise throughout the import supply chain process.*

as a security specialist, however, compliance is the nucleus of global security. The more compliant an importer/exporter remains, the more globally secure that same entity will be. Compliance management should include C-TPAT partnership participation.

Penalties

Customs can fine violators in amounts as high as the goods entire resale value, impose liquidated damages, seize and keep goods, and restrict future imports. The importer remains ultimately liable for compliance with the import regulations. Following are the most common fines and penalties issued by customs:

Recordkeeping: $100,000 per willful violation and $10,000 per negligent violation

Negligence: Twice the revenue loss, or if no revenue loss, 20 percent of the goods' dutiable value

Gross Negligence: Four times the revenue loss, or if no revenue loss, 40 percent of the goods' dutiable value

Fraud: Market or resale value of the goods seized and forfeited

Criminal: Goods seized and forfeited plus $500,000 fine plus five years in prison

Import Case Studies

CASE STUDY 1: THE WRONG WAY

A German manufacturer of industrial washing machine parts and accessories Schnizel Ltd., recently imported a shipment of machine parts into the United States in the name of Schnizel USA, their U.S. subsidiary. The shipment consisted of all German-made components made by Schnizel. The shipment consisted of fans, blowers, motors, brackets, rubber molding, and plastic fittings. The plastic fittings were specially designed by an Italian manufacturer and provided to Schnizel free of charge, due to a special arrangement between Schnizel and the Italian plastics company. Schnizel USA did not declare the value of the plastic fittings because they were provided free of charge and truly did not have a price-listed value.

Edward Kettles, compliance manager for Schnizel USA, noticed the packing list itemizing the plastic articles and wondered if he should declare them to his broker with a value or not. Mr. Kettles sent an E-mail to the parent company inquiring about the valuation criteria for the molds. He received a reply from his parent company that the plastic fittings would have been valued at $8,000.00, if purchased. After carefully weighing his options, Mr. Kettles decided not to inform his broker but to rather wait and see if his broker noticed the lack of information on the invoice themselves. The brokerage provider did not notice the itemized description and only made entry classifying and declaring the value for the fans, blowers, motors, and rubber molding excluding the plastic fittings. The entry cleared customs and the shipment was delivered.

Then, 215 days later, Mr. Kettles received a CF28 request for information from customs in reference to the itemized value of the imported shipment. Mr. Kettles was nervous about this letter and decided to tell customs the truth about the undervalued shipment in an attempt to submit a prior disclosure to customs to mitigate any possible penalties. Mr. Kettles offered to pay customs the duty originally due at the time of importation.

Customs issued several penalties in addition to the demand for payment of duties due. Schnizel USA was issued a fraud penalty for knowingly and intentionally trying to defraud the government out of revenue in the form of duties and taxes in the amount of value of the merchandise. Schnizel USA was also issued a penalty for lack of reasonable care for failing to provide the broker with complete information sufficient enough to make proper entry and a duty bill for the amount of duties originally due plus interest.

> **The upfront cost would have been less then $1500.00, but now the actual cost with fines and penalties exceeds $10,000.00.**

It is clear that shortcuts and misinformation do not make good sense related to the import declaration process. Pay now or pay much more later is the lesson learned. In addition to the increased amount of fines and penalties assessed, Schnizel has a bad mark on their compliance record, which will affect their import profile for years to come.

The proper thing for Mr. Kettles to do was to declare the $8,000.00 value as a dutiable assists and pay duty accordingly at the time of entry (CFR 152.102).

CASE STUDY 2: THE RIGHT WAY

Bullock Studios, a high-end photography studio, imported a shipment of cameras. There were 1,500 cameras in total contained in the imported shipment.

Bullock Studios also imported 1,500 camera cases in the same shipment. There was a concern as how to classify the cameras and the cases. There is one Harmonized Tariff Schedule (HTS) for the cameras and another HTS classification number for the cases.

These cases were specially designed and manufactured to carry and store these cameras and suitable for long-term use. After careful review of the general rules of interpretation, Bullock Studios consulted with the broker of record for their opinion. The broker suggested that Bullock Studios obtain a binding ruling for clarification from the Bureau of Customs and Border Protection.

Bullock Studios did not feel comfortable with that advice and sought additional advice from a third party customs consultant, who advised them that based on the General Rule of Interpretation 5a, they could classify the cameras and the cases together as cameras.

The broker further clarified that there was no need for a binding ruling as long as the importer used the rules and principles of classification provided by customs by referencing the Global Reporting Initiatives (GRIs).

Bullock Studios properly decided to enter the cameras and camera cases together based on the advice of the consultant.

Bullock Studios did several things that warrant merit. First, Bullock sought the advice of industry experts prior to making any decision. Second, Bullock did not rely on the one opinion from their broker. Due to an uncomfortable feeling about the advice and a level of informed compliance, Bullock Studios sought additional advice, demonstrating further levels of reasonable care and due diligence.

Customs liquidated the entry as entered.

Bioterrorism Act of 2002

In June 2002, President Bush signed the Bioterrorism Act. This law went into effect December 12, 2003, and provided the FDA with new authority in protecting the nation's food supply against terrorist acts and other threats. Food articles include: food packaging, beverages, dietary supplements, and animal food products. There are four provisions to this law: registration, prior notice, administrative detention, and recordkeeping.

The FDA required that domestic and foreign facilities that manufacture, process, pack, or hold food articles for human and animal consumption in the United States register with the FDA by December 12, 2003. Registration information included: name and address of facility, contact information like telephone, fax, and E-mail addresses, U.S. agent information, and details on the manner in which the food is processed, stored, packed, or produced at the foreign facility.

One of the regulations concerns the advance notification by U.S. food importers to the FDA by noon of the calendar day before the arrival day of the food. The prior notification includes but is not limited to the entry number and entry type, location where product will be held at the port of entry for failure to submit adequate notice, identification of food article including FDA product code, common product name, market product name, quantity, lot numbers, identification or manufacturer, identification of shipper, country from which shipped, identification of importer, consignee, carrier information.

Much of this information is the usual data provided to customs on the commercial invoice submitted on arrival into the United States. However, this advance notification allows FDA time to review, evaluate, and assess the import information before the food product arrives to ensure that a safe food product is going to consumers. Any food article, found during inspection, that presents a threat of serious health consequences, whether to animals or humans, will be detained. The detention order will include the detention order number, hour and date of the order, identification of the detained article, detention period, reason for detention, and location where the article is to be detained. The detention period may not exceed thirty days. Detention orders will be terminated by release by FDA or expiration of the detention period.

The final provision of the Bioterrorism Act covers recordkeeping. Records must be maintained by domestic persons and foreign facilities that manufacture, process, pack, transport, distribute, receive, hold, or import food intended for human and animal consumption.

Records must be established and maintained to identify sources of all food (including names, faxes, addresses, delivery dates, food quantities and types), identifying every mode of transportation used (company truck, rail/air/ocean carrier), and the individual responsible from when the food was first received until it was delivered.

Records must be retained at the establishment where the activities as described in the records occurred. Records may be kept in any format as long as they contain all of the required information.

Engagement

CBP expects companies who import to fully engage themselves in the numerous iniatitives and programs that they offer to inform, train, educate and influence.

Programs which are voluntary, such as the C-TPAT program are an excellent engagement option that should be considered.

CBP outreach programs annually on a national basis and locally on a more frequent basis should be attended by all serious importers.

Concluding Remarks

We cannot emphasize enough the importance of maintaining a specific compliance and security strategy for your import business. This strategy will work more successfully when integrating the components of security and compliance management as outlined in detail in this chapter.

The import supply chain or purchasing manager that thinks and acts proactively with a security and compliance mindset will have the most success in inbound logistics.

14

Bureau of Customs and Border Protection
Compliance and Security
Expectations: Post 9/11

The focus of this chapter is to provide a detailed overview of just what expectations the Bureau of Customs and Border Protection (CBP) has of the importing community in securing the supply chain since the terrorist attacks of September 11, 2001.

Pre 9/11

In this book, we have covered the subject of customs enforcement before and post 9/11. The focus of U.S. Customs (as it was called then) before 9/11 was revenue, collection, and compliance. Programs like informed compliance, focused assessment were in effect from 1993 to 2002.

Securing the inbound supply chain became the number one priority of the CBP. New buzzwords became relevant, such as Customs Trade Partnership Against Terrorism (C-TPAT), Container Security Initiative (CSI), 24-Hour Manifest, etc., and all of which have been discussed in preceding chapters.

Customs has a very specific agenda, post 9/11, which is making sure that the inbound supply chains are secure and compliant. Inbound documentation and compliance issues such as classification, valuation, origin, etc. are all still critical, but the focus is in the security of the "supply chain." Every customs seminar we attended after 9/11 broached this subject with this articulation.

Also keep in mind that CBP was moved from reporting to the Treasury to the Office of Homeland Security.

One presentation we attended with CBP in 2003 provided insight into its then new responsibilities, with the officer advising the following:

1. Most importers should consider joining C-TPAT. It will expedite their clearances and in the event of a new terrorist attack, when the borders reopen, there will be clear advantages to the importer that is a member of C-TPAT.
2. Larger importers (over 10 million in value), and eventually all, should consider the new Customs Program, **Internal Self-Assessment (ISA)**. This pro-

gram affords the importer to be classified as a "low risk" to customs. This provides an advantage to the importer by reducing the opportunity for a "focused assessment" audit from the CBP—specifically meaning that the importer by using a process of completing applications and passing an audit proves they have developed an internal set of operating procedures with a clear and precise paper and audit trail in place.

An importer gains access to the ISA program by validating that they can internally make sure they are following customs regulations.

3. The officer also worked through the CBP **"Account Management Program"** from a question and answer perspective (see below).

CBP Account Management Program

Customs is working with more and more businesses as accounts rather than transaction by transaction. The Account Management Program is an example of this effort.

Q: What is account management?
A: Account management is a program designed to increase importer compliance and improve customer service by using one-on-one interaction with a specially designated customs representative called an *Account Manager.*

Q: What is the account management's mission?
A: The mission is to use account-based methods consistent with risk management principles to develop and maintain the highest levels of trade compliance, which incorporate supply chain integrity with border security to enforce, regulate, and administer U.S. trade laws, while fostering the flow of lawful international trade.

Q: How does account management relate to the C-TPAT program?
A: For companies that currently do not have an account manager, being designated as an account and having an assigned account manager is one potential benefit of joining C-TPAT. If you are already an account, you can contact your account manager for more information about C-TPAT and gain assistance in joining this program.

Q: How did my company become an account?
A: Accounts are selected by the Customs Headquarters Account Management Branch. Importers are selected based on the value and volume of imports. In addition, account managers are assigned to C-TPAT partners as available.

Q: Does participation in this program mean increased scrutiny by U.S. Customs?
A: No. In fact, one of the goals of the Account Management Program is to help importers achieve the highest level of compliance so that they can enjoy the lowest number of customs examinations possible.

Q: How can having an account manager improve my compliance?
A: Your account manager is an experienced customs officer who can offer you expert advice on a wide variety of topics including valuation of merchandise and improving your internal control systems. In addition, your account manager has frequent contact with subject matter experts in all levels of customs so that any questions can be answered in an expedited manner.

Q: What are the benefits to being an account?
A: There are many benefits to being an account, including increased access to company data relating to customs examinations and receiving advance notice of

customs programs and policy changes. The account manager acts as your primary point of contact for all customs issues. This personal attention streamlines communication on important and time-sensitive issues and provides you with the best customer service possible.

CBP and Managing Import Trade Risk

Import supply chain risk management concentrates on identifying and controlling events that have the potential to cause significant problems. In customs trade terms, that means identifying imports that represent the greatest risk of noncompliance so that we can focus our resources in those areas. The key to risk management is to systematically isolate and treat risk identified throughout the trade compliance process.

Q: Is risk management a new program? What does it do?
A: Risk management does not create any new work, but rather combines existing programs to maximize resources. Risk management requires clear responsibility and accountability for each program or action. Some of the programs that are currently being used to manage risk include compliance measurement, compliance assessment, selectivity, and account management. Risk management also shows field personnel how their work affects the work of the agency.
Q: How is risk management achieved in the customs service?
A: This is done using a seven-step process:

1. **Collect Data and Information:** Proper risk management requires a structured approach to collecting data.
2. **Analyze and Assess Risk:** Analyze the data and determine the likelihood of noncompliance.
3. **Prescribe Action:** Once the potential risk has been identified and analyzed, it is time to design the appropriate action and dedicate the necessary resources.
4. **Track and Report:** Once the appropriate action is designed, ownership for the action must be assigned and its results tracked and fed back into the risk management process.
5. **Direct Support:** Customs needs direct support from importers in securing the supply chain.
6. **The CBP when auditing importers looks for five key areas:**
   1. Management Communication
   2. Risk Assessment
   3. Policies and Procedures
   4. Information and Communication
   5. Monitoring
7. **Compliance and Security Areas:** There are approximately nine focus areas in a corporation for which customs expect compliance and security audits. Following are the "red flag" or "points of scrutiny" issues:
   1. The freight on piece goods that may originate in one country and transit through another before entering the United States.
   2. Tooling expense and/or depreciation expense on machines sent overseas to assist foreign suppliers with manufacturing of goods that will come into the United States.
   3. Commissions paid to sales or purchasing agents.
   4. Where are the imported goods designed?

5. Where is the research and development accomplished?
6. Where is the engineering done on imported products?
7. Are there any loans payable between the parties?
8. Are there agreements in place which contain management fee structures?
9. Is there an "inter-company" account set up for things like returns, currency conversions, claims, etc. for "to and from."

CBP in an audit, which it now attempts to accomplish quickly, uses the above outlined areas as guidelines to catch an importer in a regulatory faux pas. Companies should heed these points in establishing internal operating guidelines to prevent the potential of fines and penalties (Figure 14-1).

Under Title 19, section 1467, of the United States Code (19 USC 1467), customs has a right to examine any shipment imported into the United States—and it is important to know that you, the importer, must bear the cost of such cargo exams. Per the customs regulations, it is the responsibility of the importer to make the goods available for examination. "The importer shall bear any expense involved in preparing the merchandise for customs examination and in the closing of packages" (19 CFR 151.6). Household effects are not exempt. No distinction is made between commercial and personal shipments.

In the course of normal operations, customs does not charge for cargo examinations. However, there may still be costs involved for the importer. For example, if your shipment is selected for examination, it will generally be moved to a Centralized Examination Station (CES) for the customs exam to take place. A CES is a privately operated facility, not in the charge of a customs officer, at which merchandise is made available to customs officers for physical examination. The CES facility will unload (devan) your shipment from its shipping container and will reload it after the exam. The CES will bill you for their services. There are also costs associated with moving the cargo to and from the exam site and with storage. Rates will vary across the country.

A complete devanning may cost several hundred dollars. The CES concept fulfills the needs of customs and the importer by providing an efficient means to conduct exams in a timely manner. CES is discussed in part 118 of the Customs Regulations.

Concluding Remarks

U.S. CBP is the major player in managing the security and compliance controls on inbound freight to the United States. This chapter was structured to emphasize its role and provide valuable insight to its mindset.

CBP's entire focus changed on September 11, 2001. Security of the supply chain became a dominant force in how it managed its day-to-day activities along with the other key responsibilities of revenue collection and compliance management.

> *You may receive a bill if your shipment is examined by customs.*

Customs-Trade Partnership Against Terrorism (C-TPAT)

In order to develop, enhance, and maintain effective security processes throughout the global supply chain, U.S. Customs and Border Protection (CBP) continues to accept applications in various international supply chain categories.

Customs and Border Protection (CBP) Transition—On The Line Communication Series

On The Line is a series of brief broadcasts that provide up-to-date information on important transition issues.

Container Security Initiative

Every year some 200 million sea cargo containers move among the world's top seaports. In the U.S., nearly 50 percent of the value of all imports arrive via sea container. In January of 2002, U.S. Customs launched the Container Security Initiative (CSI) to help prevent global containerized cargo from being exploited by terrorists. Now within the Department of Homeland Security, Customs and Border Protection (CBP) continues to implement CSI at major ports around the world.

Safe Explosives Act (25 KB.—doc)

The Act amends several provisions of the Federal explosives law to include, among other things, additional categories of persons who may not lawfully pos-

Importers Security Filing Program (ISF)

CBP now requires importers to file advanced manifest security information in addition to the carrier requirements outlined in the CSI's 24 hour manifest rule for carriers. Importers must submit information in a timely and accurate manner to avoid costly fines and penalties and structured at $5,000.00 USD per errant or late filing.

The Bioterrorism Act—Public Health Security and Bioterrorism Preparedness and Response Act of 2002

Agricultural Quarantine Inspections

Safe Explosives Act (25 KB.—doc)

The Act amends several provisions of the Federal explosives law to include, among other things, additional categories of persons who may not lawfully possess or receive explosive materials.

Figure 14-1. CBP import spotlight.

15

Getting on Top of the Regulatory Challenges of the Future

You are not alone if you are wondering when the government pendulum will shift away from increased regulatory enforcement and focus on trade facilitation. Unfortunately, it seems that as I am writing this in 2011, the government will not buck the current enforcement trend. In this chapter, we have constructively addressed the actions your company can take today to address the top ten regulatory challenges and opportunities we expect the trade community to face over the next few years.

Imports

1. DEVELOP INTERNAL PROCEDURES TO WITHSTAND A CUSTOMS BROKER AUDIT

ISSUE: After many years, CBP has resurrected its customs broker audit program. This year more brokers can expect a call and visit from CBP's Office of Regulatory Audit to assess compliance.

RATIONALE: While the broker visits are designed to increase compliance, CBP always maintains the right to assess broker penalties of up to $30,000 (and higher penalties in cases of fraud or financial gain) if it uncovers violations of the customs laws and/or a lack of responsible supervision or control.

ACTIONS:

✓ Carefully review CBP's *Broker Compliance Handbook*, particularly the list of items CBP typically considers when conducting a site visit.
✓ Review, or as needed, develop a written compliance manual addressing all critical issues such as: Power of Attorneys (POAs), reference materials, document processing/filing, other government agency requirements, payment/financial controls, recordkeeping, etc.
✓ Assess risky shipments involving high-value or duty preference claims, as well as those that involved a post entry adjustment or CBP inquiry. Also, identify imports where you may have served as the importer of record.

2. Scrutinize the Documentation Necessary to Support Duty Preference Claims

ISSUE: This year, expect CBP to more frequently verify the sufficiency of preference claims. Imports declared as duty free under a free or preferential trade program present a major revenue risk to CBP, particularly for apparel, which accounts for more than 40 percent of all collected duties.

RATIONALE: CBP consistently has found that many importers and their brokers cannot substantiate preference claims. Often, the merchandise actually meets the requirements of the program, but mandatory supporting documentation is inaccurate or unavailable, a circumstance which often motivates importers to suggest that their brokers (or their brokers' E&O carrier) pay the increased duty bills.

ACTIONS:

- ✓ Match the origin requirements for the applicable preference program(s) to bills of materials for the goods initially to determine if the merchandise meets the necessary criteria.
- ✓ Confirm that all supporting documents exist and are internally consistent, including Certificates of Origin, affidavits, proof of purchase and sale, etc., as required by applicable CBP directives.
- ✓ Establish procedures requiring producers and/or providers of the finished goods and components/materials to present the necessary documentation as a condition of sale.

3. Develop an Effective Strategy for the Release of Goods Seized for Trademark or Copyright Infringement

ISSUE: In fiscal year 2009, CBP logged 14,841 seizures of counterfeit and pirated goods with a total domestic value of $260.7 million. While these figures may seem high, the administration, Congress, and trademark and copyright owners claim that a great deal more escapes detection. It is one of CBP's highest priorities to increase its seizures in 2010/11/12.

RATIONALE: Consistent with customs regulations and some case law, CBP generally follows the instruction of the trademark owner as to whether imports are counterfeit or piratical, warranting seizure, destruction, and often the issuance of a fine. Frequently, this leaves importers of genuine merchandise or those unknowingly purchasing fakes feeling there are no alternatives but to abandon the merchandise.

ACTIONS:

- ✓ Understand the difference between counterfeit, confusingly similar, and gray market (restricted and unrestricted) merchandise to ascertain whether the goods may be classified as other than counterfeit.
- ✓ Confirm whether the trademark or copyright has been recorded with CBP. If not, there may be a greater chance to have the goods released.
- ✓ If plausible, attempt to obtain authorization to import from the trademark owner.
- ✓ Alternatively, consider establishing a paper trail to the authorized manufacturer.
- ✓ Distinguish between products claiming to be "compatible with" a brand as opposed to knocking off the brand itself.

4. Remain Vigilant on Import Safety Requirements to Avoid Border Delays

ISSUE: CBP increasingly has been coordinating with agencies such as the FDA, USDA, and CPSC to prevent the importation of contaminated, diseased, infested, unsafe, or adulterated products that could harm individuals or the economy.

RATIONALE: The numerous cases of tainted products entering the United States will continue to spark an unprecedented wave of enforcement and legislation, which means increased scrutiny and delays at the border.

ACTIONS:

- ✓ Confirm that appropriate facility registration numbers exist for food and pharmaceutical/device manufacturers and shippers.
- ✓ Obtain New Drug Applications or Codes for pharmaceuticals.
- ✓ Check for SID/FCE numbers for acidified foods.
- ✓ Keep current with FDA Import Alerts.
- ✓ Verify that the appropriate FDA product code is submitted via the OASIS system.
- ✓ Familiarize yourself with FDA and CPSC labeling requirements.
- ✓ Keep abreast of CPSC lead requirements and recent penalty actions particularly for toys and child care articles.

5. *Assess Your Current 10 + 2 Progress to Minimize Exposure to Potential Liquidated Damages Claims*

ISSUE: The 10 + 2 rule, which took effect in 2010, requires that an importer submit an electronic Importer Security Filing, as we discussed in detail in Chapter 12.

RATIONALE: In order to work with importers and filers to achieve compliance, CBP began by providing warning letters and progress reports instead of issuing liquidated damages claims or "No Load" messages. However, in 2010, CBP started holding cargo and issuing claims for more high-risk, serious errors particularly those that are repetitious. They promise special treatment for those repeatedly failing to comply during the generous "gradual enforcement approach" period.

ACTIONS:

- ✓ Carefully analyze and track ISF progress reports to identify recurring errors so you can reach out to your supply chain to improve compliance.
- ✓ Adopt language with your business partners requiring cooperation in providing the necessary data elements, including bill of lading information, in a timely fashion.
- ✓ Apply recordkeeping requirements in the 10 + 2 context. The documentation may assist in mitigating potential claims.
- ✓ Leverage 10 + 2 information to improve supply chain efficiency and lower transaction costs.

Exports

1. *Identify Drawback Opportunities*

ISSUE: Drawback allows companies to receive a refund of 99 percent of the duties paid on imports based on exports (or destruction) of the same or similar articles, their components, or materials. Although the program has been in place for over 200 years, exporters (or their designees) currently claim less than 15 percent of all available duty drawback refunds.

Rationale: Florida businesses more than ever should focus on drawback because this state ranks fifth in total value of exports. Also, the South Florida CBP district maintains the highest export surplus nationally. Additionally, new drawback laws simplifying the claims process passed Congress in late 2010.

Actions:

✓ Identify top exporters and determine whether their exported goods can be matched with the same or similar imported goods, or their components or materials, which carry a significant duty rate or with such goods imported in high volumes carrying a lower duty rate.

✓ Familiarize yourself with the various types of drawback, e.g., unused, same condition, and manufacturing.

✓ Understand who can claim drawback and the necessary endorsements as well as certificates of transfer.

✓ Work with a qualified drawback specialist to ensure appropriate documentation is available to demonstrate the import and timely export of the same or similar merchandise within appropriate time frames.

2. File Accurate EEIs (Electronic Export Information) to Avoid Census Penalties

Issue: Based on guidelines established in February, 2009 CBP is issuing penalties of up to $10,000 per transaction (that can be mitigated) for untimely and/or inaccurate EEI/SED violations. CBP will continue to assess penalties against U. S. parties (USPPIs), foreign parties (FPPIs), agents, and/or carriers for the failure to file EEIs, late filing of EEIs, and/or providing incorrect information.

Rationale: The Census regulations and the CBP penalty guidelines are designed to encourage the trade community to provide appropriate filing citations to the carrier and to timely file EEIs prior to export. EEIs must contain critical information, such as the appropriate parties to the transaction and the merchandise description, classification, and value.

Actions:

✓ As a forwarder, understand and recognize cases involving routed transactions where FPPIs, not USPPIs, are authorizing the filing. Ensure this is properly reflected on the EEIs.

✓ Always require a Shipper's Letter of Instruction (SLI) demonstrating that you are exercising due diligence in obtaining all necessary information from the party in interest.

✓ Be sure to include the Internal Transaction Number (ITN) on export documentation and format the ITN appropriately, avoiding reuse of ITNs.

3. Make Smart Business Decisions to Avoid Export Seizures

Issue: Section §1595a(d) of the customs laws provides that merchandise exported or sent from the United States (or attempted to be exported or sent) contrary to law, shall be seized and forfeited. Congress intended this law to provide seizure authority primarily to combat federal money laundering and terrorist offenses.

Rationale: For the first time, CBP now has its own export seizure authority and is using that authority more frequently to stop exports that do *not* involve smuggling or more serious infractions.

ACTIONS:

✓ In all cases avoid declaring on the EEI a lower value for the merchandise than invoiced and paid by the parties to the transaction. These schemes may result in paying less duty to foreign customs administrations and can violate U.S. money laundering laws.

✓ Check updated lists of denied and blocked parties published by the BIS, OFAC, and the Directorate of Defense Trade Controls (DDTC). Consider subscribing to software that conducts the screening, because denied parties are located throughout the world in countries you would least expect.

✓ Question your customers' knowledge of the licensing requirements to assess whether they are accurately declaring no licensed required (NLR) for typically controlled commodities.

4. *Properly Handle International Traffic in Arms Regulations (ITAR) Commodities*

ISSUE: The State Department's Directorate of Defense Trade Controls (DDTC) administers ITAR. The regulations set forth specific registration and licensing requirements for the export, reexport, and temporary import of defense-related articles, services, and technical data. Such items are designated on the U.S. Munitions List and are controlled because they are specifically designed, developed, configured, adapted, or modified for the military, with no predominant civil application.

RATIONALE: CBP detains or seizes many shipments of defense articles because they often are not properly declared as licensed or exempt. Until recently, CBP had not issued uniform instructions for handling imports and exports subject to ITAR.

ACTIONS:

✓ Parties, regardless of registration with the DDTC, should file a commodity jurisdiction (CJ) request to confirm the proper licensing authority for an item. And, of course, it still is necessary to obtain the appropriate license.

✓ Ensure that manufacturers, exporters, importers, or brokers of U.S. defense articles or services are currently registered with the DDTC. Registrations are valid for one year only and renewal requests must be timely submitted (at least thirty days, but no more than sixty days, prior to the expiration date).

✓ Present and retain licenses consistent with CBP requirements. Follow CBP's recent instructions (February 2010) requiring temporary imports and exports to include a hard copy of CBP Form 3461 along with the license for review. Also, ensure that entry documents refer to any applicable exemptions along with required ITAR statements, citing the exemption on the EEI.

5. *Decide How You Will Approach the TSA Screening Mandate*

ISSUE: As of August 2010 all passenger air carriers of outbound and domestic cargo will be required to perform 100 percent security screenings.

RATIONALE: TSA feels that more entities need to become Certified Cargo Screening Facilities (CCSFs) or delays and logjams will occur when 100 percent screening is required; the carriers alone cannot conduct all the screening themselves. TSA stresses that all entities are eligible as long as they meet the appropriate requirements. (See the full discussion of CCSFs in Chapter XX of this book.)

ACTIONS:

- ✓ Become familiar with the equipment, processes, and training necessary to meet the CCSF requirements.
- ✓ Assess the costs and potential revenue to conduct the screening at your facility.
- ✓ Consider your ability to comply with requirements because screeners are subject to inspection and possibly penalties (although ultimate responsibility is on the carrier).
- ✓ Talk to your business partners to understand how they each handle and move their shipments.
- ✓ Also, stay aware of developing CBP and TSA requirements for bonded cargo as these currently are being addressed.

In 2011/12, all indications are that the government will heighten its enforcement of the laws and regulations designed to promote the health, safety, and security of the United States. More vigorous enforcement is also expected to be the case for commercial transactions, especially where the government feels companies are not playing by the rules and are creating an unlevel playing field. Finding just the right blend of perseverance and diplomacy to address these challenging issues as they arise will serve your business well when dealing with any of the numerous government agencies inquiring, auditing, or questioning the imports or exports of your company and your clients.

16

Concluding Remarks

The events of September 11, 2001 changed our lives forever.

Having been in international business for almost forty years, I have never witness any one single event that so greatly affected our own personal family lives; but for the focus of this book, it has also affected the parts of our lives that interface with global trade.

As I write this in 2012, the impact of 9/11 still rings loud and clear. . . . Trade Compliance and Security is as important in global supply chain management as negotiating international freight rates.

The companies that succeed in managing international business and that master the skillsets of freight, trade compliance, Incoterms and competitive tools will be the ones that will thrive into the future. The path to success is three-pronged:

1. Master the Skillsets

Master the skillsets and you will succeed. This book pays attention to providing every single skill set an import/export supply chain executive may need and how to best master it.

One of the most important skill sets is learning not to cut corners and dotting the i's and crossing the t's. Failure to do so will cause havoc in the supply chain and produce potential insurmountable losses.

2. Connecting the Dots of All the Supply Chain Responsibilities

What we mean is that, as links in a chain, all the issues and functions must work in concert. Having one or several things right is not sufficient; they must all work.

Documentation, freight, clearance, insurance, finance are some of the "things" or skillsets of import/export supply chains. If the documentation is done correctly and the freight is handled properly, but there is loss or damaged goods and someone forgot to insure the shipment, it will result in financial loss and a dissatisfied customer. Having two parts out of three correct results in little value.

If the freight arrives in good condition, but the exporter is unable to get paid, then all the prior steps were for naught. So, at the end of the day, the importer/

exporter must align all the operational steps and make sure they are in order to best assure success.

A theme throughout this book is "mitigate the risks and maximize the opportunities." In other words, one can mitigate the risks by making sure they do all the things necessary to make sure the import/export transaction goes well. To make sure all goes well, one must master the skill sets and assure all the functions are done right.

3. Integrate Compliance and Security Into Your Global Supply Chain

If you read this book, by now you certainly know that post-9/11 changed how freight moves from and to the United States. You know that there are significant convolutions of regulatory mandates that come into play in the supply chain decisions.

The world is a very competitive market. Those companies that survive and prosper are those that manage the most cost-effective supply chains and have opened up the entire globe to new suppliers and markets. The key ingredient of being competitive post-9/11 is to keep the costs of compliance and security in balance. The key to keeping these in balance is to be proactive and upfront, rather than reactionary. Preparation, planning, and concise budgeting will help to assure competitive landed costs and open trade lanes.

Those companies that do the following in developing a Global Policy will be the most competitive in their global supply chains:

1. Learn and keep updated on new regulations.
2. Obtain senior management commitment.
3. Train and educate staff.
4. Create functional standard operating procedures.
5. Work to achieve high levels of compliance and security.
6. Manage the supply chain cost-effectively.
7. Know all your options.
8. Think out of the box, sometimes the solution is not where you expect it or maybe more "stones" have to be turned over.
9. Be proactive and not reactive: plan, prepare, and budget.
10. Develop resources.
11. Assign responsibility and accountability.
12. Engage in government initatives.

We cannot emphasize enough the importance and critical nature of developing a Global Policy that incorporates all of these factors, which this book and author advocate comprehensively, concisely, and passionately.

Follow this book: Not only will the global supply chain survive, but it will prosper greatly. Mitigate risk . . . maximize profits is a key and central theme that, if followed, will lead to favorable results.

Appendix

Contents

Glossary

Abandonment: Refusing delivery of a shipment that is so badly damaged in transit that it has little or no value.

Acceptance: An international banking instrument known as a time draft or bill of exchange that the drawee has accepted and is unconditionally obligated to pay at maturity.

Ad valorem: A tariff that is calculated based on a percentage of the value of the product.

Advising bank: A bank operating in the exporter's country that handles letters of credit for a foreign bank by notifying the exporter that the credit has been opened in their favor.

Agency for International Development (AID) shipments: The Agency for International Development is a U.S. governmental agency created to provide relief to developing countries who must purchase products and services via U.S. companies. Specialized export documentation is necessary to complete the transactions.

All-inclusive: Term of sale used to notate "all charges are included."

Allowance: Typically afforded to a consignee as a "credit" or "deduction" on a specific export transaction.

All-risk cargo insurance: A clause included in marine insurance policies to cover loss and damage from external causes during the course of transit within all the terms and conditions agreed to by the underwriters.

Arbitration: Wording included in export contracts introducing an independent third party negotiator into the dispute resolution in lieu of litigation.

Arrival notice: Advice to a consignee on inbound freight, sometimes referred to as a prealert, that contains details of the shipment arrival schedule and bill of lading data.

"As is": An international term denoting that the buyer accepts the goods as is. It is a connotation that there may be something wrong with the merchandise, and the seller limits their future potential liability.

Automated broker Interface (ABI): The electronic transmission and exchange of data between a customhouse broker and Customs and Border Protection (CBP).

Automated Export System (AES): The electronic transmission of the electronic export information to census, Bureau of Industry and Security (BIS), and Customs and Border Protection (CBP).

Automated Manifest System (AMS): The electronic transmission of a carrier/ vessel's manifest between the carrier/steamship line and Customs and Border Protection (CBP).

Balance of trade: The difference between a country's total imports and exports. If the exports exceed the imports, a favorable balance of trade, or trade surplus, exists; if not, a trade deficit exists.

Barter: The direct exchange of goods and/or services without the use of money as a medium of exchange and without third party involvement.

Bill of lading: A document that establishes the terms of a contract between a shipper and a transportation company under which freight is to be moved between specified points for a specified charge. It is usually prepared by the shipper on forms issued by the carrier, and it serves as a document of title, a contract of carriage, and a receipt of goods.

Bond: A form of insurance between two parties obligating a surety to pay against a performance or obligation.

Bonded warehouse: A warehouse authorized by customs authorities for storage of goods on which payment of duties is deferred until the goods are cleared and removed.

Break bulk cargo: Loose cargo that is loaded directly into a conveyance's hold.

Bretton Woods Conference: A meeting under the auspices of the United Nations at Bretton Woods, New Hampshire, in 1944, that was held to develop some degree of cooperation in matters of international trade and payments and to devise a satisfactory international monetary system to be in operation after World War II. The particular objectives intended were stable exchange rates and convertibility of currencies for the development of multilateral trade. The Bretton Woods Conference established the International Monetary Fund and the World Bank.

Bunker adjustment fee (BAF): Fuel surcharge issued by a steamship line.

Bureau of Industry and Security (BIS): Department of Commerce agency responsible for Export Administration Regulations, formerly known as the Bureau of Industry and Security.

Carnet: A customs document permitting the holder to carry or send merchandise temporarily into certain foreign countries without paying duties or posting bonds.

Certificate of Origin: A document used to certify the country of origin for a product.

Clingage: When shipping bulk liquids, the residue remaining inside the conveyance after discharge.

Combi: An aircraft with pallet or container capacity on its main deck and belly holds.

Commission agent: An individual, company, or governmental agent that serves as the buyer of overseas goods on behalf of another buyer.

Commodity specialist: An official authorized by the U.S. Treasury to determine proper tariff and value of imported goods.

Consignment: Delivery of merchandise from an exporter (the consignor) to an agent (the consignee) under the agreement that the agent sells the merchandise for the account of the exporter. The consignor retains the title to the goods until the consignee has sold them. The consignee sells the goods for commission and remits the net proceeds to the consignor.

Consolidator: An agent who brings together a number of shipments for one destination to qualify for preferential rates.

Cost, insurance, freight (CIF): A system of valuing imports that includes all costs, insurance, and freight involved in shipping the goods from the port of embarkation to the destination.

Countertrade: The sale of goods or services that are paid for in whole or part by the transfer of goods or services from a foreign country.

Credit risk insurance: Insurance designed to cover risks of nonpayment for delivered goods.

Currency: National form for payment medium: dollars, pesos, rubles, naira, pounds, etc.

Destination control statement: Specific wording included on a commercial invoice and bill of lading advising goods are subject to export control laws and diversion contrary to U.S. law is prohibited.

Distributor: A foreign agent who sells for a supplier directly and maintains an inventory of the supplier's products.

Dock receipt: Documented receipt that the shipment has been received by the steamship line.

Domestic International Sales Corporation (DISC): Established in 1971 by U.S. legislation, DISCs were designed to help exporters by offering income tax deferrals on export earnings. DISCs were phased out in 1984.

Draft: A negotiable instrument presented to the buyer's bank for payment.

Drawback: duties to be refunded by government when previously imported goods are exported or used in the manufacture of exported products.

Dumping: Exporting or importing merchandise into a country below the costs incurred in production and shipment.

Duty: A tax imposed on imports by the customs authority of a country. Duties are generally based on the value of the goods (*ad valorem* duties), some other factor like weight or quantity (specified duties), or a combination of value and other factors (compounded duties).

Embargo: A prohibition on imports or exports as a result of a political eventuality.

European Union (EU): The twenty-seven nations of Europe that have combined to form the world's largest single market of more than twenty-seven million consumers. The EU includes Austria, Belgium, Bulgaria, Cyprus, Czech Republic, Denmark, Estonia, Finland, France, Germany, Greece, Hungary, Ireland, Italy, Latvia, Lithuania, Luxémbourg, Malta, Netherlands, Poland, Portugla, Romania, Slovakia, Slovenia, Spain, Sweden, and the United Kingdom.

Export: To send or transport goods out of a country for sale in another country. In international sales, the exporter is usually the seller or the seller's agent.

Export-Import Bank of the United States (Ex-Im Bank): Ex-Im Bank facilitates and aids the financing of exports of U.S. goods and services through a variety of programs created to meet the needs of the U.S. exporting community. Programs, which are tailored to the size of a transaction, can take the form of direct lending or loan guarantees.

Export management company: A private company that serves as the export department for several manufacturers, soliciting and transacting export business on behalf of its clients in return for a commission, salary, or retainer plus commission.

Export trading company: An organization designed to facilitate the export of goods and services. It can be a trade intermediary that provides export-related services to producers or can be established by the producers themselves, though typically export trading companies do not take title to goods.

Ex works (EXW) from factory: The buyer accepts goods at the point of origin and assumes all responsibility for transportation of the goods sold. Also: Ex Warehouse, Ex Mine, Ex Factory as defined in International Commercial (INCO) Terms, Chapter 6.

Fair trade: A concept of international trade in which some barriers are tolerable as long as they are equitable. When barriers are eliminated, there should be reciprocal action by all parties.

Federal Maritime Commission (FMC): The agency issuing rules and regulations for ocean transportation.

Force majeure: Expressed as "acts of God." Conditions found in some marine contracts exempting certain parties from liability for occurrences out of their control, like earthquakes and floods.

Foreign Commercial Service: Department of Commerce agency assisting in promoting exports of U.S. products

Foreign Corrupt Practices Act of 1977: U.S. legislation with stringent antibribery provisions and guidelines for recordkeeping and internal accounting control requirements for all publicly held corporations. The act makes it illegal to offer, pay, or agree to pay money or any item of value to a foreign official for the purpose of getting or retaining business.

Foreign Credit Insurance Association (FCIA): An insurance program, previously managed and underwritten by the government, now privately held, that insures commercial and political risks for U.S. exporters.

Foreign sales agent: An individual or company that serves as the foreign representative of a domestic supplier and seeks sales abroad for the supplier.

Forfaiting: The selling, at a discount, of a longer-term receivable or promissory note of a buyer.

Franchising: A form of licensing by the service sector for companies that want to export their trademark, methods, or personal services.

Free alongside (FAS): A system of valuing imports that includes inland transportation costs involved in delivery of goods to a port in the exporting country but excludes the cost of ocean shipping, insurance, and the cost of loading the merchandise on the vessel.

Free domicile: Terminology used for "door to door" deliveries.

Free on board (FOB): A system of valuing imports that includes inland transportation costs involved in delivery of goods to a port in the exporting country and the cost of loading the merchandise on the vessel, but excludes the cost of ocean shipping and insurance.

Free port: An area like a port city into which merchandise may legally be moved without payment of duties.

Free trade: A theoretical concept to describe international trade unhampered by governmental barriers like tariffs or nontariff measures. Free trade typically favors the reduction or elimination of all tariff and nontariff barriers to trade.

Free Trade Zone (FTZ): A port designated by the government of a country for duty-free entry of any nonprohibited goods. Merchandise may be stored, displayed, or used for manufacturing within the zone, and re-exported without the payment of duties.

Freight all kinds (FAK): A mix of cargoes traveling as one.

General Agreement on Tariffs and Trade (GATT): A multilateral treaty to which 85 nations (or more than 80 percent of world trade) subscribe; it is designed to reduce trade barriers and promote trade by tariff concessions, thereby contributing to global economic growth and development.

Generalized System of Preferences (GSP): Notes duty free/reduced tariffs on imports from the countries listed on the GSP list.

Harmonized Tariff Schedule of the United States (HTSUS): A system of classifying products imported into the United States by number.

Harter Act: Legislation protecting a ship owner from certain types of claims that are due to actions of the crew.

Haz-mat: Hazardous materials regulated by various governmental agencies, Department of Transportation (DOT)/Code of Regulations (CFR) Title 49, International Air Transportation Association (IATA), (IMCO), Coast Guard, etc. Personnel who interface with Haz-mat cargoes need to be certified to do so.

Hedging: A mechanism that allows an exporter to take a position in a foreign currency to protect against losses due to wide fluctuations in currency exchange rates.

Hold: The space below deck inside an ocean-going vessel.

Igloo: Container used in airfreight.

Import license: Government license issued for particular products and required by the importer prior to importation.

In bond: Transportation of merchandise under custody of a bonded carrier.

INCO terms: Terms of sale issued by the International Chamber of Commerce.

Inherent vice: capability of a product to produce damage to itself. Example: metal will rust; fruit will spoil.

Integrated carrier: A carrier acting as the pickup agent, airfreight carrier, customs clearance agent, and delivery agent. Examples: United Parcel Service (UPS), Federal Express.

Intermodal: Covering more than one mode of transportation.

Irrevocable letter of credit: A letter of credit in which the specified payment is guaranteed by the bank if all terms and conditions are met by the drawee (buyer). *See also* Revocable letter of credit.

ISO 9000: Issued in 1987 by the International Organization for Standardization, ISO 9000 is a series of five international standards that establish requirements for the quality control systems of companies selling goods in the European community. It now includes many additional countries and companies throughout the world.

Joint venture: A business undertaking in which more than one company shares ownership and control.

Known shipper: Federal Aviation Administration (FAA) ruling requiring forwarders and carriers to know the shipper of a product before accepting goods for shipment.

Letter of credit: A document is issued by a bank per instructions from a buyer of goods that authorizes the seller to draw a specified sum of money under specified terms, usually the receipt by the bank of certain documents within a given period of time.

Licensing: A business arrangement in which the manufacturer of a product (or a company with proprietary rights over certain technology, trademarks, etc.) grants permission to some other group or individual to manufacture that product (or make use of that proprietary material) in return for specified royalties or other payment.

Limits of liability: When goods are insured, they are subject to the limits of liability set forth within the policy and/or contract.

Logistics: The science of transportation covering the planning and implementation of specific strategies to move materials at a desired cost.

Mala fide: Misrepresentation or in bad faith.

Maquiladora: A tax-free program allowing the import of materials into Mexico for manufacturing of goods for export back to the United States.
Now declining in importance as a result of the North American Free Trade Agreement (NAFTA).

Marine insurance: Insurance covering loss or damage of goods during transit. It covers all modes of transport.

Market research: Specific intelligence about the market in which a seller proposes to sell goods or services. This information is gathered using interviews, commissioned surveys, and direct contact with potential customers or their representatives.

Marks and numbers: The references made in writing to identify a shipment on the exterior packing, typically referenced in the documentation.

No license required (NLR): Designation of a product not found on the Commerce Control List and/or a product that does not require a license authorization prior to export.

Nonvessel operating common carrier (NVOCC): An ocean freight consolidator.

North American Free Trade Agreement (NAFTA): An agreement that creates a single unified market of the United States, Canada, and Mexico.

Office of Foreign Asset Controls (OFAC): Department of Treasury office issuing regulations on transfers/funding of money.

Open account: A trade arrangement in which goods are shipped to a foreign buyer without guarantee of payment. The obvious risk this method poses to the supplier makes it essential that the buyer's integrity be unquestionable.

Order bill of lading: Negotiable bill of lading made out to the order of the shipper.

Overseas Private Investment Corporation (OPIC): A government-sponsored organization that promotes investment in plans and equipment in less developed countries by offering guarantees comparable to the Export-Import Bank of the United States.

Paperless release: An electronic release of a shipment by CBP prior to hard copies being presented.

Phytosanitary: Type of certificate issued for particular commodities.

Political risk: In exporting, the risk of loss due to causes like currency inconvertibility, government action preventing entry of goods, expropriation, confiscation, or war.

Power of attorney: A document that authorizes a customs broker or freight forwarder to act on the exporter's/importer's behalf on issues relative to customs clearance, transportation, documentation, etc.

Premium: Insurance dollars paid to an underwriter to accept a transfer of risk.

Prima facie: At face value.

Product registration: Requirement to register a product with a particular governmental agency prior to import.

Proforma invoice: (1) Invoice prepared by the supplier to the buyer, usually as a means to secure financing. (2) Invoice prepared by an importer when the supplier's invoice does not mean the invoice requirements set forth by Customs and Border Protection.

Protectionism: The setting of trade barriers high enough to discourage foreign imports or to raise the prices sufficiently to enable relatively inefficient domestic producers to compete successfully with foreign producers.

Purchasing agent: An individual or company that purchases goods in their own country on behalf of foreign importers, like governmental agencies or large private concerns.

Remarketers: Export agents, merchants, or foreign trading companies that purchase products from an exporter to resell them under their own name.

Revocable letter of credit: A letter of credit that can be cancelled or altered by the drawee (buyer) after it has been issued by the drawee's bank. Compared to an irrevocable letter of credit, which is totally binding without both parties written agreement.

Security endorsement: Affirmative document issued by exporter/forwarder to carrier stating goods meet security guidelines.

SGS inspection: Preinspection performed by Societe Generales Surveillance prior to export of goods to designated countries.

Tariff: A tax on imports or the rate at which imported goods are taxed.

Terminal handling charge: A fee assessed by a terminal for handling a shipment.

Through bill of lading: A bill of lading signifying various modes of transportation will be used to destination.

Time draft: A draft that matures in a certain number of days from acceptance or date of draft.

Tracking: A forwarder or carrier's system of recording movement intervals of shipments from origin through to final destination.

Trade acceptance: *See* Acceptance.

Transfer risk: The risk associated with converting a local foreign currency into U.S. dollars.

Transmittal letter: Cover communication outlining details of an export transaction and accompanying documentation.

Twenty-foot equivalent (TEU): Twenty-foot equivalent or standard measure for a twenty-foot ocean freight container. Two TEUs represent one forty-foot standard container.

Ullage: Measuring the amount of liquid or dry bulk freight in the hold of a vessel by measuring the height of the stow from the opening on deck.

Uniform Customs and Practice: International rules governing documentary collections.

United States Agency for International Development (USAID): A U.S. governmental agency that carries out assistance programs designed to help the people of certain lesser developed countries develop their human and economic resources, increase production capacities, and improve the quality of human life and promote the economic or potential stability in friendly countries.

Value-added tax (VAT): An indirect tax assessed on the increase in value of goods from the raw material stage through the production process to final consumption. The tax to processors or merchants is levied on the amount by which they have increased the value of items that were purchased by them for use or resale. This system is used in the European Community.

Warehouse receipt: A receipt given to signify goods have been received into a warehouse

Weight breaks: Discounts to freight charges are given as the total weight increases at various weight breaks: 50 pounds, 100 pounds, 500 pounds, etc.

Wharfage: Charges assessed for handling freight near a dock or pier.

With average: A marine insurance term meaning that shipment is protected for partial damage whenever the damage exceeds an agreed percentage.

Zone: Freight tariffs are often determined by certain geographic areas called zones.

Credits and Support Reference Material

American River International
American Management
Association
The Atlas Group
Bank of New York
Bureau of Export
Administration
Chemical Bank
Chubb
CIGNA
Council of Logistics
Management
Department of Commerce
Ex-Im Bank
Export America
Export Practitioner
Export/Import Procedures &
Documentation
The Exporter
FSI Global Logistics

International Chamber of Commerce
Journal of Commerce
Institute of Management and
Administration
Manufacturer's Hanover
Marine Midland Bank
NatWest
PriceWaterhouseCoopers
Rene Alston
RHDC
Sealand
Shipping Digest
Small Business Association
Unz & Co.
U.S. Customs
U.S. Council for International
Business
World Trade Institute
World Trade Magazine
World Trade Press

Key Telephone Numbers

Organization and Number

ABP International (212) 490-3999
Air Consolidators International (516) 872-1490/(310) 337-0181
American Institute of Marine Underwriters (212) 233-0550
American River International (1-800) 524-2493
Bureau of National Affairs, *International Trade Reporter,*
Export Reference Manual (202) 452-4200
BIS (202) 482-3332
Credit Report Latin America & World (718) 729-4906
D&B (201) 605-6455
Department of Agriculture (202) 720-1340
Department of Commerce (1-800) USA-Trade
Documents Instruction/Unz & Co. 800-631-3098
Econo Caribe (201) 656-4555
Ex-Im Bank (202) 566-2117
Foreign Credit Insurance Association (212) 306-5000
Graydon America (888) Graydon
Graydon America (908) 709-9499
IBB (202) 260-9052
ICC Publication Corporation Incorporated (212) 354-4480
INCO Terms publications by ICC Publications NYC (212) 354-4480
INCO Terms for Americans International Projects (419) 865-6201
International SOS Assistance (800) 523-8662
J.I. International (860) 589-1698
Kreller Business Information (800) 444-6361
Lin Henry (619) 222-5721
Mexico Desk Office (202) 482-2332
National Customs Brokers & Forwarders Association
(212) 432-0050
National Institute for World Trade (631) 582-9102
National Technical Information Service (NAFTA Facts)
(202) 482-4464
Owens Online (800) 745-4656
President of Great American Marine Division (212) 510-0115
RHDC (1-800) 468-3627
Rose Container Line (800) 444-3433
Sea Lion Shipping (908) 206-0056
SGS U.S. (212) 482-8700
Shippers Association (610) 458-0823
SOS Assistant Corporation Pennsylvania (215) 678-9000
Status Credit Report (292) 544-333
TIC 1 (800) USA-TRAD(E)
U.S. Council (212) 354-4480/(708) 381-1558
Uniform Rules of Contact Guarantees (212) 354-4480
U.S. Department of State (202) 647-1942
U.S. Small Business Administration (202) 205-6720
Veritas Group of Companies (203) 781-3800

Government Resources

Directory of Export Assistance Centers in the United States

Alabama
Birmingham (205) 731-1331

Alaska
Anchorage (907) 271-6237

Arizona
Phoenix (602) 640-2513
Tucson (520) 670-5540

California
Fresno (559) 325-1619
Inland Empire (909)
466-4134
Long Beach Export
Assistance Center (562)
980-4550
Downtown Los Angeles
(213) 894-8784
West Los Angeles (310)
235-7206
Monterey (831) 641-9850
Novato (415) 883-1966
Oakland (510) 273-7350
Orange County (949)
660-1688
Sacramento (916) 498-5155
Santa Clara (408) 970-4610
San Diego (619) 557-5395
San Francisco (415) 705-2300
San Jose U.S. Export
Assistance Center (408)
271-7300
Ventura County (805)
676-1573

Colorado
Denver U.S. Export Center
(303) 844-6623

Connecticut
Middletown (860) 638-6950

Delaware
Served by the Philadelphia
U.S. Export Assistance
Center

Florida
Clearwater (727) 893-3738
Miami U.S. Export
Assistance Center (305)
526-7425
Ft. Lauderdale North

Campus (954) 356-6640
Orlando (407) 648-6235
Tallahassee (850) 488-6469

Georgia
Atlanta U.S. Export
Assistance Center (404)
657-1900
Savannah (912) 652-4204

Hawaii
Honolulu (808) 522-8040

Idaho
Boise (208) 334-3857

Illinois
Chicago U.S. Export
Assistance Center (217)
466-5222
Peoria (309) 671-7815
Rockford (815) 987-8123

Indiana
Indianapolis (317) 582-2300

Iowa
Des Moines (515) 288-8614

Kansas
Wichita (316) 263-4067

Kentucky
Louisville (502) 582-5066
Somerset (606) 677-6160

Louisiana
Delta U.S. Export Assistance
Center (504) 589-6546
Shreveport (318) 676-3064

Maine
Portland (207) 541-7400

Maryland
Baltimore U.S. Export
Assistance Center (410)
962-4539

Massachusetts
Boston U.S. Export
Assistance Center (617)
424-5990
Marlborough (508) 624-6000

Michigan
Detroit U.S. Export
Assistance Center (313)

226-3650
Ann Arbor (734) 741-2430
Grand Rapids (616) 458-3564
Pontiac (248) 975-9600

Minnesota
Minneapolis U.S. Export
Assistance Center (612)
348-1638

Mississippi
Mississippi (601) 857-0128

Missouri
St. Louis U.S. Export
Assistance Center (314)
425-3302
Kansas City (816) 410-9201

Montana
Missoula (406) 243-2098

Nebraska
Omaha (402) 221-3664

Nevada
Reno (702) 784-5203

New Hampshire
Portsmouth (603) 334-6074

New Jersey
Trenton (609) 989-2100
Newark (973) 645-4682

New Mexico
New Mexico (505) 827-0350

New York
Buffalo (716) 551-4191
Harlem (212) 860-6200
Long Island (516) 739-1765
New York U.S. Export
Assistance/Westchester
(914) 682-6712

North Carolina
Carolinas U.S. Export
Assistance Center (704)
333-4886
Greensboro (336) 333-5345
Raleigh (919) 715-7373 x515

North Dakota
Served by the Minneapolis
U.S. Export Assistance
Center

Ohio
Cincinnati (513) 684-2944
Cleveland U.S. Export
Assistance Center (216)
522-4750
Columbus (614) 365-9510
Toledo (419) 241-0683

Oklahoma
Oklahoma City (405)
608-5302
Tulsa (918) 581-6263

Oregon
Eugene (541) 484-1314
Portland (503) 326-3001

Pennsylvania
Harrisburg (717) 221-4510
Philadelphia U.S. Export
Assistance Center (215)
597-6101
Pittsburgh (412) 395-5050

Puerto Rico
San Juan (787) 766-5555

Rhode Island
Providence (401) 528-5104

South Carolina
Charleston (843) 760-3794
Columbia (803) 765-5345
Upstate (864) 271-1976

South Dakota
Siouxland (605) 330-4264

Tennessee
Knoxville (865) 545-4637
Memphis (901) 323-1543
Nashville (615) 736-5161

Texas
Austin (512) 916-5939
Dallas U.S. Export Assistance
Center (214) 767-0542
Fort Worth (817) 212-2673
Houston (713) 718-3062
San Antonio (210) 228-9878

Utah
Salt Lake City (801) 524-5116

Vermont
Montpelier (802) 828-4508

Virginia
Highland Park (847) 681-8010
Richmond (804) 771-2246

Washington
Seattle U.S. Export Assistance
Center (206) 553-5615
Spokane (509) 353-2625
Tacoma (253) 593-6736

West Virginia
Charleston (304) 347-5123
Wheeling (304) 243-5493

Wisconsin
Milwaukee (414) 297-3473

Wyoming
Served by the Denver U.S.
Export Assistance Center

General Export Sample with Definitions and Instructions

Export Transaction File

Pro Forma Invoice

Upon receiving a purchase order from a buyer overseas, a "pro forma" invoice is usually then prepared and sent to the buyer for approval. The buyer will check the pro forma to make sure only those items on the purchase order are listed. The approximate weights and value should be listed as well as terms and conditions of sale. In some cases, the buyer needs the pro forma to obtain import permits or foreign exchange permits.

Once the buyer approves the pro forma invoice, the seller (or exporter) begins to ready the order. Upon having the order completed, a commercial invoice and packing list is usually prepared.

Commercial Invoice

This document is a "bill" that the seller prepares for the buyer. It should contain all pertinent details of the sale, including the shipping terms and other information such as:

- Name, address, and phone number of export/shipper
- Name and address of buyer, or "sold to" party
- Name, address, and phone number of "ship to" party, if other than "sold to" party
- Date
- Invoice number
- Buyer's purchase order number
- Terms of payment
- Terms of sale
- Quantity, description of goods, unit price, and extended prices
- Total value of goods (specify currency)
- Country of origin
- Signature of exporter
  The commercial invoice travels with the air waybill (or ocean bill of lading). Note: there may be certain countries that require additional specific information, so it is always best to check with the buyer for any documentation instructions.
  Some countries require that the commercial invoice be "legalized" by the local chamber of commerce and the specific country's consulate. See page 261 for an example of a "legalized" commercial invoice.

Packing List

This document describes the physical packaging of the goods. It should list the following information:

- Date
- "Ship to" party
- Buyer purchase order number
- How many packages
- Type of packing (e.g., crate, drum, fiberboard box, cases)
- Contents of packages
- Gross and net weight
- Dimensions (length _ width _ height)
- Any marks or labels on the packages

Although not all countries require this document, it is certainly instrumental with regard to filing a cargo insurance claim. It is recommended that every cargo movement be accompanied by a packing list.

Certificate of Origin

Some countries require goods to be shipped with a certificate of origin. This document certifies the country of manufacture, and the manufacturer's name and address. This document is signed by the exporter, notarized by an official notary public, and usually is required to be certified by the local chamber of commerce.

Your freight forwarder can advise if your consignment needs a certificate of origin, but it is always recommended that the exporter check with the buyer for a list of all documents required to enable customs clearance in the country of destination.

When shipping between North America (Canada, Mexico, and the United States), there is a specific certificate of origin called North American Free Trade Agreement (NAFTA) that may be filled out by the manufacturer, or the seller if he has intimate knowledge of the product composition. This document allows preferential duty rates to be applied to the shipment for goods qualifying under the applicable NAFTA rules of origin.

Air Waybill

This document is a bill of lading for air transportation. It identifies the pieces, weight, commodity, shipper, and consignee.

This document must be tendered to the airline with the cargo. It also serves as a receipt of tender.

Electronic Export Information (EEI)—

This document is only required when:

a. Goods are valued at $2500.00 or more. (Exports from Canada do not require an EEI.)

b. Goods are licensable by State or Commerce department.

The main function of this document is to compile census information regarding trade and exports from the United States.

Insurance Certificate

Insurance certificates are used as evidence that the shipment has proper coverage. The standard is to insure for 110 percent of the cost-insurancefreight (CIF) value. This certificate is not always required so it is best to check the conditions and terms of sale and to see who the responsible party is.

Straight Bill of Lading Form

This document is used as a receipt of carriage for inland freight from the origin point to the airport or port of departure or the consolidation warehouse.

It lists the pieces, weight, and a short description of the goods.

Whoever is receiving goods against this inland freight form should always check the cargo they are receiving and sign any exceptions such as broken seals, crushed corners, tear in boxes etc

Ocean Bill of Lading

This document is issued by the ocean freight carrier as evidence that they acknowledge receipt of your goods and that they agree to transport it to the destination that is indicated and becomes the contract and agreement of carriage between the exporter and the carrier.

Quality Certificate

This document is used as evidence that the product complies with all U.S. Food and Drug Regulations, that it is offered for sale in the United States, and that it is fit for human consumption. Some products require more specific information regarding how the processing was done, etc.

It cannot be stressed enough that you should always check with the buyer for their country's requirements.

Export License

There are certain commodities that cannot be exported from the United States without having prior authorization by the U.S. Department of State.

The Bureau of Industry & Security and the Department of State issue licenses for dual use items and items for military enduse as well as technology for these items.

Airfreight Export
(Cash Against Documents)

020	JFK 1234 5678		MAWB# 020 1234 5678

Shipper's Name and Address	Shipper's Account Number

AMANDA RICARDO PET SERVICES INC.
1322 ORCHID CIRCLE
BELLPORT , NY 11713

Air Waybill LUFTHANSA CARGO AG
Issued by LANGER KORNWEG 34I
D-65451 KELSTERBACH

Copies 1, 2 and 3 of this Air Waybill are originals and have the same validity.

Consignee's Name and Address	Consignee's Account Number

SLOAN KEATING GMBH
AM WEIGER 7 STRASSE
65452 FRANKFURT GERMANY
FRANKFURT

It is agreed that the goods described herein are accepted in apparent good order and condition (except as noted) for carriage SUBJECT TO THE CONDITIONS OF CONTRACT ON THE REVERSE HEREOF. ALL GOODS MAY BE CARRIED BY ANY OTHER MEANS INCLUDING ROAD OR ANY OTHER CARRIER UNLESS SPECIFIC CONTRARY INSTRUCTIONS ARE GIVEN HEREON BY THE SHIPPER, AND SHIPPER AGREES THAT THE SHIPMENT MAY BE CARRIED VIA INTERMEDIATE STOPPING PLACES WHICH THE CARRIER DEEMS APPROPRIATE. THE SHIPPER'S ATTENTION IS DRAWN TO THE NOTICE CONCERNING CARRIER'S LIMITATION OF LIABILITY. Shipper may increase such limitation of liability by declaring a higher value for carriage and paying a supplemental charge if required.

Issuing Carrier's Agent Name and City	Accounting Information

AMERICAN RIVER LOGISTICS, LTD.
1229 Old Walt Whitman Road
Melville, NY 11747   Account No.

NO SED REQUIRED AES
113145116-SAMPLE1

Agents IATA Code
01-1-9112/0011

Airport of Departure (Addr. of First Carrier) and Requested Routing		Reference Number		Optional Shipping Information

FRANKFURT

To	By First Carrier	Routing and Destination	to	by	to	by	Currency	CHGS Code	WT/VAL PPD COLL	Other PPD COLL	Declared Value for Carriage	Declared Value for Customs
FRA	LH						US$		X	X	N.V.D.	N.V.D.

Airport of Destination	Requested Flight/Date	Amount of Insurance	INSURANCE - If carrier offers insurance, and such insurance is requested in accordance with the conditions thereof, indicate amount to be insured in figures in box marked "Amount of Insurance".
FRANKFURT	020/6	NIL	

Handling Information

NOTIFY: NATIONAL BANK OF FRANKFURT
FRANKFURT BRANCH 0123451?2345

These commodities, technology or software were exported from the U.S. in accordance with the Export Administration Regulations. Ultimate destination GERMANY

Diversion contrary to
U.S. law prohibited.

SCI

No. of Pieces RCP	Gross Weight	kg lb	Rate Class / Commodity Item No.	Chargeable Weight	Rate / Charge	Total	Nature and Quantity of Goods (incl. Dimensions or Volume)
10	235 KG			235 KG	2.25	528.75	10 BOXES: DOG HARNESSES AND PET TOYS ORDER #122 INVOICE #3353 **CASH AGAINST DOCUMENTS**
10	235 KG					528.75	

Prepaid	Weight Charge	Collect	Other Charges
	528.75		

Valuation Charge

Tax

Total Other Charges Due Agent

Shipper certifies that the particulars on the face hereof are correct and that insofar as any part of the consignment contains dangerous goods, such part is properly described by name and is in proper condition for carriage by air according to the applicable Dangerous Goods Regulations.

Total Other Charges Due Carrier

AMERICAN RIVER LOGISTICS, LTD
Joseph Pisano   as agent for shipper
Signature of Shipper or his Agent

Total Prepaid	Total Collect
558.75	

Currency Conversion Rates	CC Charges in Dest. Currency

06/06/03   AMERICAN RIVER LOGISTICS, LTD
Joseph Pisano JFK   , as agent for carrier
Executed on (date)   at (place)   Signature of Issuing Carrier or his Agent

For Carriers Use only at Destination	Charges at Destination	Total Collect Charges

APPERSON F7333 (11/02)   ORIGINAL 3 (FOR CONSIGNEE)   MAWB# 020 1234 5678

U.S. DEPARTMENT OF COMMERCE — U.S. CENSUS BUREAU – Economics and Statistics Administration — BUREAU OF EXPORT ADMINISTRATION

FORM **7525-V** (7-25-2000) **SHIPPER'S EXPORT DECLARATION** OMB No. 0607-0152

1a. U.S. PRINCIPAL PARTY IN INTEREST (USPPI) *(Complete name and address)*
Amanda Ricardo Pet Services Inc.
1322 Orchid Circle
Bellport, New York

ZIP CODE 11713	**2.** DATE OF EXPORTATION 6/6/03

3. TRANSPORTATION REFERENCE NO.
020-1234-5678

b. USPPI EIN (IRS) OR ID NO.
90-7649813

c. PARTIES TO TRANSACTION
__ Related XX Non-related

4a. ULTIMATE CONSIGNEE *(Complete name and address)*
Sloan Keating GMBH
AM Weiger 7 Strasse _ _ _ _ _ _ _ _ _
b. INTERMEDIATE CONSIGNEE *(Complete name and address)*
65452 Frankfurt, Germany

5. FORWARDING AGENT *(Complete name and address)*
American River Intl.
1229 Old Walt Whitman Road
Melville, NY 11747

6. POINT (STATE) OF ORIGIN OR FTZ NO.
New York

7. COUNTRY OF ULTIMATE DESTINATION
Germany

8. LOADING PIER *(Vessel only)*

9. METHOD OF TRANSPORTATION *(Specify)*
Air

14. CARRIER IDENTIFICATION CODE
LH

15. SHIPMENT REFERENCE NO.
Sample 1

10. EXPORTING CARRIER
Lufthansa

11. PORT OF EXPORT
JFK, New YHrk

16. ENTRY NUMBER

17. HAZARDOUS MATERIALS
Yes XXX No

12. PORT OF UNLOADING *(Vessel and air only)*
Frankfurt

13. CONTAINERIZED *(Vessel only)*
Yes | No

18. IN BOND CODE

19. ROUTED EXPORT TRANSACTION
__ Yes XXX No

20. SCHEDULE B DESCRIPTION OF COMMODITIES *(Use columns 22–24)*

D/F or M (21)	SCHEDULE B NUMBER (22)	QUANTITY – SCHEDULE B UNIT(S) (23)	SHIPPING WEIGHT (Kilograms) (24)	VIN/PRODUCT NUMBER/ VEHICLE TITLE NUMBER (25)	VALUE (U.S. dollars, omit cents) (Selling price or cost if not sold) (26)
D	4201.0030.00 DOG LEASHES, HARNESSES, COLLARS AND SIMILAR DOG EQUIPMENT	x	200 kgs		$ 2763

27. LICENSE NO./LICENSE EXCEPTION SYMBOL/AUTHORIZATION
NLR

28. ECCN *(When required)*

29. Duly authorized officer or employee
Amanda Ricardo

The USPPI authorizes the forwarder named above to act as forwarding agent for export control and customs purposes.

30. I certify that all statements made and all information contained herein are true and correct and that I have read and understand the instructions for preparation of this document, set forth in the **"Correct Way to Fill Out the Shipper's Export Declaration."** I understand that civil and criminal penalties, including forfeiture and sale, may be imposed for making false or fraudulent statements herein, failing to provide the requested information or for violation of U.S. laws on exportation (13 U.S.C. Sec. 305; 22 U.S.C. Sec. 401; 18 U.S.C. Sec. 1001; 50 U.S.C. App. 2410).

Signature *Kelly Kae*
as agent for Amanda Ricardo

Confidential – For use solely for official purposes authorized by the Secretary of Commerce (13 U.S.C. 301 (g)).

Export shipments are subject to inspection by U.S. Customs Service and/or Office of Export Enforcement.

6/6/03

31. AUTHENTICATION *(When required)*

Telephone No. *(Include Area Code)*
800-524-2493

E-mail address
kelly@worldest.com

This form may be printed by private parties provided it conforms to the official form. For sale by the Superintendent of Documents, Government Printing Office, Washington, DC 20402, and local Customs District Directors. The **"Correct Way to Fill Out the Shipper's Export Declaration"** is available from the U.S. Census Bureau, Washington, DC 20233.

Amanda Ricardo Pet Services Inc.
1322 Orchid Circle
Bellport, New York 11713
Tel: (631)555-1054 Fax: (631)555-1055

Invoice No.   **3353**

INVOICE

Customer

Name	Sloan Keating GMBH		Date	6/6/2003
Address	AM Weiher 7, 65452 Frankfurt Germany		Order No.	122
City	Frankfurt Country DE		Rep	
Phone	(49)234500900		CIF	Frankfurt Airport

Qty	Description	Unit Price	TOTAL
50	Dog Harness (Size Large) #2355	$22.50	$1,125.00
25	Dog Harness (Size Medium) #2365	$18.50	$462.50
55	Dog Harness (Size Small) #2375	$15.00	$825.00
25	Dog Harness (Size Extra Small) #2385	$14.00	$350.00
50	Pet Toys (Assorted Sizes) #2395	$4.50	$225.00

These commodities, technology or software were
exported from the United States in accordance with the
Export Administration Regulations. Diversion contrary
to U.S. law prohibited.

Goods made in the U.S.

SubTotal	$2,987.50
Shipping & Handling	
Taxes State	
TOTAL	$2,987.50

Payment Details

◉ Cash against Documents
○
○

Customer Order #122
Ship Via Airfreight

Office Use Only

Amanda Ricardo Pet Services Inc.
1322 Orchid Circle
Bellport, New York 11713
631-555-1054

PACKING LIST

Sold to:

Sloan Keating GMBH
AM Weiher 7
Frankfurt Germany 65452
(49)234500900

Quantity	Description	Weight	Style No.
50	Dog Harness (lg)	75 kgs	#2355
25	Dog Harness (med)	50 kgs	#2365
55	Dog Harness (small)	40 kgs	#2375
25	Dog Harness (extra small)	35 kgs	#2385
50	Pet Toys	35 kgs	#2395

Packed in ten (10) Cartons

Shipment by
Airfreight

Terms of Payment
Cash Against Documents

Country of Origin
U.S.A.

CERTIFICATE OF ORIGIN for general use and for the following countries

ARGENTINA AUSTRIA BRAZIL COLOMBIA CYPRUS ECUADOR EGYPT ERITREA GERMANY (Western)
GREECE INDIA IRAN ITALY KUWAIT LIBYA NETHERLANDS PAKISTAN SAUDI ARABIA VIET-NAM

The undersigned KELLY RAIA, AS AGENT
                          (Owner or Agent, or DC)

for AMANDA RICARDO PET SERVICES INC., 1322 ORCHID CIRCLE, BELLPORT , NY 11713,,   declares
                          (Name and Address of Shipper)

that the following mentioned goods shipped on S/S   LUFTHANSA CARGO AG   020 1234 5678
                                                              (Name of Ship)

on the date of   06/06/2003   consigned to SLOAN KEATING GMBH, AM WEIGER 7 STRASSE

65452 FRANKFURT GERMANY FRANKFURT ,   are the product of the United States of America.

| MARKS AND NUMBERS | NO. OF PKGS., BOXES OR CASES | WEIGHT IN KILOS | | DESCRIPTION |
		GROSS	NET	
ADDR:	10	215	235	DOG HARNESS & PET TOYS
				CERTIFIED TRUE AND CORRECT

Sworn before me

this _____ 6th ____ day of JUNE _____ 20 03

Dated at   NEW YORK   on the   6th day of JUNE, 2003

Kelly Raia
(Signature of Owner or Agent)

The _____ , a recognized Chamber of Commerce under the laws of the State of

_____ , has examined the manufacturer's invoice or shipper's affidavit concerning the origin of the merchandise and,
according to the best of its knowledge and belief, finds that the products named originated in the United States of North America.

Secretary _____

U.S. $ 2987.50   June 6   2 003

Cash against documents   of this **FIRST** of Exchange (Second unpaid)

Pay to the Order of AMANDA RICARDO PET SERVICES INC.

--Two thousand nine hundred and eighty-seven/50/100 ---   **United States Dollars**

for Value received and charge the same to account of

To Sloan Keating GMBH

AM Weiger 7 Strasse, 65452 Frankfurt, Germany   Kelly Raia

No. Invoice #3353, Order #122

Amanda Ricardo Pet Services Inc.
Authorized Signature

FRANKFURT BANK
AM AULD 35, 65452, FRANKFURT, GERMANY   June 6, 2003
                                                                    Date

Gentlemen: ☒ for collection,

We enclose Draft Number Sample 1 _____ and documents below   ☐ for

                                                        ☐ for payment/negotiation under L/C

BILLS OF LADING	B/L COPY	COMM. INV.	INS. CTF.	CTF. ORIG.	CONS. INV.	PKNG. LIST	WGT. CTF.	OTHER DOCUMENTS
1 awb	1 awb	1	-	x	-	-	-	

Please handle in accordance with instructions marked "X"

☐ Deliver all documents in one mailing.

☐ Deliver documents in two mailings.

☐ Deliver documents against payment if sight draft, or acceptance if time draft.

☐ All charges for account of drawee.

☐ Do not waive charges.

☐ Protest for non-payment / non-acceptance

☐ Do not protest.

☐ Present on arrival of goods.

☐ Advise non-payment / non-acceptance by airmail / cable giving reasons.

☐ Advise payment / acceptance by airmail / cable

IN CASE OF NEED refer to:

Name Kelly Raia, American River Intl.

Address 1229 Old Walt Whitman Road, Melville, NY 11747

who is empowered by us:

a ☐ To act fully on our behalf, i.e., authorize reductions; extensions, free delivery, waiving of protest, etc.

b ☒ To assist in obtaining acceptance or payment of draft, as drawn, but not to alter its terms in any way.

OTHER INSTRUCTIONS:

Please remit proceeds direction to:
Amanda Ricardo Pet Services Inc.
Cash Against Documents

Please refer all questions concerning this collection to:

☐ Shipper   Kelly Raia

☒ Freight Forwarder:

American River International
1229 Old Walt Whitman Road   Amanda Ricardo Pet Services Inc.
Melville, New York 11747
(800)524-2493   Authorized Signature

Form 20-015 Printed and Sold by *UNICO* 700 Central Ave., New Providence, NJ 07974 ● (800) 631-3098

Airfreight Export
(Hazardous Materials)

179 JFK 8765 4321

Shipper's Name and Address	Shipper's Account Number

MAWB# 179 8765 4321

Not Negotiable

Air Waybill AIR GLOBAL INTERNATIONAL

Issued by P.O BOX 02-5114

DETONATION BY FRANK
275 BROOKLYN AVENUE
MASSAPEQUA , NY 11794

MIAMI, FL 33102-5114

Copies 1, 2 and 3 of this Air Waybill are originals and have the same validity.

Consignee's Name and Address	Consignee's Account Number

It is agreed that the goods described herein are accepted in apparent good order and condition (except as noted) for carriage SUBJECT TO THE CONDITIONS OF CONTRACT ON THE REVERSE HEREOF. ALL GOODS MAY BE CARRIED BY ANY OTHER MEANS INCLUDING ROAD OR ANY OTHER CARRIER UNLESS SPECIFIC CONTRARY INSTRUCTIONS ARE GIVEN HEREON BY THE SHIPPER, AND SHIPPER AGREES THAT THE SHIPMENT MAY BE CARRIED VIA INTERMEDIATE STOPPING PLACES WHICH THE CARRIER DEEMS APPROPRIATE. THE SHIPPER'S ATTENTION IS DRAWN TO THE NOTICE CONCERNING CARRIER'S LIMITATION OF LIABILITY. Shipper may increase such limitation of liability by declaring a higher value for carriage and paying a supplemental charge if required.

CONNIE'S CANISTERS INTERNATIONAL
6835 CALLE GRANDE

SAN JUAN , 22355

Issuing Carrier's Agent Name and City

Accounting Information

AMERICAN RIVER LOGISTICS, LTD.
1229 Old Walt Whitman Road
Melville, NY 11747   Account No.

NO SED REQUIRED AES
TY3T45116 SAMPLE10

01-1-9112/0011

Airport of Departure (Addr. of First Carrier) and Requested Routing

Reference Number	Optional Shipping Information

SAN JUAN PR

To	By First Carrier	Routing and Destination	to	by	to	by	Currency	CHGS Code	WT/VAL		Other		Declared Value for Carriage	Declared Value for Customs
									PPD	COLL	PPD	COLL		
SJU	5Y						US$		X	Y			N.V.D.	N.V.D.

Airport of Destination	Requested Flight/Date	Amount of Insurance	INSURANCE - If carrier offers insurance, and such insurance is requested in accordance with the conditions thereof, indicate amount to be insured in figures in box marked "Amount of Insurance".
SAN JUAN, PR	601/16	NIL	

Handling Information

DANGEROUS GOODS AS PER ATTACHED SHIPPERS DECLARATION
CARGO AIRCRAFT ONLY

These commodities, technology or software were exported from the United States in accordance with the Export Administration Regulations. Ultimate destination USA

Diversion contrary to U.S. law prohibited.

SCI

No. of Pieces RCP	Gross Weight	kg lb	Rate Class / Commodity Item No.	Chargeable Weight	Rate / Charge	Total	Nature and Quantity of Goods (Incl. Dimensions or Volume)
300	725 KG			725	KG 3.00	2175.00	DETONATOR ASSEMBLIES
							1.4B, UN 0361, PG II
							CUSTOMER REF #4321
300	725 KG					2175.00	

Prepaid	Weight Charge	Collect	Other Charges
	2175.00		

Valuation Charge

2175.00

Tax

Total Other Charges Due Agent

Shipper certifies that the particulars on the face hereof are correct and that insofar as any part of the consignment contains dangerous goods, such part is properly described by name and is in proper condition for carriage by air according to the applicable Dangerous Goods Regulations.

Total Other Charges Due Carrier

2175.00

Joseph Pisano   AMERICAN RIVER LOGISTICS, LTD
Signature of Shipper or his Agent   as agent for shipper

Total Prepaid	Total Collect

Currency Conversion Rates	CC Charges in Dest. Currency

06/16/03   AMERICAN RIVER LOGISTICS, LTD
Joseph Pisano JFK   , as agent for carrier
Executed on (date)   at (place)   Signature of Issuing Carrier or its Agent

For Carriers Use only at Destination	Charges at Destination	Total Collect Charges

APPERSON F7333 (11/02)

MAWBA 179 8765 4321

Detonation by Frank Inc.

275 Brooklyn Avenue
Massapequa, New York 11794
631-555-1212 fax 631-555-1213

Invoice No.   **1234**

INVOICE

Customer

Name	Connie's Canisters International
Address	6835 Calle Grande
City	San Juan Country Puerto Rico
Phone	22-355

Date	6/16/2003
Order No.	4321
Rep	
CIF	San Juan

Qty	Description	Unit Price	TOTAL
3000	Assembly #2445 for Detonators Packed in 300 cases, 10 units per case Class 1.4B, UN0361, PG II Cargo Aircraft Only	$5.00	$15,000.00
1	Inland Freight	$700.00	$700.00
1	Airfreight	$2,800.00	$2,800.00
1	Insurance	$155.00	$155.00
	These commodities, technology or software were exported from the United States in accordance with the Export Administration Regulations. Diversion contrary to U.S. law prohibited. Goods made in the U.S.A.		

SubTotal	$18,655.00
Shipping & Handling	
Taxes	
TOTAL	$18,655.00

Payment Details

◉ Net 90 Days
○
○

Customer Order #4321
Ship Via Airfreight

Office Use Only

U.S. DEPARTMENT OF COMMERCE — U.S. CENSUS BUREAU – Economics and Statistics Administration — BUREAU OF EXPORT ADMINISTRATION

FORM **7525-V** (7-25-2000)

SHIPPER'S EXPORT DECLARATION

OMB No. 0607-0152

1a. U.S. PRINCIPAL PARTY IN INTEREST (USPPI) *(Complete name and address)*
DETONATION BY FRANK
275 BROOKLYN AVENUE
MASSAPEQUA, NEW YORK   ZIP CODE 11794

2. DATE OF EXPORTATION 6/16/03

3. TRANSPORTATION REFERENCE NO. 179-8765-4321

b. USPPI EIN (IRS) OR ID NO. 34-1234567

c. PARTIES TO TRANSACTION ___ Related   XX Non-related

4a. ULTIMATE CONSIGNEE *(Complete name and address)*
CONNIE'S CANISTERS INTERNATIONAL
6835 CALLE GRANDE

b. INTERMEDIATE CONSIGNEE *(Complete name and address)*
PUERTO RICO, SAN JUAN 22355

5. FORWARDING AGENT *(Complete name and address)*
AMERICAN RIVER LOGISTICS LTD.
1229 OLD WALT WHITMAN ROAD
MELVILLE, NEW YORK 11747

6. POINT (STATE) OF ORIGIN OR FTZ NO. NEW YORK

7. COUNTRY OF ULTIMATE DESTINATION PUERTO RICO

8. LOADING PIER *(Vessel only)* JFK, NEW YORK

9. METHOD OF TRANSPORTATION *(Specify)* AIR

14. CARRIER IDENTIFICATION CODE 5Y

15. SHIPMENT REFERENCE NO. SAMPLE 10

10. EXPORTING CARRIER AIR GLOBAL

11. PORT OF EXPORT JFK, NEW YORK

16. ENTRY NUMBER

17. HAZARDOUS MATERIALS XX Yes   ___ No

12. PORT OF UNLOADING *(Vessel and air only)* SAN JUAN

13. CONTAINERIZED *(Vessel only)* Yes | No

18. IN BOND CODE

19. ROUTED EXPORT TRANSACTION ___ Yes   XX No

20. SCHEDULE B DESCRIPTION OF COMMODITIES *(Use columns 22–24)*

D/F or M (21)	SCHEDULE B NUMBER (22)	QUANTITY – SCHEDULE B UNIT(S) (23)	SHIPPING WEIGHT (Kilograms) (24)	VIN/PRODUCT NUMBER/ VEHICLE TITLE NUMBER (25)	VALUE (U.S. dollars, omit cents) (Selling price or cost if not sold) (26)
D	3603.0000.00	600 ths	725		$15000.00

27. LICENSE NO./LICENSE EXCEPTION SYMBOL/AUTHORIZATION NLR

28. ECCN *(When required)*

29. Duly authorized officer or employee R. Rala

The USPPI authorizes the forwarder named above to act as forwarding agent for export control and customs purposes.

30. I certify that all statements made and all information contained herein are true and correct and that I have read and understand the instructions for preparation of this document, set forth in the "Correct Way to Fill Out the Shipper's Export Declaration." I understand that civil and criminal penalties, including forfeiture and sale, may be imposed for making false or fraudulent statements herein, failing to provide the requested information or for violation of U.S. laws on exportation (13 U.S.C. Sec. 305; 22 U.S.C. Sec. 401; 18 U.S.C. Sec. 1001; 50 U.S.C. App. 2410).

Signature

Title as agent for

Date 6/16/03

Telephone No. *(include Area Code)* 631-555-1212

Confidential – For use solely for official purposes authorized by the Secretary of Commerce (13 U.S.C. 301 (g)).

Export shipments are subject to inspection by U.S. Customs Service and/or Office of Export Enforcement.

31. AUTHENTICATION *(When required)*

E-mail address kelly@worldest.com

This form may be printed by private parties provided it conforms to the official form. For sale by the Superintendent of Documents, Government Printing Office, Washington, DC 20402, and local Customs District Directors. The "Correct Way to Fill Out the Shipper's Export Declaration" is available from the U.S. Census Bureau, Washington, DC 20233.

SHIPPER'S DECLARATION FOR DANGEROUS GOODS   (Provide at least two copies to the airline.)

Shipper

DETONATION BY FRANK
275 BROOKLYN AVENUE
MASSAPEQUA, NEW YORK   11794

Air Waybill No.

Page **1** of **1**   Pages

Shipper's Reference Number #1234
  (optional)

Consignee

CONNIE'S CANISTERS INTERNATIONAL
6835 CALLE GRANDE
SAN JUAN, PUERTO RICO 22-355

Two completed and signed copies of this Declaration must be handed to the operator

TRANSPORT DETAILS

This shipment is within the limitations prescribed for:
(delete non-applicable)

~~PASSENGER AND CARGO AIRCRAFT~~	CARGO AIRCRAFT ONLY

Airport of Departure

JFK, NEW YORK

Airport of Destination: **SAN JUAN, PR**

WARNING

Failure to comply in all respects with the applicable Dangerous Goods Regulations may be in breach of the applicable law, subject to legal penalties. This Declaration must not, in any circumstances, be completed and/or signed by a consolidator, a forwarder or an IATA cargo agent.

Shipment type: (delete non-applicable)
NON-RADIOACTIVE ~~RADIOACTIVE~~

NATURE AND QUANTITY OF DANGEROUS GOODS (see Subsections 6.6 and 8.1 of IATA Dangerous Goods Regulations)

Dangerous Goods Identification

Proper Shipping Name	Class or Division	UN or ID No.	Packing Group	Subsidiary Risk	Quantity and Type of packing	Packing Inst.	Authorization
DETONATOR ASSEMBLIES, NON_ELECTRIC	1.4B	UN0361	II		60 FIBREBOARD BOXES X 5.21 KG/BX NET WT, 5.66 KG/BX GROSS WT, NET EXPLOSIVE CONTENT PER BOX: 0.05 KG	131	XYZ

Additional Handling Information ALL PREPARED IN ACCORDANCE WITH I.C.A.O.
SHIPPED FROM
DETONATION BY FRANK
275 BROOKLYN AVENUE
MASSAPEQUA, NEW YORK 11794

IN USA: 1-800-424-9300
24 hr. Emergency Contact Tel. No. INTERNATIONAL: 01-703-527-3887

I hereby declare that the contents of this consignment are fully and accurately described above by the proper shipping name and are classified, packaged, marked and labelled/placarded, and are in all respects in proper condition for transport according to applicable international and national governmental regulations.

Name/Title of Signatory
FRANK IEEE
Place and Date
MASSAPEQUA, NY 6/15/03
Signature
(see warning above)

Style F83R Labelmaster, An American Labelmark Co., Chicago, IL 60846 (800) 621-5808

Airfreight Export
(Department of State License)

Shipper's Name and Address 5555 7777	Shipper's Account Number	Not Negotiable **Air Waybill** Issued by	MAWB# 000 5555 7177 FENWICK NATIONAL AIRLINES

COME FLY WITH ME SERVICES LTD.
2366 SMITHFIELD CORNER
SMITHFIELD , RI 98788

Copies 1, 2 and 3 of this Air Waybill are originals and have the same validity.

Consignee's Name and Address	Consignee's Account Number

FENWICK AIR NATIONAL GUARD
AVENUE OF THE DUKES
FENWICK CITY , FENWICK

It is agreed that the goods described herein are accepted in apparent good order and condition (except as noted) for carriage SUBJECT TO THE CONDITIONS OF CONTRACT ON THE REVERSE HEREOF. ALL GOODS MAY BE CARRIED BY ANY OTHER MEANS INCLUDING ROAD OR ANY OTHER CARRIER UNLESS SPECIFIC CONTRARY INSTRUCTIONS ARE GIVEN HEREON BY THE SHIPPER, AND SHIPPER AGREES THAT THE SHIPMENT MAY BE CARRIED VIA INTERMEDIATE STOPPING PLACES WHICH THE CARRIER DEEMS APPROPRIATE. THE SHIPPER'S ATTENTION IS DRAWN TO THE NOTICE CONCERNING CARRIER'S LIMITATION OF LIABILITY. Shipper may increase such limitation of liability by declaring a higher value for carriage and paying a supplemental charge if required.

Issuing Carrier's Agent Name and City	Accounting Information

AMERICAN RIVER LOGISTICS, LTD.
1229 Old Walt Whitman Road
Melville, NY 11747

Account No.

91-1-9112/9911

Airport of Departure (Addr. of First Carrier) and Requested Routing	Reference Number	Optional Shipping Information

JFK AIRPORT

To	By First Carrier Routing and Destination	to	by	to	by	Currency	CHGS Code	WT/VAL PPD COLL	Other PPD COLL	Declared Value for Carriage	Declared Value for Customs
FEN	NEV					US$		X	Y	N.V.D.	N.V.D.

Airport of Destination	Requested Flight/Date	Amount of Insurance
FENWICK INTERNATIO	928/20	NIL

INSURANCE - If carrier offers insurance, and such insurance is requested in accordance with the conditions thereof, indicate amount to be insured in figures in box marked "Amount of Insurance".

Handling Information

FREIGHT COLLECT

These commodities, technology or software were exported from the United States in accordance with the Export Administration Regulations. Ultimate destination FENWICK

Diversion contrary to U.S. law prohibited.

SCI

No. of Pieces RCP	Gross Weight	kg	Rate Class Commodity Item No.	Chargeable Weight	Rate Charge	Total	Nature and Quantity of Goods (Incl. Dimensions or Volume)
3	91 KG			91 KG	3.00	273.00	C 130 AIRCRAFT PARTS

These commodities are authorized by the US Government for export only to FENWICK for the use by FENWICK AIR NATIONAL GUARD. They may not be transferred, transshipped, on a non-continuous voyage or otherwise be disposed of in any other country, either in their original form or after being incorporated into other end-items, without the prior written approval of the U.S. Department of State.

DSP5
LICENSE #000111
EXPIRES 01/16/05

| 3 | 91 KG | | | | | 273.00 | |

Prepaid	Weight Charge	Collect	Other Charges
	Valuation Charge 273.00		
	Tax		
	Total Other Charges Due Agent		

Shipper certifies that the particulars on the face hereof are correct and that insofar as any part of the consignment contains dangerous goods, such part is properly described by name and is in proper condition for carriage by air according to the applicable Dangerous Goods Regulations.

Total Other Charges Due Carrier	

AMERICAN RIVER LOGISTICS, LTD
Joseph Pisano   as agent for shipper
Signature of Shipper or his Agent

Total Prepaid	Total Collect

Currency Conversion Rates	CC Charges in Dest. Currency 273.00

06/16/03   AMERICAN RIVER LOGISTICS, LTD
Joseph Pisano JFK   ,as agent for carrier
Executed on (date)   at (place)   Signature of Issuing Carrier or its Agent

For Carrier's Use only at Destination	Charges at Destination	Total Collect Charges

APPERSON F7333 (11/02)

ORIGINAL 3 FOR SHIP

MAWB# 000 5555 7177

Come Fly With Me Services Ltd.
2366 Smithfield Corner
Smithfield, Rhode Island 98788
415-999-0099 fax 415-999-0100

Invoice No.   **1234**

— *INVOICE* —

Customer

Name	Fenwick Air National Guard
Address	Avenue of the Dukes
City	Fenwick City Country Fenwick
Phone	

Date	6/16/2003
Order No.	999
Rep	
FCA	JFK Airport

Qty	Description	Unit Price	TOTAL
3	C-130 Aircraft Parts	$400.00	$1,200.00
	DSP 5, license #000111		
	These commodities are authorized by the U.S. government for export only to Fenwick, for use by the Fenwick Air National Guard. They may not be transferred, transhipped on a non-continuous voyage or otherwise be disposed of in any other country, either in their original form or after being incorporated into other end items without the prior written approval of the U.S. Department of State.		
	Goods made in the U.S.A.		

SubTotal	$1,200.00
Shipping & Handling	
Taxes	
TOTAL	$1,200.00

Payment Details

◉ Net 30 Days
○
○

Customer Order #999
Ship Via Airfreight

Office Use Only

U.S. DEPARTMENT OF COMMERCE — U.S. CENSUS BUREAU – Economics and Statistics Administration — BUREAU OF EXPORT ADMINISTRATION

FORM **7525-V** (7-25-2000)

SHIPPER'S EXPORT DECLARATION

OMB No. 0607-0152

1a. U.S. PRINCIPAL PARTY IN INTEREST (USPPI) *(Complete name and address)*
COME FLY WITH ME SERVICES LTD.
2366 SMITHFIELD CORNER
SMITHFIELD, RHODE ISLAND

ZIP CODE 98788

2. DATE OF EXPORTATION
6/20/03

3. TRANSPORTATION REFERENCE NO.
000-5555-7777

b. USPPI EIN (IRS) OR ID NO.
98-2345987

c. PARTIES TO TRANSACTION
___ Related   XXX Non-related

4a. ULTIMATE CONSIGNEE *(Complete name and address)*
FENWICK AIR NATIONAL GUARD
AVENUE OF THE DUKES

b. INTERMEDIATE CONSIGNEE *(Complete name and address)*
FENWICK CITY, FENWICK

5. FORWARDING AGENT *(Complete name and address)*
AMERICAN RIVER LOGISTICS LTD.
1229 OLD WALT WHITMAN ROAD
MELVILLE, NEW YORK   11747

6. POINT (STATE) OF ORIGIN OR FTZ NO.
RHODE ISLAND

7. COUNTRY OF ULTIMATE DESTINATION
FENWICK

8. LOADING PIER *(Vessel only)*

9. METHOD OF TRANSPORTATION *(Specify)*
AIR

14. CARRIER IDENTIFICATION CODE
FEN

15. SHIPMENT REFERENCE NO.
SAMPLE 110

10. EXPORTING CARRIER
FENWICK

11. PORT OF EXPORT
JFK, NEW YORK

16. ENTRY NUMBER

17. HAZARDOUS MATERIALS
Yes ___   XXX No

12. PORT OF UNLOADING *(Vessel and air only)*
FENWICK CITY

13. CONTAINERIZED *(Vessel only)*
Yes | No

18. IN BOND CODE

19. ROUTED EXPORT TRANSACTION
___ Yes   XXX No

20. SCHEDULE B DESCRIPTION OF COMMODITIES *(Use columns 22–24)*

D/F or M (21)	SCHEDULE B NUMBER (22)	QUANTITY – SCHEDULE B UNIT(S) (23)	SHIPPING WEIGHT *(Kilograms)* (24)	VIN/PRODUCT NUMBER/ VEHICLE TITLE NUMBER (25)	VALUE (U.S. dollars, omit cents) *(Selling price or cost if not sold)* (26)
D	8803.30.0050	x	100kgs		$1200.00
	C130 AIRCRAFT PARTS				

THESE COMMODITIES ARE AUTHORIZED BY THE U.S. GOVERNMENT FOR EXPORT ONLY TO FENWICK FOR THE USE BY FENWICK AIR NATIONAL GUARD. THEY MAY NOT BE TRANSFERRED, TRANSSHIPPED, ON A NON-CONTINUOUS VOYAGE OR OTHERWISE BE DISPOSED OF IN ANY OTHER COUNTRY, EITHER IN THEIR ORIGINAL FORM OR AFTER BEING INCORPORATED INTO OTHER END-ITEMS, WITHOUT THE PRIOR WRITTEN APPROVAL OF THE U.S. DEPARTMENT OF STATE.

27. LICENSE NO./LICENSE EXCEPTION SYMBOL/AUTHORIZATION
DSP 5, LICENSE #000111 EXP:1/16/2003

28. ECCN *(When required)*

29. Duly authorized officer or employee
The USPPI authorizes the forwarder named above to act as forwarding agent for export control and customs purposes.

30. I certify that all statements made and all information contained herein are true and correct and that I have read and understand the instructions for preparation of this document, set forth in the "Correct Way to Fill Out the Shipper's Export Declaration." I understand that civil and criminal penalties, including forfeiture and sale, may be imposed for making false or fraudulent statements herein, failing to provide the requested information or for violation of U.S. laws on exportation (13 U.S.C. Sec. 305; 22 U.S.C. Sec. 401; 18 U.S.C. Sec. 1001; 50 U.S.C. App. 2410).

Signature

Title as agent for

Date 6/16/03

Telephone No. *(Include Area Code)* 513-999-9999

Confidential – For use solely for official purposes authorized by the Secretary of Commerce (13 U.S.C. 301 (g)).

Export shipments are subject to inspection by U.S. Customs Service and/or Office of Export Enforcement.

31. AUTHENTICATION *(When required)*

E-mail address kelly@worldest.com

This form may be printed by private parties provided it conforms to the official form. For sale by the Superintendent of Documents, Government Printing Office, Washington, DC 20402, and local Customs District Directors. The "Correct Way to Fill Out the Shipper's Export Declaration" is available from the U.S. Census Bureau, Washington, DC 20233.

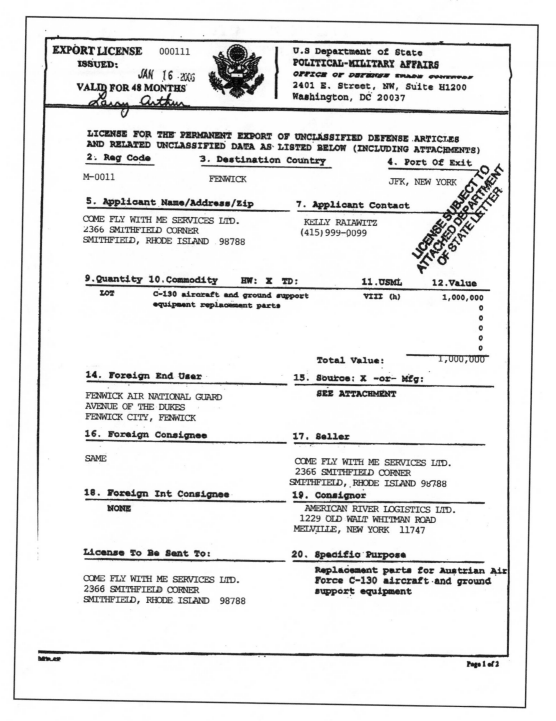

EXPORT LICENSE 000111

ISSUED: JAN 16 2005

VALID FOR 48 MONTHS
Larry Arthur

U.S Department of State
POLITICAL-MILITARY AFFAIRS
OFFICE OF DEFENSE TRADE CONTROLS
2401 E. Street, NW, Suite H1200
Washington, DC 20037

LICENSE FOR THE PERMANENT EXPORT OF UNCLASSIFIED DEFENSE ARTICLES
AND RELATED UNCLASSIFIED DATA AS LISTED BELOW (INCLUDING ATTACHMENTS)

2. Reg Code   **3. Destination Country**   **4. Port Of Exit**

M-0011   FENWICK   JFK, NEW YORK

LICENSE SUBJECT TO ATTACHED DEPARTMENT OF STATE LETTER

5. Applicant Name/Address/Zip   **7. Applicant Contact**

COME FLY WITH ME SERVICES LTD.
2366 SMITHFIELD CORNER
SMITHFIELD, RHODE ISLAND 98788

KELLY RAIAWITZ
(415) 999-0099

9. Quantity	10. Commodity HW: X TD:	11. USML	12. Value
LOT	C-130 aircraft and ground support equipment replacement parts	VIII (h)	1,000,000
			0
			0
			0
			0
			0
	Total Value:		1,000,000

14. Foreign End User   **15. Source: X -or- Mfg:**

FENWICK AIR NATIONAL GUARD
AVENUE OF THE DUKES
FENWICK CITY, FENWICK

SEE ATTACHMENT

16. Foreign Consignee   **17. Seller**

SAME

COME FLY WITH ME SERVICES LTD.
2366 SMITHFIELD CORNER
SMITHFIELD, RHODE ISLAND 98788

18. Foreign Int Consignee   **19. Consignor**

NONE

AMERICAN RIVER LOGISTICS LTD.
1229 OLD WALT WHITMAN ROAD
MELVILLE, NEW YORK 11747

License To Be Sent To: **20. Specific Purpose**

COME FLY WITH ME SERVICES LTD.
2366 SMITHFIELD CORNER
SMITHFIELD, RHODE ISLAND 98788

Replacement parts for Austrian Air
Force C-130 aircraft and ground
support equipment

Truck Export
(NAFTA)

954672/028750

3-PART STOCK FORM NO. B-3876

STRAIGHT BILL OF LADING— SHORT FORM

ORIGINAL—NOT NEGOTIABLE

Shipper's No. _____3350_____

Carrier's Name: _____BESTWAY TRUCK_____

Carrier's No. _____EW #9988_____

RECEIVED, subject to the classifications and tariffs in effect on the date of the issue of this Bill of lading,

at _____BELLPORT, NEW YORK_____ (Date)._____06/16/03_____ 19____ FROM _____AMANDA RICARDO PET SERVICES INC._____

the property described below, in apparent good order, except as noted (contents and condition of contents of packages unknown), marked, consigned, and destined as shown below, which said company (the word company being understood throughout this contract as meaning any person or corporation in possession of the property under the contract) agrees to carry to its usual place of delivery at said destination, if on its own railroad, water line, highway route or routes, or within the territory of its highway operation, otherwise to deliver to another carrier on the route to said destination. It is mutually agreed, as to each carrier of all or any of said property over all or any portion of said route to destination, and as to each party at any time interested in all or any of said property, that every service to be performed hereunder shall be subject to all the terms and conditions of the Uniform Domestic Straight Bill of Lading set forth (1) in the Uniform Freight Classification in effect on the date hereof, if this is a rail or rail-water shipment, or (2) in the applicable motor carrier classification or tariff if this is a motor carrier shipment. Shipper hereby certifies that he is familiar with all the terms and conditions of the said bill of lading, including those on the back thereof, set forth in the classification or tariff which governs the transportation of this shipment, and the said terms and conditions are hereby agreed to by the shipper and accepted for himself and his assigns.

Consigned TO _____SLOAN KEATING CANADA, 1200 KEATING INDUSTRIAL PARK, TORONTO, CA_____

On Collect on Delivery Shipments, the letters "COD" must appear before consignee's name or as otherwise provided in Item 430, Sec. 1.

Destination _____TORONTO, CANADA_____ Street_____1200 KEATING INDUSTRIAL PARK_____ City_____

County_____ Delivery Address ★ _____SAME_____ State_____CANADA_____ Zip_____

Route_____

Delivering Carrier _____BESTWAY TRUCK_____ Car or Vehicle Initials and No._____

Collect on Delivery $_____ And Remit to_____

Subject to Section 7 of conditions, if this shipment is to be delivered to the consignee without recourse on the consignor, the consignor shall sign the following statement:

The carrier shall not make delivery of this shipment without payment of freight and all other lawful charges.

_____
(Signature of consignor.)

C. O. D. Charges to be.

Paid by

☐ Shipper   ☐ Consignee

If charges are to be prepaid, write or stamp here, "To be Prepaid."

PREPAID, BILL ARPS IN

Received $ _____ to apply in prepayment of the charges on the property described" hereon.

_____
Agent or Cashier

Per_____
(The signature here acknowledges only the amount prepaid.)

Charges Advanced:

$_____

No. Package	H.M.	Kind of Package, Description of Articles, Special Marks, and Exceptions	*Weight (Subject to Correction)	Class or Rate	Check Column
FIVE		(5) CASES DOG HARNESSES (#2365)	1275#	55	
		NOTIFY: SLOAN KEATING CANADA			
		1200 KEATING INDUSTRIAL PARK			
		TORONTO, CANADA			
		NO SED REQUIRED 15CFR30.58			

†The fibre containers used for this shipment conform to the specifications set forth in the box maker's certificate thereon, and all other requirements of Rule 41 of the Uniform Freight Classification and Rule 5 of the National Motor Freight Classification.

†Shipper's imprint in lieu of stamp; not a part of bill of lading approved by the Interstate Commerce Commission.

"If the shipment moves between two ports by a carrier by water, the law requires that the bill of lading shall state whether it is carrier's or shipper's weight.

NOTE — Where the rate is dependent on value, shippers are required to state specifically in writing the agreed or declared value of the property.

The agreed or declared value of the property is hereby specifically stated by the shipper to be not exceeding

_____ per _____

_____ Shipper, Per _____

Permanent post-office address of shipper.

_____ Agent

Per _____

Amanda Ricardo Pet Services Inc.
1322 Orchid Circle
Bellport, New York 11713
Tel: (631)555-1054 Fax: (631)555-1055

Invoiçe No.   3317

INVOICE

Customer		Date	6/16/2003
Name	Sloan Keating Canada	Order No.	082
Address	1200 Keating Industrial Park	Rep	
City	Toronto Country CA	FCA	Toronto
Phone	919-123-1234		

Qty	Description	Unit Price	TOTAL
255	Dog Harness (Size Medium) #2365	$18.50	$4,717.50
	These commodities, technology or software were exported from the United States in accordance with the Export Administration Regulations. Diversion contrary to U.S. law prohibited. Goods made in the U.S.		

	SubTotal	$4,717.50
	Shipping & Handling	
	Taxes	
	TOTAL	$4,717.50

Payment Details
● Net 30 days
○
○

Customer Order #082
Ship Via Bestway Truck

Office Use Only

DEPARTMENT OF THE TREASURY
UNITED STATES CUSTOMS SERVICE

OMB No. 1515-0204
See back of form for
Paperwork Reduction
Act Notice.

NORTH AMERICAN FREE TRADE AGREEMENT
CERTIFICATE OF ORIGIN

Please print or type   19 CFR 181.11, 181.22

1. EXPORTER NAME AND ADDRESS	2. BLANKET PERIOD (DD/MM/YY)
AMANDA RICARDO PET SERVICES INC. 1322 ORCHID CIRCLE, BELLPORT, NY 11713	01/01/03
TAX IDENTIFICATION NUMBER: 90-7649813	FROM 12/31/03 03/0 01/01/03
	TO 12/31/03
3. PRODUCER NAME AND ADDRESS SAME	4. IMPORTER NAME AND ADDRESS SLOAN KEATING CANADA 1200 KEATING INDUSTRIAL PARK, TORONTO CANADA
TAX IDENTIFICATION NUMBER:	TAX IDENTIFICATION NUMBER: 99-2345678

5. DESCRIPTION OF GOOD(S)	6. HS TARIFF CLASSIFICATION NUMBER	7. PREFERENCE CRITERION	8. PRODUCER	9. NET COST	10. COUNTRY OF ORIGIN
DOG HARNESS (#2365) SIZE MEDIUM	4201.00	B	YES	NO	U.S.A.

I CERTIFY THAT:

· THE INFORMATION ON THIS DOCUMENT IS TRUE AND ACCURATE AND I ASSUME THE RESPONSIBILITY FOR PROVING SUCH REPRESENTATIONS. I UNDERSTAND THAT I AM LIABLE FOR ANY FALSE STATEMENTS OR MATERIAL OMISSIONS MADE ON OR IN CONNECTION WITH THIS DOCUMENT;

· I AGREE TO MAINTAIN, AND PRESENT UPON REQUEST, DOCUMENTATION NECESSARY TO SUPPORT THIS CERTIFICATE, AND TO INFORM, IN WRITING, ALL PERSONS TO WHOM THE CERTIFICATE WAS GIVEN OF ANY CHANGES THAT COULD AFFECT THE ACCURACY OR VALIDITY OF THIS CERTIFICATE;

· THE GOODS ORIGINATED IN THE TERRITORY OF ONE OR MORE OF THE PARTIES, AND COMPLY WITH THE ORIGIN REQUIREMENTS SPECIFIED FOR THOSE GOODS IN THE NORTH AMERICAN FREE TRADE AGREEMENT, AND UNLESS SPECIFICALLY EXEMPTED IN ARTICLE 411 OR ANNEX 401, THERE HAS BEEN NO FURTHER PRODUCTION OR ANY OTHER OPERATION OUTSIDE THE TERRITORIES OF THE PARTIES; AND

· THIS CERTIFICATE CONSISTS OF _____ PAGES, INCLUDING ALL ATTACHMENTS.

11.	11a. AUTHORIZED SIGNATURE AMANDA RICARDO	11b. COMPANY AMANDA RICARDO PET SERVICES INC.
	11c. NAME *(Print or type)* AMANDA RICARDO	11d. TITLE PRESIDENT
	11e. DATE (DD/MM/YY) 06/16/03	11f. TELEPHONE > NUMBER *(Voice)* 631-555-1054	*(Facsimile)* 631-555-1055

Customs Form 434 (040397)

Oceanfreight Export
(Registration, No SED Required)

SEA LION SHIPPING, LTD. *(New York)*

Sea Lion Shipping, Ltd. (of New York) 1229 Old Walt Whitman Road, Melville, NY 11747

SHIPPER (Principal or Seller licencee and address) AMANDA RICARDO PET SERVICES INC. 1322 ORCHID CIRCLE BELLPORT, NEW YORK 11713	**BOOKING NUMBER** ELZ/BDA/C02387	**Master No.:** **Control No.:**
	EXPORT REFERENCES Ref Number : V305305 Sail Date 06/16/03	

CONSIGNEE (Non-Negotiable unless consigned to order) SLOAN KEATING ENTERPRISES BERMUDA P.O. BOX DV985 DEVONSHIRE, BERMUDA ATTN: MR. SLOAN	**FORWARDING AGENT** (References) SEA LION SHIPPING LTD. FMC #4124 1229 OLD WALT WHITMAN ROAD MELVILLE, NEW YORK 11747
	PORT AND COUNTRY OF ORIGIN ELIZABETH

VESSEL BERMUDA QUEEN	**PORT OF LOADING** ELIZABETH	**NOTIFY PARTY:** SAME AS ABOVE
PORT OF DISCHARGE HAMILTON	**FOR TRANSSHIPMENT TO**	

PARTICULARS FURNISHED BY SHIPPER

MARKS AND NUMBERS	NO.	DESCRIPTION OF PACKAGES AND GOODS	WEIGHT	MEASUREMENT
ADDRESSED: (1) CARTON INVOICE #3393 ORDER #095 **NO SED REQUIRED SECTION 30.55(h) FTSR**	1	DOG HARNESSES FREIGHT PREPAID EXPRESS RELEASE ON BOARD: 6/16/03	155 lbs.	65x25x25

FREIGHT RATES, CHARGES, WEIGHTS AND/OR MEASUREMENTS
SUBJECT TO CORRECTION

	US Rate	PREPAID	COLLECT
FREIGHT CHARGE		120.00	

Received by Carrier for shipment by ocean vessel between port of loading and port of discharge, and for arrangement or procurement of pre-carriage from place of receipt and on-carriage to place of delivery, where stated above, the goods specified above in apparent good order and condition unless otherwise stated. The goods to be delivered at the above mentioned port of discharge or place of delivery, whichever applicable, subject always to exeptions, limitations, conditions, and liberties as posted at the office of the agent, to which the Shipper and/or Consignees agree to by accepting this Cargo Control Document.

DATED AT: _____

BY: _____

TOTAL PREPAID	120.00	#############
TOTAL COLLECT	#############	
TOTAL USD DOLLAR$		120.00

FOR DELIVERY, APPLY TO:
BERMUDA CUSTOM BROKERS
TEL.: 44-12345667
FAX: 44-12345665

Amanda Ricardo Pet Services Inc.
1322 Orchid Circle
Bellport, New York 11713
Tel: (631)555-1054 Fax: (631)555-1055

Invoice No.   **3393**

INVOICE

Customer

Name	Sloan Keating Enterprises Bermuda
Address	P.O. Box DV985
City	Devonshire Country Bermuda
Phone	441-555-1212

Date	6/16/2003
Order No.	095
Rep	
FCA	Elizabeth, NJ

Qty	Description	Unit Price	TOTAL
100	Dog Harnesses (Size Extra Small) #2399	$18.50	$1,850.00
	Harnesses being shipped for temporary use abroad by Sloan Keating. Shipment will be registered with U.S. Customs prior to export from the U.S.		
	These commodities, technology or software were exported from the United States in accordance with the Export Administration Regulations. Diversion contrary to U.S. law prohibited.		
	Made in Japan.		

	SubTotal	$1,850.00
	Shipping & Handling	
	Taxes	
	TOTAL	$1,850.00

Payment Details

◉ Net 30 days
○
○

Customer Order #095
Ship Ocean Freight

Office Use Only

American River Logistics, Ltd.

1229 Old Walt Whitman Road
Melville, New York 11747
Tel:1-(631)-396-6800 Fax:1-(631)-396-6801

BOOKING CONFIRMATION

TO   :   AMANDA RICARDO PET SERVICES INC.   ATTN   : AMANDA

FROM : ARI, NY   DATE   : Jun 16, 2003

We are pleased to provide the following booking confirmation and details:

SHIPPER   : AMANDA RICARDO PET SERVICES INC.   BOOKING # BCLU23454

                                                         CONTAINER
COMMODITY   : DOG HARNESSES
LINE   : BERMUDA LINES
VESSEL   : BERMUDA QUEEN
VOYAGE   : 023
               :

PICKUP DATE   :
PICKUP ORIG   : BELLPORT, NY
ETD   : 06/16/03   ETA   : 06/21/03
EXPORT PORT   : ELIZABETH   ULT DEST : BERMUDA

CUT OFF   : 06/15/03   PORT   :

PACKAGES	COMMODITY DESCRIPTION	WEIGHT LBS	MEASURE CBM	OVERSIZE LxWxH
1	CARTON COTG. (100) quantity dog harnesses	155 lbs.		65x25x25

Any questions regarding this booking, please notify us at the number below immediately.

Very truly yours,

Roseann Esposito
Phone:(631) 396-6800

```
                        D O C K   R E C E I P T
            T R U C K E R  /  L O A D   I N S T R U C T I O N S

TO:   AMANDA RICARDO PET SERVICES INC.        ATTN: AMANDA
FROM: AMERICAN RIVER LOGISTICS, LTD.          DATE: Jun 16, 2003
```

Please arrange trucking for the account of American River Int'l (800) 524-2493
as per the following:

SHIPPER: AMANDA RICARDO PET SERVICES INC.
PICKUP @: AMANDA RICARDO PET SERVICES INC.
          1322 ORCHID CIRCLE   **PICK-UP DATE** : 06/10/03
          BELLPORT, NY 11713

STEAMSHIP LINE: BERMUDA LINES   **BOOKING NUMBER:** BCLU23454
DEST PORT: HAMILTON
CUT OFF AT PIER: 06/15/03   **VESSEL:** BERMUDA QUEEN
                                              VOYAGE: 023
COMMODITY: DOG HARNESSES
CONTAINERS: **SIZE:**   **TYPE:**

Packages	Commodity Description	Weight	Measure	Oversize LxWxH
1	CARTON COTG. 100 (QTY) DOG HARNESSES	155 lbs.		65x25x25

ARI #V305305

PICKUP AND DELIVERY INSTRUCTIONS:

LOADED CONTAINERS TO BE DRAYED TO:
**THIS IS TO CERTIFY THAT THE ABOVE NAMED MATERIAL ARE PROPERLY CLASSIFIED,
DESCRIBED, PACKAGED, MARKED AND LABELED AND ARE IN PROPER CONDITION FOR
TRANSPORTATION ACCORDING TO THE APPLICABLE REGULATION OF THE DEPARTMENT OF
TRANSPORTATION.**
Very Truly Yours
Roseann Esposito
AMERICAN RIVER LOGISTICS, LTD.
MELVILLE, NY 11747

(631) 396-6800
(631) 396-6801

DEPARTMENT OF THE TREASURY
United States Customs Service

CERTIFICATE OF REGISTRATION

Form Approved. OMB No. 1515-0042

NO.

19 CFR 10.8, 10.9, 10.68,
148.1, 148.8, 148.32, 148.37

(NOTE: Number of copies to be submitted varies with type of transaction. Inquire at Port Director's office as to number of copies required.)

VIA *(Carrier)*	B/L or INSURED NO.	DATE
BERMUDA LINES, VESSEL BERMUDA QUEEN	ELZ/BDA/C02387	6/10/03

NAME, ADDRESS, AND ZIP CODE TO WHICH CERTIFIED FORM IS TO BE MAILED *(If Applicable)*

AMANDA RICARDO PET SERVICES LTD.
1322 ORCHID CIRCLE
BELLPORT, NEW YORK 11713

ARTICLES EXPORTED FOR:

☐ ALTERATION*
☐ REPAIR*
☒ USE ABROAD
☐ REPLACEMENT

☐ PROCESSING*
☐ OTHER, *(specify)*

_____

*** NOTE:** The cost or value of alterations, repairs, or processing abroad is subject to customs duty.*

LIST ARTICLES EXPORTED

Number Packages	Kind of Packages	Description
1	1 carton	DOG HARNESSES (EXTRA SMALL #2399) ORDER #095/INVOICE #3393 100 pieces in 1 carton

SIGNATURE OF OWNER OR AGENT *(Print or Type and Sign)*	DATE
AMANDA RICARDO PET SERVICES INC. AMANDA RICARDO	6/10/03

The Above-Described Articles Were:

EXAMINED		LADEN under my supervision	
DATE	PORT	DATE	PORT
SIGNATURE OF CUSTOMS OFFICER		SIGNATURE OF CUSTOMS OFFICER	

CERTIFICATE ON RETURN

Duty-free entry is claimed for the described articles as having been exported without benefit of drawback and are returned unchanged except as noted: (use reverse if needed)

SIGNATURE OF IMPORTER *(Print or Type and Sign)*	DATE

NOTE: *Certifying officers shall draw lines through all unused spaces with ink or indelible pencil*

Paperwork Reduction Act Notice: This request is in accordance with the Paperwork Reduction Act of 1995. The information to be provided is submitted by importers/exporters. Completion of this form is mandatory and to your benefit. The estimated average burden associated with this collection of information is 3 minutes per respondent depending on individual circumstances. Comments concerning the accuracy of this burden estimates and suggestions for reducing this burden should be directed to U.S. Customs Service, Information Service Branch, Washington, DC 20229, and to the Office of Management and Budget, Paperwork Reduction Project (1515-0042), Washington, DC 20503.

Customs Form 4455 (06/00)

Oceanfreight Export
(Letter of Credit)

SEA LION SHIPPING, LTD. *(New York)*

Sea Lion Shipping, Ltd. (of New York) 1229 Old Walt Whitman Road, Melville, NY 11747

SHIPPER (Principal or Seller licencee and address) SWEEP IT UNDER THE RUG 122 BLIND TIGER BLVD. NEW YORK, NEW YORK 10017	BOOKING NUMBER NYF1252678	Master No.: Control No.:

	EXPORT REFERENCES LC #152137617
	Ref Number : LCE01/0512
	Sail Date : 6/16/03

CONSIGNEE (Non-Negotiable unless consigned to order) BANGKOK BANK PUBLIC COMPANY LIMITED SIAM SQUARE BRANCH, 990 RAMA 4 ROAD BANGKOK, THAILAND 10330	FORWARDING AGENT (References) AMERICAN RIVER LOGISTICS LTD. 1229 OLD WALT WHITMAN ROAD MELVILLE, NEW YORK 11747
	PORT AND COUNTRY OF ORIGIN ELIZABETH, NEW JERSEY, U.S.A.

VESSEL EDDIE TWO	PORT OF LOADING BANGKOK	NOTIFY PARTY: NOTIFY APPLICANT MASTER NEAT CLEANING COMPANY 77 RAMA ROAD, BANGPONGPANG BANGKOK, THAILAND 10120
PORT OF DISCHARGE BANGKOK	FOR TRANSSHIPMENT TO	

PARTICULARS FURNISHED BY SHIPPER

MARKS AND NUMBERS	NO.	DESCRIPTION OF PACKAGES AND GOODS	WEIGHT	MEASUREMENT
ADDR: 1 20' CONTAINER	25	FEATHER DUSTERS	18493	
NO SED REQUIRED AES				

FREIGHT RATES, CHARGES, WEIGHTS AND/OR MEASUREMENTS SUBJECT TO CORRECTION			Received by Carrier for shipment by ocean vessel between port of loading and port of discharge, and for arrangement or procurement of pre-carriage from place of receipt and on-carriage to place of delivery, where stated above, the goods specified above in apparent good order and condition unless otherwise stated. The goods to be delivered at the above mentioned port of discharge or place of delivery, whichever applicable, subject always to exceptions, limitations, conditions, and liberties as posted at the office of the agent, to which the Shipper and/or Consignees agree to by accepting this Cargo Control Document.
	US Rate	PREPAID	COLLECT
FREIGHT CHARGE			

DATED AT: _____

BY: _____

TOTAL PREPAID		###############	FOR DELIVERY, APPLY TO:
TOTAL COLLECT	###############		
TOTAL USD DOLLAR$			

Sweep It Under The Rug

122 Blind Tiger Blvd.
New York, New York   10017
212-678-9876 fax 212-678-9877

Invoice No.   55

= INVOICE =

Customer

Name	Master Neat Cleaning Company	Date	6/16/2003
Address	77 Rama Rd, Bangpongpang	Order No.	2344
City	Bangkok Country Thailand	Rep	
Phone	10120	FOB	New York

Qty	Description	Unit Price	TOTAL
6755	Feather Dusters	$4.50	$30,397.50
	Packed in 25 Cartons		
	LC #152137617 LC Ref #LCE01/0512		
	Made in the U.S.A.		
	Contact Rosandrea with any questions… 212-678-9876		

SubTotal	$30,397.50
Shipping & Handling	
Taxes	
TOTAL	$30,397.50

Payment Details

◉ Letter of Credit
○
○

Customer Order #2344
Ship Via Oceanfreight

Office Use Only

U.S. DEPARTMENT OF COMMERCE — U.S. CENSUS BUREAU – Economics and Statistics Administration — BUREAU OF EXPORT ADMINISTRATION

FORM **7525-V** (7-25-2000)   **SHIPPER'S EXPORT DECLARATION**   OMB No. 0607-0152

1a. U.S. PRINCIPAL PARTY IN INTEREST (USPPI) *(Complete name and address)*
SWEEP IT UNDER THE RUG
122 BLIND TIGER BLVD.
NEW YORK, NEW YORK

ZIP CODE: 10017

2. DATE OF EXPORTATION: 6/16/03

3. TRANSPORTATION REFERENCE NO.: NYF1252678

b. USPPI EIN (IRS) OR ID NO.: 097549831

c. PARTIES TO TRANSACTION: __ Related   XX Non-related

4a. ULTIMATE CONSIGNEE *(Complete name and address)*
MASTER NEAT CLEANING COMPANY
77 RAMA RD, BANGPONGPANG, BANGKOK, THAILAND

b. INTERMEDIATE CONSIGNEE *(Complete name and address)*
10120

5. FORWARDING AGENT *(Complete name and address)*
AMERICAN RIVER LOGISTICS LTD.
1229 OLD WALT WHITMAN ROAD
MELVILLE, NEW YORK   11747

6. POINT (STATE) OF ORIGIN OR FTZ NO.: NEW YORK

7. COUNTRY OF ULTIMATE DESTINATION: THAILAND

8. LOADING PIER *(Vessel only)*: ELIZABETH, NJ

9. METHOD OF TRANSPORTATION *(Specify)*: OCEAN

14. CARRIER IDENTIFICATION CODE: RSTU

15. SHIPMENT REFERENCE NO.: NYF1252678

10. EXPORTING CARRIER: EDDIE TWO

11. PORT OF EXPORT: ELIZABETH, NJ

16. ENTRY NUMBER:

17. HAZARDOUS MATERIALS: __ Yes   XX No

12. PORT OF UNLOADING *(Vessel and air only)*: BANGKOK, THAILAND

13. CONTAINERIZED *(Vessel only)*: XX Yes | __ No

18. IN BOND CODE:

19. ROUTED EXPORT TRANSACTION: __ Yes   XX No

20. SCHEDULE B DESCRIPTION OF COMMODITIES *(Use columns 22–24)*

D/F or M (21)	SCHEDULE B NUMBER (22)	QUANTITY – SCHEDULE B UNIT(S) (23)	SHIPPING WEIGHT (Kilograms) (24)	VIN/PRODUCT NUMBER/ VEHICLE TITLE NUMBER (25)	VALUE (U.S. dollars, omit cents) (Selling price or cost if not sold) (26)
D	9603.90.4000 FEATHER DUSTERS	x	9135 kgs		30398

27. LICENSE NO./LICENSE EXCEPTION SYMBOL/AUTHORIZATION: NLR

28. ECCN *(When required)*:

29. Duly authorized officer or employee: K. KALA

The USPPI authorizes the forwarder named above to act as forwarding agent for export control and customs purposes.

30. I certify that all statements made and all information contained herein are true and correct and that I have read and understand the instructions for preparation of this document, set forth in the **"Correct Way to Fill Out the Shipper's Export Declaration."** I understand that civil and criminal penalties, including forfeiture and sale, may be imposed for making false or fraudulent statements herein, failing to provide the requested information or for violation of U.S. laws on exportation (13 U.S.C. Sec. 305; 22 U.S.C. Sec. 401; 18 U.S.C. Sec. 1001; 50 U.S.C. App. 2410).

Signature:

Title: as agent for

Date: 6/16/03

Confidential – For use solely for official purposes authorized by the Secretary of Commerce (13 U.S.C. 301 (g)).

Export shipments are subject to inspection by U.S. Customs Service and/or Office of Export Enforcement.

31. AUTHENTICATION *(When required)*:

Telephone No. *(Include Area Code)*: 631-396-6801

E-mail address: kelly@worldest.com

This form may be printed by private parties provided it conforms to the official form. For sale by the Superintendent of Documents, Government Printing Office, Washington, DC 20402, and local Customs District Directors. The **"Correct Way to Fill Out the Shipper's Export Declaration"** is available from the U.S. Census Bureau, Washington, DC 20233.

<u>*American River Logistics, Ltd.*</u>

1229 Old Walt Whitman Road
Melville, New York 11747
Tel: 631-396-6800
Fax: 631-396-6801

<u>BOOKING CONFIRMATION</u>

TO: ROSANDREA
FROM: ARI, NY
DATE: 6/16/03

WE ARE PLEASED TO PROVIDE YOU WITH THE FOLLOWING BOOKING CONFIRMATION
AND DETAILS:

SHIPPER: SWEEP IT UNDER THE RUG

BOOKING #NYF1252678
VESSEL: EDDIE TWO
VOYAGE: 234   LC #152137617
                                    LC REF #LCE01/0512

1 20' CONTAINER: PONU 090944-8

EXPORT REF: #SAMPLE 225

PICKUP DATE: 6/10/03
PICKUP ORIGIN: NEW YORK CITY

ULTIMATE DESTINATION: THAILAND
PORT: BANGKOK

CUT OFF: 6/15/03

PACKAGES

1 – 20' CONTAINER COTG. FEATHER DUSTERS

ANY QUESTIONS REGARDING THIS BOOKING, PLEASE NOTIFY US AT THE NUMBER BELOW
IMMEDIATELY.

VERY TRULY YOURS,

KELLY RAIA
631-396-6819

Certificate of Origin

AMERICAN RIVER LOGISTICS

The undersigned _____
(Owner or Agent)

for _____ SWEEP IT UNDER THE RUG _____
(Name and Address of Shipper)

declares the following listed goods shipped on _____ EDDIE TWO _____
(Name of Carrier)

on _____ 6/16/03 _____ consigned to TO ORDER OF BANGKOK PUBLIC BANK
(Shipment Date)   (Recipient's Name)

NOTIFY: APPLICANT MASTER NEAT CLEANING COMPANY
_____
(Recipient's Name and Address)

are the products of the United States of America.

Marks & Numbers	No. of Packages, Boxes or Cases	Weight in Kilos		Full Description of Item
		Gross	Net	
ADDR:	25 cartons	18493	18000	1 20' container / feather dusters
				LETTER OF CREDIT #152137617
				LC REF #LCE01/0512

State of _____ New York _____ County of _____ Suffolk _____

Sworn to me _____

this _____ day of _____, 20____ _____
(Signature of Owner or Agent)

_____

The _____, a recognized Chamber of Commerce Under

the laws of the State of _____, has examined the manufacturer's

invoice or shipper's affidavit concerning the origin of the merchandise and, according to the best

of its knowledge and belief, finds that the products named originated in the United States of North

America.

Secretary _____

Sweep It Under The Rug

122 Blind Tiger Blvd.
New York, New York 10017
212-678-9876 fax 212-678-9877

PACKING LIST

Customer

Name	Master Neat Cleaning Company
Address	77 Rama Rd, Bangpongpang
City	Bangkok Country Thailand
Phone	10120

Date	6/16/2003
Order No.	2344
Rep	
FOB	New York

Qty	Description	GROSS WT	NET WT
6755	Feather Dusters Packed in 25 Cartons LC #152137617 LC Ref #LCE01/0512 Made in the U.S.A. Contact Rosandrea with any questions… 212-678-9876	18493 #	18000#

Payment Details

◉ Letter of Credit
○
○

Customer Order #2344
Ship Via Oceanfreight

Office Use Only

Sweep It Under The Rug
122 Blind Tiger Blvd.
New York, New York 10017

BENEFICIARIES CERTIFICATE

DATE: JUNE 10, 2003

TO: BANGKOK BANK PUBLIC COMPANY LIMITED
        SIAM SQUARE BRANCH, 990 RAMA 4 ROAD
        BANGKOK, THAILAND 10330

RE: LETTER OF CREDIT #152137617
        LC REF #LCE01/0512

GENTLEMEN:

WE HEREBY CERTIFY THAT ONE SET OF NON-NEGOTIABLE SHIPPING DOCUMENTS
HAVE BEEN SENT BY COURIER TO THE APPLICANT AFTER SHIPMENT.

RESPECTFULLY YOURS,

KELLY RAIA

_____

U.S. $ 30397.50   June 16,   2,003

~~LETTER OF CREDIT~~   of this *FIRST* of Exchange (Second unpaid)

Pay to the Order of   SWEEP IT UNDER THE RUG

-- Thirty thousand three hundred and ninety-seven 50/100 ------   **United States Dollars**

for Value received and charge the same to account of   LC #152137617
LC REF #LCE01/0512

To BANGKOK BANK PUBLIC COMPANY LIMITED

SIAM SQUARE BRANCH, 990 RAMA 4 ROAD   SWEEP IT UNDER THE RUG

No. BANGKOK, THAILAND 10330   Authorized Signature

BANGKOK BANK PUBLIC COMPANY LIMITED
SIAM SQUARE BRANCH, 990 RAMA 4 ROAD   June 16, 2003
BANGKOK, THAILAND 10330   Date

Gentlemen: ☐ for collection,
We enclose Draft Number 9491 _____ and documents below   ☐ for
                                              ☐ for payment/negotiation under L/C

BILLS OF LADING	B/L COPY	COMM. INV.	INS. CTF.	CTF. ORIG.	CONS. INV.	PKNG. LIST	WGT. CTF.	OTHER DOCUMENTS
3/3	3	8	2	2	-	2	-	BENEFICIARIES CERTIFICATE

Please handle in accordance with instructions marked "X"

☐ Deliver all documents in one mailing.
☐ Deliver documents in two mailings.
☐ Deliver documents against payment if sight draft, or acceptance if time draft.
☐ All charges for account of drawee.
☐ Do not waive charges.
☐ Protest for non-payment / non-acceptance
☐ Do not protest.
☐ Present on arrival of goods.
☐ Advise non-payment / non-acceptance by airmail / cable giving reasons.
☐ Advise payment / acceptance by airmail / cable

IN CASE OF NEED refer to:

Name **AMERICAN RIVER INTERNATIONAL**

Address 1229 OLD WALT WHITMAN ROAD, MELVILLE, NEW YORK 11747

who is empowered by us:

a ☐ To act fully on our behalf, i.e., authorize reductions; extensions, free delivery, waiving of protest, etc.

b ☒ To assist in obtaining acceptance or payment of draft, as drawn, but not to alter its terms in any way.

OTHER INSTRUCTIONS:

PLEASE CONTACT AMERICAN RIVER INTL. IF THERE ARE ANY QUESTIONS PERTAINING TO THESE DOCUMENTS. KINDLY WIRE PAYMENT TO NORTH FORK BANK, MELVILLE, NEW YORK BENEFICIARY'S ACCOUNT #12345000, ABA TRANSIT #02124321

Please refer all questions concerning this collection to:
☐ Shipper
☒ Freight Forwarder:

                                            Authorized Signature

Form 20-015 Printed and Sold by UNZCO 700 Central Ave., New Providence, NJ 07974 ● (800) 631-3098

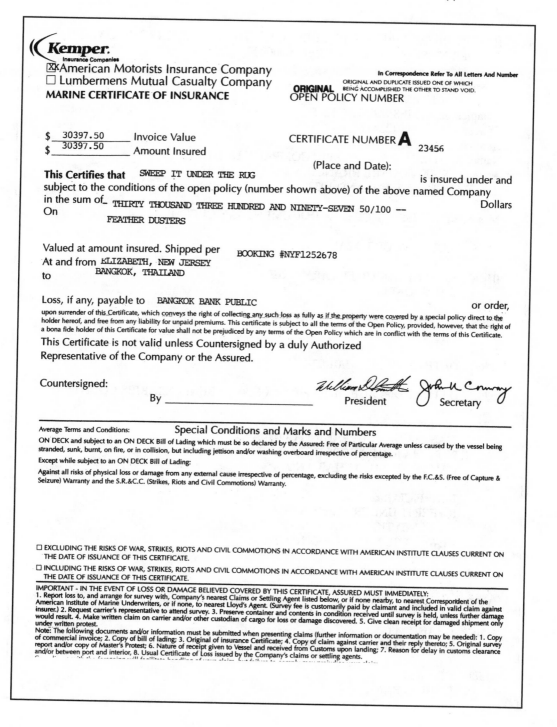

Kemper.
Insurance Companies
☒ American Motorists Insurance Company
☐ Lumbermens Mutual Casualty Company
MARINE CERTIFICATE OF INSURANCE

In Correspondence Refer To All Letters And Number
ORIGINAL AND DUPLICATE ISSUED ONE OF WHICH
ORIGINAL BEING ACCOMPLISHED THE OTHER TO STAND VOID.
OPEN POLICY NUMBER

$___30397.50___ Invoice Value
$___30397.50___ Amount Insured

CERTIFICATE NUMBER A 23456

(Place and Date):

This Certifies that SWEEP IT UNDER THE RUG   is insured under and
subject to the conditions of the open policy (number shown above) of the above named Company
in the sum of_ THIRTY THOUSAND THREE HUNDRED AND NINETY-SEVEN 50/100 --   Dollars
On   FEATHER DUSTERS

Valued at amount insured. Shipped per   BOOKING #NYF1252678
At and from ELIZABETH, NEW JERSEY
to   BANGKOK, THAILAND

Loss, if any, payable to BANGKOK BANK PUBLIC   or order,
upon surrender of this Certificate, which conveys the right of collecting any such loss as fully as if the property were covered by a special policy direct to the
holder hereof, and free from any liability for unpaid premiums. This certificate is subject to all the terms of the Open Policy, provided, however, that the right of
a bona fide holder of this Certificate for value shall not be prejudiced by any terms of the Open Policy which are in conflict with the terms of this Certificate.

This Certificate is not valid unless Countersigned by a duly Authorized
Representative of the Company or the Assured.

Countersigned:

By _____

President   Secretary

Average Terms and Conditions: Special Conditions and Marks and Numbers
ON DECK and subject to an ON DECK Bill of Lading which must be so declared by the Assured: Free of Particular Average unless caused by the vessel being
stranded, sunk, burnt, on fire, or in collision, but including jettison and/or washing overboard irrespective of percentage.

Except while subject to an ON DECK Bill of Lading:

Against all risks of physical loss or damage from any external cause irrespective of percentage, excluding the risks excepted by the F.C.&S. (Free of Capture &
Seizure) Warranty and the S.R.&C.C. (Strikes, Riots and Civil Commotions) Warranty.

☐ EXCLUDING THE RISKS OF WAR, STRIKES, RIOTS AND CIVIL COMMOTIONS IN ACCORDANCE WITH AMERICAN INSTITUTE CLAUSES CURRENT ON
THE DATE OF ISSUANCE OF THIS CERTIFICATE.
☐ INCLUDING THE RISKS OF WAR, STRIKES, RIOTS AND CIVIL COMMOTIONS IN ACCORDANCE WITH AMERICAN INSTITUTE CLAUSES CURRENT ON
THE DATE OF ISSUANCE OF THIS CERTIFICATE.

IMPORTANT - IN THE EVENT OF LOSS OR DAMAGE BELIEVED COVERED BY THIS CERTIFICATE, ASSURED MUST IMMEDIATELY:
1. Report loss to, and arrange for survey with, Company's nearest Claims or Settling Agent listed below, or if none nearby, to nearest Correspondent of the
American Institute of Marine Underwriters, or if none, to nearest Lloyd's Agent. (Survey fee is customarily paid by claimant and included in valid claim against
insurer.) 2. Request carrier's representative to attend survey. 3. Preserve container and contents in condition received until survey is held, unless further damage
would result. 4. Make written claim on carrier and/or other custodian of cargo for loss or damage discovered. 5. Give clean receipt for damaged shipment only
under written protest.
Note: The following documents and/or information must be submitted when presenting claims (further information or documentation may be needed): 1. Copy
of commercial invoice; 2. Copy of bill of lading; 3. Original of insurance Certificate; 4. Copy of claim against carrier and their reply thereto; 5. Original survey
report and/or copy of Master's Protest; 6. Nature of receipt given to Vessel and received from Customs upon landing; 7. Reason for delay in customs clearance
and/or between port and interior, 8. Usual Certificate of Loss issued by the Company's claims or settling agents.

!!!! LIVE !!!! LIVE !!!! LIVE !!!! LIVE !!!! LIVE !!!! LIVE !!!! LIVE !!!! LIVE !!!!
AUTOPRINT SEQUENCE NUMBER: 000002

Message Type: RECEIVED
Time Created: 05/01/03   07:32
Completion: MESSAGE ACTIVE
Correspondent: 00012341111
Amount: 30,397.50
Name: BANGKOK BANK PUBLIC COMPANY LIMITED
Address: SIAM SQUARE BRANCH, 990 RAMA 4 ROAD
City: BANGKOK, THAILAND 10330

Message Type: ISSUANCE OF A DOCUMENTARY CREDIT

072 /   SEQUENCE OF TOTAL

070A   FORM OF DOCUMENTARY CREDIT
       IRREVOCABLE

070B   DOCUMENTARY CREDIT NUMBER
       152137617

070C   DATE OF ISSUE: 05/01/03

070D   DATE AND PLACE OF EXPIRY: 06/30/03 BENEFICIARIES COUNTRY

124   APPLICANT:
       MASTER NEAT CLEANING COMPANY
       77 RAMA RD. BANGPONGPANG
       BANGKOK, 10120 THAILAND

136   BENEFICIARY:
       SWEEP IT UNDER THE RUG
       122 BLIND TIGER BLVD.
       NEW YORK, NEW YORK 10017

148B   AMOUNT: 30,397.50 US DOLLAR

148D   AVAILABLE WITH....BY....ANY BANK IN U.S.A. BY NEGOTIATION

156C   DRAFTS AT ...:
       SIGHT IN DUPLICATE INDICATING THIS LC NUMBER

158D   DRAWEE:
       ISSUING BANK

!!!! LIVE !!!! LIVE !!!! LIVE !!!! LIVE !!!! LIVE !!!! LIVE !!!! LIVE !!!! LIVE !!!!
AUTOPRINT SEQUENCE NUMBER: 000002

166C   PARTIAL SHIPMENT:
         NOT ALLOWED

166F   TRANSSHIPMENT:
         ALLOWED

244A   LOAD ON BRD/DISPATCH/TAKING IN CHARGE AT/FROM..NEW YORK

250B   FOR TRANSPORTATION TO...: BANGKOK

254C   LATEST DATE OF SHIPMENT: 06/25/03

258A   DESCRIPTION OF GOODS AND/OR SERVICES:

         FEATHER DUSTERS

262A   DOCUMENTS REQUIRED:
         COMMERCIAL INVOICE IN ONE ORIGINAL PLUS 6 COPIES,
         INDICATING VALUE, ALL OF WHICH MUST BE MANUALLY SIGNED
         FULL SET OF 3/3 CLEAN ON BOARD OCEAN BILLS OF LADING AND
         TWO NON-NEGOTIABLE COPIES MADE OUT
         Made out BANGKOK BANK PUBLIC COMPANY LIMITED, MARKED
         FREIGHT PAYABLE AT DESTINATION AND NOTIFY APPLICANT AND
         INDICATING THIS L/C NUMBER.
         PACKING LIST IN ONE ORIGINAL PLUS 4 COPIES, ALL OF WHICH
         MUST BE MANUALLY SIGNED.
         CERTIFICATE OF ORIGIN IN TRIPLICATE.
         BENEFICIARIES CERTIFICATE CERTIFYING THAT ONE SET OF
         NON-NEGOTIABLE SHIPPING DOCUMENTS HAVE BEEN SENT BY
         COURIER TO THE APPLICANT AFTER SHIPMENT.

347A   ADDITIONAL CONDITIONS:
         A DISCREPANCY FEE OF USD50.00 WILL BE IMPOSED ON EACH SET
         DOCUMENTS PRESENTED FOR NEGOTIATION UNDER THIS L/C WITH
         DISCREPANCY. THE FEE WILL BE DEDUCTED FROM THE BILL
         AMOUNT.

371B   CHARGES:
         ALL BANK CHARGES OUTSIDE THAILAND INCLUDING REIMBURSING
         BANK COMMISSION AND DISCREPANCY FEE (IF ANY) ARE FOR
         BENEFICIARIES ACCOUNT.

!!!! LIVE !!!! LIVE !!!! LIVE !!!! LIVE !!!! LIVE !!!! LIVE !!!! LIVE !!!! LIVE !!!!
AUTOPRINT SEQUENCE NUMBER: 000002

378A   PERIOD FOR PRESENTATION:
        PRESENTATION OF DOCUMENTS MUST BE MADE WITHIN 21 DAYS
        AFTER SHIPMENT.

382D   CONFIRMATION INSTRUCTIONS:
        DO NOT CONFIRM CREDIT

386B   REIMBUSRING BANK
        BANKGKOK BANK PUBLIC COMPANY LIMITED
        NEW YORK BRANCH

Airfreight Import

057	CDG	2345 6547		MAWB# 057 2345 6547

057 CDG 2345 6547

Shipper's Name and Address	Shipper's Account Number

CHEZ BLANCHE
RUE DU TROIS
PARIS, FRANCE   R24 9 ,

Not Negotiable

Air Waybill AIR FRANCE

1 SQUARE MAX HYMANS

Issued by

Copies 1, 2 and 3 of this Air Waybill are originals and have the same validity.

Consignee's Name and Address	Consignee's Account Number

MANNY'S MANNEQUINS CORP.
1233 123RD STREET

JERSEY CITY , NJ 10017

It is agreed that the goods described herein are accepted in apparent good order and condition (except as noted) for carriage SUBJECT TO THE CONDITIONS OF CONTRACT ON THE REVERSE HEREOF. ALL GOODS MAY BE CARRIED BY ANY OTHER MEANS INCLUDING ROAD OR ANY OTHER CARRIER UNLESS SPECIFIC CONTRARY INSTRUCTIONS ARE GIVEN HEREON BY THE SHIPPER, AND SHIPPER AGREES THAT THE SHIPMENT MAY BE CARRIED VIA INTERMEDIATE STOPPING PLACES WHICH THE CARRIER DEEMS APPROPRIATE. THE SHIPPER'S ATTENTION IS DRAWN TO THE NOTICE CONCERNING CARRIER'S LIMITATION OF LIABILITY. Shipper may increase such limitation of liability by declaring a higher value for carriage and paying a supplemental charge if required.

Issuing Carrier's Agent Name and City

AMERICAN RIVER LOGISTICS, LTD.
1229 Old Walt Whitman Road
Melville, NY 11747

Agent's IATA Code   Account No.

01-1-9112/0011

Accounting Information

Airport of Departure (Addr. of First Carrier) and Requested Routing

PARIS

Reference Number   Optional Shipping Information

To	By First Carrier	Routing and Destination	to	by	to	by	Currency	CHGS Code	WT/VAL PPD / COLL	Other PPD / COLL	Declared Value for Carriage	Declared Value for Customs
EWR	AF						US$		X	X	N.V.D.	N.V.D.

Airport of Destination	Requested Flight/Date		Amount of Insurance
NEWARK, NJ	929/16		NIL

INSURANCE - If carrier offers insurance, and such insurance is requested in accordance with the conditions thereof, indicate amount to be insured in figures in box marked "Amount of Insurance".

Handling Information

NOTIFY AMERICAN BROKERAGE UPON ARRIVAL

These commodities, technology or software were exported from the United States in accordance with the Export Administration Regulations. Ultimate destination **USA**

Diversion contrary to U.S. law prohibited.   SCI

No. of Pieces RCP	Gross Weight	kg / lb	Rate Class / Commodity Item No.	Chargeable Weight	Rate / Charge	Total	Nature and Quantity of Goods (Incl. Dimensions or Volume)
5	134 KG			134 KG	3.00	402.00	DISPLAY MANNEQUINS FIVE BOXES COTG 550 PIECES
5	134 KG					402.00	

Prepaid	Weight Charge	Collect	Other Charges
	Valuation Charge		402.00
	Tax		
	Total Other Charges Due Agent		
	Total Other Charges Due Carrier		

Shipper certifies that the particulars on the face hereof are correct and that insofar as any part of the consignment contains dangerous goods, such part is properly described by name and is in proper condition for carriage by air according to the applicable Dangerous Goods Regulations.

AMERICAN RIVER LOGISTICS, L'

Joseph Pisano   as agent for shipper

Signature of Shipper or his Agent

Total Prepaid	Total Collect

Currency Conversion Rates	CC Charges in Dest. Currency
	402.00

06/16/03   AMERICAN RIVER LOGISTICS, L'

Joseph Pisano CDG   , as agent for carrier

Executed on (date)   at (place)   Signature of Issuing Carrier or its Agent

For Carriers Use only at Destination	Charges at Destination	Total Collect Charges

MAWB# 057 2345 6547

Chez Blanche

Rue du trois
Paris, France R24 987
43 555-2345 fax 43 555-2346

Invoice No. 35

INVOICE

Customer

Name	Manny's Mannequins Corp.
Address	1233 123rd Street
City	Jersey City Country New Jersey USA
Phone	10017

Date	6/16/2003
Order No.	9876
Rep	
FOB	Paris Airport

Qty	Description	Unit Price	TOTAL
550	Mannequins	$11.00	$6,050.00
	Packed in Five (5) Boxes 110 pieces per box		
	Mannequin #KAM2544		
	Made in France		
	Contact Mme Blanche for any questions (43)555-2345		

	SubTotal	$6,050.00
	Shipping & Handling	
	Taxes	
	TOTAL	$6,050.00

Payment Details

◉ Net 90 Days
○ Port of Newark, NJ
○

Customer Order #9876
Ship Via Airfreight

Office Use Only

United States Customs Service

Form Approved
OMB No. 1515-0069

ENTRY/IMMEDIATE DELIVERY

AMERICAN RIVER BROKERAGE SERVICE LTD.
614 PROGRESS STREET
ELIZABETH, NEW JERSEY   07201

CST #420

19 CFR 142.3, 142.16, 142.22, 142.24

1. ARRIVAL DATE 06/16/03	2. ELECTED ENTRY DATE 06/16/03	3. ENTRY TYPE CODE/NAME 01	4. ENTRY NUMBER KH5-2345678
5. PORT 4601	6. SINGLE TRANS. BOND	7. BROKER/IMPORTER FILE NUMBER 20032865	

	8. CONSIGNEE NUMBER 09-23456789		9. IMPORTER NUMBER 09-23456789

10. ULTIMATE CONSIGNEE NAME MANNY'S MANNEQUINS CORP. 1233 123rd Street Jersey City, New Jersey 10017	11. IMPORTER OF RECORD NAME SAME
12. CARRIER CODE AF	13. VOYAGE/FLIGHT/TRIP 929	14. LOCATION OF GOODS-CODE(S)/NAME(S) F253 - Air France Cargo
15. VESSEL CODE/NAME		

16. U.S. PORT OF UNLADING 4601	17. MANIFEST NUMBER	18. G. O. NUMBER	19. TOTAL VALUE 6050

20. DESCRIPTION OF MERCHANDISE
DISPLAY MANNEQUINS

21. IT/BL/ AWB CODE	22. IT/BL/AWB NO.	23. MANIFEST QUANTITY	24. H.S. NUMBER	25. COUNTRY OF ORIGIN	26. MANUFACTURER NO.
M	057-2345-6547	5	9618.00.0000	FR	FRCHEBLARUE

27. CERTIFICATION	28. CUSTOMS USE ONLY
I hereby make application for entry/immediate delivery. I certify that the above information is accurate, the bond is sufficient, valid, and current, and that all requirements of 19 CFR Part 142 have been met. SIGNATURE OF APPLICANT X AMERICAN RIVER BROKERAGE SERVICE	☐ OTHER AGENCY ACTION REQUIRED, NAMELY:
PHONE NO. 631-396-6800 DATE 6/16/03	☐ CUSTOMS EXAMINATION REQUIRED.
29. BROKER OR OTHER GOVT. AGENCY USE	☐ ENTRY REJECTED, BECAUSE:

ELECTRONIC ENTRY - NEWARK, NJ DISTRICT
I certify that this cargo has been authorized
for delivery by U.S. Customs

DELIVERY AUTHORIZED: | SIGNATURE | DATE

American River Brokerage Service
Signature   Date

Customs Form 3461 (010189)

Trade Forms: Import

American River Brokerage Svc **CF 7501 – ENTRY SUMMARY**
614 Progress Street
Elizabeth, NJ 07201

DEPARTMENT OF THE TREASURY
UNITED STATES CUSTOMS SERVICE

ENTRY SUMMARY

Form Approved OMB No. 1515-0065

1. Entry No.	2. Entry Type Code	3. Entry Summary Date
315-2345678	01 ABI	06/30/03

4. Entry Date	5. Port Code	
06/16/03	4601	PAPERLESS

6. Bond No.	7. Bond Type Code	8. Broker/Importer File No.
422	8	20032865

9. Ultimate Consignee Name and Address	10. Consignee No.	11. Importer of Record Name and Address	12. Importer No.
	09-23456789	Manny's Mannequins Corp. 1233 123rd Street Jersey City, NJ 10017	09-23456789

	13. Exporting Country	14. Export Date
	France FR	06/15/03
NJ	15. Country of Origin	16. Missing Documents
	France FR	
State	17. I.T. No.	18. I.T. Date

19. B/L or AWB No.	20. Mode of Transportation	21. Manufacturer I.D.	22. Reference No.
057-2345-6547	40	FRCHEBLARUE	

23. Importing Carrier	24. Foreign Port of Lading	25. Location of Goods/G.O. No.
AF		FIRMS: F253 – AIR FRANCE CARGO

26. U.S. Port of Unlading	27. Import Date	
4601	06/16/03	FLT: 929

28. Line No.	29. Description of Merchandise					
	30.A T.S.U.S.A. No. B. ADA/CVD Case No.	31.A Gross Weight B. Manifest Qty.	32. Net Quantity in T.S.U.S.A. Units	33.A Entered Value B. CHGS C. Relationship	34.A T.S.U.S.A. Rate ADA/CVD Rate C. I.R.C. Rate D. Visa No.	35. Duty and I.R. Tax
						Dollars / Cents
001	INVOICE #00001 9618.00.0000 110kgs DISPLAY MANNEQUINS		x	6050 C125	4.4%	266 20
	MERCHANDISE PROCESSING FEE				0.21%	112 71
	BLOCK 39 SUMMARY: MPF 123		25.00	TEV$6050.00		

Declaration of Importer of Record (Owner or Purchaser) or Authorized Agent

I declare that I am the importer of record and that the actual owner, purchaser, or consignee for customs purposes is as shown above. OR ☐ owner or purchaser or agent thereof.

I further declare that the merchandise ☐ was obtained pursuant to a purchase or agreement to purchase and that the prices set forth in the invoices are true. OR ☐ was not obtained pursuant to a purchase or agreement to purchase or agreement to purchase and the statements in the invoices as to value or price are true to the best of my knowledge and belief.

I also declare that the statements in the documents herein filed fully disclose to the best of my knowledge and belief the true prices, values, quantities, rebates, drawbacks, fees, commissions, and royalties and are true and correct, and that all goods or services provided to the seller of the merchandise either free or at reduced cost are fully disclosed. I will immediately furnish to the appropriate customs officer any information showing a different state of facts.

Notice required by Paperwork Reduction Act of 1980: This information is needed to ensure that importers/exporters are complying with U.S. customs laws, to allow us to compute and collect the right amount of money, to enforce other agency requirements, and to collect accurate statistical information on imports. Your response is mandatory. (Continued on back of form.)

▼ U.S. CUSTOMS USE ▼		TOTALS
A. Liq. Code	B. Ascertained Duty	37. Duty 266 20
	C. Ascertained Tax	38. Tax
	D. Ascertained Other	39. Other 25 00
	E. Ascertained Total	40. Total 291 20

41. Signature of Declarant, Title, and Date

PART 1 – RECORD COPY   Customs Form 7501 (112295)

ARRIVAL NOTICE

FLIGHT NUMBER: 929

ARRIVAL DATE: 6/16/03

MAWB: 057-2345-6547

PCS: 5

WEIGHT: 110 kgs

TERMINAL SERVICE CHARGE: $22.00

TOTAL CHARGES DUE AIR FRANCE: $22.00

Storage begins on 6/19/03.......................

All charges are due prior to cargo being released by Air France.

Miscellaneous Documents: Export

U.S. $ _____   _____ 19 ____

_____ of this *FIRST* of Exchange (Second unpaid)

Pay to the Order of

United States Dollars

for Value received and charge the same to account of

To _____

No. _____   Authorized Signature

_____
Date

Gentlemen: ☐ for collection,

We enclose Draft Number _____ and documents below   ☐ for

                                                     ☐ for payment/negotiation under L/C

BILLS OF LADING	B/L COPY	COMM. INV.	INS. CTF.	CTF. ORIG.	CONS. INV.	PKNG. LIST	WGT. CTF.	OTHER DOCUMENTS

Please handle in accordance with instructions marked "X"

☐ Deliver all documents in one mailing.

☐ Deliver documents in two mailings.

☐ Deliver documents against payment if sight draft, or acceptance if time draft.

☐ All charges for account of drawee.

☐ Do not waive charges.

☐ Protest for non-payment / non-acceptance

☐ Do not protest.

☐ Present on arrival of goods.

☐ Advise non-payment / non-acceptance by airmail / cable giving reasons.

☐ Advise payment / acceptance by airmail / cable

IN CASE OF NEED refer to:

Name _____

Address _____

who is empowered by us:

a ☐ To act fully on our behalf, i.e., authorize reductions; extensions, free delivery, waiving of protest, etc.

b ☐ To assist in obtaining acceptance or payment of draft, as drawn, but not to alter its terms in any way.

OTHER INSTRUCTIONS:

Please refer all questions concerning this collection to:

☐ Shipper

☐ Freight Forwarder:

ICAT Logistics, Inc.
PO Box 28952
BWI Airport, MD 21240

_____
Authorized Signature

Form 20-015 Printed and Sold by *UNZ&CO* 700 Central Ave., New Providence, NJ 07974 ● (800) 631-3098

DEPARTMENT OF THE TREASURY
United States Customs Service

CERTIFICATE OF REGISTRATION

Form Approved. OMB No. 1515-0042

NO.

19 CFR 10.8, 10.9, 10.68,
148.1, 148.8, 148.32, 148.37

(NOTE: Number of copies to be submitted varies with type of transaction.
Inquire at Port Director's office as to number of copies required.)

VIA (Carrier)	B/L or INSURED NO.	DATE

NAME, ADDRESS, AND ZIP CODE TO WHICH CERTIFIED FORM IS TO BE MAILED (If Applicable)

ARTICLES EXPORTED FOR:

☐ ALTERATION*
☐ REPAIR*
☐ USE ABROAD
☐ REPLACEMENT

☐ PROCESSING*
☐ OTHER, (specify)

* NOTE: The cost or value of alterations, repairs, or processing abroad is subject to customs duty.

LIST ARTICLES EXPORTED

Number Packages	Kind of Packages	Description

SIGNATURE OF OWNER OR AGENT (Print or Type *and* Sign)

DATE

The Above-Described Articles Were:

	EXAMINED		LADEN under my supervision	
DATE	PORT	DATE		PORT

SIGNATURE OF CUSTOMS OFFICER

SIGNATURE OF CUSTOMS OFFICER

CERTIFICATE ON RETURN

Duty-free entry is claimed for the described articles as having been exported without benefit of drawback and are returned unchanged except as noted: (use reverse if needed)

SIGNATURE OF IMPORTER (Print or Type *and* Sign)

DATE

NOTE: Certifying officers shall draw lines through all unused spaces with ink or indelible pencil

Paperwork Reduction Act Notice: This request is in accordance with the Paperwork Reduction Act of 1995. The information to be provided is submitted by importers/exporters. Completion of this form is mandatory and to your benefit. The estimated average burden associated with this collection of information is 3 minutes per respondent depending on individual circumstances. Comments concerning the accuracy of this burden estimates and suggestions for reducing this burden should be directed to U.S. Customs Service, Information Service Branch, Washington, DC 20229, and to the Office of Management and Budget, Paperwork Reduction Project (1515-0042), Washington, DC 20503.

Customs Form 4455 (06/00)

Certificate of Origin

The undersigned ———————————————————————————
(Owner or Agent)

for ————————————————————————————————
(Name and Address of Shipper)

declares the following listed goods shipped on ————————————
(Name of Carrier)

on ————————————————————— consigned to ——————————
(Shipment Date)   (Recipient's Name)

————————————————————————————————
(Recipient's Name and Address)

are the products of the United States of America.

Marks & Numbers	No. of Packages, Boxes or Cases	Weight in Kilos		Full Description of Item
		Gross	Net	

State of ————————————— County of ———————————————

Sworn to me ————————————————————————————

this ————— day of ———— , 20——— ———————————————
(Signature of Owner or Agent)

————————————————————————————————

The ————————————————— , a recognized Chamber of Commerce Under

the laws of the State of ————————————— , has examined the manufacturer's

invoice or shipper's affidavit concerning the origin of the merchandise and, according to the best

of its knowledge and belief, finds that the products named originated in the United States of North

America.

Secretary ———————————————————————————

U.S. DEPARTMENT OF COMMERCE – Economics and Statistics Administration – U.S. CENSUS BUREAU – BUREAU OF EXPORT ADMINISTRATION

FORM **7525-V** (7-18-2003)   **SHIPPER'S EXPORT DECLARATION**   OMB No. 0607-0152

1a. U.S. PRINCIPAL PARTY IN INTEREST (USPPI)(Complete name and address)

ZIP CODE

2. DATE OF EXPORTATION

3. TRANSPORTATION REFERENCE NO.

b. USPPI'S EIN (IRS) OR ID NO.

c. PARTIES TO TRANSACTION
☐ Related ☐ Non-related

4a. ULTIMATE CONSIGNEE *(Complete name and address)*

b. INTERMEDIATE CONSIGNEE *(Complete name and address)*

5a. FORWARDING AGENT *(Complete name and address)*

5b. FORWARDING AGENT'S EIN (IRS) NO.

6. POINT (STATE) OF ORIGIN OR FTZ NO.

7. COUNTRY OF ULTIMATE DESTINATION

8. LOADING PIER *(Vessel only)*

9. METHOD OF TRANSPORTATION *(Specify)*

14. CARRIER IDENTIFICATION CODE

15. SHIPMENT REFERENCE NO.

10. EXPORTING CARRIER

11. PORT OF EXPORT

16. ENTRY NUMBER

17. HAZARDOUS MATERIALS
☐ Yes ☐ No

12. PORT OF UNLOADING *(Vessel and air only)*

13. CONTAINERIZED *(Vessel only)*
☐ Yes ☐ No

18. IN BOND CODE

19. ROUTED EXPORT TRANSACTION
☐ Yes ☐ No

20. SCHEDULE B DESCRIPTION OF COMMODITIES *(Use columns 22–24)*

D/F or M (21)	SCHEDULE B NUMBER (22)	QUANTITY – SCHEDULE B UNIT(S) (23)	SHIPPING WEIGHT (Kilograms) (24)	VIN/PRODUCT NUMBER/ VEHICLE TITLE NUMBER (25)	VALUE (U.S. dollars, omit cents) (Selling price or cost if not sold) (26)

27. LICENSE NO./LICENSE EXCEPTION SYMBOL/AUTHORIZATION

28. ECCN *(When required)*

29. Duly authorized officer or employee

The USPPI authorizes the forwarder named above to act as forwarding agent for export control and customs purposes.

30. I certify that all statements made and all information contained herein are true and correct and that I have read and understand the instructions for preparation of this document, set forth in the **"Correct Way to Fill Out the Shipper's Export Declaration."** I understand that civil and criminal penalties, including forfeiture and sale, may be imposed for making false or fraudulent statements herein, failing to provide the requested information or for violation of U.S. laws on exportation (13 U.S.C. Sec. 305; 22 U.S.C. Sec. 401; 18 U.S.C. Sec. 1001; 50 U.S.C. App. 2410).

Signature

Confidential – Shipper's Export Declarations (or any successor document) wherever located, shall be exempt from public disclosure unless the Secretary determines that such exemption would be contrary to the national interest (Title 13, Chapter 9, Section 301 (g)).

Title

Export shipments are subject to inspection by U.S. Customs Service and/or Office of Export Enforcement.

Date

31. AUTHENTICATION *(When required)*

Telephone No. (Include Area Code)

E-mail address

This form may be printed by private parties provided it conforms to the official form. For sale by the Superintendent of Documents, Government Printing Office, Washington, DC 20402, and local Customs District Directors. The **"Correct Way to Fill Out the Shipper's Export Declaration"** is available from the U.S. Census Bureau, Washington, DC 20233.

Francis Food Services
45 Denver Ave.
Detroit, California 00987

Health & Sanitary Certificate

To whom it may concern,

We herby certify that the products described on the attached invoices are manufactured in our factory in the USA; that all of the ingredients contained in each of the products to be exported are approved for food use in a regulation of the United States FDA or appear on the GRAS List. Further, we hereby certify that each product is offered for sale and sold in the USA; that said product is perfectly fit and intended for human consumption when utilized in accordance with good manufacturing practices.

All our products are free of heavy metals, radiation and all kinds of disease including cholera.

The products shown on the attached invoices meet and/or exceed the Food and Sanitary regulations promulgated by all applicable all federal and state authorities.

This product was inspected and certified by FFS internal quality control personnel, as identified below and meet or exceed all internal quality control standards.

Bob Bobbo
3 March 1998

Sample of Consularization Stamp on the Back of the Invoice

Revenue Revenu
Canada Canada

CANADA CUSTOMS INVOICE
FACTURE DES DOUANES CANADIENNES

Page ____ of ____
de

1. Vendor (Name and Address) - Vendeur (Nom et adresse)	2. Date of Direct Shipment to Canada - Date d'expédition directe vers le Canada
	3. Other References (Include Purchaser's Order No.) Autres références (Inclure le n° de commande de l'acheteur)

4. Consignee (Name and Address) - Destinataire (Nom et adresse)	5. Purchaser's Name and Address (if other than Consignee) Nom et adresse de l'acheteur (S'il diffère du destinataire)
	6. Country of Transhipment - Pays de transbordement
	7. Country of Origin of Goods Pays d'origine des marchandises / IF SHIPMENT INCLUDES GOODS OF DIFFERENT ORIGINS ENTER ORIGINS AGAINST ITEMS IN 12. SI L'EXPÉDITION COMPREND DES MARCHANDISES D'ORIGINES DIFFÉRENTES, PRÉCISER LEUR PROVENANCE EN 12.

8. Transportation: Give Mode and Place of Direct Shipment to Canada	9. Conditions of Sale and Terms of Payment (i.e. Sale, Consignment Shipment, Leased Goods, etc.) Conditions de vente et modalités de paiement (p. ex. vente, expédition en consignation, location de marchandises, etc.)
	10. Currency of Settlement - Devises du paiement

11. No of Pkgs N° de	12. Specification of Commodities (Kind of Packages, Marks and Numbers, General Description and Characteristics, i.e. Grade, Quality) Désignation des articles (Nature des colis, marques et numéros, description générale et caractéristiques, p. ex. classe, qualité)	13. Quantity (State Unit) Quantité (Préciser	Selling Price - Prix de vente	
			14. Unit Price Prix unitaire	15. Total

18. If any of fields 1 to 17 are included on an attached commercial invoice, check this box Si tout renseignement relativement aux zones 1 à 17 figure sur une ou des factures commerciales ci-attachées, cocher cette case Commercial Invoice No. / N° de la facture _____	☐	16. Total Weight - Poids total		17. Invoice Total Total de la facture
		Net	Gross - Brut	

19. Exporter's Name and Address (if other than Vendor) Nom et adresse de l'exportateur (s'il diffère du vendeur)	20. Originator (Name and Address) - Expéditeur d'origine (Nom et

21. Departmental Ruling (if applicable) - Décision du Ministère (s'il y a	22. If fields 23 to 25 are not applicable, check this box ☐ Si les zones 23 à 25 sont sans objet, cocher cette case

23. If included in field 17 indicate amount: Si compris dans le total à la zone 17, préciser	24. If not included in field 17 indicate amount: Si non compris dans le total à la zone 17, préciser :	25. Check (if applicable): Cocher (s'il y a lieu) :
(i) Transportation charges, expenses and insurance from the place of direct shipment to Canada Les frais de transport, dépenses et assurances à partir du point d'expédition directe vers le Canada	(i) Transportation charges, expenses and insurance to the place of direct shipment to Canada Les frais de transport, dépenses et assurances jusqu'au point d'expédition directe vers le Canada	(i) Royalty payments or subsequent proceeds are paid or payable by the purchaser Des redevances ou produits ont été ou seront versés par l'acheteur ☐
(ii) Costs for construction, erection and assembly incurred after importation into Canada Les coûts de construction, d'érection et d'assemblage après importation au Canada	(ii) Amounts for commissions other than buying commissions Les commissions autres que celles versées pour l'achat	(ii) The purchaser has supplied goods or services for use in the production of these goods L'acheteur a fourni des marchandises ou des ☐
(iii) Export packing Le coût de l'emballage d'exportation _____	(iii) Export packing Le coût de l'emballage d'exportation _____	

C11 (95/01) Printed in Canada - Imprimé au Canada

A466

DROP-SHIPMENT CERTIFICATE

TO:

Name of Consignee: _____ (the "Consignee")

I, the [authorized officer/agent of the Consignee]/[the Consignee (if an individual)], hereby certify and acknowledge [on behalf of the Consignee (if agent or officer of a corporation)] as follows:

1. (a) The Consignee has or will receive physical possession of [describe tangible personal property in sufficient detail to identify specific shipment of tangible personal property] (the "Property") ordered from you by [name of unregistered non-resident]; **OR**

   (b) During the period from _____ to _____ the Consignee has or will receive physical possession of [describe tangible personal property in sufficient detail to identify specific shipment of tangible personal property] (the "Property") ordered from you by unregistered non-residents.

2. The Consignee is acquiring possession of the Property for the purpose of supplying a commercial service(s) (as defined in the *Excise Tax Act and the Québec Sales Tax Act*) in respect of the Property, or for consumption, use or supply in the course of its commercial activities.

3. If the Consignee subsequently transfers physical possession of the Property to a person who is not registered for the purposes of the Goods and Services Tax, otherwise than for export, or to another person who is registered for purposes of the Goods and Services Tax who does not provide to the Consignee a drop-shipment certificate under subsection 179(2) of the *Excise Tax Act*, and section 327.1 of the *Québec Sales Tax Act*, the Consignee will be required to account for the Goods and Services Tax and the Québec Sales Tax on the fair market value of the Property at that time.

4. If the Consignee is not acquiring the Property for consumption, use or supply exclusively in the course of its commercial activities, or if the Property is a passenger vehicle that is acquired for use as capital property, where the cost of the vehicle exceeds the vehicle's capital cost for income tax purposes, the Consignee is required to self-assess the Goods and Services Tax and the Québec Sales Tax.

DATE: _____   _____

                                        (Signature of individual who is
GST/QST REG. NO._____   Consignee of officer of Consignee)

NOTE: Part 1(a) is for use in the case of one or more deliveries relating to orders by the same unregistered non-resident.

Part 1(b) is for general use in the case of shipments, over a specified period of time, of tangible personal property of a particular description or class — not necessarily restricted to orders placed by the same unregistered non-resident.

When one Canadian company sells to another Canadian company, this form is filled out and kept on file to avoid paying the GST.

- These goods are eventually exported.
- Rarely used because most companies apply for a refund.
- Is used when there are huge amounts of taxes to be paid.

CERTIFICAT DE LIVRAISON DIRECTE

À: (Nom du fournisseur)

Nom du consignataire : _____ (le "consignataire")

Je, [le mandataire ou le représentant du consignataire]/[le consignataire (s'il s'agit d'un particulier)], certifie et reconnaît par le présent certificat [au nom du consignataire (s'il est le mandataire ou le représentant d'une personne morale)] ce qui suit :

1. a) le consignataire a ou aura la possession matérielle du [décrire le bien meuble corporel avec suffisamment de détails pour que puisse être identifiée une livraison précise de ce bien] (le "bien") commandé auprès de vous par [nom de la personne non résidante qui n'est pas inscrite]; OU

    b) pendant la période du _____ au _____, le consignataire a ou aura la possession matérielle du [décrire le bien meuble corporel avec suffisamment de détails pour que puisse être identifiée une livraison précise de ce bien] (le "bien") commandé auprès de vous par des personnes non résidantes qui ne sont pas inscrites.

2. Le consignataire acquiert la possession du bien en vue de fournir un service commercial (défini dans la *Loi sur la taxe de vente du Québec*) à l'égard de ce bien, ou pour le consommer, l'utiliser ou le fournir dans le cadre de ses activités commerciales.

3. Si le consignataire transfère par la suite la possession matérielle du bien à une personne qui n'est pas inscrite sous le régime de la taxe de vente du Québec, sauf en ce qui concerne l'exportation, ou à une autre personne qui est inscrite sous le régime de la taxe de vente du Québec et qui ne fournit pas au consignataire un certificat de livraison directe aux termes du paragraphe 327.1 de la *Loi sur la taxe de vente du Québec*, le consignataire est tenu de déclarer la taxe de vente du Québec sur la juste valeur marchande du bien à ce moment.

4. Si le consignataire n'acquiert pas le bien pour le consommer, l'utiliser ou le fournir exclusivement dans le cadre de ses activités commerciales, ou si le bien est une voiture de tourisme achetée pour servir d'immobilisation, si le coût de la voiture dépasse le coût en capital de la voiture aux fins de l'impôt sur le revenu, le consignataire est tenu d'établir lui-même le montant de la taxe de vente du Québec en application de la *Loi sur la taxe de vente du Québec*.

DATE: _____   _____

NO. INSCRIPT. TVQ_____   (Signature du particulier qui est
                                            consignataire ou mandataire du
                                            consignataire)

NOTE : La partie 1a) sert lorsqu'il y a une ou plusieurs livraisons relatives à des commandes effectuées par la même personne non résidante qui n'est pas inscrite.

La partie 1b) sert à des fins plus générales dans le cas de livraisons, au cours d'une période précise, d'un bien meuble corporel d'une description ou d'une catégorie particulière - sans être nécessairement limitée aux commandes passées par la même personne non résidante qui n'est pas inscrite.

DEPARTMENT OF THE TREASURY
UNITED STATES CUSTOMS SERVICE

OMB No. 1515-0204
See back of form for
Paperwork Reduction
Act Notice.

NORTH AMERICAN FREE TRADE AGREEMENT
CERTIFICATE OF ORIGIN

Please print or type   19 CFR 181.11, 181.22

1. EXPORTER NAME AND ADDRESS	2. BLANKET PERIOD (DD/MM/YY)
TAX IDENTIFICATION NUMBER:	FROM TO

3. PRODUCER NAME AND ADDRESS	4. IMPORTER NAME AND ADDRESS
TAX IDENTIFICATION NUMBER:	TAX IDENTIFICATION NUMBER:

5. DESCRIPTION OF GOOD(S)	6. HS TARIFF CLASSIFICATION NUMBER	7. PREFERENCE CRITERION	8. PRODUCER	9. NET COST	10. COUNTRY OF ORIGIN

I CERTIFY THAT:

· THE INFORMATION ON THIS DOCUMENT IS TRUE AND ACCURATE AND I ASSUME THE RESPONSIBILITY FOR PROVING SUCH REPRESENTATIONS. I UNDERSTAND THAT I AM LIABLE FOR ANY FALSE STATEMENTS OR MATERIAL OMISSIONS MADE ON OR IN CONNECTION WITH THIS DOCUMENT;

· I AGREE TO MAINTAIN, AND PRESENT UPON REQUEST, DOCUMENTATION NECESSARY TO SUPPORT THIS CERTIFICATE, AND TO INFORM, IN WRITING, ALL PERSONS TO WHOM THE CERTIFICATE WAS GIVEN OF ANY CHANGES THAT COULD AFFECT THE ACCURACY OR VALIDITY OF THIS CERTIFICATE;

· THE GOODS ORIGINATED IN THE TERRITORY OF ONE OR MORE OF THE PARTIES, AND COMPLY WITH THE ORIGIN REQUIREMENTS SPECIFIED FOR THOSE GOODS IN THE NORTH AMERICAN FREE TRADE AGREEMENT, AND UNLESS SPECIFICALLY EXEMPTED IN ARTICLE 411 OR ANNEX 401, THERE HAS BEEN NO FURTHER PRODUCTION OR ANY OTHER OPERATION OUTSIDE THE TERRITORIES OF THE PARTIES; AND

· THIS CERTIFICATE CONSISTS OF _____ PAGES, INCLUDING ALL ATTACHMENTS.

11.	11a. AUTHORIZED SIGNATURE		11b. COMPANY	
	11c. NAME *(Print or type)*		11d. TITLE	
	11e. DATE *(DD/MM/YY)*	11f. TELEPHONE > NUMBER	*(Voice)*	*(Facsimile)*

Customs Form 434 (040397)

NORTH AMERICAN FREE TRADE AGREEMENT CERTIFICATE OF ORIGIN INSTRUCTIONS

For purposes of obtaining preferential tariff treatment, this document must be completed legibly and in full by the exporter and be in the possession of the importer at the time the declaration is made. This document may also be completed voluntarily by the producer for use by the exporter. Please print or type:

FIELD 1: State the full legal name, address (including country) and legal tax identification number of the exporter. Legal taxation number is: in Canada, employer number or importer/exporter number assigned by Revenue Canada; in Mexico, federal taxpayer's registry number (RFC); and in the United States, employer's identification number or Social Security Number.

FIELD 2: Complete field if the Certificate covers multiple shipments of identical goods as described in Field # 5 that are imported into a NAFTA country for a specified period of up to one year (the blanket period). "FROM" is the date upon which the Certificate becomes applicable to the good covered by the blanket Certificate (it may be prior to the date of signing this Certificate). "TO" is the date upon which the blanket period expires. The importation of a good for which preferential treatment is claimed based on this Certificate must occur between these dates.

FIELD 3: State the full legal name, address (including country) and legal tax identification number, as defined in Field #1, of the producer. If more than one producer's good is included on the Certificate, attach a list of additional producers, including the legal name, address (including country) and legal tax identification number, cross-referenced to the good described in Field #5. If you wish this information to be confidential, it is acceptable to state 'Available to Customs upon request'. If the producer and the exporter are the same, complete field with "SAME". If the producer is unknown, it is acceptable to state "UNKNOWN".

FIELD 4: State the full legal name, address (including country) and legal tax identification number, as defined in Field #1, of the importer. If the importer is not known, state "UNKNOWN"; if multiple importers, state "VARIOUS".

FIELD 5: Provide a full description of each good. The description should be sufficient to relate it to the invoice description and to the Harmonized System (H.S.) description of the good. If the Certificate covers a single shipment of a good, include the invoice number as shown on the commercial invoice. If not known, indicate another unique reference number, such as the shipping order number.

FIELD 6: For each good described in Field #5, identify the H.S. tariff classification to six digits. If the good is subject to a specific rule of origin in Annex 401 that requires eight digits, identify to eight digits, using the H.S. tariff classification of the country into whose territory the good is imported.

FIELD 7: For each good described in Field #5, state which criterion (A through F) is applicable. The rules of origin are contained in Chapter Four and Annex 401. Additional rules are described in Annex 703.2 (certain agricultural goods), Annex 300-B, Appendix 6 (certain textile goods) and Annex 308.1 (certain automatic data processing goods and their parts). **NOTE: In order to be entitled to preferential tariff treatment, each good must meet at least one of the criteria below.**

Preference Criteria

    A.)   The good is "wholly obtained or produced entirely" in the territory of one or more of the NAFTA countries as referenced in Article 415. **Note: The purchase of a good in the territory does not necessarily render it "wholly obtained or produced".** If the good is an agricultural good, see also criterion F and Annex 703.2. *(Reference: Article 401(a) and 415)*

    B.)   The good is produced entirely in the territory of one or more of the NAFTA countries and satisfies the specific rule of origin, set out in Annex 401, that applies to its tariff classification. The rule may include a tariff classification change, regional value-content requirement, or a combination thereof. The good must also satisfy all other applicable requirements of Chapter Four. If the good is an agricultural good, see also criterion F and Annex 703.2. *(Reference: Article 401(b))*

    C.)   The good is produced entirely in the territory of one or more of the NAFTA countries exclusively from originating materials. Under this criterion, one or more of the materials may not fall within the definition of "wholly produced or obtained", as set out in Article 415. All materials used in the production of the good must qualify as "originating" by meeting the rules of Article 401 (a) through (d). If the good is an agricultural good, see also criterion F and Annex 703.2. *(Reference: Article 401(c)).*

    D.)   Goods are produced in the territory of one or more of the NAFTA countries but do not meet the applicable rule of origin, set out in Annex 401, because certain non-originating materials do not undergo the required change in tariff classification. The goods do nonetheless meet the regional value-content requirement specified in Article 401 (d). This criterion is limited to the following two circumstances:

        1.   The good was imported into the territory of a NAFTA country in an unassembled or disassembled form but was classified as an assembled good, pursuant to H.S. General Rule of Interpretation 2(a), or

        2.   The good incorporated one or more non-originating materials, provided for as parts under the H.S., which could not undergo a change in tariff classification because the heading provided for both the good and its parts and was not further subdivided into subheadings, or the subheading provided for both the good and its parts and was not further subdivided.

        NOTE: This criterion does not apply to Chapters 61 through 63 of the H.S. *(Reference: Article 401(d))*

    E.)   Certain automatic data processing goods and their parts, specified in Annex 308.1, that do not originate in the territory are considered originating upon importation into the territory of a NAFTA country from the territory of another NAFTA country when the most-favored-nation tariff rate of the good conforms to the rate established in Annex 308.1 and is common to all NAFTA countries. *(Reference: Annex 308. 1)*

    F.)   The good is an originating agricultural good under preference criterion A, B, or C above and is not subject to a quantitative restriction in the importing NAFTA country because it is a "qualifying good" as defined in Annex 703.2, Section A or B (please specify). A good listed in Appendix 703.2B.7 is also exempt from quantitative restrictions and is eligible for NAFTA preferential tariff treatment if it meets the definition of "qualifying good" in Section A of Annex 703.2. **NOTE 1: This criterion does not apply to goods that wholly originate in Canada or the United States and are imported into either country. NOTE 2: A tariff rate quota is not a quantitative restriction.**

FIELD 8: For each good described in Field #5, state "YES" if you are the producer of the good. If you are not the producer of the good, state "NO" followed by (1), (2), or (3), depending on whether this certificate was based upon: (1) your knowledge of whether the good qualifies as an originating good; (2) your reliance on the producers written representation (other than a Certificate of Origin) that the good qualifies as an originating good; or (3) a completed and signed Certificate for the good, voluntarily provided to the exporter by the producer.

FIELD 9: For each good described in field #5, where the good is subject to a regional value content (RVC) requirement, indicate "NC" if the RVC is calculated according to the net cost method; otherwise, indicate "NO". If the RVC is calculated over a period of time, further identity the beginning and ending dates (DD/MM/YY) of that period. *(Reference: Articles 402.1, 402.5).*

FIELD 10: Identify the name of the country ("MX" or "US" for agricultural and textile goods exported to Canada; "US" or "CA" for all goods exported to Mexico; or "CA" or "MX" for all goods exported to the United States) to which the preferential rate of customs duty applies, as set out in Annex 302.2, in accordance with the Marking Rules or in each party's schedule of tariff elimination.

        For all other originating goods exported to Canada, indicate appropriately "MX" or "US" if the goods originate in that NAFTA country, within the meaning of the NAFTA Rules of Origin Regulations, and any subsequent processing in the other NAFTA country does not increase the transaction value of the goods by more than seven percent; otherwise "JNT" for joint production. *(Reference: Annex 302.2)*

FIELD 11: This field must be completed, signed, and dated by the exporter. When the Certificate is completed by the producer for use by the exporter it must be completed, signed, and dated by the producer. The date must be the date the Certificate was completed and signed.

Customs form 434 (040397) (Back)

DEPARTMENT OF THE TREASURY
United States Customs Service

OMB No. 1515-0204. See
Customs Form 434 for Paperwork Reduction Act Notice.

NAFTA VERIFICATION OF ORIGIN QUESTIONNAIRE

19 CFR 181.72

This questionnaire is sent to you pursuant to 19 CFR 181.72, The questionnaire will be used in

determining if the ....

described on the NAFTA Certificate of Origin (CO) dated .... and signed by ....

originates under the NAFTA. If necessary, additional information may be requested at a later date.

☐ **EXPORTER**	☐ **PRODUCER OF GOOD**
If this box is checked, you are being sent this questionnaire as the exporter of the imported good. If you relied upon a Certificate of Origin or written representation from the Producer to prepare your Certificate of Origin provide a copy of what it was that you relied upon, and then go directly to Section V and complete it. If you relied upon your knowledge of the good, complete the questionnaire.	If this box is checked, you are being sent this questionnaire as the producer of the imported good. The good was exported by .... Complete the questionnaire.
☐ **EXPORTER/PRODUCER**	☐ **PRODUCER OF MATERIAL**
If this box is checked, you are being sent this questionnaire as the exporter and also the producer of the imported good. Complete the questionnaire.	If this box is checked, you are being sent this questionnaire because .... identified you as the producer of the material(s) used in the production of the good described above. Complete the questionnaire.

You have until...to return the completed and signed questionnaire to the requesting Customs office. You may fax your response. If a reply cannot be made by this date, please contact the Customs office by mail, telephone, or fax. If additional space is needed for your response, attach additional pages as needed. When the verification is completed, the exporter/producer will receive a written determination of the findings. The producer of a verified material will also be notified of the results of the verification of the material. The confidential business information collected on the questionnaire may only be disclosed to those authorities responsible for the administration and enforcement of determinations of origin, and of customs and revenue matters.

The questionnaire must be signed and dated by an individual who can certify as to the accuracy of the information provided in the questionnaire. Failure to complete and return this questionnaire may result in the denial of preferential treatment under the NAFTA.

SECTION I ▶   **PRODUCTION PROCESS**

Provide a *brief* description of the production process for the good/material being verified.

SECTION II ▶   **NON-ORIGINATING/UNKNOWN MATERIALS OR COMPONENTS**

Provide the following information for each *non-originating* material or component and for each material or component whose origin is unknown, used to produce the good being verified. If none were used, state "NONE".

Description of the material or component	HS#
....	....
....	....
....	....
....	....
....	....
....	....

HS# — Provide the six digit Harmonized System number or if the rule of origin of the good requires eight digits, supply eight.

Customs Form 446 (040397)

SECTION III ▶   ORIGINATING MATERIALS OR COMPONENTS

Provide the following information for each *originating* material or component used to produce the good being verified. If none were used, state "NONE".

Description of the material or component	Basis of Originating Status	Name and Address of the Supplier or, **If known**, Name & Address of the Manufacturer

Description of the Material or Component:

If the material or component is self-produced (**Self-Produced material** or component is a material or component that is produced by the producer of a good and used in the production of that good) and designated as an intermidiate material (**Intermediate material** is a self-produced material or component, designated by the producer, that meets the rules of origin and that is incorporated into the final good), place the letter 'D' before the name of the material or component in the table.   If the material or component is self-produced but designated as an intermediate material, then each material used in the production of this self-produced material or component must be identified separately.

Basis of Originating Status:

Describe type of information (i.e. certificate of origin, affadavit, etc.) which was relied upon to determine the originating status of the material or component.

SECTION IV ▶   ADDITIONAL QUESTIONS

1.Has a classification ruling been issued with respect to any of the materials or components produced?	☐ Yes	☐ No
2.Was the de minimis provision used to determine whether the good being verified was originating?	☐ Yes	☐ No
3.Is the good being verified an originating fungible good? If yes, check below which inventory management method you used: ☐ LIFO ☐ FIFO ☐ Average ☐ Specific Identification	☐ Yes	☐ No
4.Did any of the originating materials used in the production of the good qualify as an originating fungible material? If yes, attach a list of the materials that qualify as originating materials under the fungible materials provisions, and check below which inventory management method you used: ☐ LIFO ☐ FIFO ☐ Average ☐ Specific Identification	☐ Yes	☐ No
5.Was the sale of the good/material to a related person?	☐ Yes	☐ No
6.If a Regional Value Content (RVC) was used in ascertaining whether the good being verified originates,	☐ Transaction Value	☐ Net Cost
7.What was the estimated qualifying percentage for RVC? **%**		
8.Was the RVC calculated using accumulation? If yes, provide the name and address of each supplier.	☐ Yes	☐ No

SECTION V ▶   CERTIFICATION

I certify that the information on this document is true and accurate and I assume the responsibility for proving such representations. I understand that I am liable for any false statements or relevant omissions made on or in connection with this document.

Authorized Signature	Company Name *(Print or Type)*
Name *(Print or Type)*	Title *(Print or Type)*
Telephone	Date *(MM/DD/YYYY)*

Customs Form 446 (040397)(Back)

FORM BXA-621P
(REV 10-89)

U.S. DEPARTMENT OF COMMERCE
BUREAU OF EXPORT ADMINISTRATION

REPORT OF REQUEST FOR RESTRICTIVE TRADE PRACTICE OR BOYCOTT SINGLE TRANSACTION

(For reporting requests described in Part 769 of the Export Administration Regulations)

NOTICE OF RIGHT TO PROTECT CERTAIN INFORMATION FROM DISCLOSURE

The Export Administration Act permits you to protect from public disclosure information regarding the quantity, description, and value of commodities or technical data supplied in Item 11 of this report and in any accompanying documents. *If you do not claim this protection, all of the information in your report and in accompanying documents will be made available for public inspection and copying.*

You can obtain this protection by certifying, in Item 10 of the report, that disclosure of the information referred to above would place a United States company or individual involved in the report at a competitive disadvantage. If you make such a certification in Item 10, you may remove information regarding the quantity, description, and value of the commodities or technical data supplied by you from Item 11 of the inspection copy of the report form and from the public inspection copies of the accompanying documents.

The withholding of this information will be honored by the Department unless the Secretary determines that disclosure of the information would not place a United States company or individual at a competitive disadvantage or that it would be contrary to the national interest to withhold the information.

THIS SPACE FOR BXA USE

A BATCH

MONTH/YEAR

RSN | SUBSET

RTP

CLASS | FILING | TAG

This report required by law (50 U.S.C. App. §2407 (b) (2) P.L. 96-72; E.O. 12214; 15 C.F.R. Part 769). Failure to report can result both in criminal penalties, including fines or imprisonment, and administrative sanctions.

Instructions: 1. Complete all items that apply. 2. Assemble original report form and accompanying documents as a unit, and submit intact and unaltered. 3. Assemble and submit the duplicate copy of report form (marked Duplicate (Public Inspection Copy)) and additional copies of accompanying documents (marked with the legend "Public Inspection Copy.") 4. *If you certify, in Item 10, that the disclosure of the information specified there would cause competitive disadvantage, edit the "Public Inspection Copy: of the documents submitted to exclude the specified information and remove the bottom of the Duplicate "Public Inspection Copy" of the report form relating to Item 11.*

Public reporting for this collection of information is estimated to average one hour per request, including the time for reviewing instructions, searching existing data sources, gathering and maintaining the data needed, and completing and reviewing the collection of information. Send comments regarding this burden estimate or any other aspect of this collection of information, including suggestions for reducing this burden, to Office of Security and Management Support, Bureau of Export Administration, U.S. Department of Commerce, Washington, D.C. 20230; and to the Office of Management and Budget, Paperwork Reduction Project (0694-0012), Washington, D.C. 20503

1a. Identify firm submitting this report:	Specify firm type:	1b. Check any applicable box:
Name:	☐ Exporter	☐ Revision of a previous report (attach two copies of the previously submitted report)
Address:	☐ Bank	
City, State and ZIP:	☐ Forwarder	☐ Resubmission of a deficient report returned by BXA (attach form letter that was returned with deficient report)
Country (if other than USA):	☐ Carrier	
Telephone:	☐ Insurer	☐ Report on behalf of the person identified in Item 2
Firm Identification No. (if Known): 29-34	☐ Other 35	☐ Dual report on behalf of self and the person identified in Item 2

2. If you are authorized to report and are reporting on behalf of another U.S. person, identify that person (e.g., domestic subsidiary, controlled Foreign subsidiary, exporter, beneficiary):	3. Identify exporting firm, unless same as Item 1a or 2:
Name	Name:
Address:	Address:
City, State and ZIP:	City, State and ZIP:
Country (if other than USA):	Country (if other than USA):
Type of firm: (see list in Item 1a)	Firm Identification No. (if known): 36-41 42
Firm Identification No. (if known):	

4. (a) Name of boycotting country from which request originated: (b) Name of country directing inclusion of request, if different from (a) above: 43-44	5. Name of country or countries against which request is directed: 45-46

6. Reporting firm's reference number (e.g., letter of credit, customer order, invoice): 71-77	7. Date firm received request: (use digits for month/day/year) 47-52

8. Specify type(s) of document conveying the request:

☐ Request to carrier for blacklist certificate (submit two copies of blacklist certificate or transcript of request)

☐ Unwritten, not otherwise provided for (make transcript of request and submit copies) 53-54

☐ Letter of credit

☐ Requisition/purchase order/accepted contract/shipping instruction

☐ Bid invitation/tender/proposal/trade opportunity

☐ Questionnaire (not related to a particular dollar value transaction)

☐ Other written (specify)_____

Submit two copies of each document or relevant page in which the request appears

9. Decision on request: (Check one)

☐ Have not taken and will not take the action requested.

☐ Have taken or will take the action requested.

☐ Have taken or will take the action requested and claim it is subject to a grace period (attached detailed explanation). 56-57

☐ Have taken or will take the action requested but in a modified for (attach detailed explanation).

☐ Unable to report ultimate decision on the request at this time and will inform the Bureau of Export Administration of the decision within ten days after decision is made.

Additional Information: The firm submitting this report may, if it so desires, state on a separate sheet any additional information relating to the request reported or the response to that request. This statement will constitute a part of the report and will be made available for public inspection and copying, subject to the right to protect certain confidential information from disclosure described in Item 10.

10. Protection of Certain Information from Disclosure: (Check appropriate boxes and sign below)

1. ☐ I (We) certify that disclosure to the public of the information regarding quantity, description, and value of the commodities or technical data contained in:
   ☐ Item 11 below (if you check this box, be sure to remove the bottom of the Duplicate (Public Inspection Copy) of the report form relating to Item 11.)
   ☐ Attached documents (if you check this box, be sure to edit the "Public Inspection Copy" of the documents submitted to exclude the specified information.) would place a United States person involved at a competitive disadvantage, and I (We) request that it be kept confidential.

2. ☐ I (we) authorize public release of all information contained in the report and in any attached documents. I (We) certify that all statements and information contained in this report are true and correct to the best of my (our) knowledge and belief.

Sign here in ink_____ Type or print _____ Date_____

11. Describe the commodities or technical data involved, and specify quanity and value:

Description	Quantity:
	Value to nearest whole dollar $
	58-69

ORIGINAL Subject to Office of Antiboycott Compliance, BXA, U.S. Department of Commerce, Room 6099-C, Washington, D.C. 20230

Form Approved: OMB No. 0694-0016

FORM BXA 647P
(REV. 4-98)

U.S. DEPARTMENT OF COMMERCE
BUREAU OF EXPORT ADMINISTRATION

DELIVERY VERIFICATION CERTIFICATE

Public reporting burden for this collection of information is estimated to average 30 minutes per response, including the time for reviewing instruments, searching existing data sources, gathering and maintaining the data needed, and completing and reviewing the collection of information. Send comments regarding this burden estimate or any other aspect of this collection of information, including suggestions for reducing this burden, to The Director of Administration, room 3889, Bureau of Export Administration, U.S. Department of Commerce, Washington, D.C., 20230; and to the Office of Management and Budget Paperwork Reduction Project (0694-0016) Washington, D.C. 20503

Notwithstanding any other provision of law, no person is required to respond to nor shall a person be subject to a penalty for failure to comply with a collection of information subject to the requirements of the Paperwork Reduction Act unless that collection of information displays a currently valid OMB Control Number.

Instructions - When required to obtain a delivery verification, the U.S. Importer shall submit this form in duplicate, to the Customs Office. U.S. importer is required to complete all items on this form except the portion to be completed by the U.S. Customs Service. The Customs Office will certify a Delivery Verification Certificate only after the import has been delivered to the U.S. importer. The duly certified form shall then be dispatched by the U.S. importer to the foreign exporter or otherwise disposed of in accordance with instructions of the exporting country.

No delivery verification may be obtained unless a completed application form has been received. (50 U.S.C. App § 2401 et seq., 15 C.F.R.§ 748)

EXPORTER *(Name and address)*	This certification applies to the goods described below, shown on U.S. Department of Commerce International Import Certificate No._____
	ARRIVED *(Name of port)* / DATE OF ARRIVAL
IMPORTER *(Name and address)*	NAME OF SHIP, AIRCRAFT, OR CARRIER *(Include numbers on bills of lading, airway bills, etc.)*

DESCRIPTION OF GOODS	QUANTITY	VALUE (FOB, CIF, etc)

TO BE COMPLETED BY U.S. CUSTOMS SERVICE	REGION NO:
(Customs's Seal)	CERTIFICATION – It is hereby certified that the importer has produced evidence that the goods specified above have been delivered and brought under the Export Administration Regulations of the United States.
	Signature Date

ENTRY	☐ WAREHOUSE ☐ CONSUMPTION	NUMBER	DATE

FORM BXA-645P/ATF-4522/DPS-53 (REV 3/96)

Form Approved: OMB No. 0694-0017 - Modele approuvé: OMB No. 0694-0017

U.S. DEPARTMENT OF COMMERCE
Bureau of Export Administration
U.S. DEPARTMENT OF THE TREASURY
Bureau of Alcohol, Tobacco and Firearms
U.S. DEPARTMENT OF STATE
Office of Munitions Control

INTERNATIONAL IMPORT CERTIFICATE
(CERTIFICAT INTERNATIONAL D'IMPORTATION)

NOTE: Read instructions on the reverse side before completing and submitting this form. (Lire les instructions au verso avant de remplir et de presenter la présente formule.)

Certificate Number

1. U.S. Importer/Importateur (Name and address—Nom et adresse)

FOR U.S. GOVERNMENT USE (Réservé pour le Gouvernment des Etats-Unis)

2. Exporter/Exportateur (Name and address—Nom et adresse)

If this form has been approved by the Department of Commerce or the Department of State, it is not valid unless the official seal of the Department of Commerce, or the Department of State, appears in this space. If this form is approved by the Treasury Department, a seal is not required. (Si ce formulaire a été approuvé par le Ministère du Commerce, ou le Ministère des Affaires Etrangères, il n'est pas valide à moins qu'un sceau officiel du Ministère du Commerce ou du Ministère des Affaires Etrangères soit apposé sur le document. Si ce formulaire est approuvé par le Ministère des Finances, un sceau officiel n'est pas nécessaire.

3.

Description of goods (Désignation de la Marchandise)	TSUS Anno. No. (Numéro de la liste)	Quantity (Quantité)	Value (Valeur) (FOB, CIF, etc.)

4. Representation and undertaking of U.S. importer or principal

The undersigned hereby represents that he has undertaken to import into the United States of America under a U.S. Consumption Entry or U.S. Warehouse Entry the commodities in quantities described above, or, if commodities are not so imported into the United States of America, that he will not divert, transship, or reexport them to another destination except with explicit approval of the Department of Commerce, the Department of State, or the Department of the Treasury, as appropriate. The undersigned also undertakes to notify the appropriate Department immediately of any changes of fact or intention set forth herein. If a delivery verification is required, the undersigned undertakes to obtain such verification and make disposition of it in accordance with such requirement. Any false statement willfully made in this declaration is punishable by fine and imprisonment. (See experts from U.S. Code on reverse side.)

Déclaration et engagement de l'importateur ou du commettant des Etats-Unis

Le soussigné déclare par la présente qu'il a pris l'engagement d'importer aux Etats-Unis d'Amérique, en vertu d'une Déclaration américaine de Mise en Consommation, ou d'une Déclaration américaine d'Entrée en entrepôt, la quantité de produits ci-dessus et que, dans le cas ou ces produits ne seraient pas ainsi importés aux Etats-Unis d'Amérique, il ne le détournera, ne les transbordera, ni les réexportera a destination d'un autre lieu, si ce n'est avec l'approbation explicite du Ministère du Commerce, du Ministère des Affaires Etrangères ou du Ministère des Finances, comme il est requis. Le soussigné prend également l'engagement d'aviser le Ministère intéressé des Etats-Unis de tous changements survenus dans les actes ou les intentions énoncés dans la présente déclaration. Si demande est faite d'une confirmation de la livraison le soussigné prend également l'engagement d'obtenir cette confirmation et d'en disposer de la manière prescrite par cette demande. Toute fausse déclaration faite intentionnellement expose l'auteur aux pénalités prévues par la loi. (Voir Extrait du Code des Etats-Unis au verso.)

Type or Print
(Prière d'écrire
a la machine ou
en caractères
d'imprimerie)

Type or Print
(Prière d'écrire
a la machine ou
en caractères
d'imprimerie)

Name of Firm or Corporation
(Nom de la Firme ou de la Societé)

Name and Title of Authorized Official
(Nom et titre de l'agent ou employé autorisé)

Signature of Authorised Official
(Signature de l'agent ou employé autorisé)

Date of Signature
(Date de la signature)

This document ceases to be valid unless presented to the competent foreign authorities within six months from its date of issue. (Le présent document perd sa validité s'il n'est pas remis aux autorités étrangères compétentes dans un délai de six mois à compter de sa délivrance.)

No import certification may be obtained unless this International Import Certificate has been completed and filed with the appropriate U.S. Government agency (Department of Commerce: 50 U.S.C. app. §2411, E.O. 12214 15 C.F.R. §368; Department of the Treasury; 22 U.S.C. §2778, E.O. 11959, 27 C.F.R. §47; Department of State: 22 U.S.C. 2778, 2779, E.O. 11958, 22 C.F.R. §123). Information furnished herewith is subject to the provisions of Section 12(c) of the Export Administration Act of 1979, 50 U.S.C. app. 2411(c), and its unauthorized disclosure is prohibited by law.

FOR U.S. GOVERNMENT USE (Réservé au Gouvernement des Etats-Unis)

Certification: This is to certify that the above declaration was made to the U.S. Department of Commerce, State, or Treasury through the undersigned designated official thereof and a copy of this certification is placed in the official files.

Certification : Il est certifié par la présente que la déclaration ci-dessus a été faite au Ministère du Commerce, des Affaires Etrangères, ou des Finances des Etats-Unis par l'intermédiaire du fonctionnaire autorisé soussigné de ce Ministère et qu'une copie de ce certificat a été conservée dans les archives officielles.

Designated Commerce, State, or Treasury Official (Fonctionnaire competent du Ministère du Commerce, d'Etat, ou du Trésor)   Date

USOOMM DC 99-24414

ORIGINAL COPY

Form Approved: OMB No. 0625-0005

FORM BXA-648P
(REV. 2-88)

U.S. DEPARTMENT OF COMMERCE
BUREAU OF EXPORT ADMINISTRATION

Date

Export License No.

NOTIFICATION OF
DELIVERY VERIFICATION REQUIREMENT

Applicant's Reference No.

Information furnished herewith is subject to the provisions of Section 12 (c) of the Export Administration Act of 1979, 50 U.S.C. app. 2411 (c), and its unauthorized disclosure is prohibited by law. Your failure to complete and return this form along with required delivery verification(s) may subject you to administrative action under the Export Administration Act.

International Import Certificate No.

IMPORTANT NOTICE

LICENSEE: You are required to provide the Office of Export Licensing with a document verifying the delivery of each shipment made against the attached license. For your information, instructions on what you must do about obtaining and submitting delivery verification documents will be found on the reverse side of the Duplicate Copy of this Form.

AGENT OR FREIGHT FORWARDER: When this Form BXA-648P is attached to a license which has been forwarded by the Office of Export Licensing to an agent or freight forwarder of the licensee, it is the responsibility of the agent or freight forwarder to notify the licensee that verification of delivery is required for exports made against the license.

Check Item 1, 2, or 3, as applicable, and complete Item. The ORIGINAL of this form must be return to the Office of Export Licensing, P.O. Box 273, Washington, D.C. 20044, as soon as you have received all delivery verification documents for shipments made against the attached License. (See paragraph A3 on the back of the Duplicate Copy.)

1. ☐ The total quantity authorized for export by this license has been exported and all delivery verification documents are attached hereto.

2. ☐ A part of the quantity authorized for export by this license will not be exported. Delivery verification documents covering all commodities exported are attached hereto.

3. ☐ No shipment has been made against this license and none is contemplated.

4. The License:

a. ☐ is returned herewith for cancellation.

b. ☐ Was returned to the Office of Export Licensing as required by 386.2(d) (4) of the Export Administration Regulations.

Remarks:

Print or type name of licensee

Print or type name and title of authorized representative

Date signed

Signature of authorized representative

USCOMM-DC 88-24089

(See Instructions on reverse side of Duplicate Copy)

ORIGINAL

INSTRUCTIONS

A. Under the Export Administration Regulations of the United States you are required to:

1. At the time of making each shipment under the attached license, send to your foreign importer a written request for delivery verification. Include in your request the import certificate number shown on the front of this form and ask the foreign importer to make sure that this import certificate number appears on the delivery import verification he receives from his government. Where possible, you shall submit this request together with the related shipping documents.

    The foreign importer shall be advised of the terms of the commodity description as shown on the export license, including the unit of measure (i.e., pounds, number, etc.) and/or value of commodities (as applicable) and should be requested to make sure that these same terms are used on the delivery verification. If the Office of Export Licensing is unable to relate the terms shown on the completed delivery verification with the terms on the export license, the delivery verification may be returned to you for clarification.

2. Obtain from the foreign importer a delivery verification which has been issued to him by his government for the commodities described in the attached export license.

Where the full amount licensed has not been or will not be exported, the delivery verification shall be obtained for the amount actually shipped.

If the commodities are exported in partial shipments, you are required to obtained a delivery verification for each partial shipment. Delivery verications covering partial shipments shall be retained in your files until you have received delivery verifications for all partial shipments made against the attached license.

3. Send the original copies of all delivery verifications covering shipments made under the attached license together with the signed completed original of this Form BXA-648P, in one parcel, to the U.S. Department of Commerce, Bureau of Export Administration, Office of Export Licensing, P.O. Box 273, Washington, D.C. 20044.

    If you are unable to obtain a delivery verification within 60 days after the last shipment under this license, immediately notify the Office of Export Licensing, by letter, giving a full explanation and the approximate date you expect to submit the document to the Office of Export Licensing.

B. Please note the following provisions and requirements of the Export Administration Regulations:

1. Paragraph 375.7(a) requires that documents in a foreign language shall be accompanied by an accurate English translation.

2. Paragraph 375.3(i) contains the delivery verification requirement provisions.

A list of addresses where foreign importers may obtain import Certificates and Delivery Verifications is included in Supplement No.1 to Part 375 of the Export Administration Regulations.

* The U.S. Department of Commerce Export Administration Regulations is a compilation of official regulations and policies governing the export licensing of commodities and technical data. This publication and supplementary Export Administration Bulletins may be examined free of charge at any ITA District Office, U.S. Department of Commerce. Paid subscriptions may be placed with the Superintendent of Documents, U.S. Government Printing Office, Washington, D.C. 20402

FORM BXA-648P (REV. 2-88)

FORM BXA-711 FORM APPROVED: OMB NO. 0694-0088	U.S. DEPARTMENT OF COMMERCE Bureau of Export Administration Information furnished herewith is subject to the provisions of Section 12(c) of the Export Administration Act of 1979, as amended, 50 U.S.C. app. 2411(c), and its unauthorized disclosure is prohibited by law.	DATE RECEIVED (Leave Blank)

STATEMENT BY ULTIMATE CONSIGNEE AND PURCHASER

1. ULTIMATE CONSIGNEE	CITY
ADDRESS LINE 1	COUNTRY
ADDRESS LINE 2	POSTAL CODE	TELEPHONE OR FAX

2. DISPOSITION OR USE OF ITEMS BY ULTIMATE CONSIGNEE NAMED IN BLOCK 1
We certify that the items:

A. ☐ Will be used by us (as capital equipment) in the form in which received in a manufacturing process in the country named in Block 1 and will not be reexported or incorporated into an end product.

B. ☐ Will be processed or incorporated by us into the following product(s) _____
to be manufactured in the country named in Block 1 for distribution in _____

C. ☐ Will be resold by us in the form in which received in the country named in Block 1 for use or consumption therein.
The specific end-use by my customer will be _____

D. ☐ Will be reexported by us in the form in which received to _____

E. ☐ Other (describe fully) _____

NOTE: If BOX (D) is checked, acceptance of this form by the Bureau of Export Administration as a supporting document for license applications shall not be construed as an authorization to reexport the items to which the form applies unless specific approval has been obtained from the Bureau of Export Administration for such reexport.

3. NATURE OF BUSINESS OF ULTIMATE CONSIGNEE NAMED IN BLOCK 1
A. The nature of our usual business is _____
B. Our business relationship with the U.S. exporter is _____
and we have had this business relationship for _____ year(s).

4. ADDITIONAL INFORMATION

5. ASSISTANCE IN PREPARING STATEMENT

STATEMENT OF ULTIMATE CONSIGNEE AND PURCHASER
We certify that all of the facts contained in this statement are true and correct to the best of our knowledge and we do not know of any additional facts which are inconsistent with the above statement. We shall promptly send a supplemental statement to the U.S. Exporter, disclosing any change of facts or intentions set forth in this statement which occurs after the statement has been prepared and forwarded. Except as specifically authorized by the U.S. Export Administration Regulations (15 CFR Parts 730-774), or by prior written approval of the Bureau of Export Administration, we will not reexport, resell, or otherwise dispose of any items approved on a license supported by this statement: (1) to any country not approved for export as brought to our attention by means of a bill of lading, commercial invoice, or any other means; or (2) to any person if we know that it will result directly or indirectly, in disposition of the items contrary to the representations made in this statement or contrary to Export Administration Regulations.

6. SIGNATURE OF OFFICIAL OF ULTIMATE CONSIGNEE	7. NAME OF PURCHASER
NAME OF OFFICIAL	SIGNATURE OF OFFICIAL OF PURCHASER
TITLE OF OFFICIAL	NAME OF OFFICIAL
DATE	TITLE OF OFFICIAL

CERTIFICATION FOR USE OF U.S. EXPORTER We certify that no corrections, additions, or alterations were made on this form by us after the form was signed by the (ultimate consignee)(purchaser).	DATE
8. NAME OF EXPORTER	SIGNATURE OF PERSON AUTHORIZED TO CERTIFY FOR EXPORTER
NAME OF PERSON SIGNING THIS DOCUMENT	TITLE OF PERSON SIGNING THIS DOCUMENT	DATE

We acknowledge that the making of any false statements or concealment of any material fact in connection with this statement may result in imprisonment or fine, or both and denial, in whole or in part, of participation in U.S. exports and reexports.

Public reporting burden for this collection of information is estimated to average 15 minutes per response plus one minute for recordkeeping, including the time for reviewing instruments, searching existing data sources, gathering and maintaining the data needed, and completing and reviewing the collection of information. Send comments regarding this burden estimate or any other aspect of this collection of information, including suggestions for reducing this burden, to The Director of Administration, Room 3889, Bureau of Export Administration, U.S. Department of Commerce, Washington, D.C. 20230; and to the Office of Management and Budget Paperwork Reduction Project (0694-0021), Washington, D.C. 20503.

Notwithstanding any other provision of law, no person is required to respond to nor shall a person be subject to a penalty for failure to comply with a collection of information subject to the requirements of the Paperwork Reduction Act unless that collection of information displays a currently valid OMB Control Number.

USCOMM-DC 96-24082

B

FORM BXA-748P
FORM APPROVED: OMB NO. 0694-0088, 0694-0089

U.S. DEPARTMENT OF COMMERCE
Bureau of Export Administration

MULTIPURPOSE APPLICATION

Information furnished herewith is subject to the provisions of Section 12(c) of the Export Administration Act of 1979, as amended, 50 U.S.C. app. 2411(c), and its unauthorized disclosure is prohibited by law.

APPLICATION CONTROL NUMBER
This is NOT an export license number

DATE RECEIVED
(Leave Blank)   **X**

1. CONTACT PERSON

2. TELEPHONE

3. FACSIMILE

4. DATE OF APPLICATION

5. TYPE OF APPLICATION
- ☐ EXPORT
- ☐ REEXPORT
- ☐ CLASSIFICATION REQUEST
- ☐ SPECIAL COMPREHENSIVE LICENSE
- ☐ OTHER

6. DOCUMENTS SUBMITTED WITH APPLICATION
- ☐ BXA-748P-A
- ☐ BXA-748P-B
- ☐ BXA-711
- ☐ IMPORT/END-USER CERTIFICATE
- ☐ TECH. SPECS.
- ☐ LETTER OF EXPLANATION
- ☐ FOREIGN AVAILABILITY
- ☐ OTHER

7. DOCUMENTS ON FILE WITH APPLICANT
- ☐ BXA-711
- ☐ LETTER OF ASSURANCE
- ☐ IMPORT/END-USER CERTIFICATE
- ☐ NUCLEAR CERTIFICATION
- ☐ OTHER

8. SPECIAL COMPREHENSIVE LICENSE
- ☐ BXA-752 OR BXA-752-A
- ☐ INTERNAL CONTROL PROGRAM
- ☐ COMPREHENSIVE NARRATIVE
- ☐ CERTIFICATIONS
- ☐ OTHER

9. SPECIAL PURPOSE

10. RESUBMISSION APPLICATION CONTROL NUMBER

11. REPLACEMENT LICENSE NUMBER

12. FOR ITEM(S) PREVIOUSLY EXPORTED, PROVIDE LICENSE EXCEPTION SYMBOL OR LICENSE NUMBER

13. IMPORT/END-USER CERTIFICATE COUNTRY: NUMBER:

14. APPLICANT
- ADDRESS LINE 1
- ADDRESS LINE 2
- CITY | POSTAL CODE
- STATE/COUNTRY | EMPLOYER IDENTIFICATION NUMBER

15. OTHER PARTY AUTHORIZED TO RECEIVE LICENSE
- ADDRESS LINE 1
- ADDRESS LINE 2
- CITY | POSTAL CODE
- STATE/COUNTRY | TELEPHONE OR FAX

16. PURCHASER
- ADDRESS LINE 1
- ADDRESS LINE 2
- CITY | POSTAL CODE
- COUNTRY | TELEPHONE OR FAX

17. INTERMEDIATE CONSIGNEE
- ADDRESS LINE 1
- ADDRESS LINE 2
- CITY | POSTAL CODE
- COUNTRY | TELEPHONE OR FAX

18. ULTIMATE CONSIGNEE
- ADDRESS LINE 1
- ADDRESS LINE 2
- CITY | POSTAL CODE
- COUNTRY | TELEPHONE OR FAX

19. END-USER
- ADDRESS LINE 1
- ADDRESS LINE 2
- CITY | POSTAL CODE
- COUNTRY | TELEPHONE OR FAX

20. ORIGINAL ULTIMATE CONSIGNEE
- ADDRESS LINE 1
- ADDRESS LINE 2
- CITY | POSTAL CODE
- COUNTRY | TELEPHONE OR FAX

21. SPECIFIC END-USE

22. (a) ECCN | (b) CTP | (c) MODEL NUMBER | (d) CCATS NUMBER
(e) QUANTITY | (f) UNITS | (g) UNIT PRICE | (h) TOTAL PRICE | (i) MANUFACTURER
(j) TECHNICAL DESCRIPTION

23. TOTAL APPLICATION DOLLAR VALUE
$

24. ADDITIONAL INFORMATION

Per all applications: I certify that to the best of my knowledge, all the information on this form is true and correct, and that it conforms to the instructions accompanying this form and the Export Administration Regulations. Per license applications: I certify or agree, as appropriate that (a) to the best of my knowledge all statements in this application, including the description of the commodities, software or technology and their end-uses, and any documents submitted in support of this application are correct and complete and that they fully and accurately disclose all the terms of the order and other facts of the transaction; (b) I will report promptly to the Bureau of Export Administration any material changes in the terms of the order or other facts or intentions of the transaction as them available as required by the Export Administration Regulations; (c) I will retain records pertaining to this transaction and make them available to the Export Administration Regulations; (c) I will retain records pertaining to this transaction and make them available to the Export Administration and supporting documents, whether the application is still under consideration or a license has been granted; and (d) if the license is granted, I will be amply accountable for its use in accordance with the Export Administration Regulations and all the terms and conditions of the license. A number of the parts of this form include certifications based on a person's knowledge. As defined in Part 748 of the Export Administration Regulations, "knowledge" of a circumstance includes not only positive knowledge that the circumstance exists or is substantially certain to occur, but also an awareness of a high probability of its existence or future occurrence. Such awareness is inferred from evidence of the conscious disregard of facts known to a person and is also inferred from a person's willful avoidance of facts.

25. SIGNATURE (of person authorized to execute this application) | NAME OF SIGNER | TITLE OF SIGNER

This license application and any license issued pursuant thereto are expressly subject to all rules and regulations of the Bureau of Export Administration. Making any false statement or concealing any material fact in connection with this application or altering in any way the license issued is punishable by imprisonment or fine, or both, and by denial of export privileges under the Export Administration Act of 1979, as amended, and any other applicable Federal statutes. No license will be issued unless this form is completed and submitted in accordance with Export Administration Regulation.

X   **X**   **ORIGINAL B**

USCOMM-DO 96-24024

FORM BXA-748P
FORM APPROVED: OMB NO. 0694-0088,0694-0089

U.S. DEPARTMENT OF COMMERCE
Bureau of Export Administration

MULTIPURPOSE APPLICATION FORM

GENERAL INSTRUCTIONS

A. USE OF THIS FORM. Use this form to submit either a Classification request or an application for a license to Export or Reexport items subject to the export licensing authority of the U. S. Department of Commerce.

B. WHO MAY APPLY. Anyone may submit a classification request or a license application for the reexport of commodities, software, or technology. License applications for the export of items from the United States may be made only by a person subject to the jurisdiction of the United States. An application may be made on behalf of a person not subject to the jurisdiction of the United States by an authorized agent in the United States. Refer to §748.5 of the Export Administration Regulations (EAR) for additional information.

C. WHAT TO SUBMIT. Consult part 748 of the EAR for instructions on documentation that you may need to submit with your application. Remove this cover page along with the last page of this application and firmly attach any required support documentation. (Do not separate the remaining pages in this package and note the Application Control Number on all attached support documents.) This last page contains your Application Control Number, necessary to track your application during processing at the Bureau of Export Administration (BXA). Refer to §750.5 of the EAR for additional information on these services.

D. DUPLICATE APPLICATIONS. You may not submit a second application for a license covering the same proposed transaction while your first application is pending with BXA.

E. ASSISTANCE AND ADDITIONAL COPIES. To order small quantities of this form, or to request assistance on this or other export control matters, contact the Exporter Counseling Division on (202) 482-4811 or BXA's Western Regional Office in Newport Beach, California on (714) 660-0144 or Santa Clara, California on (408) 748-7450. Copies may also be obtained from any U.S. Department of Commerce, International Trade Administration District Office. To order large quantities of this form, write BXA's Operations Support Division, P.O. Box 273, Washington, D.C. 20044, telephone (202) 482-3332, or fax (202) 219-9179.

F. COMPLIANCE WITH THE EAR. Additional information necessary to properly complete and file this application is contained in the EAR, codified at 15 CFR 730 et seq, with changes published in the Federal Register. BXA also publishes a looseleaf version of the EAR, with changes issued in the form of supplements titled Export Administration Bulletins and offers the EAR on-line. If you wish to subscribe to the print or electronic version of the EAR, contact the United States Government Information, Superintendent of Documents, P.O. Box 371954, Pittsburgh, PA 15250-7954; or by telephone (202) 512-1800; or by facsimile (202) 512-2250.

SPECIFIC INSTRUCTIONS

This application will be processed using an Optical Character Recognition (OCR) System. Type using 10 or 12 pitch. Do not use script type faces. Information must be placed within the space provided. Do not go through or outside lines. Failure to complete the form as requested will significantly delay processing of the form and could result in the return of your application. If a Block or Box does not apply to your application, leave it blank.

All information must be legibly typed within the lines for each Block or Box except where a signature is required. Enter only one typed line of text per block or line. Where there is a choice of entering telephone numbers or facsimile numbers, and you wish to provide a facsimile number instead of a telephone number, identify the facsimile number with the letter "F" immediately after the number (e.g., 011-358-0-123456F).

If you are completing this form to request classification of your item, you must complete Blocks 1 through 5, 14, 22(a), (b), (c), (d), and (i), 24 and 25 only.

Block 1: CONTACT PERSON. Enter the name of the person who can answer questions concerning the application.

Block 2: TELEPHONE. Enter the telephone number of the person who can answer questions concerning the application.

Block 3: FACSIMILE. Enter the facsimile number, if available, of the person who can answer questions concerning the application.

Block 4: DATE OF APPLICATION. Enter the current date.

Block 5: TYPE OF APPLICATION. **Export.** If the items are located within the United States, and you wish to export those items, mark the Box labeled "Export" with an (X). **Reexport.** If the items are located outside the United States, mark the Box labeled "Reexport" with an (X). **Classification.** If you are requesting BXA to classify your item against the Commerce Control List (CCL), mark the Box labeled "Classification Request" with an (X). **Special Comprehensive License.** If you are submitting a Special Comprehensive License in accordance with procedures described in part 752 of the EAR, mark the Box labeled "Special Comprehensive License" with an (X).

Block 6: DOCUMENTS SUBMITTED WITH APPLICATION. Review the documentation you are required to submit with your application in accordance with the provisions of part 748 of the EAR, and mark all applicable Boxes with an (X).

Mark the "Foreign Availability" Box with an (X) if you are submitting an assertion of foreign availability with your license application. See part 768 of the EAR for instructions on foreign availability submissions.

Mark the "Tech. Specs." Box with an (X) if you are submitting descriptive literature, brochures, technical specifications, etc. with your application.

Block 7: DOCUMENTS ON FILE WITH APPLICANT. Certify that you have retained on file all applicable documents as required by the provisions of part 748 of the EAR by placing an (X) in the appropriate Box(es).

Block 8: SPECIAL COMPREHENSIVE LICENSE. Complete this Block only if you are submitting an application for a Special Comprehensive License in accordance with part 752 of the EAR.

Block 9: SPECIAL PURPOSE. Complete this Block for certain items or types of transactions only if specifically required in Supplement No. 2 to part 748 of the EAR.

Block 10: RESUBMISSION APPLICATION CONTROL NUMBER. If your original application was returned without action (RWA), provide the Application Control Number and complete Blocks 1 through 25. This does not apply to applications returned for additional information.

Block 11: REPLACEMENT LICENSE NUMBER. If you have received a license for identical items to the same ultimate consignee, but would like to make a modification that is not excepted in §750.7(c) of the EAR, to the license as originally approved, enter the original license number and complete remaining Blocks 12 through 25, whichever applicable.

Block 12: ITEMS PREVIOUSLY EXPORTED. This Block should be completed only if you have marked the "Reexport" box in Block 5. Enter the License number, License Exception symbol (for exports under General Licenses, enter the appropriate General License symbol), or other authorization under which the items were originally exported, if known.

Block 13: IMPORT/END-USER CERTIFICATE. Enter the name of the country and number of the Import or End-user Certificate obtained in accordance with the provisions of part 748 of the EAR.

Block 14: APPLICANT. Enter the applicant's name, street address, city, state/country, and postal code. Provide a complete street address. P.O. Boxes are not acceptable. Refer to §748.5(a) of EAR for a definition of "Applicant". If you have marked "Export" in Block 5, you must include your company's Employer Identification Number unless you are filing as an individual or as an agent on behalf of the exporter. The Employer Identification Number is assigned by the Internal Revenue Service for tax identification purposes. Accordingly, you should consult your company's financial officer or accounting division to obtain this number.

Block 15: OTHER PARTY AUTHORIZED TO RECEIVE LICENSE. If you would like BXA to transmit the approved license to another party designated by you, complete all information in this Block, including name, street address, city, state/country, postal code and telephone number. Leave this space blank if the license is to be sent to the applicant. Designation of another party to receive the license does not alter the responsibilities of the applicant.

Block 16: PURCHASER. Enter the purchaser's complete name, complete street address, city, country, postal code and telephone or facsimile number. Refer to §748.5(c) of the EAR for a definition of "purchaser". If the purchaser is also the ultimate consignee, enter complete name and address.

SEE CONTINUATION OF SPECIFIC INSTRUCTIONS ON REVERSE SIDE

Block 17: INTERMEDIATE CONSIGNEE. Enter the intermediate consignee's name, street address, city, country, postal code and telephone or facsimile number. Refer to §748.5(d) of the EAR for a definition of "intermediate consignee". If this party is identical to that listed in Block 16, enter complete name and address. If your proposed transaction involves use of more than one intermediate consignee, provide the same information in Block 24 for each additional intermediate consignee.

Block 18: ULTIMATE CONSIGNEE. This Block must be completed if you are submitting a license application. Enter the ultimate consignee's complete name, street address, city, country, postal code and telephone or facsimile number. Provide a complete street address. P.O. Boxes are not acceptable. The ultimate consignee is the party who will actually receive the material for the end-use designated in Block 21. Refer to §748.5(e) of the EAR for the definition of "ultimate consignee". A bank, freight forwarder, forwarding agent, or other intermediary may not be identified as the ultimate consignee. Government purchasing organizations are the sole exception to this requirement. This type of entity may be identified as the government entity that is the actual ultimate consignee in those instances when the items are to be transferred to a government entity that is the actual end-user, provided the actual end-use and end-user is clearly identified in Block 21 or in additional documentation attached to the application.

If your application is for the reexport of items previously exported, enter the new ultimate consignee's complete name, street address, city, country, postal code and telephone or facsimile number. Provide a complete street address. P.O. Boxes are not acceptable. If your application involves a temporary export, or reexport, the applicant should be shown as the ultimate consignee in care of (i.e.C/O) a person or entity who will have control over the items abroad.

Block 19: END-USER. Complete this Block only if the ultimate consignee identified in Block 18 is not the actual end user. If there will be more than one end-user, use Form BXA-748-P-B to identify each additional end-user. Enter each end-user's complete name, street address, city, country, postal code and telephone or facsimile number. Provide a complete street address. P.O. Boxes are not acceptable.

Block 20: ORIGINAL ULTIMATE CONSIGNEE. If your application involves the reexport of items previously exported, enter the original ultimate consignee's complete name, street address, country, postal code and telephone or facsimile number. Provide a complete street address. P.O. Boxes are not acceptable. The original ultimate consignee is the entity identified in the original application for export as the ultimate consignee or the party currently in possession of the items.

Block 21: SPECIFIC END-USE This Block must be completed if you are submitting a license application. Provide a complete and detailed description of the end-use intended by the ultimate consignee and/or end-user(s). If you are requesting approval of a reexport, provide a complete and detailed description of the end-use intended by the new ultimate consignee or end-user(s) and indicate any other countries for which resale or reexport is requested. If additional space is necessary, use Block 21 on Form BXA-748P-A or B. Be specific. Such vague descriptions as "research", "manufacturing", or "scientific uses" are not acceptable.

Block 22: FOR A LICENSE APPLICATION YOU MUST COMPLETE EACH OF THE SUB-BLOCKS CONTAINED IN THIS BLOCK. If you are submitting a classification request, you need not complete Blocks (e), (f), (g), and (h). If you wish to export, reexport or have BXA classify more than one item, use Form, BXA-748P-A for additional items.

   (a) ECCN. Enter the Export Control Classification Number (ECCN) that corresponds to the item you wish to export or reexport. If you are asking BXA to classify your item, provide a recommended classification for the item in this Block.

   (b) CTP. You must complete this Block if your application involves a digital computer or equipment containing a digital computer as described in Supplement No. 2 to part 748 of the EAR. Instructions on calculating the CTP are contained in a Technical Note at the end of Category 4 in the CCL.

   (c) MODEL NUMBER. Enter the correct model number for the item.

   (d) CCATS NUMBER. If you have received a classification for this item from BXA, provide the CCATS number, shown on the classification issued by BXA.

   (e) QUANTITY. Identify the quantity to be exported or reexported, in terms of the "Unit" identified for the ECCN entered in Block 22(a). If the "Unit" for an item is "$ Value", enter the units commonly used in trade.

   (f) UNITS. The "Unit of Measure" paragraph within each ECCN will list a specific "Unit" for those items controlled by the entry. The "Unit" must be entered on all license applications submitted to BXA. If an item is licensed in terms of "$ Value", the unit of quantity commonly used in the trade must also be shown on the license application. This may be left blank on license applications only if the "Unit" for the ECCN entered in Block 22(a) is shown as "N/A" on the CCL.

   (g) UNIT PRICE. Provide the fair market value of the items you wish to export or reexport. Round all prices to the nearest whole dollar amount. Give the exact unit price only if the value is less than $0.50. If normal trade practices make it impractical to establish a firm contract price, state in Block 24 the precise items upon which the price is to be ascertained and from which the contract price may be objectively determined.

   (h) TOTAL PRICE. Provide the total price of the item(s) described in Block 22(j).

   (i) MANUFACTURER. Provide the name only of the manufacturer, if known, for each of the items you wish to export, reexport, or have BXA classify, if different from the applicant.

   (j) TECHNICAL DESCRIPTION. Provide a description of the item(s) you wish to export, reexport, or have BXA classify. Provide details when necessary to identify the applicable item(s), and include all characteristics or parameters shown in the applicable ECCN using measurements identified in the ECCN (e.g., basic ingredients, composition, electrical parameters, size gauge, grade, horsepower, etc.). These characteristics must be identified for the items in the proposed transaction when they are different from the characteristics described in a promotional brochure.

Block 23: TOTAL APPLICATION VALUE. Enter the total value of all items contained on the application in U.S. Dollars. The use of other currencies is not acceptable.

Block 24: ADDITIONAL INFORMATION. Enter additional data pertinent to the application as required in the EAR. Include special certifications, names of parties in interest not disclosed elsewhere, explanation of documents attached, etc. Do not include information concerning Block 22 in this space.

If your application represents a previously denied application, you must provide the Application Control Number from the original application.

If you are asking BXA to classify your product, use this space to explain why you believe the ECCN entered in Block 22(a) is appropriate. This explanation must contain an analysis of the item in terms of the technical control parameters specified in the appropriate ECCN. If you have not identified a recommended classification in Block 22(a), you must state the reason you cannot determine the appropriate classification, identifying any ambiguities or deficiencies in the regulations that precluded you from determining the correct classification.

If additional space is necessary, use Block 24 on Form BXA-748P-A or B.

Block 25: SIGNATURE. You as the applicant, or a duly authorized agent of the applicant, must manually sign in this Block. Rubber-stamped or automated signatures are not acceptable. If you are an agent of the applicant, in addition to providing your name in this Block you must enter your company's name in Block 24. Type both your name and title in the spaces provided.

MAIL APPLICATION TO: OFFICE OF EXPORTER SERVICES P.O. BOX 273 WASHINGTON, D.C. 20044	**COURIER DELIVERIES TO:** OFFICE OF EXPORTER SERVICES ROOM 2705 14TH & PENNSYLVANIA AVE., N.W. WASHINGTON, D.C. 20230

Public reporting burden for this collection of information is estimated to average 45 minutes per response, including the time for reviewing instructions, searching existing data sources, gathering and maintaining the data needed, and completing and reviewing the collection of information. Send comments regarding this burden estimate or any other aspect of this collection of information, including suggestions for reducing this burden, to Robert F. Kugleman, Director of Administration, U.S. Department of Commerce, Bureau of Export Administration, Room 3889, Washington, D.C. 20230

INCOMPLETE APPLICATIONS WILL BE RETURNED FOR THE NECESSARY INFORMATION AND/OR DOCUMENTATION. DETACH THIS SHEET AT PERFORATION

EXPORT LICENSE

EXPORT LICENSE NO.: A030043 VALIDATED: 7/19/88 EXPIRATION DATE: 7/31/90	UNITED STATES DEPARTMENT OF COMMERCE BUREAU OF EXPORT ADMINISTRATION P.O. BOX 273 BEN FRANKLIN STATION WASHINGTON, D.C. 20044

CONSIGNEE IN COUNTRY OF ULTIMATE DESTINATION: ABU DHABI TRADING ESTABLISHMENT 2345 LIAN DUK WAY ABU DHABI, UNITED ARAB EMIRATES	APPLICANT'S REFERENCE NO.: A030043 PURCHASER: AEG TELEFUNKEN STEINHOEFT 9 HAMBURG, WEST GERMANY
LICENSEE: A P CIRCUIT CORPORATION 513 EAST 86 STREET NEW YORK, NY 10028	INTERMEDIATE CONSIGNEE: ZINCOR INFOSYSTEMS, INC. 4456 PASQUATCH LET BOMBAY, INDIA

PROCESSING CODE: CS

COMMODITIES:

QUANTITY	DESCRIPTION	ECCN	UNIT PRICE	TOTAL PRICE
50 EACH	MODEL 2345 6.50 MATH COPROCESSORS	1565	14000.00	700000.00
2 EACH	MCS68 3.40 HUMPHREY ANALYZERS	1565	30000.00	60000.00

VOID

TOTAL: 760000

THE EXPORT ADMINISTRATION REGULATIONS REQUIRE YOU TO TAKE THE FOLLOWING ACTIONS WHEN EXPORTING UNDER THE AUTHORITY OF THIS LICENSE.

A.   RECORD THE EXPORT CONTROL COMMODITY NUMBER IN PARENTHESES DIRECTLY BELOW THE CORRESPONDING SCHEDULE B NUMBER ON EACH SHIPPERS EXPORT DECLARATION (SED).

B.   RECORD YOUR LICENSE NUMBER IN THE COMMODITY DESCRIPTION COLUMN ON EACH SED.

C.   PLACE A DESTINATION CONTROL STATEMENT ON ALL BILLS OF LADING, AIRWAY BILLS, AND COMMERCIAL INVOICES.

THIS LICENSE AUTHORIZES THE LICENSEE TO CARRY OUT THE EXPORT TRANSACTION DESCRIBED ON THE LICENSE (INCLUDING ALL ATTACHMENTS). IT MAY NOT BE TRANSFERRED WITHOUT PRIOR WRITTEN APPROVAL OF THE BUREAU OF EXPORT ADMINISTRATION. THIS LICENSE HAS BEEN GRANTED IN RELIANCE ON REPRESENTATIONS MADE BY THE LICENSEE AND OTHERS IN CONNECTION WITH THE APPLICATION FOR EXPORT AND IS EXPRESSLY SUBJECT TO ANY CONDITIONS STATED ON THE LICENSE, AS WELL AS ALL APPLICABLE EXPORT CONTROL LAWS, REGULATIONS, RULES, AND ORDERS. THIS LICENSE IS SUBJECT TO REVISION, SUSPENSION, OR REVOCATION WITHOUT PRIOR NOTICE.

C		U.S. DEPARTMENT OF COMMERCE		DATE RECEIVED	X
FORM BXA-748P-A FORM APPROVED: OMB NO. 0694-0088,0694-0089		Bureau of Export Administration **ITEM APPENDIX**		(Leave Blank)	
1. APPLICATION CONTROL NUMBER (Insert from BXA-748P)		Information furnished herewith is subject to the provisions of Section 12(c) of the Export Administration Act of 1979, as amended, 50 U.S.C. app. 2411(c), and its unauthorized disclosure is prohibited by law.		2. SUBTOTAL	

22. (a) ECCN	(b) CTP	(c) MODEL NUMBER		(d) CCATS NUMBER	
(e) QUANTITY	(f) UNITS	(g) UNIT PRICE	(h) TOTAL PRICE	(i) MANUFACTURER	
(j) TECHNICAL DESCRIPTION					

22. (a) ECCN	(b) CTP	(c) MODEL NUMBER		(d) CCATS NUMBER	
(e) QUANTITY	(f) UNITS	(g) UNIT PRICE	(h) TOTAL PRICE	(i) MANUFACTURER	
(j) TECHNICAL DESCRIPTION					

22. (a) ECCN	(b) CTP	(c) MODEL NUMBER		(d) CCATS NUMBER	
(e) QUANTITY	(f) UNITS	(g) UNIT PRICE	(h) TOTAL PRICE	(i) MANUFACTURER	
(j) TECHNICAL DESCRIPTION					

22. (a) ECCN	(b) CTP	(c) MODEL NUMBER		(d) CCATS NUMBER	
(e) QUANTITY	(f) UNITS	(g) UNIT PRICE	(h) TOTAL PRICE	(i) MANUFACTURER	
(j) TECHNICAL DESCRIPTION					

22. (a) ECCN	(b) CTP	(c) MODEL NUMBER		(d) CCATS NUMBER	
(e) QUANTITY	(f) UNITS	(g) UNIT PRICE	(h) TOTAL PRICE	(i) MANUFACTURER	
(j) TECHNICAL DESCRIPTION					

21. CONTINUATION OF SPECIFIC END-USE INFORMATION

24. CONTINUATION OF ADDITIONAL INFORMATION

X		X	ORIGINAL	C

D

FORM BXA-748P-B
FORM APPROVED; OMB NO. 0694-0088,0694-0089

1. APPLICATION CONTROL NUMBER
(Insert from BXA-748P)

U.S. DEPARTMENT OF COMMERCE
Bureau of Export Administration

END-USER APPENDIX

Information furnished herewith is subject to the provisions of Section 12(c) of the Export Administration Act of 1979, as amended, 50 U.S.C. app. 2411(c) and its unauthorized disclosure is prohibited by law.

DATE RECEIVED
(Leave Blank)   **X**

19. END-USER		19. END-USER	
ADDRESS LINE 1		ADDRESS LINE 1	
ADDRESS LINE 2		ADDRESS LINE 2	
CITY	POSTAL CODE	CITY	POSTAL CODE
COUNTRY	TELEPHONE OR FAX	COUNTRY	TELEPHONE OR FAX

19. END-USER		19. END-USER	
ADDRESS LINE 1		ADDRESS LINE 1	
ADDRESS LINE 2		ADDRESS LINE 2	
CITY	POSTAL CODE	CITY	POSTAL CODE
COUNTRY	TELEPHONE OR FAX	COUNTRY	TELEPHONE OR FAX

19. END-USER		19. END-USER	
ADDRESS LINE 1		ADDRESS LINE 1	
ADDRESS LINE 2		ADDRESS LINE 2	
CITY	POSTAL CODE	CITY	POSTAL CODE
COUNTRY	TELEPHONE OR FAX	COUNTRY	TELEPHONE OR FAX

19. END-USER		19. END-USER	
ADDRESS LINE 1		ADDRESS LINE 1	
ADDRESS LINE 2		ADDRESS LINE 2	
CITY	POSTAL CODE	CITY	POSTAL CODE
COUNTRY	TELEPHONE OR FAX	COUNTRY	TELEPHONE OR FAX

19. END-USER		19. END-USER	
ADDRESS LINE 1		ADDRESS LINE 1	
ADDRESS LINE 2		ADDRESS LINE 2	
CITY	POSTAL CODE	CITY	POSTAL CODE
COUNTRY	TELEPHONE OR FAX	COUNTRY	TELEPHONE OR FAX

21. CONTINUATION OF SPECIFIC END-USE INFORMATION

24. CONTINUATION OF ADDITIONAL INFORMATION

X   **X**   **ORIGINAL** **D**

USCOMM-DC 90-24080

F

FORM BXA-752
FORM APPROVED: OMB NO. 0694-0089

U.S. DEPARTMENT OF COMMERCE
Bureau of Export Administration

DATE RECEIVED
(Leave Blank) **X**

STATEMENT BY CONSIGNEE IN SUPPORT OF
SPECIAL COMPREHENSIVE LICENSE

1. APPLICATION CONTROL NUMBER (Insert from BXA-748P)	2. CONSIGNEE ID NUMBER (Leave Blank)	Information furnished herewith is subject to the provisions of Section 12(c) of the Export Administration Act of 1979, as amended, 50 U.S.C. app. 2411(c), and its unauthorized disclosure is prohibited by law.

3. TYPE OF REQUEST

A. ☐ ADD A NEW CONSIGNEE   B. ☐ CHANGE AN EXISTING CONSIGNEE   C. ☐ DELETE A CONSIGNEE

4. ULTIMATE CONSIGNEE	5. SCL HOLDER	
ADDRESS LINE 1	ADDRESS LINE 1	
ADDRESS LINE 2	ADDRESS LINE 2	
CITY / POSTAL CODE	CITY	ZIP CODE
COUNTRY / CONSIGNEE NUMBER	STATE	SCL CASE NUMBER

6. DESCRIPTION OF ITEMS
We expect to use, sell, install, or reexport the following items:

7. CONSIGNEE'S BUSINESS AND RELATIONSHIP WITH SCL HOLDER NAMED IN BLOCK 5

A. Nature of Business	B. Our relationship with the exporter is:	C. We have had this business relationship for _____ years.	D. Past Sales Volume $	E. Projected Sales Volume $

8. DISPOSITION OR USE OF ITEMS BY ULTIMATE CONSIGNEE NAMED IN BLOCK 4
We certify that the items:

A. ☐ Used by us (as capital equipment) in the form in which received in the country named in Block 4 and will not be reexported or incorporated into an end product.

B. Will be processed or incorporated by us into the following product(s) for distribution in the countries authorized on the attached BXA-752-A.

C. Will be used to service the following commodities in the countries authorized on the attached BXA-752-A.

D. Will be resold by us in the form in which received in the country named in Block 4 for use or consumption therein. The specific end-use by my customer(s) will be:

E. ☐ Will be reexported by us in the form in which received to countries authorized on the attached BXA-752-A.

F. Other

9. ADDITIONAL INFORMATION

CERTIFICATION OF CONSIGNEE
We certify that all of the facts contained in this statement are true and correct to the best of our knowledge and belief and we do not know of any additional facts which are inconsistent with the above statement. We shall promptly send a supplemental statement to the SCL Holder named in Block 5, disclosing any change of facts or intentions set forth in this statement which occurs after the statement has been prepared and forwarded, except as specifically authorized by the U.S. Export Administration Regulations (15 CFR Parts 730-774). We (a) will not use, reexport, sell, distribute, install or otherwise dispose of any items covered by this statement contrary to U.S. Export Administration Regulations; and (b) will not sell or otherwise dispose of any of these items to any person or firm listed on the Bureau of Export Administration Denied Persons List or where there is reason to believe that the items will be reexported to destinations or activities not authorized by the Bureau of Export Administration.

10. SIGNATURE OF OFFICIAL OF ULTIMATE CONSIGNEE	DATE SIGNED
NAME OF OFFICIAL OF ULTIMATE CONSIGNEE	TITLE OF PERSON SIGNING THIS DOCUMENT

REQUEST AND CERTIFICATION OF SCL HOLDER
We request that the firm named in Block 4 be approved as an ultimate consignee to whom we may export items, under the Special Comprehensive License Case Number specified in Block 5. We understand that all undertakings, commitments, obligations, and responsibilities under the special comprehensive licensing procedure, and the Export Administration Regulations related thereto, are fully applicable to any export to the above mentioned ultimate consignee if this form is validated by the Bureau of Export Administration. No corrections, additions, or alterations were made on this form by us after the form was signed by the official named in Block 10 above. We certify that we will not export or otherwise dispose of any items covered by the Special Comprehensive License to the ultimate consignee named in Block 4, until this form has been validated or after it has expired or been revoked.

SIGNATURE OF PERSON AUTHORIZED TO CERTIFY FOR SCL HOLDER	NAME OF PERSON SIGNING THIS DOCUMENT	
NAME OF SCL HOLDER FIRM	TITLE OF PERSON SIGNING THIS DOCUMENT	DATE SIGNED

We acknowledge that the making of any false statements or concealment of any material fact in connection with this statement may result in imprisonment or fine, or both and denial, in whole or in part, of participation in U.S. exports and reexports.

X   **X**   ORIGINAL **F**

USCOMM-DC 99-34022

G

FORM BXA-752-A
FORM APPROVED: OMB NO. 0694-0089

U.S. DEPARTMENT OF COMMERCE
Bureau of Export Administration

DATE RECEIVED   **X**
(Leave Blank)

REEXPORT TERRITORIES

1. APPLICATION CONTROL NUMBER (Insert from BXA-748P)	2. SCL LICENSE NUMBER	3. CONSIGNEE NUMBER	4. CONTINUATION OF BXA-752 QUESTION NUMBER:

☐ 6B   ☐ 6C   ☐ 6E   ☐ 6F

☐ AFGHANISTAN	☐ CANADA	☐ GERMANY	☐ LIBERIA	☐ PAKISTAN	☐ SWAZILAND
☐ ALBANIA	☐ CAPE VERDE	☐ GHANA	☐ LIECHTENSTEIN	☐ PALAU	☐ SWEDEN
☐ ALGERIA	☐ CENTRAL AFRICAN REPUBLIC	☐ GREECE	☐ LITHUANIA	☐ PANAMA	☐ SWITZERLAND
☐ ANDORRA	☐ CHAD	☐ GRENADA	☐ LUXEMBOURG	☐ PAPUA NEW GUINEA	☐ TAIWAN
☐ ANGOLA	☐ CHILE	☐ GUATEMALA	☐ FYROM (MACEDONIA)	☐ PARAGUAY	☐ TAJIKISTAN
☐ ANTIGUA & BARBUDA	☐ CHINA (PRC)	☐ GUINEA	☐ MADAGASCAR	☐ PERU	☐ TANZANIA
☐ ARGENTINA	☐ COLOMBIA	☐ GUINEA-BISSAU	☐ MALAWI	☐ PHILIPPINES	☐ THAILAND
☐ ARMENIA	☐ COMOROS	☐ GUYANA	☐ MALAYSIA	☐ POLAND	☐ TOGO
☐ AUSTRALIA	☐ CONGO	☐ HAITI	☐ MALDIVES	☐ PORTUGAL	☐ TONGA
☐ AUSTRIA	☐ COSTA RICA	☐ HONDURAS	☐ MALI	☐ QATAR	☐ TRINIDAD & TOBAGO
☐ AZERBAIJAN	☐ COTE d'IVOIRE	☐ HONG KONG	☐ MALTA	☐ ROMANIA	☐ TUNISIA
☐ BAHAMAS, THE	☐ CROATIA	☐ HUNGARY	☐ MARSHALL ISLANDS	☐ RUSSIA	☐ TURKEY
☐ BAHRAIN	☐ CYPRUS	☐ ICELAND	☐ MAURITANIA	☐ RWANDA	☐ TURKMENISTAN
☐ BANGLADESH	☐ CZECH REPUBLIC	☐ INDIA	☐ MAURITIUS	☐ ST KITTS & NEVIS	☐ TUVALU
☐ BARBADOS	☐ DENMARK	☐ INDONESIA	☐ MEXICO	☐ ST. LUCIA	☐ UGANDA
☐ BELARUS	☐ DJIBOUTI	☐ IRELAND	☐ MICRONESIA	☐ ST. VINCENT & GRENADINES	☐ UKRAINE
☐ BELGIUM	☐ DOMINICA	☐ ISRAEL	☐ MOLDOVA	☐ SAN MARINO	☐ UNITED ARAB EMIRATES
☐ BELIZE	☐ DOMINICAN REPUBLIC	☐ ITALY	☐ MONACO	☐ SAO TOME & PRINCIPE	☐ UNITED KINGDOM
☐ BENIN	☐ ECUADOR	☐ JAMAICA	☐ MONGOLIA	☐ SAUDI ARABIA	☐ URUGUAY
☐ BHUTAN	☐ EGYPT	☐ JAPAN	☐ MOROCCO	☐ SENEGAL	☐ UZBEKISTAN
☐ BOLIVIA	☐ EL SALVADOR	☐ JORDAN	☐ MOZAMBIQUE	☐ SEYCHELLES	☐ VANUATU
☐ BOSNIA & HERZEGOVINA	☐ EQUATORIAL GUINEA	☐ KAZAKHSTAN	☐ NAMIBIA	☐ SIERRA LEONE	☐ VATICAN CITY
☐ BOTSWANA	☐ ERITREA	☐ KENYA	☐ NAURU	☐ SINGAPORE	☐ VENEZUELA
☐ BRAZIL	☐ ESTONIA	☐ KIRIBATI	☐ NEPAL	☐ SLOVAKIA	☐ VIETNAM
☐ BRUNEI	☐ ETHIOPIA	☐ KOREA, SOUTH	☐ NETHERLANDS	☐ SLOVENIA	☐ WESTERN SAHARA
☐ BULGARIA	☐ FIJI	☐ KUWAIT	☐ NEW ZEALAND	☐ SOLOMON ISLANDS	☐ WESTERN SAMOA
☐ BURKINA FASO	☐ FINLAND	☐ KYRGYZSTAN	☐ NICARAGUA	☐ SOMALIA	☐ YEMEN
☐ BURMA	☐ FRANCE	☐ LAOS	☐ NIGER	☐ SOUTH AFRICA	☐ ZAIRE
☐ BURUNDI	☐ GABON	☐ LATVIA	☐ NIGERIA	☐ SPAIN	☐ ZAMBIA
☐ CAMBODIA	☐ GAMBIA, THE	☐ LEBANON	☐ NORWAY	☐ SRI LANKA	☐ ZIMBABWE
☐ CAMEROON	☐ GEORGIA	☐ LESOTHO	☐ OMAN	☐ SURINAM	

☐ OTHER SPECIFY: ☐ OTHER SPECIFY: ☐ OTHER SPECIFY:

X   **X**   ORIGINAL   **G**

U.S. DEPARTMENT OF STATE

STATEMENT OF REGISTRATION

(INSTRUCTIONS ON REVERSE SIDE)
(Attach additional sheet if necessary)

OMB APPROVAL NO. 1405-002
EXPIRATION DATE: 01/31/2002
*ESTIMATED BURDEN: 1 HOUR

PM/DTC DATE RECEIVED

NEW REGISTRANT CODE

1. REGISTRANT'S NAME AND ADDRESS:	2. CURRENT REGISTRANT CODE:

3.
$ _____ ENCLOSED FOR 1   2   3   4   (CIRCLE ONE) YEARS REGISTRATION.

4. REGISTRANT IS: ☐ INDIVIDUAL ☐ PARTNERSHIP ☐ COMPANY ☐ CORPORATION

5. REGISTRANT IS: ☐ MANUFACTURER AND/OR   ☐ EXPORTER OF MUNITIONS LIST
☐ EXPORTER OF DEFENSE SERVICE   ☐ BROKER

6. INCORPORATION OR COMMENCEMENT OF BUSINESS: DATE *(mm-dd-yyyy)* _____
IN _____
(City, country, and state)

TELEPHONE NUMBER:

7. DIRECTORS, OFFICERS, PARTNERS, OWNERS:

NAME *(Last, First, Middle)*	POSITION	DATE *(mm-dd-yyyy)* AND PLACE OF BIRTH	SOCIAL SECURITY NUMBER	HOME ADDRESS	CITIZENSHIP

8. U.S. MUNITIONS LIST ARTICLES MANUFACTURED AND/OR EXPORTED, OR DEFENSE SERVICES PROVIDED:

CATEGORY	COMMODITY/SERVICE	PURCHASING U.S. GOVERNMENT AGENCY *(IF ANY)*

9. NAMES AND ADDRESSES OF REGISTRANT'S WHOLLY AND PARTIALLY-OWNED U.S. SUBSIDIARIES: YES (SPECIFY) ☐   NO ☐

10. NAMES AND ADDRESSES OF REGISTRANT'S WHOLLY AND PARTIALLY-OWNED FOREIGN SUBSIDIARIES   YES (SPECIFY) ☐   NO ☐

11. NAME, ADDRESS AND TELEPHONE NUMBERS OF REGISTRANT'S PARENT COMPANY *(IF ANY)*

12. IS THE REGISTRANT OWNED ☐ AND/OR CONTROLLED ☐ BY FOREIGN PERSONS (See § 122.2(2)(C)) OF ITAR   YES (SPECIFY) ☐   NO ☐

13. DOES REGISTRANT SUBMIT FEDERAL INCOME TAX FORMS SEPARATELY FROM COMPANY IN BLOCK 11?   YES ☐   NO ☐

14. REGISTRANT'S STATEMENT:
UNDER PENALTY ACCORDING TO FEDERAL LAW *(See § 22 CFR 127; 22 USC 2778; 18 USC 1001)*

I, _____ WARRANT THE TRUTH OF ALL STATEMENTS MADE HEREIN
(TYPE FULL NAME)

_____   _____
(SIGNATURE)   *(DATE (mm-dd-yyyy)*

_____
(TITLE POSITION)

DS-2032   *(DESTROY PREVIOUS EDITIONS)*

INSTRUCTIONS
STATEMENT OF REGISTRATION

1. Complete all items. If "none" applies to an item, so state. If more space is required to complete an item, use plain white paper.

2. **Item 1.** Show the business name, home office address and telephone number of the parent company, as it appears on federal income tax forms.

3. **Item 2.** If you have been in the past, or are currently registered with the Directorate of Defense Trade Controls (DDTC), give your DDTC registrant code number.

4. **Item 3.** Circle the number of years required and enter the amount of fee enclosed. Fee schedule:

1 year	$ 600
2 years	$1,200
3 years	$1,800
4 years	$2,200

   You are encouraged to register for the maximum period of four years to reduce administrative overhead and take advantage of the reduced fees. **Do Not Send Cash.** Make your check or money order payable to "U.S. Department of State."

5. **Item 4.** Give the most applicable organizational description.

6. **Item 5.** Indicate the nature of your business.

7. **Item 6.** Enter the date *(mm-dd-yyyy)*, city, county and state where your organization commenced doing business.

8. **Item 7.** Enter the name, title, date *(mm-dd-yyyy)* and place of birth *(city & state)*, social security number, residential address, and country of citizenship for all directors, officers, partners and owners.

9. **Item 8.** Enter U.S. Munitions List (USML) category (part 121 of the International Traffic In Arms Regulations (ITAR)), generic name, and U.S. Government agency *(if applicable)* for which manufactured.

10. **Item 9.** List U.S. subsidiaries, wholly or partially owned by registrant, manufacturing and/or exporting USML articles or services.

11. **Item 10.** List foreign subsidiaries, wholly or partially owned by registrant, that manufacture, export, and/or broker USML articles, technical data or services.

12. **Item 11.** Give complete name, address, and telephone number of parent company.

13. **Item 12.** Is the registrant owned and/or controlled by foreign person(s)? See § 122.2(2)(c) of the ITAR for definition of ownership or control.

14. **Item 13.** Company or corporate divisions or subsidiaries may not register separately unless they are required by law to file separate federal tax returns.

15. **Item 14.** The individual signing this form must be a senior official empowered by the intending registrant. Violations and penalties are explained in Part 127 of the ITAR.

16. DTC will acknowledge in writing receipt of your application and fee, and assign a new registrant code number.

17. **IMPORTANT:** Changes in the information contained in this application by law must be reported promptly to: (See § 122.4 of the ITAR).

> **Office of Defence Trade Controls Compliance (Registration)**
> **Directorate of Defense Trade Controls,**
> **SA-1, Suite H1300**
> **U.S. Department of State**
> **Washington, DC 20522-0112**

PRIVACY ACT AND PAPERWORK REDUCTION ACT STATEMENTS

AUTHORITIES: U.S. Department of State's authorities to register persons engaged in the business of manufacturing, exporting, or importing any defense article or defense service are 22 U.S.C. 2778 (b) (1) (A) (i) and 22 CFR Part 122. The authorities to register brokers are 22 U.S.C. 2778 (b) (1) (A) (ii) (I) and 22 CFR 129.3 and 129.4

PURPOSE: The purpose of registration is to provide the U.S. Government with necessary information on individuals and entities engaged in certain manufacturing, exporting and brokering activities.

ROUTINE USES: The information solicited on this form is made available as a routing use to appropriate agencies whether federal, state, local or foreign, for intelligence, law enforcement and administrative purposes or pursuant to a court order. It may also be used to send required reports to Congress about certain defense trade transactions.

SOCIAL SECURITY NUMBER: Disclosure of the social security number(s) is voluntary and for the purpose of facilitating coordination with the Department of Treasury to review the registration statement for law enforcement concerns in accord with 22 U.S.C. 2778 (b) (1) (B). Refusal to provide requested social security number, by itself, will not result in registration being denied, but may result in delays in the processing of a registration request.

*Public reporting burden for this collection of information is estimated to average 2 hours per response, including time required for searching existing data sources, gathering the necessary data, providing the information required, and reviewing the final collection. Send comments on the accuracy of this estimate of the burden and recommendations for reducing it to: U.S. Department of State (A/RPS/DIR) Washington, DC 20520.

DS-2032

(U.S. DEPARTMENT OF STATE USE ONLY)

SEAL

SAMPLE
Signature

COPY
LICENSE NO.

License is hereby granted to the applicant for the described commodity to be permanently exported from the United States. This license may be revoked, suspended or amended by the Secretary of State without prior notice whenever the Secretary deems such action advisable.

LICENSE VALID FOR
MONTHS FROM ABOVE DATE

UNITED STATES OF AMERICA   DEPARTMENT OF STATE

APPLICATION/LICENSE FOR PERMANENT EXPORT OF UNCLASSIFIED DEFENSE ARTICLES AND RELATED UNCLASSIFIED TECHNICAL DATA

1. Date Prepared	2. PM/DTC Applicant/Registrant Code	3. Country of Ultimate Destination	4. Probable Port of Exit from U.S.

5. Applicant's Name, Address, ZIP Code, Tel. No.
Applicant is: ☐ Government ☐ Manufacturer ☐ Exporter/freight forwarder

6. Names, agency and telephone numbers of U.S. Government personnel (not PM/DTC) familiar with the commodity
☐ Army ☐ Air Force
☐ Navy ☐ Other

7. Name and telephone number of applicant contact if U.S. Government needs additional information.

TELEPHONE NUMBER:

8. Description of Transaction
   a. This application represents: ☐ ONLY completely new shipment; ☐ ONLY the unshipped balance of license no. _____ .
   b. The IDENTICAL commodity ☐ was licensed to the country in block 3 under license no. _____ ; ☐ was licensed to other countries under license no. _____ ; ☐ was returned without action under voided license no. _____ ; ☐ was denied to the country in block 3 under voided license no. _____ ; ☐ was never licensed for this applicant.
   c. If commodity is being financed under ☐ Foreign Military Sale (FMS); ☐ Foreign Military Financing (FMF) or; ☐ Grant Aid Program (GAD), give the case number:

9. QUANTITY	10. COMMODITY ☐ Hardware ☐ Technical Data		11. USML CAT.	12. VALUE
			13. TOTAL VALUE: $	

14. Name and address of foreign end-user	15. ☐ Source or ☐ Manufacturer of Commodity

16. Name and address of foreign consignee	17. Name and address of seller in United States

18. Name and address of foreign intermediate consignee	19. Name and address of consignor and/or freight forwarder in United States

20. Specific purpose for which the material is required, including specific program/end item	21. APPLICANT'S STATEMENT (See instructions)

21. APPLICANT'S STATEMENT (See instructions)
I, _____ (Typed name) , hereby apply for a license to complete the transaction described above; warrant the truth of all statements made herein; and acknowledge, understand and will comply with the provisions of Title 22 CFR 120 – 130, and any conditions and limitations imposed.
CHECK ALL THAT APPLY:
☐ I am a responsible official empowered by the applicant to certify that the conditions of 22 CFR 126.13 and 22 CFR 130 as listed on the reverse of this form have been met in full.
☐ This applicant, or another party to this export cannot meet one or more of the conditions in 22 CFR 126.13. A request for an exception to policy is attached.
☐ U.S. consignor(s) and/or freight forwarder list(s) is/are attached.
☐ I am not empowered by the applicant to certify that the conditions of 22 CFR 126.13 and 22 CFR 130 as listed on the reverse of this form have been met in full. Please see the attached letter for such certification.
Signature *SAMPLE COPY*

22. LICENSE TO BE SENT TO: Name, address, ZIP code

FORM DSP-5
10-95

1 – APPLICATION/LICENSE
UNLESS OTHERWISE EXEMPT IN THE ITAR, APPROVED LICENSE MUST BE PRESENTED TO U.S. CUSTOMS OR POST OFFICE PRIOR TO EXPORT/MAILING

OMB APPROVAL NO. 1405-0003
EXPIRATION DATE: 12-31-98
*ESTIMATED BURDEN: 1/2 HOUR

*Public reporting burden for this collection of information is estimated to average 1/2 hour per response, including time required for searching existing data sources, gathering the necessary data, providing the information required, and reviewing the final collection. Send comments on the accuracy of this estimate of the burden and recommendations for reducing it to: Department of State (DS/RAOR) Washington, D.C. 20520-0954, and to the Office of Information and Regulatory Affairs, Office of Management and Budget, Paperwork Reduction Project (1405-0003), Washington, D. C. 20503

Miscellaneous Documents: Import

CUSTOMS POWER OF ATTORNEY

E.I.N. # _____

Check appropriate box:
- ☐ Individual
- ☐ Partnership
- ☐ Corporation
- ☐ Sole Proprietorship

KNOW ALL MEN BY THESE PRESENTS: That _____

(Full Name of person, partnership, or corporation or sole proprietorship (Identify)

a corporation doing business under the laws of the State of _____ or a _____

(Indicate state in which you are incorporated)   *(If not incorporated state Individual or Partnership)*

doing business as _____ residing at _____

(Enter the name of the partnership or fictitious business name)   *(If an individual, fill in your home address.)*

having an office and place of business at _____

,hereby constitutes and appoints : **American River Brokerage Services Ltd.**

as a true and lawful agent and attorney of the grantor named above for and in the name, place, and stead of said grantor from this date and in all Customs Districts, and in no other name, to make, endorse, sign, declare, or swear to any entry, withdrawal, declaration, certificate, bill of lading, carnet or other document required by law or regulation in connection with the importation, transportation, or exportation, of any merchandise shipped or consigned by or to said grantor; to perform any act or condition which may be required by law or regulation in connection with such merchandise; to receive any merchandise deliverable to said grantor;

     To make endorsements on bills of lading conferring authority to transfer title, make entry or collect drawback, and to make, sign, declare, or swear to any statement, supplemental statement, schedule, supplemental schedule, certificate of delivery, certificate of manufacturer, certificate of manufacture and delivery, abstract of manufacturing records, declaration of proprietor on drawback entry, declaration of exporter on drawback entry, or any other affidavit or document which may be required by law or regulation for drawback purposes, regardless of whether such bill of lading, sworn statement, schedule, certificate, abstract, declaration, or other affidavit or document is intended for filing in any customs district;

     To sign, seal, and deliver for and as the act of said grantor any bond required by law or regulation in connection with the entry or withdrawal of imported merchandise or merchandise exported with or without benefit of drawback, or in connection with the entry, clearance, lading, unlading or navigation of any vessel or other means of conveyance owned or operated by

said grantor, and any and all bonds which may be voluntarily given and accepted under applicable laws and regulations, consignee's and owner's declarations provided for in section 485, Tariff Act of 1930, as amended, or affidavits in connection with the entry of merchandise;

To sign and swear to any document and to perform any act that may be necessary or required by law or regulation in connection with the entering, clearing, lading, unlading, or operation of any vessel or other means of conveyance owned or operated by said grantor;

To authorize other Customs Brokers to act as grantor's agent; to receive, endorse and collect checks issued for Customs duty refunds in grantor's name drawn on the Treasurer of the United States; if the grantor is a nonresident of the United States, to accept service of process on behalf of the grantor;

And generally to transact at the customhouses in any district any and all customs business, including making, signing, and filing of protests under section 514 of the Tariff Act of 1930, in which said grantor is or may be concerned or interested and which may properly be transacted or performed by an agent and attorney, giving to said agent and attorney full power and authority to do anything whatever requisite and necessary to be done in the premises as fully as said grantor could do if present and acting, hereby ratifying and confirming all that the said agent and attorney shall lawfully do by virtue of these presents; the foregoing power of attorney to remain in full force and effect until the _____ day of , _____ 20 _____
or until notice of revocation in writing is duly given to and received by a District Director of Customs. If the donor of this power of attorney is a partnership, the said power shall in no case have any force or effect after the expiration of 2 years from the date of its execution.

IN WITNESS WHEREOF, the said _____

has caused these presents to be sealed and signed: (Signature) _____

(Signature of an officer of the corporation or another employee specifically designated by the articles of incorporation or resolution of the board of directors to sign power of attorney for that corporation; if a partnership, a signature of a partner; if an individual, the signature of that individual.)

(Capacity) _____ (Date) _____

(Title of the person signing item 11.)

WITNESS: _____ _____

(Name of witness)   *(Signature of witness.)*

(Corporate Seal)

Power of Attorney. Instructions

Item 1. If you are a U.S. corporation or partnership, fill in your firms E.I.N. If you are a foreign corporation, fill in your firms customs assigned I.D. number. If you are acting as an individual doing business under a fictitious name without an E.I.N., then fill in your social security number.

Item 2. Check the appropriate box that pertains to your business, Individual, Partnership, Corporation or Sole Proprietorship.

Item 3. Fill in the name of the corporation, partnership or person who will be the importer-of-record and/or owner/operator.

Item 4. If you are a corporation, then indicate here the state in which you are incorporated.

Item 5. If you are not a corporation, then indicate here if you are an individual or a partnership.

Item 6. The name of the partnership or fictitious business name of the individual should be placed here.

Item 7. If an individual, fill in your home address.

Item 8. Corporations, partnerships and individuals fill in your business street address.

Item 9. Put in the phrase "UNTIL REVOKED" or an expiration date. The expiration date should be at least one year.

Item 10. Enter the legal name of the company to which the power of attorney covers.

Item 11. Signature of an officer of the corporation or another employee specifically designated by the articles of incorporation or resolution of the board of directors to sign power of attorney for that corporation; if a partnership, a signature of a partner; if an individual, the signature of that individual.

Item 12. Title of the person signing at 11.

Item 13. Enter the date signed.

Item 14. Name of witness.

Item 15. Signature of witness named in 14.

Item 16. Affix the corporate seal if applicable.

USFWS Form 3-177
(Revised 10/17/2000)
O.M.B. No. 1018-0012
Expiration Date: 10/31/2003

U.S. FISH AND WILDLIFE SERVICE

Page ___ of ___

**DECLARATION FOR IMPORTATION
OR EXPORTATION OF
FISH OR WILDLIFE**

Please Type or Print Legibly

1. Date of Import/Export: (mm/dd/yyyy)

___ ___ / ___ ___ / ___ ___ ___ ___

2. I/E License Number:

3. Indicate One: ☐ Import ☐ Export

4. Port of Clearance:

5. Purpose Code:

6. Customs Entry Number:

7. Name of Carrier:

8. Air Way Bill or Bill of Lading Number:
Master:
House:

9. Transportation Code:
___
License   State

10. Bonded Location for Inspection:

11. Number of Cartons Containing Wildlife:

12. Package Markings Containing Wildlife:

13. (indicate one) (complete name / address / phone number)
☐ U.S. Importer of Record
☐ U.S. Exporter

14a. Foreign Supplier / Receiver:
(complete name / address / phone number)

14b. ___ ___

15. Customs Broker, Shipping Agent or Freight Forwarder:

Phone Number / Fax Number: Contact Name:

Species Code (Official Use)	16a. Scientific Name / 16b. Common Name	17a. Foreign CITES Permit Number / 17b. U.S. CITES Permit Number	18a. Description Code / 18b. Source	19a. Quantity / Unit / 19b. Total Monetary Value	20. Country of Origin of Animal

Knowingly making a false statement in a Declaration for Importation or Exportation of Fish or Wildlife may subject the declarant to the penalty provided by 18 U.S.C 1001 and 16 U.S.C. 3372 (d)

21. I certify under penalty of perjury that the information furnished is true and correct:

Signature   Date

Type or Print Name

FOR OFFICIAL USE ONLY

Action/Comments:

Wildlife Inspected:

None / Partial / Full

CLICK HERE   FOR PRIVACY ACT NOTICE

United States Customs Service

Form Approved
OMB No. 1515-0069

ENTRY/IMMEDIATE DELIVERY

19 CFR 142.3, 142.16, 142.22, 142.24

1. ARRIVAL DATE	2. ELECTED ENTRY DATE	3. ENTRY TYPE CODE/NAME	4. ENTRY NUMBER
5. PORT	6. SINGLE TRANS. BOND	7. BROKER/IMPORTER FILE NUMBER	
	8. CONSIGNEE NUMBER		9. IMPORTER NUMBER
10. ULTIMATE CONSIGNEE NAME		11. IMPORTER OF RECORD NAME	
12. CARRIER CODE	13. VOYAGE/FLIGHT/TRIP	14. LOCATION OF GOODS-CODE(S)/NAME(S)	
15. VESSEL CODE/NAME			
16. U.S. PORT OF UNLADING	17. MANIFEST NUMBER	18. G. O. NUMBER	19. TOTAL VALUE
20. DESCRIPTION OF MERCHANDISE			

21. IT/BL/ AWB CODE	22. IT/BL/AWB NO.	23. MANIFEST QUANTITY	24. H.S. NUMBER	25. COUNTRY OF ORIGIN	26. MANUFACTURER NO.

27. CERTIFICATION	28. CUSTOMS USE ONLY
I hereby make application for entry/immediate delivery. I certify that the above information is accurate, the bond is sufficient, valid, and current, and that all requirements of 19 CFR Part 142 have been met.	☐ OTHER AGENCY ACTION REQUIRED, NAMELY:

SIGNATURE OF APPLICANT

X

PHONE NO.	DATE

☐ CUSTOMS EXAMINATION REQUIRED.

29. BROKER OR OTHER GOVT. AGENCY USE

☐ ENTRY REJECTED, BECAUSE:

DELIVERY AUTHORIZED:	SIGNATURE	DATE

Statement Required by 5 CFR 1320.21: The estimated average burden associated with this collection of information is 15 minutes per respondent or recordkeeper depending on individual circumstances. Comments concerning the accuracy of this burden estimate and suggestions for reducing this burden should be directed to U.S. Customs Service, Information Services Branch, Washington, DC 20229, and to the Office of Management and Budget, Paperwork Reduction Project (1515-0069) Washington, DC 20503.

Paperwork Reduction Act Notice: This information is needed to determine the admissibility of imports into the United States and to provide the necessary information for the examination of the cargo and to establish the liability for payment of duties and taxes. Your response is necessary.

Customs Form 3461 (010189)

Trade Forms: Import

CF 7501 – ENTRY SUMMARY

DEPARTMENT OF THE TREASURY UNITED STATES CUSTOMS SERVICE	**ENTRY SUMMARY**		Form Approved OMB No. 1515-0065

① Entry No.	② Entry Type Code	3. Entry Summary Date
4. Entry Date	⑤ Port Code	
6. Bond No.	7. Bond Type Code	8. Broker/Importer File No.

9. Ultimate Consignee Name and Address	10. Consignee No.	⑪ Importer of Record Name and Address	⑫ Importer No.

⑬ Exporting Country	14. Export Date
⑮ Country of Origin	16. Missing Documents
⑰ I.T. No.	⑱ I.T. Date

State

⑲ B/L or AWB No.	20. Mode of Transportation	21. Manufacturer I.D.	22. Reference No.
㉓ Importing Carrier	24. Foreign Port of Lading	25. Location of Goods/G.O. No.	
26. U.S. Port of Unlading	㉗ Import Date		

㉘ Line No.	30. Ⓐ T.S.U.S.A. No. Ⓑ ADA/CVD Case No.	31. Ⓐ Gross Weight Ⓑ Manifest Qty.	㉙ Description of Merchandise		
			㉜ Net Quantity in T.S.U.S.A. Units	33. Ⓐ Entered Value Ⓑ CHGS Ⓒ Relationship	34. Ⓐ T.S.U.S.A. Rate Ⓑ ADA/CVD Rate Ⓒ I.R.C. Rate Ⓓ Visa No.

	㉟ Duty and I.R. Tax	
	Dollars	Cents

㊱ Declaration of Importer of Record (Owner or Purchaser) or Authorized Agent

I declare that I am the
☐ importer of record and that the actual owner, purchaser, or consignee for customs purposes is as shown above.

OR

☐ owner or purchaser or agent thereof.

I further declare that the merchandise
☐ was obtained pursuant to a purchase or agreement to purchase and that the prices set forth in the invoices are true.

OR

☐ was not obtained pursuant to a purchase or agreement to purchase and the statements in the invoices as to value or price are true to the best of my knowledge and belief.

I also declare that the statements in the documents herein filed fully disclose to the best of my knowledge and belief the true prices, values, quantities, rebates, drawbacks, fees, commissions, and royalties and are true and correct, and that all goods or services provided to the seller of the merchandise either free or at reduced cost are fully disclosed. I will immediately furnish to the appropriate customs officer any information showing a different state of facts.

Notice required by Paperwork Reduction Act of 1980: This information is needed to ensure that importers/exporters are complying with U.S. customs laws, to allow us to compute and collect the right amount of money, to enforce other agency requirements, and to collect accurate statistical information on imports. Your response is mandatory. (Continued on back of form.)

▼ U.S. CUSTOMS USE ▼		TOTALS	
A. Liq. Code	B. Ascertained Duty	㊲ Duty	
	C. Ascertained Tax	㊳ Tax	
	D. Ascertained Other	㊴ Other	
	E. Ascertained Total	㊵ Total	

㊶ Signature of Declarant, Title, and Date

PART 1 – RECORD COPY

Customs Form 7501 (112295)

DEPARTMENT OF THE TREASURY
United States Customs Service

NOTICE OF INTENT TO EXPORT, DESTROY OR RETURN MERCHANDISE FOR PURPOSES OF DRAWBACK

19 CFR 191

OMB 1515-0213

PAPERWORK REDUCTION ACT NOTICE: This request is in accordance with the Paperwork Reduction Act of 1995. We ask for the information in order to enforce the laws of the United States, to fulfill the Customs Regulations, to ensure that the claimant is entitled to drawback, and to have the necessary information which permits Customs to calculate and refund (or increase) the correct amount of duty and/or tax. Your response is required to obtain a benefit. The estimated average burden associated with this collection of information is 10 minutes per respondent depending on individual circumstances. Comments concerning the accuracy of this burden estimates and suggestions for reducing this burden should be directed to U.S. Customs Service, Information Services Branch, Washington, DC 20229, and to the Office of Management and Budget, Paperwork Reduction Project (1515-0213) Washington, DC 20503

1. Exporter or Destroyer		2. Drawback Entry No.	3. Intended Action	4. Intended Date of Action	5. Drawback Center
Name			☐ Export ☐ Destroy		
Address					
I.D. Number					**DATE RECEIVED**

6. Contact Name	
Address	
Phone	Ext.
FAX	

7. Location of Merchandise	8. Method of Destruction/Location	9. Exporting Carrier Name (if known)	10. Intended Port of Export	11. Unique Identifier No.

14. Import Entry No.	15. Description of Merchandise (include part number(s))	12. T & E No.	13. Country of Ultimate Destination
		16. Drawback Amount	17. Quantity & Unit of Measure
			18. HTSUS No./Schedule B

19. Drawback to be filled as:
- ☐ Unused Merchandise Drawback
  - ☐ J1 ☐ J2
- ☐ Manufacturing Drawback
- ☐ Rejected Merchandise
- ☐ Same Condition Drawback under NAFTA
- ☐ Distilled Spirits, Wine or Beer under
- ☐ Shipped without Consent
- ☐ Defective at Time of Importation
- ☐ Not Conforming to Sample or Specifications

THIS FORM MUST BE SUBMITTED WITH THE DRAWBACK CLAIM

20. Preparer		
Printed Name	X Signature	Title	Date

21. Examination ☐ Waived ☐ Required
(Additional information may be required if exam requested, T & E may be required)

22. Present Merchandise to Customs at:

23. Destruction to be Witnessed by Customs ☐ Yes ☐ No

CUSTOMS USE ONLY

24. Printed Name	28. Comments/Results of Examination or Witnessing of Destruction.
Phone Number	(Merchandise matches invoice description)

25. Signature & Badge No.	29. Date Destroyed or Exam Conducted
X	30. Printed Name of Examining Officer	31. Signature & Badge No.

26. Date	27. Port	Phone Number	Ext.	X	Date

Customs Form 7553 (08/01)

DEPARTMENT OF THE TREASURY
United States Customs Service

DRAWBACK ENTRY

19 CFR 191

OMB 1515-0213

PAPERWORK REDUCTION ACT NOTICE: This request is in accordance with the Paperwork Reduction Act of 1995. We ask for the information in order to carry out U.S. Department of Treasury laws and regulations, to determine the eligibility for refund of taxes on domestic alcohol (if applicable), and to determine the proper amount of drawback. Your response is required to obtain or retain a benefit. The estimated average burden associated with this collection of information is 10 minutes per respondent depending on individual circumstances. Comments concerning the accuracy of this burden estimate and suggestions for reducing this burden should be directed to U.S. Customs Service, Information Services Branch, Washington, DC 20229, and to the Office of Management and Budget, Paperwork Reduction Project (1515-0213), Washington, DC 20503.

Section I - Claim Header

1. Drawback Entry Number		2. Entry Type Code	3. Port Code	4. Surety Code	5. Bond Type
6. Claimant ID Number		7. Broker ID Number (CF4811)	8. DBK Ruling Number		9. Total MPF Claimed
10. Total Drawback Claimed		11. Puerto Rico Drawback Claimed	12. Total I.R. Tax Claimed		
13. Method of Filing ☐ Manual ☐ Disk ☐ ABI	14. NAFTA DBK ☐ Yes ☐ No	15. ESP ☐ Yes ☐ No	16. Privilege Authorized ☐ Accelerated Payment ☐ WPN		17. Drawback Section
18. Name and Address of Claimant	19. Contact Name, Address, Phone & Fax Numbers of Preparer				

Section II - Imported Duty Paid, Designated Merchandise or Drawback Product

20. Import Entry Or CM&D Number(s)	21. Port Code	22. Import Date	23. CD	24. (If using 1313(b)) A. Date(s) Received / B. Date(s) Used	25. HTSUS No.	26. Description of Merchandise (Include Part Numbers)	27. Quantity & Unit of Measure	28. Entered Value Per Unit	29. Duty Rate	30. 99% Duty
									31. Total	

U.S. CUSTOMS SERVICE USE ONLY

Class Code	Accelerated	Liquidated	Net
364 Drawback			
365 Tax			
369 Puerto Rico			
399 MPF			

32. STATUS - The import entries as listed on this form are subject to:
(Must be identified on claim or coding sheet)
☐ Reconciliation   ☐ Protest
☐ 520 (c) (1)   ☐ 520 (d)

DATE RECEIVED

Reason Code   ☐ Bill   ☐ Refund   ☐ No Change   Specialist Code

Customs Form 7551 (08/01)

Section III - Manufactured Articles

33. Quantity & Description of Merchandise Used	34. Date(s) of Manufacture or Production	35. Description of Articles Manufactured or Produced	36. Quantity and Unit of Measure	37. Factory Location

38. Exhibits to be attached for the following:

☐ Relative Value   ☐ Petroleum   ☐ Domestic Tax Paid Alcohol   ☐ Piece Goods   ☐ Waste Calculation   ☐ Recycled   ☐ Merchandise Processing Fee

Section IV - Information on Exported or Destroyed Merchandise

PERIOD COVERED _____ TO _____

39. Date	40. Action Code	41. Unique Indentifier No.	42. Name of Exporter/Destroyer	43. Description of Articles (Include part number(s))	44. Quantity and Unit of Measure	45. Export Destination	46. HTSUS No.

Same condition to NAFTA countries - The undersigned herein certifies that the merchandise herein described is in the same condition as when it was imported under above import entry(ies) and further certifies that this merchandise was not subjected to any process of manufacturer or other operation except the following allowable operations:

☐ The undersigned hereby certifies that the merchandise herein described is unused in the United States and further certifies that this merchandise was not subjected to any process of manufacture or other operation except the following allowable operations:

☐ The undersigned hereby certifies that the merchandise herein described is commercially interchangeable with the designated imported merchandise and further certifies that the substituted merchandise is unused in the United States and that the substituted merchandise was in our possession prior to exportation or destruction.

☐ Merchandise does not conform to sample or specifications.   ☐ Merchandise was defective at time of importation.   ☐ Merchandise was shipped without consent of the consignee.

☐ The undersigned hereby certifies that the merchandise herein described is the same kind and quality as defined in 19 U.S.C. 1313(p)(3)(B), with the designated imported merchandise or the article manufactured or produced under 1313(a) or (b), as appropriate.

☐ The article(s) described above were manufactured or produced and disposed of as stated herein in accordance with the drawback ruling on file with Customs and in compliance with applicable laws and regulations.

The undersigned acknowledges statutory requirements that all records supporting the information on this document are to be retained by the issuing party for a period of three years from the date of payment of the drawback claim. The undersigned is fully aware of the sanctions provided in 18 U.S.C. 1001 and 18 U.S.C. 560 and 19 U.S.C. 1593a.

I declare that according to the best of my knowledge and belief, all of the statements in this document are correct and that the exported article is not to be relanded in the United States or any of its possessions without paying duty.

☐ Member of Firm with Power of Attorney   ☐ Officer of Corporation   ☐ Broker with Power of Attorney

Printed Name and Title	Signature and Date

Customs Form 7551 (Back)(08/01)

DEPARTMENT OF THE TREASURY
United States Customs Service

DELIVERY CERTIFICATE FOR PURPOSES OF DRAWBACK
19 CFR 191

OMB 1515-0213

PAPERWORK REDUCTION ACT NOTICE: This request is in accordance with the Paperwork Reduction Act of 1995. We ask for the information in order to carry out U.S. Department of Treasury laws and regulations, to determine the eligibility for refund of taxes on domestic alcohol (if applicable), and to determine the proper amount of drawback. Your response is required to obtain or retain a benefit. The estimated average burden associated with this collection of information is 10 minutes per respondent depending on individual circumstances. Comments concerning the accuracy of this burden estimates and suggestions for reducing this burden should be directed to U.S. Customs Service, Information Services Branch, Washington, DC 20229, and to the Office of Management and Budget, Paperwork Reduction Project (1515-0213) Washington, DC 20503

	Certificate of Delivery		
		1. CM&D No.	2. Port Code	3. DBK Ruling No.

	Certificate of Manufacture and Delivery	4. Type Code	5. ID No. of Transferor

6. FROM TRANSFEROR:
Company Name and Complete Address

7. TO TRANSFEREE:
Company Name
Complete Address

RECEIVED DATE

IMPORTED DUTY PAID, DESIGNATED MERCHANDISE OR DRAWBACK PRODUCT

8. Use	9. Import Entry or CM&D Number	10. Port Code	11. Import Date (mm/dd/yyyy)	12. CD	13. (If using 1313(b)) A. Date(s) Received	B. Date(s) Used	14. Date Delivered	15. HTSUS No.	16. Description Of Merchandise (Include Part Numbers)	17. Quantity & Unit of	18. Entered Value Per Unit	19. 100% Duty

		20. **Total**

21. Contact Name and Address

PREPARER
Phone Number _____ Ext. _____
FAX Number

Customs Form 7552 (08/01)

22. Quantity & Description of Merchandise Used

23. Date(s) of Manufacture

24. Description of Articles Manufactured or Produced (Include Part Numbers)

25. Quantity & Unit of Measure

26. Date Delivered

27. Duty Available on Manufacture Articles (Total of Duties in Block 20)

28. Drawback Available Per Unit of Measure on Manufactured Article

29. Factory Location

30. Exhibits to be attached for the following:

☐ Relative Value ☐ Petroleum ☐ Domestic Tax Paid Alcohol ☐ Piece Goods ☐ Waste Calculation ☐ Recycled ☐ Merchandise Processing Fee

31. STATUS - Import Entries listed on this form are subject to (If CD, identify on this form; if CM&D, identify on coding sheet):

☐ Reconciliation ☐ Protest, 514 ☐ 520 (c) (1) ☐ 520 (d)

☐ This Certificate of Delivery is a subsequent transfer and the merchandise is the same as received.

☐ The article(s) described above were manufactured or produced and delivered as stated herein in accordance with the Drawback ruling on file with Customs and in compliance with applicable laws and regulations.

☐ The merchandise transferred on this CD is pursuant to 19 U.S.C. 13130)(2) and will not be designated for any other Drawback purposes.

☐ The merchandise transferred on this CD is the imported merchandise.

DECLARATIONS

The undersigned acknowledges statutory requirements that all records supporting the information on this document are to be retained by the issuing party for a period of three years from the date of payment of the related drawback entry.

Assignment of Rights is transferred when this form is prepared as a CD or CM&D.

I declare that according to the best of my knowledge and belief, all of the statements in this document are correct and I am fully aware of the sanctions provided in 18 U.S.C. 1001 and 18 U.S.C. 650 and 19 U.S.C. 1593a.

☐ Member of Firm with Power of Attorney ☐ Officer of Corporation ☐ Broker with Power of Attorney

Printed Name and Title

Signature and Date

Customs Form 7552 (Back) (08/01)

DEPARTMENT OF THE TREASURY
UNITED STATES CUSTOMS SERVICE

Form Approved
OMB No. 1515-0043

DECLARATION FOR FREE ENTRY OF RETURNED AMERICAN PRODUCTS

19 CFR 7.8, 10.1, 10.5, 10.6, 10.66, 10.67, 12.41, 123.4, 143.23, 145.35

1. PORT	2. DATE	3. ENTRY NO. & DATE
4. NAME OF MANUFACTURER		5. CITY AND STATE OF MANUFACTURE

6. REASON FOR RETURN	7. U.S. DRAWBACK PREVIOUSLY ☐ CLAIMED ☐ UNCLAIMED
	8. PREVIOUSLY IMPORTED UNDER TSUSA 864.05? ☐ YES ☐ NO

9. MARKS, NUMBERS, AND DESCRIPTION OF ARTICLES RETURNED	10. VALUE*

* If the value of the article is $10,000 or more and the articles are not clearly marked with the name and address of U.S. manufacturer, please attach copies of any documentation or evidence that you have that will support or substantiate your claim for duty free status as American Goods Returned.

11. I declare that the information given above is true and correct to the best of my knowledge and belief; that the articles described above are the growth, production, and manufacture United States and are returned without having been advanced in value or improved in condition by any process of manufacture or other means; that no drawback bounty, or allowanc been paid or admitted thereon, or on any part thereof; and that if any notice(s) of exportation of articles with benefit of drawback ☐ was ☐ were filed upon exportation of th merchandise from the United States, such notice(s) ☐ has ☐ have been abandoned.

12. NAME OF DECLARANT	13. TITLE OF DECLARANT
14. NAME OF CORPORATION OR PARTNERSHIP (If any)	15. SIGNATURE (See note)

16. SIGNATURE OF AUTHORIZING CUSTOMS OFFICER

NOTE: If the owner or ultimate consignee is a corporation, this form must be signed by the president, vice president, secretary, or treasurer of the corporation, or by any employee or a of the corporation who holds a power of attorney and a certificate by the corporation that such employee or agent has or will have knowledge of the pertinent facts.

Notice required by Paperwork Reduction Act of 1980: This information is needed to ensure that importers/exporters are complying with U.S. customs laws, to allow us to compute and cc the right amount of money, to enforce other agency requirements, and to collect accurate statistical information on imports. Your response is mandatory.

Statement Required by 5 CFR 1320.21: The estimated average burden associated with this collection of information is 6 minutes per respondent or recordkeeper depending on individua cumstances. Comments concerning the accuracy of this burden estimate and suggestions for reducing this burden should be directed to U.S. Customs Service, Paperwork Managem Branch, Washington DC 20229, and to the Office of Management and Budget, Paperwork Reduction Project (1515-0043), Washington DC 20503.

Customs Form 3311 (062496)

OMB No. 1515-0144

United States Customs Service

CUSTOMS BOND

19 CFR Part 113

CUSTOMS USE ONLY	BOND NUMBER 1 (Assigned by Customs)
	FILE REFERENCE

In order to secure payment of any duty, tax or charge and compliance with law or regulation as a result of activity covered by any condition referenced below, we, the below named principal(s) and surety(ies), bind ourselves to the United States in the amount or amounts, as set forth below.

Execution Date

SECTION I--Select Single Transaction OR Continuous Bond (not both) and fill in the applicable blank spaces.

☐ SINGLE TRANSACTION BOND	Identification of transaction secured by this bond (e.g., entry no., seizure no., etc.)	Date of transaction	Port code

☐ CONTINUOUS BOND	Effective date	This bond remains in force for one year beginning with the effective date and for each succeeding annual period, or until terminated. This bond constitutes a separate bond for each period in the amounts listed below for liabilities that accrue in each period. The intention to terminate this bond must be conveyed within the period and manner prescribed in the Customs Regulations.

SECTION II-- This bond includes the following agreements. 2 (Check one box only, except that, 1a may be checked independently or with 1, and 3a may be checked independently or with 3. Line out all other parts of this section that are not used.

Activity Code	Activity Name and Customs Regulations in which conditions codified	Limit of Liability	Activity Code	Activity Name and Customs Regulations in which conditions codified	Limit of Liability
☐ 1	Importer or broker......................113.62		☐ 5	Public Gauger.........................113.67	
☐ 1a	Drawback Payments Refunds.........113.65		☐ 6	Wool & Fur Products Labeling Acts Importation (Single Entry Only)...........113.68	
☐ 2	Custodian of bonded merchandise.........113.63 (Includes bonded carriers, freight forwarders, cartmen and lightermen, all classes of warehouse, container station operators)		☐ 7	Bill of Lading (Single Entry Only) 113.69	
☐ 3	International Carrier.....................113.64		☐ 8	Detention of Copyrighted Material (Single Entry Only)......................113.70	
☐ 3a	Instruments of International Traffic......113.66		☐ 9	Neutrality (Single Entry Only) 113.71	
☐ 4	Foreign Trade Zone Operator............113.73		☐ 10	Court Costs for Condemned Goods (Single Entry Only)....................113.72	

SECTION III-- List below all tradenames or unincorporated divisions that will be permitted to obligate this bond in the principal's name including their Customs identification Number(s). 3 (If more space is needed, use Section III (Continuation) on back of form.)

Importer Number	Importer Name	Importer Number	Importer Name
		Total number of importer names listed in Section III:	

Principal and surely agree that any charge against the bond under any of the listed names is as though it was made by the principal(s).

Principal and surety agree that they are bound to the same extent as if they executed a separate bond covering each set of conditions incorporated by reference into the Customs Regulations into this bond.

If the surety fails to appoint an agent under Title 6, United States Code, Section 7, surety consents to service on the Clerk of any United States District Court or the U.S. Court of International Trade, where suit is brought on this bond. That clerk is to send notice of the service to the surety at:

Mailing Address Requested by the Surety

Name and Address	Importer No. 3	
	SIGNATURE 5	**SEAL**
Name and Address	Importer No. 3	
	SIGNATURE 5	**SEAL**
Name and Address 6	Surety No. 7	
	SIGNATURE 5	**SEAL**
Name and Address 6	Surety No. 7	
	SIGNATURE 5	**SEAL**

SURETY AGENTS	Name 8	Identification No. 9	Name 8	Identification No. 9

PART 1 - U.S. CUSTOMS   **Customs Form 301 (050798)**

Note: Turn carbons over before writing on back of form.

SECTION III (Continuation)

Importer Number	Importer Name	Importer Number	Importer Name

WITNESSES	SIGNED, SEALED, and DELIVERED in the PRESENCE OF:	
Two witnesses are required to authenticate the signature of any person who signs as an individual or partner; however a witness may authenticate the signatures of both such non-corporate principals and sureties. No witness is needed to authenticate the signature of a corporate official or agent who signs for the corporation.	Name and Address of Witness for the Principal	Name and Address of Witness for the Surety
	SIGNATURE:	SIGNATURE:
	Name and Address of Witness for the Principal	Name and Address of Witness for the Surety
	SIGNATURE:	SIGNATURE:

EXPLANATIONS AND FOOTNOTES

1. The Customs Bond Number is a control number assigned by Customs to the bond contract when the bond is approved by an authorized Customs official.
2. For all bond coverage available and the language of the bond conditions refer to Part 113, subpart G, Customs Regulations.
3. The Importer Number is the Customs identification number filed pursuant to section 24.5, Customs Regulations. When the Internal Revenue Service employer identification number is used the two-digit suffix code must be shown.
4. If the principal or surety is a corporation, the name of the State in which incorporated must be shown.
5. See witness requirement above.

6. Surety Name, if a corporation, shall be the company's name as it is spelled in the Surety Companies Annual List published in the Federal Register by the Department of the Treasury (Treasury Department Circular 570).
7. Surety Number is the three digit identification code assigned by Customs to a surety company at the time the surety company initially gives notice to Customs that the company will be writing Customs bonds.
8. Surety Agent is the individual granted a Corporate Surety Power of Attorney, CF 5297, by the surety company executing the bond.
9. Agent Identification No. shall be the individual's Social Security number as shown on the Corporate Surety Power of Attorney, CF 5297, filed by the surety granting such power of attorney.

Paperwork Reduction Act Notice: The Paperwork Reduction Act of 1995 says we must tell you why we are collecting this information, how we will use it, and whether you have to give it to us. We ask for this information to carry out the Customs Service laws and regulations of the United States. We need it to ensure that persons transacting business with Customs have the proper bond coverage to secure their transactions as required by law and regulation. Your response is required to enter into any transaction in which a bond is a prerequisite under the Tariff Act of 1930, as amended.

Privacy Act Statement: The following notice is given pursuant to section 7(b) of the Privacy Act of 1974 (5 U.S.C. 552a). Furnishing the information of this form, including the Social Security Number, is mandatory. The primary use of the Social Security Number is to verify, in the Customs Automated System, at the time an agent submits a Customs bond for approval that the individual was granted a Corporate Surety Power of Attorney by the surety company. Section 7 of Act of July 30, 1947, chapter 390, 61 Stat. 646, authorizes the collection of this information.

Customs Form 301 (050798)(Back)

United States Customs Service

REQUEST FOR INFORMATION
19 CFR 151.11

OMB No. 1515-0068

1. Date of Request	
2. Date of Entry and Importation	

3. Manufacturer/Seller/Shipper	4. Carrier	5. Entry No.

5a. Invoice Description of Merchandise	5b. Invoice No.	6. HTSUS Item No.

7. Country of Origin/Exportation	8. Customs Broker and Reference or File No.

9. TO:	10. FROM:

Production of Documents and/or Information Required by Law: If you have provided the information requested on this form to U.S. Customs at other ports, please indicate the port of entry to which it was supplied, and furnish a copy of your reply to this office, if possible.

11a. Port	11b. Date Information Furnished

General Information and Instructions on Reverse

12. Please Answer Indicated Question(s)	13. Please Furnish Indicated Item(s)

☐ A. Are you related (see reverse) in any way to the seller of this merchandise? If you are related, please describe the relationship, and explain how this relationship affects the price paid or payable for the merchandise.	☐ A. Copy of contract (or purchase order and seller's confirmation thereof) covering this transaction, and any revisions thereto.
	☐ B. Descriptive or illustrative literature or information explaining what the merchandise is, where and how it is used, and exactly how it operates.
	☐ C. Breakdown of components, materials, or ingredients by weight and the actual cost of the components at the time of assembly into the finished article.
☐ B. Identify and give details of any additional costs/expenses incurred in this transaction, such as:	☐ D. Submit samples: Article number and description _____
☐ (1) packing	
☐ (2) commissions	from container _____
☐ (3) proceeds that accrue to the seller	mark(s) and number _____
☐ (4) assists	Samples consumed in analysis, and other samples whose return is not specifically requested, will not normally be returned.
☐ (5) royalties and/or license fees	☐ E. See item 14 below.

14. Customs Officer Message

15. Reply Message (Use additional sheets if more space is needed.)

16. CERTIFICATION	It is required that an appropriate corporate/company official execute this certificate and/or endorse all correspondence in response to the information requested. (**NOTE:** NOT REQUIRED IF FOREIGN FIRM COMPLETES THIS FORM.)

I hereby certify that the information furnished herewith or upon this form in response to this inquiry is true and correct, and that any samples provided were taken from the shipment covered by this entry.	16a. Name and Title/Position of Signer (Owner, Importer, or Corporate/Company Official)	16b. Signature
		16c. Telephone No.
		16d. Date

17. Customs Officer	18. Team Designation	19. Telephone No.

Customs Form 28 (02/02)

GENERAL INFORMATION AND INSTRUCTIONS

1. The requested information is necessary for proper classification and/or appraisement of your merchandise and/or for insuring import compliance of such merchandise. Your reply is required in accordance with section 509(a), Tariff Action of 1930, as amended (19 U.S.C. 1509).

2. All information, documents, and samples requested must relate to the shipment of merchandise described on the front of this form

3. Please answer all indicated questions to the best of your knowledge.

4. All information submitted will be treated confidentially.

5. If a reply cannot be made within 30 days from the date of this request or if you wish to discuss any of the questions designated for your reply, please contact the Customs officer whose name appears on the front of this form.

6. Return a copy of this form with your reply.

DEFINITIONS OF KEY WORDS IN BLOCK 12

Question A: RELATED - The persons specified below shall be treated as persons who are related:

(A) Members of the same family, including brothers and sisters (whether by whole or half blood), spouse, ancestors, and lineal descendants.

(B) Any officer or director of an organization and such organization.

(C) An officer or director of an organization and an officer or director of another organization, if each such individual is also an officer or director in the other organization.

(D) Partners.

(E) Employer and employee.

(F) Any person directly or indirectly owning, controlling, or holding with power to vote, 5 percent or more of the outstanding voting stock or shares of any organization and such organization.

(G) Two or more persons directly or indirectly controlling, controlled by or under common control with, any person.

PRICE PAID OR PAYABLE - This term is defined as the total payment (whether direct or indirect and exclusive of any costs, charges, or expenses incurred for transportation, insurance, and other C.I.F. charges) made, or to be made, for imported merchandise by the buyer to, or for the benefit of, the seller.

Question B: ASSISTS - The term "assist" means any of the following if supplied directly or indirectly, and free of charge or at reduced cost, by the buyer of the imported merchandise for use in connection with the production or the sale for export to the United States of the merchandise:

(1) Materials, components, parts, and similar items incorporated in the imported merchandise.

(2) Tools, dies, molds, and similar items used in the production of the imported merchandise.

(3) Merchandise consumed in the production of the imported merchandise.

(4) Engineering, development, artwork, design work, and plans and sketches that are undertaken elsewhere than in the United States and are necessary for the production of the imported merchandise.

PROCEEDS THAT ACCRUE TO THE SELLER - This term is defined as the amount of any subsequent resale, disposal, or use of the imported merchandise that accrues, directly or indirectly, to the seller.

ROYALTIES AND/OR LICENSE FEES - This term relates to those amounts that the buyer is required to pay, directly or indirectly, as a condition of the sale of the imported merchandised for exportation to the United States.

PAPERWORK REDUCTION ACT NOTICE: This request is in accordance with the Paperwork Reduction Act of 1995. We ask for the information to carry out the laws of the United States. We need it to ensure importers/brokers are complying with these laws and to allow us to properly appraise and classify imported merchandise or correct duties and determine import admissibility, where appropriate. Your response is mandatory. The estimated average burden associated with this collection of information is 33 minutes per respondent or recordkeeper depending on individual circumstances. Comments concerning the accuracy of this burden estimate and suggestions for reducing this burden should be directed to the U.S. Customs Service, Information Services Branch, Washington, DC 20229, and to the Office of Management and Budget Paperwork Reduction Project (1515-0068), Washington, DC 20503.

Customs Form 28 (Back) (02/02)

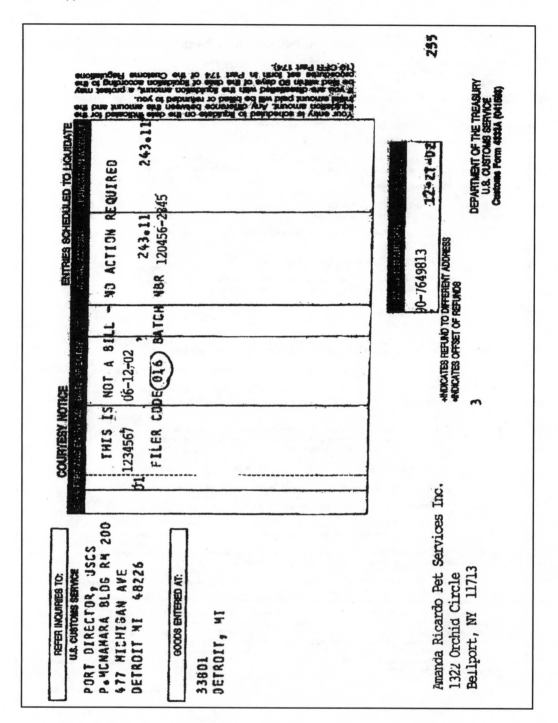

Amanda Ricardo Pet Services Inc.
1322 Orchid Circle
Bellport, NY 11713

REFER INQUIRIES TO:

U.S. CUSTOMS SERVICE

PORT DIRECTOR, JSCS
P. MCNAMARA BLDG RM 200
477 MICHIGAN AVE
DETROIT MI 48226

GOODS ENTERED AT:

33801
DETROIT, MI

COURTESY NOTICE   ENTRIES SCHEDULED TO LIQUIDATE

THIS IS NOT A BILL - NO ACTION REQUIRED

1234567   06-12-02   243.11   243.11

FILER CODE 016   BATCH NBR 120456-2345

Your entry is scheduled to liquidate on the date indicated for the
liquidation amount. Any difference between this amount and the
paid amount paid will be billed or refunded to you.
If you are dissatisfied with the liquidation amount, a protest may
be filed within 90 days of the date of liquidation according to the
procedures set forth in Part 174 of the Customs Regulations
(19 CFR Part 174).

90-7649813   12-12-02

*INDICATES REFUND TO DIFFERENT ADDRESS
*INDICATES OFFSET OF REFUNDS

3

DEPARTMENT OF THE TREASURY
U.S. CUSTOMS SERVICE
Customs Form 4333A (041600)

255

Miscellaneous Documents: Resource Guides

Commerce Control List Overview and the Country Chart

Supplement No. 1 to Part 738 page 1

Commerce Country Chart
Reason for Control

Countries	Chemical & Biological Weapons			Nuclear Nonproliferation		National Security		Missile Tech	Regional Stability		Firearms Convention	Crime Control			Anti-Terrorism	
	CB 1	CB 2	CB 3	NP 1	NP 2	NS 1	NS 2	MT 1	RS 1	RS 2	FC 1	CC 1	CC 2	CC 3	AT 1	AT 2
Afghanistan	X	X	X	X		X	X	X	X	X		X		X		
Albania [2,3]	X	X		X		X	X	X	X	X						
Algeria	X	X		X		X	X	X	X	X		X		X		
Andorra	X	X		X		X	X	X	X	X		X		X		
Angola	X	X		X		X	X	X	X	X		X		X		
Antigua & Barbuda	X	X				X	X	X	X	X	X	X		X		
Argentina	X					X	X	X	X	X	X	X		X		
Armenia	X	X	X	X		X	X	X	X	X		X	X			
Aruba	X	X		X		X	X	X	X	X		X		X		
Australia [3]	X					X	X	X	X			X				
Austria [3,4]	X	X	X	X		X	X	X	X	X		X	X			
Azerbaijan	X	X		X		X	X	X	X	X		X		X		
Bahamas, The	X	X		X		X	X	X	X	X	X	X		X		

Export Administration Regulations   Bureau of Industry and Security   September 6, 2011

Commerce Control List Overview and the Country Chart

Supplement No. 1 to Part 738 page 2

Commerce Country Chart

Reason for Control

Countries	Chemical & Biological Weapons			Nuclear Nonproliferation		National Security		Missile Tech	Regional Stability		Firearms Convention	Crime Control			Anti-Terrorism	
	CB 1	CB 2	CB 3	NP 1	NP 2	NS 1	NS 2	MT 1	RS 1	RS 2	FC 1	CC 1	CC 2	CC 3	AT 1	AT 2
Bahrain	X	X	X	X		X	X	X	X	X		X		X		
Bangladesh	X	X		X		X	X	X	X	X		X		X		
Barbados	X	X		X		X	X	X	X	X	X	X		X		
Belarus	X	X	X			X	X	X	X	X			X			
Belgium[3]	X					X		X	X							
Belize	X	X		X		X	X	X	X	X	X	X		X		
Benin	X	X		X		X	X	X	X	X		X		X		
Bhutan	X	X		X		X	X	X	X	X		X		X		
Bolivia	X	X		X		X	X	X	X	X	X	X		X		
Bosnia & Herzegovina	X	X		X		X	X	X	X	X		X		X		
Botswana	X	X		X		X	X	X	X	X	X	X		X		
Brazil	X	X				X	X	X	X	X		X		X		
Brunei	X	X		X		X	X	X	X	X		X		X		

Commerce Control List Overview and the Country Chart

Supplement No. 1 to Part 738 page 3

Commerce Country Chart

Reason for Control

Countries	Chemical & Biological Weapons CB 1	CB 2	CB 3	Nuclear Nonproliferation NP 1	NP 2	National Security NS 1	NS 2	Missile Tech MT 1	Regional Stability RS 1	RS 2	Firearms Convention FC 1	Crime Control CC 1	CC 2	CC 3	Anti-Terrorism AT 1	AT 2
Bulgaria[3]	X					X			X							
Burkina Faso	X	X		X		X	X	X	X	X		X		X		
Burma	X	X	X	X		X	X	X	X	X		X		X		
Burundi	X	X		X		X	X	X	X	X		X		X		
Cambodia	X	X		X		X	X	X	X	X		X	X			
Cameroon	X	X		X		X	X	X	X	X		X		X		
Canada	X															
Cape Verde	X	X		X		X	X	X	X	X	X	X		X		
Central African Republic	X	X		X		X	X	X	X	X		X		X		
Chad	X	X		X		X	X	X	X	X		X		X		
Chile	X	X		X		X	X	X	X	X	X	X		X		
China	X	X	X	X		X	X	X	X	X		X		X		
Colombia	X	X		X		X	X	X	X	X	X	X		X		

Export Administration Regulations

Bureau of Industry and Security

September 6, 2011

Commerce Control List Overview and the Country Chart

Commerce Country Chart

Reason for Control

Countries	Chemical & Biological Weapons CB 1	CB 2	CB 3	Nuclear Nonproliferation NP 1	NP 2	National Security NS 1	NS 2	Missile Tech MT 1	Regional Stability RS 1	RS 2	Firearms Convention FC 1	Crime Control CC 1	CC 2	CC 3	Anti-Terrorism AT 1	AT 2
Comoros	X	X		X		X	X	X	X	X		X		X		
Congo (Democratic Republic of the)	X	X		X		X	X	X	X	X		X		X		
Congo (Republic of the)	X	X		X		X	X	X	X	X		X		X		
Costa Rica	X	X		X		X	X	X	X	X	X	X		X		
Cote d'Ivoire	X	X		X		X	X	X	X	X		X		X		
Croatia [3]	X			X		X		X	X							
Cuba	See part 746 of the EAR to determine whether a license is required in order to export or reexport to this destination.															
Curaçao	X	X		X		X	X	X	X	X		X				
Cyprus [2,3,4]	X					X	X	X	X	X		X		X		
Czech Republic [3]	X					X	X	X	X							
Denmark [3]	X					X			X							
Djibouti	X	X		X		X	X	X	X	X	X	X		X		
Dominica	X	X		X		X	X	X	X	X		X		X		

Commerce Control List Overview and the Country Chart

Commerce Country Chart
Reason for Control

Countries	Chemical & Biological Weapons			Nuclear Nonproliferation		National Security		Missile Tech	Regional Stability		Firearms Convention	Crime Control			Anti-Terrorism	
	CB 1	CB 2	CB 3	NP 1	NP 2	NS 1	NS 2	MT 1	RS 1	RS 2	FC 1	CC 1	CC 2	CC 3	AT 1	AT 2
Dominican Republic	X	X		X		X	X	X	X	X	X	X		X		
Ecuador	X	X		X		X	X	X	X	X	X	X		X		
Egypt	X	X	X	X		X	X	X	X	X		X		X		
El Salvador	X	X		X		X	X	X	X	X	X	X		X		
Equatorial Guinea	X	X		X		X	X	X	X	X		X		X		
Eritrea	X	X		X		X	X	X	X	X		X		X		
Estonia[3]	X					X		X	X	X		X				
Ethiopia	X	X		X		X	X	X	X	X		X		X		
Fiji	X	X		X		X	X	X	X	X		X		X		
Finland[3,4]	X					X		X	X	X		X		X		
France[3]	X	X				X		X	X	X		X				
Gabon	X	X		X		X	X	X	X	X		X		X		
Gambia, The	X	X		X		X	X	X	X	X		X		X		

Export Administration Regulations   Bureau of Industry and Security

Commerce Country Chart
Reason for Control

Commerce Control List Overview and the Country Chart

Supplement No. 1 to Part 738 page 6

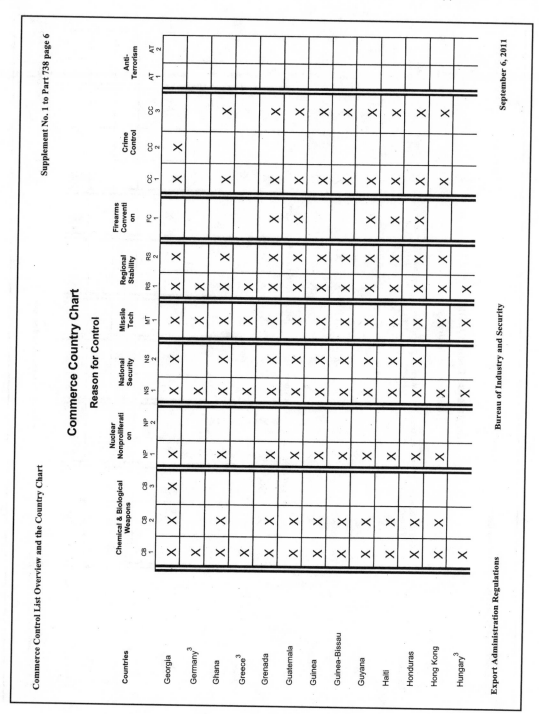

Countries	Chemical & Biological Weapons CB 1	CB 2	CB 3	Nuclear Nonproliferation NP 1	NP 2	National Security NS 1	NS 2	Missile Tech MT 1	Regional Stability RS 1	RS 2	Firearms Convention FC 1	Crime Control CC 1	CC 2	CC 3	Anti-Terrorism AT 1	AT 2
Georgia	X	X	X	X		X	X	X	X	X		X	X			
Germany[3]	X					X		X	X	X						
Ghana	X	X		X		X	X	X	X			X		X		
Greece[3]	X					X		X	X							
Grenada	X	X		X		X	X	X	X	X		X		X		
Guatemala	X	X		X		X	X	X	X	X	X	X		X		
Guinea	X	X		X		X	X	X	X	X	X	X		X		
Guinea-Bissau	X	X		X		X	X	X	X	X		X		X		
Guyana	X	X		X		X	X	X	X	X		X		X		
Haiti	X	X		X		X	X	X	X	X		X		X		
Honduras	X	X		X		X	X	X	X	X	X	X		X		
Hong Kong	X	X		X		X		X	X		X	X		X		
Hungary[3]	X			X		X		X	X		X	X		X		

Export Administration Regulations

Bureau of Industry and Security

September 6, 2011

Commerce Control List Overview and the Country Chart

Supplement No. 1 to Part 738 page 7

Commerce Country Chart

Reason for Control

Countries	Chemical & Biological Weapons			Nuclear Nonproliferation		National Security		Missile Tech	Regional Stability		Firearms Convention	Crime Control			Anti-Terrorism	
	CB 1	CB 2	CB 3	NP 1	NP 2	NS 1	NS 2	MT 1	RS 1	RS 2	FC 1	CC 1	CC 2	CC 3	AT 1	AT 2
Iceland[3]	X			X		X		X	X							
India	X	X		X		X	X	X	X	X		X		X		
Indonesia	X	X		X	X	X	X	X	X	X		X		X		
Iran	See part 746 of the EAR to determine whether a license is required in order to export or reexport to this destination.															
Iraq[1]	X	X	X	X	X	X	X	X	X	X		X				
Ireland[3,4]	X	X	X	X		X		X	X			X		X		
Israel	X	X		X	X	X	X	X	X	X		X				
Italy[3]	X			X		X		X	X							
Jamaica	X	X		X		X	X	X	X	X	X	X		X		
Japan[3]	X	X		X		X		X	X			X				
Jordan	X	X	X	X		X	X	X	X	X		X		X		
Kazakhstan	X	X	X			X	X	X	X	X		X	X			
Kenya	X	X		X		X	X	X	X	X		X		X		

Export Administration Regulations

Bureau of Industry and Security

September 6, 2011

Commerce Control List Overview and the Country Chart

Supplement No. 1 to Part 738 page 8

Commerce Country Chart

Reason for Control

Countries	Chemical & Biological Weapons			Nuclear Nonproliferation		National Security		Missile Tech	Regional Stability		Firearms Convention	Crime Control			Anti-Terrorism	
	CB 1	CB 2	CB 3	NP 1	NP 2	NS 1	NS 2	MT 1	RS 1	RS 2	FC 1	CC 1	CC 2	CC 3	AT 1	AT 2
Kiribati	X	X		X		X	X	X	X	X		X		X		
Korea, North	See Sections 742.19 and 746.4 of the EAR to determine whether a license is required in order to export or reexport to this destination.															
Korea, South[3,4]	X	X	X	X		X	X	X	X	X		X		X		
Kosovo	X	X		X		X	X	X	X	X		X		X		
Kuwait	X	X	X	X		X	X	X	X	X		X		X		
Kyrgyzstan	X	X	X	X		X	X	X	X	X		X		X		
Laos	X	X		X		X	X	X	X	X		X	X			
Latvia[3]	X			X		X	X	X	X	X		X	X			
Lebanon	X	X	X	X		X	X	X	X	X		X		X		
Lesotho	X	X		X		X	X	X	X	X		X		X		
Liberia	X	X		X		X	X	X	X	X		X		X		
Libya	X	X	X	X	X	X	X	X	X	X		X		X		
Liechtenstein	X	X		X		X	X	X	X	X		X		X		

Export Administration Regulations

Bureau of Industry and Security

September 6, 2011

Commerce Control List Overview and the Country Chart

Commerce Country Chart

Reason for Control

Countries	Chemical & Biological Weapons			Nuclear Nonproliferation		National Security		Missile Tech	Regional Stability		Firearms Convention	Crime Control			Anti-Terrorism	
	CB 1	CB 2	CB 3	NP 1	NP 2	NS 1	NS 2	MT 1	RS 1	RS 2	FC 1	CC 1	CC 2	CC 3	AT 1	AT 2
Lithuania[3]	X			X		X		X	X							
Luxembourg[3]	X			X		X		X	X							
Macau	X	X	X	X		X	X	X	X	X		X		X		
Macedonia (The Former Yugoslav Republic of)	X	X		X		X	X	X	X	X		X		X		
Madagascar	X	X		X		X	X	X	X	X		X		X		
Malawi	X	X		X		X	X	X	X	X		X		X		
Malaysia	X	X		X		X	X	X	X	X		X		X		
Maldives	X	X		X		X	X	X	X	X		X		X		
Mali	X	X		X		X	X	X	X	X		X		X		
Malta[2,3,4]	X	X		X		X	X	X	X	X		X		X		
Marshall Islands	X	X		X		X	X		X	X		X		X		
Mauritania	X	X		X		X	X	X	X	X		X		X		
Mauritius	X	X		X		X	X	X	X	X		X		X		

Export Administration Regulations

Bureau of Industry and Security

September 6, 2011

Commerce Control List Overview and the Country Chart

Supplement No. 1 to Part 738 page 10

Commerce Country Chart

Reason for Control

Countries	Chemical & Biological Weapons			Nuclear Nonproliferation		National Security		Missile Tech	Regional Stability		Firearms Convention	Crime Control			Anti-Terrorism	
	CB 1	CB 2	CB 3	NP 1	NP 2	NS 1	NS 2	MT 1	RS 1	RS 2	FC 1	CC 1	CC 2	CC 3	AT 1	AT 2
Mexico	X	X		X		X	X	X	X	X	X	X		X		
Micronesia (Federated States of)	X	X		X		X	X	X	X	X		X		X		
Moldova	X	X	X	X		X	X	X	X	X		X	X			
Monaco	X	X		X		X	X	X	X	X		X		X		
Mongolia	X	X	X	X		X	X	X	X	X		X	X			
Montenegro	X	X		X		X	X	X	X	X		X	X	X		
Morocco	X	X		X		X	X	X	X	X		X		X		
Mozambique	X	X		X		X	X	X	X	X		X		X		
Namibia	X	X		X		X	X	X	X	X		X		X		
Nauru	X	X		X		X	X	X	X	X		X		X		
Nepal	X	X		X		X	X	X	X	X		X		X		
Netherlands[3]	X					X	X	X	X							

Export Administration Regulations

Bureau of Industry and Security

September 6, 2011

Commerce Control List Overview and the Country Chart

Supplement No. 1 to Part 738 page 11

Commerce Country Chart

Reason for Control

Countries	Chemical & Biological Weapons			Nuclear Nonproliferation		National Security		Missile Tech	Regional Stability		Firearms Convention	Crime Control			Anti-Terrorism	
	CB 1	CB 2	CB 3	NP 1	NP 2	NS 1	NS 2	MT 1	RS 1	RS 2	FC 1	CC 1	CC 2	CC 3	AT 1	AT 2
New Zealand[3]	X					X	X	X	X							
Nicaragua	X	X		X		X	X	X	X	X		X		X		
Niger	X	X		X		X	X	X	X	X	X	X		X		
Nigeria	X	X		X			X	X	X	X		X		X		
Norway[3]	X					X			X							
Oman	X	X	X	X		X	X	X	X	X		X		X		
Pakistan	X	X	X	X	X	X	X	X	X	X		X		X		
Palau	X	X		X		X	X	X	X	X		X		X		
Panama	X	X		X		X	X	X	X	X		X		X		
Papua New Guinea	X	X		X		X	X	X	X	X	X	X		X		
Paraguay	X	X		X		X	X	X	X	X	X	X		X		
Peru	X	X		X		X	X	X	X	X		X		X		
Philippines	X	X		X		X	X	X	X	X		X		X		

Export Administration Regulations

Bureau of Industry and Security

September 6, 2011

Commerce Control List Overview and the Country Chart

Supplement No. 1 to Part 738 page 12

Commerce Country Chart

Reason for Control

Countries	Chemical & Biological Weapons			Nuclear Nonproliferation		National Security		Missile Tech	Regional Stability		Firearms Convention	Crime Control			Anti-Terrorism	
	CB 1	CB 2	CB 3	NP 1	NP 2	NS 1	NS 2	MT 1	RS 1	RS 2	FC 1	CC 1	CC 2	CC 3	AT 1	AT 2
Poland[3]	X					X			X							
Portugal[3]	X					X		X	X							
Qatar	X	X	X	X		X	X	X		X		X		X		
Romania[3]	X					X		X	X							
Russia	X	X	X			X	X	X	X	X						
Rwanda[1]	X	X		X		X	X	X	X	X		X		X		
St. Kitts & Nevis	X	X		X		X	X	X	X	X	X	X		X		
St. Lucia	X	X		X		X	X	X	X	X	X	X	X	X		
Saint Vincent and the Grenadines	X	X		X		X	X	X	X	X	X	X	X	X		
Samoa	X	X		X		X	X	X	X	X		X		X		
San Marino	X	X		X		X	X	X	X	X		X		X		
Sao Tome & Principe	X	X		X		X	X	X	X	X		X		X		
Saudi Arabia	X	X	X	X		X	X	X	X	X		X		X		

Commerce Control List Overview and the Country Chart

Supplement No. 1 to Part 738 page 13

Commerce Country Chart

Reason for Control

Countries	Chemical & Biological Weapons			Nuclear Nonproliferation		National Security		Missile Tech	Regional Stability		Firearms Convention	Crime Control			Anti-Terrorism	
	CB 1	CB 2	CB 3	NP 1	NP 2	NS 1	NS 2	MT 1	RS 1	RS 2	FC 1	CC 1	CC 2	CC 3	AT 1	AT 2
Senegal	X	X		X		X	X	X	X	X		X		X		
Serbia	X	X		X		X	X	X	X	X		X	X	X		
Seychelles	X	X		X		X	X	X	X	X		X		X		
Sierra Leone	X	X		X		X	X	X	X	X		X		X		
Singapore	X	X		X		X	X	X	X	X		X		X		
Sint Maarten (the Dutch two-fifths of the island of Saint Martin)	X	X		X		X	X	X	X	X		X		X		
Slovakia[3]	X					X		X	X							
Slovenia[3]	X					X		X	X							
Solomon Islands	X	X		X		X	X	X	X	X		X		X		
Somalia	X	X		X		X	X	X	X	X		X		X		
South Africa[2,3,4]	X	X				X	X	X	X	X		X		X		
South Sudan, Republic of	X	X		X		X	X	X	X	X		X		X		

Commerce Control List Overview and the Country Chart

Export Administration Regulations

Bureau of Industry and Security

September 6, 2011

Commerce Control List Overview and the Country Chart

Commerce Country Chart

Reason for Control

Countries	Chemical & Biological Weapons			Nuclear Nonproliferation		National Security		Missile Tech	Regional Stability		Firearms Convention	Crime Control			Anti-Terrorism	
	CB 1	CB 2	CB 3	NP 1	NP 2	NS 1	NS 2	MT 1	RS 1	RS 2	FC 1	CC 1	CC 2	CC 3	AT 1	AT 2
Spain[3]	X					X		X	X							
Sri Lanka	X	X		X		X	X	X	X	X		X		X		
Sudan	X	X		X		X	X	X	X	X		X		X	X	X
Suriname	X	X		X		X	X	X	X	X	X	X		X		
Swaziland	X	X		X		X	X	X	X	X		X		X		
Sweden[3,4]	X			X		X		X	X							
Switzerland[3,4]	X					X		X	X			X		X		
Syria	X					X		X	X			X		X		
Taiwan	X	X	X	X		X	X	X	X	X		X		X		
Tajikistan	X	X	X	X		X	X	X	X	X		X	X			
Tanzania	X	X		X		X	X	X	X	X		X		X		
Thailand	X	X		X		X	X	X	X	X		X		X		
Timor-Leste	X	X		X		X	X	X	X	X		X		X		

Syria: See General Order No. 2 in Supplement No. 2 to Part 736 of the EAR to determine whether a license is required in order to export or reexport to this destination.

Export Administration Regulations   Bureau of Industry and Security   September 6, 2011

Commerce Control List Overview and the Country Chart

Commerce Country Chart
Reason for Control

Supplement No. 1 to Part 738 page 15

Countries	Chemical & Biological Weapons			Nuclear Nonproliferation		National Security		Missile Tech	Regional Stability		Firearms Convention	Crime Control			Anti-Terrorism	
	CB 1	CB 2	CB 3	NP 1	NP 2	NS 1	NS 2	MT 1	RS 1	RS 2	FC 1	CC 1	CC 2	CC 3	AT 1	AT 2
Togo	X	X		X		X	X	X	X	X		X		X		
Tonga	X	X		X		X	X	X	X	X		X		X		
Trinidad & Tobago	X	X		X		X	X	X	X	X	X	X		X		
Tunisia	X	X		X		X	X	X	X	X		X		X		
Turkey[3]	X		X			X		X	X							
Turkmenistan	X	X		X		X	X	X	X	X		X		X		
Tuvalu	X	X		X		X	X	X	X	X		X		X		
Uganda	X	X		X		X	X	X	X	X		X	X			
Ukraine	X					X	X	X	X	X		X	X			
United Arab Emirates	X	X		X		X	X	X	X	X		X		X		
United Kingdom[3]	X		X			X			X							

Export Administration Regulations

Bureau of Industry and Security

September 6, 2011

Commerce Control List Overview and the Country Chart

Supplement No. 1 to Part 738 page 16

Commerce Country Chart
Reason for Control

Countries	Chemical & Biological Weapons			Nuclear Nonproliferation		National Security		Missile Tech	Regional Stability		Firearms Convention	Crime Control			Anti-Terrorism	
	CB 1	CB 2	CB 3	NP 1	NP 2	NS 1	NS 2	MT 1	RS 1	RS 2	FC 1	CC 1	CC 2	CC 3	AT 1	AT 2
Uruguay	X	X		X		X	X	X	X	X	X	X		X		
Uzbekistan	X	X	X	X		X	X	X	X	X		X	X			
Vanuatu	X	X		X		X	X	X	X	X		X		X		
Vatican City	X	X		X		X	X	X	X	X		X		X		
Venezuela	X	X	X	X		X	X	X	X	X	X	X		X		
Vietnam	X	X		X		X	X	X	X	X		X	X			
Western Sahara	X	X		X		X	X	X	X	X		X		X		
Yemen	X	X	X	X		X	X	X	X	X		X		X		
Zambia	X	X		X		X	X	X	X	X		X		X		
Zimbabwe	X	X		X		X	X	X	X	X		X		X		

Commerce Control List Overview and the Country Chart

[1] This country is subject to sanctions implemented by the United Nations Security Council.   See '746.3 for license requirements for exports and reexports to Iraq or transfer within Iraq, as well as regional stability licensing requirements not included in the Country Chart.   See '746.8 for license requirements for exports and reexports to Rwanda.

[2] See '742.4(a) for special provisions that apply to exports and reexports to these countries of certain thermal imaging cameras.

[3] See '742.6(a)(3) for special provisions that apply to Amilitary commodities@ that are subject to ECCN 0A919.

[4] See '742.6(a)(2) and (4)(ii) regarding special provisions for exports and reexports of certain thermal imaging cameras to these countries.

Export Administration Regulations

Bureau of Industry and Security

September 6, 2011

Country Group A

Country	[A:1]	[A:2] Missile Technology Control Regime	[A:3] Australia Group	[A:4] Nuclear Suppliers Group
Argentina		X	X	X
Australia	X	X	X	X
Austria[1]		X	X	X
Belarus				X
Belgium	X	X	X	X
Brazil		X		X
Bulgaria		X	X	X
Canada	X	X	X	X
Croatia			X	
Cyprus			X	X
Czech Republic		X	X	X
Denmark	X	X	X	X
Estonia			X	
Finland[1]		X	X	X
France	X	X	X	X
Germany	X	X	X	X
Greece	X	X	X	X
Hong Kong[1]				
Hungary		X	X	X
Iceland		X	X	
India		X		
Ireland[1]		X	X	X
Italy	X	X	X	X
Japan	X	X	X	X
Kazakhstan				X
Korea, South[1]		X	X	X
Latvia			X	X
Lithuania			X	
Luxembourg	X	X	X	X
Malta			X	

Country	[A:1]	[A:2] Missile Technology Control Regime	[A:3] Australia Group	[A:4] Nuclear Suppliers Group
Netherlands	X	X	X	X
New Zealand[1]		X	X	X
Norway	X	X	X	X
Poland		X	X	X
Portugal	X	X	X	X
Romania			X	X
Russia		X		X
Slovakia			X	X
Slovenia			X	X
South Africa		X		X
Spain	X	X	X	X
Sweden[1]		X	X	X
Switzerland[1]		X	X	X
Turkey	X	X	X	X
Ukraine		X	X	X
United Kingdom	X	X	X	X
United States	X	X	X	X

[1] Cooperating Countries

Country Group B
Countries

Afghanistan	El Salvador	Mali	island of Saint
Albania	Equatorial Guinea	Malta	Martin)
Algeria	Eritrea	Marshall Islands	Slovakia
Andorra	Estonia	Mauritania	Slovenia
Angola	Ethiopia	Mauritius	Solomon Islands
Antigua and Barbuda	Fiji	Mexico	Somalia
Argentina	Finland	Micronesia, Federated	South Africa
Aruba	France	States of	South Sudan,
Australia	Gabon	Monaco	(Republic of)
Austria	Gambia, The	Montenegro	Spain
The Bahamas	Germany	Morocco	Sri Lanka
Bahrain	Ghana	Mozambique	Surinam
Bangladesh	Greece	Namibia	Swaziland
Barbados	Grenada	Nauru	Sweden
Belgium	Guatemala	Nepal	Switzerland
Belize	Guinea	Netherlands	Taiwan
Benin	Guinea-Bissau	New Zealand	Tanzania
Bhutan	Guyana	Nicaragua	Thailand
Bolivia	Haiti	Niger	Timor-Leste
Bosnia & Herzegovina	Honduras	Nigeria	Togo
Botswana	Hong Kong	Norway	Tonga
Brazil	Hungary	Oman	Trinidad & Tobago
Brunei	Iceland	Pakistan	Tunisia
Bulgaria	India	Palau	Turkey
Burkina Faso	Indonesia	Panama	Tuvalu
Burundi	Ireland	Papua New Guinea	Uganda
Cameroon	Israel	Paraguay	United Arab
Canada	Italy	Peru	Emirates
Cape Verde	Jamaica	Philippines	United Kingdom
Central African Republic	Japan	Poland	United States
Chad	Jordan	Portugal	Uruguay
Chile	Kenya	Qatar	Vanuatu
Colombia	Kiribati	Romania	Vatican City
Comoros	Korea, South	Rwanda	Venezuela
Congo (Democratic	Kosovo	Saint Kitts & Nevis	Western Sahara
Republic of the)	Kuwait	Saint Lucia	Yemen
Congo (Republic of the)	Latvia	Saint Vincent and the	Zambia
Costa Rica	Lebanon	Grenadines	Zimbabwe
Cote d'Ivoire	Lesotho	Samoa	
Croatia	Liberia	San Marino	
Curaçao	Liechtenstein	Sao Tome & Principe	
Cyprus	Lithuania	Saudi Arabia	
Czech Republic	Luxembourg	Senegal	
Denmark	Macedonia, The Former	Serbia	
Djibouti	Yugoslav Republic of	Serbia	
Dominica	Madagascar	Seychelles	
Dominican Republic	Malawi	Sierra Leone	
Ecuador	Malaysia	Singapore	
Egypt	Maldives	Sint Maarten (the Dutch	
		two-fifths of the	

Country Group C

[RESERVED]

Country Group D

Country	[D: 1] National Security	[D: 2] Nuclear	[D: 3] Chemical & Biological	[D: 4] Missile Technology
Afghanistan			X	
Armenia	X		X	
Azerbaijan	X		X	
Bahrain			X	X
Belarus	X		X	
Burma	X		X	
Cambodia	X			
China (PRC)	X		X	X
Cuba		X	X	
Egypt			X	X
Georgia	X		X	
Iran		X	X	X
Iraq	X	X	X	X
Israel		X	X	X
Jordan			X	X
Kazakhstan	X		X	
Korea, North	X	X	X	X
Kuwait			X	X
Kyrgyzstan	X		X	
Laos	X			
Lebanon			X	X
Libya	X	X	X	X
Macau	X		X	X
Moldova	X		X	
Mongolia	X		X	
Oman			X	X
Pakistan		X	X	X
Qatar			X	X
Russia	X		X	
Saudi Arabia			X	X

Country	[D: 1] National Security	[D: 2] Nuclear	[D: 3] Chemical & Biological	[D: 4] Missile Technology
Syria			X	X
Taiwan			X	
Tajikistan	X		X	
Turkmenistan	X		X	
Ukraine	X			
United Arab Emirates			X	X
Uzbekistan	X		X	
Vietnam	X		X	
Yemen			X	X

Country Group E [1]

Country	[E:1] Terrorist Supporting Countries [2]	[E:2] Unilateral Embargo
Cuba	X	X
Iran	X	
Korea, North	X	
Sudan	X	
Syria	X	

[1] In addition to the controls maintained by the Bureau of Industry and Security pursuant to the EAR, note that the Department of the Treasury administers:

    (a) A *comprehensive embargo* against Cuba, Iran, and Sudan; and

    (b) An *embargo against certain persons,* e.g., Specially Designated Terrorists (SDT), Foreign Terrorist Organizations (FTO), Specially Designated Global Terrorists (SDGT), and Specially Designated Narcotics Traffickers (SDNT). Please see part 744 of the EAR for controls maintained by the Bureau of Industry and Security on these and other persons.

[2] The President made inapplicable with respect to Iraq provisions of law that apply to countries that have supported terrorism.

When the items are purchased or obtained for export, it is the exporter (U.S. principal party in interest) and must be listed as the U.S. principal party in interest on the SED or AES record (see §30.4(a)(1)).

Note to paragraph (a)(1): The EAR defines the "exporter" as the person in the United States who has the authority of a principal party in interest to determine and control the sending of items out of the United States (see 15 CFR Part 772 of the EAR). For statistical purposes the Foreign Trade Statistics Regulations (FTSR) have a different definition of "exporter" from the Export Administration Regulations (EAR). Under the FTSR the "exporter" will always be the U.S. principal party in interest. For purposes of licensing responsibility under the EAR, the U.S. agent of the foreign principal party in interest may be the "exporter" or applicant on the license, in certain routed export transactions (see 15 CFR §758.3).

(2) Forwarding or other agent. The forwarding or other agent is that person in the United States who is authorized by a principal party in interest to perform the services required to facilitate the export of items from the United States. The forwarding or other agent must be authorized by the exporter (U.S. principal party in interest) or, in the case of a routed export transaction, the foreign principal party in interest to prepare and file the SED or the AES record. In a routed export transaction, the forwarding or other agent can be the exporter for export control purposes under the EAR. However, the forwarding or other agent is never the "U.S. principal party in interest" in the U.S. principal party in interest block on the paper SED or in the "U.S. principal party in interest" field of the AES record unless the forwarding or other agent acts as an "order party." (See paragraph (a)(1)(iii) for definition of order party)

(3) Principal parties in interest. Those persons in a transaction that receive the primary benefit, monetary or otherwise, of the transaction. Generally, the principals in a transaction are the seller and the buyer. In most cases, a forwarding or other agent is not a principal party in interest.

(b) Responsibilities of parties in export transactions

(1) Exporter (U.S. principal party in interest) responsibilities.

(i) The exporter (U.S. principal party in interest) can prepare and file the SED or AES record itself, or it can authorize a forwarding or other agent to prepare and file the SED or AES record on its behalf. If the exporter (U.S. principal party in interest) prepares the SED or AES record itself, the exporter (U.S. principal party in interest) is responsible for the accuracy of all the export information reported on the SED or AES record, for signing the paper SED, filing the paper SED with U.S. Customs, or transmitting the AES record to U.S. Customs.

(ii) When the exporter (U.S. principal party in interest) authorizes a forwarding or other agent to complete the SED or AES record on its behalf, the exporter (U.S. principal party in interest) is responsible for:

(A) Providing the forwarding or other agent with the export information necessary to complete the SED or AES record;

(B) Providing the forwarding or other agent with a power of attorney or written authorization to complete the SED or AES record, or signing the authorization block printed on the paper SED (block 23 on Commerce Form 7525-V and block 29 on Commerce Form 7525-V-ALT); and

(C) Maintaining documentation to support the information provided to the forwarding or other agent for completion of the SED or AES record, as specified in § 30.11.

(2) Forwarding or other agent responsibilities. The forwarding or other agent, when authorized by an exporter (U.S. principal party in interest) to

prepare and sign the SED or prepare and file the AES record in an export transaction, is responsible for:

(i) Accurately preparing the SED or AES record based on information received from the exporter (U.S. principal party in interest) and other parties involved in the transaction;

(ii) Obtaining a power of attorney or written authorization to complete the SED or AES record, or obtaining a paper SED with a signed authorization from the exporter (U.S. principal party in interest);

(iii) Maintaining documentation to support the information reported on the SED or AES record, as specified in § 30.11; and

(iv) Upon request, providing the exporter (U.S. principal party in interest) with a copy of the export information filed in the form of a completed SED, an electronic facsimile, or in any other manner prescribed by the exporter (U.S. principal party in interest).

(c) Responsibilities of parties in a routed export transaction

(1) Exporter (U.S. principal party in interest) responsibilities. In a routed export transaction where the foreign principal party in interest authorizes a U.S. forwarding or other agent to prepare and file the SED or AES record, the exporter (U.S. principal party in interest) must maintain documentation to support the information provided to the forwarding or other agent for preparing the SED or AES record as specified in § 30.11, and provide such forwarding or other agent with the following information to assist in preparing the SED or AES record:

(i) Name and address of the U.S. principal party in interest;

(ii) U.S. principal party in interest's, IRS, EIN;

(iii) Point of origin (State or FTZ);

(iv) Schedule B description of commodities;

(v) Domestic (D), foreign (F), or FMS (M) code;

(vi) Schedule B Number;

(vii) Quantity/unit of measure;

(viii) Value;

(ix) Upon request from the foreign principal party in interest or its agent, the Export Control Classification Number (ECCN) or sufficient technical information to determine the ECCN; and

(x) Any information that it knows will affect the determination of license authority.

Note to paragraph (c)(1): For items in paragraph (c)(1)(ix) and (x) of this section, where the foreign principal party in interest has assumed responsibility for determining and obtaining license authority, the EAR sets forth the information sharing requirements that apply at 15 CFR 758.3(c) of the EAR.

(2) Forwarding or other agent responsibilities. In a routed export transaction, the forwarding or other agent is responsible for; obtaining a power of attorney or written authorization from the foreign principal party in interest to prepare and file the SED or AES record on its behalf; preparing, signing, and filing the SED or AES record based on information obtained from the exporter (U.S. principal party in interest) or other parties involved in the transaction; maintaining documentation to support the information reported on the SED or AES record, and upon request by the exporter (U.S. principal party in interest), provide appropriate documentation to the exporter (U.S. principal party in interest) verifying that the information provided by the exporter (U.S. principal party in interest) was accurately reported on the SED or AES record. The forwarding or other agent must also provide the following export

medium (except indelible pencil). The use of duplicating processes, as well as the overprinting of selected items of information, is acceptable.

(g) Copies of SEDs

All copies of the SEDs must contain all of the information called for in the signature space as to name of firm, address, name of signer, and capacity of signer. The original SED must be signed in ink, but signature on other copies is not required. The use of signature stamps is acceptable. A signed legible carbon or other copy of the export declaration is acceptable as an "original" of the SED.

§30.5

NUMBER OF COPIES OF SHIPPER'S EXPORT DECLARATION REQUIRED

(a) Except as provided elsewhere in these regulations the Shipper's Export Declaration shall be delivered to the carrier or postmasters, as specified in §§ 30.12 and 30.15, in the following number of copies:

(1) In duplicate for shipments, except by mail, destined to all foreign countries except Canada.

(2) One copy only for shipments to Canada (see §30.58 for exemption for shipments from theUnited States to Canada) and nonforeign areas.

(3) One copy only for mail shipments to all destinations.

(b) In addition to the standard requirements set forth in paragraph (a) of this section, additional copies of Shipper's Export Declarations may be required for export control purposes by the regulations of the Office of Export Administration or other Government agencies or in particular circumstances by the Customs Director or by the postmaster.

January 2002

§30.6

REQUIREMENTS AS TO SEPARATE SHIPPER'S EXPORT DECLARATIONS

Except as specifically provided in subpart C, a separate Shipper's Export Declaration (in the required number of copies--see §30.5) is required for each shipment (consisting of one or more kinds of merchandise) from one consignor to one consignee on a single carrier. In addition, more than one declaration is required for an individual shipment as follows:

(a) For consignments by rail, truck, or other vehicle, requiring more than one rail car, truck, or other vehicle, a separate export declaration is required for the merchandise carried in each such rail car, truck, or other vehicle. However, Customs Directors are authorized to waive this requirement where multiple car shipments are made under a single bill of lading or other loading document and are cleared simultaneously.

(b) [Reserved]

Procedures for Imported Electrical Appliances, Equipment and Accessories

Please note that for any imported electrical appliances, equipment and accessories from the United States to the Kingdom of Saudi Arabia, the requirement of the Saudi Arabian Standards Organization must be completed in order to be accepted by technical representatives present at the customs house in Saudi Arabia.

Encl.:

Requirements of Saudi Arabian Standards Organization

(SASO).

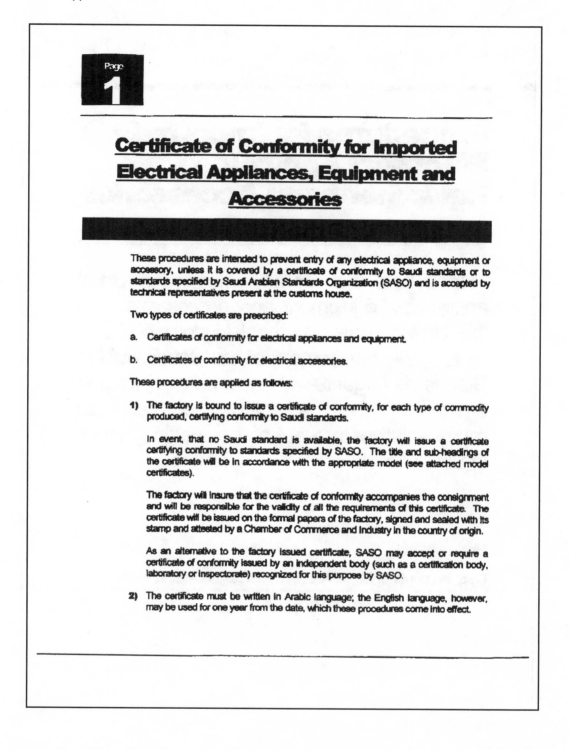

Page
1

Certificate of Conformity for Imported Electrical Appliances, Equipment and Accessories

These procedures are intended to prevent entry of any electrical appliance, equipment or accessory, unless it is covered by a certificate of conformity to Saudi standards or to standards specified by Saudi Arabian Standards Organization (SASO) and is accepted by technical representatives present at the customs house.

Two types of certificates are prescribed:

a.   Certificates of conformity for electrical appliances and equipment.

b.   Certificates of conformity for electrical accessories.

These procedures are applied as follows:

1)   The factory is bound to issue a certificate of conformity, for each type of commodity produced, certifying conformity to Saudi standards.

In event, that no Saudi standard is available, the factory will issue a certificate certifying conformity to standards specified by SASO. The title and sub-headings of the certificate will be in accordance with the appropriate model (see attached model certificates).

The factory will insure that the certificate of conformity accompanies the consignment and will be responsible for the validity of all the requirements of this certificate. The certificate will be issued on the formal papers of the factory, signed and sealed with its stamp and attested by a Chamber of Commerce and Industry in the country of origin.

As an alternative to the factory issued certificate, SASO may accept or require a certificate of conformity issued by an independent body (such as a certification body, laboratory or inspectorate) recognized for this purpose by SASO.

2)   The certificate must be written in Arabic language; the English language, however, may be used for one year from the date, which these procedures come into effect.

3) The Directorate General for Quality Control and Inspection (Ministry of Commerce), in collaboration with SASO will undertake examination, inspection and release of consignments.

4) The technical representative of the authority concerned has the right to draw samples for inspection and test whenever he deems this necessary to ensure conformity of electrical appliances, equipment and accessories to the applicable standards.

5) SASO will provide the Directorate General for Quality Control and Inspection and the customs authority with lists of commodities subject to these procedures and the relevant approved Saudi standards for these commodities or other standards defined by SASO for this purpose.

6) The authority concerned may request annexure of a report on t4st results made in the factory on the commodity identified in the certificate of conformity.

Attached are models of the certificates.

<u>Certificate of Conformity of Electrical Appliances</u>
<u>And Equipment issued by the factory in execution</u>
<u>OF SASO Board of Directors' decision</u>
<u>No. 58 dated 17/9/1405 H.</u>

Name of appliance and category: Quantity:

Type: Unique designation*:

Name of Manufacturer:

Country of Origin:

Principal technical information for this appliance is as follows:

 Rated voltage: Rated frequency:

Rated current: Rated power:

Power coefficient (if any):

Rated period of operation:

Appliance capacity: Dimensions:

Mass (weight):

Other information:

We certify that the supplied consignment of the above-mentioned
appliance, was produced by our factory and conform to the following
Saudi standards and/or to the following standards approved by SASO:

Name & Position of responsible manager

Signature and Date

Stamp of factory

                                    Attestatin of the Chamber
                                         of Commerce & Industry

_____

* Unique designation or identifier (such as the range of serial
  numbers) which unambiguously identifies uniits within the
  certified consignment.

THIS PAGE MUST BE ON THE MANAFUCTER'S LETTER HEAD

The Export Finance Matchmaker (EFM)

Website at:

www.doc.gov/td/efm helps you:

Match with financing firms that are likely to facilitate your overseas sales.

Understood export financing terminology and techniques.

Link to other U.S. Government and State export finance websites.

Contact other U.S. Government agencies for more information.

Provides a variety of financial products:

Pre-export capital: Financing to fill export orders

Direct loans to foreign buyers: Financing the overseas buyer

Forfaiting: Converting a foreign buyer's medium and long-term receivables to cash

Export factoring: Converting short-term foreign account receivables to cash

Documentary products: Facilitating collections from overseas buyers using various bank products

Export credit insurance: Reducing an exporter's credit and political risk with insurance

Miscellaneous types: Offering collection activity, foreign exchange, purchase order financing, and structured trade finance/offsets, among others

EFM's five simple steps to financing:

GO TO: www.ita.doc.gov/td/efm.

Click "ENTER."

Click "EXPORTERS" on the left menu.

Complete the "exporter query" and click "SUBMIT."

Review the results and choose the option to have EFM send an e-mail to all, a select few, or only one matched firm!

Export Management Systems (EMS) and BIS Guidelines

Contents

Background—History of Export Management System (EMS)

The events of the early 1990s in Europe and the former Soviet Union have resulted in a significant easing of the U.S. and multilateral export controls on West-East trade. At the same time, developments in other areas of the world, such as the Middle East, have underscored the importance of nonproliferation controls on chemical, biological, and nuclear weapons and missile technology.

The Commerce Department's Bureau of Industry & Security (BIS) has responded to the changing world events by focusing much of its attention on items and services that could be used to develop or deliver weapons of mass destruction. Regulations issued pursuant to the President's Enhanced Proliferation Control Initiative (EPCI) were published in 1991 and place greater emphasis on the end-use or end-user of exported items.

As a result, exporters need to be more vigilant in screening their customers and transactions.

Before the EPCI regulation changes, license requirements were identified primarily by checking the item and country of destination against the Commerce Control List (CCL). Items not specifically identified on the CCL as controlled to a given destination could, in most instances, be exported under a General License. The export of General License eligible items did not require prior approval from the Department of Commerce except for certain nuclear end-uses and persons denied export privileges.

Under the EPCI controls, a third element, the end-use or end-user, has become critical in determining whether an export requires a license.

Under the nonproliferation regulations, items that might not otherwise require a license based on a review of the CCL and country requirements, could require a license from the Department of Commerce because of the nature of the end-use/user.

The first EMS Guidelines were published in September 1992 to assist companies with the establishment of internal procedures for screening exports.

The Guidelines provided steps for exporters to determine whether a license is required because of item/country identification on the CCL.

The Guidelines also focused on screening mechanisms that a company could use to determine whether an export required a license because of the nature of the end-use or end-user.

In March 1996, BIS published a complete rewrite of the Export Administration Regulations (EAR), which restructured and reorganized the EAR. While the old EAR had a binary structure, requiring either a "General License" or a "Validated License" for every transaction, the new EAR has a decision tree format. The simplification dropped the term "General License." Items previously exported under the broadest of the old General License, General Destination or G-DEST, may now be exported under "No License Required" (NLR). Those General Licenses that allowed export of items that would otherwise have required a license became "License Exceptions." The 1997 revised EMS Guidelines incorporate changes necessary to be consistent with the 1996 publication of the Export Administration Regulations.

In response to requests from the business community, BIS has prepared these detailed Export Management System Guidelines to assist firms wishing to establish an internal procedure for screening exports. The information contained in the Guidelines is not meant to modify or interpret the Export Administration Regulations, and no action should be taken based solely on what is contained in the EMS Guidelines.

What Is an EMS?

An EMS is an optional program a company can consider establishing to ensure that their exports and export decisions are consistent with the EAR.

An EMS is based on a corporate philosophy that says: "We want to maximize our export sales while ensuring that we comply with the U.S. export laws and regulations." Just as it is vital for a firm to have a system that ensures its tax returns are submitted accurately and on time, an EMS can be an important part of an exporting firm's operation to be sure that it complies with export control requirements. A vital part of an EMS is the establishment of mechanisms within the company that provide checks and safeguards at key steps in the order processing system, helping to better manage the overall export process. Such checks and safeguards help to ensure that the right questions are being asked to preclude exporters from making shipments that are contrary to U.S. export controls and therefore inconsistent with the company's best interests.

How Can an EMS Be Helpful?

An EMS can be a useful tool to help companies comply with export control requirements. The implementation of EPCI and the changing world situation have increased the need for such systems.

The regulations require the exporter to assume greater responsibility in screening export transactions against the prohibitions of exports, re-exports, and selected transfers to certain end-users and uses:

- Denied persons list (General Prohibition Four): Engaging in actions prohibited by a denial order.
- End-use/users (General Prohibition Five): Export or re-export to prohibited end-uses or end-users.
- Activities of U.S. persons (General Prohibition Seven): Activities of U.S. persons in relation to proliferation activities.

Exporters should also have a procedure in place to screen transactions to ensure that they do not conduct business with persons/firms where BIS has "informed" the exporter or the public at large that the transaction involves an unacceptable risk of use in, or diversion to, prohibited proliferation activities anywhere in the world.

Firms/Persons that act contrary to General Prohibitions could lose their export privileges, be fined, or even be criminally prosecuted.

An EMS is *not* a U.S. Government mandated requirement. However, in a changing export control environment, it is a program that companies should consider establishing to ensure their actions are handled in a way that is consistent with the EAR.

The establishment of an EMS, in and of itself, will not relieve an exporter of criminal and administrative liability under the law if a violation occurs. However, the implementation of an EMS, coupled with good and sound judgment, can greatly reduce the risk of inadvertently exporting to an unauthorized party or for an unauthorized end-use.

Preliminary Steps in Developing an EMS

There are certain steps that companies will need to address as they begin to develop an EMS.

Know the customer. A key objective of an effective EMS is to be able to detect and react to information that raises questions about the legitimacy of a customer or transaction. The "Know Your Customer Guidance" help all persons avoid an illegal activity under the EAR.

The EAR also prohibits specific activities with "knowledge" that a violation is about to occur. These duties require a certain standard of care. The optional screening suggestions in the Guidelines can help the exporter understand his/her responsibilities.

BIS's "Know Your Customer" Guidance as defined in Supplement 1 to Part 732 of the EAR is included in the booklet as appendix II.

This Guidance refers to the provisions in the regulations that require a license when an exporter "knows" that a proscribed end-use, enduser, destination, activity, or other violation is involved. It is important that the exporter have an established procedure for reviewing proposed transactions in accordance with this Guidance. For your convenience, a Checklist of the Red Flag indicators is included with Element 3.

Understanding the EAR. Companies should have a clear understanding of the EAR. Exporters, as well as firms that facilitate exports or engage in other controlled activities, need a working knowledge of the regulations and their applications. It is strongly recommended that to develop such an understanding you send company personnel responsible for export controls to one of the many seminars offered by BIS. (For further information, contact the Export Seminar Staff at (202) 482-6031).

Identifying the factors that will form the foundation for the system. Each firm should provide examples, i.e., steps, scope, prohibitions, recordkeeping, etc. of the export regulations that apply to the firm's specific activities. The company's management team should look at a number of factors as it plans the development of its EMS.

A company's EMS should be appropriate to the scope of its export and re-export markets and to its business situation. Several factors can affect how an EMS can be structured. All of the factors that follow are important to consider, however, the most significant are exporter size, location of customers, product sensitivity or restrictions, and order processing system.

A. Exporter type
–Manufacturer
–Trading company
–Purchasing agent
–Original equipment manufacturer (OEM)
–Systems integrator
–Servicing Agent
–Other (i.e., banks, transportation, freight forwarder, etc.)

B. U.S. person participation
–Direct export
–Financing
–Shipping
–Service
–Employment
–Other assistance or facilitation

C. Nature of item exported
–Production material or capital equipment
–Part or component
–End item:
    for retail consumption
    for use by customer
–Software
–Technical data
–Service (i.e., financing, freight forwarding, legal, technical, engineering, architectural assistance, etc.)

D. Source of item exported
–Own manufacture:
    at one location
    at multiple locations
–Purchase from manufacturer(s)
–Purchase from distributor(s)

E. Item sensitivity of restrictions
  –Authorized for export/re-export to all destinations (except embargoed or terrorist countries)
  –License exception eligibility or likelihood of approval under a license to Country Group D (Supp. 1 Part 740)
  –Subject to the missile technology restrictions
  –Subject to the nuclear restrictions
  –Subject to the chemical and biological weapons restrictions
  –Potential for use by restricted nuclear, missile technology, and chemical and biological weapon end-uses/users

F. Exporter size
  –Small
  –Medium
  –Large

G. Customer type
  –Reseller:
    Distributor
    Sales agent
    Systems integrator
    Original equipment manufacturer (OEM), i.e., assembler
  –End-use:
    Government entity
    Manufacturer
    OEM
    Purchaser of capital equipment regardless of nature
    Banks

H. Use of product by customer
  –Capital or other equipment exclusively for own use
  –Resale to retail customers
  –Resale to manufacturers or OEMs for own use
  –Incorporation into new product of manufacture for resale
  –Support equipment for foreign product for resale
  –Servicing
  –Warehousing for further distribution
  –Systems integration activities
  –Assembling finished product from kit form
  –Other

I. Location of customers
  –Country group A (see Part 740, Supplement No. 1, to the EAR)
  –Country group B
  –Country group D:1
  –Country group D:2
  –Country group D:3
  –Country group E

J. Activity of customers
  –Disposition in country in which located
  –Re-exports to countries listed in Section I

–Exports of foreign manufactured products incorporating U.S. origin parts and components
–Exports of foreign manufactured products produced using U.S. origin technical data

K. Exporter/customer relationships
–Customer is a foreign branch of a U.S. company
–Customer is a foreign subsidiary or affiliate under effective control of U.S. company
–U.S. exporter is the subsidiary/branch of customer
–Independent relationship
–Company is a new customer

L. Product flow
–Exported from U.S. manufacturing site(s)
–Exported/re-exported from off-shore manufacturing site(s)
–Direct shipments to an end-customer
–Shipments direct from a nonaffiliated manufacturing entity to a customer

M. Order processing system
–Order received at:
  One location
  Several locations
  Regional international sales or headquarters office
–Records maintained at:
  One central location
  Several locations

The various elements described in the Guidelines, and as noted in the Menu of EMS Elements with specific Objectives identified in appendix III, constitute compliance options. The elements are *not* minimum requirements that every exporting company must follow regardless of its size, products, destinations, and methods of distribution. Rather, the Guidelines provide a "menu" of options a company may choose from to shape a compliance program uniquely suited to its particular operational features. No one compliance program will be appropriate for every company.

Referring to the factors described previously can help a company select elements it believes are appropriate. Some examples may help to illustrate this point.

A small company with only two or three employees will probably not need a list with the names, phone numbers, and responsibilities of all persons involved in export control issues. However, such a list may be very useful for large firms.

Likewise, a small company will not necessarily develop its own formalized training program. Rather, the company's employees or owners may familiarize themselves with the EAR and one of the employees will take on export compliance duties in addition to several other duties. In contrast, a large company might find it extremely valuable to develop its own ongoing training program to educate a large number of employees on evolving export control requirements.

A company that exports bacterial agents may develop a compliance program that includes an extensive screen of end-uses. The company would want to ensure that no exports/re-exports of the bacterial agents will be used in any of the prohibited end-uses described in Section 744.4. However, a compliance program for such an exporter need not necessarily include a screen to identify, for instance, nuclear end-uses, because their transactions do not involve prohibited nuclear end-uses.

A firm may have determined that no end-uses/end-users activities described in Part 744 apply to its transactions. Therefore, it does not need to include extensive nuclear, missile, or chemical, and biological screens. However, it should still set up a procedure for Denied Persons screening and Diversion Risk screening.

A bank or other financial institution need only be concerned with end-use and end-user screens to avoid prohibited financing or other participation in the design, development, production, stockpiling, and use of missiles or chemical/biological weapons and financing certain transactions with Denied Persons.

The size, organizational structure, and production/distribution network of a company will determine the location of activities required to implement and maintain an EMS. In small companies, one individual at one location may perform almost all of the activities. In large or medium-size companies, these activities may be performed in different organizational areas (comptroller, accounting, sales, marketing, contracts, general counsel, customer service, traffic, corporate audits, order processing, etc.) and/or at different geographical locations (product center, regional office, headquarters, shipping points, etc.).

Some companies choose to designate a single employee as responsible for the administration, performance, and coordination of these activities (e.g., EMS Administrator). Some large companies decentralize export control responsibilities throughout the organization, but with corporate oversight to ensure essential standards are set and maintained.

Regardless of the method of export control coordination or the size of the exporting company, the person or entity responsible should be sufficiently high in the management hierarchy to maintain and impose a strong commitment to export control activities for the entire company. In instances where export control activities are decentralized, it is paramount to have knowledgeable staff trained in export control issues at each location or in each function where orders are received and from which items are shipped.

Many companies centralize the administration of training, recordkeeping, dissemination of regulatory material, notification of noncompliance, and internal reviews. However, the actual screening activities in some companies of the denied persons lists, end-use and end-user activities, and diversion-risk may be performed by personnel throughout the company, (e.g., sales and marketing, order entry, or shipping) where first-hand knowledge and information on the consignee is available.

If a company decides to adopt an EMS, BIS recommends that the export control program be formalized into a written format. This format, an EMS Manual, should describe what elements the company has identified as necessary to include in its program. Further, it should address "who," "how," "when," and "where," export control checks are conducted.

An exporter clearly benefits from an EMS that:

- Protects employees through training and awareness programs from inadvertently violating the EAR.
- Protects the company through on-going control and review systems against inadvertent violations of the EAR.

- Demonstrates to the U.S. Government, and a company's employees, a strong commitment to comply with U.S. export laws and regulations.
- Instills confidence that the company is complying with the letter of the law.

How Do I Develop an EMS?

Sometimes the toughest part of any job is getting started. This section is intended to offer you a starting point that has worked for many companies and to give you steps to proceed with the development of your EMS.

The following five types of facts determine how your EMS should be crafted:

1. What is it (the item)?
2. Where is it going (country)?
3. Who will receive it (end-user)?
4. What will they do with it (end-use)?
5. What else do they do (activity)?

Developing Administrative Elements

The administrative elements are considered to be the foundation of the EMS. These elements may be developed simply by answering questions about your company and the company personnel.

Step One. Determine which employees are involved in the day-to-day export functions and identify specific responsibilities of each employee.

Step Two. Identify the most experienced employee(s) in the area of export controls and appoint an export control administrator.

Step Three. Evaluate any training programs that you currently have in place and formally detail the type of training that is being done.

Step Four. Review export control documents (records) and evaluate how they are kept and specifically what is kept.

Step Five. Refer to the specific elements within the EMS guidelines for a more detailed description of the administrative elements. Formalize your written procedures including the necessary details that apply to your company.

Developing Screening Elements

An ideal place to start in developing the screening elements necessary to perform export control functions is with the order processing element.

This screen will assist companies in combining all of the various screens into a comprehensive flow chart and will allow a company to demonstrate what screens are addressed during order processing.

Starting with the order processing element is like building the foundation of a puzzle. Once the order processing system (foundation) has been established and formalized, it will be easy to fit all of the other pieces in their appropriate place. The following steps should help you place the screening elements into your written procedures/EMS manual:

Step One. In narrative form, describe each step of the company's order entry operation to the point of shipment.

Step Two. Create a flow chart that visually displays company's order processing system narrative (see step one).

Step Three. On the flow chart, fill in any missing pieces with the screening elements described in the EMS, identifying at what point(s) the various screenings take place. Keep in mind that Companies should adapt those elements necessary to meet their particular exporting requirements.

Screening elements include the following:

1. Denied persons screen/entities list screening
2. Product classification/licensing determination screen
3. Diversion-risk screen
4. Nuclear screen
5. Missile screen
6. Chemical and biological weapons screen
7. Anti boycott screen (if performed)

Step Four. Ensure consistent processing of all orders with appropriate "Hold" and "Release" functions.

Step Five. Once all relevant screening elements have been placed on the flow chart, a more detailed description of those elements may be described and formalized within the individual element of the EMS.

Assistance for Developing an EMS

Due to the wide diversity of export transactions, companies may still have questions after studying the EAR and reading these guidelines. BIS's Office of Exporter Services (OEXS) seminars may provide assistance in gaining proficiency in the regulations and valuable insights into developing and refining an EMS. Finally, where additional guidance is desired, BIS's Special License and Compliance Division should be consulted. For additional guidance, or one-on-one counseling, telephone or send your EMS program to one of the following offices for review to:

The Office of Exporter Services
Attention: SLCD
P.O. Box 273
Washington, D.C. 20044
(202) 482-4524 or (202) 482-3541 phone
(202) 501-6750 fax

or

Western Regional Office
3300 Irvine Avenue
Suite 345
Newport Beach, CA 92660-3198
(714) 660-0144 phone
(714) 660-9347 fax

or

Northern California Office
101 Park Center Plaza
Suite 1001
San Jose, CA 95113
(408) 998-7402 phone
(408) 998-7470 fax

Administrative Elements: Introduction

The administrative elements have been developed to assist companies to ensure that documents attesting to the completion of the various checks are maintained along with other pertinent records. These elements also ensure that the personnel responsible for compliance are given authority commensurate with their responsibilities and receive all necessary training.

The content of these elements can be incorporated easily into a company's existing office procedures. Such elements help establish a concept that export control issues play an important role in company's day-to-day operation.

Although the implementation of an EMS is entirely optional, as are most of the administrative elements, any exporting company is required to maintain records relevant to all its export transactions. Consequently, the objective of Administrative Element 3: Recordkeeping is a regulatory *requirement* for all exporters. The administrative elements consist of the following:

1. Management policy
2. Responsible officials
3. Recordkeeping
4. Training
5. Internal reviews
6. Notification

Element 1: Management Policy

A clear statement of management policy communicated to all levels of the firm involved in export/re-export sales, traffic and related functions, emphasizing the importance of compliance with the Export Administration Regulations.

Objective. To convey a clear commitment of compliance with the EAR from senior management to all employees involved with U.S. export controls.

An important component of this commitment consists of providing sufficient time, money, and personnel to make the compliance program effective.

Procedure. One way of demonstrating strong management support of compliance with export control regulations is to prepare and distribute a policy statement. If a company decides to adopt an EMS, the written statement should convey a clear commitment to comply with the EAR. This formal statement should be included in the EMS manual and disseminated to all employees who work in export-related functions.

Senior management, preferably the president, owner of the company, or the chief executive officer, should be the responsible party for issuance of the statement. Senior management is also responsible for providing the relevant corporate policies, organizational structure, and resources to carry out an effective EMS.

The policy statement of commitment to export controls may include the following types of policies:

- Under no circumstances will sales be made contrary to U.S. export regulations. Special care should be taken to prevent transactions with entities involved in the proliferation of weapons of mass destruction.
- Any question concerning the legitimacy of a transaction or potential violations should be referred to: (responsible official).

- A description of penalties (corporate, criminal, and administrative) applied in instances of compliance failure.

The policy statement can be reinforced through a continuing education program. (See Administrative Element 4.) Other important vehicles for the communication of the policy statement of commitment to export controls are:

- New employee orientation
- In-house publications
- Training and/or procedures manuals

Important recipients of the policy statement of commitment to export controls are all employees of the company, specifically those dealing with:

- International sales
- Customer service
  Marketing
- Contracts
- Finance and accounting
- Legal counsel
- Field services
- Export administration
- Order entry
- Shipping
- Traffic
- Engineering (those involved in item classifications)

Comments. To be effective, the policy statement included in any EMS manual should be communicated to employees on a regular basis and would:

- Be prepared on company letterhead.
- Be dated.
- Be signed (including the name and title of the signer).
- Include policy statements referring to those factors in the preceding list.

If the names of any other individuals identified in the management policy statement change, the statement should be reissued. However, one way to avoid constant reissuing of the policy statement due to personnel changes is to use the title of the "responsible official" within the statement and refer all export control personnel to a company web page that posts current names and phone numbers.

Issuance of a policy statement by management or owners of even a small company shows employees the importance of complying with export control requirements. For exporting companies of all sizes, it highlights the fact that compliance with export regulations is essential to protecting a company's future.

Element 2: Responsible Officials

Identification of positions and specific individuals responsible for compliance with the Export Administration Regulations.

Objective: To ensure that all compliance-related functions, duties, and responsibilities in the company are clearly identified and assigned, the positions and incumbents are known, and the list is routinely updated.

Procedure: Initially, each company involved in the export or re-export of controlled items may wish to analyze its current organizational structure and operations to determine the effective placement of these functions.

Effort should be made, where practicable, to assign export responsibility separately from the sales function to prevent a conflict of objectives. However, sales staff should communicate, to the export control staff, information on the end-user, intended end-use, or end destination of the export. Where possible, the organizational structure of the company should centralize the key export functions and coordinate export activities with other departments that may become involved in export-related issues (e.g., legal counsel, credit, shipping, or contracts).

Personnel assigned export control functions should be given authority commensurate with their responsibilities. Formal lines of communication between the key personnel and others with export-related functions should be established.

Once the export control responsibilities have been assigned, the company adopting an EMS may want to document the following information:

- A list and/or organizational chart identifying the employee(s) responsible for each export and export-related function. General export control responsibilities should be listed in brief and the formal coordination between the various functions clearly set forth.
- A list of the personnel responsible, identified by name, title, and telephone number or extension. To ensure ongoing compliance in cases of absence, backup personnel should be formally assigned for all key export control-related functions. Telephone numbers or extensions should also be provided for these individuals.
- The list or chart of personnel with export and export-related functions should be distributed throughout the organization.
- A list identifying the EMS administrator (or persons with equivalent responsibilities) at the firm's consignees or customers. This may prove especially useful in instances where customers receive a variety of items or are authorized to resell controlled items in approved re-export territories. If this information is maintained, procedures can be developed to ensure that this list of contacts is updated promptly when changes occur.

Comments: The exporter may accomplish these objectives in a variety of ways. The following is provided to assist in development:

- At large or medium-size companies, the initial analysis of positions and individuals responsible for export compliance may include the development of an Export Control Unit.
- Information should be maintained in the form of lists and/or organizational charts. Use of lists are superior for presenting specific export control duties, while organizational charts are preferable for illustrating reporting lines and structures. A combination may be most practical. Responsible individuals should be identified by name and/or title.
- Policies, procedures, and job descriptions should be written to ensure smooth transitions during personnel turnover. Of key importance during these events is the assignment of backup personnel. A backup should be identified for each position with export-related responsibilities. This information should be promptly updated and disseminated when changes occur.

- Consignees and customers should also be made aware of the name and position of the exporter's EMS administrator. These companies should be encouraged to direct questions or problems to the administrator as they arise.

The amount of detail provided in the list of responsible officials may depend on the size of the exporting company. At a small company, it is probably not necessary to go into a great amount of detail. However, at a large company that has many players involved in export control issues, it is very important to clearly identify responsible parties in detail.

Introduction to the Order Processing System Element

This optional element has been developed to assist companies in combining all of the various screens into a comprehensive flow chart or narrative. This will allow a company to demonstrate what screens are addressed during order processing.

Order Processing System

An order processing system that documents employee clearance of transactions in accordance with the requirements of the firm's EMS.

Objective. To set forth in written procedures the order processing system used to screen and document the checks required by the firm's EMS.

Procedure. The EMS administrator should determine the nature and frequency of export checks through the use of these guidelines and analysis of the company's operational system. This should be completed prior to designing a company's particular order processing flow chart or narrative. An EMS should contain a formal flow chart or narrative description of the order processing system. The flow chart or narrative should include export checks equivalent to those listed in the optional screening elements that determine the type(s) of license(s) to be used by the company. The order processing system should be supported by documentation to leave a trail to verify export control compliance.

It is recommended that the flow chart or narrative include descriptions for the processing of the following shipping documents:

- Commercial/billing invoices
- Shipper's export declarations/shipper's letter of instructions (SED/SLI)
- Air waybills (AWB) and/or bills of lading

Comments. The order processing system, whether it is manual or automated, should have "hold" functions that ensure adherence to sign-off procedures and prevent the preparation of commercial invoices and shipping documents prior to review and sign-off. Each individual with responsibility for performing a control check(s) should be held accountable for orders processed. All special transactions should receive supervisory sign-off.

The EMS administrator and all order processing personnel should be aware that the chosen optional screening elements should be performed on all intermediate parties involved in a transaction. This is particularly true for denied persons screening. This is to ensure that items exported under in-transit shipments and shipments to bonded warehouses and free trade zones are disposed of as authorized, thereby reducing the possibility of diversion. The company should determine whether any of its transactions with its consignees involve these types of activities.

The party with control over the items should be assigned responsibility for monitoring the items. For example, control over items that are intransit remains the responsibility of the company until such time that the title is transferred to the customer.

However, control over shipments to bonded warehouses or free trade zones may not rest with the exporter. The question of control therefore depends on the point at which title passes from the company to the ultimate customer. The export clearance and retention of records requirements for these types of shipments are no different from any ordinary export transaction.

Menu of EMS Elements with Objectives

Administrative Elements

The administrative elements are designed to help exporters establish a foundation upon which the Export Management System (EMS) is built.

All of the following elements are optional with the exception of Administrative Element # 3-Recordkeeping.

1. Management Policy. A clear statement of management policy communicated to all levels of the firm involved in export/re-export sales, traffic and related functions, emphasizing the importance of compliance with the Export Administration Regulations (EAR).

Objective. To convey a clear commitment of compliance with the EAR from senior management to all employees involved with U.S. export controls.

An important component of this commitment consists in providing sufficient time, money, and personnel to make the compliance program effective.

2. Responsible Officials. Identification of positions and specific individuals responsible for compliance with the EAR.

Objective. To ensure that all compliance-related functions, duties, and responsibilities in the firm are clearly identified and assigned, and that the positions and incumbents are known.

3. Recordkeeping. A program for recordkeeping as required by the EAR.

Objective. To ensure documents are maintained in an accurate and consistent manner and are available for inspection as required by the EAR.

4. Training. A continuing program for educating people who require knowledge of the EAR.

Objective. To ensure training and education are provided on a regular basis to all employees involved in export-related activities.

5. Internal Reviews. An internal review program to verify compliance with the company's EMS and the EAR.

Objective. To ensure compliance at all the company's export-related locations with the EMS and EAR.

6. Notification. A system for consulting the BIS when questions arise regarding the propriety of specific export transactions.

Objective. To ensure that all exports and re-exports are conducted in accordance with the EAR.

Order Processing System Element

An optional order processing element is recommended to help clarify when and where exports are appropriately screened.

Order Processing System. An order processing system that documents employee clearance of transactions in accordance with the requirements of the company's EMS.

Objective. To set forth in written procedures the order processing system used to screen and document the checks required by the firm's EMS.

Screening Elements

The optional screening elements are designed to provide a mechanism to help exporters evaluate export transactions.

1. Denied Persons Screen. A system for screening all customers against the most current list of denied persons.

Objective. To ensure that transactions involving U.S. origin items covered by the EAR do not involve persons or entities whose export privileges have been denied by the U.S. Department of Commerce.

2. Product Classification/License Determination Screen. A system for classifying products by Export Control Classification Number (ECCN) to determine what export authorization may potentially be used for the intended destination.

Objective. To ensure that the export license or license exception to be used authorizes the transfer of the items to the intended country.

3. Diversion-Risk Screen. A system for assessing proposed transactions against a diversion risk profile (DPL) that takes into account the factors outlined in Screening Element 3 of the EMS.

Objective. To establish procedures to adequately screen orders for "red flag" indicators using the diversion-risk profile (DRP).

4. Nuclear Screen. A system for assuring compliance with the restrictions on prohibited nuclear end-uses/end-users.

Objective. To ensure that transactions do not involve prohibited nuclear end-uses/end-users without authorization from the U.S. Government.

5. Missile Screen. A system for assuring compliance with the restrictions on prohibited missile end-uses/end-users.

Objective. To ensure that transactions do not involve prohibited missile end-uses/end-users without authorization from the U.S. Government.

6. Chemical and Biological Weapons Screen. A system for assuring compliance with the restrictions on prohibited chemical and biological weapons end-uses/end-users.

Objective. To ensure that transactions do not involve prohibited chemical or biological weapons end-uses/end-users without authorization from the U.S. Government.

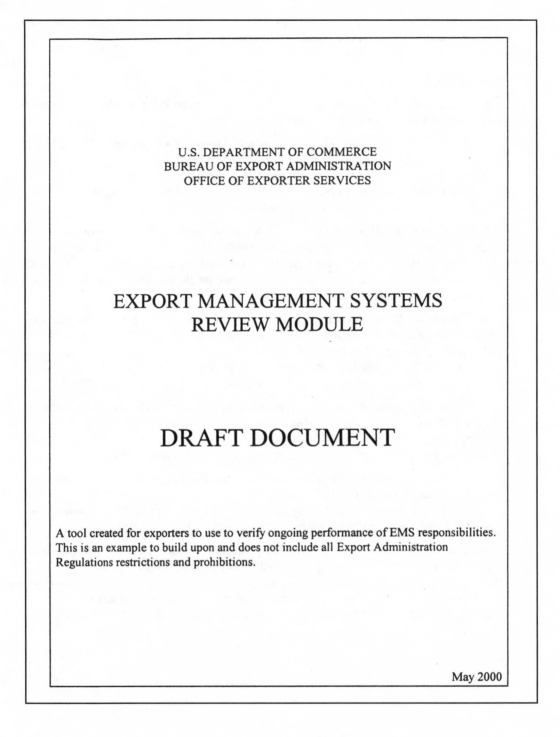

U.S. DEPARTMENT OF COMMERCE
BUREAU OF EXPORT ADMINISTRATION
OFFICE OF EXPORTER SERVICES

EXPORT MANAGEMENT SYSTEMS REVIEW MODULE

DRAFT DOCUMENT

A tool created for exporters to use to verify ongoing performance of EMS responsibilities. This is an example to build upon and does not include all Export Administration Regulations restrictions and prohibitions.

May 2000

Administrative Element　　　　　　　　　Written Review **Element 1: Management Policy Statement**　·　Date_____	Y	N	Operational Review　　　　　　　　Date 　―――― Comments
Clear commitment to export control from upper management to all employees involved with export related activities.	–	–	――――――――――――――――――
1. Are there written procedures to ensure consistent, ongoing maintenance of this Element?	–	–	
A. Is a responsible person designated to update the statement when management changes or at least annually?	–	–	
B. Is the policy included in employee training in:			
1) Orientation programs?	–	–	
2) Refresher training?	–	–	
3) Electronic training modules?	–	–	
4) Employee procedures manuals?	–	–	
C. Is the statement distributed to all export-related personnel?	–	–	
D. Is the statement communicated on an ongoing basis by:			
1) Company publications?	–	–	
2) Company awareness posters?	–	–	
3) Daily operating procedures?	–	–	
4) Other means, i.e. bulletin boards, in meetings, etc.?	–	–	
2. Is there a statement from management that communicates clear commitment to export control?	–	–	
A. Is it from current senior management? Signed? Dated?	–	–	
B. Does it explain why corporate commitment is important?	–	–	
C. Does it indicate that no sales will be made contrary to the US EAR?	–	–	
D. Does it convey the dual-use risk of the items to be exported?	–	–	
E. Does it address weapons of mass destruction activities concerns?	–	–	
1) nuclear proliferation?	–	–	
2) missile technology proliferation?	–	–	
3) chemical and biological proliferation?			
F. Does it contain a description of penalties applied in instances of compliance failure?	–	–	
1) Imposed by Department of Commerce?	–	–	
2) Imposed by your company?			
G. Does it include the name, position, e-mail address & telephone number of the person to contact with questions concerning the legitimacy of a transaction or possible violations?	–	–	
3. Are adequate resources dedicated to the maintenance of the EMS program?	–	–	
4. Did export-related personnel have a copy of the statement?	–	–	
5. Is the statement part of the new employee orientation training and refresher training?	–	–	

Administrative Element **Element 2: Responsible Officials** Written Review Date_____	Y	N	Operational Review *Date_____ Comments
Identification of personnel for all export control related functions, duties, responsibilities, positions, and employees in the firm.	–	–	
1. Are there written procedures to identify all export control related personnel in the company?	–	–	
2. Is there a list that identifies individuals, their positions, addresses, telephone numbers, e-mail addresses, and their respective export control related activities?	–	–	
A. Does it include all domestic sites?	–	–	
B. Does it include all international sites?	–	–	
3. Has an EMS Administrator been designated for oversight of the program?	–	–	
4. Is there a system of back up personnel identified?	–	–	
5. Are export-related tasks clearly defined in written procedures?	–	–	
6. Does each export control person understand the importance of his/her function related to export compliance and where he/she fits in the overall flow?	–	–	
7. Are there any conflicts of interest in responsible offices (or individuals) and tasks?	–	–	

Administrative Element Element 3: Recordkeeping Written Review Date_____ A program for recordkeeping required by the EAR as well as other administrative records.	Y	N	Operational Review Comments	Date_____
1. Are there written procedures to ensure compliance with Export Administration Regulations requirements?	–	–		
A. Is an individual designated as responsible?	–	–		
B. Is the retention period defined?	–	–		
C. Is the physical location for storage defined?	–	–		
2. Is there a list of records to maintain within the procedure?	–	–		
A. Does the list include the following **Administrative Records**:	–	–		
1) Commodity Classification records?				
2) Commodity Jurisdiction Letters?	–	–		
3) Advisory Opinion Letters?	–	–		
4) BXA 748P, Multipurpose Application Form?	–	–		
5) BXA 748P-A, Item Appendix?	–	–		
6) BXA 748P-B, End-User Appendix?	–	–		
7) BXA 711, Statement by Ultimate Consignee and Purchaser?	–	–		
8) Accompanying attachments, riders, or conditions?	–	–		
9) International Import Certificates?	–	–		
10) End-User Certificates?	–	–		
11) License Exception TSR Written Assurances?	–	–		
12) AES electronic filing authorization?	–	–		
13) NDAA Reports?	–	–		
14) High Performance Computer Records?	–	–		
15) Transmittal and acknowledgment of license conditions?	–	–		
16) Log administering control over use of Export/Reexport license?	–	–		
17) Is a log maintained to ensure return or commodities previously exported under the License Exception TMP?	–	–		
18) Is a log maintained to ensure License Exception LVS limits are not exceeded?	–	–		
19) Humanitarian Donations GFT Records?	–	–		
B. Are there instructions for the accurate completion and filing for the following **Transaction Records**:	–	–		
1) Commercial Invoices (with Destination Control Statement)?	–	–		
2) Shippers Export Declarations?	–	–		
a) Description of item(s)?	–	–		
b) Export Control Classification Number(s)?	–	–		
c) License Number(s)	–	–		
d) License Exception Symbol(s)?	–	–		
e) Schedule B Number(s)?				
3) Air Waybills and/or Bills of Lading?	–	–		
C. Is there conformity of the above documents?				
D. Does the list include Export Management System Manual and changes as well as EMS operating procedures?	–	–		
E. Does the list include a current copy of EAR with Export Administration Bulletin (EAB) Updates?	–	–		
F. Does the list include a copy of the current Denied Persons List	–	–		

Administrative Element Element 4. Training	Written Review Date_____	Y	N	Operational Review Comments	Date_____
An ongoing program of training and education to all employees, domestically and internationally, regarding the EAR requirements and EMS procedures.		–	–		
1. Are there written procedures that describe an ongoing program of export control/compliance training and education?		–	–		
		–	–		
A. Is a qualified individual designated to conduct training?					
B. Is there a schedule to conduct training (including date, time, place?)		–	–		
C. What training materials are used (module, videos, manuals)?		–	–		
D. Are training materials current and accurate?					
E. Are attendance logs used for documentation which include, agenda, date, trainer, trainees, and subjects?		–	–		
F. Is frequency of training defined?		–	–		
G. Is a list of employees/positions defined who should receive export control/compliance training?		–	–		
2. Do training methods include:		–	–		
A. Orientation of new employee(s)?		–	–		
B. Formal (structured setting, agendas, modules used)?					
C. Informal (less structured basis, verbal, daily, on-the-job exchanges)?		–	–		
D. Circulation of written memoranda and e-mails to a small number of personnel., (usually group specific instruction)?		–	–		
E. Refresher courses and update sessions scheduled?		–	–		
F. Back up personnel training?		–	–		
3. Does content of training materials include: A. Organizational structure of export-related departments and functions?		–	–		
B. The role of the EMS Administrator and Key Contacts?		–	–		
C. U.S. export/reexport regulatory requirements?		–	–		
D. EMS company operating procedures?		–	–		
E. The purpose and scope of export controls?		–	–		
F. Licenses & Conditions/License Exceptions & parameters?		–	–		
G. Regulatory changes and new requirements?		–	–		
H. Destination and item restrictions?					
I. Order processing screens (i.e., Denied Persons List (" DPL"), Diversion-Risk etc.)?		–	–		
J. Procedure concerning exports/reexports with documented checks?		–	–		
K. New customer review procedures?		–	–		
L. Identification and description of non-compliance?					

Administrative Element **Element 5: Internal Reviews**	Written Review Date_____	Y	N	Operational Review	Date_____
An internal audit system or compliance review program.				Comments	
		–	–		

1. Are written procedures established to verify ongoing compliance? — —
2. Is there a qualified individual (or auditing group) designated to conduct internal reviews? — —
3. Is there a schedule for reviews? —
4. Is there a description of the review process? —
5. Is a review module or self-assessment tool used? — —
   If yes, does the review tool evaluate:
   A. Corporate management commitment in all aspects of the review--not just the Written Policy Statement Element? —
   B. Formalized, written EMS procedures compared to operational procedures? —
   C. A set of questions for each Element in the EMS written program to verify compliance? —
   D. Accuracy & conformity of export transaction documents? —
   E. Maintenance of documents, as required in the written EMS program. —
   F. Correct authorization used? —
   G. Are export control screens documented? — —
   H. Whether there is a current, accurate product/license determination matrix consistent with the current EAR and *Federal Register* notices? — —
   I. Whether there is a flow chart of the order processing system that clearly communicates export control screens? —
   J. Whether there is a procedure to stop/hold transactions if problems arise? — —
   K. Whether all key export-related personnel are interviewed? —
   L. Whether there are clear, open communication between all export-related divisions? — —
   M. How is the performance of export control checks verified on a daily basis? — —
   N. Does it include sampling of the completed screens performed during the order processing? — —
   O. Whether export control procedures and EMS manuals are consistent with EAR changes that have been published? — —
   P. Whether the company's training module and procedures are current with EAR and *Federal Register* notices? — —
5. Is there a written report of each internal review? — —
   A. Are there written results of the review? — —
   B. Is the appropriate manager notified if action is needed? —
   C. Are internal reviews performed annually, every six months, quarterly, etc.? —
   D. Are spot checks/informal self-assessments performed? —
   E. Are they documented? —
6. Is there evidence of a conflict of interest between the reviewer and the division being reviewed? — —
7. Is a history maintained of reviews to monitor repeated deficiencies? —
8. Is there a "best practice" that should be shared with other divisions in the company to improve effectiveness and efficiency of export controls and promote consistency of procedures? — —
9. Are other Departments aware of their export control-related responsibilities, i.e., legal dept., human resources, information management., etc.) — —

Administrative Element **Element 6: Notification** A system for notifying designated officials of possible non-compliance with the EAR	Written Review Date_____	Y	N	Operational Review Date_____ Comments
		–	–	
1. Does the company have an on-going procedure for monitoring compliance of consignees, end-users and other responsible parties involved in export transactions?		–	–	
2. Are there internal procedures in place to notify management within the company if a responsible party is determined to be in non-compliance?		–	–	
3. Are there internal procedures in place to notify the appropriate U.S. Government officials when non-compliance is determined? (i.e., Export Administration's Office of Exporter Services ("OEXS"), Export Enforcement, etc.)		–	–	
4. Do all employees receive export control awareness training (think about potential deemed exports and hand-carry scenarios)?		–	–	
5. Has corporate policy been implemented which stresses to all employees an affirmative duty to notify export control officials in the event of possible non-compliance?		–	–	

Order Processing Element	Written Review Date_____	Y	N	Operational Review	Date_____
An Order Processing System affixing responsibility for all required export control checks/reviews.				Comments	

1. Are there written procedures to ensure that checks and safeguards are in place within the order processing flow and responsibility for all checks are assigned?

2. Is the Order Processing System displayed visually in an order flow chart?

3. Is there a narrative that describes the process?

4. Are the following screens included in the order process?
   A. Are pre-order entry screen checks performed (i.e., know your customer red flags)?
   B. Is the DPL screen described?
   C. Is the Entity List screen described?
   D. Are the Antiboycott red flags considered?
   E. Is the nuclear screen performed?
   F. Is the missile technology screen performed?
   G. Is the chemical & biological weapons screen performed?
   H. Is the product/country licensing determination screen performed?
   I. Is the diversion risk screen performed?
   J. Does the Order Processing System procedure include a description of administrative control over the following documents:
   Shipper's Export Declaration (SED), Shippers'Letter of Instruction (SLI)? Airwaybills (AWB) and/or Bills of Lading?

5. Does the procedure explain the order process from receipt of order to actual shipment?

6. Does the procedure include who is responsible for each screen throughout the flow?

7. Does the procedure describe when and what screening is performed (frequency of screening)?

8. Are hold and cancel functions implemented?

9. Does the procedure clearly indicate who has the authority to make classification decisions?

10. Are supervisory or Export Control Administrator ("ECA") sign-off procedures implemented at high risk points?

Screening Element **Element 1: Denied Persons Screen (DPL)**	Written Review Date_____	Y	N	Operational Review Comments	Date_____
A methodology for review of orders/shipments/transactions against the DPL.		–	–	_____	
1. Is there a written procedure to ensure screening of orders/shipments to customers covering servicing, training, and sales of items against the DPL?		–	–		
2. Are persons/positions identified who are responsible for DPL screening (consider domestic and international designees)?		–	–		
3. Is there a procedure to stop orders if a customer and/or other parties are found on the DPL?		–	–		
4. Is there a procedure to report all names of customers and/or other parties found on the DPL?		–	–		
5. Do the procedures include a process of what is used to perform the screening and if distribution of hard copies is required, who is responsible for their update and distribution?		–			

6. Is the DPL checked against a customer base?
  A. Are both the customer name and principal checked?
  B. Is there a method for keeping the customer base current?
  C. Is there a method for screening new customers?
		–
		–
		–
			–
			
			–		

7. Is the DPL checked on a transaction base?
  A. Is the name of ordering party's firm and principal checked?
  B. Is the end-user identity available? If so, is a DPL check done on the end-user?
  C. Is the check performed at the time an order is accepted and/or received?
  D. Is the check performed at the time of shipment?
  E. Is the check performed against backlog orders when a new or updated DPL is published?
		–
		–
		–
		
		–
		
		–
		–
			–
			–
			
			–
			
			–		

8. Does documentation of screen (whether hard copy or electronic signature) include:
  A. Name of individual performing the check?
  B. Date of screen performed?
  C. Date of current denied persons information used to perform the check?
  D. Is the date of the DPL used to check the transaction documented? Is it current?
		–
		–
		–
		–
			–
			–
			
			–		

9. Are other trade-related sanctions, embargoes and debarments imposed by agencies other than the Department of Commerce checked?
  A. Department of Treasury (Office of Foreign Assets Control):
    1) Specially Designated Terrorists?
    2) Specially Designated Nationals and Foreign Terrorist Organizations?
  B. Department of State:
    1) Trade-related sanctions (Bureau of Politico-Military Affairs)?
    2) Suspensions & debarments (Center for Defense Trade, Office of Defense Trade Controls)?
		–
		–
		
		–
		–
		
		–
			–
			–
			
			–
			–
			
				744.13
				744.14	

10. Are domestic transactions screened against the DPL?		–	–		

Screening Element	Written Review Date_____	Y	N	Operational Review Comments	Date_____
Element 2. Product/Country License Determination Screen					
A system for assuring compliance with export licensing decisions, product/country restrictions, License Exception Parameters, and License Conditions.					

1. Are there written procedures for assuring compliance with product and country export restrictions?

2. Do procedures include reexport guidelines?

3. Is there a written procedure that describes how items (including commodities, software, and technology) are <u>classified</u> under ECCNs on the CCL?
   A. Does a technical expert within the company classify the items?
   B. Does the manufacturer of the item classify the item?
   C. Is there a written procedure that describes when a classification will be submitted to BXA and who will be responsible?
       D. Is there a written procedure that describes commodity jurisdiction determinations?

4. Is an individual designated to ensure that Product/Country License determination guidance is current and updated?

5. Is a Matrix or Decision Table used?
   A. Are instructions provided easily understood and applied?
   B. Do instructions provided specify who, when, where and how to check each shipment against the matrix?
   C. Does the matrix/table display ECCNs and product descriptions?
   D. Appropriate shipping authorizations, License Required, License Exception(specify which) EAR 99, NLR?
   E. Does the matrix communicate License Exception parameters/restrictions?
   F. Are license conditions and restrictions included within the matrix/table?
   G. Does the matrix/table cross reference items to be exported with license exceptions normally available (based on item description and end destination?
   H. Does the matrix/table clearly define what license exceptions may be available for each item (also clearly state which license exceptions may not be used due to General Prohibitions)?
   I. Are country restrictions displayed?
   J. Is country information up-to-date?
   K. Are item restrictions displayed? (i.e., technical parameter limitations, end-user limitations.)
   L. Are reporting prompts built into the matrix/table?
   M. Are Wassenaar reports required? When?
   N. Is National Defense Authorization Act Notification (NDAA) required?   750.7(d) 742.15 and 740.7
   O. Are NDAA Post shipment verifications required?
   P. Is the matrix automated?
   Q. Is the matrix manually implemented?
   R. Is there a distribution procedure to ensure all appropriate users receive the tool and instructions for use?
   S. Is there a list to indicate the name of the person responsible for using the tool?

Screening Element	Written Review Date_____	Y	N	Operational Review Comments	Date_____
Element 2. Product/Country License Determination Screen (contd.)		–	–		
6. Is there a " hold" function to prevent shipments, if needed, during processing?		–	–		
7. Is there a procedure to distribute and verify receipt of license conditions?		–	–		
A. Is there someone designated to distribute and follow-up with acknowledgment verification?		–	–		
B. Is there a response deadline defined when conditions are distributed?		–	–		

Screening Element **Element 3: Diversion Risk Screen**	Written Review Date _____	Y	N	Operational Review Comments	Date_____
To review orders against a Diversion Risk Profile (DRP).		–	–	_____	
1. Are there procedures to screen orders for diversion risk red flag indicators?		–	–		
2. Is a checklist used based upon the red flag indicators?		–	–	Part 732, Supplement 3	
3. Does the written screening procedure identify the responsible individual who performs the screen check?		–			
4. Is the DRP considered at all phases of the order processing system?		–	–		
5. Is DRP performed on a transaction basis?		–	–		
6. Is DRP performed on a customer base?		–	–		
7. Is a checklist documented and maintained on file for each and _every order?_		–	–		
8. Is a checklist documented and maintained on file in the _customer profile?_		–	–		
9. Is the customer base checked at least annually against the red flag indicators or when a customer's activities change?		–			
10. General Prohibition 6 - Prohibits export/reexport of items to embargoed destinations without proper license authority. Are embargoed destination prohibitions communicated on the product/country matrix and part of the red flag indicators?		–	–		
11. General Prohibition 10 - prohibits an exporter from proceeding with transactions with knowledge that a violation has occurred or is about to occur. Is there anything that is suspect regarding the legitimacy of the transactions?		–	–		
12. Are Missile Technology, Chemical and Biological Weapons, and Nuclear Screens performed? (See Screening Elements 4, 5, & 6 in the EMS Guidelines.)		–	–		

Screening Element Element 4: Nuclear Screen Written Review Date_____ A system for assuring compliance with the prohibited nuclear end uses/users in Part 744.2 and 744.6 of the EAR and 744, Supplement 4.	Y	N	Operational Review Date_____ Comments
	_	_	_____
1. Prior to exporting, is there a written procedure for reviewing exports and reexports of all items subject to the EAR to determine whether they might be destined to be used directly or indirectly in any one or more of the prohibited of nuclear activities?	_	_	744.2
2. Is a person/position identified who is responsible for ensuring screening of customers and their activities against the prohibited end-uses/users?	_	_	
3. Does the procedure describe when the nuclear screen should be performed?	_	_	
4. Does the procedure include a check against the Entity List?	_	_	744, Supplement 4
5. If yes, is there a procedure to maintain documented Entity List screen decisions on file to verify consistent, operational review?	_	_	
6. Is your nuclear screen completed on a: A. transaction basis? B. against a customer base? C. before new customers are approved?	_ _ _	 _ _	
7. Does the check include documentation of the signature/initial of the person performing the check, and the date performed to verify consistent, operational performance of the check?	_	_	
8. Is the customer base checked and the check documented at least annually in the Customer Profiles? (See EMS Guidelines, Screening Element 3, Diversion Risk Screen).	_	_	
9. Is it clear who is responsible for the annual check?	_		
10. Is there a list of all employees responsible for performing nuclear screening?	_	_	
11. Is there a procedure to verify that all responsible employees are performing the screening?	_	_	
12. Are nuclear checklists (or other tool) distributed to appropriate export control personnel for easy, efficient perfomance of the review?	_	_	
13. Have export/sales personnel been instructed on how to recognize prohibited nuclear end-use activities?	_	_	744.6
14. Does the procedure include a review of U.S. person activities against prohibited activities?	_	_	
15. Does the procedure include what to do if it is known that an item is destined to a prohibited end-use/user?	_	_	

Screening Element Written Review Date_____	Y	N	Operational Review Comments ⁻ Date_____
Element 5: Missile Technology (MT) Screen A system for assuring compliance with the prohibited missile end-uses/users in part 744.3 and 744.6 and 744, Supplement 4.	–	–	
1. Prior to exporting, is there a written procedure for reviewing exports and reexports of all items subject to the EAR to determine whether the items:			744.3
A. are destined to or for a project listed in the footnote to Country Group D:4?	–	–	740, Supplement No. 1
B. or can be used in the design, development, production or use of missiles in or by a country listed in Country Group D:4, whether or not that use involves a listed project?	–	–	
C. If D:4 countries are listed with the EMS procedures, are they current?	–		
2. Is a person/position identified who is responsible for ensuring screening of customers and their activities against the prohibited end-uses/users?	– –	–	
3. Does the procedure describe when the missile technology screen should be performed?	–	–	
4. Does the procedure include a check against the Entity List?	–	–	744, Supplement 4
5. If yes, is there a procedure to maintain documented Entity List screen decisions on file to verify consistent, operational review?	–	–	

6. Is your missile screen completed on a:
  A. transaction basis?
  B. against a customer base?
  C. before new customers are approved?
	–
	–
	–
		–
		–	

7. Does the check include documentation of the signature/initial of the person performing the check, and the date performed to verify consistent, operational performance of the check?	– –		
8. Is the customer base checked and the check documented at least annually in the Customer Profiles?	–	–	
9. Is it clear who is responsible for the annual check?	– –		
10. Is there a list of all employees responsible for performing missile screening?	–	–	
11. Is there a procedure to verify that all responsible employees are performing the screening?	–		
12. Are missile checklists (or other tool) distributed to appropriate export control personnel for easy, efficient perfomance of the review?	– –		
13. Have export/sales personnel been instructed on how to recognize prohibited missile end-use activities?	–		
14. Does the procedure include a review of U.S. person activities against prohibited activities?	– –		744.6

Screening Element Written Review Date_____	Y	N	Operational Review Date_____ Comments
Element 6: Chemical & Biological Weapons (CBW) Screen			
A system for assuring compliance with the prohibited chemical & biological weapons end-uses/users in Part 744.4 and 744.6 and 744, Supplement 4.	–	–	
1. Prior to exporting, is there a written procedure for reviewing exports and reexports of all items subject to the EAR for license requirements if the item can be used in the design, development, production, stockpiling, or use of chemical or bilogical weapons in or by a country listed in Country Group D:3?	–	–	744.4 Part 740, Supplement No. 1
NOTE: If D:3 countries are listed within the EMS procedures, are they current?	–	–	
2. Is a person/position identified who is responsible for ensuring screening of customers and their activities against the prohibited end-uses/users?	–	–	
3. Does the procedure describe when the chemical & biological weapons screen should be performed?	–	–	Part 744, Supplement 4
4. Does the procedure include a check against the Entity List?	–	–	
5. If yes, is there a procedure to maintain documented Entity List screen decisions on file to verify consistent, operational review?	–	–	
6. Is your chemical & biological weapons screen completed on a: A. transaction basis? B. against a customer base? C. before new customers are approved?	–	–	
7. Does the check include documentation of the signature/initial of the person performing the check, and the date performed to verify consistent, operational performance of the check?	–	–	
8. Is the customer base checked and the check documented at least annually in the Customer Profiles?	–	–	
9. Is it clear who is responsible for the annual check?	–	–	
10. Is there a list of all employees responsible for performing chemical & biological weapons screening?	–	–	
11. Is there a procedure to verify that all responsible employees are performing the screening?	–	–	
12. Are chemical & biological weapons checklists (or other tools) distributed to appropriate export control personnel for easy, efficient perfomance of the review?	–	–	
13. Have export/sales personnel been instructed on how to recognize prohibited chemical & biological weapons end-use activities?	–	–	744.6
14. Does the procedure include a review of U.S. person activities against prohibited activities?	–	–	

Screening Element	Written Review Date_____	Y	N	Operational Review	Date_____
Element 7: Antiboycott Compliance Screen				Comments	
A Method to Review Orders Against Antiboycott Compliance Red Flags.		–	–		
1. Is there a written procedure to screen transactions and orders/shipping documents against antiboycott red flags?		–	–	Part 760	
2. Are persons/positions identified who are responsible for performing this screen?		–	–		
3. Is the antiboycott screening performed by using a profile check list?		–	–		
4. Does the checklist include the following: A. the firm's name? B. name/initials of individual performing the screen check? C. date screen check is performed?		– – –	– – –		
5. Is there a procedure to "hold" orders if there is a red flag during the processing of orders?		–	–		
6. Is a person designated to resolve red flags or report them to the Office of Antiboycott Compliance?		–	–		
7. Have all units that might possibly come into contact with the red flags been trained to identify the red flags?		–	–		
8. Are antiboycott red flags included in training materials in Element 4?		–	–		

Screening Element	Written Review Date_____	Y	N	Operational Review Comments	Date_____
Element 8: Informed Letter/Entity List Screen					
A Procedure to Review Customers and Other Parties Against the Entity List.		–	–		
1. Is there a written procedure to screen transactions against the Entity List to determine whether a license is required for exports or reexports of specified items to specified end-users, because BXA has determined that there is an unacceptable risk of use in, or diversion to prohibited proliferation activities?		–	–		Part 744, Supplement 4
2. Is the screening documented, including the following?		–	–		
A. the firm's name?		–	–		
B. name/initials of individual performing the check?		–	–		
C. date check is performed?					
D. is screen check combined and performed with another check (i.e., Denied Persons List check)?		–	–		
3. Is the *Federal Register* monitored daily for the addition of new entities to the Entity List?		–	–		
4. If matches occur, is there a "hold" function implemented within the order processing system that stops the order until a decision is made as to whether a license is required?		–	–		

Overall Evaluation

Was management commitment demonstrated throughout the system? Adequate resources to do the tasks?

Was ongoing export control communication demonstrated?

Are the written procedures current?

Are the written procedures consistent with operational procedures? If not, which needs to be amended..written or operational?

Were designated responsible persons (names current?) well trained in export control tasks?

Were there gaps in performance of export management procedures or was a smooth "SYSTEM" in place?

Was adequate documentation in place to verify performance of all export control tasks?

Assess the stability of the environment: recent company-wide changes? New export control personnel?

Import Compliance Issues Review and Customs and Border Protection Guidelines

Three Major Players in the Import Process

1. Importer of Record. Person or party who is responsible for duties and penalties to Customs and Border Protection.

2. U.S. Customs Service. Division of the Department of Homeland Security responsible for protecting the U.S. borders against illegal importation of commodities, persons, and contraband. Revenue collection agency.

3. Customs Broker. Person or party licensed by the Department of Treasury to conduct "customs business" on behalf of an importer of record.

Customs and Border Protection is collecting less and less funds each year in the form of duties and taxes due to special tariff treatment programs and yearly rate reductions of general duties and taxes. To offset this reduction in funds collected, customs is aggressively pursuing fines and penalties from importers through the customs audit process.

The Customs Modernization Act of 1993 was passed to encourage the following:

1. Reasonable care standards
2. Informed compliance standards
3. Supervision and control standards
4. Recordkeeping standards
5. Proper valuation of imported goods

Every U.S. importer will be audited by Customs and Border Protection. There is no importer that is totally compliant. Most importers do not understand their responsibility to Customs and Border Protection and their total liability pending a customs audit.

Most importers rely on their customs broker for compliance standards. However, most customs brokers do not have the operational expertise to properly operate in a compliant manner themselves. As a result, most customs brokers give improper advice to importers.

Reasonable Care

The Modernization Act mandated and passed into law the concept of reasonable care, so defined as. . . .

That degree of care which a person of ordinary prudence would exercise in the same or similar circumstances.

Reasonable care is the "legal responsibility" to fix the final classification and value.

Meeting Reasonable Care Standards

Customs Brokers

A broker shall not withhold information relative to any "customs business" from a client who is entitled to the information.

A broker shall exercise due diligence to ascertain the correctness of any and all information which he or she imparts to a client.

A broker shall not knowingly impart to a client false information relative to any customs business.

Importers of Record

Following are some of the responsibilities of importers of record:

Should seek guidance from customs for proper compliance through the formal rulings program.

Should consult with **qualified experts** such as a customs broker, customs consultant, or customs attorney who specializes in customs law.

If using a broker, must provide such broker with full and complete information sufficient enough for the broker to make an entry properly or for the broker to provide advice on how to make an entry.

When appropriate, obtain analyses from accredited labs to determine the technical qualities of imported merchandise.

Use in-house employees such as counsel, customs administrators, and customs managers who have experience in customs law proceedings.

Follow any customs binding rulings requested and received from customs.

Cannot classify own identical merchandise in different ways.

Notify customs when receiving different treatment by customs for the same goods in different ports of entry.

To examine Import Declarations CF 3461 prepared by the broker to determine the accuracy of information in relation to classification and valuation.

Customs Bonds

A customs bond is a contract that obligates the importer to perform certain functions in the importing process. These, among others, include:

1. The obligation to pay duties and related charges on a timely basis
2. To pay as demanded by customs, all additional duties, taxes, and charges subsequently found due

3. To file complete entries
4. To produce documents where customs releases merchandise conditionally
5. To hold the merchandise at the place of examination until the merchandise is properly released
6. To redeliver merchandise in a timely fashion to customs custody; where, for example, the merchandise is inadmissible (e.g., product of convict labor, non-compliance automobile, etc) or, more commonly, where it does not comply with the country-of-origin marking rules

The requirement for a bond is found in 19 U.S.C1623. This section of the U.S. code allows Customs to take bonds or other security (other security meaning cash deposits, U.S. bonds (except saving bonds), treasury notes, or treasury bills) in an amount equal to the amount of the bond.

Parties to a Bond

- Principal (importer)
- Surety (insurance company)
- The beneficiary–Customs and Border Protection

A bond is not designed or intended to protect the importer (rather it protects the government of the United States), nor does it relieve the importer of any of their obligations.

The surety (insurance) company by bonding the importer assumes the same duties and responsibilities of the importer. If an importer fails to honor any condition of the bond, surety can be compelled to do so in their place.

Types of Bonds

1. **Single Transaction.** Covers a particular entry (declaration) at a particular port.
2. **Continuous.** Covers all entries (declarations) at all ports in the United States.

Amount of Bond

1. **Single transaction.**
   - **Unrestricted Merchandise.** Entered value, plus all duties, taxes, fees.
   - **Restricted Merchandise.** Entered value × 3. (Restricted merchandise is that subject to other government agency requirements where failure to redeliver could pose a threat to the public health and safety).

2. **Continuous Bond.** Ten percent of all duties, taxes, and fees paid in the preceding calendar year. If no duties, taxes, and fees were paid in the preceding calendar year, then 10 percent of all duties, taxes, and fees, estimated to be paid in the current calendar year.

Breach of Bond (Failure to comply with bond conditions)

Liquidated damages assessed in the following amounts:

- **Unrestricted Merchandise.** Entered value, plus all duties, taxes, and fees.
- **Restricted Merchandise.** Three (3) times the entered value.

Requirements to Issue

Because the bond is a guarantee by surety (insurance company) of performance by the importer, prior approval from surety must be obtained in the following situations:

1. For importers who previously have not paid estimated duties timely.
2. For foreign principals (individuals and corporations).
3. For importers in bankruptcy or any insolvency proceedings.
4. For bond covering the importation of an automobile.
5. For bond covering merchandise subject to food and drug regulations.
6. Financial statement may be required.

Invoice Requirements

Invoice requirements as set forth in the CFR 19 Pt 141.86 are crucial element of the customs clearance process. Many penalty case situations develop and stem from incorrect invoices submitted on behalf of imported merchandise. It is the importer's responsibility to present to the broker a proper invoice as established in the mentioned customs regulations.

It is the broker's responsibility to ensure that a proper invoice is received from the importer for presentation purposes to U.S. Customs. If the invoice is incomplete or in violation of the rules and regulatory standards in Pt 141.86 of the CFR, the broker is to request from the importer a corrected invoice. Failure to do so is a violation of lack of reasonable care on behalf of the broker. The broker then would possibly face a penalty for the submission of incomplete or incorrect documentation in connection to an import clearance.

Carefully review CFR 141.86 to ensure all levels of understanding of the proper and regulatory invoicing requirements. You will note that most invoices used on a common practice basis are incomplete or contain a basic error. Avoid future penalties and correct this situation immediately.

Invoice Requirements

General Information

Each invoice of imported merchandise must set forth the following information:

1. The port of entry to which the merchandise is destined.
2. If merchandise is sold or agreed to be sold, the time, place, names of buyer and seller. If consigned, the time and origin of shipment, and names of shipper and receiver.
3. A detailed description of the merchandise including:
   - The name by which each item is known
   - The grade or quality
   - Marks, numbers, and symbols under which sold by the seller or manufacturer to the trade in the country of exportation
   - Marks and numbers of the packages in which the merchandise is packed
4. The quantities in weights and measures.
5. If sold or agreed to be sold, the purchase price of each item in the currency of the sale.
6. If the merchandise is shipped on consignment, the value of each item in

the currency in which the transactions are usually made or, in the absence of such value, the price in such currency that the manufacturer, seller, shipper, or owner would have received or was willing to receive, for such merchandise if sold in the ordinary course of trade and in the usual wholesale quantities in the country of exportation.

7. The kind of currency (yen/U.S. dollars, etc.).
8. All charges upon the merchandise, itemized by name and amount including:
   - Actual amount of freight
   - Actual amount of insurance
   - Actual amount of any commission paid
   - Actual cost of packing
   - All charges, costs, and expenses incurred in bringing the merchandise from alongside the carrier at the port of exportation in the country of exportation and placing it alongside the carrier at the first U.S. port of entry
9. All rebates, drawbacks, and bounties, separately itemized, allowed upon the exportation.
10. The country of origin (manufacture).
11. All cost for goods or services furnished for the production of the merchandise not included in the invoice price. These costs are termed "assists" and defined as dies, molds, tooling, printing plates, artwork, engineering work, design, and development, financial assistance, etc.
12. Must state in adequate detail the packing information (what merchandise is contained in each individual package).
13. Set forth in detail for each class or kind of merchandise every discount from list or other base price that has been or may be allowed in fixing each price or value.
14. Must be in the English language or shall have attached thereto an accurate English translation containing adequate information for examination of the merchandise and determination of duties.
15. Shall identify by name a responsible employee of the exporter who has knowledge or who can readily obtain knowledge of the transaction.

Additional Information

Special information is required on certain goods or classes of goods in addition to the general information outlined previously.

Frequent Errors in Invoicing

The fundamental rule is that the shipper and importer must furnish customs with all pertinent information with respect to each import transaction to assist customs in determining the tariff status of the goods. Some examples of omissions and inaccuracies to be avoided are:

1. On CIF transactions, actual prepaid amounts for freight and insurance are not shown. In many situations only estimated amounts are shown. In others, none are shown.
2. The shipper assumes that a commission, royalty, or other charges against the goods is a so-called nondutiable item and omits it from the invoice.

3. A foreign shipper who purchases goods and sells them to a U.S. importer at a delivered price shows on the invoice the cost of the goods to him instead of the delivered price.

Valuation Verifications

Transaction value

Transaction value of identical or similar value

Deductive value

Computed value

Derived value

Methods of valuation are contained in the preceeding hierarchy.

Knowledge of this order is essential in the comprehension of proper valuation concepts as outlined in CFR 152.

All transactions contain a term of sale:

CIF duty paid

CIF

CF

FOB

FAS

Ex-Works

Verifications must be made to determine the correct term of sale for every invoice and every import declaration of merchandise.

Proper deductions from price can only be calculated after categorizing the proper term of sale through solid identification from the commercial or proforma invoice. For example, prepaid freight, insurance, duty paid calculations, are non-dutiable charges. Foreign loading and foreign inland freight and packing are subject to duty charges.

Customs and Border Protection Regulatory Audit General Compliance Assessment Questionnaire for Importer Audits

A. General Organizational Information.

Please provide the following information on the organization of your company:

1. Description of overall organization structure, organization charts, and similar information.
2. Company's full name and IRS identification number(s).
3. Name and title of the company's officers.
4. Name, title, and telephone number of the person who will be the Customs and Border Protection contact during the review.
5. Name, title, and telephone number of the official(s) preparing information for this questionnaire.
6. General information on company operations such as a description of busi-

ness operations, number of employees, location of facilities and related operations, products, divisions, and customers.

7. Names and addresses of any other U.S. and foreign-related companies (as defined in section 152.102(g) of the Customs Regulations).

8. Similar material as items 1 through 6 for the company's parent, sister, subsidiary, and joint venture organizations and relationships.

9. Name and contact person for internal preparer of year end financial statements.

10. Name and contact person for external financial auditors, such as a certified public accountant, and authorization to contact those auditors.

B. Customs-Related Activities.

1. Identify the organizational element (departments, divisions, subsidiaries, etc.) involved in customs-related operations.

2. List names under which the company imports. Does the company import under a broker's bond?

3. List customs identification numbers and suffixes (importer ID numbers) applicable to customs-related business and the organizational element that imports under each number or suffix.

4. List the names and locator information for key individuals associated with customs-related operations.

5. List the name(s) and addresses of broker(s) your company uses.

6. Provide the names and addresses of all foreign sellers and suppliers.

7. Describe the disposition of imported products (manufacturing, resale, etc.).

8. Identify and explain situations in which the company *exports* merchandise from the United States.

9. Identify situations in which the company *imports* merchandise in accordance with binding rulings received from customs.

C. Recordkeeping System.

The Tariff Act of 1930 as amended (Title 19 USC 1508) establishes recordkeeping requirements for organizations dealing in customs operations. Organizations conducting customs-related operations are required to maintain and produce records that are normally kept in the ordinary course of business. During the audit, specific recordkeeping requirements that are being defined in accordance with the Customs Modernization Act will be discussed. Describe the recordkeeping system supporting customs-related operations, including accounting and financial recordkeeping systems, documents, and information. This information may be available in the company's internal procedures manuals.

Include the following:

1. The identity of the source records and information used to prepare customs information. Please explain how they are created, maintained, and transferred to and from originating, using, and storing organizations. Please provide other information necessary to understand operating procedures and associated internal controls over record production and retention.

2. Location of records. If records are maintained at multiple locations, list each location by address and identify documents and information at each.

Include the name and telephone number of the contact person at each location.

3. Procedures or techniques to link records and information to customs entry submissions.
4. Retention period. Length of time records are retained within department before moving to storage and length of time retained in storage.
5. Storage medium.
6. Retrieval procedures with contact names and phone numbers.
7. Description of alternative storage procedures (conversion and maintenance of information in other than original formats), if applicable.
8. Internal and management controls concerning recordkeeping practices.
9. Other appropriate information.
10. A description of the company's accounting and financial system as it relates to and supports customs-related operations.
11. The company's fiscal year.
12. General ledger accounts typically used to record customs-related transactions.

D. Internal Controls.
1. Provide the company's formal policies and procedures manuals or other written directives related to the handling of customs matters and documents. If there are no formal written procedures, provide a written summary of your procedures for ensuring compliance with customs laws, regulations, and rulings.
2. If transaction value is the method of appraisement, explain procedures to ensure that import values reported to customs accurately reflect the price actually paid or payable for the imported merchandise. Explain procedures to assure that indirect and additional payments are included in the transaction value.
3. Explain procedures to ensure that assists, commissions, royalties, license fees, freight, and other dutiable costs are correctly reported to customs.
4. Explain procedures to ensure that import quantities reported to customs are accurate. Include procedures for reporting overages and shortages of merchandise receipts.
5. Explain procedures to ensure that nondutiable costs such as international freight and insurance are accurate and fully supported by documentation.
6. Explain procedures to ensure that harbor maintenance fees and merchandise processing fees are accurately calculated and timely paid on imports. Explain procedures to ensure that harbor maintenance fees are accurately calculated and timely paid on admissions to the foreign trade zones, domestic shipments, and exports. See section 24.24 of the Customs Regulations.
7. Explain procedures to ensure that imported merchandise is accurately classified and all admissibility requirements are met. List other agencies for which compliance requirements on importations must be met.
8. If different procedures are used for nonrelated and related foreign sellers, explain the procedures used for each.
9. Explain the company's merchandise entry procedures. For example, does the company rely exclusively on a customs broker to fulfill all of the company's responsibilities related to customs, or does the company maintain

an internal staff responsible for conducting customs entry operations? If an internal staff is maintained, provide the names of the individuals, a description of the job performed by each, and identify those who have a customs license and provide the license number.

10. Provide and explain results of evaluations of the effectiveness of the company's system of internal controls, particularly with respect to customs-related operations. Please include evaluations by internal or independent parties.

E. Customs Value Information and Company Internal Procedures for Import-Related Operations

1. Identify the method of appraisement, as prescribed in sections 152.103 through 152.108 of the Customs Regulations, used to value imported merchandise from each of your major suppliers (consider any supplier who provides 10 percent or more of the total value of your importations as a major supplier).

2. If transaction value is used for importations from related parties, do the importations qualify for transaction value based on the circumstances of the sale or on the basis of test values? Provide an explanation and support documentation for the method that you use to support transaction value.

3. Describe how prices for imported merchandise from major suppliers are determined.

4. If the company is an exclusive U.S. importer of merchandise from foreign suppliers, explain the circumstances of sale and relationships with the foreign suppliers. Provide written agreements, if applicable.

5. If applicable, identify situations in which foreign *related* suppliers sell the same or similar merchandise to other U.S. companies.

6. Explain how and when the company takes title to the imported merchandise. Explain differences that may exist between different importing situations.

7. Explain transportation procedures and responsibilities for foreign, international, and domestic transportation of merchandise from the foreign plant to the place of international shipment, to the port of importation, and to the final U.S. destination. Include explanations and information concerning responsibilities for foreign inland freight charges. For example, is foreign inland freight included on the invoice with the merchandise or is it invoiced separately? If included on the invoice with the merchandise, is it separately identified or included with the charge for international freight? Identify general ledger accounts used to record the various freight charges.

8. Explain contractual agreements between the company or foreign suppliers with shippers or freight forwarders. Identify and explain any rebates received by the company or foreign affiliate from shippers or freight forwarders. Identify general ledger accounts used to record rebates, if any.

9. Identify and explain loans payable to or receivable from foreign suppliers and sellers.

10. Identify situations in which the merchandise price from the foreign seller does not include all costs plus a profit.

11. Identify and explain retroactive price increases or adjustments for imported merchandise at the end of the accounting period or other times

that are paid to or accrue to the company and/or the foreign supplier. Identify the general ledger accounts used to record the transactions.

12. Explain procedures and accounting for foreign currency fluctuations. Identify general ledger accounts used to record the fluctuations.

13. Identify and explain situations in which the company receives price adjustments, variances, rebates, or allowances directly or indirectly from foreign exporters or sellers. Identify the general ledger accounts used to record the transactions.

14. Identify and explain payments to foreign companies for expenses other than imported merchandise, such as management fees, research and development, tooling, and similar matters. Identify general ledger accounts used to record the transactions.

15. Identify and explain situations in which the foreign seller influences or controls the resale price of merchandise imported into the United States.

16. Identify and explain situations in which prices for imported merchandise are subject to restrictions or conditions as explained in sections 152.103(j)(1)(i–iv) of the Customs Regulations.

17. Describe how packing costs are calculated and declared to customs in accordance with section 152.103(b)(1)(i) of the Customs Regulations. Identify general ledger accounts where packing costs are recorded.

18. Identify and explain situations in which the company uses the services of foreign selling agents. Explain procedures for declaring selling commissions on entries in accordance with section 152.103(b)(1)(ii) of the Customs Regulations. Provide names and addresses of agents and agency agreements, and identify the general ledger accounts used to record commissions and related transactions.

19. Identify and explain situations in which the company provides assists to foreign suppliers in accordance with 152.103(b)(1)(iii) and 152.103(d) of the Customs Regulations. Describe the form of any assists (tools, molds, fabrics, loans, design and engineering costs, machinery used in production, etc.), their values, and identify general ledger accounts used to record the transactions.

20. Identify and explain situations in which *third parties* provide assists to foreign suppliers in accordance with 152.103(b)(1)(iii) and 152.103(d) of the Customs Regulations. Describe the form of any assists (tools, molds, fabrics, loans, design and engineering costs, machinery used in production, etc.), their values, and identify general ledger accounts in which the transactions are recorded.

21. Identify and explain situations in which royalties or license fees were paid for importer merchandise. Provide copies of the royalty or license agreement. Identify the general ledger accounts used to record the transactions.

22. Identify and explain situations in which proceeds of any subsequent resale, disposal, or use of the imported merchandise accrue directly or indirectly to the seller. Identify the general ledger accounts used to record the transaction and provide documentation on how the proceeds are calculated.

23. Identify and explain situations in which the company makes indirect payments to foreign sellers as covered by section 152.103(a)(2) of the Customs Regulations? Include supporting documentation, agreements, and the identity of general ledger accounts used to record the transactions.

24. Identify and explain the company's usual form of payment (e.g., letters of credit, wire transfers, checks, open accounts, etc.) for imported merchandise. Explain whether the payment is made in U.S. dollars or in a foreign currency, frequency of payments made to foreign sellers, and the identity of general ledger accounts used to record the payments.

25. If applicable, explain circumstances and responsibilities for obtaining and paying for quota, visa, and licenses. Identify general ledger accounts used to record the payments.

§ 141.86 Contents of invoices and general requirements.

⬆ top

(a) *General information required on the invoice.* Each invoice of imported merchandise, must set forth the following information:

(1) The port of entry to which the merchandise is destined;

(2) The time when, the place where, and the person by whom and the person to whom the merchandise is sold or agreed to be sold, or if to be imported otherwise than in pursuance of a purchase, the place from which shipped, the time when and the person to whom and the person by whom it is shipped;

(3) A detailed description of the merchandise, including the name by which each item is known, the grade or quality, and the marks, numbers, and symbols under which sold by the seller or manufacturer to the trade in the country of exportation, together with the marks and numbers of the packages in which the merchandise is packed;

(4) The quantities in the weights and measures of the country or place from which the merchandise is shipped, or in the weights and measures of the United States;

(5) The purchase price of each item in the currency of the purchase, if the merchandise is shipped in pursuance of a purchase or an agreement to purchase;

(6) If the merchandise is shipped otherwise than in pursuance of a purchase or an agreement to purchase, the value for each item, in the currency in which the transactions are usually made, or, in the absence of such value, the price in such currency that the manufacturer, seller, shipper, or owner would have received, or was willing to receive, for such merchandise if sold in the ordinary course of trade and in the usual wholesale quantities in the country of exportation;

(7) The kind of currency, whether gold, silver, or paper;

(8) All charges upon the merchandise itemized by name and amount, including freight, insurance, commission, cases, containers, coverings, and cost of packing; and if not included above, all charges, costs, and expenses incurred in bringing the merchandise from alongside the carrier at the port of exportation in the country of exportation and placing it alongside the carrier at the first United States port of entry. The cost of packing, cases, containers, and inland freight to the port of exportation need not be itemized by amount if included in the invoice price, and so identified. Where the required information does not appear on the invoice as originally prepared, it must be shown on an attachment to the invoice;

(9) All rebates, drawbacks, and bounties, separately itemized, allowed upon the exportation of the merchandise;

(10) The country of origin of the merchandise; and,

(11) All goods or services furnished for the production of the merchandise (e.g., assists such as dies, molds, tools, engineering work) not included in the invoice price. However, goods or services furnished in the United States are excluded. Annual reports for goods and services, when approved by the port director, will be accepted as proof that the goods or services were provided.

(b) *Nonpurchased merchandise shipped by other than manufacturer.* Each invoice of imported merchandise shipped to a person in the United States by a person other than the manufacturer and otherwise than pursuant to a purchase or agreement to purchase must set forth the time when, the place where, the person from whom such merchandise was purchased, and the price paid therefor in the currency of the purchase, stating whether gold, silver, or paper.

(c) *Merchandise sold in transit.* If the merchandise is sold on the documents while in transit from the port of exportation to the port of entry, the original invoice reflecting the transaction under which the merchandise actually began its journey to the United States, and the resale invoice or a statement of sale showing the price paid for each item by the purchaser, must be filed as part of the entry, entry summary, or withdrawal documentation. If the original invoice cannot be obtained, a pro forma invoice showing the values and transaction reflected by the original invoice must be filed together with the resale invoice or statement.

(d) *Invoice to be in English.* The invoice and all attachments must be in the English language, or must have attached thereto an accurate English translation containing adequate information for examination of the merchandise and determination of duties.

(e) *Packing list.* Each invoice must state in adequate detail what merchandise is contained in each individual package.

(f) *Weights and measures.* If the invoice or entry does not disclose the weight, gage, or measure of the merchandise which is necessary to ascertain duties, the consignee must pay the expense of weighing, gaging, or measuring prior to the release of the merchandise from CBP custody.

(g) *Discounts.* Each invoice must set forth in detail, for each class or kind of merchandise, every discount from list or other base price which has been or may be allowed in fixing each purchase price or value.

(h) *Numbering of invoices and pages* —(1) *Invoices.* Except when electronic invoice data are transmitted to CBP under the provisions of part 143 of this chapter, when more than one invoice is included in the same entry, each invoice with its attachments must be numbered consecutively by the importer on the bottom of the face of each page, beginning with No. 1.

(2) *Pages.* Except when electronic invoice data are transmitted to CBP under the provisions of part 143 of this chapter, if the invoice or invoices filed with one entry consist of more than two pages, each page must be numbered consecutively by the importer on the bottom of the face of each page, with the page numbering beginning with No. 1 for the first page of the first invoice and continuing in a single series of numbers through all the invoices and attachments included in one entry.

(3) *Both invoices and pages.* Except when electronic invoice data are transmitted to CBP under the provisions of part 143 of this chapter, both the invoice number and the page number must be shown at the bottom of each page when applicable. For example, an entry covering one invoice of one page and a second invoice of two pages must be paginated as follows:

Inv. 1, p. 1.

Inv. 2, p. 2.

Inv. 2, p. 3

(i) *Information may be on invoice or attached thereto.* Any information required on an invoice by any provision of this subpart may be set forth either on the invoice or on an attachment thereto.

(j) *Name of responsible individual.* Each invoice of imported merchandise must identify by name a responsible employee of the exporter, who has knowledge, or who can readily obtain knowledge, of the transaction.

[T.D. 73–175, 38 FR 17447, July 2, 1973, as amended by T.D. 79–221, 44 FR 46820, Aug. 9, 1979; T.D. 85–39, 50 FR 9612, Mar. 11, 1985; CBP Dec. 09–47, 74 FR 69019, Dec. 30, 2009]

Harmonized Tariff Schedule of the United States (HTSUS)

Explanation and Use Exercise

The HTSUS is a very thick reference and guide to proper classification of merchandise upon entry into the United States. All articles subject to customs clearance needs to be properly classified prior to such clearance. The customs service takes great care in the annual preparation and update of this book and expects reasonable care to be used in referencing this book for classification purposes.

Book Format

The HTSUS has many key components to assist you in obtaining proper harmonize classifications. Lets take a look at these components now!

General Rules of Interpretation (GRI)

The GRI is found at the front of the book and is relied upon greatly in the determination of proper classification techniques. Classification itself is not an exact science. In many cases, an entry writer is asked to interpret the determining factors of what is being imported to properly classify the imported goods. Because different individuals may "interpret" imported items of description and usage in many different ways as to effect the classification, customs uses the GRI as a formal guide of interpretation. Read the GRI carefully and memorize them. It is essential to proper classification to do so.

General Notes

General Notes are located next in the HTSUS to provide ease in the usage of the book as well as provide a definitive explanation and analysis to special tariff treaty programs. It is important to be familiar with these notes to ensure proper classification techniques. Each general note is essential to classification clarity and understanding.

Chapters and Chapter Notes

The HTSUS is formatted in numerical order by chapters. Each chapter deals with a specific class of commodities. Each chapter is preceded by **chapter notes,** which provide a more defined level of understanding on individual chapters, for classification purposes. Inclusions to and exclusions from a chapter are found here. Key definitions to terms and descriptions are also outlined in the chapter notes. Prior to selecting any HTSUS ten-digit number it is essential to read the related chapter note for any required reference to the imported or classifiable items.

Alphabetical Index

The alphabetical index is located in the back of the book and is the guide to quickly and correctly access the proper chapter for classification purposes.

The index contains commodity descriptions of everything that you could possible think of. To classify an item, look in this index to reference the description. The index provides at least the first two letters of the ten-digit HTSUS number. In most cases the first four digits are provided.

Techniques of Usage of the HTSUS

The most difficult task in proper HTSUS classification is to determine what it is that you are classifying. In that determination, one must consider the GRI for interpretation. Once you have decided what you are classifying, reference the alphabetical index for a "hint or clue" (the first four digits of the HTSUS). This will direct you to the numerical chapter in the HTSUS where the goods are described. Next, reference the chapter notes to verify any exclusions or inclusions to the chapter. The HTSTS number is a ten-digit number. You have not properly classified something until you have reached a tenth digit in its classification.

HTSUS Page Outline/Description

Heading and subheading = the first eight digits of the HTSUS number.

Statistical suffix = the last two digits in the HTSUS number.

Article description = A detailed description of articles for classification purposes.
Rates of duty
General column = rate of duty originating in a most-favored nation (see the general notes for a detailed analysis).
Special column = rate of duty originating in a county under a special tariff treaty program.
Column 2 = rate of duty on goods originating in an unfavored nation (see the General notes for detailed analysis).

Harmonized Tariff Schedule of the United States (2003)
Annotated for Statistical Reporting Purposes

Gen.Rs.Int.

GENERAL RULES OF INTERPRETATION

Classification of goods in the tariff schedule shall be governed by the following principles:

1. The table of contents, alphabetical index, and titles of sections, chapters and sub-chapters are provided for ease of reference only; for legal purposes, classification shall be determined according to the terms of the headings and any relative section or chapter notes and, provided such headings or notes do not otherwise require, according to the following provisions:

2. (a) Any reference in a heading to an article shall be taken to include a reference to that article incomplete or unfinished, provided that, as entered, the incomplete or unfinished article has the essential character of the complete or finished article. It shall also include a reference to that article complete or finished (or falling to be classified as complete or finished by virtue of this rule), entered unassembled or disassembled.

    (b) Any reference in a heading to a material or substance shall be taken to include a reference to mixtures or combinations of that material or substance with other materials or substances. Any reference to goods of a given material or substance shall be taken to include a reference to goods consisting wholly or partly of such material or substance. The classification of goods consisting of more than one material or substance shall be according to the principles of rule 3.

3. When, by application of rule 2(b) or for any other reason, goods are, *prima facie*, classifiable under two or more headings, classification shall be effected as follows:

    (a) The heading which provides the most specific description shall be preferred to headings providing a more general description. However, when two or more headings each refer to part only of the materials or substances contained in mixed or composite goods or to part only of the items in a set put up for retail sale, those headings are to be regarded as equally specific in relation to those goods, even if one of them gives a more complete or precise description of the goods.

    (b) Mixtures, composite goods consisting of different materials or made up of different components, and goods put up in sets for retail sale, which cannot be classified by reference to 3(a), shall be classified as if they consisted of the material or component which gives them their essential character, insofar as this criterion is applicable.

    (c) When goods cannot be classified by reference to 3(a) or 3(b), they shall be classified under the heading which occurs last in numerical order among those which equally merit consideration.

4. Goods which cannot be classified in accordance with the above rules shall be classified under the heading appropriate to the goods to which they are most akin.

5. In addition to the foregoing provisions, the following rules shall apply in respect of the goods referred to therein:

    (a) Camera cases, musical instrument cases, gun cases, drawing instrument cases, necklace cases and similar containers, specially shaped or fitted to contain a specific article or set of articles, suitable for long-term use and entered with the articles for which they are intended, shall be classified with such articles when of a kind normally sold therewith. This rule does not, however, apply to containers which give the whole its essential character;

    (b) Subject to the provisions of rule 5(a) above, packing materials and packing containers entered with the goods therein shall be classified with the goods if they are of a kind normally used for packing such goods. However, this provision is not binding when such packing materials or packing containers are clearly suitable for repetitive use.

6. For legal purposes, the classification of goods in the subheadings of a heading shall be determined according to the terms of those subheadings and any related subheading notes and, *mutatis mutandis*, to the above rules, on the understanding that only subheadings at the same level are comparable. For the purposes of this rule, the relative section, chapter and subchapter notes also apply, unless the context otherwise requires.

Harmonized Tariff Schedule of the United States (2003)
Annotated for Statistical Reporting Purposes

Add.U.S.Rs.Int.

ADDITIONAL U.S. RULES OF INTERPRETATION

1.   In the absence of special language or context which otherwise requires—

    (a)   a tariff classification controlled by use (other than actual use) is to be determined in accordance with the use in the United States at, or immediately prior to, the date of importation, of goods of that class or kind to which the imported goods belong, and the controlling use is the principal use;

    (b)   a tariff classification controlled by the actual use to which the imported goods are put in the United States is satisfied only if such use is intended at the time of importation, the goods are so used and proof thereof is furnished within 3 years after the date the goods are entered;

    (c)   a provision for parts of an article covers products solely or principally used as a part of such articles but a provision for "parts" or "parts and accessories" shall not prevail over a specific provision for such part or accessory; and

    (d)   the principles of section XI regarding mixtures of two or more textile materials shall apply to the classification of goods in any provision in which a textile material is named.

Harmonized Tariff Schedule of the United States (2003)
Annotated for Statistical Reporting Purposes

GENERAL NOTES

1. <u>Tariff Treatment of Imported Goods and of Vessel Equipments, Parts and Repairs</u>. All goods provided for in this schedule and imported into the customs territory of the United States from outside thereof, and all vessel equipments, parts, materials and repairs covered by the provisions of subchapter XVIII to chapter 98 of this schedule, are subject to duty or exempt therefrom as prescribed in general notes 3 through 18, inclusive.

2. <u>Customs Territory of the United States</u>. The term "<u>customs territory of the United States</u>", as used in the tariff schedule, includes only the States, the District of Columbia and Puerto Rico.

3. <u>Rates of Duty</u>. The rates of duty in the "Rates of Duty" columns designated 1 ("General" and "Special") and 2 of the tariff schedule apply to goods imported into the customs territory of the United States as hereinafter provided in this note:

   (a) <u>Rate of Duty Column 1</u>.

      (i) Except as provided in subparagraph (iv) of this paragraph, the rates of duty in column 1 are rates which are applicable to all products other than those of countries enumerated in paragraph (b) of this note. Column 1 is divided into two subcolumns, "General" and "Special", which are applicable as provided below.

      (ii) The "<u>General</u>" subcolumn sets forth the general or normal trade relations (NTR) rates which are applicable to products of those countries described in subparagraph (i) above which are not entitled to special tariff treatment as set forth below.

      (iii) The "<u>Special</u>" subcolumn reflects rates of duty under one or more special tariff treatment programs described in paragraph (c) of this note and identified in parentheses immediately following the duty rate specified in such subcolumn. These rates apply to those products which are properly classified under a provision for which a special rate is indicated and for which all of the legal requirements for eligibility for such program or programs have been met. Where a product is eligible for special treatment under more than one program, the lowest rate of duty provided for any applicable program shall be imposed. Where no special rate of duty is provided for a provision, or where the country from which a product otherwise eligible for special treatment was imported is not designated as a beneficiary country under a program appearing with the appropriate provision, the rates of duty in the "General" subcolumn of column 1 shall apply.

      (iv) <u>Products of Insular Possessions</u>.

         (A) Except as provided in additional U.S. note 5 of chapter 91 and except as provided in additional U.S. note 2 of chapter 96, and except as provided in section 423 of the Tax Reform Act of 1986, and additional U.S. note 3(e) of chapter 71, goods imported from insular possessions of the United States which are outside the customs territory of the United States are subject to the rates of duty set forth in column 1 of the tariff schedule, except that all such goods the growth or product of any such possession, or manufactured or produced in any such possession from materials the growth, product or manufacture of any such possession or of the customs territory of the United States, or of both, which do not contain foreign materials to the value of more than 70 percent of their total value (or more than 50 percent of their total value with respect to goods described in section 213(b) of the Caribbean Basin Economic Recovery Act), coming to the customs territory of the United States directly from any such possession, and all goods previously imported into the customs territory of the United States with payment of all applicable duties and taxes imposed upon or by reason of importation which were shipped from the United States, without remission, refund or drawback of such duties or taxes, directly to the possession from which they are being returned by direct shipment, are exempt from duty.

         (B) In determining whether goods produced or manufactured in any such insular possession contain foreign materials to the value of more than 70 percent, no material shall be considered foreign which either--

            (1) at the time such goods are entered, or

            (2) at the time such material is imported into the insular possession,

            may be imported into the customs territory from a foreign country, and entered free of duty; except that no goods containing material to which (2) of this subparagraph applies shall be exempt from duty under subparagraph (A) unless adequate documentation is supplied to show that the material has been incorporated into such goods during the 18-month period after the date on which such material is imported into the insular possession.

         (C) Subject to the limitations imposed under sections 503(a)(2), 503(a)(3) and 503(c) of the Trade Act of 1974, goods designated as eligible under section 503 of such Act which are imported from an insular possession of the United States shall receive duty treatment no less favorable than the treatment afforded such goods imported from a beneficiary developing country under title V of such Act.

Harmonized Tariff Schedule of the United States (2003)
Annotated for Statistical Reporting Purposes

(D)   Subject to the provisions in section 213 of the Caribbean Basin Economic Recovery Act, goods which are imported from insular possessions of the United States shall receive duty treatment no less favorable than the treatment afforded such goods when they are imported from a beneficiary country under such Act.

(E)   Subject to the provisions in section 204 of the Andean Trade Preference Act, goods which are imported from insular possessions of the United States shall receive duty treatment no less favorable than the treatment afforded such goods when they are imported from a beneficiary country under such Act.

(F)   No quantity of an agricultural product that is subject to a tariff-rate quota that exceeds the in-quota quantity shall be eligible for duty-free treatment under this paragraph.

(v)   Products of the West Bank, the Gaza Strip or a qualifying industrial zone.

(A)   Subject to the provisions of this paragraph, articles which are imported directly from the West Bank, the Gaza Strip, a qualifying industrial zone as defined in subdivision (G) of this subparagraph or Israel and are--

(1)   wholly the growth, product or manufacture of the West Bank, the Gaza Strip or a qualifying industrial zone; or

(2)   new or different articles of commerce that have been grown, produced or manufactured in the West Bank, the Gaza Strip or a qualifying industrial zone, and the sum of--

(I)   the cost or value of the materials produced in the West Bank, the Gaza Strip, a qualifying industrial zone or Israel, plus

(II)   the direct costs of processing operations (not including simple combining or packaging operations, and not including mere dilution with water or with another substance that does not materially alter the characteristics of such articles) performed in the West Bank, the Gaza Strip, a qualifying industrial zone or Israel,

is not less than 35 percent of the appraised value of such articles;

shall be eligible for duty-free entry into the customs territory of the United States. For purposes of subdivision (A)(2), materials which are used in the production of articles in the West Bank, the Gaza Strip or a qualifying industrial zone, and which are the product of the United States, may be counted in an amount up to 15 percent of the appraised value of such articles.

(B)   Articles are "imported directly" for the purposes of this paragraph if--

(1)   they are shipped directly from the West Bank, the Gaza Strip, a qualifying industrial zone or Israel into the United States without passing through the territory of any intermediate country; or

(2)   they are shipped through the territory of an intermediate country, and the articles in the shipment do not enter into the commerce of any intermediate country and the invoices, bills of lading and other shipping documents specify the United States as the final destination; or

(3)   they are shipped through an intermediate country and the invoices and other documents do not specify the United States as the final destination, and the articles--

(I)   remain under the control of the customs authority in an intermediate country;

(II)   do not enter into the commerce of an intermediate country except for the purpose of a sale other than at retail, but only if the articles are imported as a result of the original commercial transactions between the importer and the producer or the producer's sales agent; and

(III)   have not been subjected to operations other than loading, unloading or other activities necessary to preserve the articles in good condition.

(C)   The term "new or different articles of commerce" means that articles must have been substantially transformed in the West Bank, the Gaza Strip or a qualifying industrial zone into articles with a new name, character or use.

Harmonized Tariff Schedule of the United States (2003)
Annotated for Statistical Reporting Purposes

GN 3(a)(v)(D)--3(a)(v)(E)

(D) (1) For the purposes of subdivision (A)(2)(I), the cost or value or materials produced in the West Bank, the Gaza Strip or a qualifying industrial zone includes--

   (I) the manufacturer's actual cost for the materials;

   (II) when not included in the manufacturer's actual cost for the materials, the freight, insurance, packing and all other costs incurred in transporting the materials to the manufacturer's plant;

   (III) the actual cost of waste or spoilage, less the value of recoverable scrap; and

   (IV) taxes or duties imposed on the materials by the West Bank, the Gaza Strip or a qualifying industrial zone, if such taxes are not remitted on exportation.

(2) If a material is provided to the manufacturer without charge, or at less than fair market value, its cost or value shall be determined by computing the sum of--

   (I) all expenses incurred in the growth, production or manufacturer of the material, including general expenses;

   (II) an amount for profit; and

   (III) freight, insurance, packing and all other costs incurred in transporting the material to the manufacturer's plant.

(3) If the information necessary to compute the cost or value of a material is not available, the Customs Service may ascertain or estimate the value thereof using all reasonable methods.

(E) (1) For purposes of this paragraph, the "direct costs of processing operations performed in the West Bank, the Gaza Strip or a qualifying industrial zone" with respect to an article are those costs either directly incurred in, or which can be reasonably allocated to, the growth, production, manufacture or assembly of that article. Such costs include, but are not limited to, the following to the extent that they are includible in the appraised value of articles imported into the United States:

   (I) All actual labor costs involved in the growth, production, manufacture or assembly of the article, including fringe benefits, on-the-job training and costs of engineering, supervisory, quality control and similar personnel;

   (II) Dies, molds, tooling and depreciation on machinery and equipment which are allocable to such articles;

   (III) Research, development, design, engineering and blueprint costs insofar as they are allocable to such articles; and

   (IV) Costs of inspecting and testing such articles.

(2) Those items that are not included as direct costs of processing operations with respect to an article are those which are not directly attributable to the article or are not costs of manufacturing the article. Such items include, but are not limited to--

   (I) profit; and

   (II) general expenses of doing business which are either not allocable to the article or are not related to the growth, production, manufacture or assembly of the article, such as administrative salaries, casualty and liability insurance, advertising and salesmen's salaries, commissions or expenses.

Harmonized Tariff Schedule of the United States (2003)
Annotated for Statistical Reporting Purposes

GN 3(a)(v)(F)–3(b)

(F)   Whenever articles are entered with a claim for the duty exemption provided in this paragraph–

   (1)   the importer shall be deemed to certify that such articles meet all of the conditions for duty exemption; and

   (2)   when requested by the Customs Service, the importer, manufacturer or exporter submits a declaration setting forth all pertinent information with respect to such articles, including the following:

      (I)   A description of such articles, quantities, numbers and marks of packages, invoice numbers and bills of lading;

      (II)   A description of the operations performed in the production of such articles in the West Bank, the Gaza Strip, a qualifying industrial zone or Israel and an identification of the direct costs of processing operations;

      (III)   A description of the materials used in the production of such articles which are wholly the growth, product or manufacture of the West Bank, the Gaza Strip, a qualifying industrial zone, Israel or the United States, and a statement as to the cost or value of such materials;

      (IV)   A description of the operations performed on, and a statement as to the origin and cost or value of, any foreign materials used in such articles which are claimed to have been sufficiently processed in the West Bank, the Gaza Strip, a qualifying industrial zone or Israel so as to be materials produced in the West Bank, the Gaza Strip, a qualifying industrial zone or Israel; and

      (V)   A description of the origin and cost or value of any foreign materials used in the article which have not been substantially transformed in the West Bank, the Gaza Strip or a qualifying industrial zone.

(G)   For the purposes of this paragraph, a "qualifying industrial zone" means any area that--

   (1)   encompasses portions of the territory of Israel and Jordan or Israel and Egypt;

   (2)   has been designated by local authorities as an enclave where merchandise may enter without payment of duty or excise taxes; and

   (3)   has been designated by the United States Trade Representative in a notice published in the Federal Register as a qualifying industrial zone.

(b)   Rate of Duty Column 2. 1/ Notwithstanding any of the foregoing provisions of this note, the rates of duty shown in column 2 shall apply to products, whether imported directly or indirectly, of the following countries and areas pursuant to section 401 of the Tariff Classification Act of 1962, to section 231 or 257(e)(2) of the Trade Expansion Act of 1962, to section 404(a) of the Trade Act of 1974 or to any other applicable section of law, or to action taken by the President thereunder:

      Cuba   Laos   North Korea

1/   Pursuant to Pub.L. 102–420, Oct. 16, 1992 (106 Stat. 2149), nondiscriminatory treatment was withdrawn from goods that are products of Serbia or Montenegro effective Oct. 31, 1992.

Harmonized Tariff Schedule of the United States (2003)
Annotated for Statistical Reporting Purposes

GN 3(c)--3(d)(ii)(C)

(c) Products Eligible for Special Tariff Treatment.

(i) Programs under which special tariff treatment may be provided, and the corresponding symbols for such programs as they are indicated in the "Special" subcolumn, are as follows:

Generalized System of Preferences	A, A* or A+
Automotive Products Trade Act	B
Agreement on Trade in Civil Aircraft	C
North American Free Trade Agreement:	
Goods of Canada, under the terms of	
general note 12 to this schedule	CA
Goods of Mexico, under the terms of	
general note 12 to this schedule	MX
African Growth and Opportunity Act	D
Caribbean Basin Economic Recovery Act	E or E*
United States-Israel Free Trade Area	IL
Andean Trade Preference Act or	
Andean Trade Promotion and Drug Eradication Act	J, J* or J+
United States-Jordan Free Trade Area Implementation Act	JO
Agreement on Trade in Pharmaceutical Products	K
Uruguay Round Concessions on Intermediate	
Chemicals for Dyes	L
United States-Caribbean Basin Trade Partnership Act	R

(ii) Articles which are eligible for the special tariff treatment provided for in general notes 4 through 14 and which are subject to temporary modification under any provision of subchapters I, II and VII of chapter 99 shall be subject, for the period indicated in the "Effective Period" column in chapter 99, to rates of duty as follows:

(A) if a rate of duty for which the article may be eligible is set forth in the "Special" subcolumn in chapter 99 followed by one or more symbols described above, such rate shall apply in lieu of the rate followed by the corresponding symbol(s) set forth for such article in the "Special" subcolumn in chapters 1 to 98; or

(B) if "No change" appears in the "Special" subcolumn in chapter 99 and subdivision (c)(ii)(A) above does not apply, the rate of duty in the "General" subcolumn in chapter 99 or the applicable rate(s) of duty set forth in the "Special" subcolumn in chapters 1 to 98, whichever is lower, shall apply.

(iii) Unless the context requires otherwise, articles which are eligible for the special tariff treatment provided for in general notes 4 through 14 and which are subject to temporary modification under any provision of subchapters III or IV of chapter 99 shall be subject, for the period indicated in chapter 99, to the rates of duty in the "General" subcolumn in such chapter.

(iv) Whenever any rate of duty set forth in the "Special" subcolumn in chapters 1 to 98 is equal to or higher than, the corresponding rate of duty provided in the "General" subcolumn in such chapters, such rate of duty in the "Special" subcolumn shall be deleted; except that, if the rate of duty in the "Special" subcolumn is an intermediate stage in a series of staged rate reductions for that provision, such rate shall be treated as a suspended rate and shall be set forth in the "Special" subcolumn, followed by one or more symbols described above, and followed by an "s" in parentheses. If no rate of duty for which the article may be eligible is provided in the "Special" subcolumn for a particular provision in chapters 1 to 98, the rate of duty provided in the "General" subcolumn shall apply.

(d) Certain Motor Vehicles Manufactured in Foreign Trade Zones.

(i) Duty imposed. Notwithstanding any other provision of law, the duty imposed on a qualified article shall be the amount determined by multiplying the applicable foreign value content of such article by the applicable rate of duty for such article.

(ii) Qualified article. For purposes of this subdivision, the term "qualified article" means an article that is--

(A) classifiable under any of subheadings 8702.10 through 8704.90 of the Harmonized Tariff Schedule of the United States,

(B) produced or manufactured in a foreign trade zone before January 1, 1996,

(C) exported therefrom to a NAFTA country (as defined in section 2(4) of the North American Free Trade Agreement Implementation Act (19 U.S.C. 3301(4)), and

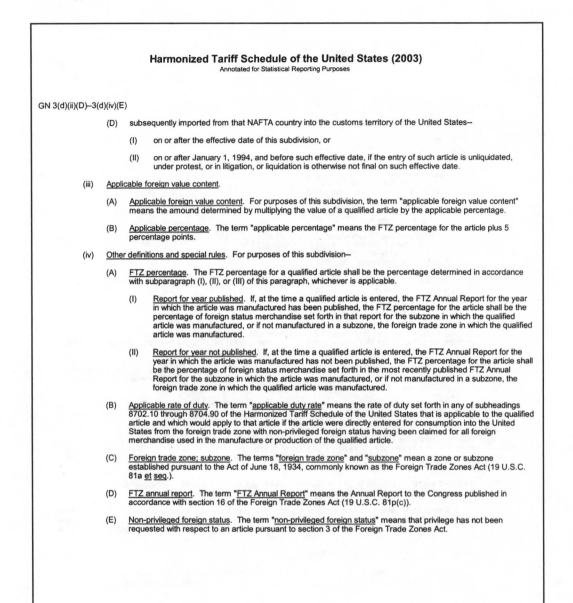

Harmonized Tariff Schedule of the United States (2003)
Annotated for Statistical Reporting Purposes

GN 3(d)(ii)(D)–3(d)(iv)(E)

  (D) subsequently imported from that NAFTA country into the customs territory of the United States--

    (I) on or after the effective date of this subdivision, or

    (II) on or after January 1, 1994, and before such effective date, if the entry of such article is unliquidated, under protest, or in litigation, or liquidation is otherwise not final on such effective date.

 (iii) Applicable foreign value content.

  (A) Applicable foreign value content. For purposes of this subdivision, the term "applicable foreign value content" means the amound determined by multiplying the value of a qualified article by the applicable percentage.

  (B) Applicable percentage. The term "applicable percentage" means the FTZ percentage for the article plus 5 percentage points.

 (iv) Other definitions and special rules. For purposes of this subdivision--

  (A) FTZ percentage. The FTZ percentage for a qualified article shall be the percentage determined in accordance with subparagraph (I), (II), or (III) of this paragraph, whichever is applicable.

    (I) Report for year published. If, at the time a qualified article is entered, the FTZ Annual Report for the year in which the article was manufactured has been published, the FTZ percentage for the article shall be the percentage of foreign status merchandise set forth in that report for the subzone in which the qualified article was manufactured, or if not manufactured in a subzone, the foreign trade zone in which the qualified article was manufactured.

    (II) Report for year not published. If, at the time a qualified article is entered, the FTZ Annual Report for the year in which the article was manufactured has not been published, the FTZ percentage for the article shall be the percentage of foreign status merchandise set forth in the most recently published FTZ Annual Report for the subzone in which the article was manufactured, or if not manufactured in a subzone, the foreign trade zone in which the qualified article was manufactured.

  (B) Applicable rate of duty. The term "applicable duty rate" means the rate of duty set forth in any of subheadings 8702.10 through 8704.90 of the Harmonized Tariff Schedule of the United States that is applicable to the qualified article and which would apply to that article if the article were directly entered for consumption into the United States from the foreign trade zone with non-privileged foreign status having been claimed for all foreign merchandise used in the manufacture or production of the qualified article.

  (C) Foreign trade zone; subzone. The terms "foreign trade zone" and "subzone" mean a zone or subzone established pursuant to the Act of June 18, 1934, commonly known as the Foreign Trade Zones Act (19 U.S.C. 81a et seq.).

  (D) FTZ annual report. The term "FTZ Annual Report" means the Annual Report to the Congress published in accordance with section 16 of the Foreign Trade Zones Act (19 U.S.C. 81p(c)).

  (E) Non-privileged foreign status. The term "non-privileged foreign status" means that privilege has not been requested with respect to an article pursuant to section 3 of the Foreign Trade Zones Act.

Harmonized Tariff Schedule of the United States (2003)
Annotated for Statistical Reporting Purposes

ALPHABETICAL INDEX

CHAPTER 89

SHIPS, BOATS AND FLOATING STRUCTURES

Note

1. A hull, an unfinished or incomplete vessel, assembled, unassembled or disassembled, or a complete vessel unassembled or dissassembled, is to be classified in heading 8906 if it does not have the essential character of a vessel of a particular kind.

Additional U.S. Note

1. Vessels if in use in international trade or commerce or if brought into the customs territory of the United States by nonresidents thereof for their own use in pleasure cruising shall be admitted without formal customs consumption entry or the payment of duty.

Harmonized Tariff Schedule of the United States (2003)
Annotated for Statistical Reporting Purposes

XVII
89-2

Heading/ Subheading	Stat. Suf- fix	Article Description	Unit of Quantity	Rates of Duty		
				1		2
				General	Special	
8901		Cruise ships, excursion boats, ferry boats, cargo ships, barges and similar vessels for the transport of persons or goods:				
8901.10.00	00	Cruise ships, excursion boats and similar vessels principally designed for the transport of persons; ferry boats of all kinds	No.	Free		Free
8901.20.00	00	Tankers	No.	Free		Free
8901.30.00	00	Refrigerated vessels, other than those of subheading 8901.20	No.	Free		Free
8901.90.00	00	Other vessels for the transport of goods and other vessels for the transport of both persons and goods ..	No.	Free		Free
8902.00.00	00	Fishing vessels; factory ships and other vessels for processing or preserving fishery products	No.	Free		Free
8903		Yachts and other vessels for pleasure or sports; row boats and canoes:				
8903.10.00		Inflatable	....	2.4%	Free (A,CA,E,IL,J, JO,MX)	25%
	15	Valued over $500: With attached rigid hull	No.			
	45	Other	No.			
	60	Other	No.			
		Other:				
8903.91.00		Sailboats, with or without auxiliary motor	....	1.5%	Free (A,CA,E,IL,J, JO,MX)	30%
	25	With auxiliary motor: Not exceeding 9.2 m in length	No.			
	35	Exceeding 9.2 m in length	No.			
	45	Other: Not exceeding 4 m in length	No.			
	60	Exceeding 4 but not exceeding 6.5 m in length	No.			
	75	Exceeding 6.5 m but not exceeding 9.2 m in length	No.			
	85	Exceeding 9.2 m in length	No.			
8903.92.00		Motorboats, other than outboard motorboats	....	1.5%	Free (A,CA,E,IL,J, JO,MX)	30%
	15	Inboard/outdrive: Not exceeding 6.5 m in length	No.			
	30	Exceeding 6.5 m in length: Cabin cruisers	No.			
	35	Other	No.			
	50	Other: Not exceeding 8 m in length	No.			
	65	Exceeding 8 m in length: Cabin cruisers	No.			
	70	Other	No.			

Harmonized Tariff Schedule of the United States (2003)
Annotated for Statistical Reporting Purposes

Heading/ Subheading	Stat. Suf-fix	Article Description	Unit of Quantity	Rates of Duty 1 General	Special	2
8903 (con.)		Yachts and other vessels for pleasure or sports; row boats and canoes (con.): Other (con.):				
8903.99		Other: Row boats and canoes which are not of a type designed to be principally used with motors or sails:				35%
8903.99.05	00	Canoes	No.	Free		
8903.99.15	00	Other	No.	2.7%	Free (A,CA,E,IL,J, JO,MX)	45%
8903.99.20		Outboard motorboats		1%	Free (A,CA,E,IL,J, JO,MX)	30%
		With hulls of metal:				
	15	Not exceeding 5 m in length	No.			
	30	Exceeding 5 m in length	No.			
		With hulls of reinforced plastics:				
	45	Not exceeding 5 m in length	No.			
	60	Exceeding 5 m in length	No.			
	75	Other	No.			
8903.99.90	00	Other	No.	1%	Free (A,CA,E,IL,J, JO,MX)	30%
8904.00.00	00	Tugs and pusher craft	No.	Free		Free
8905		Light-vessels, fire-floats, dredgers, floating cranes, and other vessels the navigability of which is subsidiary to their main function; floating docks; floating or submersible drilling or production platforms:				Free
8905.10.00	00	Dredgers	No.	Free		Free
8905.20.00	00	Floating or submersible drilling or production platforms	t No.	Free		Free
8905.90		Other:				35%
8905.90.10	00	Floating docks	t No.	Free		
8905.90.50	00	Other	No.	Free		Free
8906		Other vessels, including warships and lifeboats other than row boats:				
8906.10.00	00	Warships	No.	Free		Free
8906.90.00		Other		Free		Free
	10	Hulls	t No.			
	90	Other	X			
8907		Other floating structures (for example, rafts, tanks, cofferdams, landing-stages, buoys and beacons):				
8907.10.00	00	Inflatable rafts	No.	Free		45%
8907.90.00		Other		Free		45%
	30	Buoys	X			
	60	Tanks	X			
	90	Other	X			
8908.00.00	00	Vessels and other floating structures for breaking up (scrapping)	t	Free		Free

ATA Carnet

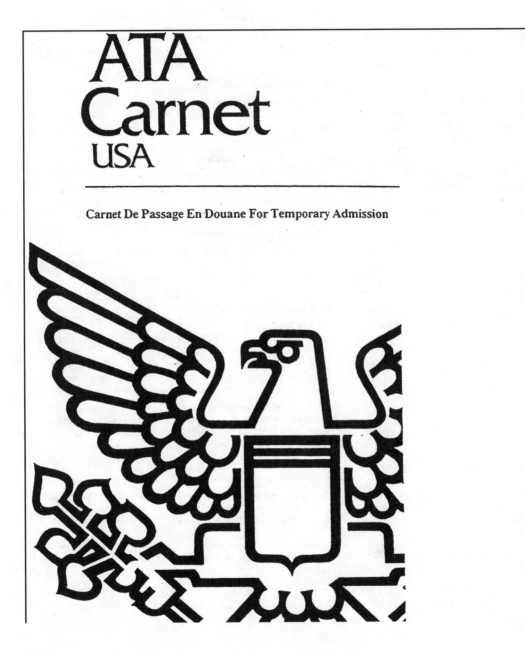

ATA Carnet

Holder	Customs Inspector
Front Green Cover	
Holder must sign in the lower right hand box, on the line between the two "X's, marked "Signature of Holder."	**Customs and Border Protection** should complete and stamp the lower left hand box, "Certificate by Customs Authorities."
Yellow Exportation Certificate	
On the voucher, complete sections D–F, located on the left hand column, as well as the lower right corner, below the shaded box.	**Customs and Border Protection** should complete and stamp the counterfoil and the "For Customs Use Only" section of the voucher. Generally, USCS does **not** remove the voucher.
White Importation Certificate	
On the voucher, the Holder must complete sections D–F, located on the left hand column, as well as the lower right corner, below the shaded box.	**Foreign Customs** should complete and stamp the counterfoil and the "For Customs Use Only," secton of the voucher. The customs inspector should then remove the voucher. **Note:** Be sure to comply with "Final Date for Re-exportation" on the counterfoil.
White Re-Exportation Certificate	
On the voucher, the Holder must complete sections D–F, located on the left hand column, as well as the lower right corner, below the shaded box.	**Foreign Customs** should complete and stamp the counterfoil and the "For Customs Use Only," section of the voucher. The customs inspector should then remove the voucher.
Blue Transit Certificates	
Holders must complete sections D–F, located on the left hand column, as well as the lower right corner, below the shaded box.	**At the time of Entry** **Foreign Customs** will complete and stamp the sections of the counterfoil and voucher entitled, "Clearance for Transit," indicating which goods have entered, the port to which the goods are being dispatched, final date that the goods must exit that port. The customs inspector will then remove the voucher. **At the time of Departure** **Foreign Customs** at the port of discharge will complete and stamp the sections of both the counterfoil and voucher entitled, "Certificate of Discharge." The customs inspector will then remove the second voucher.
Yellow Re-Importation Certificate	
On the voucher, the Holder must complete sections D–F, as well as the lower right corner below the shaded box.	**Customs and Border Protection** will complete the counterfoil and the section of the voucher entitled "For Customs Use Only." The customs inspector should then remove the voucher.

Complete details on the handling of a Carnet are located on the inside of the blue jacket of the ATA Carnet.

For more information contact:
USCIB ATA Carnet Customer Service Department
212-354-4480 or atacarnet@uscib.org

INTERNATIONAL GUARANTEE CHAIN -------------- -------------- INTERNATIONAL GUARANTEE CHAIN
CHAINE DE GARANTIE INTERNATIONALE *CHAINE DE GARANTIE INTERNATIONALE*

GENERAL LIST / *LISTE GENERALE*
(May be used for Continuation Sheets / *Feuille Supplementaire*)

X X

Signature of Holder / *Signature du titulaire*

....
Signature of authorized official and stamp of the Issuing Association /
Signature du delegué et timbre de L'association emettrice

| VOUCHER No. .... | CONTINUATION SHEET No. .... | A.T.A. Carnet No. |
| *VOLET DE No.* | *FEUILLE SUPPLEMENTAIRE No.* | *Carnet A.T.A. No.* |

Item No./ No. d'ordre	Trade description of goods and marks and numbers, if any/ *Désignation commerciale des marchandises et, le cas échéant, marques et numéros*	Number of Pieces/ Nombre de Pièces	Weight or Volume/ *Poids ou Volume*	**Country of origin/ *Value/ Valeur*	For Customs Use/ Pays d'origine	Réservé à la douane
1	2	3	4	5	6	7
	TOTAL CARRIED OVER / *REPORT*					

General List includes ———— *(number)* "Continuation Sheets".

TOTAL or CARRIED OVER / *TOTAL ou A REPORTER*

*Commercial value in country of issue and in the currency, unless stated differently. / *Valeur commerciale dans le pays d'émission et dans sa monnaie sauf indication contraire.*
**Show country of origin if different from country of issue of theCarnet, using ISO country codes. / *Indiquer le pays d'origine s'il est différent du pays d'émission du Carnet en utilisant le code international des pays ISO.*
6/99

General List Instructions

The General List is an itemized list of *all* the items covered by the Carnet. Careful completion of this form is essential to ensure entry and exit from foreign countries with a minimum of time and trouble.

Each item must be accurately described and accompanied by a stated value. Be sure to include serial numbers whenever appropriate. If your General List exceeds one page then use Continuation Sheets. (Continuation Sheets may be obtained by photocopying a blank General List.)

Make sure to put the total number of Continuation Sheets in the space provided at the bottom of the first General List page. Individuals applying for the Carnet, or applying on behalf of a corporation must sign the original General List page and all Continuation Sheets in the space marked Holder's Signature. *Only typed lists will be accepted*! Do not list such consumable items as bottle fluids, food, paper goods, pamphlets, or giveaways.

Carnets cannot be issued for consumables.

To Complete the General List

Column 1—Item No.: Each item of the shipment must be given an item number. Items answering to the same description may be grouped together.

Column 2—Trade Description of Goods: This column must contain a complete and specific description of each line item of merchandise, including the manufacturer's name, serial number, and/or model number.

Column 3—Number of Pieces: Indicate the quantity of each particular item.

Column 4—Weight or Volume: This column should include the total weight for each item number. (Example: if an item consists of three pieces each weighing five pounds, then a total weight of fifteen pounds be shown.) Make sure to indicate the correct unit of measure, e.g., pounds, ounces, kilograms.

Column 5—Value: Show total cost for each line item. Example: Four pieces with a value of $400 each should be listed at a total value of $1,600. Be sure to use the insured value of the goods.)

Column 6—Country of Origin: Country in which the goods were *originally* manufactured.

Note: In order to close the General List, columns 3 and 5 *must* be totaled.

Temporary Importation and the Benefits of an ATA Carnet

All countries have procedures allowing for the temporary importation of goods across their borders. Such importations are generally valid for less than 12 months.

Importers may choose from three options when considering a temporary importation: (1) duty drawback, (2) temporary importation under bond (TIB), and (3) ATA Carnet.

1. Duty drawback is the process by which an importer registers the goods at the time of entry, and deposits the applicable duties and taxes. In Europe,

duty and taxes range from 20–30 percent of the value of the goods. At the time of departure, the exporter presents the goods and appropriate paperwork to the customs inspector. Exporters can expect to receive a full refund of the duties and taxes posted at some future point. (For Europe, refunds are generally made two to six months after departure.)

2. To use a TIB, importers are required to secure the TIB from a customhouse broker at the time of entry into the foreign country. The purchase of a TIB is required for each country visited on every trip. Fees for TIBS vary widely.

3. The ATA Carnet was created by international convention thirty years ago. ATA Carnets:

   - May be used for **unlimited exits** from and entries into the U.S. and foreign countries. (Carnet are valid for one year.)

   - Are **accepted in** over 50 countries and territories.

   - **Eliminate** value-added taxes (VAT), duties, and the posting of security normally required at the time of importation.

   - **Simplify** customs procedures. Carnets allow a temporary exporter to use a single document for all customs transactions, make arrangements in advance and at a predetermined cost.

   - **Facilitate** reentry into the United States by eliminating the need to register goods with U.S. Customs at the time of departure.

Merchandise Covered by ATA Carnets

Virtually all goods, including commercial samples, professional equipment, and goods for tradeshows and exhibitions.

Ordinary goods such as computers, tools, cameras and video equipment, industrial machinery, automobiles, gems and jewelry, and wearing apparel. **Extraordinary items,** for example, Van Gogh Self-portrait, Ringling Brothers tigers, Cessna jets, Paul McCartney's band instruments, World Cup class yachts, satellites, human skulls, and the New York Philharmonic.

Carnets do not cover consumable goods (food and agriculture products), disposable items, or postal traffic.

Carnet Countries

ATA Carnets are accepted in:

Algeria	Iceland	Norway
Andorra	India	Pakistan
Antarctica	Ireland	Poland
Aruba	Isle of Man	Portugal
Australia	Israel	Puerto Rico
Austria	Italy	Reunion Is.
Balearic Is.	Ivory Coast	Romania
Belarus	Japan	Russia
Belgium	Jersey	Seychelles
Botswana	Korea	Senegal
Bosnia-	Latvia	Serbia
Herzegovina$_2$	Lebanon	Singapore
Bulgaria	Lesotho	Slovakia
Canada	Liechtenstein	Slovenia
Canary Is.	Lithuania	South Africa
Ceuta	Luxembourg	Spain
Chile	Macao	Sri Lanka
China	Macedonia	St. Barthelemy
Corsica	Malaysia	St. Martin (French side)
Croatia	Malta	St. Pierre
Curacao	Martinique	Swaziland
Cyprus	Mauritius	Sweden
Czech Rep.	Mayotte	Switzerland
Denmark	Melilla	Tahiti
Estonia	Mexico$_2$	Taiwan*
Finland	Miquelon	Tasmania
France	Moldova	Thailand
French Guiana	Monaco	Tunisia
Germany	Mongolia	Turkey
Gibraltar	Montenegro	Ukraine
Greece	Morocco	United Arab Emirates
Guadeloupe	Namibia	United Kingdom
Guernsey	Netherlands	United States
Hong Kong	New Caledonia	Wallis & Futuna
Hungary	New Zealand	Members of the European Union

*TECRO/AIT Carnets are accepted for goods traveling between Taiwan and the U.S. only. Countries are added to the ATA system periodically. Call to determine if the country to which you are traveling accepts Carnets.

Fees and Processing Time

There are **three basic components to the Carnet application** process:

1. Preparation of the *General List*
2. Completion of the *Carnet application*
3. Provision of a *security deposit*

The normal processing time for a Carnet is five working days. Basic processing fees ($120–$250) are determined by the value of the shipment.

Expedited service ($35–$150). Payment can be made in the form of a check or money order.

For more information contact:

USCIB ATA Carnet Customer Service Department
212-354-4480 or atacarnet@uscib.org

All Contents 1996–1998 U.S. Council for International Business. All Rights Reserved. (With permission from USCIB/NYC.)

ATA Carnet Service Bureaus

The first point of contact should be the New York office.

ATA Carnet Headquarters and Service Bureau:
1212 Avenue of the Americas
New York, NY 10036
Tel: (212) 354-4480
Fax: (212) 944-0012

Regional Service Bureaus:
New England
185 Devonshire Street, Suite 800
Boston, MA 02110
Tel: (800) 233-3620/(617) 728-9199
Fax: (617) 728-9830

Mid-Atlantic
61 Broadway, Suite 2700 Executive Plaza I, Suite 105
New York, NY 10006 11350 McCormick Road
Tel: (888) 571-1675/(212) 747-1800 Hunt Valley, MD 21031
Fax: (212) 747-1948 Tel: (800) 422-9944/(410) 771-6100
Fax: (410) 771-6104

Southeast
7205 N.W. 19th Street, Suite 104
Miami, FL 33126
Tel: (800) 468-5467/(305) 592-6929
Fax: (305) 592-9537

Mid-West
1501 East Woodfield Road, 118 Barrington Commons Plaza,
Suite 302N Suite 236
Schaumburg, IL 60173 Barrington, IL 60010
Tel: (800) 762-6653/(847) 969-8211 Tel: (800) ATA-2900/(847) 381-1558
Fax: (847) 969-8200 Fax: (847) 381-3857

Southwest
5112 Morningside Drive
Houston, TX 77005
Tel: (800) 227-6387
Fax: (281) 847-0700

Northern California
425 California Street, Suite 700
San Francisco, CA 94104
Tel: (800) 255-4994/(415) 765-6636
Fax: (415) 391-2716

Southern California
100 West Broadway, Suite 100
Long Beach, CA 90802
Tel: (800) 421-9324/(562) 628-9306
Fax: (562) 590-8523

For more information contact:
USCIB ATA Carnet Customer Service Department
(212) 354-4480 or atacarnet@uscib.org

Options in Export Finance

Exporters control the options for their payment. Often, the option chosen will determine the exporter's competitiveness.

The terms of sale in an export transaction are arranged between the buyer and the seller prior to shipment. Typically, the actual collection of payments internationally is accomplished through the facilities of a commercial bank. The payment method, or financial instrument used, is dependent on such factors as the credit standing of the buyer (importer), any existing exchange restrictions in the buyer's country, competitive pressure that the seller faces, and the political and economic condition of the country of import.

Most merchandise sales by U.S. exporters to overseas buyers are made on the basis of one of the following methods of payment:

1. Cash in advance
2. Open account
3. Documentary collection
4. Letter of credit

A. Open Account

Open account sales in international trade may be defined as one in which no financial institutions act as intermediaries between buyer and seller.

This mode of payment is usually dictated by custom and competitive terms. The seller must be confident of the buyer's creditworthiness and ability to pay promptly.

In an open account transaction, the seller is sending the buyer goods without any negotiable instrument evidencing the obligation and is dependent solely upon the buyer to make payment. The advantages of selling on an open account basis are simplicity and reduced banking charges.

The seller has little legal recourse in cases of dishonored transactions and typically has a harder time getting dollar exchange from a defaulted buyer. For these reasons, this sales method is used primarily when sellers are dealing with buyers they know well, to established markets, and for sales to foreign branches or subsidiaries.

B. Documentary Collection

Export collections require that the seller forward documents and instructions to his bank which will pass them to a foreign bank for collection. Various banks provide a direct collection service to their customers. Under this method, the exporter or his or her forwarder sends collection instructions directly to the buyer's bank and a copy to their bank for follow-up.

A collection does not eliminate the market risk associated with the buyer (failure of buyer to take title of material purchased; not uncommon in a period of falling market prices) or the country risk associated with the buyer's country. When asked for payment by a bank, the buyer could refuse. The bank or banks involved in the collection assumes no liability for payment requested on a collection basis. A sight draft ensures that documents do not pass to the buyer until payment is made. Neither a time draft nor a clean draft provides this protection.

C. Letter of Credit

Except for cash in advance, the letter of credit affords the seller the highest degree of protection. A letter of credit is issued by the opening bank assuring that certain payments will be made under specified conditions.

Normally, letter of credit transactions involve two banks: one in the exporter's country and one in the buyer's.

An irrevocable letter of credit replaces the commercial risk associated with the Buyer with that of the bank issuing the letter of credit. Hence, the seller is no longer relying on the buyer's promise to pay; he or she is relying on the promise and the ability to pay of a bank located in a foreign country. If the seller wishes to reduce the risk of nonpayment further, he or she can request that the bank confirm the letter of credit. From the seller's viewpoint, this eliminates the foreign country risk and replaces the commercial risk of the buyer's bank with that of the confirming bank. Payment against a confirmed letter of credit is assured by the confirming bank when documents in good order are submitted.

It is crucial to understand that a letter of credit is not an unconditional guarantee of payment; rather, payment will be made only after the terms of the letter of credit have been precisely fulfilled. Anyone using collections or letters of credit have been precisely fulfilled. Anyone using collections or letters of credit should very carefully read the segment on documents, "How a Letter of Credit Works" because discrepancies that can delay payment often arise upon inspection of the documents.

Foreign trade normally presents the following uncertainties:

A. Country Risk

Country risk is the risk associated with the buyer's country. This covers the country's financial condition, stability of currency, social and political climate, and availability of foreign exchange.

B. Commercial Risk

Commercial risk is the risk associated with the individual or institution responsible for payment. Because the purchase is in another country, the seller generally not only has less reliable information regarding his financial condition and integrity, but also typically has few avenues of redress should the buyer fail to pay or otherwise violate the agreed upon terms of sale.

The existence of greater commercial and country risk explains why few international transactions are made on an open account or consignment basis.

Completing the Export Transaction

The initial step in a foreign sales transaction may be taken by the buyer or the seller. A buyer may approach the seller with a request for a quotation, or he may dispatch an offer to buy at stipulated prices and on certain terms and conditions, or the seller may extend his quotation to potential buyers on his own initiative. Regardless of the approach and the formality of such exchanges, once an offer has been accepted by the other party, a contract, known as a sales contract, has been created.

Given the complexities that arise in a foreign transaction where language, customs, and practices may differ, the importance of the sales contract is readily apparent. Hence, companies engaged in foreign trade should have a sales contract form fitted to their basic requirements encompassing all the necessary details to assure a satisfactory conclusion to the transaction. Following is a list of some of the more important items that should be included in such a form:

Merchandise. A complete description specifying standards of grade or quality, catalog numbers or other descriptive terms.

Quantity. The exact number in units or specific weight, measurement or volume. Care should be taken as to different weight and measurement systems.

Price. Unit price specifying the currency in which the unit price is expressed.

Terms of Sale (INCO). Normally are expressed as FOB, CIF, etc., with named points or ports to which they apply. These terms indicate the duties and responsibilities of both buyer and seller with respect to point of delivery, costs, and risks to be assumed by each.

Packing. The type of packing is usually determined by the nature of the merchandise, conditions at sea, at the ports, and in transit in the interior as well as by customs regulations.

Marking. Usually are dictated by the customs regulations of the importing country and the requirements of the buyer.

Insurance. The extent of coverage required and who is to provide it should be stated.

Shipping Instructions. Method of transportation and consignment, documents required, and time of shipment should be explicit.

Method of Payment. Whether payment will be effected against cash in advance, on open account, on a collection basis, against a letter of credit, etc.

This list should not be considered complete, but rather used as a guide that can be adapted to fit the needs of individual transactions.

Letters of Credit

For new trading entities, a letter of credit is often an excellent means to arrange payment. It compromises the exposures on both sides of the trade.

A letter of credit is used to reduce the risk in international trade. It is a contract in letter form, written by a bank (issuing bank) on behalf of the buyer (applicant). The issuing bank then forwards the letter of credit, which is transmitted through a bank. If you are the exporter, you must have your foreign buyer specify your bank to be the advising bank. Similarly, if you want to have the letter of credit confirmed, you should have your buyer include the request for confirmation on the application for the letter of credit.

Because the advising bank has no contact with the buyer but takes the instructions from the issuing bank, it is, therefore, important that the seller (beneficiary) examine the letter of credit carefully to ensure that it is consistent with the agreed upon terms of sale and that the seller can comply with its terms and conditions. If changes are needed, the seller should contact the buyer immediately to request an amendment to the letter of credit. A credit cannot be amended without the agreement of both parties.

The documents required under letters of credit may vary, but most often call for the presentation of a draft, commercial invoices, packing lists, and bills of lading. It is the responsibility of the bank making payments to examine those documents with care to be certain that they appear on their face to comply with the terms and conditions of the credit. It must be understood that in documentary credit operations all parties concerned deal in documents and not in goods. Because credits advised by the bank are subject to the Uniform Customs and Practice for Documentary Credit, its provisions will be applied to documents presented under such credits in determining whether payment will be made.

It is important to remember that all terms and conditions should be consistent with the sales contracts, since an irrevocable letter of credit cannot be modified or canceled without the consent of all parties concerned.

If a situation arises where a letter of credit has to be amended, the buyer submits a written request, whereupon the credit may be amended. Once the amendment is accepted by the seller, the amendment will become an integral part of the credit.

A letter of credit may be payable at sight against presentation of documents in accordance with the credit or at a future date.

Letters of credit may be issued in U.S. dollars or foreign currency. The credit may also be transmitted by full text teletransmission, short cable/telex, and airmail or courier.

A Review of the Standard Incoterms 2010

The International Chamber of Commerce's *Incoterms 2010* includes eleven trade terms that specify the buyer's and seller's responsibilities, and transfer of risks and costs when those terms are made part of the international transaction.

Ex Works: EXW (insert named place of delivery) Incoterms 2010: Any mode of transport; seller makes goods available to buyer at seller's premises or other location, not cleared for export and not loaded on any collecting vehicle. The buyer bears all risks and costs involved in taking the goods from the seller's premises and thereafter.

Free Carrier: FCA (insert named place of delivery) Incoterms 2010: Any mode transport; seller delivers goods, cleared for export, to the carrier named by the buyer at the specified place. If delivery occurs at the seller's premises, the seller is responsible for loading. If delivery occurs elsewhere, the seller must load the conveyance but is not responsible for unloading. The seller is responsible to clear the goods for export.

Free Alongside Ship: FAS (insert named port of shipment) Incoterms 2010: Sea and inland waterway only; seller delivers when the goods are placedalongside the vessel at the named port of shipment. The seller also clears the goods for export.

Free on Board: FOB (insert named port of shipment) Incoterms 2010: Sea and inland waterway only; seller delivers when the goods are loaded on board the vessel at the named port. The seller clears the goods for export.

Cost and Freight: CFR (insert named port of destination) Incoterms 2010: Sea and inland waterway only; seller delivers when the goods are loaded on board the vessel. The seller pays for bringing the goods to the foreign port and clears the goods for export, however the risk passes at the point of delivery to the carrier.

Cost, Insurance, and Freight: CIF (insert named port of destination) Incoterms 2010: Sea and inland waterway only; seller delivers when the goods are loaded on board the vessel. The seller pays CFR for bringing the goods to the foreign port, obtains insurance against the buyer's risk of loss or damage, and clears the goods for export, however the risk passes at the point of delivery to the carrier.

Carriage and Insurance Paid To: CIP (insert name place of destination) Incoterms 2010: Any mode of transport; seller delivers the goods to the carrier at an agreed place and it also pays the cost of bringing the goods to the named destination. The seller also obtains insurance against the buyer's risk of loss or damage during carriage and clears the goods for export. The risk passes at the point of delivery to the carrier.

Carriage Paid To: CPT (insert named place of destination) Incoterms 2010: Any mode of transport; seller delivers goods to carrier at an agreed place and pays costs of bringing goods to the named destination. The seller also clears the goods for export. The risk passes at the point of delivery to the carrier.

Delivered at Terminal: DAT (insert named terminal at port or place of destination) Incoterms 2010: Any mode of transport; seller delivers the goods once unloaded from the arriving means of transport and placed at the disposal of the buyer at a named terminal at the named port or place of destination. The seller clears the goods for export.

Delivered at Place: DAP (insert named place of destination) Incoterms 2010: Any mode of transport; seller delivers when the goods are placed a the disposal of the buyer on the arriving means of transport ready for unloading at the named place of destination. The seller clears the goods for export.

Delivered Duty Paid: DDP (insert named place of destination) Incoterms 2010: Any mode of transport; seller delivers goods to the buyer, cleared for import (including import license, duties, and taxes) but not unloaded from the means of transport.

Types of Letters of Credit

Documentary Credits

Irrevocable Letter of Credit. One in which the issuing bank irrevocably undertakes to pay or accept drafts presented with documents in compliance with the credit terms. Can only be modified/canceled with the agreement of all parties concerned. Virtually all import credits are issued irrevocably by the bank.

Irrevocable Unconfirmed Letter of Credit. The same as an irrevocable letter of credit, except it is being advised through another bank that does not add any obligation of its own. Most import credits are advised by foreign banks on an unconfirmed basis.

Irrevocable Confirmed Letter of Credit. A credit that adds the obligation of the second (confirming) bank to the irrevocable undertaking of the first (issuing) bank. The beneficiary has protection to two banks, however, protection is only as good as the banks giving it.

Revocable Letter of Credit. Contains the undertaking of no one and can be revoked anytime prior to payment being effected. Rarely issued.

Red Clause Credit. A special notation that the beneficiary may draw advances up to a stipulated amount to purchase and pay for the merchandise before shipping against presentation of "Undertaking to Ship" or of a similar document. When issuing a red clause credit, the issuing bank, on behalf of applicant, undertakes to repay the foreign bank for advances made even if shipment did not take place.

Revolving Credit. Allows the beneficiary to make multiple shipments and draw a specific amount of money on a specified periodic basis. The amount drawn becomes available to the beneficiary as the shipments and drawings are made and continues up to the expiration of the letter of credit.

Transferable Letter of Credit. One that expressly authorizes transfers to be made to other parties by a bank as directed by the beneficiary. The transfer credit must contain the identical conditions as the original letter of credit except that the amount transferred may be less and the dates indicated may be earlier.

Back to Back Letter of Credit Arrangement. One in which a beneficiary under an original confirmed letter of credit utilizes this letter of credit issued in his or her favor as collateral to open another letter of credit in favor of a supplier. A back to back letter of credit must contain the same conditions, merchandise, and documents as the original letter of credit with the exception of the invoice, unit prices, amount of drawing and shipping, and validity dates that must be prior to the dates stipulated in the original letter of credit.

Time or Usance Credit. Allows payment at a future specified time.

Stand by Letter of Credit. Does not involve the direct purchase of merchandise or the presentation of title documents. Rather, it is similar to performance or bid bonds. The bank's obligation to pay should arise only upon the presentation of a draft or other documents as specified in the letter of credit, and the bank must not be called upon to determine questions of fact or law at issue between the applicant and the beneficiary. The applicant for a standby letter of credit must trust the beneficiary. If the beneficiary presents documents in accordance with the terms of the standby credit, the bank must pay irrespective of any extenuating circumstances brought to its attention. The applicant is legally bound to reimburse the bank. Standby letters of credit are versatile instruments and can be used for the following:

- Payments for merchandise shipped on open account
- Bid and performance bonds
- Advance payment guarantees
- Other financial obligations

Assignments Under Letters of Credit. The beneficiary of a letter of credit may, at his or her discretion, assign the proceeds of a letter of credit to another party. An assignment of a credit should not be construed as a transfer of the instrument. By an assignment, the beneficiary does not transfer the credit, but only directs the bank involved in the payment or negotiation of documents to pay the assignee a certain portion of the beneficiary's proceeds. An assignment of proceeds may be made against any letter of credit; it need not be designated as "transferable." The assignment of proceeds has no monetary value until the proceeds come into existence. In other words, receipt of an assignment does not guarantee payment; it ensures payment only if the beneficiary presents the documents against the credit, and the credit terms are satisfied. For the assignee to receive payment directly from the bank, the assignment of proceeds must be made directly through the bank.

Letter of Credit Checklist

On receipt of the letters of credit, the beneficiary should check the following:

1. Name and address of beneficiary and applicant. All documents presented under the credit must show names and addresses consistent with those in the credit.
2. The type of credit and its terms and conditions conform to the sales contract or purchase order, if not, request amendment.
3. All conditions are acceptable.
4. The documents can be obtained in the form stated.
5. The description of the merchandise or commodity and any unit price conforms with the sales contract.
6. The amount of the credit is sufficient to cover all costs permitted by the terms of the contract.
7. The shipping and expiration dates and the period of time allowed for presentation of the shipping documents following their date of issuance and making presentation of the documents to the bank for payment, acceptance, or negotiation.

8. The points of shipment and destination are as agreed.
9. The provision for insurance is in accordance with the terms of the sale.
10. Country in which credit is payable.
11. The credit is subject to Uniform Customs and Practice for Documentary Credits, International Chamber of Commerce, Paris, France, that are in effect on the issue date.

Parties to Commercial Credits

1. *Direct Parties*
   The Buyer—Bank Customer/Applicant/Importer

   - Applies for letter of credit from bank.

   - Creditworthiness must be satisfactory to bank.

   The Beneficiary—Party to Be Paid/Seller/Exporter/Shipper

   - Party to whom letter of credit is issued/addressed.

   - Party who arranges compliance with terms and presentation of documents to the paying bank.

   Issuing Bank

   - Buyer's bank that issues the letter of credit to the beneficiary.

   - Examines documents to insure conformity to letter of credit.

   - Arranges for financing of transactions, if requested.

   - Releases documents to buyer and charges his or her account.

   Advising Bank

   - Bank that advises the beneficiary of the opening of the credit. May be the issuing bank, negotiating bank, or a third bank.

   Confirming Bank

   - The advising bank, which adds its obligation to that of the issuing bank.

   Negotiating Bank

   - Bank, usually unnamed in credit, that agrees to purchase draft of beneficiary.

   - Pays beneficiary immediately, usually with recourse.

2. *Indirect Parties*
   Steamship Company

   - Receives merchandise from exporter/shipper/forwarder and arranges for transport of merchandise.

   - Issues bills of lading that serve as the title document, receipt of goods, contract between shipper and steamship company.

Air Carrier

- Receives merchandise from exporter/shipper/forwarder and arranges for transport of merchandise.

- Issues airway bill that serves as the receipt of goods and the contract between shipper and carrier.

Freight Forwarder

- Acts as the agent for exporter.

- Assists exporter to expedite shipments.

- Prepares necessary documents and makes other arrangements for the movement of merchandise.

Customs Broker

- Acts as the agent for the importer.

- Receives shipping documentation from the bank or importer.

- Clears merchandise upon arrival.

- Arranges for delivery of merchandise to the importer.

Insurance Company

- Insures shipment for value requested.

- Issues policy/certificate covering risks requested.

- Settles claims, if any.

Comparison Method of Export Payment Options

Method	Risk to Exporter	Goods Available to Buyer	Usual Time of Payment	Risk to Importer
Cash in advance	None	After payment	Before shipment	Maximum, relies on exporter to ship goods
Letter of credit: Confirmed Unconfirmed	Virtually none	After payment	When documents are available at shipment	Assured of quantity and other particulars
Documentary collection sight draft documents against acceptance	If draft unpaid, goods must be returned or disposed of	After payment	On presentation of draft to importer	Assured of quantity and quality
Documentary collection time draft documents against acceptance	Relies on importer to pay draft if unpaid goods must be returned or disposed of	Before payment	On maturity of draft	Minimal, can check shipment for quantity and quality before payment
Consignment	Substantial risk	Before payment exporter retains title until goods are sold or used	After use	None
Open	Relies on importer to pay account as agreed. Complete risk	Before payment	As agreed	None

Examples of Volume Weight vs. Gross Weight

Transportation carriers will charge a shipper for the gross weight or the volume weight, whichever is greater. The formula for international volume calculations is length $\times$ width $\times$ height (divided by) 166. For the purpose of the following examples, assume the air freight cost is $1.50 per pound.

Example # 1 (cargo that is voluminous)
    One (1) skid @ 660 pounds gross weight
    Dimensions in inches: l 48 $\times$ w 48 $\times$ h 63
    Calculation: 48 $\times$ 48 $\times$ 63 divided by 166 = 874 pounds
    ***Volume weight: 874 pounds
    ***Chargeable weight: 874 pounds
    874 pounds $\times$ 1.50 per pound = $1,311 = air freight
Example # 2 (cargo that is not voluminous)
    One (1) skid @ 660 pounds gross weight
    Dimensions in inches: l 48 $\times$ w 48 $\times$ h 35
    Calculation: 48 $\times$ 48 $\times$ 35 divided by 166 = 486
    ***Volume weight: 486 pounds
    ***Chargeable weight: 660 pounds
    660 pounds $\times$ 1.50 per pound = $990 = air freight
Differences in freight
    Example #1: $1,311
    Example #2: $990
    Difference in freight charges: $321
    (Difference is only because of change in dimensions.)

Resources for Export Credit Insurance

Export-Import Bank of the United States (U.S. Ex-Im Bank)
811 Vermont Avenue NW
Washington DC 20571 USA
Tel: (+1) 202-565-3946
Fax: (+1) 202-565-3380
Internet: http://www.exim.gov
Ownership structure: 100 percent sovereign.

Overview: Provides medium- and long-term guarantees and loans and short- and medium-term insurance.

General Description: The Export-Import Bank of the United States (U.S. Ex-Im Bank) provides guarantees, insurance, and loans. The main programs offered are short-term supplier credit and medium- and long-term buyer credit. Policies cover up to 100 percent for political and commercial risks. The CIRR is offered for loans. Overseas investment insurance is not offered. The U.S. Ex-Im Bank carries the full faith and credit of the U.S. Government. The bank is bound by OECD consensus and has a dedicated project finance department. Commercial banks provide a source for lending. The bank works with many institutions, including commercial banks, insurance brokers, and state and local governments and organizations.

Overseas Private Investment Corporation (OPIC)
1100 New York Avenue NW
Washington, DC 20527 USA
Tel: (+1) 202-336-8484
Fax: (+1) 202-218-0235
Contact for guarantee information: Alfredo M. Rodriguez. Fax: (+1) 202-408-9866.
Contact for insurance information: Julie Martin. Tel: (+1) 202-336-8586;
Fax: (+1) 202-408-5142.
Ownership structure: 100 percent sovereign.

Overview: Provides medium- and long-term guarantees, insurance, and finance to support U.S. investment in emerging markets.

General Description: The Overseas Private Investment Corporation (OPIC) is a self-sustaining federal agency that operates at no net cost to taxpayers. The agency sells investment services to U.S. businesses of all sizes. OPIC-backed projects strengthen the U.S. economy by promoting investment by American companies and American-made exports that support and create American jobs. OPIC only supports projects that take steps to protect the local environment and respect workers rights. OPIC provides insurance and guarantees. The agency is not bound by OECD consensus, except in certain instances when it insures loans tied to the U.S. government. OPIC carries the full faith and credit of the government and has a dedicated project finance department.

American International Group, Inc. (AIG)
70 Pine Street
New York, NY 10270 USA
Tel: (+1) 212-770-7261
Fax: (+1) 212-269-3387
Contact for trade credit: Des DeSwart (New York); Ed Brittenham (AIG Europe-London).
Contact for political risk: John Hegeman (New York); Julian Edwards (AIG Europe-London).
Ownership structure: 100 percent private.

Overview: Provides short-term export credit and political risk insurance.

General Description: American International Group, Inc. (AIG) members underwrite property, casualty, marine, life, and financial services insurance in approximately 130 countries and jurisdictions and are involved in a range of financial services businesses. AIG is rated AAA by Standard & Poor's and AAA by Moody's. AIG Global Trade and Political Risk Insurance comprises the trade credit division and the political and commercial risks. AIG is not bound by the OECD consensus. No interest support is offered. AIG is a member of the Berne Union.

C N A Credit Insurance (C N A)
1100 Cornwall Road
PO Box 905
Monmouth Junction, NJ 08852 USA
Tel: (+1) 732-398-4463
Fax: (+1) 732-398-5106
Contact: Jim Higgins.
Internet: http://www.CAN-CREDIT.com
E-mail: James.Higgins@CAN.com
Ownership structure: 100 percent private.

Overview: Provides short-term insurance.

General Description: C N A Credit is a division of C N A, one of the largest insurance groups in the United States. C N A is the second largest commercial insurer in the United States, providing a variety of insurance products to business. Policies cover up to 90 percent for political and commercial risks. C N A is not bound by OECD consensus, does not carry the full faith and credit of the government, and does not have a project finance department.

ISLAND CAPITAL LTD.
(F/K/A EXPORTERS INSURANCE COMPANY, LTD.)
6th Floor, Cumberland House
1 Victoria Street
P.O. Box HM 3033

Hamilton HM 11, Bermuda
Telephone: 441-292-7505
Facsimile: 441-292-1243
Website: http://www.Isle-Capital.com
Paul M. Mooney
President & CEO
PMooney@Isle-Capital.com
Telephone: 212-805-8377

General Description: Island Capital, LTD., is a group captive insurance company. Its policies cover up to 90 percent for political and commercial risks. Interest support is offered, but the CIRR is not. Island Capital is not bound by OECD consensus, does not carry the full faith and credit of any government, and does not have a separate project finance department.

FCIA Management Company Inc. (FCIA)
40 Rector Street
New York, NY 10006 USA
Tel: 212-306-5000
Fax: 212-306-5218
Contact: Lindley Franklin.
http://www.FICA.com
Ownership structure: 100 percent private.

Overview: Provides credit and political risks insurance.

General Description: FCIA Management Company, Inc. provides the underwriting and administrative services for the worldwide credit insurance businesses of Great American Insurance Company and Foreign Credit Insurance Association. FCIA offers a broad line of credit insurance and political risks products. Great American insurance Company heads one of the largest property/casualty groups in the United States, and provides a wide variety of specialty coverages to U.S. customers. Foreign Credit Insurance Association was established in 1961 and has continuously provided export credit insurance to U.S. companies since that time—longer than any other insurer.

Local Contacts of the Export Import Bank

Northeast Region
New York City, New York
6 World Trade Center, Suite 635
New York, NY 10048
Tel: (212) 466-2950
Fax: (212) 466-2959

Mid-Atlantic Region
Washington, DC
Ex-Im Bank Headquarters
811 Vermont Ave., NW, Suite 911
Washington, DC 20571
Tel: (800) 565-3946, ext. 3908
(202) 565-3940
Fax: (202) 565-3932

Southeast Region
Miami, Florida
777 NW 72nd Ave., Suite 3M2
Miami, FL 33126
Tel: (305) 526-7436
Fax: (305) 526-7435

Midwest Region
Chicago, Illinois
55 W. Monroe St., Suite 2440
Chicago, IL 60603
Tel: (312) 353-8081
Fax: (312) 353-8098

Southwest Region
Houston, Texas
1880 South Dairy Ashford II,
Suite 585
Houston, TX 77077
Tel: (281) 721-0465
Fax: (281) 679-0156

West Region
Long Beach, California
1 World Trade Center, Suite 1670
Long Beach, CA 90831
Tel: (562) 980-4580
Fax: (562) 980-4590
Orange County Satellite Office
3300 Irvine Ave., Suite 305
Newport Beach, CA 92660
Tel: (949) 660-1688 ext. 150
Fax: (949) 660-8039
San Francisco Satellite Office
250 Montgomery Street,
14th Floor
San Francisco, CA 94104
Tel: (415) 705-2285
Fax: (415) 705-1156

Or contact Michael J. Spivey, Director Business Development, at (202) 565-3459;
E-mail: mike.Spivey@exim.gov.; www.exim.gov/contacts.html
Local contacts of the Export Import Bank can also be found at www.exim.gov/
regional.gtml

Legalization Prices and Requirements

CONSULATE	MINIMUM DOCUMENTS REQUIRED*	MINIMUM CHARGES, INCL. HANDLING & CHAMBER FEES	Cost/page of addl. Doc. (Submitted w/originals)	EST. TIME IN CONSULATE**
Argentina	1 C/O (send 1 & 3)	$65.00	$65.00	Depends on jurisdiction of Consulate office. Normally 3-5 working days
Bahrain	1 C/O & 1 C/I (send 1 & 3)	Based on bottom line "Grand Total" of your invoice. See below: **Invoice Total** — **Cost** Up to $2650.00 — $97.00 $2650.01 to $13245.00 — $109.00 $13245.01 to $26490.00 — $145.00 $26490.01 to $52980.00 — $205.00 $52980.01 to $264900.00 — $265.00 over $264900.00 — $385.00	Depends on whether the doc is an invoice or a certificate. Please call 1-800-468-3627	24 – 48 hours
Costa Rica	1 original AWB or B/L & 1 C/I (1 & 3)	$135.00	$55.00	48 – 72 hours
Cyprus	1 C/O & 1 C/I (send 1 & 3)	The bottom line "Grand Total" of your invoice X 0.004 (round "up" to nearest $1.00), plus $72.00. The min. cost for 1 set of docs is $86.00	Depends on whether the doc is an invoice or a certificate. Please call 1-800-468-3627	24 – 48 hours
Dominican Republic	1 original AWB or B/L & 1 C/I (send 1 & 5)	$181.00 all Ports of Loading but Miami. $241.00 for Miami Port of Loading	Please call 1-800-468-3627	Same Day All Ports of Loading but Miami. 48 hours for Miami
Egypt	1 C/O & 1 C/I (send 1 & 3)	$235.00	$105.00	Based on jurisdiction 3 – 5 working days
Jordan	1 C/O & 1 C/I (send 1 & 3)	Based on bottom line "Grand Total" of your invoice. See Below: **Invoice Value** — **Cost** Up to $15000.00 — $223.00 $15001.00 to $30000.00 — $319.00 $30001.00 to $75000.00 — $359.00 $75001.00 to $150000.00 — $419.00 Over $150001.00 — Please Call	Depends on whether the document is an invoice or a certificate. Please call 1-800-468-3627	24 - 48 hours
Kuwait	1 C/O & 1 C/I (send 1 & 3)	$147.00	Inv.=$55.00, Other=$49.00	48 – 72 hours
Lebanon	1 C/O & 1 C/I (send 1 & 3)	Consular legalization NO LONGER REQUIRED! U.S. Arab Chamber Only $55.00	Depends on whether the doc is an invoice or a certificate. Please call 1-800-468-3627.	24 hours

CONSULATE	MINIMUM DOCUMENTS REQUIRED*	MINIMUM CHARGES, INCL. HANDLING & CHAMBER FEES	COST PER PAGE OF EA. ADD'L DOC.	EST. TIME IN CONSULATE**
Oman	1 C/O & 1 C/I (send 1 & 3)	Cost is $121.00 for invoices under $10000.00 and $136.00 for invoices $10000.00 and over.	Depends on whether the doc is an invoice or a certificate. Please call 1-800-468-3627.	48 – 72 hours
Paraguay	1 original AWB or B/L & 1 C/I & C/O (send 1 & 5)	$215.00	Depends on whether the doc is an invoice or a certificate. Please call 1-800-468-3627	48 – 72 hours
Qatar	1 C/O & 1 C/I (send 1 & 4)	Based on bottom line "Grand Total" of your invoice. See below: Invoice Total / Cost Up to $1373.00 / $125.00 $1373.01 to $4120.00 / $152.00 $4120.01 to $13736.00 / $235.00 $13736.01 to $27472.00 / $345.00 $27472.01 to $41208.00 / $454.00 $41208.01 to $68681.00 / $592.00 $68681.01 to $137362.00 / $702.00 $137362.01 to $274725.00 / $922.00 over $274725.00 / Please call	Please call 1-800-468-3627.	24 -- 48 hours
Saudi Arabia	1 C/O & 1 C/I (send 1 & 3)	$72.00	$24.00 EIS Form req'd. Please call.	Based on jurisdiction 24 -- 72 hours
Spain	1 Spanish C/O & 1 C/I (1 & 3)	$124.00 - Includes Spanish C/O & Prep.	Please call 1-800-468-3627.	24 – 48 hours
Syria	1 C/O & 1 C/I (send 1 & 3)	The bottom line "Grand Total" of your invoice X 1% (round "up" to nearest $1.00), plus $102.00.	Depends on whether the doc is an invoice or a certificate. Please call 1-800-468-3627.	24 – 72 hours
Tunisia	1 C/O & 1 C/I (send 1 & 3)	$86.00	$30.00	24 -- 48 hours
Turkey	1 C/O & 1 C/I (send 1 & 3) Please do NOT notarize documents	The bottom line "Grand Total" of your invoice X 0.006 (round "up" to nearest $1.00), plus $80.00. The min. cost for 1 set of documents is $99.00	Depends on whether the doc is an invoice or a certificate. Please call 1-800-468-3627.	48 – 72 hours
U.A.E.	1 C/O & 1 C/I (send 1 & 3)	Based on bottom line "Grand Total" of your invoice. See below: Invoice Total / Cost Up to $2702.00 / $99.00 $2702.01 to $8108.00 / $130.00 $8108.01 to $16216.00 / $190.00 $16216.01 to $24324.00 / $250.00 $24324.01 to $40540.00 / $310.00 $40540.01 to $67567.00 / $370.00 $67567.01 to $135135.00 / $460.00 $135135.01 to $270270.00 / $520.00 over $270270.00 / max. $675.00	Depends on whether the doc is an invoice or a certificate. Please call 1-800-468-3627.	48 – 72 hours
Yemen	1 C/O & 1 C/I (send 1 & 3)	$155.00	$65.00	24 - 48 hours

SGS Inspection Countries

SGS Government Programs Inc. New York, New York
Preshipment Inspection Countries
Countries Currently Mandating SGS Preshipment Inspection
SES INSPECTION COUNTRIES

Bolivia	Guinea	Mauritania
Burkina Faso	Haiti	Mexico
Burundi	India	Moldova
Cambodia	Indonesia	Nigeria
Cameroon	Iran	Peru
Central African Republic	Ivory Coast	Uzbekistan
Democratic Republic of the Congo	Malawi	Venezuela
Ecuador	Madagascar	Zanzibar
Ethiopia	Mali	

*Selected Mexican Government Purchases only.
**Voluntary participation by importers.
***Presently suspended but may activate at any time.
SGS is pleased to furnish this information as an accomodation, but without
responsibility, as countries frequently update their requirements.

International Commercial (INCO) Terms

INCO Terms are internationally recognized terms of sale used to determine responsibility for shipping arrangements and transfer of goods shipped in international trade. These standard terms help eliminate or reduce legal disputes and misinterpretation of responsibilities to the export transaction. There are four term categories:

E Terms. The seller makes the goods available at the seller's facility.

F Terms. The seller is required to deliver the goods to a carrier specified by the buyer.

C Terms. The seller contracts for carriage, but does not assume the risk of loss or damage to the goods after delivery to the carrier.

D Terms. The seller is responsible for all costs and risks required to bring the shipment to the destination country.

A Review of the Standard Incoterms 2010

The International Chamber of Commerce's *Incoterms 2010* includes eleven trade terms that specify the buyer's and seller's responsibilities, and transfer of risks and costs when those terms are made part of the international transaction.

Ex Works: EXW (insert named place of delivery) Incoterms 2010: Any mode of transport; seller makes goods available to buyer at seller's premises or other location, not cleared for export and not loaded on any collecting vehicle. The buyer bears all risks and costs involved in taking the goods from the seller's premises and thereafter.

Free Carrier: FCA (insert named place of delivery) Incoterms 2010: Any mode transport; seller delivers goods, cleared for export, to the carrier named by the buyer at the specified place. If delivery occurs at the seller's premises, the seller is responsible for loading. If delivery occurs elsewhere, the seller must load the conveyance but is not responsible for unloading. The seller is responsible to clear the goods for export.

Free Alongside Ship: FAS (insert named port of shipment) Incoterms 2010: Sea and inland waterway only; seller delivers when the goods are placed alongside the vessel at the named port of shipment. The seller also clears the goods for export.

Free on Board: FOB (insert named port of shipment) Incoterms 2010: Sea and inland waterway only; seller delivers when the goods are loaded on board the vessel at the named port. The seller clears the goods for export.

Cost and Freight: CFR (insert named port of destination) Incoterms 2010: Sea and inland waterway only; seller delivers when the goods are loaded on board the vessel. The seller pays for bringing the goods to the foreign port and clears the goods for export, however the risk passes at the point of delivery to the carrier.

Cost, Insurance, and Freight: CIF (insert named port of destination) Incoterms 2010: Sea and inland waterway only; seller delivers when the goods are loaded on board the vessel. The seller pays CFR for bringing the goods to the foreign port, obtains insurance against the buyer's risk of loss or damage, and clears the goods for export, however the risk passes at the point of delivery to the carrier.

Carriage and Insurance Paid To: CIP (insert name place of destination) Incoterms 2010: Any mode of transport; seller delivers the goods to the carrier at an agreed place and it also pays the cost of bringing the goods to the named destination. The seller also obtains insurance against the buyer's risk of loss or damage during carriage and clears the goods for export. The risk passes at the point of delivery to the carrier.

Carriage Paid To: CPT (insert named place of destination) Incoterms 2010: Any mode of transport; seller delivers goods to carrier at an agreed place and pays costs of bringing goods to the named destination. The seller also clears the goods for export. The risk passes at the point of delivery to the carrier.

Delivered at Terminal: DAT (insert named terminal at port or place of destination) Incoterms 2010: Any mode of transport; seller delivers the goods once unloaded from the arriving means of transport and placed at the disposal of the buyer at a named terminal at the named port or place of destination. The seller clears the goods for export.

Delivered at Place: DAP (insert named place of destination) Incoterms 2010: Any mode of transport; seller delivers when the goods are placed a the disposal of the buyer on the arriving means of transport ready for unloading at the named place of destination. The seller clears the goods for export.

Delivered Duty Paid: DDP (insert named place of destination) Incoterms 2010: Any mode of transport; seller delivers goods to the buyer, cleared for import (including import license, duties, and taxes) but not unloaded from the means of transport.

WTO Agreement on Rules of Origin

What is this Agreement and what does it do?

Who benefits from this Agreement?

How can this Agreement help my company?

Can the U.S. Government help me if I have a problem?

How can I get more information?

What is this Agreement and what does it do?

The Rules of Origin Agreement of the World Trade Organization (WTO) requires that WTO members apply their rules of origin in an impartial, transparent, and consistent manner. The Agreement also requires that rules of origin not restrict, distort, or disrupt international trade.

Rules of origin are the laws, regulations, and administrative guidelines that governments use to determine an imported product's country of origin; not always an easy matter when the raw materials, manufacturing, processing, or assembly of a product can be provided in several different countries. Rules of origin have many applications—for example in setting duty rates (including anti-dumping and countervailing duties), granting tariff preferences, administering government procurement policies, and applying safeguards.

All WTO members are parties to this Agreement.

The Agreement entered into force on January 1, 1995. It has no expiration date.

Who benefits from this Agreement?

Any company involved in international trade can benefit from clear and predictable rules of origin.

How can this Agreement help my company?

The Agreement requires WTO members to permit companies interested in exporting a product requiring an origin determination to request an assessment of the origin of the product, normally from that country's customs service. Requests must be accompanied by the appropriate documentation. Under the WTO Rules of Origin Agreement, the importing country must issue its origin assessment within 150 days. Assessments are valid for three years, and changes in origin rules cannot be applied retroactively. Information of a confidential nature that is provided to government officials for the purpose of assessing origin must be treated as confidential by the authorities concerned.

If you need further information on whether your product requires an origin determination and how to obtain one, you can contact the Trade Information Center at the U.S. Department of Commerce.

The WTO Agreement provides for the establishment of a Committee on Rules of Origin, where member countries consult on matters relating to the operation of the Agreement. This Committee and a Technical Committee on Rules of Origin of the World Customs Organization (WCO) have been charged with developing a permanent, harmonized set of product-specific origin rules that will apply to all trade in goods—except preferential trade—among WTO members. (Preferential trade is trade that is carried out within free trade areas or other regional trading arrangements, such as the North American Free Trade Agreement, or trade preference programs like the U.S. Generalized System of Preferences.) Both Committees are still working on this project. Once it is completed, exporters will be able to determine exactly which origin criteria will be applied to their product lines when exporting to any WTO member country.

Can the U.S. Government help me if I have a problem?

Yes, but first, if you disagree with an importing country's origin determination, or if that country is not complying with the provisions of the WTO Agreement, you or your importer should contact the customs service of that country and try to resolve the problem. If this attempt fails, the Agreement requires WTO member countries to permit a prompt review by an independent judicial or administrative tribunal in the importing country, which would have the authority to modify or reverse a customs official's ruling.

If these courses of action prove fruitless, then contact the U.S. Commerce Department's Trade Compliance Center hotline, which can provide you with the information and assistance you need to understand your rights under this Agreement. The Center can also activate the U.S. Government to help you resolve your exporting problem. If appropriate, U.S. officials can make official inquiries with the government of the other country involved. The World Trade Organization's dispute settlement process, which is described in the Exporter's Guide to the WTO Understanding on the Settlement of Disputes, can also be used by the U.S. Government, in certain circumstances, when WTO member countries fail to comply with a WTO Agreement.

How can I get more information?

The complete text of the WTO Rules of Origin Agreement is available from the Trade Compliance Center's web site.

If you have questions about this Agreement or how to use it, you can e-mail the Trade Compliance Center which will forward your message to the Commerce Department's Designated Monitoring Officer for the Agreement. You can also contact the Designated Monitoring Officer at the following address:

Designated Monitoring Officer
WTO Rules of Origin Agreement
Office of Multilateral Affairs
International Trade Administration
Room 3027
U.S. Department of Commerce
14th Street & Constitution Avenue, N.W.
Washington, D.C. 20230
Tel: (202) 482-3681
Fax: (202) 482-5939

WTO Agreement on Anti-Dumping

What is this Agreement and what does it do?

Who benefits from this Agreement?

How can this Agreement help my company?

Can the U.S. Government help me if I have a problem?

How can I get more information?

What is this Agreement and what does it do?

The Anti-Dumping Agreement of the World Trade Organization (WTO), commonly known as the AD Agreement, governs the application of antidumping measures by WTO member countries.

A product is considered to be "dumped" if it is exported to another country at a price below the normal price of a like product in the exporting country. Anti-dumping measures are unilateral remedies (the imposition of anti-dumping duties on the product in question) that the government of the importing country may apply after a thorough investigation has determined that the product is, in fact, being dumped, and that sales of the dumped product are causing material injury to a domestic industry that produces a like product.

All members of the WTO are parties to this Agreement, whose full name is the "Agreement on Implementation of Article VI of the General Agreement on Tariffs and Trade 1994". It went into effect on January 1, 1995. It has no expiration date.

Who benefits from this Agreement?

Any company involved in international trade can benefit from clear and predictable rules for the application of anti-dumping measures.

How can this Agreement help my company?

The AD Agreement ensures that WTO members will not apply antidumping measures arbitrarily. It provides detailed substantive requirements for determining whether dumping and injury are, in fact, taking place, and sets forth elaborate procedures that governments must follow when they conduct anti-dumping investigations and impose anti-dumping duties. The Agreement ensures that all proceedings will be transparent and that all interested parties have a full opportunity to defend their interests.

Substantive Requirements

Since a determination of dumping requires a comparison between the export price of a product and its normal value in the exporting country, the AD Agreement sets forth rules for the calculation of export price and normal value. It then explains how a "fair comparison" is made between the two. The government conducting an anti-dumping investigation uses this fair comparison as the basis for determining the "margin of dumping."

The Agreement then sets forth rules for determining whether dumped imports are causing injury to a domestic industry that produces a like product. Injury is defined to mean material injury itself, the threat of material injury or material retardation in the establishment of a domestic industry. The government authorities must establish injury to the domestic industry and that the dumped imports are a cause of that injury. The AD Agreement provides for "cumulative assessments" of the effects of imports on a domestic industry when imports of a product from more than one country are simultaneously subject to anti-dumping investigations.

Investigations

A government normally initiates an anti-dumping investigation on the basis of a written application by a domestic industry, although in special circumstances the government itself can initiate the investigation on the industry's behalf. The application must provide evidence of dumping, injury and a causal link between the two. It must include a complete description of the allegedly dumped product, information on the like product produced by the applicant, evidence regarding export price and normal value, an assessment of the impact of the imports on the domestic industry, and information concerning industry support for the application.

The rules set forth in the Agreement for the collection of evidence state that as soon as government authorities initiate an investigation, they must provide the full text of the written application to all known exporters. All interested parties are given access to nonconfidential information and the opportunity to meet with the parties that have adverse interests, so that opposing views can be presented and rebuttal arguments offered. Before they make a final determination of whether dumping has occurred, the government authorities must inform all interested parties of the essential facts under consideration, giving them sufficient time to defend their interests.

An application will be rejected, according to the Agreement, and an investigation promptly terminated if the government authorities conclude that there is insufficient evidence of either dumping or injury. The Agreement provides that unless there are special circumstances, investigations will be concluded within one year and will continue in no case more than 18 months after their initiation.

Price Undertakings

The Agreement provides that government authorities can suspend or terminate an anti-dumping proceeding if they receive voluntary undertakings from an exporter that it will revise its prices or cease exporting to the area in question at dumped prices. Investigating authorities have the option of accepting price increases that are less than the margin of dumping if they are adequate to remove the injury to the domestic industry.

Imposition of Anti-Dumping Duties

Under the Agreement, it is up to the government of the importing country to decide whether or not to impose anti-dumping duties. (The Agreement provides an option of not imposing duties in cases where all requirements for imposing such duties have been fulfilled, but not all authorities allow such an option.) The amount of the duty set by the government cannot exceed the margin of dumping, but the Agreement permits it to be lower if it is adequate to remove the injury to the domestic industry.

Normally anti-dumping duties are applied to all imports of the subject merchandise made on or after the date on which their is a preliminary determination of dumping, injury, and causality.

The Agreement states that an anti-dumping duty shall remain in force as long as necessary to counteract dumping that is causing injury. It contains a "sunset" provision that provides that the duty will be terminated five years from the date of its imposition unless the government authorities determine in a review that termination of the duty would lead to continuation or recurrence of dumping and injury.

The Committee; Notifications

The Agreement established a Committee on Anti-dumping Practices, composed of representatives of each WTO member country. This Committee meets not less than twice a year and affords members the opportunity to consult on any matters relating to the operation of the Agreement. Member countries are required to notify this Committee of their anti-dumping legislation and/or regulations, their anti-dumping actions, and the names, addresses and contact numbers of officials responsible for anti-dumping matters.

Can the U.S. Government help me if I have a problem?

Yes. If your export business is being adversely affected because another WTO member country is not complying with the Anti-Dumping Agreement, contact the Trade Compliance Center's hotline at the U.S. Department of Commerce. The Center can help you understand your rights under this Agreement and can alert the relevant U.S. Government officials to make inquiries, if appropriate, with the other country involved that could help you resolve your exporting problem.

Disputes under the Anti-dumping Agreement can also, in certain circumstances, be resolved by the U.S. Government through the WTO's dispute settlement process, which is described in the *Exporter's Guide to the WTO Understanding on the Settlement of Disputes.*

How can I get more information?

The complete text of the WTO Anti-Dumping Agreement is available from the Trade Compliance Center's web site.

If you have questions about this Agreement or how to use it, you can e-mail the Trade Compliance Center, which will forward your message to the Commerce Department's Designated Monitoring Officer for the Agreement. You can also contact the Designated Monitoring Officer at the following address:

Designated Monitoring Officer—
WTO Anti-Dumping Agreement
Office of Policy—Import Administration

International Trade Administration
Room 3713
U.S. Department of Commerce
14th Street & Constitution Avenue, N.W.
Washington, D.C. 20230
Tel: (202) 482-4412
Fax: (202) 482-2308

(Census Bureau) Foreign Trade Division Contacts

Commodity Classification

(Schedule B Number) Assistance Schedule B

Food, animal, and wood 301-457-3484 Chapters 1–24; 41; 43–49
products (Including paper
and printed matter)
Minerals 301-457-3484 Chapters 25–27; 68–71
Metals 301-457-3259 Chapters 72–83
Textiles and apparel 301-457-3484 Chapters 41–43; 50–67
Machinery and vehicles 301-457-3259 Chapters 84–85; 86–89
(including computers, other electronic
equipment and transportation)
Chemical and sundries 301-457-3259 Chapters 28–40; 90–98
Foreign Trade Statistics Regulations 301-457-2238
Automated Export System (AES) 1-800-549-0595

Other Agency Export Control Telephone Contacts

Bureau of Export Administration, Department of Commerce:
<www.bxa.doc.gov>

Washington, D.C.: 202-482-4811 or 202-482-2642
Newport Beach, California 949-660-0144
San Jose, California 408-998-7402

International Trade Administration, Export Assistance Center

1-800-872-8723; *www.ita.doc.gov*

Department of State, Office of Defense Trade Controls (ODTC)

(International Traffic in Arms Regulations (ITAR)) 202-663-2714;
www.pmdtc.org

Department of the Treasury, Office of Foreign Assets Control (OFAC)

(Sanctioned countries and trade restrictions) 202-622-2490;
www.treas.gov/ofac

*U.S. Customs Import (Inbound) Questions (Summary Management
Office)* 202-927-0625; *www.customs.treas.gov*

U.S. Customs Export (Outbound) Questions (Outbound Programs)
202-927-6060; *www.customs.treas.gov*

NAFTA (hotline) 972-574-4061; *www.mac.doc.gov/nafta/nafta2.htm*

To order paper SEDs contact the: Government Printing Office (GPO),
Publication Order & Information Office: 202-512-1800

Sample Fines and Penalties on Export Transactions from the Bureau of Industry & Security (BIS) Archives

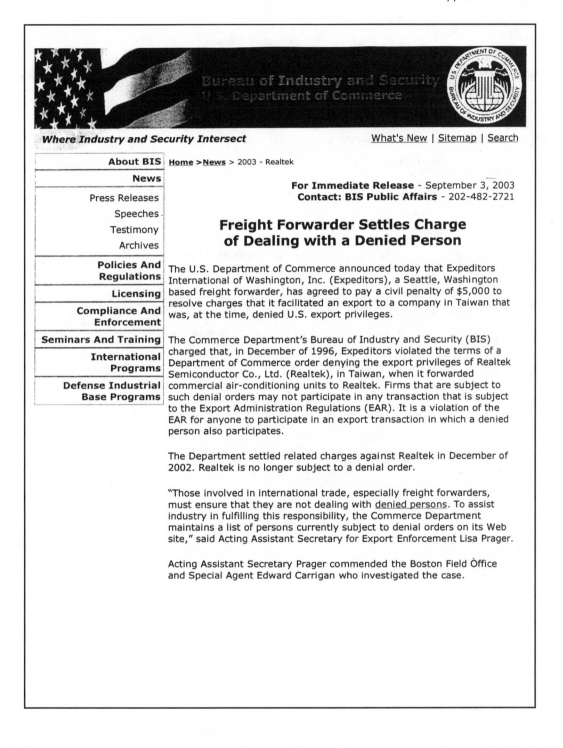

Where Industry and Security Intersect

What's New | Sitemap | Search

About BIS	Home >News > 2003 - Realtek
News	
Press Releases	
Speeches	
Testimony	
Archives	
Policies And Regulations	
Licensing	
Compliance And Enforcement	
Seminars And Training	
International Programs	
Defense Industrial Base Programs	

For Immediate Release - September 3, 2003
Contact: BIS Public Affairs - 202-482-2721

Freight Forwarder Settles Charge of Dealing with a Denied Person

The U.S. Department of Commerce announced today that Expeditors International of Washington, Inc. (Expeditors), a Seattle, Washington based freight forwarder, has agreed to pay a civil penalty of $5,000 to resolve charges that it facilitated an export to a company in Taiwan that was, at the time, denied U.S. export privileges.

The Commerce Department's Bureau of Industry and Security (BIS) charged that, in December of 1996, Expeditors violated the terms of a Department of Commerce order denying the export privileges of Realtek Semiconductor Co., Ltd. (Realtek), in Taiwan, when it forwarded commercial air-conditioning units to Realtek. Firms that are subject to such denial orders may not participate in any transaction that is subject to the Export Administration Regulations (EAR). It is a violation of the EAR for anyone to participate in an export transaction in which a denied person also participates.

The Department settled related charges against Realtek in December of 2002. Realtek is no longer subject to a denial order.

"Those involved in international trade, especially freight forwarders, must ensure that they are not dealing with denied persons. To assist industry in fulfilling this responsibility, the Commerce Department maintains a list of persons currently subject to denial orders on its Web site," said Acting Assistant Secretary for Export Enforcement Lisa Prager.

Acting Assistant Secretary Prager commended the Boston Field Òffice and Special Agent Edward Carrigan who investigated the case.

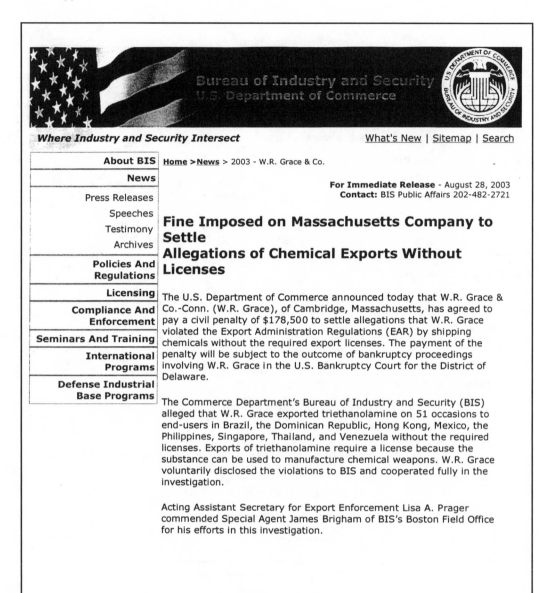

About BIS	Home >News > 2003 - W.R. Grace & Co.
News	
Press Releases	**For Immediate Release** - August 28, 2003
Speeches	**Contact:** BIS Public Affairs 202-482-2721
Testimony	
Archives	
Policies And Regulations	
Licensing	
Compliance And Enforcement	
Seminars And Training	
International Programs	
Defense Industrial Base Programs	

Fine Imposed on Massachusetts Company to Settle
Allegations of Chemical Exports Without Licenses

The U.S. Department of Commerce announced today that W.R. Grace & Co.-Conn. (W.R. Grace), of Cambridge, Massachusetts, has agreed to pay a civil penalty of $178,500 to settle allegations that W.R. Grace violated the Export Administration Regulations (EAR) by shipping chemicals without the required export licenses. The payment of the penalty will be subject to the outcome of bankruptcy proceedings involving W.R. Grace in the U.S. Bankruptcy Court for the District of Delaware.

The Commerce Department's Bureau of Industry and Security (BIS) alleged that W.R. Grace exported triethanolamine on 51 occasions to end-users in Brazil, the Dominican Republic, Hong Kong, Mexico, the Philippines, Singapore, Thailand, and Venezuela without the required licenses. Exports of triethanolamine require a license because the substance can be used to manufacture chemical weapons. W.R. Grace voluntarily disclosed the violations to BIS and cooperated fully in the investigation.

Acting Assistant Secretary for Export Enforcement Lisa A. Prager commended Special Agent James Brigham of BIS's Boston Field Office for his efforts in this investigation.

Home >News > 2003 - E&M Computing

About BIS

News

Press Releases

Speeches

Testimony

Archives

Policies And Regulations

Licensing

Compliance And Enforcement

Seminars And Training

International Programs

Defense Industrial Base Programs

For Immediate Release
August 18, 2003

E & M Computing Ltd. of Israel
Fined for Unauthorized Computer Sales

The U.S. Department of Commerce announced today the imposition of a $165,000 fine and a three-year denial of export privileges on E & M Computing Ltd. (E&M), of Ramat-Gan, Israel, to settle multiple charges that the company violated the Export Administration Regulations (EAR) when it sold and serviced computers and computer components to three customers in Israel, including a nuclear research center. The denial period was suspended for three years, and will thereafter be waived if the company does not violate U.S. export control laws during the period of suspension.

The Commerce Department's Bureau of Industry and Security (BIS) charged that E&M caused the export of central processing units (CPUs), a workstation, a server, and a high performance computer to Israel without the required export licenses. BIS also charged that E&M evaded the EAR by purchasing computers from another vendor after learning that BIS would deny the first vendor's license application to export the items.

In addition, BIS charged that E&M "loaned" a computer to a customer until a BIS license could be obtained, and then provided false and misleading information in support of the license application. E&M later attempted to avoid detection of this loan by removing the computer from the end-user when they were notified that BIS officials were planning to conduct a post-shipment verification.

In other instances, E&M upgraded computers above the export control threshold with CPUs from its own warehouse. E&M also sold or loaned a server to a customer without authorization, after learning that a BIS license was required. Finally, E&M failed to disclose these upgrades to BIS when filing notifications required by the National Defense Authorization Act of 1998.

"This case demonstrates that companies may not evade the license requirements on exports of computer equipment by making illegal upgrades and transfers in-country. BIS will continue to pursue efforts by companies to circumvent U.S. export controls," said Acting Assistant Secretary of Commerce for Export Enforcement Lisa Prager.

Acting Assistant Secretary Prager commended Special Agent Erin Kelly of BIS's San Jose Field Office for her efforts in this investigation.

**United States
Department of
Justice**

ROSCOE C. HOWARD, JR.
United States Attorney for the
District of Columbia

Judiciary Center
555 Fourth St. N.W.
Washington, D.C. 20530

For Information Contact
DOJ Public Affairs
Channing Phillips (202) 514-6933
or BIS Public Affairs
(202) 482-2721

FOR IMMEDIATE RELEASE - Tuesday, August 5, 2003

Bushnell Corporation fined $650,000
as part of sentence for
illegally exporting night vision equipment

Washington, D.C. - United States Attorney Roscoe C. Howard,
Jr. and Acting Assistant Secretary of Commerce for Export
Enforcement Lisa A. Prager today announced that Worldwide
Sports & Recreation, Inc., which does business as Bushnell
Corporation, was sentenced to a $650,000 criminal fine and
five years of probation in the U.S. District Court for the District
of Columbia for exporting, between September 1995 and
December 1997, over 500 Night Ranger night vision devices to
Japan and 14 other countries, without the required
Department of Commerce export licenses. Under a separate
agreement with the Department of Commerce, Bushnell
agreed to pay a civil fine of $223,000 and receive a one year
denial of export privileges (suspended). Bushnell's sentence
was imposed by the Honorable Richard W. Roberts.

United States Attorney Howard heralded the sentence as a
warning to manufacturers, distributors, and exporters of night
vision equipment that has potential military use. "Export
licensing requirements and restrictions are not to be
deliberately evaded or blindly ignored. Our national security is
put at risk when export compliance is not taken seriously,"
said Mr. Howard.

Acting Assistant Secretary Prager stated, "the Night Rangers
that Bushnell exported are optical imaging binoculars and
monoculars. These illegal exports can be diverted to countries
and end-users that pose a direct threat to U.S. national
security interests."

Under the International Emergency Economic Powers Act,

optical sensors, such as the Night Rangers, are controlled for national security and foreign policy reasons. While some optical sensors, whose value is less than $3,000, may be exported to some destinations without a license, that exception does not apply to Night Rangers, which must be licensed to all countries, except Canada, regardless of the value of the shipment.

Bushnell was informed by the manufacturer and its own lawyers of the comprehensive export licensing requirement when it entered into a distributorship agreement in 1994. In 1996, Bushnell received notification from the Department of Commerce, which stated that the Night Ranger models it was selling - that is, Model 150 (a monocular) and 250 (a binocular) - required licenses for each individual shipment to all countries (except Canada), and were not subject to the license exception for low-value shipments.

Bushnell began selling Night Ranger night vision equipment in 1995. Although it obtained export licenses for five shipments of 11 Night Rangers that it shipped directly overseas, it did not obtain export licenses for the bulk of its international shipments that required export licenses, in particular for shipments to Japan and for certain low-value shipments to other countries.

With regard to the Japanese sales, Bushnell arranged to deliver Night Rangers to a company in the United States that was conspiring with the Japanese purchase. The U.S. company exported the Night Rangers to Japan. Bushnell exported 11 shipments, totaling 471 Night Rangers, valued at over $300,000, to the Japanese company without obtaining an export license for those exports from the Department of Commerce in Washington, D.C. The dates and details of the transactions are stated in the Information to which defendant pleaded guilty on April 16, 2003.

With regard to shipments made to other countries, a Bushnell mid-level manager of the International Sales Department told her staff that low-value shipments of Night Rangers under $3,000 could be shipped internationally without an export license. Even after a Commodity Classification explicitly stating that an export license was required for all shipments and that no exception applied was received and distributed to the International Sales Department, Bushnell continued, from July 19, 1996, to February 13, 1997, to ship Night Rangers without an export license even if the value of the shipment was under $3,000. As set forth in the Information, 15 of these shipments were made, totaling 37 Night Rangers, valued at $33,290.

In announcing today's sentence, U.S. Attorney Howard and Acting Assistant Secretary of Commerce for Export Enforcement Prager commended the work of Senior Special Agent David Poole and Senior Special Agent Christopher Tafe as well as the U.S. Customs Service Office of Investigations-Boston. They also praised Assistant United States Attorney Wendy Wysong.

BIS Home > BIS Press Page

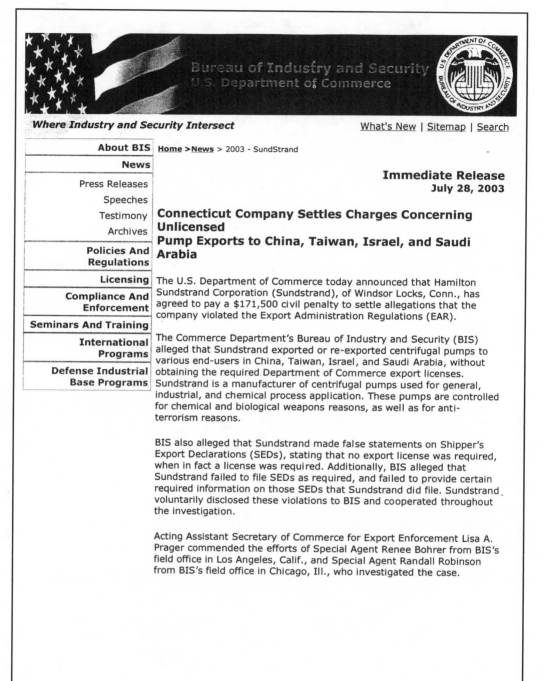

Where Industry and Security Intersect

What's New | Sitemap | Search

About BIS

News

Press Releases

Speeches

Testimony

Archives

Policies And Regulations

Licensing

Compliance And Enforcement

Seminars And Training

International Programs

Defense Industrial Base Programs

Home >News > 2003 - SundStrand

Immediate Release
July 28, 2003

Connecticut Company Settles Charges Concerning Unlicensed Pump Exports to China, Taiwan, Israel, and Saudi Arabia

The U.S. Department of Commerce today announced that Hamilton Sundstrand Corporation (Sundstrand), of Windsor Locks, Conn., has agreed to pay a $171,500 civil penalty to settle allegations that the company violated the Export Administration Regulations (EAR).

The Commerce Department's Bureau of Industry and Security (BIS) alleged that Sundstrand exported or re-exported centrifugal pumps to various end-users in China, Taiwan, Israel, and Saudi Arabia, without obtaining the required Department of Commerce export licenses. Sundstrand is a manufacturer of centrifugal pumps used for general, industrial, and chemical process application. These pumps are controlled for chemical and biological weapons reasons, as well as for anti-terrorism reasons.

BIS also alleged that Sundstrand made false statements on Shipper's Export Declarations (SEDs), stating that no export license was required, when in fact a license was required. Additionally, BIS alleged that Sundstrand failed to file SEDs as required, and failed to provide certain required information on those SEDs that Sundstrand did file. Sundstrand voluntarily disclosed these violations to BIS and cooperated throughout the investigation.

Acting Assistant Secretary of Commerce for Export Enforcement Lisa A. Prager commended the efforts of Special Agent Renee Bohrer from BIS's field office in Los Angeles, Calif., and Special Agent Randall Robinson from BIS's field office in Chicago, Ill., who investigated the case.

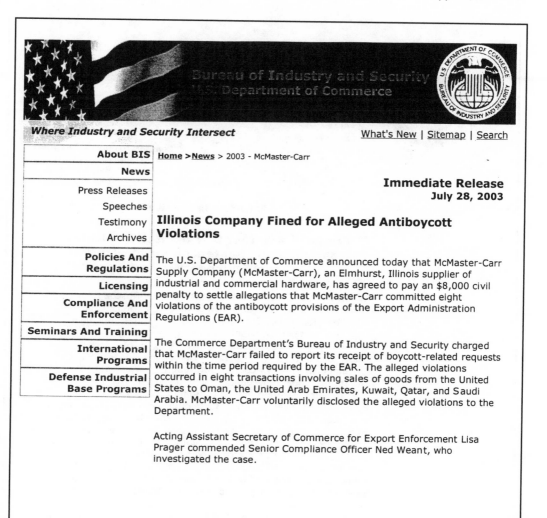

Home >News > 2003 - McMaster-Carr

Immediate Release
July 28, 2003

Illinois Company Fined for Alleged Antiboycott Violations

The U.S. Department of Commerce announced today that McMaster-Carr Supply Company (McMaster-Carr), an Elmhurst, Illinois supplier of industrial and commercial hardware, has agreed to pay an $8,000 civil penalty to settle allegations that McMaster-Carr committed eight violations of the antiboycott provisions of the Export Administration Regulations (EAR).

The Commerce Department's Bureau of Industry and Security charged that McMaster-Carr failed to report its receipt of boycott-related requests within the time period required by the EAR. The alleged violations occurred in eight transactions involving sales of goods from the United States to Oman, the United Arab Emirates, Kuwait, Qatar, and Saudi Arabia. McMaster-Carr voluntarily disclosed the alleged violations to the Department.

Acting Assistant Secretary of Commerce for Export Enforcement Lisa Prager commended Senior Compliance Officer Ned Weant, who investigated the case.

**United States
Department of
Justice**

ROSCOE C. HOWARD, JR.
United States Attorney for the
District of Columbia

Judiciary Center
555 Fourth St. N.W.
Washington, D.C. 20530

Contact DOJ Public Affairs
Channing Phillips (202) 514-6933
or **BIS Public Affairs**
(202) 482-2721

For Immediate Release - July 17, 2003

Freight Forwarder DSV Samson Transport Pleads Guilty and Sentenced for forwarding 30 Illegal Shipments to India

Washington, D.C. - United States Attorney Roscoe C. Howard, Jr. and Department of Commerce Acting Assistant Secretary for Export Enforcement Lisa A. Prager announced that DSV Samson Transport, a freight-forwarding company based in New Jersey, pleaded guilty today in U.S. District Court for the District of Columbia before the Honorable Royce C. Lamberth to a two-count Information, charging violations of the International Emergency Economic Powers Act and the Export Administration Act. In pleading guilty, DSV Samson admitted to forwarding over 30 shipments to India, between November 1999 and May 12, 2001, despite being warned by Special Agents from the Office of Export Enforcement on at least three occasions that such shipments would be in violation of Department of Commerce export controls designed to prevent nuclear proliferation. DSV Samson Transport was immediately sentenced by the Court to a $250,000 fine, an $800 special assessment and five years of probation.

Separately, the Department of Commerce's Bureau of Industry and Security and DSV Samson have tentatively agreed that DSV Samson will pay a civil penalty of $399,000 to resolve related administrative charges.

In announcing today's guilty plea and sentencing, United States Attorney Howard warned that "freight forwarders are the last link in the export chain and must not knowingly make shipments from the United States that do not comply with the export laws for the safety and protection of our national interests. Because of the position that freight forwarders hold in the chain of international commerce, they have a unique opportunity to ensure export compliance. Freight forwarders, and anyone else with responsibility for compliance with U.S. export laws, will be held responsible for such compliance, particularly when our national security is at issue."

Acting Assistant Secretary of Commerce for Export Enforcement Prager stated, "this case demonstrates that the Department of Commerce will hold freight forwarders accountable for fulfilling their responsibilities under our export control laws. Forwarders play a key role in the global supply chain. As such, it is important that they be extremely attentive to their export control obligations."

Freight forwarders are in the business of forwarding shipments for their exporting customers. A freight forwarder does not itself manufacture or sell goods, but provides the service of arranging and monitoring the intermediate stages of air, sea, or ground transport necessary for an exporting customer's shipment to reach its intended destination. The law imposes upon all parties, including freight forwarders, an obligation to refrain from knowingly participating in illegal export transactions.

In May 1998, India detonated a nuclear test device. In response to this test, in November 1998, the Department of Commerce expanded the "Entity List," a list of organizations published in the Export Administration Regulations ("EAR"), to include end-users of concern in India, thereby imposing a licensing requirement on virtually all exports to these organizations.

According to the government's evidence, from December 1998 to June 1999, DSV Samson Transport, Inc. caused six illegal exports of items, valued in total over $13,500, such as radio frequency test equipment, a pulse generator, and an oscillator to the Government of India, Directorate of Purchase and Stores, Department of Atomic Energy, in India, which was an organization listed on the Entity List, without the required Department of Commerce licenses.

On June 29, 1999, a Special Agent from the Department of Commerce's Office of Export Enforcement ("OEE") warned the sales manager at DSV Samson Transport, Inc. in New Jersey that Bharat Heavy Electricals was listed on the Entity List, and gave the sales manager OEE outreach materials that included a description of the civil and criminal penalties that can be assessed for violations of the EAR. This information also included phone numbers for questions or self-disclosures of previous violations. Shortly thereafter, the sales manager sent an e-mail to his staff specifically addressing the Entity List and warning that shipments to India, among other countries, must be checked against the Entity List and if the consignee of the shipment appeared on the list, an export license would be required "regardless if the shipper is sending a paper clip or just documents."

In August 1999, a different OEE agent, on a routine outreach visit, met with the sales coordinator and export supervisor of DSV's California office, who denied knowledge of the Entity List and the EAR. The agent warned the DSV employee of the firm's obligations and the potential penalties for violations. Thereafter, the sales coordinator and export supervisor sent a memorandum to DSV sales and export personnel referencing a shipment DSV had forwarded to a listed entity, that was later found to be illegal, warning of potential fines and jail terms for future violations, and referring them to the Department of Commerce web page for the EAR and further information about licensing and compliance.

In October 1999, an OEE Special Agent contacted a DSV export supervisor in New Jersey regarding a possible illegal export by DSV in May 1999. The export supervisor acknowledged that there may have been illegal shipments prior to the June 1999 visit, but told the agent that DSV was in compliance thereafter.

From November 13, 1999, to February 17, 2000, DSV forwarded nine illegal shipments of items, valued in total over $36,800, such as lenses, electronic equipment, and instruments to the Government of India, Directorate of Purchase and Stores, Department of Atomic Energy, to Bharat Heavy Electricals, and to the Nuclear Power Corporation of India, which were organizations listed on the Entity List, for which export licenses were required. DSV forwarded these shipments with the knowledge that its customers, who were exporting the items, had not obtained the required export licenses.

On March 17, 2000, the Department of Commerce changed its policy of presumption of denial for certain items being exported to organizations in India on the Entity List, but a license was still required for exports to such entities and was subject to case-by-case basis review.

From April 2000 to May 2001, DSV forwarded 21 illegal shipments of items, valued in total over $102,200, such as a power supply, software, a transducer, a radioisotope, and oscillators to the Government of India, Directorate of Purchase and Stores, Department of Atomic Energy, to Bharat Electronics, Ltd., and to Bharat Heavy Electricals in India, all organizations then on the Entity List. Again, DSV forwarded these shipments with the knowledge that its customers, who were exporting the items, had not obtained the required export licenses.

In addition, DSV representatives have made assurances to the U.S. Department of Commerce that an extensive export compliance program has been implemented that it intends to be a model for the international freight forwarding business.

In announcing today's conviction, U.S. Attorney Howard and

Acting Assistant Secretary of Commerce for Export Enforcement Prager commended the work of OEE Special Agents Michael Imbrogna and Scott Dunberg. They also praised Assistant United States Attorney Wendy Wysong.

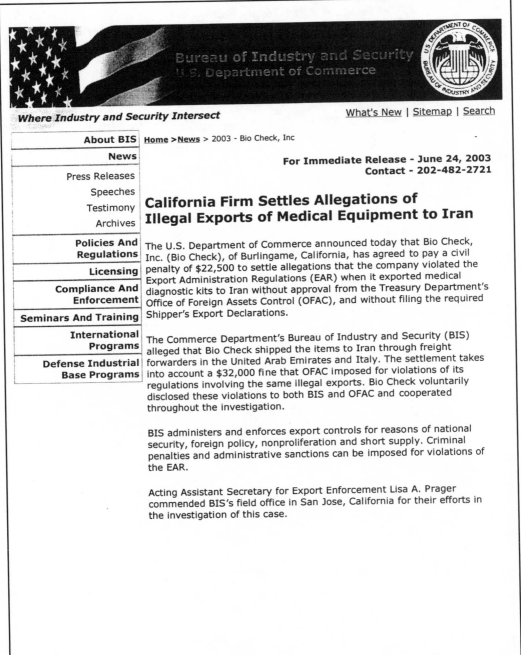

Where Industry and Security Intersect

What's New | Sitemap | Search

About BIS

News

Press Releases

Speeches

Testimony

Archives

Policies And Regulations

Licensing

Compliance And Enforcement

Seminars And Training

International Programs

Defense Industrial Base Programs

Home >News > 2003 - Bio Check, Inc

For Immediate Release - June 24, 2003
Contact - 202-482-2721

California Firm Settles Allegations of Illegal Exports of Medical Equipment to Iran

The U.S. Department of Commerce announced today that Bio Check, Inc. (Bio Check), of Burlingame, California, has agreed to pay a civil penalty of $22,500 to settle allegations that the company violated the Export Administration Regulations (EAR) when it exported medical diagnostic kits to Iran without approval from the Treasury Department's Office of Foreign Assets Control (OFAC), and without filing the required Shipper's Export Declarations.

The Commerce Department's Bureau of Industry and Security (BIS) alleged that Bio Check shipped the items to Iran through freight forwarders in the United Arab Emirates and Italy. The settlement takes into account a $32,000 fine that OFAC imposed for violations of its regulations involving the same illegal exports. Bio Check voluntarily disclosed these violations to both BIS and OFAC and cooperated throughout the investigation.

BIS administers and enforces export controls for reasons of national security, foreign policy, nonproliferation and short supply. Criminal penalties and administrative sanctions can be imposed for violations of the EAR.

Acting Assistant Secretary for Export Enforcement Lisa A. Prager commended BIS's field office in San Jose, California for their efforts in the investigation of this case.

Bureau of Industry and Security
U.S. Department of Commerce

Where Industry and Security Intersect

What's New | Sitemap | Search

About BIS

News

Press Releases

Speeches

Testimony

Archives

Policies And Regulations

Licensing

Compliance And Enforcement

Seminars And Training

International Programs

Defense Industrial Base Programs

Home >News > 2003 - Zooma Enterprises

For Immediate Release - June 24, 2003
Contact - 202-482-2721

California Company, President Penalized for Making False Statements in Connection with an Attempted Export to Iraq

The U.S. Department of Commerce announced today that Zooma Enterprises, Inc. (Zooma), of San Diego, California, and its president, Issa Salomi, have agreed to pay $32,000 in civil penalties to settle charges that they made false statements to the U.S. Government in connection with an attempted export of medical equipment to Iraq. Mr. Salomi will pay a $24,000 fine and Zooma will pay an $8,000 fine.

The Commerce Department's Bureau of Industry and Security (BIS) charged that Zooma violated the Export Administration Regulations (EAR) by listing the country of ultimate destination on a Shipper's Export Declaration as Jordan, when the destination was, in fact, Iraq. BIS also charged that Issa Salomi committed three violations of the EAR by filing a petition with the U.S. Customs Service that falsely represented facts about the sale of the medical equipment, an ampul filling and sealing machine, including its ultimate destination.

Acting Assistant Secretary for Export Enforcement Lisa A. Prager commended Special Agent Michael Imbrogna of the Office of Export Enforcement's field office in Boston, Massachusetts, who investigated this case.

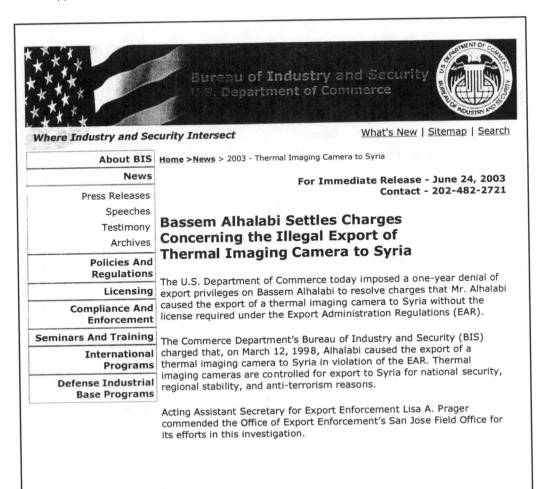

About BIS

News

Press Releases

Speeches

Testimony

Archives

Policies And
Regulations

Licensing

Compliance And
Enforcement

Seminars And Training

International
Programs

Defense Industrial
Base Programs

Home >News > 2003 - Thermal Imaging Camera to Syria

For Immediate Release - June 24, 2003
Contact - 202-482-2721

Bassem Alhalabi Settles Charges Concerning the Illegal Export of Thermal Imaging Camera to Syria

The U.S. Department of Commerce today imposed a one-year denial of export privileges on Bassem Alhalabi to resolve charges that Mr. Alhalabi caused the export of a thermal imaging camera to Syria without the license required under the Export Administration Regulations (EAR).

The Commerce Department's Bureau of Industry and Security (BIS) charged that, on March 12, 1998, Alhalabi caused the export of a thermal imaging camera to Syria in violation of the EAR. Thermal imaging cameras are controlled for export to Syria for national security, regional stability, and anti-terrorism reasons.

Acting Assistant Secretary for Export Enforcement Lisa A. Prager commended the Office of Export Enforcement's San Jose Field Office for its efforts in this investigation.

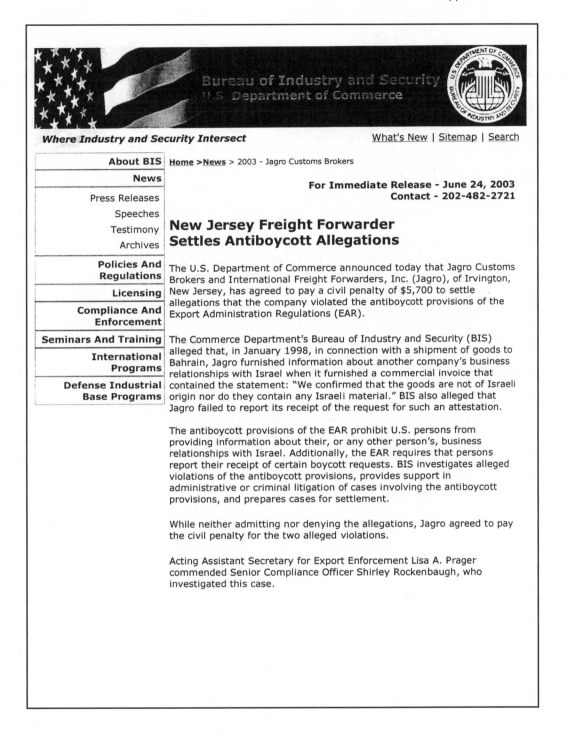

Bureau of Industry and Security
U.S. Department of Commerce

Where Industry and Security Intersect

What's New | Sitemap | Search

About BIS

News

Press Releases

Speeches

Testimony

Archives

Policies And Regulations

Licensing

Compliance And Enforcement

Seminars And Training

International Programs

Defense Industrial Base Programs

Home >News > 2003 - Jagro Customs Brokers

For Immediate Release - June 24, 2003
Contact - 202-482-2721

New Jersey Freight Forwarder Settles Antiboycott Allegations

The U.S. Department of Commerce announced today that Jagro Customs Brokers and International Freight Forwarders, Inc. (Jagro), of Irvington, New Jersey, has agreed to pay a civil penalty of $5,700 to settle allegations that the company violated the antiboycott provisions of the Export Administration Regulations (EAR).

The Commerce Department's Bureau of Industry and Security (BIS) alleged that, in January 1998, in connection with a shipment of goods to Bahrain, Jagro furnished information about another company's business relationships with Israel when it furnished a commercial invoice that contained the statement: "We confirmed that the goods are not of Israeli origin nor do they contain any Israeli material." BIS also alleged that Jagro failed to report its receipt of the request for such an attestation.

The antiboycott provisions of the EAR prohibit U.S. persons from providing information about their, or any other person's, business relationships with Israel. Additionally, the EAR requires that persons report their receipt of certain boycott requests. BIS investigates alleged violations of the antiboycott provisions, provides support in administrative or criminal litigation of cases involving the antiboycott provisions, and prepares cases for settlement.

While neither admitting nor denying the allegations, Jagro agreed to pay the civil penalty for the two alleged violations.

Acting Assistant Secretary for Export Enforcement Lisa A. Prager commended Senior Compliance Officer Shirley Rockenbaugh, who investigated this case.

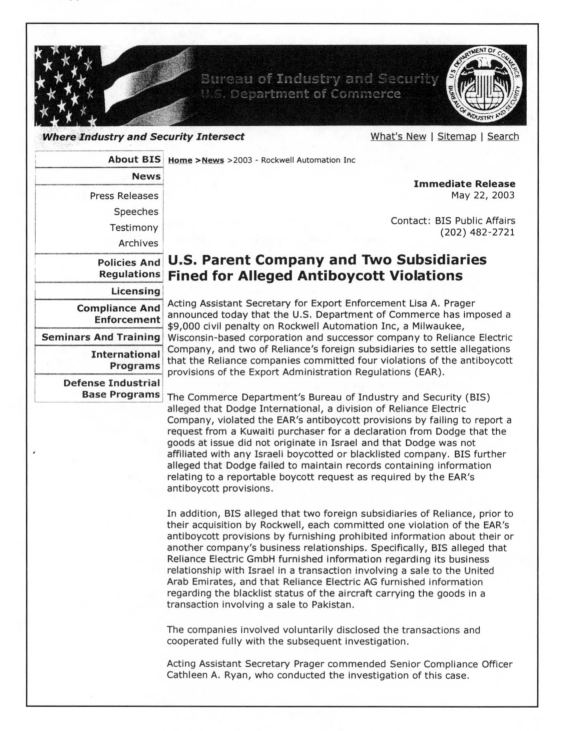

Where Industry and Security Intersect

What's New | Sitemap | Search

| About BIS | Home >News >2003 - Rockwell Automation Inc |

News

Press Releases

Speeches

Testimony

Archives

Immediate Release
May 22, 2003

Contact: BIS Public Affairs
(202) 482-2721

Policies And
Regulations

Licensing

Compliance And
Enforcement

Seminars And Training

International
Programs

Defense Industrial
Base Programs

U.S. Parent Company and Two Subsidiaries Fined for Alleged Antiboycott Violations

Acting Assistant Secretary for Export Enforcement Lisa A. Prager announced today that the U.S. Department of Commerce has imposed a $9,000 civil penalty on Rockwell Automation Inc, a Milwaukee, Wisconsin-based corporation and successor company to Reliance Electric Company, and two of Reliance's foreign subsidiaries to settle allegations that the Reliance companies committed four violations of the antiboycott provisions of the Export Administration Regulations (EAR).

The Commerce Department's Bureau of Industry and Security (BIS) alleged that Dodge International, a division of Reliance Electric Company, violated the EAR's antiboycott provisions by failing to report a request from a Kuwaiti purchaser for a declaration from Dodge that the goods at issue did not originate in Israel and that Dodge was not affiliated with any Israeli boycotted or blacklisted company. BIS further alleged that Dodge failed to maintain records containing information relating to a reportable boycott request as required by the EAR's antiboycott provisions.

In addition, BIS alleged that two foreign subsidiaries of Reliance, prior to their acquisition by Rockwell, each committed one violation of the EAR's antiboycott provisions by furnishing prohibited information about their or another company's business relationships. Specifically, BIS alleged that Reliance Electric GmbH furnished information regarding its business relationship with Israel in a transaction involving a sale to the United Arab Emirates, and that Reliance Electric AG furnished information regarding the blacklist status of the aircraft carrying the goods in a transaction involving a sale to Pakistan.

The companies involved voluntarily disclosed the transactions and cooperated fully with the subsequent investigation.

Acting Assistant Secretary Prager commended Senior Compliance Officer Cathleen A. Ryan, who conducted the investigation of this case.

United States Department of Justice

U.S. Attorney's Office Northern District of Illinois

Press Contacts:
AUSA George Jackson III
(312)886-7645
AUSA/PIO Randall Samborn
(312)353-5318

FOR IMMEDIATE RELEASE
Thursday April 10, 2003

U.S Charges Wheeling Firm with Violating Export Ban to Iran

CHICAGO – A Wheeling firm that manufactures pipe-cutting tools was charged today with two federal felony offenses for allegedly violating a foreign trade embargo against Iran, announced Patrick J. Fitzgerald, United States Attorney for the Northern District of Illinois. The defendant, E.H. Wachs Company, allegedly shipped pipe cutters and related equipment in 1995 and 1996 from its warehouse in Wheeling, through Canada, knowing that the products were destined for the National Iranian Gas Company (NIGC) in Iran, in violation of the Iranian embargo barring exports of such goods. Wachs manufactures pipe-cutting tools, including Trav-L-Cutters, and related parts and other items used in the construction and repair of gas and oil pipelines, which it sells worldwide.

The company was charged with one count each of violating the International Emergency Economic Powers Act and the Iranian Transactions Regulations in a two-count criminal information that was filed today in U.S. District Court. No individuals were charged. Through its lawyers, E.H. Wachs, has authorized the government to disclose that it has agreed to plead guilty to the charges at a later date, which has not yet been set.

An Executive Order issued in May 1995, pursuant to the International Emergency Economic Powers Act, prohibited the unauthorized exportation from the United States to Iran or the financing of such exportation, of any goods, technology or services except items intended to relieve human suffering. The prohibition, commonly known as the Iranian embargo, was also made part of the Code of Federal Regulations.

According to the charges, in 1993 and 1994, the NIGC invited bids to purchase approximately 50 pipe-cutting machines, related blades and other specified items. The bid invitations required that the successful bidder have an agent located in Iran in order to provide service for the pipe-cutting machines and to provide training for NIGC personnel on the use of the machines. In 1994, the NIGC initiated negotiations with Wachs and an unnamed Canadian company that had a subsidiary in Iran to purchase two Trav-L-Cutters from Wachs to use to train NIGC employees. The Canadian company was Wachs' exclusive dealer for Iran, and their agreement provided that Wachs would pay the Canadian company a 10 percent commission on all sales of Wachs' goods to companies located in Iran, even if the Canadian company did not participate in the transaction.

In late 1994, the Canadian company, on behalf of the NIGC, issued purchase and sales orders for two of Wach's Trav-L-Cutters and related parts for $26,271. After the Iranian trade embargo took effect in May 1995, Wachs allegedly continued with plans to contract with the NIGC to sell pipe cutters and related items. In July 1995, the charges allege that Wachs wilfully violated the Iranian embargo by exporting pipe-cutting equipment from the United States to Canada, when Wachs employees were aware that the goods ultimately were destined for the NIGC in Iran without the required export authorization.

The charges further allege that in January 1995, Wachs issued to NIGC a quote of $4,669,643.90 for 50 Trav-L-Cutters and related items. Six months later, after the effective date of the trade embargo, a Wachs international sales coordinator issued a quote of $236,569.20 for 14 Trav-L-Cutters and other items, through a European Pakistan as the ultimate destination for the items, when the Wachs employee knew that the ultimate destination was Iran. After further negotiations over the price and amount of the pipe cutters, in September 1996, Wachs allegedly violated the Iranian embargo and the Export Administration Regulations by shipping pipe cutters and related parts and items from the United States to Canada, knowing the goods were destines for the NIGC in Iran, without the required export authorization.

Mr. Fitzgerald announced the charges with Elissa A. Brown, Special Agent-in-Charge in Chicago of the Homeland Security Department's Bureau of Immigration and Customs Enforcement, and Wendy B. Hauser, Special Agent-in-Charge in Chicago of the U.S. Commerce Department's Bureau of Industry and Security, which togther conducted the investigation. The government is being represented by Assistant U.S. Attorney George Jackson III.

Upon conviction, E.H. Wachs faces a maximum penalty on each count of five years probation and a $500,000 fine. The Court, however, will determine the appropriate sentence to be imposed under the United States Sentencing Guidelines. The public is reminded that an information contains only charges and is not evidence of guilt. The defendant is presumed innocent and is entitled to a fair trial at which the government has the burden of proving guilt beyond a reasonable doubt.

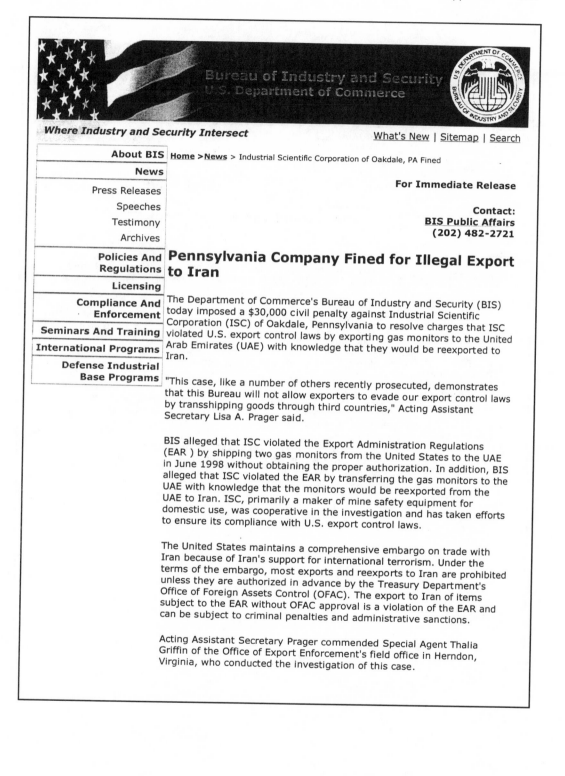

Bureau of Industry and Security
U.S. Department of Commerce

Where Industry and Security Intersect

What's New | Sitemap | Search

About BIS | Home >News > Industrial Scientific Corporation of Oakdale, PA Fined

News

Press Releases

Speeches

Testimony

Archives

Policies And
Regulations

Licensing

Compliance And
Enforcement

Seminars And Training

International Programs

Defense Industrial
Base Programs

For Immediate Release

Contact:
BIS Public Affairs
(202) 482-2721

Pennsylvania Company Fined for Illegal Export to Iran

The Department of Commerce's Bureau of Industry and Security (BIS) today imposed a $30,000 civil penalty against Industrial Scientific Corporation (ISC) of Oakdale, Pennsylvania to resolve charges that ISC violated U.S. export control laws by exporting gas monitors to the United Arab Emirates (UAE) with knowledge that they would be reexported to Iran.

"This case, like a number of others recently prosecuted, demonstrates that this Bureau will not allow exporters to evade our export control laws by transshipping goods through third countries," Acting Assistant Secretary Lisa A. Prager said.

BIS alleged that ISC violated the Export Administration Regulations (EAR) by shipping two gas monitors from the United States to the UAE in June 1998 without obtaining the proper authorization. In addition, BIS alleged that ISC violated the EAR by transferring the gas monitors to the UAE with knowledge that the monitors would be reexported from the UAE to Iran. ISC, primarily a maker of mine safety equipment for domestic use, was cooperative in the investigation and has taken efforts to ensure its compliance with U.S. export control laws.

The United States maintains a comprehensive embargo on trade with Iran because of Iran's support for international terrorism. Under the terms of the embargo, most exports and reexports to Iran are prohibited unless they are authorized in advance by the Treasury Department's Office of Foreign Assets Control (OFAC). The export to Iran of items subject to the EAR without OFAC approval is a violation of the EAR and can be subject to criminal penalties and administrative sanctions.

Acting Assistant Secretary Prager commended Special Agent Thalia Griffin of the Office of Export Enforcement's field office in Herndon, Virginia, who conducted the investigation of this case.

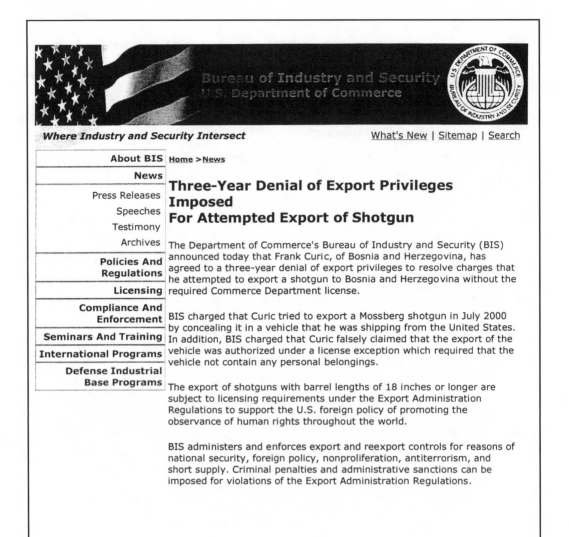

About BIS	Home >News
News	
Press Releases	
Speeches	
Testimony	
Archives	
Policies And Regulations	
Licensing	
Compliance And Enforcement	
Seminars And Training	
International Programs	
Defense Industrial Base Programs	

Three-Year Denial of Export Privileges Imposed
For Attempted Export of Shotgun

The Department of Commerce's Bureau of Industry and Security (BIS) announced today that Frank Curic, of Bosnia and Herzegovina, has agreed to a three-year denial of export privileges to resolve charges that he attempted to export a shotgun to Bosnia and Herzegovina without the required Commerce Department license.

BIS charged that Curic tried to export a Mossberg shotgun in July 2000 by concealing it in a vehicle that he was shipping from the United States. In addition, BIS charged that Curic falsely claimed that the export of the vehicle was authorized under a license exception which required that the vehicle not contain any personal belongings.

The export of shotguns with barrel lengths of 18 inches or longer are subject to licensing requirements under the Export Administration Regulations to support the U.S. foreign policy of promoting the observance of human rights throughout the world.

BIS administers and enforces export and reexport controls for reasons of national security, foreign policy, nonproliferation, antiterrorism, and short supply. Criminal penalties and administrative sanctions can be imposed for violations of the Export Administration Regulations.

DEPARTMENT OF HEALTH AND HUMAN SERVICES

Food and Drug Administration
Southwest Import District
4040 North Central XPY
Suite 300
Dallas, Texas 75204
Telephone: (214) 253-5200
FAX: (214) 253-6316

May 22, 2003

Ref: FY03-SWID-WL-010

WARNING LETTER

VIA FED-EX

Donald Palmer, President
Morven Partners, LP
9210 Arboretum Parkway, Suite 100
Richmond, VA 23236

Dear Mr. Palmer,

The Food and Drug Administration (FDA), on 3/4/03, was informed by Ms. Chaga Villanueva, of Brown, Alcantar & Brown, Inc, El Paso, TX, your broker for entry 328-0332606-8, line 1/1, that the entry was not held intact by your firm pending FDA review and release. On 4/23/03, the FDA was informed by US Customs and Border Protection that this entry was not redelivered pursuant to a Demand for Redelivery and that your firm was in violation of the entry bond agreement.

Entry Number 328-0332606-8 1/1, shelled pecans, ~~███████████████~~, was imported into the United States by your firm on 12/5/02. The entry was detained under Food, Drug and Cosmetic Act 21 USC 342(a)(1) and 381(a)(3) in that FDA laboratory analysis found *Salmonella*; additional charges included 21 USC 343(b) and 381(a)(3) in that the pecans were offered for sale under the name of another food, "AZUCAR REFINADA" (refined sugar); and, 21 USC 343(f) and 381(a)(3) in that the required label or labeling was not in English. This detention status and the violations were communicated to you through our Notice of FDA Action, dated 1/7/03, a copy of which is enclosed.

On 1/29/03, FDA Compliance Officer Catherine Vieweg contacted Ms. Villanueva and asked about your firm's intended actions regarding this detained shipment. Ms. Villanueva replied that your firm intended to export the product. C.O. Vieweg responded on 1/29/03:

> This is a significant health hazard in a ready to eat food…At the very least I would expect the FDA to inform Mexico that the pecans might be exported to Mexico. In the past, when we had made such notification, Mexico has refused to accept the product.

Ms. Villanueva responded that you would be informed and C.O. Vieweg would be contacted back with your intentions   Since no response was received, C.O. Vieweg contacted Ms. Villanueva on 2/24/03 again asking your intentions. Ms. Villanueva responded that the information would be provided on that same day (2/24/03). The response was finally received on 3/4/03 from ▮▮▮▮▮▮▮▮▮▮▮▮▮▮▮▮▮▮▮ ▮▮▮▮▮▮▮ (where you had held the pecans in question) informing FDA that the goods had already been exported to Mexico. However, the reported exportation occurred without being overseen by either FDA or Customs. The documentation your firm presented to substantiate the purported exportation reflects that ▮▮▮▮▮▮▮▮ of pecans with a total weight of ▮▮▮▮▮▮▮ were exported. This exportation cannot be reconciled with your entry of ▮▮▮▮▮▮ of pecans, total weight of ▮▮▮▮▮▮▮.

Failure to hold an entry intact pending an FDA release is a violation of 21 CFR Section 1.90, which requires the importer to hold a sampled imported article intact pending a release notice from FDA.

Failure to promptly correct this situation and prevent future premature distribution of imported products may result in requiring that future shipments be held in secured storage. Secured storage will be under the supervision and direction of U.S. Customs and Border Protection, such as in a bonded warehouse. You will be responsible for all costs incurred in secured storage.

It is your responsibility, as the importer, to ensure that imported products meet all the requirements of the Federal Food, Drug, and Cosmetic Act and the regulations promulgated thereunder.

We have requested that U.S. Customs and Border Protection order redelivery of the goods which were distributed without a FDA release. Failure to redeliver the entire shipment to Customs custody may result in assessment of liquidated damages at a later date.

We request a response in writing within fifteen(15) working days of receipt of this letter outlining the specific steps you have taken to correct the violation, including an explanation of each step being taken to prevent recurrence. In the event that the product is still available for examination, you should inform Customs and FDA if and when redelivery is accomplished.

Your written reply should be addressed to the Food and Drug Administration, Attention: Catherine L. Vieweg, Compliance Officer, Southwest Import District, 4040 North Central Expressway, Suite 300, Dallas, Texas 75204.

Sincerely,

Robert J. Deininger

Robert J. Deininger
District Director

DEPARTMENT OF HEALTH AND HUMAN SERVICES

Food and Drug Administration
Florida District
555 Winderley Place
Suite 200
Maitland Florida 32751
Telephone: 407-475-4700

VIA FEDERAL EXPRESS

Reference: Customs Entry No.DM4-0085887-2 and DM4-0085886-4
Product: Snow Peas

<u>WARNING LETTER</u>

FLA-02-58

September 10, 2002

Mr. Stanley F. Yu
Transamerica Food Enterprises
11077 NW 36th Avenue
Miami, Florida 33167

Dear Mr. Yu:

On June 1, 2002, your firm offered for import into the United States 246 cartons of snow peas
under U. S. Customs Service (Customs) entries DM4-0085887-2 and DM4-0085886-4. On June
20, 2002, the U. S. Food and Drug Administration (FDA) issued a Notice of Refusal because the
product contained chlorothalonil.[1]

Section 801(a) [21 U.S.C. § 381(a)] of the Federal Food, Drug, and Cosmetic Act ("the Act")
directs the Secretary of the Treasury to issue a Notice of Refusal when it appears from
examination of samples, or otherwise, that an imported shipment is in violation. This Section
also orders the destruction of any such shipment refused admission, unless it is exported within
90 days of the date of the notice, or within such additional time as may be permitted pursuant to
such regulations. Under the Act, the product under entries DM4-0085887-2 and DM4-0085886-4
are subject to refusal of admission pursuant to Section 801(a)(3) in that it appears to contain
pesticide chemicals, which is in violation of Section 402(a)(2)(B) [21 U.S.C. § 342(a)(2)(B)].

On July 12, 2002, FDA documented the substitution of the refused product upon examination of the
refused merchandise at the South Dade County Landfill, located at 24000 SW 97th Avenue,
Homestead, FL 30032. The product offered for destruction was labeled with an air waybill number
that did not correspond with the original air waybill number (American Airlines AWB #001-
99470615) for the refused entries DM4-0085887-2 and DM4-0085886-4. FDA investigated the
history of the air waybills and found that the product offered for destruction actually arrived nine

---

[1] There is no tolerance for chlorothalonil pursuant to 40 CFR § 180.275.

days after the original FDA refused product (entries DM4-0085887-2 and DM4-0085886-4). On July 16, 2002, you provided FDA with a signed affidavit and supporting invoices demonstrating the sale, into interstate commerce, of at least ●cartons of the refused shipment.[2]

This is a violation of Title 21, Code of Federal Regulations, Section 1.90, which requires the importer to hold an entry intact pending receipt of a May Proceed or Release Notice from FDA. Since the articles were not held and there was an attempt to evade regulation, FDA has requested Customs to increase your bond, and require future entries from your firm to be held in a bonded warehouse until FDA makes a final decision as to admissibility. You will be responsible for all costs incurred at secured storage. In addition, FDA is requesting that Customs assess liquidated damages for failure to redeliver the entry noted above.

It is your responsibility, as the importer, to ensure that imported products meet all requirements of the Act, and the regulations promulgated thereunder. We wish to remind you that making fraudulent misrepresentations or false statements to federal officials are criminal offences under Title 18, United States Code (18 U.S.C.), sections 542 and 1001. When evidence demonstrates the article presented to FDA for examination is not from the original entry, but was substituted for the entry, the article may be seized under Title 19 section 1595a. Criminal charges of entry contrary to law (18 U.S.C. § 545) may result in addition to the charges mentioned above.

Failure to promptly correct this violation and prevent future violations may result in regulatory action without further notice such as seizure, injunction, or detention without examination of future shipments. Please notify this office in writing within 15 working days of receipt of this letter, of the specific steps you have taken to correct the violation, including an explanation of each step being taken to prevent the recurrence of the violation. In addition, you should inform Customs and FDA if and when redelivery is accomplished.

Your written reply should be addressed to the Food and Drug Administration, Attention: Christine M. Humphrey, Compliance Officer, 6601 NW 25th Street, P.O. Box 59-2256, Miami, Florida 33159-2256. If you have any questions related to this matter, you may contact Ms. Humphrey at (305) 526-2800, ext. 932.

Sincerely,

Elizabeth W. Ormond

for Emma R. Singleton
Director, Florida District

---

[2] Invoice # 14722 (copy attached)

DEPARTMENT OF HEALTH & HUMAN SERVICES

Public Health Service

Food and Drug Administration
555 Winderley Pl., Ste. 200
Maitland, Fl   32751

<u>**VIA FEDERAL EXPRESS**</u>

Ref: Customs Entry No. 406-0318899-2 /001
      Product: Frozen Langostinos (shrimp)

<u>**WARNING LETTER**</u>

FLA-02-59

September 10, 2002

Mr. Mario Gatica, President
Nico's Seafood & Products Corp.
13860 S.W. 100 Lane
Miami, Florida 33186

Dear Mr. Gatica:

On May 14, 2002, the Food and Drug Administration ("FDA") issued a Notice of FDA Action to you, advising you that it would be examining the shipment of langostinos that was being offered by you for import into the United States under Customs Entry No. 406-0318899-2/001. On May 28, 2002, FDA attempted to examine this entry.

Upon examination, FDA Investigators found that the product presented by you for examination was not the product received under entry number 406-0318899-2. When the FDA Investigators informed you of this fact, you told them that you had distributed the entry. This is a serious violation of Title 21, Code of Federal Regulations, Section 1.90, which requires you to hold an entry intact and to not distribute it when FDA has notified you that it will be examining the shipment, as it did in this instance. Since the entry was not held, FDA has requested U.S. Customs to issue a Demand for Redelivery of this entry.

It is your responsibility, as the importer, to ensure that imported products meet all requirements of the Federal Food, Drug and Cosmetic Act, and the regulations promulgated thereunder. We also remind you that knowingly filing a false import entry and knowingly making fraudulent misrepresentations or false statements to federal officials are criminal offenses under Title 18, United States Code, sections 542 and 1001, respectively, and under Title 18, Section 545. Further, when evidence demonstrates that an article presented to FDA for examination is not from the original entry, but was substituted for the entry, the article may be seized by U. S. Customs Service under Title 19, section 1595a (c) and civil monetary penalties may be assessed under Title 19 section 1595a(b). Liquidated damages may also be assessed for articles not redelivered.

Your failure to promptly correct this situation and prevent future premature distribution of imported product may result in regulatory action without further notice, such as seizure, injunction, or detention of future entries without examination. In addition, such failure may result in FDA recommending to the U. S. Customs Service that it is requiring that future entries by you be held in secured storage. Secured storage would be under the supervision and direction of the U. S. Customs Service, such as in a bonded warehouse and you would be responsible for all costs incurred for such storage.

Please notify this office in writing within 15 working days of receipt of this letter, of the specific steps you have taken to correct the violation, including an explanation of each step being taken to prevent the recurrence of the violation. In addition, if the U. S. Customs Service orders you to redeliver the entry, please inform this office in writing when redelivery is accomplished. Your written reply should be addressed to the Food and Drug Administration, Attention: Carlos W. Hernandez, Compliance Officer, P.O. Box 59-2256, Miami, Florida 33159-2256.

Sincerely,

Elizabeth W. Opmand

for Emma R. Singleton
Director, Florida District

cc: Thomas Winkowski
Port Director
U. S. Customs Service
P. O. Box 02-580
Miami, Florida   33102-5280

DEPARTMENT OF HEALTH AND HUMAN SERVICES

Food and Drug Administration
Florida District
555 Winderley Place
Suite 200
Maitland Florida 32751
Telephone: 407-475-4700
FAX: 407-475-4768

VIA FEDERAL EXPRESS

Reference: Customs Entry No.DM4-0086124-9.
Product: Fresh Produce

WARNING LETTER

FLA-02-57

September 6, 2002

Alan Michael Parr, President
Team Produce International, Inc.
8850 NW 20th Street
Miami, Florida 33172

Dear Mr. Parr:

On June 12, 2002, your firm offered for import into the United States 200 cartons of French Beans, 20 cartons of Green Zucchini and 20 cartons of Sunburst Squash under U. S. Customs Service entry DM4-0086124-9. On June 12, 2002, the U. S. Food and Drug Administration (FDA) detained the products without physical examination because the product appeared to be adulterated due to the presence of pesticides. On June 28, 2002, the products were refused entry into the United States.

Section 801(a) of the Federal Food, Drug, and Cosmetic Act ("Act") directs the Secretary of the Treasury to issue a Notice of Refusal when it appears from examination of samples, or otherwise, that an imported shipment is in violation. This Section also orders the destruction of any such shipment refused admission, unless it is exported within 90 days of the date of the notice, or within such additional time as may be permitted pursuant to such regulations. Under the Act, the product under entry DM4-0086124-9 is subject to refusal of admission pursuant to Section 801(a)(3) in that it appears to contain pesticide chemicals, which is in violation of Section 402(a)(2)(B).

On June 28, 2002, FDA documented the substitution of the refused product (under entry #DM4-0086124-9). On July 10, 2002, you provided FDA with a signed affidavit and supporting invoices demonstrating the sale, into interstate commerce, of the refused shipment.

This is a violation of Title 21, Code of Federal Regulations, Section 1.90, which requires the importer to hold an entry intact pending receipt of a May Proceed or Release Notice from FDA. Since the articles were not held and there was an attempt to evade regulation, the FDA has requested U.S. Customs to increase your bond, and require future entries from your firm to be held in a bonded warehouse until FDA makes a final decision as to admissibility.

It is your responsibility, as the importer, to ensure that imported products meet all requirements of the Federal Food, Drug and Cosmetic Act, and the regulations promulgated thereunder. We wish to remind you that making fraudulent misrepresentations or false statements to federal officials are criminal offences under Title 18, United States Code (18 USC), 542 and 1001. When evidence demonstrates the article presented to FDA for examination is not from the original entry, but was substituted for the entry, the article may be seized under Title 19 section 1595a (c). Liquidated damages may also be assessed for articles not redelivered. Criminal charges of entry contrary to law (18 USC 545) may result in addition to the charges mentioned above. Criminal offenses can result in imprisonment or fines or both.

Failure to promptly correct this violation and prevent future violations may result in regulatory action without further notice such as seizure, injunction, or detention without examination of future shipments. Please notify this office in writing within 15 working days of receipt of this letter, of the specific steps you have taken to correct the violation, including an explanation of each step being taken to prevent the recurrence of the violation. In addition, you should inform Customs and FDA if and when redelivery is accomplished. Your written reply should be addressed to the Food and Drug Administration, Attention: Christine M. Humphrey, Compliance Officer, 6601 NW 25th Street, P.O. Box 59-2256, Miami, Florida 33159-2256.

Sincerely,

for Emma R. Singleton
Director, Florida District

DEPARTMENT OF HEALTH & HUMAN SERVICES

Public Health Service
Food and Drug Administratio

San Francisco District
1431 Harbor Bay Parkway
Alameda. CA 94502-7070
Telephone: 510/337-6700

VIA FEDERAL EXPRESS

June 20, 2002

Our Reference: Entry Number MA7-0708834-4, lines 001/001 and 005/001

Yaswant Singh, CEO / President
Pioneer International
8017 36th Avenue
Sacramento, CA 95824-3310

WARNING LETTER

Dear Mr. Singh:

On May 21, 2002, we attempted to sample a shipment of mahi-mahi and duruka (entered as "asparagus"), in accordance with Notice of FDA Action dated May 15, 2002 and found the shipment was not available, having already been sold. The shipment was offered for import into the United States by your firm on May 14, 2002 under entry number MA7-07078834-4.

The action taken by your firm is a violation of Title 21, Code of Federal Regulations, Section 1.90 (21CFR 1.90), which requires the importer to hold an entry intact pending receipt of a May Proceed or Release Notice. We are hereby requesting U. S. Customs to order redelivery of the part of this shipment that was not held (copy enclosed).

Failure to promptly correct this violation and prevent future premature distribution of imported products may result in requiring that future shipments be held in secured storage. Secured storage will be under the supervision and direction of the U.S. Customs Service, such as in a bonded warehouse. You would be responsible for all costs incurred in secured storage.

Within fifteen working days of receipt of this letter, notify this office in writing of the specific steps you have taken to correct the violation, including an explanation of each step being taken to prevent the recurrence of the violation. In addition, you should inform U.S. Customs and FDA if and when redelivery is accomplished.

Your written reply should be addressed to:

> Charles D. Hoffman, Compliance Officer
> U.S. Food and Drug Administration
> 1431 Harbor Bay Parkway
> Alameda, CA 94502

You may fax your response to Mr. Hoffman at: 510-337-6707.

Sincerely,

Janet Codor

for

Dennis K. Linsley
District Director
San Francisco District

Enclosure: Request to Customs to issue Redelivery Notice

DEPARTMENT OF HEALTH & HUMAN SERVICES

Public Health Service

Food and Drug Administration
555 Winderley Pl., Ste. 200
Maitland, Fl 32751

VIA FEDERAL EXPRESS

Ref: Customs Entry No. WKV-0036537-4
        Product: Frozen Lobster Tails (23,320 lbs.)

WARNING LETTER

FLA-02-46

June 3, 2002

Cauley Dennis, President
Patriot Foods, L.L.C.
800 Brickell Avenue
Suite 201
Miami, Florida 33131

Dear Mr. Dennis:

The Food and Drug Administration (FDA), on February 12, 2002, attempted to examine a shipment of frozen lobster tails in accordance with our Notice of FDA Action, dated February 12, 2002. The shipment was offered for entry into the United States by your firm on February 12, 2002, under the above referenced entry number. Although FDA requested documents for this entry on February 13, 2002, 50 cases of the adulterated product were shipped on March 8, 2002, into interstate commerce.

FDA collected physical samples of the lobster tails that revealed the presence of Salmonella. A Notice of FDA Action (refusal) was issued on April 3, 2002.

On April 18, 2002, U. S. Customs Service (Customs) notified FDA that 10 cases (▮▮ lbs.) of frozen lobster tails were not redelivered into Customs' custody pursuant to the Notice of FDA Action (refusal) dated April 3, 2002. The consignee, Penguin Frozen Foods, Inc., confirmed by letter dated April 19, 2002, that 10 cases of the original shipment could not be recovered and redelivered to Customs custody. In addition, FDA examination of the remaining portion of the lobster tails in this entry on April 23, 2002, revealed that 10 master cartons and 1 partial case (a total of ▮▮ lbs.) were unavailable. This is in violation of Title 21, Code of Federal Regulations, Section 1.90, which requires the importer to hold an entry intact pending receipt of a "May Proceed Notice" or "Notice of Release" from FDA.

Failure to promptly correct this situation and prevent future premature distribution of imported products may result in requiring that future shipments be held in secured storage. Secured storage will be under the supervision and direction of U.S. Customs Service, such as in a bonded warehouse. You will be responsible for all costs incurred in secured storage.

We request a response in writing within fifteen (15) working days of receipt of this letter outlining the specific steps you have taken to correct the violation, including an explanation of each step being taken to prevent recurrence.   In the event that the product is still available for examination, you should inform Customs and FDA if and when redelivery is accomplished.

Your written reply should be addressed to the Food and Drug Administration, Attention: Christine M. Humphrey, Compliance Officer, P.O. Box 59-2256, Miami, Florida 33159-2256.

Sincerely,

Emma R. Singleton
Director, Florida District

cc: Thomas Winkowski
        Port Director
        U. S. Customs Service
        P. O. Box 02-580
        Miami, Florida 33102-5280

DEPARTMENT OF HEALTH & HUMAN SERVICES   Public Health Service

---

Food and Drug Administration
555 Winderley Pl., Ste. 200
Maitland, Fl 32751

VIA FEDERAL EXPRESS

Ref: Customs Entry No. EJ7-0027236-5/001
       Product: Whole Pompano Fish (1000 lbs.)

WARNING LETTER

FLA-02-48

June 6, 2002

Jose Gomez, Owner
Tip Top Trading
910 N.W. 128th Court
Miami, Florida 33182

Dear Mr. Gomez:

The Food and Drug Administration (FDA), on May 10, 2002, attempted to examine a shipment of whole pompano fish in accordance with our Notice of FDA Action, dated May 8, 2002. The shipment was offered for entry into the United States by your firm on May 8, 2002, under the above referenced entry number.

On May 10, 2002, the FDA inspector noted that the shipment was unavailable for FDA examination. The product had been distributed prior to the FDA examination. Since your firm voluntarily decided to redeliver the shipment, FDA conducted a second examination of the lot at Guanabo Seafood, Miami, Florida. As per your request, on May 17, 2002, the FDA investigator conducted another examination of the product redelivered. FDA examination revealed that you were not successful in redelivering 1000 lbs. of pompano fish from this entry. This is in violation of Title 21, Code of Federal Regulations, Section 1.90, which requires the importer to hold an entry intact pending receipt of a "May Proceed Notice" or "Notice of Release" from FDA. We have requested the U. S. Customs Service (Customs) to order redelivery of 1000 lbs. of the whole pompano fish referenced above.

Failure to promptly correct this situation and prevent future premature distribution of imported product may result in U. S. Customs requiring that future shipments be held in secured storage, such as in a bonded warehouse. You would also be responsible for all costs incurred in obtaining secured storage.

We request a response in writing within fifteen (15) working days of receipt of this letter outlining the specific steps you have taken to correct the violation, including an explanation of each step being taken to prevent recurrence. In the event that the product is still available for examination, you should inform Customs and FDA, if and when redelivery is accomplished.

Your written reply should be addressed to the Food and Drug Administration, Attention: Paul R. Bagdikian, Compliance Officer, P. O. Box 59-2256, Miami, Florida 33159-2256.

Sincerely,

Emma R. Singleton
Director, Florida District

cc: Thomas Winkowski
       Port Director
       U. S. Customs Service
       P. O. Box 02-580
       Miami, Florida   33102-5280

About BIS

News

Press Releases

Speeches

Testimony

Publications

Electronic FOIA

Archives

Policies And Regulations

Licensing

Compliance And Enforcement

Seminars And Training

International Programs

Defense Industrial Base Programs

Home >News > Four Companies Settle Antiboycott Charges

FOR IMMEDIATE RELEASE

Thursday, October 27, 2011

www.bis.doc.gov

BUREAU OF INDUSTRY AND SECURITY

Office of Public Affairs

202-482-2721

Four Companies Settle Antiboycott Charges

WASHINGTON – U.S. Department of Commerce Assistant Secretary for Export Enforcement, Bureau of Industry and Security, David W. Mills announced today that four companies agreed to pay a total of $ 72,000 in civil penalties to settle allegations that each violated the antiboycott provisions of the Export Administration Regulations (EAR). The companies are: ChemGuard Inc, Bank of New York Mellon (Shanghai Branch), World Kitchen LLC, and Tollgrade Communications Inc.

Case summaries and additional information:

- **ChemGuard Inc (CGI)**, located in Mansfield, TX, has agreed to pay a civil penalty of $22,000 to settle seven allegations that it violated the antiboycott provisions of the EAR. The Bureau of Industry and Security (BIS), through its Office of Antiboycott Compliance (OAC), alleged that during the period 2005 through 2007, CGI, in connection with transactions involving the sale and/or transfer of goods or services (including information) from the United States to United Arab Emirates, on two occasions, furnished prohibited information in a statement regarding the blacklist status of the carrying vessel, in violation of the antiboycott provisions of the EAR and, on five occasions, failed to report to the Department of Commerce the receipt of a request to engage in a restrictive trade practice or boycott, as required by the EAR. Further information is available at: http://efoia.bis.doc.gov/antiboycott/violations/tocantiboycott.html

- **Bank of New York Mellon (Shanghai Branch) (BNYM)** has agreed to pay a civil penalty of $30,000 to settle fifteen allegations that it violated the antiboycott provisions of the EAR. The Bureau of Industry and Security (BIS), through its Office of Antiboycott Compliance (OAC), alleged that during the year 2007, in connection with transactions involving the sale and/or transfer of goods or services (including information) from the United States to United Arab Emirates, BNYM (Shanghai Branch), on fifteen occasions, furnished prohibited information in a statement certifying that the goods were neither of Israeli origin nor contained Israeli materials. BNYM voluntarily disclosed the transactions to BIS. Further information is available at: http://efoia.bis.doc.gov/antiboycott/violations/tocantiboycott.html

- **World Kitchen LLC (WK)**, located in Greencastle, PA, has agreed to pay a civil penalty of $10,000 to settle five allegations that it violated the antiboycott provisions of the EAR. The Bureau of Industry and Security (BIS), through its Office of Antiboycott Compliance (OAC), alleged that during the years 2006 through 2008, in connection with transactions involving the sale and/or transfer of goods or services (including information) from the United States to United Arab Emirates, WK, on five occasions, failed to report to the Department of Commerce the receipt of a request to engage in a restrictive trade practice or boycott, as required by the EAR. Further information is available at: http://efoia.bis.doc.gov/antiboycott/violations/tocantiboycott.html

- **Tollgrade Communications, Inc (TCI)**, located in Cranberry Township, PA, has agreed to pay a civil penalty of $10,000 to settle four allegations that it violated the antiboycott provisions of the EAR. The Bureau of Industry and Security (BIS), through its Office of Antiboycott Compliance (OAC), alleged that during the period 2002 through 2004, TCI, in connection with transactions involving the sale and/or transfer of goods or services (including information) from the United States to Saudi Arabia, on three occasions, furnished prohibited information in a statement regarding TCI's business activities with or in Israel, and, on one occasion, failed to report to the Department of Commerce the receipt of a request to engage in a restrictive trade practice or boycott, as required by the EAR. TCI voluntarily disclosed the transactions to BIS. Further information is available at: http://efoia.bis.doc.gov/antiboycott/violations/tocantiboycott.html

BACKGROUND

The antiboycott provisions of the EAR prohibit US persons from taking certain actions with intent to comply with, further or support unsanctioned foreign boycotts, including furnishing information about business relationships with or in a boycotted country or with blacklisted persons. In addition, the EAR requires that persons report their receipt of certain boycott requests to the Department of Commerce. For more information, please visit BIS' Online Training Room at http://www.bis.doc.gov/seminarsandtraining/seminar-training.htm or contact the OAC Advice Line at (202) 482.2381.

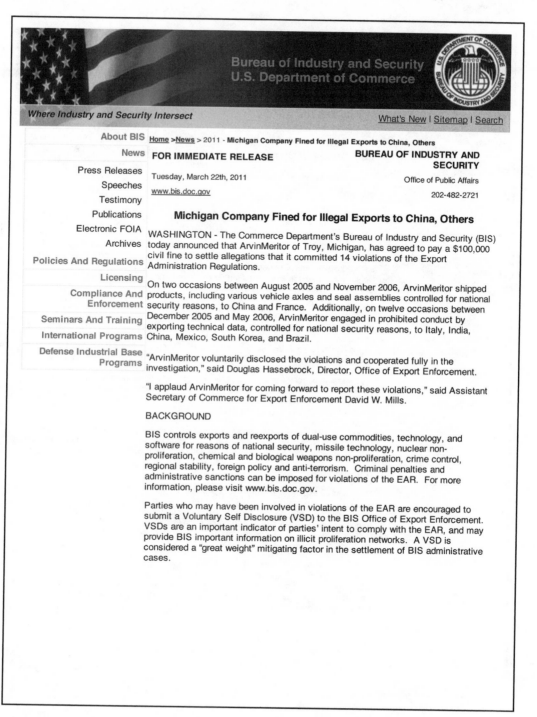

Home >News > 2011 - Michigan Company Fined for Illegal Exports to China, Others

Bureau of Industry and Security
U.S. Department of Commerce

Where Industry and Security Intersect

What's New I Sitemap I Search

About BIS
News
Press Releases
Speeches
Testimony
Publications
Electronic FOIA
Archives
Policies And Regulations
Licensing
Compliance And Enforcement
Seminars And Training
International Programs
Defense Industrial Base Programs

FOR IMMEDIATE RELEASE

Tuesday, March 22th, 2011

www.bis.doc.gov

BUREAU OF INDUSTRY AND SECURITY

Office of Public Affairs

202-482-2721

Michigan Company Fined for Illegal Exports to China, Others

WASHINGTON - The Commerce Department's Bureau of Industry and Security (BIS) today announced that ArvinMeritor of Troy, Michigan, has agreed to pay a $100,000 civil fine to settle allegations that it committed 14 violations of the Export Administration Regulations.

On two occasions between August 2005 and November 2006, ArvinMeritor shipped products, including various vehicle axles and seal assemblies controlled for national security reasons, to China and France. Additionally, on twelve occasions between December 2005 and May 2006, ArvinMeritor engaged in prohibited conduct by exporting technical data, controlled for national security reasons, to Italy, India, China, Mexico, South Korea, and Brazil.

"ArvinMeritor voluntarily disclosed the violations and cooperated fully in the investigation," said Douglas Hassebrock, Director, Office of Export Enforcement.

"I applaud ArvinMeritor for coming forward to report these violations," said Assistant Secretary of Commerce for Export Enforcement David W. Mills.

BACKGROUND

BIS controls exports and reexports of dual-use commodities, technology, and software for reasons of national security, missile technology, nuclear non-proliferation, chemical and biological weapons non-proliferation, crime control, regional stability, foreign policy and anti-terrorism. Criminal penalties and administrative sanctions can be imposed for violations of the EAR. For more information, please visit www.bis.doc.gov.

Parties who may have been involved in violations of the EAR are encouraged to submit a Voluntary Self Disclosure (VSD) to the BIS Office of Export Enforcement. VSDs are an important indicator of parties' intent to comply with the EAR, and may provide BIS important information on illicit proliferation networks. A VSD is considered a "great weight" mitigating factor in the settlement of BIS administrative cases.

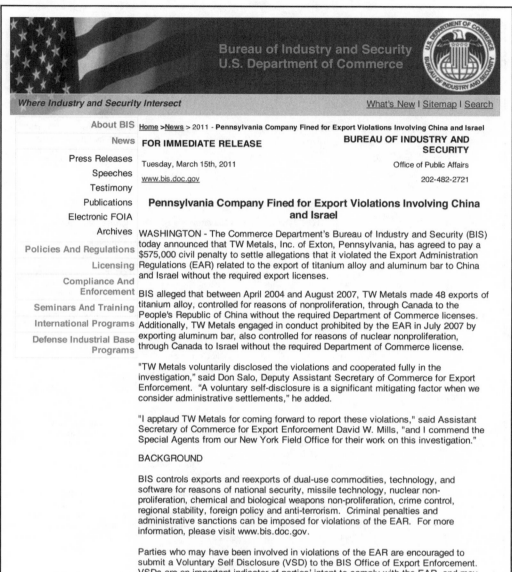

Bureau of Industry and Security
U.S. Department of Commerce

Where Industry and Security Intersect

What's New I Sitemap I Search

About BIS

News

Press Releases

Speeches

Testimony

Publications

Electronic FOIA

Archives

Policies And Regulations

Licensing

Compliance And Enforcement

Seminars And Training

International Programs

Defense Industrial Base Programs

Home >News > 2011 - Pennsylvania Company Fined for Export Violations Involving China and Israel

FOR IMMEDIATE RELEASE

Tuesday, March 15th, 2011

www.bis.doc.gov

BUREAU OF INDUSTRY AND SECURITY

Office of Public Affairs

202-482-2721

Pennsylvania Company Fined for Export Violations Involving China and Israel

WASHINGTON - The Commerce Department's Bureau of Industry and Security (BIS) today announced that TW Metals, Inc. of Exton, Pennsylvania, has agreed to pay a $575,000 civil penalty to settle allegations that it violated the Export Administration Regulations (EAR) related to the export of titanium alloy and aluminum bar to China and Israel without the required export licenses.

BIS alleged that between April 2004 and August 2007, TW Metals made 48 exports of titanium alloy, controlled for reasons of nonproliferation, through Canada to the People's Republic of China without the required Department of Commerce licenses. Additionally, TW Metals engaged in conduct prohibited by the EAR in July 2007 by exporting aluminum bar, also controlled for reasons of nuclear nonproliferation, through Canada to Israel without the required Department of Commerce license.

"TW Metals voluntarily disclosed the violations and cooperated fully in the investigation," said Don Salo, Deputy Assistant Secretary of Commerce for Export Enforcement. "A voluntary self-disclosure is a significant mitigating factor when we consider administrative settlements," he added.

"I applaud TW Metals for coming forward to report these violations," said Assistant Secretary of Commerce for Export Enforcement David W. Mills, "and I commend the Special Agents from our New York Field Office for their work on this investigation."

BACKGROUND

BIS controls exports and reexports of dual-use commodities, technology, and software for reasons of national security, missile technology, nuclear non-proliferation, chemical and biological weapons non-proliferation, crime control, regional stability, foreign policy and anti-terrorism. Criminal penalties and administrative sanctions can be imposed for violations of the EAR. For more information, please visit www.bis.doc.gov.

Parties who may have been involved in violations of the EAR are encouraged to submit a Voluntary Self Disclosure (VSD) to the BIS Office of Export Enforcement. VSDs are an important indicator of parties' intent to comply with the EAR, and may provide BIS important information on illicit proliferation networks. A VSD is considered a "great weight" mitigating factor in the settlement of BIS administrative cases.

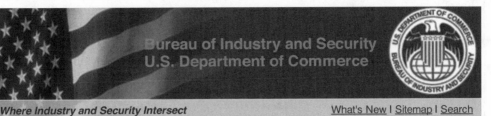

Bureau of Industry and Security
U.S. Department of Commerce

Where Industry and Security Intersect What's New I Sitemap I Search

About BIS Home > News > DOJ Press Release

News
Press Releases
Speeches
Testimony
Publications
Electronic FOIA
Archives

Policies And Regulations
Licensing
Compliance And Enforcement
Seminars And Training
International Programs
Defense Industrial Base Programs

U.S. Department of Justice
United States Attorney's Office

For Immediate Release: October 7, 2011
Contact - BIS Public Affairs: 202-482-2721

NEW YORK RESIDENT AND HIS COMPANY PLEAD GUILTY TO CONSPIRACY TO EXPORT COMPUTER-RELATED EQUIPMENT TO IRAN

WASHINGTON – Jeng "Jay" Shih, 54, a U.S. citizen, and his Queens, N.Y., company, Sunrise Technologies and Trading Corporation, pleaded guilty today in the District of Columbia to conspiracy to illegally export U.S.-origin computers from the United States to Iran through the United Arab Emirates (UAE).

The guilty pleas were announced by Lisa Monaco, Assistant Attorney General for National Security; Ronald C. Machen Jr., U.S. Attorney for the District of Columbia; John Morton, Director of U.S. Immigration and Customs Enforcement (ICE); David W. Mills, Assistant Secretary of Export Enforcement, U.S. Department of Commerce; and Adam Szubin, Director of the Office of Foreign Assets Control (OFAC), U.S. Department of the Treasury.

At a hearing today before U.S. District Judge James E. Boasberg, Shih and his company each pleaded guilty to conspiracy to violate the International Emergency Economic Powers Act (IEEPA) and to defraud the United States. The maximum sentence is five years in prison and $1 million in criminal fines. Sentencing has been scheduled for Jan. 13, 2012.

Under the terms of the plea and related civil settlements with the U.S. Department of Commerce's Bureau of Industry and Security and OFAC, Shih and his company have agreed to forfeiture of a money judgment in the amount of $1.25 million. In addition, Shih and Sunrise are denied export privileges for 10 years, although this penalty will be suspended provided that neither Shih nor Sunrise commits any export violations.

Shih was arrested on a criminal complaint on April 6, 2011. He and his company were later indicted on April 21, 2011. According to court documents filed in the case, beginning as early as about 2007, Shih conspired with a company operating in Dubai, UAE, and Tehran, Iran, to procure U.S.-origin computers through Sunrise and export those computers from the United States to Iran, through Dubai, without first obtaining a license or authorization from OFAC.

Specifically, in April 2010, the defendants caused the illegal export of 368 units of computer-related goods to Dubai, which were later sent to Iran. Later that month, the defendants caused the illegal export of 158 additional units of computer-related goods to Dubai, which were later sent to Iran. The defendants subsequently caused an additional 185 units of computer-related goods to be illegally exported to Iran via Dubai.

This investigation was conducted by the ICE-Homeland Security Investigations (HSI) field offices New York and San Diego and the Department of Commerce Office of Export Enforcement field offices in New York and Los Angeles, with assistance from ICE-HSI offices in Chicago, Newark, N.J., Los Angeles and Orange County, Calif. The Department of Homeland Security's U.S. Customs and Border Protection and OFAC's Office of Enforcement also assisted in the investigation.

Chief Counsel Attorney Gregory Michelsen and Attorney-Advisor Elizabeth Abraham from the U.S. Department of Commerce and Assistant Director of Enforcement Michael Geffroy and Enforcement Officer Elizabeth Fruzynski of the U.S. Department of Treasury handled the civil settlements for their respective agencies.

The prosecution is being handled by Assistant U.S. Attorneys T. Patrick Martin and Anthony Asuncion, from the U.S. Attorney's Office for the District of Columbia, and Trial Attorney Jonathan C. Poling from the Counterespionage Section of the Justice Department's National Security Division.

INDIVIDUALS – 31 CFR 501.801(d)(1)(ii)

(Aggregate Numbers As Of Week Ending 4/4/03)

No. Penalties Imposed and Informal Settlements Reached	Sanctions 31 CFR Part, or Executive Order	Description of Actual or Alleged Violation	Penalty Assessed, Informal Settlement, or Hearing	Aggregate Amounts of Penalties Assessed, or Settled
3	515	CTRT	A	$ 9,000.00
1	515	I	IS	$ 1,750.00

LEGEND

CTRT = Currency travel-related transaction	H = Hearing
DP = Dealing in Property	I = Import (Goods or Services)
E = Export (Goods or Services)	IS = Informal Settlement
FFR = Failure to File Report	K = Contract in which Cuba has an interest
FT = Funds Transfer	LC = Letter of Credit
F602 = Failure to Respond to .602 Request	PS = Provision of Services

PTRS = Provision of Travel-Related Services
S = Sales

OFAC Civil Penalties Enforcement Information

ENTITIES - 31 CFR 501.805(d)(1)(i)

Name	Address	Sanctions 31 CFR Part, or Executive Order	Description of Actual or Alleged Violation	Voluntary Disclosure	Amount	Assessed (A) Settled (S)
A. Kazemi & Co., Inc.	Tucson, AZ 85751	560	LC		$ 8,262.00	S
A.B.Y. Paralegal, Inc.	Miami, FL 33175	515	PTRS		$ 750.00	S
AAA Travel	Helena, MT 59604	515	PTRS		$ 500.00	S
Allfirst Financial Inc.	Baltimore, MD 21203	550	FT	v	$ 4,000.00	S
Amazon.com, Inc.	Seattle, WA 98108	515	PS		$ 1,985.68	S
Axon Corporation	Raleigh, NC 27603	560	E		$ 45,000.00	S
Banco di Napoli	New York, NY 10022	550	FT		$ 2,300.00	S
Bancomer S.A.	Los Angeles, CA 90071	515	FT		$ 5,000.00	S
Bank of New York	New York, NY 10028	585	FT		$ 24,750.00	A
Barwill Agencies (N.A.), Inc.	Houston, TX 77008	EO 13067	FT		$ 8,250.00	A
Bio Check Corp.	Burlingame, CA 94010	560	E	v	$ 32,000.00	S
The Cargill Lumber Co.	Minneapolis, MN 55440	560	FT		$ 2,000.00	S
Carrier Access Corp.	Boulder, CO 80301	560	E	v	$ 13,000.00	S
Caterpillar, Inc.	Peoria, IL 61629	515	E	v	$ 18,000.00	S
Cephar International, Inc.	Woodridge, IL 60517	550	FT		$ 2,750.00	S
Charmilles Techonologies Manufacturing Corporation	Owosso, MI 48867	538	S	v	$ 5,000.00	S
Chevron/Texaco	Concord, CA 94524	515, 575	DP, S	v	$ 14,071.07	S
Citibank, N.A.	New York, NY 10043	538	FT		$ 2,500.00	S

OFAC Civil Penalties Enforcement Information

ENTITIES - 31 CFR 501.805(d)(1)(i)

Name	Address	Sanctions 31 CFR Part, or Executive Order	Description of Actual or Alleged Violation	Voluntary Disclosure	Amount	Assessed (A) Settled (S)
Citibank, N.A.	New York, NY 10043	595	DP	V	$ 2,925.00	A
Cooper Industries, Inc.	Syracuse, NY 13221	538	E		$ 13,658.00	S
Cornell Pump Co.	Portland, OR 97222	560	E		$ 1,936.00	A
Credit Lyonnais, NY	New York, NY 10019	550	FT		$ 5,500.00	S
Dow Agrosciences, LLC	Midland MI 48641	515	K	V	$ 20,000.00	S
EMO Trans Georgia, Inc	Atlanta, GA 30354	538	E		$ 1,550.00	A
ESPN, Inc.	Bristol, CT 06010	515	K		$ 39,050.86	S
Exxon Mobil Corp.	Fairfax, VA 22037	538	E	V	$ 50,000.00	S
First Security Bank, Utah	Salt Lake City, Utah	560	FT		$63,200	S
Fleet Bank	Boston, MA 02109	560, 515	FT, E		$ 41,050.00	S
GEM Communications	New York, NY 10019	550	CTRT		$ 542.36	S
IGI, Inc.	Buena, NJ 08310	560	E		$ 225,000.00	S
International Union of Pure & Applied Chemistry (IUPAC)	Research Triangle Park, NC 27709	539	FT		$ 500.00	S
International Physicians for the Prevention of Nuclear War Inc. (IPPNW)	Cambridge, MA 02139	515	FT	V	$ 500.00	S
Metso Minerals, a/k/a Svedala Industries, Inc.	Milwaukee, WI	515	CTRT		$ 10,000.00	S
MSA Haute Couture, Inc.	New York, NY 10018	560	FT		$ 4,000.00	S
National Australia Bank	New York, NY 10166	550	FT		$ 4,779.73	S
Northern Trust, IBC	New York, NY 10040	515, 538, 586	FT		$ 18,027.00	S

OFAC Civil Penalties Enforcement Information

ENTITIES - 31 CFR 501.805(d)(1)(i)

Name	Address	Sanctions 31 CFR Part, or Executive Order	Description of Actual or Alleged Violation	Voluntary Disclosure	Amount	Assessed (A) Settled (S)
Omega World Travel	Fairfax, VA 22031	515	PTRS	V	$ 1,000.00	S
Paul Sims, Inc.	Richmond, VA 23233	EO 13121	I		$ 1,880.00	S
Royal Crown Co.	White Plains, NY 10604	538	E		$ 38,200.00	S
John Royle & Sons	Pompton Lakes, NJ 07442	EO 13088	FT		$ 3,000.00	S
Safra National Bank	New York, NY 10036	538	FT		$ 5,380.79	A
Stanadyne Automotive Corp.	Windsor, CT 06095	538	FFR		$ 1,000.00	S
Tacala, Inc.	Birmingham, AL 35243	515	I		$ 1,235.00	A
Triangle Wholesale	Racine, WI 53403	EO 13088	I		$ 11,000.00	S
Union Bank of CA	San Francisco, CA 94104	EO 13121	FT		$ 14,913.96	S
Union Bank of CA	San Francisco, CA 94104	560	E, FT		$ 12,000.00	A
Union Planters Bank	Cordova, TN 38018	538	FT		$ 4,500.00	A
Vee-Marine Int'l Corp.	Houston, TX 77002	538	E		$ 24,750.00	A
Wal-Mart Stores, Inc.	Bentonville, AR 72716	515	DP		$ 50,000.00	S
Wells Fargo Bank	San Francisco, CA 94103	538	FT		$ 5,500.00	S
Witte Travel & Tours	Grand Rapids, MI 49512	550	E		$ 1,300.00	S
World Auto Parts	Houston, TX 77091	560	I, FT		$ 5,500.00	S
Yusen Air & Sea Services (USA)	East Boston, MA 02128	560	E		$ 767.51	A
Zim American Israeli Shipping Co., Inc.	Miami, FL 33132	515	DP/CTRT		$ 250,000.00	S

OFAC Civil Penalties Enforcement Information

ENTITIES – 31 CFR 501.805(d)(1)(i)

Name	Address	Sanctions 31 CFR Part, or Executive Order	Description of Actual or Alleged Violation	Voluntary Disclosure	Amount	Assessed (A) Settled (S)
New York Yankees	Bronx, NY 10451	515	K		$ 75,000.00	S
State Bank of India	New York, NY 10022	EO 13121	FT		$ 5,500.00	S
Ruffin Company	Wichita, KS 67217	515	K		$ 42,964.18	S
Stolt-Nielson Transportation Group	Greenwich, CT 06836	538	FT		$ 95,000.00	S
Silberline Manufacturing Co., Inc.	Tamaqua, PA 18252	560	S	√	$ 2,750.00	S

OFAC Civil Penalties Enforcement Information

ENTITIES - 31 CFR 501.805(d)(1)(i)

Name	Address	Sanctions 31 CFR Part, or Executive Order	Description of Actual or Alleged Violation	Voluntary Disclosure	Amount	Assessed (A) Settled (S)
Voices in the Wilderness	Chicago, IL 60640	575	E		$ 20,000.00	A
Playboy Enterprises, Inc.	Chicago, IL 60611	515	CTRT		$ 27,500.00	S
Scientific Games, Inc.	Alpharetta, GA 30004	550	E,DP		$ 3,000.00	S

OFAC Civil Penalties Enforcement Information

ENTITIES - 31 CFR 501.805 (d) (1) (i)

Name of Entity Involved	Address	Sanctions Program	Description of Actual or Alleged Violation	Voluntary Disclosure	Amount	Assessed (A) Settled (S)
AdMarket International	Southport, CT 06490	Kosovo	2001 Funds Transfer			S
Ingersoll-Rand Co.	Woodcliff Lake, NJ 07677	Iraq	1999 Supply of goods to Iraq		$ 1,115.61	S
Bently Nevada Corporation	Minden, NV 89423	Sudan	1999 Exportation of goods to Sudan		$ 137,500.00	A
Societe Generale, New York	New York, NY 10020	Libya	2001 Funds Transfer		$ 8,250.00	A
					$ 11,000.00	A

OFAC Civil Penalties Enforcement Information
ENTITIES - 31 CFR 501.805 (d) (1) (i)

Name of Entity Involved	Address	Sanctions Program	Description of Actual or Alleged Violation	Voluntary Disclosure	Amount	Assessed (A) Settled (S)
Bank Polska Kasa Opieki SA/Bank Pekao SA	New York, NY 10016	Cuba	2001 Funds Transfer		$ 9,725.00	S
Green Peace Shipping Lines	Apple Valley, CA 92307	Sudan	2000 Attempted Exportation and Transportation of goods to Sudan		$ 4,000.00	S
National City Bank	Cleveland, OH 44101	Iran	1999 Maintenance of account		$ 5,500.00	S
National City Bank	Cleveland, OH 44101	Kosovo	1999-2000 Unblocking of funds and discrepant report		$ 250.00	S
University of California at Los Angeles	Oakland, CA 94623	Iran	2001 Funds Transfers and Execution of contract		$ 5,750.00	S
Hanjin Shipping Co., Ltd.	Jersey City, NJ 07305	Cuba	2000 Importation of goods		$ 39,160.00	A

OFAC Civil Penalties Enforcement Information

ENTITIES - 31 CFR 501.805 (d) (1) (i)

Name of Entity Involved	Address	Sanctions Program	Description of Actual or Alleged Violation	Voluntary Disclosure	Amount	Assessed (A) Settled (S)
Federal Express Corp.	Memphis, Tennessee 38132	Cuba	1999 Importation of Cuban-origin goods		$ 1,000.00	S

OFAC Civil Penalties Enforcement Information

ENTITIES - 31 CFR 501.805(d)(1)(i)

Name of Entity Involved	Address	Sanctions Program	Description of Actual or Alleged Violation	Voluntary Disclosure	Amount	Assessed (A) Settled (S)
ST Travel	Pasadena, CA 91106	Cuba	2000 Importation of Cuban-origin goods		$ 2,948.00	S

OFAC Civil Penalties Enforcement Information

ENTITIES - 31 CFR 501.805(d)(1)(i)

Name of Entity Involved	Address	Sanctions Program	Description of Actual or Alleged Violation	Voluntary Disclosure	Amount	Assessed (A) Settled (S)
American Airlines	Dallas/Ft. Worth Airport, TX 75261	Cuba	1999-2000 Provision of Travel-Related Services		$ 47,250.00	S
American Airlines	Dallas/Ft. Worth Airport, TX 75261	Iran	1997 Transportation of goods		$ 2,750.00	S

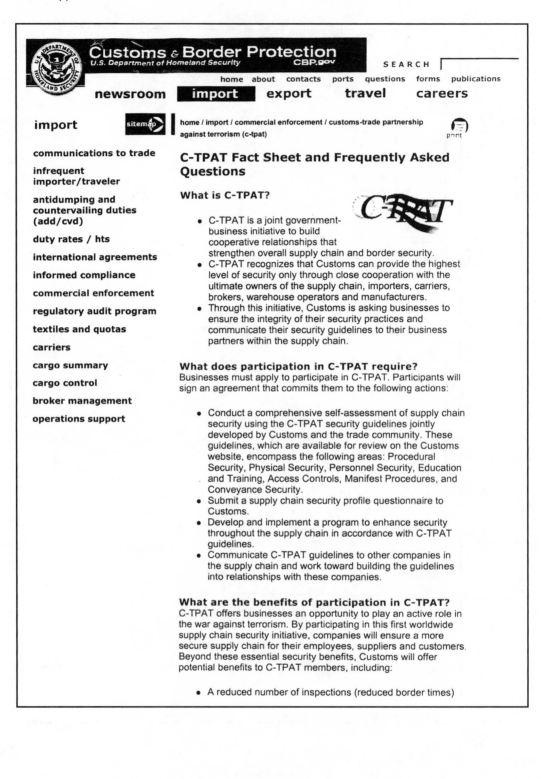

home / import / commercial enforcement / customs-trade partnership against terrorism (c-tpat)

C-TPAT Fact Sheet and Frequently Asked Questions

What is C-TPAT?

- C-TPAT is a joint government-business initiative to build cooperative relationships that strengthen overall supply chain and border security.
- C-TPAT recognizes that Customs can provide the highest level of security only through close cooperation with the ultimate owners of the supply chain, importers, carriers, brokers, warehouse operators and manufacturers.
- Through this initiative, Customs is asking businesses to ensure the integrity of their security practices and communicate their security guidelines to their business partners within the supply chain.

What does participation in C-TPAT require?

Businesses must apply to participate in C-TPAT. Participants will sign an agreement that commits them to the following actions:

- Conduct a comprehensive self-assessment of supply chain security using the C-TPAT security guidelines jointly developed by Customs and the trade community. These guidelines, which are available for review on the Customs website, encompass the following areas: Procedural Security, Physical Security, Personnel Security, Education and Training, Access Controls, Manifest Procedures, and Conveyance Security.
- Submit a supply chain security profile questionnaire to Customs.
- Develop and implement a program to enhance security throughout the supply chain in accordance with C-TPAT guidelines.
- Communicate C-TPAT guidelines to other companies in the supply chain and work toward building the guidelines into relationships with these companies.

What are the benefits of participation in C-TPAT?

C-TPAT offers businesses an opportunity to play an active role in the war against terrorism. By participating in this first worldwide supply chain security initiative, companies will ensure a more secure supply chain for their employees, suppliers and customers. Beyond these essential security benefits, Customs will offer potential benefits to C-TPAT members, including:

- A reduced number of inspections (reduced border times)

- An assigned account manager (if one is not already assigned)
- Access to the C-TPAT membership list
- Eligibility for account-based processes (bimonthly/monthly payments, e. g.)
- An emphasis on self-policing, not Customs verifications

Who is eligible for C-TPAT?

C-TPAT is currently open to all importers and carriers (air, rail, sea). Customs plans to open enrollment to a broader spectrum of the trade community in the near future. C-TPAT membership will be made available to all sectors of the supply chain. Customs will be consulting with the trade community to develop the most effective approach for each sector to participate in C-TPAT. Please refer to this site for the latest information on eligibility and application procedures.

How do I apply?

- Applicants will submit signed agreements to Customs, which will represent their commitment to the C-TPAT security guidelines.
- Applicants will also submit a supply chain security profile questionnaire at the same time they submit their signed agreements or within a specified time thereafter.
- Complete application instructions will be maintained on this site.

When will benefits begin?

Benefits will begin once Customs has completed an evaluation of the importer's C-TPAT application package and notified the importer of our findings. Customs aims to complete these evaluations within 30-60 days after the supply chain security questionnaire has been submitted.

How will the partnership work on an ongoing basis?

- Account managers will contact participants to begin joint work on establishing or updating account action plans to reflect C-TPAT commitments.
- Action plans will track participants' progress in making security improvements, communicating C-TPAT guidelines to business partners, and establishing improved security relationships with other companies.
- Failure to meet C-TPAT commitments will result in suspension of C-TPAT benefits. Benefits will be reinstated upon correcting identified deficiencies in compliance and/or security.

Where can I get more information on C-TPAT?

C-TPAT information will be maintained on this site.

Frequently Asked Questions

Q: What exactly are Customs expectations for the trade on this program?

A: To make a commitment toward the common goal of creating a more secure and efficient supply chain through partnership. Customs understands that it has entered a new era and requires the assistance of private industry to ensure increased vigilance throughout the supply chain. Customs recognizes that just as it protects the trade and our borders, businesses must ensure that their brands, employees, and customers are protected to the best of their abilities.

Q: Will the information our company provides be confidential?

A: All information on supply chain security submitted by companies applying for the C-TPAT program will be confidential. Customs will not disclose a company's participation in C-TPAT without the company's consent.

Q: As a company, we are very interested in C-TPAT but we are not interested in spending a lot of money, nor putting ourselves in a liability position if something goes wrong. Is it still possible to do this partnership?

A: Yes. Customs intent is to not impose security requirements that will be cost prohibitive. For this reason, we worked in concert with the trade community in developing security guidelines that reflect a realistic business perspective. Potential C-TPAT participants may find that they already have many of these guidelines in place.

C-TPAT is also not intended to create any new 'liabilities' for companies beyond existing trade laws and regulations. However, joining C-TPAT will commit companies to follow through on actions specified in the signed agreement. These actions include self-assessing security systems, submitting security questionnaires, developing security enhancement plans, and communicating C-TPAT guidelines to companies in the supply chain. If a company fails to uphold its C-TPAT commitments, Customs would take action to suspend benefits or cancel participation.

Q: What is the overall vision for C-TPAT in the coming months and years?

A: Customs recognizes that a safe and secure supply chain is the most critical part of our work in keeping our country safe. For this reason, Customs is seeking a strong anti-terrorism partnership with the trade community through C-TPAT. Trade partners will have a commitment to both trade security and trade compliance, which are rooted in the same business practices. Customs wants to work closely with companies whose good business practices ensure supply chain security and compliance with trade laws.

Q: How will audits work in the future?

A: Audits will continue to be used to assess overall trade compliance. Customs Regulatory Audit will apply the new "Focused Assessment" methodology, a risk-based audit program, in conducting these audits. Companies will not be required to undergo a Focused Assessment in order to participate in C-TPAT. However, to take advantage of Customs Regulatory Audit Importer Self-Assessment (ISA) program, importers must be C-TPAT participants.

Q: As a carrier, I already participate in the Customs Carrier Initiative - is it a duplication of effort in joining C-TPAT?

A: Customs will be looking for carriers to join C-TPAT to enhance existing security practices and better address the terrorism threat to international air, sea, and land shipping. We will work to ensure that C-TPAT participation does not require duplicate work for current Customs Carrier Initiative Program (CIP) participants. CIP participants already subscribe to the importance of security from a narcotics-smuggling perspective and are well positioned to expand their security focus to encompass anti-terrorism.

Q: Is the C-TPAT program a viable consideration for medium or small size companies?

A: C-TPAT is designed for the entire trade community and Customs encourages all companies to take an active role in promoting supply chain and border security. While the benefits of C-TPAT are greatest for large companies that rely heavily on international supply chains, C-TPAT is not just a big-company program. Medium and small companies may want to evaluate the requirements and benefits of C-TPAT carefully in deciding whether to apply for the program. Moreover, even without official participation in C-TPAT, companies should still consider employing C-TPAT guidelines in their security practices.

For More Information:
Contact Industry Partnership Programs at **(202) 927-0520** or email us, at industry.partnership@customs.treas.gov

FOIA | Legal Notices
Technical Questions

NEWSROOM ◼ IMPORT ◼ EXPORT ◼ TRAVEL ◼ CAREERS ◼ ENFORCEMENT
home ◼ about ◼ contacts ◼ ports ◼ questions ◼ forms
publications ◼ legal ◼ contracting

H

Customs & Border Protection | 1300 Pennsylvania Avenue, NW Washington, D.C. 20229 | (202) 354-1000

C-TPAT Validation Process
Frequently Asked Questions

What is a C-TPAT validation?

A C-TPAT validation is a process through which the Customs Service meets with company representatives and potentially visits selected domestic and foreign sites to verify that the supply chain security measures contained in the C-TPAT participant's security profile are accurate and are being followed.

What is the goal of a C-TPAT validation?

Since the decision to provide expedited release of cargo, and/or a reduced number of examinations, may be directly linked to a company's C-TPAT documentation, the principal goal of a validation for Customs is to ensure that the company's C-TPAT security profile is reliable, accurate, and effective. However, we expect that validations will also provide a forum through which Customs and a C-TPAT participant can build a stronger partnership by discussing supply chain security issues, sharing "best practices," and cooperatively developing solutions to address potential vulnerabilities. The face-to-face nature of a validation encourages both Customs and the C-TPAT participant to better understand the role each plays in securing our borders against international terrorism.

Is a C-TPAT validation an audit?

No. A validation is not a Customs audit. Whereas Customs routinely performs audits in a variety of operational areas (e.g. trade compliance, NAFTA), C-TPAT validations do not measure a company's adherence to existing government rules and regulations. Instead, the validation is focused on the reliability of the materials that a company voluntarily submits to Customs under the C-TPAT program.

How long will a validation last?

Validations will be focused and concise. Although they may extend beyond two weeks on some occasions due to Customs planning and travel, they will not involve more than ten working days of a company's time.

03/04/03

Will all companies undergo a validation?

Customs plans on validating the security profiles of all C-TPAT participants. Normally a company's initial validation will occur within three years of becoming a certified member of C-TPAT.

How will validations be scheduled?

The order in which a C-TPAT participant's profile will be selected for validation will be based on risk management principles. Validations may be initiated based on import volume, security related anomalies, strategic threat posed by geographic regions, or other risk related information. Alternatively, a validation may be performed as a matter of routine program oversight. Customs Headquarters will provide C-TPAT participants with thirty days advance written notice prior to the beginning of any validation.

How will validation findings be reported back to the company?

At the conclusion of a validation, company management will be briefed on the findings of the validation. Additionally, a Validation Report will be prepared and presented to the company shortly thereafter.

How will validation findings impact a company's participation in C-TPAT?

Ideally, the report will affirm or increase the level of benefits provided to the participant. However, depending on the findings, some or all of the participant's C-TPAT benefits may be deferred until corrective action is taken to address identified vulnerabilities. With respect to actions resulting from a validation, Customs authority will rest with the Executive Director, Border Security and Facilitation, Office of Field Operations, at Customs Headquarters.

The validation process makes reference to the C-TPAT Security Recommendations. What role do those recommendations play in the validation?

The C-TPAT security recommendations were developed jointly by Customs and the trade community as guidelines that companies should consider as they assess the effectiveness of their own supply chain security programs. With the understanding that they are not requirements and are not all-inclusive, the recommendations may help limit the scope of the validation and customize it to the C-TPAT participant involved.

03/04/03

1/23/2003

C-TPAT VALIDATION PROCESS GUIDELINES

I. Introduction

The Customs Service has developed a validation process to ensure that C-TPAT participants have implemented the security measures outlined in their Security Profile and in any supplemental information provided to Customs. The validation process will be conducted jointly by U.S. Customs personnel and a representative of the industry participant. The validation will focus on the material in the participant's C-TPAT security profile and any related materials provided by the participant and will be conducted under the guiding partnership principles of C-TPAT.

II. Objective

The purpose of the validation is to ensure that the supply chain security measures contained in the C-TPAT participant's security profile have been implemented and are being followed. In the context of the company's operations and the C-TPAT security recommendations, the validation team will evaluate the status and effectiveness of key security measures in the participant's profile and make recommendations where appropriate.

III. Validation Principles

The guiding principle of the C-TPAT program is partnership. The C-TPAT program is voluntary and designed to share information that will protect the supply chain from being compromised by terrorists and terrorist organizations.

The validation process will enable Customs and the C-TPAT participant to jointly review the participant's C-TPAT security profile to ensure that security actions in the profile are being effectively executed. Throughout the process there will also be the opportunity to discuss security issues and to share "best practices" with the ultimate goal of securing the international supply chain.

C-TPAT validations are not audits. In addition, they will be focused, concise, and will last not longer than ten work days.

Based on the participant's C-TPAT security profile and the recommendations of the validation team, Headquarters will also oversee the specific security elements to be validated.

IV. Conducting a Validation

A. Validation Selection Process

To ensure their accuracy, the security profiles of C-TPAT participants will be validated. The order in which a C-TPAT participant's profile will be selected for validation will be based on risk management principles. Validations may be initiated based on import volume, security related anomalies, strategic threat posed by geographic regions, or other risk related information. Alternatively, a validation may be performed as a matter of routine program oversight. Customs Headquarters will schedule a company's first validation within approximately three years of the company becoming a C-TPAT certified participant. Customs field offices will not initiate validations and unannounced validations will not be conducted. C-TPAT participants will be given thirty days advance written notice along with a request for any supporting documentation that is needed.

B. Partnership Validation Teams

A Partnership Validation Team (PVT), consisting of Customs Office of Field Operations personnel and a representative of the C-TPAT participant, will conduct the on-site C-TPAT validation.

Customs representatives on a PVT will be officers knowledgeable in supply chain security matters. Customs PVT members will receive supply chain security training to assist them in working with industry representatives to promote effective corporate supply chain security programs. Customs Headquarters will determine the Customs representatives for each PVT. All Customs PVT representatives will be personnel from the Office of Field Operations.

The Customs Partnership Validation Team Leader (assigned by Customs Headquarters) will be responsible for the team's reviewing the company's security profile, other security information provided by the company, and data and information retrievable from other sources to determine the focus of the validation. This will help ensure that the validation is effective and limited in duration.

C. Validation Venue

A validation is an on-site review of the participant's C-TPAT supply chain security profile. The actual site of the validation may vary depending on the aspect(s) of the participant's profile that the "C-TPAT Validation Team" will review.

Under normal circumstances the validation will begin with a briefing of company officials at the domestic corporate office or facility of the C-TPAT participant. If additional data or information is required to validate a portion of a C-TPAT participant's supply chain domestically or overseas, the PVT leader will request approval of travel through the Director, C-TPAT, at Customs Headquarters.

D. Validation Procedures

Upon receiving direction from Headquarters, Customs PVT leader will provide the company with a written notification of the scheduled validation. The notice will be issued at least thirty days prior to the start of the validation and will include a request for supporting documentation or materials, if any. The PVT leader will also contact the C-TPAT participant to establish a single point of contact at the corporate level.

Each validation will be customized for the participant involved and focused on the company's C-TPAT security profile. Prior to the on-site validation, the Customs representatives on the PVT will review the participant's C-TPAT security profile, any supplemental information received from the company, and any Customs Headquarters instructions, to determine the extent and focus of the validation.

In preparation for the on-site validation, the validation team may also consider pertinent C-TPAT security recommendations. A complete set of recommendations is included as Attachment A below. These security recommendations are a reference tool for considering the sufficiency of specific aspects of a participant's C-TPAT security profile. It is understood that the recommendations are not mandatory and are not all-inclusive with respect to effective security practices.

As noted earlier, to begin the validation, the PVT will meet with company officials to discuss the process. Upon completion of the validation, the PVT will again convene with company officers to discuss validation findings. Although not a part of the PVT, the company's Customs account manager will normally attend the company briefings that initiate and complete the validation process.

E. Validation Report

Validation findings will be documented, included in the team's final report, and forwarded to the Director of C-TPAT for final editing and sharing with the C-TPAT participant. Ideally the report will affirm or increase the level of benefits provided to the participant. However, depending on the findings, some or all of the participant's C-TPAT benefits may be deferred until corrective action is taken to address identified vulnerabilities. With respect to actions resulting from a validation, Customs authority will rest with the Executive Director, Border Security and Facilitation.

ATTACHMENT A

PREFACE

The following outlines the C-TPAT Security Recommendations that may be used by the C-TPAT Validation Team in the planning phase of an on-site validation. The recommendations are not mandatory for C-TPAT participation, but they may be helpful in the pre-validation review of key aspects of a participant's C-TPAT security profile. Therefore, prior to conducting an on-site validation, the validation team may review and discuss appropriate security recommendations contained in these attachments in the context of the participant's C-TPAT security profile. This will assist the team in limiting the scope of the validation and in customizing the validation to the C-TPAT participant involved.

IMPORTERS

Develop and implement a sound plan to enhance security procedures throughout your supply chain. Where an importer does not control a facility, conveyance or process subject to these recommendations, the importer agrees to make every reasonable effort to secure compliance by the responsible party. The following are general recommendations that should be followed on a case-by-case basis depending on the company's size and structure and may not be applicable to all.

Procedural Security: Procedures should be in place to protect against unmanifested material being introduced into the supply chain. Security controls should include the supervised introduction/removal of cargo, the proper marking, weighing, counting and documenting of cargo/cargo equipment verified against manifest documents, the detecting/reporting of shortages/overages, and procedures for verifying seals on containers, trailers, and railcars. The movement of incoming/outgoing goods should be monitored. Random, unannounced security assessments of areas in your company's control within the supply chain should be conducted. Procedures for notifying Customs and other law enforcement agencies in cases where anomalies or illegal activities are detected, or suspected, by the company should also be in place.

Physical Security: All buildings and rail yards should be constructed of materials, which resist unlawful entry and protect against outside intrusion. Physical security should include perimeter fences, locking devices on external and internal doors, windows, gates and fences, adequate lighting inside and outside the facility, and the segregation and marking of international, domestic, high-value, and dangerous goods cargo within the warehouse by a safe, caged or otherwise fenced-in area.

Access Controls: Unauthorized access to facilities and conveyances should be prohibited. Controls should include positive identification all employees, visitors, and vendors. Procedures should also include challenging unauthorized/unidentified persons.

Personnel Security: Companies should conduct employment screening and interviewing of prospective employees to include periodic background checks and application verifications.

Education and Training Awareness: A security awareness program should be provided to employees including the recognition of internal conspiracies, maintaining cargo integrity, and determining and addressing unauthorized access. These programs should offer incentives for active employee participation in security controls.

Manifest Procedures: Companies should ensure that manifests are complete, legible, accurate, and submitted in a timely manner to Customs.

Conveyance Security: Conveyance integrity should be maintained to protect against the introduction of unauthorized personnel and material. Security should include the physical search of all readily accessible areas, the securing of internal/external compartments and panels, and procedures for reporting cases in which unauthorized personnel, unmanifested materials, or signs of tampering, are discovered.

BROKERS

Develop and implement a sound plan to enhance security procedures. These are general recommendations that should be followed on a case-by-case basis depending on the company's size and structure and may not be applicable to all.

Procedural Security: Companies should notify Customs and other law enforcement agencies whenever anomalies or illegal activities related to security issues are detected or suspected.

Documentation Processing: Brokers should make their best efforts to ensure that all information provided by the importer/exporter, freight forwarder, etc., and used in the clearing of merchandise/cargo, is legible and protected against the exchange, loss or introduction of erroneous information. Documentation controls should include, where applicable, procedures for:

- Maintaining the accuracy of information received, including the shipper and consignee name and address, first and second notify parties, description, weight, quantity, and unit of measure (i.e. boxes, cartons, etc.) of the cargo being cleared.
- Recording, reporting, and/or investigating shortages and overages of merchandise/cargo.
- Safeguarding computer access and information.

Personnel Security: Consistent with federal, state, and local regulations and statutes, companies should establish an internal process to screen prospective employees, and verify employment applications. Such an internal process could include background checks and other tests depending on the particular employee function involved.

Education and Training Awareness: A security awareness program should include notification being provided to Customs and other law enforcement agencies whenever anomalies or illegal activities related to security are detected or suspected. These programs should provide:

- Recognition for active employee participation in security controls.
- Training in documentation fraud and computer security controls.

MANUFACTURERS

Develop and implement a sound plan to enhance security procedures. These are general recommendations that should be followed on a case by case basis depending on the company's size and structure and may not be applicable to all. The company should have a written security procedure plan in place that addresses the following:

Physical Security: All buildings should be constructed of materials, which resist unlawful entry and protect against outside intrusion. Physical security should include:

- Adequate locking devices for external and internal doors, windows, gates, and fences.
- Segregation and marking of international, domestic, high-value, and dangerous goods cargo within the warehouse by a safe, caged, or otherwise fenced-in area.
- Adequate lighting provided inside and outside the facility to include parking areas.
- Separate parking area for private vehicles separate from the shipping, loading dock, and cargo areas.
- Having internal/external communications systems in place to contact internal security personnel or local law enforcement police.

Access Controls: Unauthorized access to the shipping, loading dock and cargo areas should be prohibited. Controls should include:

- The positive identification of all employees, visitors and vendors.
- Procedures for challenging unauthorized/unidentified persons.

Procedural Security: Measures for the handling of incoming and outgoing goods should include the protection against the introduction, exchange, or loss of any legal or illegal material. Security controls should include:

- Having a designated security officer to supervise the introduction/removal of cargo.
- Properly marked, weighed, counted, and documented products.
- Procedures for verifying seals on containers, trailers, and railcars.
- Procedures for detecting and reporting shortages and overages.
- Procedures for tracking the timely movement of incoming and outgoing goods.
- Proper storage of empty and full containers to prevent unauthorized access.
- Procedures to notify Customs and other law enforcement agencies in cases where anomalies or illegal activities are detected or suspected by the company.

Personnel Security: Companies should conduct employment screening and interviewing of prospective employees to include periodic background checks and application verifications.

Education and Training Awareness: A security awareness program should be provided to employees including recognizing internal conspiracies, maintaining product integrity, and determining and addressing unauthorized access. These programs should encourage active employee participation in security controls.

WAREHOUSES

Develop and implement a sound plan to enhance security procedures. These are general recommendations that should be followed on a case-by-case basis depending on the company's size and structure and may not be applicable to all. Warehouses as defined in this guideline are facilities that are used to store and stage both Customs bonded and non-bonded cargo. The company should have a written security procedure plan in place addressing the following:

Physical Security: All buildings should be constructed of materials, which resist unlawful entry and protect against outside intrusion. Physical security should include:

- Adequate locking devices for external and internal doors, windows, gates and fences.
- Adequate lighting provided inside and outside the facility to include parking areas.
- Segregation and marking of international, domestic, high-value, and dangerous goods cargo within the warehouse by a safe, caged, or otherwise fenced-in area.
- Separate parking area for private vehicles separate from the shipping, loading dock, and cargo areas.
- Having internal/external communications systems in place to contact internal security personnel or local law enforcement police.

Access Controls: Unauthorized access to facilities should be prohibited. Controls should include:

- The positive identification of all employees, visitors, and vendors.
- Procedures for challenging unauthorized/unidentified persons.

Procedural Security: Procedures should be in place to protect against unmanifested material being introduced into the warehouse. Security controls should include:

- Having a designated security officer to supervise the introduction/removal of cargo.
- Properly marked, weighed, counted, and documented cargo/cargo equipment verified against manifest documents.
- Procedures for verifying seal on containers, trailers, and railcars.
- Procedures for detecting and reporting shortages and overages.
- Procedures to notify Customs and other law enforcement agencies in cases where anomalies or illegal activities are detected or suspected by the company.
- Proper storage of empty and full containers to prevent unauthorized access.

Personnel Security: Companies should conduct employment screening and interviewing of prospective employees to include periodic background checks and application verifications.

Education and Training Awareness: A security awareness program should be provided to employees including recognizing internal conspiracies, maintaining cargo integrity, and determining and addressing unauthorized access. These programs should encourage active employee participation in security controls.

AIR CARRIERS

Develop and implement a sound plan to enhance security procedures. These are general recommendations that should be followed on a case-by-case basis depending on the company's size and structure and may not be applicable to all.

Conveyance Security: Aircraft integrity should be maintained to protect against the introduction of unauthorized personnel and material. Conveyance security procedures should include the physical search of all readily accessible areas, securing all internal/external compartments and panels, and reporting cases in which unmanifested materials, or signs of tampering, are discovered.

Access Controls: Unauthorized access to the aircraft should be prohibited. Controls should include the positive identification of all employees, visitors and vendors as well as procedures for challenging unauthorized/unidentified persons.

Procedural Security: Procedures should be in place to protect against unmanifested material being introduced aboard the aircraft. Security controls should include complete, accurate and advanced lists of international passengers, crews, and cargo, as well as a positive baggage match identification system providing for the constant security of all baggage. All cargo/cargo equipment should be properly marked, weighed, counted, and documented under the supervision of a designated security officer. There should be procedures for recording, reporting, and/or investigating shortages and overages, and procedures to notify Customs and other law enforcement agencies in cases where anomalies or illegal activities are detected or suspected by the carrier.

Manifest Procedures: Companies should ensure that manifests are complete, legible, accurate, and submitted in a timely manner to Customs.

Personnel Security: Employment screening, application verifications, the interviewing of prospective employees and periodic background checks should be conducted.

Education and Training Awareness: A security awareness program should be provided to employees including recognizing internal conspiracies, maintaining cargo integrity, and determining and addressing unauthorized access. These programs should encourage active employee participation in security controls.

Physical Security: Carrier's buildings, warehouses, and on & off ramp facilities should be constructed of materials which resist unlawful entry and protect against outside intrusion. Physical security should include adequate locking devices for external and internal doors, windows, gates and fences. Perimeter fencing should also be provided, as well as adequate lighting inside and outside the facility; including parking areas. There should also be segregation and marking of international, domestic, high-value, and dangerous goods cargo within the warehouse by means of a safe, cage, or otherwise fenced-in area.

SEA CARRIERS

Develop and implement a sound plan to enhance security procedures. These are general recommendations that should be followed on a case-by-case basis depending on the company's size and structure and may not be applicable to all.

Conveyance Security: Vessel integrity should be maintained to protect against the introduction of unauthorized personnel and material. Conveyance security should include the physical search of all readily accessible areas, the securing all internal/external compartments and panels as appropriate, and procedures for reporting cases in which unmanifested materials, or signs of tampering, are discovered.

Access Controls: Unauthorized access to the vessel should be prohibited. Controls should include the positive identification of all employees, visitors, and vendors. Procedures for challenging unauthorized/unidentified persons should be in place.

Procedural Security: Procedures should be in place to protect against unmanifested material being introduced aboard the vessel. Security procedures should provide for complete, accurate and advanced lists of crews and passengers. Cargo should be loaded and discharged in a secure manner under supervision of a designated security representative and shortages/overages should be reported appropriately. There should also be procedures for notifying Customs and other law enforcement agencies in cases where anomalies or illegal activities are detected, or suspected, by the company.

Manifest Procedures: Manifests should be complete, legible, accurate and submitted in a timely manner pursuant to Customs regulations.

Personnel Security: Employment screening, application verifications, the interviewing of prospective employees and periodic background checks should be conducted.

Education and Training Awareness: A security awareness program should be provided to employees including recognizing internal conspiracies, maintaining cargo integrity, and determining and addressing unauthorized access. These programs should encourage active employee participation in security controls.

Physical Security: Carrier's buildings should be constructed of materials, which resist unlawful entry and protect against outside intrusion. Physical security should include adequate perimeter fencing, lighting inside and outside the facility, and locking devices on external and internal doors windows, gates, and fences.

LAND CARRIERS

Develop and implement a sound plan to enhance security procedures. These are general recommendations that should be followed on a case-by-case basis depending on the company's size and structure and may not be applicable to all.

Conveyance Security: Integrity should be maintained to protect against the introduction of unauthorized personnel and material. Conveyance security procedures should include the physical search of all readily accessible areas, securing all internal/external compartments and panels, and procedures for reporting cases in which unmanifested materials, or signs of tampering, are discovered.

Physical Security: All carrier buildings and rail yards should be constructed of materials, which resist unlawful entry and protect against outside intrusion. Physical security should include adequate locking devices on external and internal doors, windows, gates and fences. Perimeter fencing should be addressed, as well as adequate lighting inside and outside the facility, to include the parking areas. There should be segregation and marking of international, domestic, high-value, and dangerous goods cargo within the warehouse by a safe, caged or otherwise fenced-in area.

Access Controls: Unauthorized access to facilities and conveyances should be prohibited. Controls should include the positive identification of all employees, visitors, and vendors as well as procedures for challenging unauthorized/unidentified persons.

Procedural Security: Procedures should be in place to protect against unmanifested material being introduced aboard the conveyance. Security controls should include the proper marking, weighing, counting, and documenting of cargo/cargo equipment under the supervision of a designated security representative. Procedures should be in place for verifying seals on containers, trailers, and railcars, and a system for detecting and reporting shortages and overages. The timely movement of incoming and outgoing goods should be tracked and there should be procedures for notifying Customs and other law enforcement agencies in cases where anomalies or illegal activities are detected or suspected by the company.

Manifest Procedures: Companies should ensure that manifests are complete, legible, accurate, and submitted in a timely manner to Customs.

Personnel Security: Companies should conduct employment screening and interviewing of prospective employees to include periodic background checks and application verifications.

Education and Training Awareness: A security awareness program should be provided to employees including recognizing internal conspiracies, maintaining cargo integrity, and determining and addressing unauthorized access. These programs should encourage active employee participation in security controls.

AIR FREIGHT CONSOLIDATORS/
OCEAN TRANSPORTATION INTERMEDIARIES, AND NVOCCS

Develop and implement a sound plan to enhance security procedures. These are general recommendations that should be followed on a case-by-case basis depending on the company's size and structure and may not be applicable to all.

Procedural Security: Companies should notify Customs and other law enforcement agencies whenever anomalies or illegal activities related to security issues are detected or suspected.

Documentation Processing: Consolidators should make their best efforts to ensure that all information provided by the importer/exporter, freight forwarder, etc., and used in the clearing of merchandise/cargo, is legible and protected against the exchange, loss or introduction of erroneous information. Documentation controls should include, where applicable, procedures for:

- Maintaining the accuracy of information received, including the shipper and consignee name and address, first and second notify parties, description, weight, quantity, and unit of measure (i.e. boxes, cartons, etc.) of the cargo being cleared.
- Recording, reporting, and/or investigating shortages and overages of merchandise/cargo.
- Tracking the movement of incoming and outgoing cargo.
- Safeguarding computer access and information.

Companies should participate in the Automated Manifested System (AMS) and all data submissions should be complete, legible, accurate and submitted in a timely manner pursuant to Customs regulations.

Personnel Security: Consistent with federal, state, and local regulations and statutes, companies should establish an internal process to screen prospective employees, and verify applications. Such an internal process could include background checks and other tests depending on the particular employee function involved.

Education and Training Awareness: A security awareness program should include notification being provided to Customs and other law enforcement agencies whenever anomalies or illegal activities related to security are detected or suspected. These programs should provide:

- Recognition for active employee participation in security controls.
- Training in documentation fraud and computer security controls.

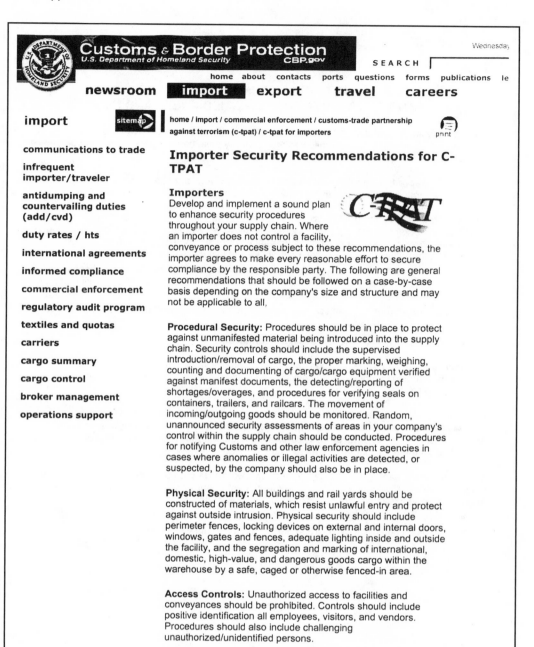

Customs & Border Protection
U.S. Department of Homeland Security   CBP.gov

Wednesday

SEARCH

home   about   contacts   ports   questions   forms   publications   le

newsroom   import   export   travel   careers

import   sitemap

home / import / commercial enforcement / customs-trade partnership
against terrorism (c-tpat) / c-tpat for importers

print

communications to trade

infrequent
importer/traveler

antidumping and
countervailing duties
(add/cvd)

duty rates / hts

international agreements

informed compliance

commercial enforcement

regulatory audit program

textiles and quotas

carriers

cargo summary

cargo control

broker management

operations support

Importer Security Recommendations for C-TPAT

Importers

Develop and implement a sound plan
to enhance security procedures
throughout your supply chain. Where
an importer does not control a facility,
conveyance or process subject to these recommendations, the
importer agrees to make every reasonable effort to secure
compliance by the responsible party. The following are general
recommendations that should be followed on a case-by-case
basis depending on the company's size and structure and may
not be applicable to all.

Procedural Security: Procedures should be in place to protect
against unmanifested material being introduced into the supply
chain. Security controls should include the supervised
introduction/removal of cargo, the proper marking, weighing,
counting and documenting of cargo/cargo equipment verified
against manifest documents, the detecting/reporting of
shortages/overages, and procedures for verifying seals on
containers, trailers, and railcars. The movement of
incoming/outgoing goods should be monitored. Random,
unannounced security assessments of areas in your company's
control within the supply chain should be conducted. Procedures
for notifying Customs and other law enforcement agencies in
cases where anomalies or illegal activities are detected, or
suspected, by the company should also be in place.

Physical Security: All buildings and rail yards should be
constructed of materials, which resist unlawful entry and protect
against outside intrusion. Physical security should include
perimeter fences, locking devices on external and internal doors,
windows, gates and fences, adequate lighting inside and outside
the facility, and the segregation and marking of international,
domestic, high-value, and dangerous goods cargo within the
warehouse by a safe, caged or otherwise fenced-in area.

Access Controls: Unauthorized access to facilities and
conveyances should be prohibited. Controls should include
positive identification all employees, visitors, and vendors.
Procedures should also include challenging
unauthorized/unidentified persons.

Personnel Security: Companies should conduct employment
screening and interviewing of prospective employees to include
periodic background checks and application verifications.

Education and Training Awareness: A security awareness program should be provided to employees including the recognition of internal conspiracies, maintaining cargo integrity, and determining and addressing unauthorized access. These programs should offer incentives for active employee participation in security controls.

Manifest Procedures: Companies should ensure that manifests are complete, legible, accurate, and submitted in a timely manner to Customs.

Conveyance Security: Conveyance integrity should be maintained to protect against the introduction of unauthorized personnel and material. Security should include the physical search of all readily accessible areas, the securing of internal/external compartments and panels, and procedures for reporting cases in which unauthorized personnel, unmanifested materials, or signs of tampering, are discovered.

FOIA | Legal Notices
Technical Questions

NEWSROOM ◼ IMPORT ◼ EXPORT ◼ TRAVEL ◼ CAREERS ◼ ENFORCEMENT
home ◼ about ◼ contacts ◼ ports ◼ questions ◼ forms
publications ◼ legal ◼ contracting

H

Customs & Border Protection | 1300 Pennsylvania Avenue, NW Washington, D.C. 20229 | (202) 354-1000

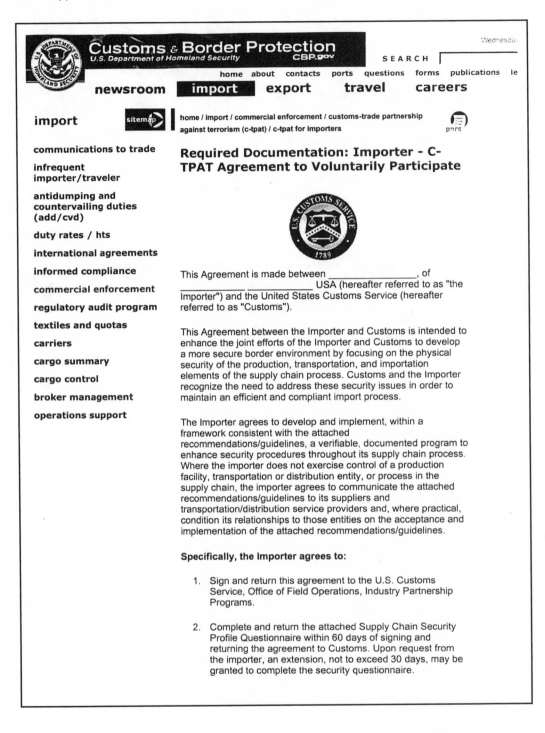

Customs & Border Protection
U.S. Department of Homeland Security   CBP.gov

SEARCH

home   about   contacts   ports   questions   forms   publications   le

newsroom   **import**   **export**   **travel**   **careers**

import   sitemap

home / import / commercial enforcement / customs-trade partnership
against terrorism (c-tpat) / c-tpat for importers   print

communications to trade

infrequent importer/traveler

antidumping and countervailing duties (add/cvd)

duty rates / hts

international agreements

informed compliance

commercial enforcement

regulatory audit program

textiles and quotas

carriers

cargo summary

cargo control

broker management

operations support

Required Documentation: Importer - C-TPAT Agreement to Voluntarily Participate

This Agreement is made between _____, of
_____ _____ USA (hereafter referred to as "the
Importer") and the United States Customs Service (hereafter
referred to as "Customs").

This Agreement between the Importer and Customs is intended to
enhance the joint efforts of the Importer and Customs to develop
a more secure border environment by focusing on the physical
security of the production, transportation, and importation
elements of the supply chain process. Customs and the Importer
recognize the need to address these security issues in order to
maintain an efficient and compliant import process.

The Importer agrees to develop and implement, within a
framework consistent with the attached
recommendations/guidelines, a verifiable, documented program to
enhance security procedures throughout its supply chain process.
Where the importer does not exercise control of a production
facility, transportation or distribution entity, or process in the
supply chain, the importer agrees to communicate the attached
recommendations/guidelines to its suppliers and
transportation/distribution service providers and, where practical,
condition its relationships to those entities on the acceptance and
implementation of the attached recommendations/guidelines.

Specifically, the Importer agrees to:

1. Sign and return this agreement to the U.S. Customs
   Service, Office of Field Operations, Industry Partnership
   Programs.

2. Complete and return the attached Supply Chain Security
   Profile Questionnaire within 60 days of signing and
   returning the agreement to Customs. Upon request from
   the importer, an extension, not to exceed 30 days, may be
   granted to complete the security questionnaire.

3. Companies will be asked to implement security and/or trade compliance improvement programs, included in their account action plans, when applicable.

Specifically, Customs agrees to:

1. Provide feedback and recommendations to the Importer on the information provided in the Supply Chain Security Profile Questionnaire within 60 days of receipt.

   Provide technical guidance when requested and when practical.

2. Consider the Importer's acceptance and implementation of the listed guidelines when making risk determinations for the purposes of cargo examinations and document reviews.

The listed recommendations/guidelines reflect the mutual understanding of the Importer and Customs of what constitutes the basic elements of supply chain security.

This Agreement will be administered pursuant to a plan jointly developed by Customs and the Importer.

This Agreement is subject to review by the Importer or Customs and may be terminated with written notice by either party.

This Agreement cannot, by law, exempt the Importer from any statutory or regulatory sanctions in the event that discrepancies are discovered during a physical examination of cargo or the review of documents associated with the Importer's Customs transactions.

All information provided by the Importer to Customs pursuant to this Agreement will remain confidential. Customs will not disclose the Importer's identity as a C-TPAT participant without the Importer's consent.

Nothing in this Agreement relieves the Importer of any responsibilities with respect to United States law, including the Customs Regulations.

_____
Assistant Commissioner
Office of Field Operations
United States Customs Service

_____
Name & Title
Company

FOIA | Legal Notices
Technical Questions

NEWSROOM ◾ IMPORT ◾ EXPORT ◾ TRAVEL ◾ CAREERS ◾ ENFORCEMENT
home ◾ about ◾ contacts ◾ ports ◾ questions ◾ forms
publications ◾ legal ◾ contracting

H

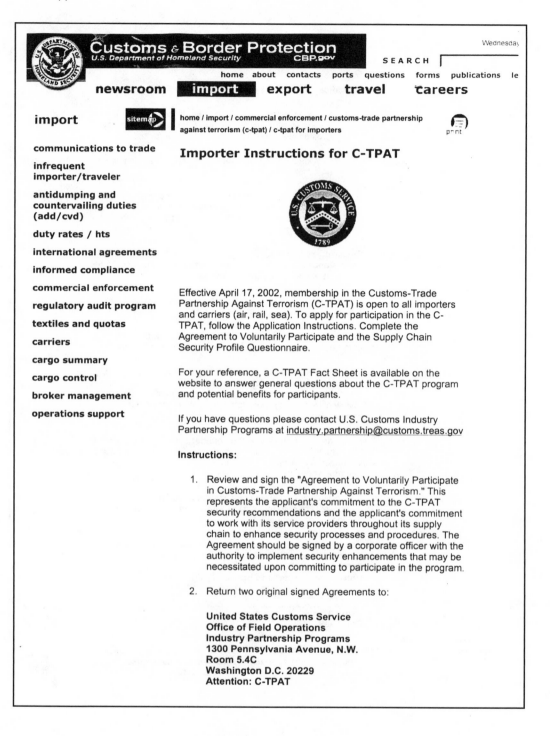

home / import / commercial enforcement / customs-trade partnership against terrorism (c-tpat) / c-tpat for importers

Importer Instructions for C-TPAT

Effective April 17, 2002, membership in the Customs-Trade Partnership Against Terrorism (C-TPAT) is open to all importers and carriers (air, rail, sea). To apply for participation in the C-TPAT, follow the Application Instructions. Complete the Agreement to Voluntarily Participate and the Supply Chain Security Profile Questionnaire.

For your reference, a C-TPAT Fact Sheet is available on the website to answer general questions about the C-TPAT program and potential benefits for participants.

If you have questions please contact U.S. Customs Industry Partnership Programs at industry.partnership@customs.treas.gov

Instructions:

1. Review and sign the "Agreement to Voluntarily Participate in Customs-Trade Partnership Against Terrorism." This represents the applicant's commitment to the C-TPAT security recommendations and the applicant's commitment to work with its service providers throughout its supply chain to enhance security processes and procedures. The Agreement should be signed by a corporate officer with the authority to implement security enhancements that may be necessitated upon committing to participate in the program.

2. Return two original signed Agreements to:

   United States Customs Service
   Office of Field Operations
   Industry Partnership Programs
   1300 Pennsylvania Avenue, N.W.
   Room 5.4C
   Washington D.C. 20229
   Attention: C-TPAT

3. Upon submission of your signed agreement, please be sure to also include (on a separate cover) the following:

   a. Official Company Name
   b. Street Address, including zip code
   c. Company Point of Contact to include:

      - Name of Point of Contact and title
      - Telephone Number
      - Fax Number
      - E-mail Address

4. Complete the Supply Chain Security Profile Questionnaire and:

   a. Mail an electronic copy contained on a 3.5" floppy disk or a CD-ROM to the address listed in item number 2.

      or

   b. E-mail a copy to industry.partnership@customs.treas.gov and include in the subject line the name of your company and "Security Questionnaire"

5. The following guidance is provided to better inform you on how to complete the Supply Chain Security Profile Questionnaire:

   a. The focus of the profile should be on the Importers Supply Chain, including the foreign countries you operate in and/or conduct business.

   b. The Security Profile should contain an executive summary outlining the process elements of the security procedures you currently have in place. The Security Profile should also identify the service providers your company utilizes and confirm that they have an active security program in place.

      NOTE: Detailed profiles of the security processes utilized by your service providers should not be forwarded to Customs as part of the profile response.

   c. Indicate if your service providers participate in Customs Industry Partnership Programs: the Customs-Trade Partnership Against Terrorism (C-TPAT), the Carrier Initiative Program (CIP), the Super Carrier Initiative Program (SCIP), the Business Anti Smuggling Coalition (BASC).

   d. Note the specific importing entities, identified by the importer number (IRS number), which are covered by the security process you detail. Specify the relationship of the listed importing entities to the company making application.

6. Upon receipt Customs will review the importers completed Supply Chain Security Profile Questionnaire. After Customs completes it's review the importer will receive a copy of the Customs-Trade Partnership Against Terrorism Agreement, signed by the Assistant Commissioner, Office of Field Operations, along with feedback on their application within 60 days.

7. An electronic confirmation indicating receipt of a signed agreement will be sent to the e-mail address provided in the application.

FOIA | Legal Notices
Technical Questions

NEWSROOM ▪ IMPORT ▪ EXPORT ▪ TRAVEL ▪ CAREERS ▪ ENFORCEMENT
home ▪ about ▪ contacts ▪ ports ▪ questions ▪ forms
publications ▪ legal ▪ contracting

H

Customs & Border Protection | 1300 Pennsylvania Avenue, NW Washington, D.C. 20229 | (202) 354-1000

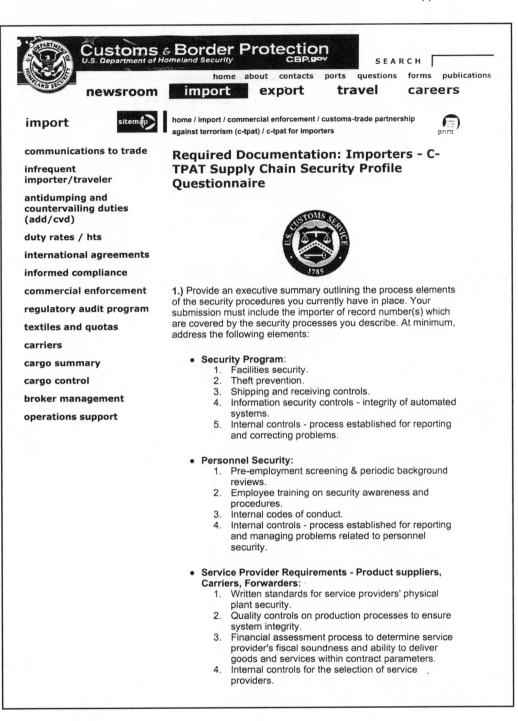

Customs & Border Protection
U.S. Department of Homeland Security — CBP.gov

SEARCH

home   about   contacts   ports   questions   forms   publications

newsroom   import   export   travel   careers

import

home / import / commercial enforcement / customs-trade partnership against terrorism (c-tpat) / c-tpat for importers

print

communications to trade

infrequent importer/traveler

antidumping and countervailing duties (add/cvd)

duty rates / hts

international agreements

informed compliance

commercial enforcement

regulatory audit program

textiles and quotas

carriers

cargo summary

cargo control

broker management

operations support

Required Documentation: Importers – C-TPAT Supply Chain Security Profile Questionnaire

1.) Provide an executive summary outlining the process elements of the security procedures you currently have in place. Your submission must include the importer of record number(s) which are covered by the security processes you describe. At minimum, address the following elements:

- **Security Program**:
  1. Facilities security.
  2. Theft prevention.
  3. Shipping and receiving controls.
  4. Information security controls - integrity of automated systems.
  5. Internal controls - process established for reporting and correcting problems.

- **Personnel Security**:
  1. Pre-employment screening & periodic background reviews.
  2. Employee training on security awareness and procedures.
  3. Internal codes of conduct.
  4. Internal controls - process established for reporting and managing problems related to personnel security.

- **Service Provider Requirements - Product suppliers, Carriers, Forwarders:**
  1. Written standards for service providers' physical plant security.
  2. Quality controls on production processes to ensure system integrity.
  3. Financial assessment process to determine service provider's fiscal soundness and ability to deliver goods and services within contract parameters.
  4. Internal controls for the selection of service providers.

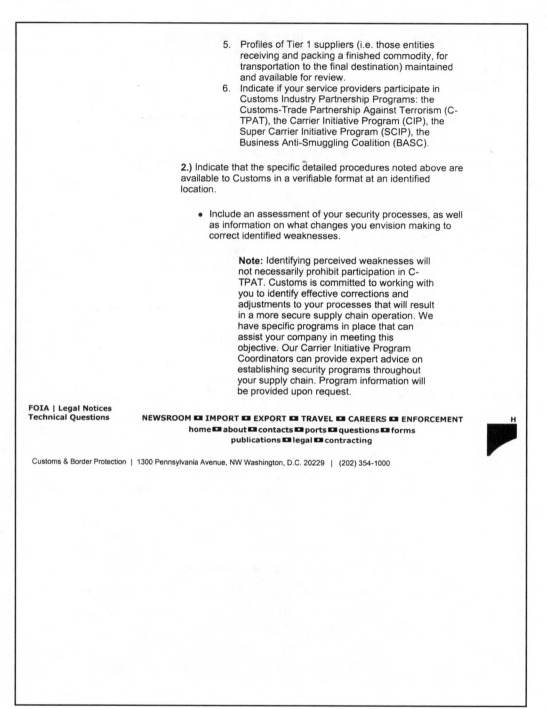

5. Profiles of Tier 1 suppliers (i.e. those entities receiving and packing a finished commodity, for transportation to the final destination) maintained and available for review.

6. Indicate if your service providers participate in Customs Industry Partnership Programs: the Customs-Trade Partnership Against Terrorism (C-TPAT), the Carrier Initiative Program (CIP), the Super Carrier Initiative Program (SCIP), the Business Anti-Smuggling Coalition (BASC).

2.) Indicate that the specific detailed procedures noted above are available to Customs in a verifiable format at an identified location.

- Include an assessment of your security processes, as well as information on what changes you envision making to correct identified weaknesses.

    Note: Identifying perceived weaknesses will not necessarily prohibit participation in C-TPAT. Customs is committed to working with you to identify effective corrections and adjustments to your processes that will result in a more secure supply chain operation. We have specific programs in place that can assist your company in meeting this objective. Our Carrier Initiative Program Coordinators can provide expert advice on establishing security programs throughout your supply chain. Program information will be provided upon request.

FOIA | Legal Notices
Technical Questions

NEWSROOM ■ IMPORT ■ EXPORT ■ TRAVEL ■ CAREERS ■ ENFORCEMENT
home ■ about ■ contacts ■ ports ■ questions ■ forms
publications ■ legal ■ contracting

H

Customs & Border Protection | 1300 Pennsylvania Avenue, NW Washington, D.C. 20229 | (202) 354-1000

CBP Officer Fact Sheet

U.S. Customs and Border Protection, Department of Homeland Security, is establishing a new frontline officer position, the CBP Officer, to serve at the Nation's ports of entry and provide the American public, travelers and the international trade community with "one face at the border." The CBP Officer will unify and integrate the work of approximately 18,000 inspectors who came together from three different agencies when CBP was formed on March 1, 2003.

Today, travelers typically encounter three uniformed government officers upon entering the U.S. However, based on an extensive job analysis, CBP has determined that <u>one integrated occupation</u> can and should be established to carry out the CBP mission at the ports of entry. The result will be "one-stop processing" and maximized efficiency for travelers and members of the trade.

The CBP Officer will perform the critical, priority mission of preventing terrorists and terrorist weapons from entering the United States, while facilitating the flow of legitimate trade and travel. In addition, building on the knowledge and skills of the consolidated workforce, the CBP Officer will continue to carry out the important traditional missions that were joined together at the ports, including interdiction of illegal drugs and other contraband, enforcing trade and immigration laws, apprehension of those attempting to enter the United States illegally, and protection of U.S. agricultural and economic interests from harmful pests and diseases.

A CBP Agriculture Specialist will support the CBP Officer in the analysis of agriculture imports and examination of cargo.

An extensive training course has been developed to support the integration and unification of the CBP workforce. The officers will receive comprehensive training in the agency's priority anti-terrorism mission and in the inspectional duties of the legacy Immigration, Agriculture Quarantine Inspection and Customs missions.

Key features of the CBP Officer:
- Recruited at the GS-5/7 level, through a rigorous battery of tests
- Career ladder through GS-11 (full performance level)
- Uniformed and armed
- Proficient in other languages as needed (Spanish will be required at some ports)
- Highly trained, with a two year program that includes basic training at the Federal Law Enforcement Training Center, extensive on-the-job training and advanced proficiency training

Implementation:
- Training of new Officer begins in October 2003.
- Legacy Customs and Immigration Inspectors will be converted to the CBP Officer position in the spring of 2004 and receive necessary cross-training.
- Agriculture Inspectors will have the opportunity to apply for CBP Officers and CBP Agriculture Specialists at the GS-11 level.

CBP Agriculture Specialist Fact Sheet

U.S. Customs and Border Protection (CBP), Department of Homeland Security, is establishing a new position, the CBP Agriculture Specialist, to play a critical role in the inspection of agricultural and related goods entering the United States. Responsibility for these inspectional functions was transferred from the U.S. Department of Agriculture (USDA) to CBP when it was formed on March 1, 2003. The CBP Agriculture Specialist will join the CBP frontline officer team in carrying out the priority mission of preventing terrorists and instruments of terrorism from entering the U.S., while expediting the flow of legitimate trade and travel. The establishment of this new position will help CBP protect the American public from agro-terrorism and bio-terrorism, while safeguarding U.S. agricultural and economic interests from the unintentional introduction of harmful pests and diseases.

The CBP Agriculture Specialist will serve as the agricultural expert at ports of entry with large volumes of cargo importation, particularly in those hubs where the agriculture industry imports much of the flowers, fruits, vegetables, and meat that are used by the American consumer. The CBP Agriculture Specialist will apply professional knowledge of the sciences to support CBP Officers in the analysis of agriculture imports and examination of cargo. Functions performed by the CBP Agriculture Specialist include pre-arrival risk analysis; cargo examination for quarantine diseases and pests; collection, preparation, and submission of pest and disease samples to USDA; seizures, safeguarding, destruction, or re-exportation of inadmissible cargo; and negotiation of compliance agreements with importers of regulated commodities.

Key features of the CBP Agriculture Specialist:
- Recruited at the GS-5/7 level
- GS-401-11 full performance level.
- Uniformed; not armed.
- Requires biological science or agriculture education.
- Maintains pesticide certification.
- Proficient in all aspects of CBP agricultural inspection.

Implementation:
- Positions will be filled competitively from among eligible Agriculture Inspectors.
- Agriculture Inspectors may also apply for promotion to the GS-11 CBP Officer position.

"One Face at the Border"
Key Questions and Answers

1.   Why is the new CBP Officer position being established?

The establishment of U.S. Customs and Border Protection (CBP) within the Department of Homeland Security brought together employees from three departments of government. Inside CBP, three different inspector occupations -- the Customs Inspector, the Immigration Inspector and the Agriculture Inspector -- joined together at the nation's ports of entry. The new CBP Officer position will unify the duties and responsibilities of these occupations, creating a corps of officers who will present "one face at the border" to travelers and the importing community. As a single inspectional workforce, they will enable CBP to effectively carry out its priority mission – preventing terrorists and terrorist weapons from entering the U.S., while facilitating the flow of legitimate trade and travel – as well as performing the traditional missions of the three legacy agencies.

While these officers are united around a common mission, they came together in CBP with different personnel and pay policies. The integration of the inspectional workforce will also eliminate disparities in personnel policies affecting employees, while creating a more effective officer corps at the air, land, and sea ports of entry.

2.   Will the CBP Officer perform all of the work of the three Inspectors?

Today's Inspectors work at airports, land border ports and seaports. The work is further divided into passenger and cargo functions, and within the passenger function, Inspectors may be stationed at "primary" or "secondary" inspection. In creating the new occupation, it is our goal to integrate the work to the extent possible, so that we could build a versatile, highly skilled workforce, able to meet the challenges of the CBP and DHS mission. However, at the same time, it was important to assure that the knowledge and skills required to perform the work could, in fact, be acquired by one officer. Therefore, an extensive job analysis was conducted to determine exactly what work could and should be incorporated into the new Officer position. This analysis showed that one Officer could perform all of the work that takes place in the passenger environment (both primary and secondary functions) and most of the work that takes place in the cargo environment. However, the complexities of cargo examination of certain kinds of agricultural products requires such a specialized background that a second position, the CBP Agriculture Specialist, is also being established to work with the CBP Officer in the cargo environment.

3.   What will the CBP Agriculture Specialist do?

The CBP Agriculture Specialist position will complement the work of the CBP Officers. These Specialists will be stationed at ports with large volumes of cargo importation, particularly in those hubs where the agriculture industry imports much of the flowers, fruits, vegetables, meat, and other products of an agricultural interest. They will apply their specialized backgrounds to support the CBP Officer in complex cargo examinations, pre-arrival risk analysis, and will be responsible for seizing, safeguarding, destroying, or re-exporting cargo. The Specialists will coordinate with USDA who will continue to manage commodity pre-clearance operations, issue export certifications, identify pests, and oversee Plant Inspection Stations as well as fumigations and cold treatments.

4.   Before DHS was formed, all of the Agriculture Inspectors were in the Department of Agriculture. Will this change to the CBP Officer detract from the agriculture inspection mission previously performed by USDA?

Not at all -- the establishment of the CBP Officer is a "force multiplier" for agriculture inspection. Now, a greatly expanded workforce of over 18,000 officers, trained to carry out important agriculture responsibilities in the processing of passengers and their baggage, will be on the frontlines to make sure that harmful pests and diseases do not enter our country. Further, the CBP Agriculture Specialists, who support the CBP Officer, will provide in-depth expertise in the analysis and examination of cargo. Plus, CBP will be unifying cargo operations so that the importer can have a "one-stop process" and cargo can be examined more quickly and more thoroughly, and released faster.

5.   Will the creation of the new positions slow down the flow of travel and trade?

Actually, trade and travel will be expedited for the vast majority of travelers and members of the trade community, who pose no threat to the American public or economy. Currently, three different inspectors are responsible for processing trade and travelers at the ports of entry. Each inspector understands his or her part of the import/ passenger process and applies this knowledge to the relevant portions. From the perspective of the traveling public, this means that they may need to interface with three different types of officers, just to complete their business or personal transactions.

With the CBP Officer, one officer will be trained in the entire import/passenger process. Thus, CBP will take advantage of a much larger, integrated workforce to carry out the responsibilities associated with the entire process. The travelling public and the trade community will have a "one-stop process" and reap the benefits of the collective resources, skills, and best practices of the combined and integrated workforces. By leveraging its resources, CBP will maximize efficiency and streamline processes that support the facilitation of lawful travel and trade. This greater efficiency will free up the CBP Officers to focus on their anti-terrorism mission as well as other risks to the American public.

6.   When will new CBP Officers be hired?

We are moving rapidly to implement "One Face at the Border". New recruits coming on board in September will be classified as Customs Inspectors for personnel and pay purposes, but we consider them our first CBP Officers because they will be the first class to attend the new, integrated CBP Officer training at the CBP Academy at the

"One Face at the Border"
Key Questions and Answers

Federal Law Enforcement Training Center.

7.   What will happen to the legacy Inspectors from Immigration, Customs and Agriculture when CBP Officers are recruited? Will they be transitioned to the new position?

During the spring of 2004, "legacy" supervisors will be reassigned to the new position, followed by legacy Immigration Inspectors, Customs Inspectors, and Canine Enforcement Officers. These legacy officers, who have the same career ladder as the CBP Officer, will be reassigned to the CBP Officer position at the same time, and at their present grade levels. However, they will not perform the full range of duties until appropriately trained in each functional area. Cross- training is already underway for legacy officers to provide them with a working knowledge of the full range of inspectional skills.

Legacy Agriculture Inspectors, whose career ladder does not currently extend to the GS-11, will be given the opportunity to apply and compete for the GS-11 CBP Officer position as well as the GS-11 CBP Agriculture Specialist position. This is because competitive procedures apply when reassigning an employee to a position with greater promotion potential than their current position. Those who do not apply, or are not selected, will remain in their current career ladders, without loss of pay, and perform Agriculture Inspection duties.

8.   What kind of training is planned to ensure that the CBP Officer can perform all of these functions?

New CBP Officers will complete a rigorous, multi-layered and comprehensive training program that includes: 10 days of Pre-Academy orientation in their home ports; 12 weeks of Basic Academy training at the Federal Law Enforcement Training Center in Glynco, Georgia; In-Port training (a combination of classroom, computer-based training and on-the-job training); and, Advanced Proficiency training.

Legacy Customs and Immigration Inspectors, who will be converted to the CBP Officer position in Spring 2004, will receive extensive cross-training in all aspects of the work of the new Officer that they have not performed in the past (e.g., Customs Inspectors will be trained in Immigration laws and vice versa). This training will take place through a series of different classes or modules. The first phase of this training is unified primary cross-training in the airport environment. Subsequent training will address airport secondary as well as cargo and land border environments.

Unlike Customs and Immigration Inspectors who attended basic Academy training at FLETC, Agriculture Inspectors have a different background; those Agriculture Inspectors who are selected to be CBP Officers will attend the complete basic training course.

"One Face at the Border"
Key Questions and Answers

9. How does the establishment of the CBP Officer relate to the DHS/OPM Human Resource Management System design project?

The Homeland Security Act provided the opportunity for a new look at a broad array of personnel practices in many areas of Federal employment. As outlined in the Act, there are specified areas which the Design Team has been charged to review, including pay rates and systems, classification, performance appraisal, labor management relations; adverse actions and appeals. The new CBP Officer occupation, which was designed to meet urgent operational needs to unify the three inspectional workforces at the ports of entry, was based on the current laws and systems governing employment in the civil service. The establishment of this position comes at an opportune time to capitalize on the work of this Design Team. Changes that result from the Design Team process will apply to CBP Officers and will enhance the ability of employees, supervisors and managers to carry out their responsibilities.

10. Why were Border Patrol Agents not included in the CBP Officer position along with inspectional officers?

Although there are many commonalities of mission, inspectional officers work in the ports of entry, while Border Patrol Agents work in the environment <u>between</u> the ports of entry. Their active patrolling of border terrain focuses on the anti-terrorism mission as well as detecting and preventing the illegal entry of persons and the smuggling of contraband. Inspectional officers perform the priority anti-terrorism mission at the over 300 ports, while facilitating the millions of legitimate travelers and conveyances passing through the ports of entry. Because of the differences in roles and geographic areas served, the Border Patrol Agent position is not being integrated with the three inspectional positions working at the ports. However, CBP Officers and Border Patrol Agents will closely coordinate their efforts in support of CBP's homeland security mission.

11. Will this change to one occupation cost the taxpayer more?

There will be no extra cost to the taxpayers. CBP plans to manage this initiative within existing resources. The ability to combine these three inspectional disciplines and to cross-train frontline officers will allow CBP to more easily handle projected workload increases and stay within present budgeted levels.

U.S. Government Contact List

U.S. DEPARTMENT OF STATE
Bureau of Political-Military Affairs   202 647-9023
Office of Defense Trade Controls   202 663-2700
(PM/DTC)

ARM LICENSING DIVISION
TIB   202 663-3618

**Licensing Officers for Applications,
Distribution Agreements and Advisory
Opinions**
Licensing Officers for Agreements   202 663-2796
Commodity Jurisdictions   202 663-2719
Compliance Division   202 663-2807
Compliance Enforcement   202 663-2809

Research and Analysis
Branch Chief   202 663-2826
Compliance Specialist   202 663-2717
Computer Support Staff   202 663-2714

System Manager, Support Staff Supervisor   202 663-2727
Access to ROBB & ALISS

Computer Specialist   202 261-8693

U.S. Customs Liaison Staff
U.S. Customs Agent   202 663-2808
Exodus Liaison Officer   202 663-2818

DTC Access & Services
Case Status   202 663-2982
Arms Licensing Division Personnel   202 663-2863

Regional Security Arms Transfer Policy
Director   202 647-9750
Deputy Director, Arms Transfer   202 647-8145
Deputy Director, Regional Security   202 647-9750

Congressional Public Affairs
Director   202 647-6968

Bureau of Non Proliferation
Deputy Assistant Secretary   202 647-6977

Export Controls & Conventional Arms
Non-Proliferation Policy

Director	202 647-2718
Deputy Director	202 647-0397

Export Control Cooperation & Sanctions

Director	202 647-1966
Deputy Director	202 647-2870
Administration	202 647-0224

Office of Chemical, Biological, & Missile
Non-Proliferation

Director	202 647-1142
Deputy Director	202 647-4009
Administration	202 647-4930

Office of Nuclear Energy Affairs

Director	202 647-3310
Deputy Director	202 647-2950

Defense Trade Advisory Group

Chairman	703 524-5522
Vice-Chairman	703 814-5549

U.S. Department of Defense-Defense
Threat Reduction Agency

Export License Status Advisory	703 602-4740
Director	703 325-3294
Secretary	703 325-3295

External Affairs & Program
Management Division

Chief	703 325-3689
Chief, External Affairs Branch	703 325-3458
Chief, Program Management Branch	703 325-3506

License Division

Chief	703 325-4108

Munitions Branch (STLM)

Chief	703 325-4108

Dual Use Branch (STLD)

Chief	703 325-4116

Technology Division

Director	703 325-3667
Military	703 325-3745
Policy	703 325-3633
Security	703 325-3631

Space Launch Monitoring Division
Chief   703 325-7085

Military Departments U.S. Army
Director   703 588-8077

U.S. Army
Security Assistance   703 617-9394
Technology   703 601-1560

U.S. Navy
Director   202 764-2352

U.S. Air Force
Division Chief   703 588-8890

**Office of the Deputy to the Under
Secretary of Defense for Policy Support**
Director, International Security   703 695-6607

**United States / Canada Joint
Certification Office**
U.S. Representative   616 961-5651

Defense Security Service
Chief   703 325-9520

**Directorate for Freedom of Information
& Security Review**
Director   703 697-4768

Defense Security Cooperation Agency
Director   703 604-6642

National Security Agency
Assistant Secretary   202 482-5491

Office of Exporter Services
Director   202 482-0436

Exporter Counseling Division
Director   202 482-4811

Export Seminar Staff
Director   202 482-6031

Regulatory Policy Division
Director   202 482-2440

Deemed Export and Short Supply Division
Director   202 501-7876

Chemical & Biological Controls Division
Director   202 482-3343

Missile Technology Controls Division
Director   202 482-3550

Nuclear Technology Controls Division
Director   202 482-1641

Treat Compliance Division
Director   703 605-4403

Inspection Management Team
Support   703 605-4405

Information Technology Team
Support   703 235-1347

Office of Strategic Industry and Economic Security
Defense Programs Division   202 482-4506
Strategic Analysis Division   202 482-4060

Office of Strategic Trade and Foreign Policy Controls
Strategic Trade Division   202 482-1837
Foreign Policy Division   202 482-0171
Encryption Division   202 482-0707

Office of Antiboycott Compliance
Director   202 482-5914

Office of Export Enforcement
Director   202 482-2252

Office of Enforcement Analysis
Export License Review Division   202 482-4255

U.S. Department of Energy—Office of Arms Control and Nonproliferation
Director   202 586-2102

U.S. Department of Treasury—Office of Foreign Assets Control
Director   202 622-2510

Bureau of Alcohol, Tobacco & Firearms

Firearms, Explosives, & Arson Service	202 927-8300
Firearms Program Division	202 927-7770
Explosives & Arson Program Division	202 927-7930
Firearms & Explosives Import Branch	202 297-8320
National Firearms Act Branch	202 927-8330
Firearms & Explosives Licensing Center	404 679-5040
United States Customs Service	202 927-2444
International Trade Compliance Division	

National Aeronautics & Space Administration

Office of External Relations	202 358-0330

U.S. Nuclear Regulatory Commission

Office of International Affairs	301 415-1780

Defense Institute of Security Assistance Management

Director	907 255-5850

Executive Office of the President - National Security Council

Nonproliferation & Export Controls	202 456-9181

Trade Events List—Export Promotion Services

Neal Burnham
Deputy Assistant Secretary
Export Promotion Services
U.S. & Foreign Commercial Service
International Trade Administration
U.S. Department of Commerce
1401 Constitution Ave., N.W. Suite 2810
Washington, D.C. 20230
Telephone: 202-482-6220
Fax: 202-482-2526
NBurnham@mail.doc.gov

DOMESTIC TRADE SHOWS – International Buyer Program

International Buyer Program (IBP) benefits U.S. companies that exhibit at domestic trade shows in that the companies are able to display their products and/or services to foreign buyers without having to travel abroad. The Commercial Service establishes an International Business Center at domestic shows were foreign buyers are welcomed and representatives of U.S. companies are given export counseling.

TRADE FAIRS – Trade Fair Certification Program

Trade Fair Certification (TFC) is a cooperative arrangement between private sector show organizers and the U.S. government to increase U.S. exports and expand U.S. participation in trade shows abroad. This program provides endorsement by the Department of Commerce, show-related services to organizers, confirmation of market viability, matchmaking services and coordination of events to recruit and promote a U.S. Pavilion at selected foreign trade shows. These shows have between 10 and over 3,000 U.S. exhibitors and host thousands of potential buyers and visitors.

TRADE MISSIONS – Commercial Service Trade Missions Program

Trade Missions introduce U.S. small and medium-sized companies to business partners in target markets abroad. Each mission usually visits two to four countries that have strong potential for U.S. goods and services. Approximately 5 to 10 people travel as a delegation with each of them representing a U.S. company.

INTERNATIONAL CATALOG EXHIBITION PROGRAM

International Catalog Exhibition Program (ICEP) works in partnership with state economic development agencies to help U.S. companies gain international market exposure for their products and/or services, and to identify potential customers and trading partners. The program allows U.S. companies to promote their products and/or services without leaving their offices. EPS and partnering states send staff to a wide range of international markets to display product literature and collect trade leads for U.S. companies.

Export Promotion Service's Trade Event List will be updated and sent to you at the beginning of each month. The list contains an explanation of each of our trade events. They are listed by the month and the type of event.

February , 2012
International Toy Fair 2012 -- Toys/Games

Location/Date: Nuremberg, Germany   2/1/2012 - 2/6/2012

Contacts:

Dagmar Winkler-Helmdach, Munich
Commercial Specialist
Phone: 49-89-2888-769
Dagmar.Winkler-Helmdach@trade.gov

Kelly A. Smith-Glover, Munich
Commercial Assistant
Phone: 49-89-2888-752
Kelly.Smith-Glover@trade.gov

Katharina Janotta, Spielwarenmesse eG

Phone: 49-911 998 13-57
k.janotta@toyfair.de

February , 2012
U.S.A. Pavilion at Taipei International Book Exhibition 2012 -- multiple industry sectors

Location/Date: Taipei City, Taiwan   2/1/2012 - 2/6/2012

Contacts:

Menny Chen, Taipei
Commercial Specialist
Phone: 886-2-2720-1550 ext 325
Menny.Chen@trade.gov

February , 2012
Brussels Holiday Show -- Travel and Tourism Industries

Location/Date: Brussels, Belgium   2/2/2012 - 2/6/2012

Contacts:

Danny Dumon, Brussels
Commercial Specialist
Phone: +32-2-811-5476
Danny.Dumon@trade.gov

Visit USA Committee, www.visitusa.org

Phone: xx
info@visitusa.org

February , 2012
Visit USA Seminar -- Travel and Tourism Industries

Location/Date: LInz, Austria   2/2/2012 - 2/2/2012

Contacts:

Ingeborg Doblinger, Vienna
Commercial Specialist
Phone: 43-1-31339-2120
Ingeborg.Doblinger@trade.gov

February , 2012
Renewable Energy Seminar -- Renewable Energy Eq.

Location/Date: Lisbon, Portugal   2/6/2012 - 2/7/2012

Contacts:

Sandillo Banerjee, Northern VA
International Trade Specialist
Phone: 703-235-0324
Dillon.Banerjee@trade.gov

Pedro Ferreira, Lisbon
Commercial Specialist
Phone: [351] (21) 770-2572
Pedro.Ferreira@trade.gov

February, 2012

International Builders' Show 2012 -- multiple industry sectors

Location/Date: Orlando, FL, United States   2/8/2012 - 2/11/2012

Contacts:

James Yi, Trade Event Programs
International Trade Specialist
Phone: 2024826482
James.Yi@trade.gov

February , 2012

Business Opportunities in Indonesia Webinar --

Register for this event

Location/Date: Philadelphia, PA, United States   2/9/2012 - 2/9/2012

Contacts:

Diego Gattesco, Wheeling
Senior International Trade Specialist
Phone: 304 243 5493
Diego.Gattesco@trade.gov

Leslie Drake, Charleston WV
USEAC Director
Phone: 304-347-5123
Leslie.Drake@trade.gov

February , 2012

Export Strategies, Tools and Techniques --

Register for this event

Location/Date: Portland, OR, United States   2/9/2012 - 2/9/2012

Contacts:

Jennifer Woods, Portland OR
Senior International Trade Specialist
Phone: 503-326-5290
Jennifer.Woods@trade.gov

February , 2012

Recreational Vehicles and Related Products Catalog Show in Japan -- Automobile/Light Truck/Vans

Location/Date: Chiba, Japan   2/10/2012 - 2/12/2012

Contacts:

Aaron Held, Tokyo
Commercial Officer
Phone: 81-3-3224-5080
Aaron.Held@trade.gov

Kevin Chambers, Tokyo
Commercial Officer
Phone: 81 (03) 3224-5092.
Kevin.Chambers@trade.gov

Koji Sudo, Tokyo
Senior Commercial Specialist
Phone: 81/3-3224-5072
Koji.Sudo@trade.gov

Sayoko Koto, Tokyo
Commercial Assistant
Phone: 81-3-3224-5079
Sayoko.Koto@trade.gov

February , 2012

SATTE 2012 -- Travel and Tourism Industries

Location/Date: New Delhi, India   2/10/2012 - 2/12/2012

                            Mumbai, India   2/15/2012 - 2/16/2012

Contacts:

Gregory O'Connor, New Delhi
Commercial Officer
Phone: +91-11-2347 2301
Greg.O'Connor@trade.gov

Helen Simpson-Davis, Trade Event Programs
Senior International Trade Specialist
Phone: 202-482-1882
Helen.Simpson-Davis@trade.gov

Marsha McDaniel, Mumbai
Commercial Officer
Phone: 91-22-2265-2511
Marsha.McDaniel@trade.gov

Sandeep Maini, New Delhi
Senior Commercial Specialist
Phone: 91-11-23472222
Sandeep.Maini@trade.gov

Smita Joshi, New Delhi
Commercial Assistant
Phone: 91-11-23472340
Smita.Joshi@trade.gov

Aliasgar Motiwala, Mumbai
Commercial Specialist
Phone: 91-22-2265-2511
aliasgar.motiwala@trade.gov

Sajid Desai, UBM India PVT, LTD

Phone: 91-22-6612-2600
sajid.desai@ubm.com

February , 2012

Aerospace Executive Service at Singapore Air Show -- multiple industry sectors

Pre-Register for this event

Location/Date: Singapore, Singapore   2/13/2012 - 2/17/2012

Contacts:

Hawcheng Ng, Singapore
Commercial Specialist
Phone: (65) 6476 9037
Hawcheng.Ng@trade.gov

Stephanie Heckel, Greensboro
Senior International Trade Specialist
Phone: 336-333-5345
Stephanie.Heckel@trade.gov

February , 2012

Singapore Air Show 2012 -- multiple industry sectors

Location/Date: Singapore, Singapore   2/14/2012 - 2/19/2012

Contacts:

Deborah Semb, Trade Event Programs
Senior International Trade Specialist
Phone: 202-482-0677
Deborah.Semb@trade.gov

Hawcheng Ng, Singapore
Commercial Specialist
Phone: (65) 6476 9037
Hawcheng.Ng@trade.gov

Gerri Cozic, Kallman Worldwide

Phone: 201/25102600, x122
gerric@kallman.com

Michael Petrassi, Kallman Worldwide

Phone: 201/251-2600, x105
mikep@kallman.com

February , 2012

BioFach 2012 and Vivaness 2012 -- multiple industry sectors

Location/Date:　　　　　　　　　Nuremberg, Germany　　　　　　　　2/15/2012 - 2/18/2012

Contacts:

Helen Simpson-Davis, Trade Event Programs
Senior International Trade Specialist
Phone: 202-482-1882
Helen.Simpson-Davis@trade.gov

Klaus Jonas, Dusseldorf
Commercial Specialist
Phone: 49-211-737-767-50
Klaus.Jonas@trade.gov

Uta Kirst, Dusseldorf
Commercial Specialist
Phone: 49 211-737-767-80
Uta.Kirst@trade.gov

Heather Kuznetz, NuernbergMesse North America, Inc

Phone: 770-618-5833
heatherk@nuernbergmesse-north-american.com

February , 2012

USG Videocon: U.S. Project/Trade Financing, Investment and Technical Assistance Support Programs -- multiple industry sectors

Location/Date:　　　　　　　　　Manila, Philippines　　　　　　　　2/15/2012 - 2/15/2012

Contacts:

Thess Sula, Manila
Commercial Specialist
Phone: DL: (632) 844-3393; (632)888-4088 x5830
Thess.Sula@trade.gov

February , 2012

U.S. Ambassador Round Table With The Canadian Auto Industry -- multiple industry sectors

Location/Date:　　　　　　　　　Toronto, Canada　　　　　　　　2/16/2012 - 2/17/2012

Contacts:

Stefan Popescu, Toronto
Commercial Specialist
Phone: 416 / 595-5412 x 223
Stefan.Popescu@trade.gov

February , 2012

ACREX India 2012 -- multiple industry sectors

Location/Date:　　　　　　　　　Bangalore, India　　　　　　　　2/23/2012 - 2/25/2012

Contacts:

James P. Golsen, Chennai
Principal Commercial Officer
Phone: 91 44 2857 4059
James.Golsen@trade.gov

Kevin Haley, Trade Event Programs
Senior International Trade Specialist
Phone: 202-482-6434
Kevin.Haley@trade.gov

Leonard Roberts, Bangalore
Senior Commercial Specialist
Phone: 91-80-2220 6402
Leonard.Roberts@trade.gov

Anna Marie Roberts, Nurnberge Messe

Phone: 770-618-5835
AnnaMarie.Roberts@nurenbergmesse-north-america.com

February , 2012

ICC China 2012 -- multiple industry sectors

Location/Date: Shenzhen, China 2/23/2012 - 2/25/2012

Contacts:

Sophie Xiao, Guangzhou
Commercial Specialist
Phone: 86-20-8667-4011 ext. 619
Sophie.Xiao@trade.gov

Sophie Xiao, CS GZ

Phone: 86 20 8667 4011
sophie.xiao@trade.gov

February , 2012

Irish Franchise Catalog Show -- Franchising

Location/Date: Dublin, Ireland 2/24/2012 - 2/25/2012

Contacts:

Finola Cunningham, Dublin
Commercial Specialist
Phone: 353-1-667-4753
Finola.Cunningham@trade.gov

February , 2012

Personal Care and Homecare Ingredients 2012 -- multiple industry sectors

Location/Date: Shanghai, China 2/27/2012 - 2/29/2012

Contacts:

Janet Li, Shanghai
Commercial Specialist
Phone: 86-21-62797630*8775; 62798775
Janet.Li@trade.gov

Lisa Huot, Trade Event Programs
Senior International Trade Specialist
Phone: 202-482-2796
Lisa.Huot@trade.gov

February , 2012

Andina Link 2012 -- multiple industry sectors

Location/Date:

Cartagena, Colombia 2/28/2012 - 3/1/2012

Contacts:

Gabriel Ramjas, Bogota
Commercial Specialist
Phone: 571-3832796
Gabriel.Ramjas@trade.gov

Graylin Presbury, Trade Event Programs
Senior International Trade Specialist
Phone: 202-482-5158
Graylin.Presbury@trade.gov

Maria F. Gomez, TDC Events International

Phone: 305-772-2549
maria@andinalink.com

February , 2012

World Smart Energy Week - 2012 -- multiple industry sectors

Location/Date: Tokyo, Japan 2/29/2012 - 3/2/2012

Contacts:

Aaron Held, Tokyo
Commercial Officer
Phone: 81-3-3224-5080
Aaron.Held@trade.gov

Kevin Haley, Trade Event Programs
Senior International Trade Specialist
Phone: 202-482-6434
Kevin.Haley@trade.gov

Takahiko Suzuki, Tokyo
Commercial Specialist
Phone: 81-3-3224-5076

March , 2012

Graphics of the Americas (GOA) 2012 -- Printing/Graphic Arts Eq.

Location/Date: Miami, FL, United States   3/1/2012 - 3/3/2012

Contacts:

Amanda Ayvaz, Trade Event Programs
International Trade Specialist
Phone: 202-482-0338
Amanda.Ayvaz@trade.gov

This International Buyer Program will be led by Adham Faltas,
Director of Trade Show Operations
Phone:

March , 2012

Security Issues Threatening U.S. Companies Working in Mexico -- multiple industry sectors

Location/Date: St. Louis, MO, United States   3/1/2012 - 3/1/2012

Contacts:

Margaret Gottlieb, St. Louis
International Trade Specialist
Phone: 314-425-3348
Margaret.Gottlieb@trade.gov

Cheryl Marty, Allied Intelligence

Phone: 314-928-0447
CMarty@alliedintel.com

March , 2012

International Hardware Fair-- multiple industry sectors

Location/Date: Cologne, Germany   3/4/2012 - 3/7/2012

Contacts:

Sabine Winkels, Dusseldorf
Commercial Specialist
Phone: 49-211-737-767-40
Sabine.Winkels@trade.gov

March , 2012

Defense & Security 2012 -- multiple industry sectors

Location/Date: Bangkok, Thailand   3/5/2012 - 3/8/2012

Contacts:

Deborah Semb, Trade Event Programs
Senior International Trade Specialist
Phone: 202-482-0677
Deborah.Semb@trade.gov

Kitisorn Sookpradist, Bangkok
Senior Commercial Specialist
Phone: 662-205-5279
Kitisorn.Sookpradist@trade.gov

Justin Webb, TNT Productions, Inc.

Phone: 703/406-0010
justin.webb@tntexpo.com

March , 2012

Russia Power 2012 -- Electrical Power Systems

Location/Date: Moscow, Russia   3/5/2012 - 3/7/2012

Contacts:

Anna Avetisyan, Moscow
Commercial Specialist
Phone: +7-495-728-53-98
Anna.Avetisyan@trade.gov

March , 2012

Visit USA Training and Workshop--Travel and Tourism Industries

Location/Date: Brussels, Belgium   3/5/2012 - 3/5/2012

Contacts:

Danny Dumon, Brussels
Commercial Specialist
Phone: +32-2-811-5476
Danny.Dumon@trade.gov

Visit USA Committee, Visit USA Committee

Phone: xx
info@visitusa.org

March , 2012

CeBIT 2012 -- multiple industry sectors

Location/Date: Hannover, Germany   3/6/2012 - 3/10/2012

Contacts:

Graylin Presbury, Trade Event Programs
Senior International Trade Specialist
Phone: 202-482-5158
Graylin.Presbury@trade.gov

Mathias Koeckeritz, Berlin
Commercial Specialist
Phone: 49-30-8305-1910
Mathias.Koeckeritz@trade.gov

Robin Estey, Hannover Fairs USA, Inc.

Phone: 609-987-1202
info@hfusa.com

March , 2012

Expo Manufactura 2012 -- multiple industry sectors

Location/Date: Monterrey, Mexico   3/6/2012 - 3/8/2012

Contacts:

Kevin Haley, Trade Event Programs
Senior International Trade Specialist
Phone: 202-482-6434
Kevin.Haley@trade.gov

Mario Vidana, Monterrey
Commerce Specialist
Phone: 528180473118
Mario.Vidana@trade.gov

John Gallagher, E.J. Krause & Associates

Phone: 301-493-5500
gallagher@ejkrause.com

March , 2012

Dental South China -- multiple industry sectors

Location/Date: Guangzhou, China   3/7/2012 - 3/10/2012

Contacts:

Jay Biggs, Guangzhou
Commercial Officer
Phone: (216) 522 - 4754
Jay.Biggs@trade.gov

Lisa Huot, Trade Event Programs
Senior International Trade Specialist
Phone: 202-482-2796
Lisa.Huot@trade.gov

Shuquan Li, Guangzhou
Senior Commercial Specialist
Phone: 86-20 8667-4011 ext.625
Shuquan.Li@trade.gov

March , 2012
Natural Products Expo West/SupplyExpo -- multiple industry sectors

Location/Date: Anaheim, CA, United States   3/8/2012 - 3/11/2012

Contacts:
Shelby Peterson, Trade Event Programs
Business and Industry Specialist
Phone: 202-482-5531
Shelby.Peterson@trade.gov
Adam Anderson, New Hope Natural Media

Phone: (303) 998-9091
aanderson@newhope.com

March , 2012
Business Opportunities in Malaysia Webinar --
Register for this event

Location/Date: Philadelphia, PA, United States   3/9/2012 - 3/9/2012

Contacts:
Diego Gattesco, Wheeling
Senior International Trade Specialist
Phone: 304 243 5493
Diego.Gattesco@trade.gov
Leslie Drake, Charleston WV
USEAC Director
Phone: 304-347-5123
Leslie.Drake@trade.gov

March , 2012
IWA & OutdoorClassics 2012 -- Sporting Goods/Recreational Eq.

Location/Date: Nuremberg, Germany   3/9/2012 - 3/12/2012

Contacts:
Moritz Holst, Munich
Commercial Assistant
Phone: 49-89-2888-754
Moritz.Holst@trade.gov

Sandra Necessary, Santa Fe
USEAC Director
Phone: 505-231-0075
Sandra.Necessary@trade.gov
Kathy Donnelly, Concord Expo Group

Phone: (801) 745 8804
conexpogrp@earthlink.net

March , 2012
SinoPack 2012 -- multiple industry sectors

Location/Date: Guangzhou, China   3/9/2012 - 3/11/2012

Contacts:
Barry Zhang, CS GZ

Phone: 86 20 8667 4011 ext. 617
barry.zhang@trade.gov

March , 2012
2012 Spring OH! Study Education Fair -- Education/Training Services

Location/Date: Taipei, Taichung and Kaohsiung, Taiwan   3/10/2012 - 3/13/2012

Contacts:
Grace Tao, Taipei
Commercial Specialist
Phone: 886-2-2720-1550 ext 383
Grace.Tao@trade.gov

March , 2012

International Home and Housewares Show 2012 -- multiple industry sectors

Location/Date: Chicago, IL, United States   3/10/2012 - 3/13/2012

Contacts:

Aditi Palli, Trade Event Programs
International Trade Specialist
Phone: 202-482-3334
Aditi.Palli@trade.gov
This International Buyer Program will be led by Derek Miller,
Vice President, International
Phone:

March , 2012

Nightclub & Bar Convention and Trade Show 2012 -- multiple industry sectors

Location/Date: Las Vegas, NV, United States   3/12/2012 - 3/14/2012

Contacts:

Vidya Desai, Trade Event Programs
International Trade Specialist
Phone: 202-482-2311
Vidya.Desai@trade.gov

March , 2012

Oceanology International 2012 -- multiple industry sectors

Location/Date: London, United Kingdom   3/13/2012 - 3/15/2012

Contacts:

Deborah Semb, Trade Event Programs
Senior International Trade Specialist
Phone: 202-482-0677
Deborah.Semb@trade.gov

John Coronado, Chicago
Commercial Officer
Phone: 312-353-4453
John.Coronado@trade.gov

Sara Jones, London
Commercial Assistant
Phone: +44 (0) 20 7894 0451
Sara.Jones@trade.gov

Alex Goodman, Reed Exhibitions Ltd

Phone: 203/840-5641
agoodman@reedexpo.com

March , 2012

U.S. Pavilion at MITT 2012 -- Travel and Tourism Industries

Location/Date: Moscow, Russia   3/13/2012 - 3/16/2012

Contacts:

Gulnara Kenzhebulatova, Moscow
Commercial Specialist
Phone: +7 495 728-5405
Gulnara.Kenzhebulatova@trade.gov

Margarita Babayan, Visit USA Russia

Phone: 7 495 935 7925
chair@visit-usa.ru

March , 2012

Globe 2012 -- multiple industry sectors

Location/Date: Vancouver, Canada, Canada   3/14/2012 - 3/16/2012

Contacts:

Cheryl Schell, Vancouver
Senior Commercial Specialist
Phone: (604) 642-6679
Cheryl.Schell@trade.gov
Jessica Arnold, Trade Event Programs
International Trade Specialist
Phone: 202-482-2026
Jessica.Arnold@trade.gov
Michael Thompson, Trade Event Programs
International Trade Specialist
Phone: 202-482-0671
Michael.Thompson@trade.gov

Trish Wuttunee, Globe Foundation
Phone: 604 633 0703
trish@globe.ca

March , 2012

Shinyway Int'l Study Fair -- Education/Training Services

Location/Date: Guangzhou, China   3/15/2012 - 3/17/2012

Contacts:

Eileen Bai, CS GZ

Phone: 86 20 8667 4011
eileen.bai@trade.gov

March , 2012

Paris Book Fair U.S. Pavilion -- multiple industry sectors

Location/Date: Paris, France   3/16/2012 - 3/19/2012

Contacts:

Dawn Bruno, New York
International Trade Specialist
Phone: 212-809-2647
Dawn.Bruno@trade.gov

Delia Valdivia, Los Angeles (West)
International Trade Specialist
Phone: 310-235-7203
Delia.Valdivia@trade.gov

Valerie Ferriere, Paris
Commercial Specialist
Phone: [33] (0)1 43 12 70 77
Valerie.Ferriere@trade.gov

March , 2012

Golf Show -- Travel and Tourism Industries

Location/Date: Beijing, China   3/18/2012 - 3/20/2012

Contacts:

Jing Wei, Beijing
Commercial Assistant
Phone: (86-10) 8531 4296
Jing.Wei@trade.gov

March , 2012

Unmanned Systems Israel 2012 -- multiple industry sectors

Pre-Register for this event

Location/Date: Tel Aviv, Israel, Israel   3/18/2012 - 3/22/2012

Contacts:

Irit van der Veur, Tel Aviv
Senior Commercial Specialist
Phone: 972-3-519-7540
Irit.Vanderveur@trade.gov

March , 2012

ISNR 2012 -- Security/Safety Eq.

Location/Date: Abu Dhabi, United Arab Emirates   3/19/2012 - 3/21/2012

Contacts:

Graylin Presbury, Trade Event Programs
Senior International Trade Specialist
Phone: 202-482-5158
Graylin.Presbury@trade.gov

John Simmons, Abu Dhabi
Senior Commercial Officer
Phone: +971 2 414 2665
John.Simmons@trade.gov

Laurie Farris, Brussels
Senior Commercial Officer
Phone: +32-2-811-5269
Laurie.Farris@trade.gov

Rula Omeish, Abu Dhabi
Commercial Specialist
Phone: 971-2-414-2217
Rula.Omeish@trade.gov

Ray Filbert, Reed Exhibitions

Phone: 203-840-4800
rfilbert@reedexpo.com

March , 2012

Ecobuild 2012 -- multiple industry sectors

Location/Date: London, United Kingdom   3/20/2012 - 3/22/2012

Contacts:

Cheryl Withers, London
Commercial Assistant
Phone: +44 (0) 20 7894 0471
Cheryl.Withers@trade.gov

Kevin Haley, Trade Event Programs
Senior International Trade Specialist
Phone: 202-482-6434
Kevin.Haley@trade.gov

Borris Murray, Atlas Marketing International
Phone: 514-802-2789
bmurray@atlasmarketing.ca

March , 2012

Hot Market Watch: Selling to Brazil, China, South Korea & Vietnam/ASEAN --

Location/Date: Cincinnati, OH, United States   3/21/2012 - 3/22/2012

Contacts:

Marcia Brandstadt, Cincinnati
USEAC Director
Phone: (513) 684-3829
Marcia.Brandstadt@trade.gov

March , 2012

Musikmesse 2012 -- Musical Instruments

Location/Date: Frankfurt, Germany   3/21/2012 - 3/24/2012

Contacts:

Volker Wirsdorf, Frankfurt
Senior Commercial Specialist
Phone: 49-69-7535 3150
Volker.Wirsdorf@trade.gov

March , 2012

Cippe 2012 -- Oil/Gas Field Machinery

Location/Date: Beijing, China   3/22/2012 - 3/24/2012

Contacts:

Jianhong Wang, Beijing
Senior Commercial Specialist
Phone: (86-10) 8531 3424
Jianhong.Wang@trade.gov

March , 2012

Hair Brasil 2012 -- Cosmetics/Toiletries

Location/Date: Sao Paulo, Brazil   3/24/2012 - 3/27/2012

Contacts:

Denise Barbosa, Sao Paulo
Commercial Specialist
Phone: 55/11/5186-7390
Denise.Barbosa@trade.gov

Helen Simpson-Davis, Trade Event Programs
Senior International Trade Specialist
Phone: 202-482-1882
Helen.Simpson-Davis@trade.gov

Daniela Yuri Tiba, Sao Paulo Feiras Comerciais Ltda

Phone: 5511 3063 2911
daniela.tiba@hairbrasil.com.br

March , 2012

JEC Composites Show Paris 2012 -- multiple industry sectors

Pre-Register for this event

Location/Date: Paris, France   3/26/2012 - 3/29/2012

Contacts:

Stephanie Pencole, Paris
Commercial Specialist
Phone: [33] (0)1 43 12 71 38
Stephanie.Pencole@trade.gov

March , 2012

ABACE 2012 -- multiple industry sectors

Location/Date: Shanghai, China   3/27/2012 - 3/29/2012

Contacts:

Deborah Semb, Trade Event Programs
Senior International Trade Specialist
Phone: 202-482-0677
Deborah.Semb@trade.gov

Landon Loomis, Beijing
Commercial Officer
Phone: +86-135-1106-1734
Landon.Loomis@trade.gov

Vivien Bao, Shanghai
Commercial Specialist
Phone: (86-21)6279-8766
Vivien.Bao@trade.gov

Kathleen Blouin, NBAA

Phone: 202/783-9000
kblouin@nbaa.org

Marc Freeman, NBAA

Phone: 202/478-7769
mfreeman@nbaa.org

March , 2012

Aircraft Interiors Expo 2012 -- Aircraft/Aircraft Parts

Location/Date: Hamburg, Germany   3/27/2012 - 3/29/2012

Contacts:

Moritz Holst, Munich
Commercial Assistant
Phone: 49-89-2888-754
Moritz.Holst@trade.gov

Tom Mapes, Reed Exhibitions

Phone: (203) 840-5526
tmapes@reedexpo.com

March , 2012

Anuga Food Tec -- Food Processing/Packaging Eq.

Location/Date: Dusseldorf, Germany   3/27/2012 - 3/30/2012

Contacts:

Klaus Jonas, Dusseldorf
Commercial Specialist
Phone: 49-211-737-767-50
Klaus.Jonas@trade.gov

March , 2012

FIDAE 2012 -- multiple industry sectors

Location/Date: Santiago, Chile   3/27/2012 - 4/1/2012

Contacts:

Deborah Semb, Trade Event Programs
Senior International Trade Specialist
Phone: 202-482-0677
Deborah.Semb@trade.gov

Isabel Margarita Valenzuela, Santiago
Commercial Specialist
Phone: 56/2/330-3421
Isabel.Valenzuela@trade.gov

Gerri Cozic, Kallman Worldwide
Phone: 201/251-2600, x
gerric@kallman.com

Justin Griffing, Kallman Worldwide
Phone: 201/251-2600, x103
justing@kallman.com

March , 2012

INTERNATIONAL SECURITY CONFERENCE (ISC-WEST) -- multiple industry sectors

Location/Date: Las Vegas, NV, United States   3/27/2012 - 3/30/2012

Contacts:

Ibrahim Ibrahim, Lagos
Commercial Specialist
Phone: 234-1-460 3400, ext 3524
Ibrahim.Ibrahim@trade.gov

March , 2012

MCE 2012 -- multiple industry sectors

Location/Date: Milan, Italy   3/27/2012 - 3/30/2012

Contacts:

Federico Bevini, Milan
Commercial Specialist
Phone: Direct +39 02 6268 8520 or Main +39 02 02 6268 851
Federico.Bevini@trade.gov

Kevin Haley, Trade Event Programs
Senior International Trade Specialist
Phone: 202-482-6434
Kevin.Haley@trade.gov

James Yarish, Reed Exhibitions, Inc.

Phone: 203-840-5420
jyarish@reedexpo.com

March , 2012

Made in America 2012 -- multiple industry sectors

Location/Date: Beirut, Lebanon   3/28/2012 - 3/31/2012

Contacts:

Maya Barhouche, Beirut
Commercial Assistant
Phone: 961-4-544860
Maya.Barhouche@trade.gov

Naaman Tayyar, Beirut
Senior Commercial Specialist
Phone: 961-4-544860
Naaman.Tayyar@trade.gov

March , 2012

FOR FAMILY Fair (includes For Pets, For Senior, and For Kids) -- multiple industry sectors

Pre-Register for this event

Location/Date: Prague, Czech Republic   3/29/2012 - 4/1/2012

Contacts:

Andrew Edlefsen, Las Vegas
USEAC Director
Phone: 702-388-6694
Andrew.Edlefsen@trade.gov

Janis Kalnins, Las Vegas
Senior International Trade Specialist
Phone: 702-219-7461
Janis.Kalnins@trade.gov

Veronika Novakova, Prague
Commercial Specialist
Phone: +420 257 022 437
Veronika.Novakova@trade.gov

April , 2012

NPE 2012 International Plastics Showcase -- multiple industry sectors

Location/Date: Orlando, FL, United States   4/1/2012 - 4/5/2012

Contacts:

James Yi, Trade Event Programs
International Trade Specialist
Phone: 2024826482
James.Yi@trade.gov

April , 2012

Marrakech Airshow 2012 -- multiple industry sectors

Location/Date: Casablanca, Morocco   4/4/2012 - 4/7/2012

Contacts:

Deborah Semb, Trade Event Programs
Senior International Trade Specialist
Phone: 202-482-0677
Deborah.Semb@trade.gov

Jane Kitson, Casablanca
Senior Commercial Officer
Phone: +212 522 26 45 50 ext 4129
Jane.Kitson@trade.gov

Maj. Kevin Minor, Deputy Chief/Office of Security Cooperation/U.S. Embassy

Phone: 212 (0) 661-09-72-31
MinorKV@state.gov

Russell Hood, Oak Overseas

Phone: 704/837-1980, x302
rhood@oakoverseas.com

April , 2012

Southwest Aerospace & Defense Trade Compliance Forum -- multiple industry sectors
Register for this event

Location/Date: Las Cruces, NM, United States   4/4/2012 - 4/5/2012

Contacts:

Sandra Necessary, Santa Fe
USEAC Director
Phone: 505-231-0075
Sandra.Necessary@trade.gov

April , 2012

Southwest Aerospace & Defense Trade Compliance Forum-DEC & ICPA MembersBoth Days -- multiple industry sectors
Register for this event

Location/Date: Las Cruces, NM, United States   4/4/2012 - 4/5/2012

Contacts:

Sandra Necessary, Santa Fe
USEAC Director
Phone: 505-231-0075
Sandra.Necessary@trade.gov

April , 2012

Southwest Aerospace & Defense Trade Compliance Forum-Day 1 (DEC & ICPA Members) -- multiple industry sectors
Register for this event

Location/Date: Las Cruces, NM, United States   4/4/2012 - 4/4/2012

Contacts:

Sandra Necessary, Santa Fe
USEAC Director
Phone: 505-231-0075
Sandra.Necessary@trade.gov

April , 2012

Southwest Aerospace & Defense Trade Compliance Forum-Day One -- multiple industry sectors

Register for this event

Location/Date:	Las Cruces, NM, United States	4/4/2012 - 4/4/2012

Contacts:

Sandra Necessary, Santa Fe
USEAC Director
Phone: 505-231-0075
Sandra.Necessary@trade.gov

April , 2012

Southwest Aerospace & Defense Trade Compliance Forum- Day 2 -- multiple industry sectors

Register for this event

Location/Date:	Las Cruces, NM, United States	4/5/2012 - 4/5/2012

Contacts:

Sandra Necessary, Santa Fe
USEAC Director
Phone: 505-231-0075
Sandra.Necessary@trade.gov

April , 2012

Southwest Aerospace & Defense Trade Compliance Forum-Day 2 (DEC & ICPA Members) -- multiple industry sectors

Register for this event

Location/Date:	Las Cruces, NM, United States	4/5/2012 - 4/5/2012

Contacts:

Sandra Necessary, Santa Fe
USEAC Director
Phone: 505-231-0075
Sandra.Necessary@trade.gov

April , 2012

CWEE6 2012 -- Renewable Energy Eq.

Location/Date:	Shanghai, China	4/6/2012 - 4/8/2012

Contacts:

Juliet Lu, Shanghai
Commercial Specialist
Phone: (86-21) 6279-7630 ext. 8780
Juliet.Lu@trade.gov

April , 2012

Expomin 2012 -- multiple industry sectors

Location/Date:	Santiago, Chile	4/9/2012 - 4/13/2012

Contacts:

Kevin Haley, Trade Event Programs
Senior International Trade Specialist
Phone: 202-482-6434
Kevin.Haley@trade.gov

Marcelo Orellana, Santiago
Commercial Specialist
Phone: 56/2/330-3455
Marcelo.Orellana@trade.gov

Matthew Hilgendorf, Santiago
Commercial Officer
Phone: 56 2 330 3315
Matthew.Hilgendorf@trade.gov

Joan Williams, Kallman

Phone: 201-251-2600x119
joanw@kallman.com

April , 2012

China Refrigeration 2012 -- multiple industry sectors

Location/Date:
Beijing, China
4/11/2012 - 4/13/2012

Contacts:

Andrew Billard, Beijing
Commercial Officer
Phone: (86) 10-8531-3589
Andrew.Billard@trade.gov

Kevin Haley, Trade Event Programs
Senior International Trade Specialist
Phone: 202-482-6434
Kevin.Haley@trade.gov

Scott Yao, Shanghai
Commercial Specialist
Phone: 011-(86-21) 6279-7630 ext. 8727
Scott.Yao@trade.gov

Jeff Malley, Events International

Phone: 203-801-0582
eiusa@optonline.net

April , 2012

InfoComm China 2012 -- multiple industry sectors

Location/Date:
Beijing, China
4/11/2012 - 4/13/2012

Contacts:

Graylin Presbury, Trade Event Programs

Senior International Trade Specialist
Phone: 202-482-5158
Graylin.Presbury@trade.gov
Yan Gao, Beijing
Commercial Specialist
Phone: 86-10-8531-3889
Yan.Gao@trade.gov

Meredith Hoydilla, InfoComm International

Phone: 703-277-2008
mhoydilla@infocomm.org

April , 2012

Mining World Russia -- multiple industry sectors

Location/Date:
Moscow, Russia
4/14/2012 - 4/16/2012

Contacts:

Irina Podsushnaya, Vladivostok
Commercial Specialist
Phone: 7-4232-30-00-70, ext. 4508, 499-381
Irina.Podsushnaya@trade.gov

April , 2012

China Medical Equipment Fair (CMEF) 2012 -- multiple industry sectors

Location/Date:
Guangzhou, China
4/16/2012 - 4/18/2012

Contacts:

Shuquan Li, CS GZ

Phone: 86 20 8667 4011
shuquan.li@trade.gov

April , 2012

London Book Fair U.S. Pavilion -- multiple industry sectors

Location/Date: London, United Kingdom   4/16/2012 - 4/18/2012

Contacts:

Dawn Bruno, New York
International Trade Specialist
Phone: 212-809-2647
Dawn.Bruno@trade.gov

Keith Yatsuhashi, Providence
USEAC Director
Phone: 401-528-5104
Keith.Yatsuhashi@trade.gov

Stewart Gough, London
Commercial Specialist
Phone: +44 (0) 20 7894 0459
Stewart.Gough@trade.gov

April , 2012

The 2012 National Association of Broadcasters (NAB) Show -- multiple industry sectors

Location/Date: Las Vegas, NV, United States   4/16/2012 - 4/19/2012

Contacts:

Shelby Peterson, Trade Event Programs
Business and Industry Specialist
Phone: 202-482-5531
Shelby.Peterson@trade.gov

Margaret Cassilly, National Association of Broadcasters

Phone: (202) 429-3189
mcassilly@nab.org

April , 2012

Analytica 2012 -- multiple industry sectors

Location/Date: Munich, Germany   4/17/2012 - 4/20/2012

Contacts:

Doris Groot, Munich
Commercial Specialist
Phone: 49-89-2888-749
Doris.Groot@trade.gov

Kirsten Hentschel, Dusseldorf
Commercial Specialist
Phone: 49 211-737-767-30
Kirsten.Hentschel@trade.gov

April , 2012

The 15th South East Asia Healthcare and Pharma Show -- multiple industry sectors

Location/Date: Kuala Lumpur, Malaysia   4/17/2012 - 4/19/2012

Contacts:

Tracy Yeoh, Kuala Lumpur
Commercial Specialist
Phone: 60-3-2168-5089
Tracy.Yeoh@trade.gov

S Singh Bhullar, ABC Exhibitions

Phone: 60-3-7954-6588
bhullar@abcex.com

April , 2012

AERO 2012 -- Aircraft/Aircraft Parts

Location/Date: Friedrichshafen, Germany 4/18/2012 - 4/21/2012

Contacts:

Moritz Holst, Munich
Commercial Assistant
Phone: 49-89-2888-754
Moritz.Holst@trade.gov

Luann Alesio, L.A. Exhibit Space Sales

Phone: (949) 489-9982
lalesio@cox.net

April , 2012

Secutech 2012 -- multiple industry sectors

Location/Date: Taipei, Taiwan 4/18/2012 - 4/20/2012

Contacts:

Cindy Chang, Taipei
Commercial Specialist
Phone: 886-2-2720-1550 ext 311
Cindy.Chang@trade.gov

Graylin Presbury, Trade Event Programs
Senior International Trade Specialist
Phone: 202-482-5158
Graylin.Presbury@trade.gov

Bridget Ferris, Messe Frankfurt Inc

Phone: 770-984-8016
bridget.ferris@usa.messefrankfurt.com

April , 2012

ExpoFranquicia Franchising Trade Fair 2012 -- Franchising

Location/Date: Madrid, Spain 4/19/2012 - 4/21/2012

Contacts:

Ellen Lenny-Pessagno, Madrid
Senior Commercial Officer
Phone: 34-91-308-1529
Ellen.Lenny-Pessagno@trade.gov

Lisa Huot, Trade Event Programs
Senior International Trade Specialist
Phone: 202-482-2796
Lisa.Huot@trade.gov

Javier Sanchez, Madrid International Business, Inc.

Phone: 212-221-5848
nyoffice@madridinternational.com

April , 2012

FIBO 2012 -- multiple industry sectors

Location/Date: Essen, Germany 4/19/2012 - 4/22/2012

Contacts:

Anette Salama, Dusseldorf
Senior Commercial Specialist
Phone: 49-211-737-767-60
Anette.Salama@trade.gov

Dagmar Winkler-Helmdach, Munich
Commercial Specialist
Phone: 49-89-2888-769
Dagmar.Winkler-Helmdach@trade.gov

Uta Kirst, Dusseldorf
Commercial Specialist
Phone: 49 211-737-767-80
Uta.Kirst@trade.gov

Olaf Tomscheit, Reed Exhibitions Germany
Phone: 49 (0) 211-90191131
olaf.tomscheit@reedexpo.de

April , 2012

IDEM Singapore - International Dental Exhibition and Meeting --

Location/Date: Singapore, Singapore   4/20/2012 - 4/22/2012

Contacts:

Lisa Huot, Trade Event Programs
Senior International Trade Specialist
Phone: 202-482-2796
Lisa.Huot@trade.gov

Luanne Theseira O'Hara, Singapore
Commercial Specialist
Phone: (65) 6476 9037 (65) 6476-9416
Luanne.Theseira@trade.gov

April , 2012

International Pow Wow -- Travel and Tourism Industries

Location/Date: Los Angeles, CA, United States   4/21/2012 - 4/26/2012

Contacts:

Diana Brandon, Buenos Aires
Commercial Specialist
Phone: (54-11) 5777-4550
Diana.Brandon@trade.gov

Michael Martin, US Travel Association

Phone: 202-218-3620
mmartin@ustravel.org

April , 2012

POW WOW 2012 -- Travel and Tourism Industries

Location/Date: Los Angeles, CA, United States   4/21/2012 - 4/25/2012

Contacts:

Ingeborg Doblinger, Vienna
Commercial Specialist
Phone: 43-1-31339-2120
Ingeborg.Doblinger@trade.gov

April , 2012

Automotive Parts and Components Business Development Mission to Russia -- multiple industry sectors

Pre-Register for this event

Location/Date: Moscow, Russia   4/23/2012 - 4/24/2012
                             St. Petersburg, Russia   4/24/2012 - 4/25/2012
                             Samara, Russia   4/26/2012 - 4/27/2012

Contacts:

Alexander Kansky, St. Petersburg
Commercial Specialist
Phone: 7 (812) 331-2881
Alexander.Kansky@trade.gov

Eduard Roytberg, Inland Empire
Senior International Trade Specialist
Phone: + 909-466-4138
Eduard.Roytberg@trade.gov

Kenneth Duckworth, St. Petersburg
Principal Commercial Officer
Phone: 7 (812) 326-2563
Kenneth.Duckworth@trade.gov

Vladislav Borodulin, Moscow
Commercial Specialist
Phone: 7 495 728-5235
Vladislav.Borodulin@trade.gov

April , 2012

Hannover Messe 2012 -- multiple industry sectors

Location/Date: Hannover, Germany   4/23/2012 - 4/27/2012

Contacts:

Kevin Haley, Trade Event Programs
Senior International Trade Specialist
Phone: 202-482-6434
Kevin.Haley@trade.gov

Volker Wirsdorf, Frankfurt
Senior Commercial Specialist
Phone: 49-69-7535 3150
Volker.Wirsdorf@trade.gov

Robin Estey, Hannover Fairs USA

Phone: 609-987-1202
restey@hfusa.com

April , 2012

Exposeguridad 2012 -- multiple industry sectors

Location/Date: Mexico City, Mexico   4/24/2012 - 4/26/2012

Contacts:

Graylin Presbury, Trade Event Programs
Senior International Trade Specialist
Phone: 202-482-5158
Graylin.Presbury@trade.gov

Silvia Cardenas, Mexico City
Commercial Specialist
Phone: 52-55-5140-2670
Silvia.Cardenas@trade.gov

George Fletcher, Giprex USA

Phone: 786-207-4769
george.fletcher@giprex.com

April , 2012

Infosecurity Europe 2012 -- multiple industry sectors

Location/Date: London, United Kingdom   4/24/2012 - 4/26/2012

Contacts:

Andrew Williams, London
Commercial Specialist
Phone: +44 20 7894 0417
Andrew.Williams@trade.gov

Graylin Presbury, Trade Event Programs
Senior International Trade Specialist
Phone: 202-482-5158
Graylin.Presbury@trade.gov

Claire Sellick, Reed Exhibitions

Phone: 44 20 8910 7907
claire.sellick@reedexpo.co.uk

Ray Filbert, Reed Exhibitions

Phone: 203-840-5821
rfilbert@reedexpo.com

April , 2012

Counter Terror Expo 2012 -- Security/Safety Eq.

Location/Date: London, United Kingdom   4/25/2012 - 4/26/2012

Contacts:

Andrew Williams, London
Commercial Specialist
Phone: +44 20 7894 0417
Andrew.Williams@trade.gov

Graylin Presbury, Trade Event Programs
Senior International Trade Specialist
Phone: 202-482-5158
Graylin.Presbury@trade.gov

Doug Schlam, Clarion Events

Phone: 203-275-8014
Doug.Schlam@clarionevents.com

Philip Hunter, Clarion Events

Phone: 44 208 524 9090
Philip.Hunter@Clarionevents.com

April , 2012

Offshore Technology Conference 2012 -- multiple industry sectors

Location/Date: Houston, TX, United States   4/30/2012 - 5/3/2012

Contacts:

Vidya Desai, Trade Event Programs
International Trade Specialist
Phone: 202-482-2311
Vidya.Desai@trade.gov

Chris Torsy, Offshore Technology Conference Inc.

Phone: 972-952-9318
ctorsy@otcnet.org

May , 2012

2012 AMI Int'l Meat, Poultry & Seafood Industry Convention and Expo, FMI 2012, NASDA, United Fresh -- multiple industry sectors

Location/Date: Dallas, TX, United States   5/1/2012 - 5/3/2012

Contacts:

Philippa Olsen, Marketing
Business and Industry Specialist
Phone: 202-482-5449
Philippa.Olsen@trade.gov

May , 2012

European Seafood Exposition -- Marine Fisheries Products (Seafood)

Location/Date: Brussels, Belgium   5/1/2012 - 5/1/2012

Contacts:

Karel Vantomme, Brussels
Commercial Assistant
Phone: +3228114733
Karel.Vantomme@trade.gov

May , 2012

Waste Expo 2012 -- multiple industry sectors

Location/Date: Las Vegas, NV, United States   5/1/2012 - 5/3/2012

Contacts:

Aditi Palli, Trade Event Programs
International Trade Specialist
Phone: 202-482-3334
Aditi.Palli@trade.gov

This International Buyer Program will be led by Rita Ugianskis-Fishman,
Managing Director, Penton Media
Phone:

May , 2012

AWS Weldmex - Fabtech - Metalform - Mexico - 2012 -- multiple industry sectors

Location/Date: Mexico City, Mexico 5/2/2012 - 5/4/2012

Contacts:

Kevin Haley, Trade Event Programs
Senior International Trade Specialist
Phone: 202-482-6434
Kevin.Haley@trade.gov

Mario Vidana, Monterrey
Commerce Specialist
Phone: 528180473118
Mario.Vidana@trade.gov

Chuck Cross, Trade Show Consulting

Phone: 410-252-1322
chuck@tradeshowconsult.com

May , 2012

DRUPA -- Printing/Graphic Arts Eq.

Location/Date: Dusseldorf, Germany 5/3/2012 - 5/16/2012

Contacts:

Nils Roeher, Dusseldorf
Commercial Specialist
Phone: 49 211 737 767 20
Nils.Roeher@trade.gov

May , 2012

The National Restaurant Association Restaurant, Hotel-Motel Show (NRA Show) 2012 -- multiple industry sectors

Location/Date: Chicago, IL, United States 5/5/2012 - 5/8/2012

Contacts:

Amanda Ayvaz, Trade Event Programs
International Trade Specialist
Phone: 202-482-0338
Amanda.Ayvaz@trade.gov

This International Buyer Program will be led by Patti Beese,
Director, Operations and Services
Phone:

May , 2012

U.S. Aerospace Supplier Mission to Canada -- multiple industry sectors
Pre-Register for this event

Location/Date: Montreal, Canada 5/7/2012 - 5/10/2012

Contacts:

Gina Bento, Montreal
Commercial Specialist
Phone: 514-908-3660
Gina.Bento@trade.gov

May , 2012

International CTIA WIRELESS® 2012 Convention -- multiple industry sectors

Location/Date: New Orleans, LA, United States 5/8/2012 - 5/10/2012

Contacts:

James Yi, Trade Event Programs
International Trade Specialist
Phone: 2024826482
James.Yi@trade.gov

May , 2012

IFT - Energy 2012 -- multiple industry sectors

| **Location/Date:** | Santiago, Chile | 5/9/2012 - 5/11/2012 |
| | Santiago, Chile | 5/9/2012 - 5/11/2012 |

Contacts:

Kevin Haley, Trade Event Programs
Senior International Trade Specialist
Phone: 202-482-6434
Kevin.Haley@trade.gov

Marcelo Orellana, Santiago
Commercial Specialist
Phone: 56/2/330-3455
Marcelo.Orellana@trade.gov

Matthew Hilgendorf, Santiago
Commercial Officer
Phone: 56 2 330 3315
Matthew.Hilgendorf@trade.gov

Joan Williams, Kallman Worldwide

Phone: 201-251-2600x116
joanw@kallman.com

Nancy Villari, Kallman Worldwide

Phone: 201-251-2600x104
nancyV@kallman.com

May , 2012

WTF (World Traver Fair) 2012 -- Travel and Tourism Industries

| **Location/Date:** | Shanghai, China | 5/11/2012 - 5/13/2012 |

Contacts:

Stellar Chu, Shanghai
Senior Commercial Specialist
Phone: 86-21-6279-7630
Stellar.Chu@trade.gov

May , 2012

PCIM Europe 2012 -- Electronic Components

| **Location/Date:** | Nuremberg, Germany | 5/14/2012 - 5/16/2012 |

Contacts:

Dagmar Winkler-Helmdach, Munich

Commercial Specialist
Phone: 49-89-2888-769
Dagmar.Winkler-Helmdach@trade.gov

Alexander Kaiser, Mesago PCIM GmbH

Phone: 49-711-6194656
alexander.kaiser@mesago.de

May , 2012

VISIT USA SHOW CHILE --

| **Location/Date:** | Santiago, Chile | 5/14/2012 - 5/15/2012 |

Contacts:

Isabel Margarita Valenzuela, Santiago
Commercial Specialist
Phone: 56/2/330-3421
Isabel.Valenzuela@trade.gov

May , 2012

VISIT USA SHOW CHILE 2012 -- Travel and Tourism Industries

Location/Date: Santiago, Chile   5/14/2012 - 5/15/2012

Contacts:

Isabel Margarita Valenzuela, Santiago
Commercial Specialist
Phone: 56/2/330-3421
Isabel.Valenzuela@trade.gov

May , 2012

Visit USA RoadShow - Southern Cone - Latin America -- Travel and Tourism Industries

Location/Date: Santiago, Buenos Aires, Montevideo, Argentina   5/14/2012 - 5/18/2012

Contacts:

Diana Brandon, Buenos Aires
Commercial Specialist
Phone: (54-11) 5777-4550
Diana.Brandon@trade.gov

Isabel Margarita Valenzuela, Santiago
Commercial Specialist
Phone: 56/2/330-3421
Isabel.Valenzuela@trade.gov

Lilian Amy, Montevideo
Commercial Specialist
Phone: (5982) 1770-2323
Lilian.Amy@trade.gov

May , 2012

Visit USA RoadShow-Southern Cone-Latin America -- Travel and Tourism Industries

Location/Date: Santiago, Montevideo, Buenos Aires, Uruguay   5/14/2012 - 5/18/2012

Contacts:

Diana Brandon, Buenos Aires
Commercial Specialist
Phone: (54-11) 5777-4550
Diana.Brandon@trade.gov

Isabel Margarita Valenzuela, Santiago
Commercial Specialist
Phone: 56/2/330-3421
Isabel.Valenzuela@trade.gov

Lilian Amy, Montevideo
Commercial Specialist
Phone: (5982) 1770-2323
Lilian.Amy@trade.gov

May , 2012

ELECTRIC POWER 2012 -- multiple industry sectors

Location/Date: Baltimore, MD, United States   5/15/2012 - 5/17/2012

Contacts:

Mark Wells, Trade Event Programs
Senior International Trade Specialist
Phone: (202) 482-0904
Mark.Wells@trade.gov

Hunter Jones, TradeFair Group, Inc.

Phone: (713) 343-1875
hunterj@TradeFairGroup.com

May , 2012
Expoaviga The Livestock Trade Fair 2012 -- multiple industry sectors

Location/Date: Barcelona, Spain   5/15/2012 - 5/17/2012

Contacts:

Angela Turrin, Madrid
International Trade Specialist
Phone: 34-91-308-1567
Angela.Turrin@trade.gov

Helen Simpson-Davis, Trade Event Programs
Senior International Trade Specialist
Phone: 202-482-1882
Helen.Simpson-Davis@trade.gov

Philippe Bazin, PB Marketing International

Phone: 212-564-0404
www.pbmarketinginternational.com

May , 2012
Orthopaedie+Rehatechnik 2012 -- multiple industry sectors

Location/Date: Leipzig, Germany   5/16/2012 - 5/18/2012

Contacts:

Anette Salama, Dusseldorf
Senior Commercial Specialist
Phone: 49-211-737-767-60
Anette.Salama@trade.gov

Jerry Kallman, Kallman Associates

Phone: 201-652-7070
jerry@kallmanexpo.com

May , 2012
Book World Prague 2012 Catalog Show -- Books/Periodicals

Location/Date: Prague, Czech Republic   5/17/2012 - 5/20/2012

Contacts:

Jana Ruckerova, Prague
Commercial Specialist
Phone: (420) 257 022 310
Jana.Ruckerova@trade.gov

May , 2012
INTEGRATED SAFETY & SECURITY -- Security/Safety Eq.

Location/Date: Moscow, Russia   5/21/2012 - 5/24/2012

Contacts:

Timur Uddin, Moscow
Commercial Specialist
Phone: +7-495-728-5526
Timur.Uddin@trade.gov

May , 2012
Hospitalar 2012 -- multiple industry sectors

Location/Date: Sao Paulo, Brazil   5/22/2012 - 5/25/2012

Contacts:

Jefferson Oliveira, Sao Paulo
Commercial Specialist
Phone: 55/11/5186-7136
Jefferson.Oliveira@trade.gov

Lisa Huot, Trade Event Programs
Senior International Trade Specialist
Phone: 202-482-2796
Lisa.Huot@trade.gov

May , 2012

Power-Gen Europe, Cologne -- multiple industry sectors

Location/Date: Cologne, Germany   5/22/2012 - 5/24/2012

Contacts:

Bettina Capurro, Munich
Commercial Specialist
Phone: 49-89-288-8751
Bettina.Capurro@trade.gov

Serdar Cetinkaya, Ankara
Senior Commercial Specialist
Phone: [90] (312) 457-7203 or [90] (312) 455-5555, ext. 7203
Serdar.Cetinkaya@trade.gov

May , 2012

Vitafoods Europe 2012 -- multiple industry sectors

Location/Date: Geneva, Switzerland   5/22/2012 - 5/24/2012

Contacts:

Elisabeth Mbitha-Schmid, Bern
Commercial Specialist
Phone: +41 31 357 7313
Elisabeth.Mbitha-Schmid@trade.gov

May , 2012

NAFSA 2012 Annual Conference & Expo -- Education/Training Services

Location/Date: Jakarta, Indonesia   5/27/2012 - 6/1/2012

Contacts:

Ignatius Indriartoto, Jakarta
Commercial Specialist
Phone: 62-21-5262850
Ignatius.Indriartoto@trade.gov

May , 2012

BeautyWorld Middle East 2012 -- Cosmetics/Toiletries

Location/Date: Dubai, United Arab Emirates   5/29/2012 - 5/31/2012

Contacts:

Ashok Ghosh, Dubai
Commercial Specialist
Phone: +971 4 309 4935
Ashok.Ghosh@trade.gov

Helen Simpson-Davis, Trade Event Programs
Senior International Trade Specialist
Phone: 202-482-1882
Helen.Simpson-Davis@trade.gov

Robert Bannerman, Dubai
Principal Commercial Officer
Phone: +971-4-309-4963
Robert.Bannerman@trade.gov

Jay Brown, Atlantic Trade Pavilions

Phone: 434-825-2800
atpi@erols.com

May , 2012

Offshore Wind Shnaghai 2012 -- Renewable Energy Eq.

Location/Date: Shanghai, China   5/30/2012 - 6/1/2012

Contacts:

Juliet Lu, Shanghai
Commercial Specialist
Phone: (86-21) 6279-7630 ext. 8780
Juliet.Lu@trade.gov

June , 2012

AcquaLiveExpo 2012 -- multiple industry sectors

Location/Date: Lisbon, Portugal   6/2/2012 - 6/5/2012

Contacts:

Pedro Ferreira, Lisbon
Commercial Specialist
Phone: [351] (21) 770-2572
Pedro.Ferreira@trade.gov

June , 2012

WINDPOWER 2012 -- Renewable Energy Eq.

Location/Date: Atlanta, GA, United States   6/3/2012 - 6/6/2012

Contacts:

Mark Wells, Trade Event Programs
Senior International Trade Specialist
Phone: (202) 482-0904
Mark.Wells@trade.gov

Jeff Anthony, American Wind Energy Association

Phone: (202) 383-2500
janthony@awea.org

June , 2012

ECWATECH 2012 -- multiple industry sectors

Pre-Register for this event

Location/Date: Moscow, Russia   6/5/2012 - 6/8/2012

Contacts:

Yuliya Vinogradova, Moscow
Commercial Specialist
Phone: + 7 (495) 728-5586
Yuliya.Vinogradova@trade.gov

June , 2012

Guangzhou Int'l Lighting Show -- multiple industry sectors

Location/Date: Guangzhou, China   6/9/2012 - 6/12/2012

Contacts:

Cathy Wang, CS GZ

Phone: 86 20 8667 4011
cathy.wang@trade.gov

June , 2012

InfoComm International 2012 -- multiple industry sectors

Location/Date: Las Vegas, NV, United States   6/9/2012 - 6/15/2012

Contacts:

Shelby Peterson, Trade Event Programs
Business and Industry Specialist
Phone: 202-482-5531
Shelby.Peterson@trade.gov

Jason McGraw, InfoComm International

Phone: (703) 279-6361
jmcgraw@infocomm.org

June , 2012

CIMES 2012 -- multiple industry sectors

Location/Date: Beijing, China   6/12/2012 - 6/16/2012

Contacts:

Kevin Haley, Trade Event Programs
Senior International Trade Specialist
Phone: 202-482-6434
Kevin.Haley@trade.gov

Zheng Xu, Beijing
Commercial Assistant
Phone: (86-10) 8531 3637
Zheng.Xu@trade.gov

James Yarish, Reed Exhibitions

Phone: 203-840-5336
jyarish@reedexpo.com

June , 2012

PECOM 2012 -- multiple industry sectors

Location/Date: Villahermosa, Mexico   6/12/2012 - 6/14/2012

Contacts:

Dennis Simmons, Mexico City
Commercial Officer
Phone: +52 55 5140 2631
Dennis.Simmons@trade.gov

Francisco Ceron, Mexico City
Senior Commercial Specialist
Phone: 52-55-5140-2640
Francisco.Ceron@trade.gov

Kevin Haley, Trade Event Programs
Senior International Trade Specialist
Phone: 202-482-6434
Kevin.Haley@trade.gov

Sandy Basler, International Exhibitions, Inc.
Phone: 713-529-1616
sbasler@ieimail.com

June , 2012

Fieldays 2012 -- multiple industry sectors

Location/Date: Wellington, New Zealand   6/13/2012 - 6/16/2012

Contacts:

Janet Coulthart, Wellington
Commercial Specialist
Phone: 644-462-6002
Janet.Coulthart@trade.gov

June , 2012

Achema 2012 -- multiple industry sectors

Location/Date: Frankfurt, Germany   6/18/2012 - 6/22/2012

Contacts:

Kirsten Hentschel, Dusseldorf
Commercial Specialist
Phone: 49 211-737-767-30
Kirsten.Hentschel@trade.gov

June , 2012

CommunicAsia2012 / BroadcastAsia2012 -- multiple industry sectors

Location/Date: Singapore, Singapore   6/19/2012 - 6/22/2012

Contacts:

Graylin Presbury, Trade Event Programs
Senior International Trade Specialist
Phone: 202-482-5158
Graylin.Presbury@trade.gov

Sweehoon Chia, Singapore
Senior Commercial Specialist
Phone: (65) 6476 9037, (65) 6476 9403
Sweehoon.Chia@trade.gov

Jerry Kallman Jr., Kallman Associates, Inc.

Phone: 201-652-7070
jerry@kallmanexpo.com

June , 2012

CommunicAsia2012/Broadcast Asia2012 -- multiple industry sectors

Location/Date: Jakarta, Indonesia   6/19/2012 - 6/22/2012

Contacts:

Kalung Riang, Jakarta
Commercial Specialist
Phone: 62-21 526 2850 Ext.3010
Kalung.Riang@trade.gov

June , 2012

HBA Global Expo -- multiple industry sectors

Location/Date: New York City, NY, United States   6/19/2012 - 6/21/2012

Contacts:

Amanda Ayvaz, Trade Event Programs
International Trade Specialist
Phone: 202-482-0338
Amanda.Ayvaz@trade.gov

This International Buyer Program will be led by Jill Birkett,
Brand Director, Beauty and Wellness Group
Phone:

June , 2012

The 28th International FISPAL 2012 Food Service Trade Show -- multiple industry sectors

Location/Date: Sao Paulo, Brazil   6/25/2012 - 6/28/2012

Contacts:

Denise Barbosa, Sao Paulo
Commercial Specialist
Phone: 55/11/5186-7390
Denise.Barbosa@trade.gov

Helen Simpson-Davis, Trade Event Programs
Senior International Trade Specialist
Phone: 202-482-1882
Helen.Simpson-Davis@trade.gov

Eric Halsten, Imex Management, Inc.
Phone: 704-365-0041
EricH@imexManagement.com

June , 2012

IFAI Expo Asia 2012 -- multiple industry sectors

Location/Date: Singapore, Singapore 6/26/2012 - 6/28/2012

Contacts:

Helen Simpson-Davis, Trade Event Programs
Senior International Trade Specialist
Phone: 202-482-1882
Helen.Simpson-Davis@trade.gov

Luanne Theseira O'Hara, Singapore
Commercial Specialist
Phone: (65) 6476 9037 (65) 6476-9416
Luanne.Theseira@trade.gov

Todd V. Lindemann, Intustrial Fabrics Association International

Phone: 651-225-6918
tvlindemann@ifai.com

July , 2012

OutDoor 2012 (European Outdoor Trade Fair) -- multiple industry sectors

Location/Date: Friedrichshafen, Germany 7/12/2012 - 7/15/2012

Contacts:

Dagmar Winkler-Helmdach, Munich
Commercial Specialist
Phone: 49-89-2888-769
Dagmar.Winkler-Helmdach@trade.gov

Uta Kirst, Dusseldorf
Commercial Specialist
Phone: 49 211-737-767-80
Uta.Kirst@trade.gov

Stefan Reisinger, Messe Friedrichshafen

Phone: 49-7541-708411
stefan.reisinger@messe-fn.de

July , 2012

Annual Meeting and Clinical Laboratory Exposition of the AACC 2012 -- multiple industry sectors

Location/Date: Los Angeles, CA, United States 7/15/2012 - 7/19/2012

Contacts:

Shelby Peterson, Trade Event Programs
Business and Industry Specialist
Phone: 202-482-5531
Shelby.Peterson@trade.gov

July , 2012

Aqua Pets Taipei 2012 -- Veterinary Medicine Eq./Supplies

Location/Date: Taipei, Taiwan 7/15/2012 - 7/18/2012

Contacts:

Rita Chen, Taipei
Commercial Specialist
Phone: 886-2-27201550 x 329
Rita.Chen@trade.gov

August , 2012

AUVSI Unmanned Systems North America 2012 -- multiple industry sectors

Location/Date: Las Vegas, NV, United States 8/7/2012 - 8/10/2012

Contacts:

Erik Hunt, Seoul
Deputy Senior Commercial Officer
Phone: [82-2] 397-4537
Erik.Hunt@trade.gov

Myoung Soo Lah, Seoul
Senior Commercial Specialist
Phone: 82-2-397-4516
MyoungSoo.Lah@trade.gov

August , 2012

China International Rail Transit Technology Exhibition -- Railroad Eq.

Location/Date: Shanghai, China   8/22/2012 - 8/24/2012

Contacts:

Vivien Bao, Shanghai
Commercial Specialist
Phone: (86-21)6279-8766
Vivien.Bao@trade.gov

August , 2012

International Woodworking Machinery & Furniture Supply Fair-USA® 2012 -- multiple industry sectors

Location/Date: Atlanta, GA, United States   8/22/2012 - 8/25/2012

Contacts:

Aditi Palli, Trade Event Programs
International Trade Specialist
Phone: 202-482-3334
Aditi.Palli@trade.gov
Jim Wulfekuhle, International Woodworking Machinery & Furniture Supply Fair-USA®

Phone: (404) 693-8333
jamesw@iwfatlanta.com

August , 2012

MAGIC Marketplace -- multiple industry sectors

Location/Date: Las Vegas, NV, United States   8/27/2012 - 8/29/2012

Contacts:

Vidya Desai, Trade Event Programs
International Trade Specialist
Phone: 202-482-2311
Vidya.Desai@trade.gov
Rob Weinstein, MAGIC International

Phone: 818-539-5000
rweinstein@magiconline.com

September , 2012

Spoga+Gafa -- multiple industry sectors

Location/Date: Cologne, Germany   9/2/2012 - 9/4/2012

Contacts:

Sabine Winkels, Dusseldorf
Commercial Specialist
Phone: 49-211-737-767-40
Sabine.Winkels@trade.gov
Darrin Stern, Koelnmesse Inc.

Phone: 773-326-9925
d.stern@koelnmessenafta.com

September , 2012

La Cumbre AmericÃ¡s' Travel Industry Summit -- Travel and Tourism Industries

Location/Date: Orlando, FL, United States   9/5/2012 - 9/8/2012

Contacts:

Diana Brandon, Buenos Aires
Commercial Specialist
Phone: (54-11) 5777-4550
Diana.Brandon@trade.gov

September , 2012

Beijing International Book Fair -- Books/Periodicals

Location/Date: Beijing, China   9/8/2012 - 9/11/2012

Contacts:

Jing Qiu, Beijing
Commercial Specialist
Phone: (86-10) 8531 4157
Jing.Qiu@trade.gov

September , 2012

AUTOMECHANIKA 2012 -- multiple industry sectors

Location/Date: Frankfurt, Germany   9/11/2012 - 9/16/2012

Contacts:

Michael Thompson, Trade Event Programs
International Trade Specialist
Phone: 202-482-0671
Michael.Thompson@trade.gov

Volker Wirsdorf, Frankfurt
Senior Commercial Specialist
Phone: 49-69-7535 3150
Volker.Wirsdorf@trade.gov

Bridget Ferris, Messe Frankfurt USA

Phone: 770-984-8016 x 426
bridget.ferris@usa.messefrankfurt.com

September , 2012

GPEC -- multiple industry sectors

Location/Date: Leipzig, Germany   9/11/2012 - 9/13/2012

Contacts:

Nils Roeher, Dusseldorf
Commercial Specialist
Phone: 49 211 737 767 20
Nils.Roeher@trade.gov

September , 2012

ILA 2012 - The Berlin Air Show 2012 -- multiple industry sectors

Location/Date: Berlin, Germany   9/11/2012 - 9/16/2012

Contacts:

Deborah Semb, Trade Event Programs
Senior International Trade Specialist
Phone: 202-482-0677
Deborah.Semb@trade.gov

Mary Boscia, Berlin
Deputy Senior Commercial Officer
Phone: 011-49-30-8305-1946
Mary.Boscia@trade.gov

Moritz Holst, Munich
Commercial Assistant
Phone: 49-89-2888-754
Moritz.Holst@trade.gov

Carl Williams, International Aerospace Consultants

Phone: 916/394-9179
cwilliams@intl-aero.net

September , 2012

Rio Oil & Gas 2012 -- multiple industry sectors

Location/Date: Rio de Janeiro, Brazil   9/17/2012 - 9/20/2012

Contacts:

Kevin Haley, Trade Event Programs
Senior International Trade Specialist
Phone: 202-482-6434
Kevin.Haley@trade.gov

Regina Cunha, Rio De Janeiro
Senior Commercial Specialist
Phone: 55-21-3823-2416
Regina.Cunha@trade.gov

Sergio Teixeira, Rio De Janeiro
Trade Event Manager/Coordinator
Phone: 55 21 3823-2419
Sergio.Teixeira@trade.gov

Joan Williams, Kallman

Phone: 201-251-2600x115
JoanW@kallman.com

September , 2012

AAD 2012 -- multiple industry sectors

Location/Date: Pretoria, South Africa   9/19/2012 - 9/23/2012

Contacts:

Johan Van Rensburg, Johannesburg
Senior Commercial Specialist
Phone: 27 11 290-3208
Johan.vanRensburg@trade.gov

September , 2012

Shanghai International Franchise Exhibition -- Franchising

Location/Date: Shanghai, China   9/19/2012 - 9/21/2012

Contacts:

Janet Li, Shanghai
Commercial Specialist
Phone: 86-21-62797630*8775; 62798775
Janet.Li@trade.gov

September , 2012

VIV China 2012 -- multiple industry sectors

Location/Date: Beijing, China   9/23/2012 - 9/25/2012

Contacts:

Helen Simpson-Davis, Trade Event Programs
Senior International Trade Specialist
Phone: 202-482-1882
Helen.Simpson-Davis@trade.gov

Zheng Xu, Beijing
Commercial Assistant
Phone: (86-10) 8531 3637
Zheng.Xu@trade.gov

Andrea Di Domenico, Imex Management, Inc

Phone: 704-365-0041
andread@imexmanagement.com

September , 2012

MINExpo International 2012 -- multiple industry sectors

Location/Date: Las Vegas, NV, United States   9/24/2012 - 9/26/2012

Contacts:

Graylin Presbury, Trade Event Programs
Senior International Trade Specialist
Phone: 202-482-5158
Graylin.Presbury@trade.gov

Moya Phelleps, National Mining Association

Phone: 202-463-2639
mphelleps@nma.org

September , 2012

Minexpo International 2012 -- Mining Industry Eq.

Location/Date: Las Vegas, NV, United States   9/24/2012 - 9/26/2012

Contacts:

John Kanawati, Sydney
Commercial Specialist
Phone: 61-2-9373 9207
John.Kanawati@trade.gov

September , 2012

Pet Fair Asia 2011 -- Pet Foods/Supp.

Location/Date: Shanghai, China   9/24/2012 - 9/27/2012

Contacts:

Janet Li, Shanghai
Commercial Specialist
Phone: 86-21-62797630*8775; 62798775
Janet.Li@trade.gov

September , 2012

IFTM Top Resa 2012 -- Travel and Tourism Industries

Location/Date: Paris, France   9/25/2012 - 9/28/2012

Contacts:

Valerie Ferriere, Paris
Commercial Specialist
Phone: [33] (0)1 43 12 70 77
Valerie.Ferriere@trade.gov

September , 2012

Security Essen -- Security/Safety Eq.

Location/Date: Essen, Germany   9/25/2012 - 9/28/2012

Contacts:

Nils Roeher, Dusseldorf
Commercial Specialist
Phone: 49 211 737 767 20
Nils.Roeher@trade.gov

September , 2012

WEFTEC 2012 - CS Korea Delegation -- multiple industry sectors

Location/Date: New Orleans, LA, United States   9/29/2012 - 10/3/2012

Contacts:

Mark OGrady, Seoul
Commercial Officer
Phone: 82-2-397-4908
Mark.OGrady@trade.gov

Young-wan Park, Seoul
Commercial Specialist
Phone: 822-397-4164
YoungWan.Park@trade.gov

October , 2012

GridWeek 2012 -- Electrical Power Systems

Location/Date: Washington, DC, United States   10/1/2012 - 10/4/2012

Contacts:

Aditi Palli, Trade Event Programs
International Trade Specialist
Phone: 202-482-3334
Aditi.Palli@trade.gov

October , 2012

2012 Graph Expo -- Printing/Graphic Arts Eq.

Location/Date: Chicago, IL, United States   10/7/2012 - 10/10/2012

Contacts:

James Yi, Trade Event Programs
International Trade Specialist
Phone: 2024826482
James.Yi@trade.gov

October , 2012

Aluminium -- Non-Ferrous Metals

Location/Date: Dusseldorf, Germany   10/9/2012 - 10/11/2012

Contacts:

Klaus Jonas, Dusseldorf
Commercial Specialist
Phone: 49-211-737-767-50
Klaus.Jonas@trade.gov

October , 2012

Chillventa 2012 -- multiple industry sectors

Location/Date: Nuernberg, Germany   10/9/2012 - 10/11/2012

Contacts:

Doris Groot, Munich
Commercial Specialist
Phone: 49-89-2888-749
Doris.Groot@trade.gov

Dirk Ebener, NuernbergMesse North America

Phone: 770-618-5830
dirk.ebener@nuernbergmesse-north.america.com

October , 2012

Rehacare 2012 -- multiple industry sectors

Location/Date: Duesseldorf, Germany   10/10/2012 - 10/13/2012

Contacts:

Anette Salama, Dusseldorf
Senior Commercial Specialist
Phone: 49-211-737-767-60
Anette.Salama@trade.gov

Ryan Klemm, Messe Duesseldorf North America

Phone: 312-781-5180
rklemm@mdna.com

October , 2012

Automotive Service & Repair Week (ASRW) 2012 -- multiple industry sectors

Location/Date: New Orleans, LA, United States 10/11/2012 - 10/13/2012

Contacts:

Shelby Peterson, Trade Event Programs
Business and Industry Specialist
Phone: 202-482-5531
Shelby.Peterson@trade.gov

Ellen Pipkin, Hanley Wood Exhibitions

Phone: (972) 563-6354
epipkin@hanleywood.com

October , 2012

2012 Fall OH! Study Education Fair -- Education/Training Services

Location/Date: Taipei, Taichung and Kaohsiung, Taiwan 10/13/2012 - 10/16/2012

Contacts:

Grace Tao, Taipei
Commercial Specialist
Phone: 886-2-2720-1550 ext 383
Grace.Tao@trade.gov

October , 2012

China Education Expo -- Education/Training Services

Location/Date: Beijing, China 10/15/2012 - 10/16/2012

Contacts:

Jing Qiu, Beijing
Commercial Specialist
Phone: (86-10) 8531 4157
Jing.Qiu@trade.gov

October , 2012

RETECH 2012 -- Renewable Energy Eq.

Location/Date: Washington, DC, United States 10/17/2012 - 10/19/2012

Contacts:

Mark Wells, Trade Event Programs
Senior International Trade Specialist
Phone: (202) 482-0904
Mark.Wells@trade.gov

Hunter Jones, TradeFair Group, Inc.

Phone: (713) 343-1875
HunterJ@TradeFairGroup.com

October , 2012

EIC Study Fair -- Education/Training Services

Location/Date: Guangzhou, China 10/18/2012 - 10/20/2012

Contacts:

Eileen Bai, CS GZ

Phone: 86 20 8667 4011
eileen.bai@trade.gov

October , 2012

Expo Comm China 2012 -- multiple industry sectors

Location/Date: Beijing, China   10/19/2012 - 10/23/2012

Contacts:

Yan Gao, Beijing
Commercial Specialist
Phone: 86-10-8531-3889
Yan.Gao@trade.gov

October , 2012

glasstec and solarpeq 2012 -- Non-Ferrous Metals

Location/Date: Dusseldorf, Germany   10/23/2012 - 10/26/2012

Contacts:

Klaus Jonas, Dusseldorf
Commercial Specialist
Phone: 49-211-737-767-50
Klaus.Jonas@trade.gov

October , 2012

AquaSur 2012 -- multiple industry sectors

Location/Date: Santiago, Chile   10/24/2012 - 10/27/2012

Contacts:

Mary Lathrop, Santiago
Commercial Specialist
Phone: (56-2) 330-3371
Mary.Lathrop@trade.gov

October , 2012

PACK EXPO International 2012 -- multiple industry sectors

Location/Date: Chicago, IL, United States   10/28/2012 - 10/31/2012

Contacts:

Vidya Desai, Trade Event Programs
International Trade Specialist
Phone: 202-482-2311
Vidya.Desai@trade.gov

Ryan Oklewicz, Packaging Machinery Manufacturers Institute

Phone: 703-516-0654
ryan@pmmi.org

October , 2012

Interpolitex 2012 -- Security/Safety Eq.

Location/Date: Moscow, Russia   10/29/2012 - 11/1/2012

Contacts:

Timur Uddin, Moscow
Commercial Specialist
Phone: +7-495-728-5526
Timur.Uddin@trade.gov

October , 2012

2012 American Film Market -- Films/Videos

Location/Date: Santa Monica, CA, United States   10/31/2012 - 11/7/2012

Contacts:

Vidya Desai, Trade Event Programs
International Trade Specialist
Phone: 202-482-2311
Vidya.Desai@trade.gov

November , 2012

USA Pavilion at 2012 Taipei International Travel Fair -- Travel and Tourism Industries

| **Location/Date:** | Taipei, Taiwan | 11/1/2012 - 11/30/2012 |

Contacts:

Wendy Tien, Taipei
Commercial Specialist
Phone: 886-2-2720-1550 ext 324
Wendy.Tien@trade.gov

November , 2012

U.S. Community College Fair in Thailand - 2012 --

Location/Date:	Bangkok, Thailand	11/3/2012 - 11/3/2012
	Chiang Mai, Thailand	11/4/2012 - 11/4/2012
	Hat Yai, Thailand	11/6/2012 - 11/6/2012

Contacts:

Nalin Phupoksakul, Bangkok
Senior Commercial Specialist
Phone: 662-205-5275
Nalin.Phupoksakul@trade.gov

November , 2012

World Travel Market -- Travel and Tourism Industries

| **Location/Date:** | London, United Kingdom | 11/5/2012 - 11/8/2012 |

Contacts:

Danny Dumon, Brussels
Commercial Specialist
Phone: +32-2-811-5476
Danny.Dumon@trade.gov

Stewart Gough, London
Commercial Specialist
Phone: +44 (0) 20 7894 0459
Stewart.Gough@trade.gov

November , 2012

Industrial Fabrics Association International, IFAI, 2012 -- multiple industry sectors

| **Location/Date:** | Boston, MA, United States | 11/7/2012 - 11/9/2012 |

Contacts:

Amanda Ayvaz, Trade Event Programs
International Trade Specialist
Phone: 202-482-0338
Amanda.Ayvaz@trade.gov

This International Buyer Program will be led by Todd Lindemann,
Vice President of Conference Management
Phone:

November , 2012

Showcase USA-Italy 2012 -- Travel and Tourism Industries

| **Location/Date:** | TBD, Italy, Italy | 11/8/2012 - 11/9/2012 |

Contacts:

Simonetta Busnelli, Milan
Commercial Specialist
Phone: Direct +39-02-62688505 or Main +39-02-6268851
Simonetta.Busnelli@trade.gov

November , 2012

U.S. Power-gen Technology Showcase at APPrO 2012 Conference and Trade Show -- multiple industry sectors

Location/Date: Toronto, Canada   11/12/2012 - 11/14/2012

Contacts:

Stefan Popescu, Toronto
Commercial Specialist
Phone: 416 / 595-5412 x 223
Stefan.Popescu@trade.gov

November , 2012

Electronica 2012 -- Electronic Components

Location/Date: Munich, Germany   11/13/2012 - 11/16/2012

Contacts:

Dagmar Winkler-Helmdach, Munich
Commercial Specialist
Phone: 49-89-2888-769
Dagmar.Winkler-Helmdach@trade.gov

Moritz Holst, Munich
Commercial Assistant
Phone: 49-89-2888-754
Moritz.Holst@trade.gov

Sabine Kallup, Munich International Trade Fairs GACC

Phone: 646-437-1012
skallup@munich-tradefairs.com

November , 2012

Eurotier/BioEnergy Decentral 2012 -- multiple industry sectors

Location/Date: Hanover, Germany   11/13/2012 - 11/16/2012

Contacts:

Andrea Stahl, Frankfurt
Commercial Specialist
Phone: 49-69-7535-3157
Andrea.Stahl@trade.gov

Bettina Capurro, Munich
Commercial Specialist
Phone: 49-89-288-8751
Bettina.Capurro@trade.gov

November , 2012

The 9th China Int'l Aviation & Aerospace Exhibition -- multiple industry sectors

Location/Date: Zhuhai, China   11/13/2012 - 11/18/2012

Contacts:

Lena Yang, Guangzhou
Senior Commercial Specialist
Phone: 86-20 8667-4011 ext.612
Lena.Yang@trade.gov

November , 2012

MEDICA 2012 -- multiple industry sectors

Location/Date: Dusseldorf, Germany   11/14/2012 - 11/17/2012

Contacts:

James Sullivan, Seoul
Senior Commercial Officer
Phone: 82-2-397-4535
Jim.Sullivan@trade.gov

Yoon Shil Chay, Seoul
Senior Commercial Specialist
Phone: 82-2-397-4439
YoonShil.Chay@trade.gov

November , 2012

MEDICA 2012: USDOC Business Center, Showcase Global and Exhibitor Outreach Event -- multiple industry sectors

Location/Date:	Dusseldorf, Germany	11/14/2012 - 11/17/2012

Contacts:

Amelia Kooistra, North Texas
International Trade Specialist
Phone: 817-310-3744
Amelia.Goeppinger@trade.gov

Anette Salama, Dusseldorf
Senior Commercial Specialist
Phone: 49-211-737-767-60
Anette.Salama@trade.gov

Nils Roeher, Dusseldorf
Commercial Specialist
Phone: 49 211 737 767 20
Nils.Roeher@trade.gov

Uta Kirst, Dusseldorf
Commercial Specialist
Phone: 49 211-737-767-80
Uta.Kirst@trade.gov

Ryan Klemm, Messe Dusseldorf North America

Phone: 312-781-5180
rklemm@mdna.com

November , 2012

Medica -- multiple industry sectors

Location/Date:	Dusseldorf, Germany	11/14/2012 - 11/17/2012

Contacts:

Danny Dumon, Brussels
Commercial Specialist
Phone: +32-2-811-5476
Danny.Dumon@trade.gov

November , 2012

Greater New York Dental Meeting 2012 -- multiple industry sectors

Location/Date:	New York, NY, United States	11/23/2012 - 11/28/2012

Contacts:

Aditi Palli, Trade Event Programs
International Trade Specialist
Phone: 202-482-3334
Aditi.Palli@trade.gov

November , 2012

Offshore South East Asia 2012 (OSEA2012) -- multiple industry sectors

Location/Date:	Singapore, Singapore	11/27/2012 - 11/30/2012

Contacts:

Kevin Haley, Trade Event Programs
Senior International Trade Specialist
Phone: 202-482-6434
Kevin.Haley@trade.gov

Yiu Kei Chan, Singapore
Commercial Specialist
Phone: (65) 6476-9029
YiuKei.Chan@trade.gov

Emily Cantwell, IMEX Management Inc.

Phone: 704.365-0041
emilyc@imexmanagment.com

December , 2012

Aeromart Toulouse 2012 -- Aircraft/Aircraft Parts

Location/Date: Toulouse, France   12/4/2012 - 12/6/2012

Contacts:

Cara Boulesteix, Paris
Commercial Specialist
Phone: [33] (0)1 43 12 70 79
Cara.Boulesteix@trade.gov

Alain Ngoie, Advanced Business Events

Phone: 33 (0) 1 41 86 41 51
ANgoie@advbe.com

December , 2012

POWER-GEN International 2012 -- multiple industry sectors

Location/Date: Orlando, FL, United States   12/11/2012 - 12/13/2012

Contacts:

Mark Wells, Trade Event Programs
Senior International Trade Specialist
Phone: (202) 482-0904
Mark.Wells@trade.gov

Melanie McGuire, PennWell Corporation

Phone: (918) 831-9180
melaniem@pennwell.com

December , 2012

U.S.A. Pavilion at 2012 Taipei International Building, Construction & Decoration Exhibition -- multiple industry sectors

Location/Date: Taipei, Taiwan   12/19/2012 - 12/23/2012

Contacts:

Allen Chien, Taipei
Commercial Specialist
Phone: 886-2-27201550 ext.331
Allen.Chien@trade.gov

Index